Testing and Counseling Services

Bunting and Lyon, Inc., administers the Independent School Entrance Exam (ISEE) and the Secondary School Admission Test (SSAT) to small groups of students one or two weekday mornings throughout the year. We also counsel families in their search for private school placement, facilitating the research of appropriate schools for their children and guiding them through the admission process.

For further information, please contact us by telephone at 203-269-3333 or by e-mail at BuntingandLyon@aol.com.

Private
Independent
Schools

Bunting and Lyon, Inc., 238 North Main Street, Wallingford, Connecticut 06492

In 1936, at the height of the Great Depression, newlyweds James and Elizabeth Webster Lyon Bunting founded Bunting and Lyon, a small company that would become one of the leading publishers of reference books in the field of private education. *Private Independent Schools* first appeared in print in 1943 and featured description of 95 schools. From those modest beginnings, the Blue Book, as it is familiarly known, has carried information on thousands of schools, from nursery and preschool through Grade 12 and a postgraduate year.

For increased convenience and availability, we feature all Blue Book entries in their entirety online at **www.BuntingandLyon.com**, offering instant, direct accessibility to every school and summer program. Bunting and Lyon also provides counseling to families seeking appropriate school placement for their children and administers on-site standardized admission tests in small groups of private school applicants.

Since the early '60s, our office has been housed in a historic homestead (photograph ca. 1860) on North Main Street in Wallingford, Connecticut, about halfway between Hartford and New Haven off Interstate 91 and the Merritt Parkway. The Davis Homestead was originally owned by cousins of Harriet Beecher Stowe, one of America's most renowned authors and civil rights advocates.

Private Independent Schools

2010
The Sixty-third Edition

Published and Distributed by
Bunting and Lyon, Inc.
238 North Main Street
Wallingford, Connecticut 06492
U.S.A.
Telephone: 1-203-269-3333
Fax: 1-203-269-8908
E-mail BuntingandLyon@aol.com
Web Site www.BuntingandLyon.com

Copyright 2010 by Bunting and Lyon, Inc.
238 North Main Street
Wallingford, Connecticut 06492
Telephone 1-203-269-3333
Fax 1-203-269-5697
Printed and Bound in U.S.A.

Library of Congress Catalog Card Number:
72-122324

International Standard Book Number:
0-913094-63-3

International Standard Series Number:
0079-5399

$115

Foreword

Leadership for Excellence

At the heart of every good private independent school lies a dedicated core of personnel whose dedication, commitment, and extraordinary breadth of skills enable the entire learning community to carry out and fulfill its mission. These capable and generous administrators are at the forefront of the school's success, its ability to shape, educate, and develop children into thoughtful scholars, artists, athletes, leaders, and citizens of the world.

Harking back to a tradition recently revived in the pages of our Blue Book, in our 63rd edition, Bunting and Lyon acknowledges the school heads, admissions directors, and directors of development and communications who, along with other key administrators, are the driving forces in the field of independent educational excellence.

Perhaps the most complex and all-encompassing role at the school is that of head, whether he or she is known as headmaster, headmistress, principal, superintendent, CEO, or any other name, this individual wears a multitude of hats, some at the same time! According to Henry M. Battle, Jr., who leads Forsyth Country Day School in Lewisville, North Carolina, "Our primary goal is that all of the students who walk through our doors in the morning are excited about the day that awaits them." This seemingly simple aim is achieved through a myriad of tasks and responsibilities. As the personification of the school itself, the head must serve as a model of integrity and inspiration to students, faculty, staff, and parents as well as the community at large. Fund-raiser, morale-builder, decision-maker, and, often, teacher *par excellence,* the head of school sets the standards and exemplifies the philosophy that distinguishes the school and realizes its objectives.

The director of admission often forms a family's first impression of the school. Ideally, this individual possesses a strong, outgoing personality, insights and intuition into children and young adults, and exceptional organizational skills. In addition to scheduling and conducting interviews with prospective candidates and their families, the hard-working admission director is a cheerleader for the school, enthusiastic about its mission, faculty and facilities and ever-ready, willing, and able to answer questions ranging from arts, athletics, and curriculum to study hall, dorm life, and financial aid. School fairs, Q&A sessions before school and parent groups, and recruitment-related overseas travel are often components of the admission director's responsibilities as he/she fulfills a job that may require being on call above and beyond the usual 9 to 5, Monday through Friday work schedule. Despite the sometimes hectic demands of the position, the rewards are great. According to Ray Diffley III, Director of Admission at Choate Rosemary Hall, the best gratification is "watching the wide-eyed parents absolutely glow with pride when they see the development of their son or daughter over a period of time that culminates on graduation day."

Communications directors provide vital information to both the school community and the world beyond. Heralding the school's strengths, assets, and benefits to students and families, these individuals create the visual and intellectual profile of the institution. All public relations—admission materials, viewbooks, newsletters, interfacing with the outside media, advertising placement, liaison with alumni and school supporters, even small details such as logos, letterheads, and banners—usually originate with the communications department. Often, the team collaborates with IT personnel, providing invaluable input into website creation and maintenance. Without this barrage of information, many schools would scarcely be known beyond the confines of the local area.

The development department plans and executes a wide variety of fund-raising campaigns, those difficult and all-important necessities required for day-to-day operations as well as extraordinary capital expenditures, such as a new library, upgraded laboratories, or new buildings. Working closely with the board of trustees, the development director determines the school's financial needs and identifies and contacts potential donors to obtain the needed funds.

Needless to say, in many schools, these departments may overlap, with the head acting as admissions coordinator or development and communications director collaborating under the same umbrella. Regardless of a school's size or reputation, we in the field of independent education recognize the hard work, talent, and commitment of school administrators who tackle the ongoing challenge of maintaining the highest standards of intellectual, ethical, artistic, athletic, and personal excellence.

Peter G. Bunting, *Publisher*
&
The Editors
2010

On Applying

Now What?

Applying to a private independent school can be a lengthy, sometimes daunting, task. Ideally, you should begin the process several seasons in advance of the desired entry year. While procedures vary from school to school, the following overview is designed to give you the general timeline of what to do when.

September–October

- So many schools—so little time.
  Figure out your priorities and criteria. Research and narrow down school choices by using guides, brochures, view books, and web sites. Consult an educational counselor. Talk with alumni as well as current students and parents, if possible. Include a "stretch" and a "safety" school in your final list.

- Ready, set, go!
  Applications and admissions packets are readily available by contacting the schools of interest. In many cases, candidates can apply directly via a school's web site as well as obtain printable forms, questionnaires, and other required materials. And, yes, there is a fee to apply.

October–January

- What's the difference?
  Many schools hold open houses that showcase student-led tours, presentations by faculty members, discussion panels with current parents, and sample classes. Go. Get a feel for the school. Poke around. Ask questions.

- Put your best foot forward.
  Schedule an on-campus interview (usually required). This may include a tour of the school and class visitation, lasting from two hours to a full day, and involves parents and the candidate. Try to do this after some of your application material has been sent in. You and the admission officer will have a much more interesting conversation. Show interest and

be prepared to ask questions that are not answered in the school's promotional material. Look your best. It's better to dress conservatively than not. Respect the school you're visiting. When you get back home, write a thank-you note to your interviewer.

- **Can't get there from here?**
  If a visit to campus is impossible, schools can often arrange for an alumni representative to hold an interview near your home. Some schools also make telephone interviews available.

- **Multiple choices.**
  Register for and take any required standardized testing. Many schools require the Secondary School Admission Test (SSAT) or the Independent School Entrance Examination (ISEE). Other schools have their own test. Candidates for Grades 11–12 and a postgraduate year may have to submit PSAT or SAT scores. International students may have to take the Secondary Level English Proficiency Test (SLEP) or the Test of English as a Foreign Language (TOEFL). Make sure the score results will arrive before your schools' application due date.

- **Applying made easy.**
  Finish your part of the application form, which usually includes student essays and a parent questionnaire. Don't leave this assignment until the last minute. Take your time; write out drafts; review, edit, rewrite. Be honest and enthusiastic. Dare to be different.

- **Reach out and touch someone.**
  Give recommendation forms to teachers, counselors, and others, as specified in the application packet, to fill out and return. Give transcript release forms to your school office. Provide everyone with stamped, addressed envelopes and a due date; then follow up! And be sure to thank your teachers.

- **Where's the money?**
  Don't let those tuition figures scare you off. All schools award financial aid, usually based on need, sometimes also on merit. Apply early, and, remember, your family will have to submit various personal financial records.

December–February

- **The longest days.**
  Be sure all application materials have been submitted. Some schools will send a postcard noting what is missing. Otherwise, call the school to check. Be proactive. Then wait while admission committees do their job.

March–April

- The good news.

  Schools send notifications of acceptance or denial. In many areas, school consortiums agree to the same mailing date and the same response deadline. You usually have a month to respond.

- Are we there yet?

  Some schools hold second visits for accepted students. Go if you can. Keep asking questions.

- Your final decision.

  Let the school of your choice know that you are coming. Your family must sign an enrollment agreement and send a deposit. And it is imperative to notify the other schools that accepted you that you are enrolling elsewhere, so they can offer the space to another candidate.

The timetable and procedures reflected in these guidelines are general in nature. No matter when you become interested in private independent education, you are encouraged to find appropriate schools and apply. It's never too late to follow your dream.

Standardized Testing Information

Most private independent schools require standardized testing as part of their admission procedure. The two most widely used admission tests are the Independent School Entrance Examination (ISEE) and the Secondary School Admission Test (SSAT). Some schools administer their own test. International students may be asked to take the Test of English as a Foreign Language (TOEFL); applicants for Grades 11–12 and a postgraduate year may have to submit ACT, SAT, or PSAT scores. You can receive information about these standardized tests through the contacts listed below.

Independent School Entrance Examination (ISEE)
    Educational Records Bureau
    220 East 42nd Street
    New York, NY 10017
    Telephone 212-672-9812; [Toll-free] 800-989-3721
    E-mail isee@erblearn.org; Web Site www.iseetest.org

Secondary School Admission Test (SSAT)
    CN 5339 (for regular mail)
    Princeton, NJ 08543
    862 Route 518 (for courier & express service)
    Skillman, NJ 08558
    Telephone 609-683-4440
    E-mail info@ssat.org; Web Site www.ssat.org

Test of English as a Foreign Language (TOEFL)
Secondary Level English Proficiency Test (SLEP)
    TOEFL Services
    Educational Testing Services
    P.O. Box 6151
    Princeton, NJ 08541-6151
    U.S.A.
    Telephone 609-771-7100; [Toll-free] 877-863-3546
    E-mail toefl@ets.org; Web Site www.ets.org/toefl

American College Test (ACT)
ACT
500 ACT Drive
P.O. Box 168
Iowa City, IA 52243-0168
Telephone 319-337-1000
Web Site www.act.org

SAT and PSAT
www.collegeboard.com

Seeking Financial Aid?

Many schools that offer financial assistance do so through the School and Student Service for Financial Aid, wholly owned by the National Association of Independent Schools. While you will find the best source of information about financial aid policies at the particular schools you are interested in, some general information may be found at NAIS.

Underserved Minorities and Independent Education

A number of organizations and foundations exist to prepare minority students for placement in private and independent schools, primarily at the secondary level. These organizations seek out academically talented and motivated students who come from economically disadvantaged, low-income, and underserved segments of society. Some agencies specify that they serve African-Americans or children of color, which may include Black, Asian, Latino, and Native American.

Goals of the various organizations include equalizing the chances for opportunity and success, motivating and supporting qualified students, developing well-educated and capable leaders, and increasing the number of students of color in independent schools.

Many programs require a rigorous application process. Those students selected to participate commit to a year or more of preparation aimed at independent school placement, which is usually ensured upon a student's successful completion of the year's requirements. Preparation may include summer academic sessions, Wednesday afternoon and Saturday classes during the school year, and extra homework. Often these programs partner with a specific consortium of private schools in student placement.

Some programs provide exposure to the world of higher education and to professional entrepreneurship and business. Others concentrate on personal growth, leadership development, and community service.

All programs offer various services designed to help students apply and gain admission to private schools. These services, which involve student and family, consist of an introduction to specific schools through fairs and tours, help with the admission process (application paperwork, interview techniques, testing information), and guidance on financial aid and financial planning. Other support services may include tutoring and mentoring, transitional counseling, summer job assistance, college guidance, internships, reunions and recognition ceremonies, and parent workshops.

A few organizations make annual tuition grants; however, most families receive financial aid from the private school in which their child enrolls.

The following list of agencies is by no means exhaustive. These particular organizations have been in contact with Bunting and Lyon, and we have gleaned our informational overview from their materials. We are pleased to present them in hope that you will contact them about their programs.

A Better Chance
240 West 35th Street, 9th Floor
New York, NY 10001
Tel. 646-346-1310
Web Site www.abetterchance.org

Baltimore Educational Scholarship
    Trust (B.E.S.T.)
808 North Charles Street, Suite 200C
Baltimore, MD 21201
Tel. 410-752-2225
Web Site www.besttrust.org

The Black Student Fund
3636 16th Street NW, 4th Floor
Washington, DC 20010-1146
Tel. 202-387-1414
Web Site www.blackstudentfund.org

The Boys' Club of New York
287 East 10th Street
New York, NY 10009
Tel. 212-533-2550
Web Site www.bcny.org

Early Steps
540 East 76th Street
New York, NY 10021
Tel. 212-288-9684
Web Site www.earlysteps.org

The Independent School Alliance
    for Minority Affairs
1545 Wilshire Boulevard, Suite 711
Los Angeles, CA 90017
Tel. 213-484-2411
Web Site www.thealliance-la.org

New Jersey SEEDS
494 Broad Street, Suite 105
Newark, NJ 07102
Tel. 973-642-6422
Web Site www.njseeds.org

Prep for Prep
328 West 71st Street
New York, NY 10023
Tel. 212-579-1390
Web Site www.prepforprep.org

Project Match
6303 Nelway Drive
McLean, VA 22101
Tel. 703-847-9677

Queen City Foundation
1 West 4th Street
Cincinnati, OH 45202
Tel. 513-241-1322

REACH Prep
2777 Summer Street
Stamford, CT 06905
Tel. 203-487-0750
Web Site www.reachprep.org

The Steppingstone Foundation
155 Federal Street, Suite 800
Boston, MA 02110
Tel. 617-423-6300
Web Site www.tsf.org

The Wight Foundation, Inc.
60 Park Place, 17th Floor
Newark, NJ 07102-3704
Tel. 973-824-1195
Web Site www.wightfoundation.org

Contents

Index of the Schools

The following Index of the Schools includes the names and locations of the private schools described in our book. The schools have made this publication possible by subscribing for full Descriptive Articles and Listings.

Schools that have subscribed for Descriptive Articles are identified with an asterisk. These articles will give you a broad feeling for private schools in general as well as an objective, in-depth definition of individual schools, both day and boarding.

Index of the Schools

Asterisk indicates a Descriptive Article.

Index of the Schools

Index of the Schools

Index of the Schools

The Schools

The Blue Book features descriptions of 1000 private schools in North America and abroad that meet our standards of acceptance. These educational institutions serve students ranging in grade levels from Nursery through Grade 12 and a postgraduate year.

For easy reference, schools in the United States are organized alphabetically within their respective states. Schools throughout the rest of the world follow and are listed alphabetically by country or territory.

The 20-line listings contain basic information and give a good idea of the philosophy and programs of the school. Descriptive Articles follow a set format and provide a school's characteristics in detail. All entries are written as "fact without opinion," allowing for clear comparisons between one school and another, from which readers may draw their own conclusions.

All entries in the book appear in their entirety online at **www.BuntingandLyon.com**. You can research schools by name, city, state, academic courses, arts offerings, sports teams, extra-curricular activities, and personnel. Direct links to schools' web sites and an e-mail inquiry form are included.

If you are interested in any of these schools, we suggest that you contact the Director of Admission or the Head of the School, the names of whom appear in the entry.

ALABAMA

Advent Episcopal School   1950

2019 Sixth Avenue North, Birmingham, AL 35203
Tel. 205-252-2535; Fax 205-252-3023

ADVENT EPISCOPAL SCHOOL in Birmingham, Alabama, was founded in 1950. Since then, this independent, equal-opportunity institution has built a reputation for academic excellence, featuring an advanced curriculum for boys and girls in four-year-old Kindergarten through Grade 8. The School's location enables students to take advantage of such resources as the Alabama Civil Rights Institute, the Alabama Symphony Orchestra, Children's Theater, and the Alabama Jazz Hall of Fame. They also attend and participate in concerts in the park, parades, and festivals.

ADVENT EPISCOPAL SCHOOL

The Advent's credo declares a dedication to "Sharing the ADVENTure" of education, while its mission promises "to offer a superior, advanced, and enriched education in a Christian environment." At a time of unsettling events and circumstances, the School draws on its Christian heritage to help provide a safe, stable, wholesome, and caring atmosphere in which students can experience the total learning process with a sense of enthusiasm. In the belief that education is a continuing adventure to be shared with students and family, the faculty develops learning concepts from day to day, emphasizing basic skills and exploring the relationships among the various disciplines.

The Advent, a nonprofit institution, was the first elementary school in Birmingham and Jefferson County to be accredited by the Southern Association of Colleges and Schools and the first independent school to integrate. It holds membership in the National Association of Independent Schools, among other organizations. School policies are established by a 13-member Board of Trustees comprised of individuals from throughout the community.

THE CAMPUS. The School is set among the modern commercial towers of Birmingham, Alabama's largest city and a major medical, educational, business, and industrial center of the American South. The campus features shaded gardens, new and period buildings, a model outdoor playground, a gymnasium, and a rooftop recreational facility. The music classroom/auditorium has been nationally recognized for its excellent acoustical properties.

The School is adjacent to the historic Cathedral Church of the Advent where many school assemblies and special programs take place. The main, three-story building, with bright, airy rooms and art-filled halls, houses fully equipped Lower and Upper School science labs, a computer lab, a 15,000-volume library, classrooms, administrative offices, and an art room equipped with a printing press, a pottery wheel, a kiln, and a darkroom. A technology center is located in the McPhillips Library. Neal Gymnasium contains basketball and volleyball courts, while the paneled refectory offers a warm atmosphere for student dining.

THE FACULTY. Una Battles, appointed Headmistress in 1969, is a graduate of the University of Alabama (B.S., M.A.). Her previous experience includes service as a teacher in Alabama public schools. Mrs. Battles and her husband, Craig, have one son.

The 29 full-time faculty members hold baccalaureates, 20 master's degrees, and 2 doctorates representing study at Auburn, Birmingham-Southern, Emory, Furman, Houston Baptist, Huntingdon, Judson, Louisiana State, Millsaps, Mississippi State, Northwestern, Samford, Spring Hill, Troy State, Tulane, Vanderbilt, and the Universities of Alabama, Mississippi, and Montevallo.

Six part-time instructors teach art, Lower School science, music, French, physical education, and literature/composition. A Red Cross-certified individual staffs the Health Room on a full-time basis.

Faculty benefits include long-term disability insurance, leaves of absence, cancer insurance, medical and dental insurance, life insurance, and a retirement plan.

STUDENT BODY. In 2009–10, the School enrolled a diverse group of 322 students from 48 zip codes located throughout the Birmingham Metropolitan area.

ACADEMIC PROGRAM. The Advent is organized into three components: Kindergarten, Lower School (Grades 1–4), and Upper School (Grades 5–8). Academics begin in four-year-old Kindergarten, and grades are departmentalized from Grade 5 upward. All children entering the Kindergartens and Grade 1 must meet the September 1 birthdate deadline. All children attend weekly chapel services.

Kindergartners have four hours of classroom instruction and play daily. Instruction consists of reading (with emphasis on phonics), mathematics, science, social studies, penmanship, art, music, French, and computer.

ADVENT EPISCOPAL SCHOOL

The schedule for Grades 1–8 is divided into 30-minute modules to accommodate approximately four morning and four afternoon class periods of varying lengths.

The basic curriculum for Grades 1–6 includes reading (with emphasis on phonics in Grades 1–3), language arts (vocabulary, composition, literature, critical thinking, and writing), penmanship (Grades 1–3), computer, French, social studies, mathematics, and science. Grades 1–4 have library periods with instruction in library skills. Social studies in Kindergarten–Grade 3 is designed to give students an awareness of the social and physical world around them. Grade 4 studies Alabama History;

Grade 5, U.S. History; and Grade 6, Ancient World History. Literature and composition, emphasizing study of the novel, short story, drama, and poetry, are added in Grade 5, as are religion and the introduction of laboratory techniques in science. Special themes explored include migration (Grades 1–2), the dynamic earth (Grades 3–4), and oceans (Grade 5). Grade 6 studies earth and space science.

First in U.S. for
BatterUp Subtraction

ADVENT EPISCOPAL SCHOOL

In Grade 7, language arts includes the study of English grammar, vocabulary, composition (including expository writing), and literature. Other subjects are French, world history and geography, modern mathematics (emphasizing geometry and the algebra of points and lines), basic life science, art, religion, and computer.

The eighth-grade curriculum consists of English grammar, composition, and literature as well as American History, French, civics, algebra, physical science, art, physical education, religion, and computer.

Regular art classes begin in Grade 3 and continue through Grade 8. All students participate in the music program, which aims toward musical literacy and appreciation as well as performance. The physical education program begins with directed play in Kindergarten and progresses to team games and dance activities for the older children. Sports included in the program are basketball, kickball, hockey, soccer, volleyball, and golf.

For students who require additional assistance, teachers are available to provide tutoring as needed for a charge.

Upon graduation from the Advent, most students elect to attend high school locally. Of these, the majority remain in independent schools. Others may choose boarding schools located throughout the eastern half of the United States.

STUDENT ACTIVITIES. The Student Council, made up of representatives from Grades 5–8 and elected by class, meets monthly with faculty advisers to discuss matters of student concern and to organize School-wide service projects for local charities. The Council also holds fund-raisers, sponsors the spring dance for Grades 7–8, and presents a leadership award to a graduating eighth grader. A Christmas Service Project is organized by the Student Council as well as a party day. A-Day activities, which include skits, sack and relay races, and a student-faculty talent show, are also planned by the Student Council.

Field trips are scheduled for all grades. Kindergarten and Lower School students have visited a bakery, a dairy, a local fire station, and the zoo. Destinations for older students may include Huntsville's Constitution Hall Village, the Birmingham-Southern planetarium, Oak Mountain State Park, McWane Science Center, City Hall, the county courthouse, and the Birmingham Museum of Art. In addition, Grades 4–8 take long trips each year to such places as the State Capitol in Montgomery, the American Village in Montevallo, and Atlanta's CNN, World of Coke, and Aquarium. The fifth grade takes a five-day trip to Washington, D.C., while sixth graders participate in a three-day environmental program at Alabama's Camp McDowell. Seventh graders travel to Dauphin Island Sea Lab near Mobile for three days, and eighth graders visit the Museum of Natural History at the University of Alabama and the Warner-Westervelt Museum of Western American Art near Tuscaloosa.

Individual classes present plays and concerts periodically.

Traditional events for the school community are a parent/teacher Open House, parent/teacher Christmas luncheon, Grandparents' Day, Art Fair, Science Fair, Services of Lessons and Carols, and the May Festival.

Activities include basketball, volleyball, golf, French Club, Math Team, Chess Team, a student newspaper, choral ensemble, and Cross and Shield service organization.

ADMISSION AND COSTS. Advent Episcopal School admits students in all grades on the basis of a standardized, School-administered entrance examination, previous academic records, and recommendations from teachers and other adults. The School admits students without regard to race, creed, or national or ethnic origin. Students currently enrolled are given priority for registration until the first of February. At that time, new students are considered with the following priorities: siblings of current students, alumni children, members of the Cathedral Church of the Advent, and the earliest applicants. If vacancies exist, students may be enrolled at midyear. There is a $25 testing fee and a $275 registration fee.

ADVENT EPISCOPAL SCHOOL

In 2010–11, tuition is $4896 for Kindergarten and $7821 for Grades 1–8. The cost of books and milk is included in the tuition; a Student Activities Fee, which is payable three times a year and varies with grade level, covers special events and materials such as novels, field trips, and seminars. The charge for before-school care is $15 per month or $1 per day; after-school care is $250 monthly or $10.50 per hour. A tuition insurance refund plan is offered.

Financial aid of approximately $190,000 is awarded annually on the basis of need and academic achievement.

Dean of Faculty: Mrs. Rosemary Ham
Alumni Secretary: Mrs. Lady Anne Buchanan
Director of Admissions: Mrs. Carolyn Neal
Director of Development: Mr. Craig Battles
Business Manager: Mr. Martin Johnson
Director of Athletics: Mr. Gene Tomlin
Director of Music: Mr. Richard Phillips

The Altamont School 1922

4801 Altamont Road, Birmingham, AL 35222
Tel. 205-879-2006; Fax 205-871-5666
Web Site www.altamontschool.org
E-mail admissions@altamontschool.org

THE ALTAMONT SCHOOL

The Altamont School is a coeducational, college preparatory day school enrolling approximately 350 students in Grades 5–12. Altamont prepares each student to live a more meaningful life and shape a more livable world. At Altamont, the arts are as important as athletics; students of different backgrounds share in the process of discovery; reading is revered; multiple language offerings include Latin, Greek, and Mandarin; and upholding the Honor Code is a source of real pride. All students take courses that follow a traditional liberal arts curriculum. Diverse electives range from creative writing and filmmaking to Model United Nations and Scholars Bowl. Senior seminar courses include such classes as The Gothic Novel and International Relations. Students may take part in 25 athletic teams, orchestra, drama, choir, school government, National Honor Society, publications, and environmental, history, music, French, Spanish, Latin, and science clubs. Fall Project Week gives every student an opportunity to travel in the U.S. and abroad. A summer program provides academic and extracurricular enrichment. Tuition: $12,348–$16,176. Financial Aid: $740,000. Jimmy Wiygul is Director of Admissions; Sarah Whiteside is Head of School. *Southern Association.*

Bayside Academy 1967

303 Dryer Avenue, Daphne, AL 36526
Tel. 251-338-6300; Fax 251-338-6310
Web Site www.baysideacademy.org
E-mail afoster@baysideacademy.org

Founded by parents to enable both average and gifted students to reach their potential, Bayside is a college preparatory day school enrolling 750 boys and girls in Pre-Kindergarten–Grade 12. The traditional academic program includes Advanced Placement courses as well as computer, fine arts, and foreign language in all grades. Teams are fielded in 11 sports; academic teams, drama, publications, and service clubs are also offered. Tuition: $6550–$8890. Extras: $1000. Financial Assistance:

$250,000. Alan Foster is Director of Admissions; Thomas Johnson (Valdosta State University, M.E. 1972) was appointed Head in 1998. *Southern Association.*

Highlands School 1958

4901 Old Leeds Road, Birmingham, AL 35213
Tel. 205-956-9731; Admissions Ext. 113; Fax 205-951-8127
Web Site www.highlandsschool.org
E-mail jmcdonald@highlandsschool.org

HIGHLANDS SCHOOL

Highlands is a coeducational day school enrolling 273 students from diverse backgrounds in Preschool–Grade 8. Its mission is to nurture each child's intellectual, physical, social, and emotional development, to instill self-confidence and a lifelong pursuit of learning, and prepare students for a future in an ever-changing world. The integrated curriculum is designed to meet individual learning styles, provide a strong foundation in the core disciplines, and educate the whole child with a focus on art, music, French, Spanish, Chinese, technology, and physical education. Activities include community outreach, student government, yearbook, photography, greenhouse, drama, scouting for girls and boys, and intramural athletics. The Family Center includes children from 6 weeks to 3 years of age. Extended-day and summer programs are available. Tuition: $8300–$10,565. Financial assistance is available. Judy Ladden McDonald is Director of Admissions; Kathryn W. Barr is Head of School.

Randolph School 1959

1005 Drake Avenue, SE, Huntsville, AL 35802
Tel. 256-799-6103; Admissions Ext. 103; Fax 256-881-1784
Web Site www.randolphschool.net
E-mail gbelow@randolphschool.net

A National School of Excellence, Randolph is a coeducational, college preparatory day school dedicated to providing a rigorous and well-rounded K–12 education within a nurturing community to its 936 students. Through a commitment to excellence in academics, the arts, and athletics, the School's program and its faculty demand diligence and discipline while encouraging creativity and discovery. Above all, the School emphasizes honor, integrity, and character. K–8 students attend the Drake Campus, while 9–12 students attend the newly opened, $27,000,000 Garth Campus less than a mile away. Students in Grades 9–12 purchase personal laptops. Graduates are consistently admitted to competitive colleges and universities. Tuition: $11,285–$13,950. Financial aid is available. Glynn Below is Director of Admissions; Dr. Byron Hulsey is Head of School. *Southern Association.*

St. Paul's Episcopal School 1947

161 Dogwood Lane, Mobile, AL 36608
Tel. 251-342-6700; Admissions 251-461-2129; Fax 251-342-1844
Web Site www.stpaulsmobile.net
Admissions E-mail jtaylor@stpaulsmobile.net

This college preparatory Episcopal school enrolls approximately 1500 girls and boys as day students in Pre-Kindergarten through Grade 12. Chapel, an honor pledge, and community service are important elements of St. Paul's program. The Upper School provides Advanced Placement in the major disciplines, while the Middle and Upper Schools offer laptop computer sections in the core courses. The program also serves a modest number of students with learning differences. Approximately 50 percent of graduates are accepted by the "most competitive," "highly competitive," and "very competitive" colleges and universities. In sports, St. Paul's has been ranked first for academic years 2006, 2007, and 2008 and first overall in the state. The fine arts program includes portrait painting, chorus, and strings, among others. Tuition: $3992–$8996. Julie L. Taylor is Director of Admissions; F. Martin Lester, Jr., is Headmaster. *Southern Association.*

ADVENT EPISCOPAL SCHOOL

ARIZONA

ARKANSAS

All Saints' Episcopal Day School   1963

6300 North Central Avenue, Phoenix, AZ 85012
Tel. 602-274-4866; Fax 602-274-5032
Web Site www.allsaints.org; E-mail dwaage@allsaints.org

An outreach ministry of All Saints' Episcopal Church, this coeducational school seeks to nurture students' minds and hearts in a close-knit community. Serving families of all faiths, All Saints' is known for its rigorous and well-rounded liberal arts curriculum in the Anglican tradition, with two chapel services a week, religion/life skill classes, and emphasis on character and values. Service to others is emphasized at all grade levels. Approximately 500 students in Prekindergarten through Grade 8 receive instruction in the core academics of language arts, math, social studies, science, and Spanish, complemented by art, music, physical education, computers, and library. Additionally, students in Grades 7 and 8 choose an elective, and Grade 8 students take Speech. Small class sizes ensure attention to the individual with the appropriate levels of challenge and support. Graduates go on to attend top-tier high schools and colleges with an impressive acceptance rate. Tuition: $12,740–$14,750. Dan Waage is Director of Admissions & Financial Aid; Leo P. Dressel is Head of School.

Phoenix Country Day School   1961

3901 East Stanford Drive, Paradise Valley, AZ 85253
Tel. 602-955-8200; Admissions Ext. 2256; Fax 602-381-4554
Web Site www.pcds.org; E-mail kelsey.neal@pcds.org

Phoenix Country Day School is a nonsectarian, college preparatory school serving 700 boys and girls in Pre-K–Grade 12. Its mission is to offer a distinguished liberal arts curriculum that fosters the growth of the whole person and establishes a foundation for success in college and in life. Intellectual, artistic, and communications skills as well as physical development share equal emphasis with self-discipline and sound moral and ethical values. In Lower School (PK–4), small classes in a nurturing environment form the basis for a strong academic program. In addition to core subjects, there are study/travel exchanges in China, Costa Rica, and Germany. AP courses are available in 14 disciplines. Experienced college counselors guide students in the application process, and virtually all graduates enroll in colleges and universities nationwide. As a "private school with a public purpose," the School encourages a culture of service to others. School government, publications, band, chorus, dramas, musicals, and more than 50 interscholastic teams are among the activities for Grades 5–12. Summer programs are available. Tuition: $17,200–$21,300. Financial Aid: $1,700,000. Kelsey Neal is Director of Admissions; Geoff Campbell is Head of School.

Episcopal Collegiate School   1996

1701 Cantrell Road, Little Rock, AR 72201
Tel. 501-372-1194; Admissions Ext. 406; Fax 501-372-2160
Web Site www.episcopalcollegiate.org
E-mail ahoneywell@episcopalcollegiate.org

EPISCOPAL COLLEGIATE SCHOOL.

Episcopal Collegiate School is an independent, college preparatory day school serving central Arkansas. As a school of 600 students in PreK3–Grade 12, Episcopal strives to mentor and nurture each individual student to reach his or her full potential. Intellectual challenge is the foundation of the liberal arts curriculum. Episcopal offers 16 Advanced Placement courses, 12 sports, 3 foreign languages, and 24 clubs and organizations. With a state-of-the-art campus, the School's educational environment fosters academic rigor, character development, artistic and athletic enrichment, as well as spiritual growth. Episcopal also offers an extensive creative arts program. Tuition: $9330. Ashley Honeywell (6–12) and Mary Jane Briggs (PK–5) are Directors of Admission; Steve Hickman is Headmaster.

CALIFORNIA

Abraham Joshua Heschel Day School   1972

17701 Devonshire Street, Northridge, CA 91325
Tel. 818-368-5781; Fax 818-360-6162
Web Site www.heschel.com; E-mail admissions@ajhds.com

Abraham Joshua Heschel Day School is an independent Jewish Community Day School serving 360 boys and girls from Transitional Kindergarten through eighth grade. Heschel offers a superior dual-curricular education that focuses on individual learners achieving their highest potential in both general and Judaic studies, thereby enabling them to attain a love of learning, sound self-esteem, and a positive Jewish identification. The individualized, experiential program permits students to become active participants in the education process as they learn how to learn. In partnership with families, the School inspires students to become active, dedicated, ethical, and informed citizens and leaders. The School has two state-of-the-art science labs, fully equipped technology centers, SMART-boards, an art studio, and an interscholastic sports program. Outdoor education and community service are important components of the educational experience. As they move into high school, graduates are ready to respond to the call to leadership and to apply the Jewish values with which they were imbued at Heschel. Tuition: $11,506–$22,560. Lara Martin is Director of Admission; Betty Winn is Head of School. *Western Association.*

All Saints' Episcopal Day School   1961

8060 Carmel Valley Road, Carmel, CA 93923
Tel. 831-624-9171; Admissions Ext. 12; Fax 831-624-3960
Web Site www.asds.org; E-mail admissions@asds.org

All Saints' Episcopal Day, affiliated with All Saints' Church parish, seeks to provide each child the opportunity to develop his or her highest potential to learn in a nurturing environment of spiritual growth and service to others. The School enrolls 220 students in Pre-kindergarten–Grade 8. The enriched curriculum includes language arts, math, science, social studies, history, French or Spanish, Latin, music, art, religion, art history, physical education, performing arts, outdoor education and an extensive outreach program. Students attend daily chapel services. After-school and summer programs are offered. Tuition: $13,577–$16,435. Financial aid is available. Michele M. Rench (University of California [Berkeley], B.A.; Notre Dame Belmont, M.A.) is Head of School; Anne Crisan is Admissions Director.

The Athenian School   1965

2100 Mount Diablo Scenic Boulevard, Danville, CA 94506-2002
Tel. 925-837-5375; Admission 925-362-7223; Fax 925-855-9342
Web Site www.athenian.org; E-mail admission@athenian.org

Dyke Brown founded The Athenian School to prepare students for the challenges of college and for lives of "purpose and personal fulfillment." Set on a 75-acre campus 32 miles east of San Francisco, Athenian enrolls approximately 450 young men and women in Grades 6–12, including 40 boarders from around the world in Grade 9 upward. Athenian's challenging curriculum includes many honors and AP courses. International students benefit from ESL classes. The curriculum features a required Athenian Wilderness Experience and service as well as options for outdoor adventure and international travel through the Round Square Conference. The Town Meeting engages students, faculty, and staff in decision making. Students engage in the visual and performing arts, varsity sports, community service, airplane construction, and robotics. The Athenian experience inspires students to become lifelong learners and confident, successful adults with a deep understanding of them-

selves, exceptional skills for achievement, and the compassion to make a positive difference in the world. Boarding Tuition: $44,500–$45,100; Day Tuition: $22,015–$28,510. Christopher Beeson is Director of Admission; Eric Niles, J.D., is Head of School. *Western Association.*

The Bay School of San Francisco   2004

35 Keyes Avenue, The Presidio of San Francisco, San Francisco,
* CA 94129-1736*
Tel. 415-561-5800; Fax 415-561-5808
Web Site www.bayschoolsf.org; E-mail admission@bayschoolsf.org

The Bay School of San Francisco, founded in 2004, is a coeducational, college preparatory high school located in the Presidio of San Francisco, overlooking San Francisco Bay and the Golden Gate Bridge. During 2009–10, the day school enrolled 274 students in Grades 9–12 and has a faculty of 42 experienced educators. The challenging, broadly based curriculum places special emphasis on study of the sciences, technology, ethics, and world religions and cultures, having the mission of uniquely preparing students for their futures as engaged citizens and leaders of the 21st-century global community. Fine arts, music, and drama course offerings are integral to the curriculum in addition to comprehensive athletics, service learning, and extracurricular clubs and programs. Students are drawn from Bay Area public, parochial, and independent middle schools comprising an inclusive community that is racially, culturally, and economically diverse. Tuition: $30,930. Annie Tsang is Director of Admission; Timothy W. Johnson is Head of School.

Bellarmine College Preparatory   1851

960 West Hedding Street, San Jose, CA 95126-1215
Tel. 408-294-9224; Fax 408-297-2072
Web Site www.bcp.org; E-mail bcolucci@bcp.org

Now in its 158th year of educating young men, Bellarmine was the first Jesuit school west of the Mississippi. While distinctly Roman Catholic in philosophy and tradition, Bellarmine welcomes approximately 1600 young men from all faiths as day students in Grades 9–12. The school adheres to the Jesuit mission of developing "men for others," guiding the mind, spirit, heart, body, and imagination of its students through a challenging and comprehensive college preparatory curriculum, broad offerings in the arts and athletics, and opportunities for service and social outreach. Course work centers on the liberal arts, sciences, and humanities, enriched by religious studies, modern and classical languages, and cutting-edge technology. Honors and Advanced Placement opportunities are available in all major disciplines, and virtually all graduates go on to higher education. Activities encompass a wide range of interests, from student government, peer tutoring, Christian service, and social justice to publications, movies, fishing, snowboarding, theater arts, ethnic clubs, and interscholastic sports. Tuition: $14,450. Financial aid is available. Bill Colucci is Director of Admissions; Chris Meyercord is Principal; Rev. Paul Sheridan, S.J., is President. *Western Association.*

The Bentley School   1920

K–8: 1 Hiller Drive, Oakland, CA 94618-2301
* Tel. 510-843-2512; Admission Ext. 2460; Fax 510-845-6516*
* Web Site www.bentleyschool.net; E-mail esilk@bentleyschool.net*
9–12: 1000 Upper Happy Valley Road, Lafayette, CA 94549
* Tel. 925-283-2101; Fax 925-299-0469*
* E-mail cting@bentleyschool.net*

Celebrating its 90th year, Bentley School is a nationally recognized coeducational, K–12, college preparatory day school, located on two campuses in Oakland and Lafayette. Its rigorous academic program, award-winning athletic and arts programs, and diverse, committed faculty serve to prepare some of the finest students in the Bay Area for lifelong learning and global citizenship. The curriculum focuses on the liberal arts, mathematics and sciences, computer technology, modern languages, and the visual and performing arts. The Upper School program includes honors and Advanced Placement courses, independent study/research projects, and off-campus senior internships. One hundred percent of Bentley graduates attend top national and international colleges and universities. Bentley is a member of the National Association of Independent Schools and the California Association of Independent Schools. Tuition: $20,510–$27,375. Cheryl Ting (9–12) and Erika Silk (K–8) are Directors of Admissions; Brian Thomas heads the Upper School; Duncan Lyon heads the Middle School; Beth Crowley heads the Lower School; Arlene Hogan is Head of School. *Western Association.*

Berkeley Hall School   1911

16000 Mulholland Drive, Los Angeles, CA 90049
Tel. 310-476-6421; Admissions Ext. 208; Fax 310-476-5748
Web Site www.berkeleyhall.org
E-mail info@berkeleyhall.org

Berkeley Hall School is committed to providing a strong, balanced education in a nurturing environment. Encompassing Preschool–Grade 8, the School enrolls 250 girls and boys. The curriculum is centered around language arts, math, science, and social studies, with numerous opportunities to develop creativity in music, drama, woodshop, photography, and studio art. Computer technology, field trips, and special cultural programs enrich and reinforce classroom instruction. Students take part in community service, sports, and student government. Character education is a vital thread running through the program. Tuition: $18,200–$21,700. Nathalie Miller is Director of Admissions; Craig Barrows is Headmaster. *Western Association.*

Besant Hill School of Happy Valley   1946

8585 Ojai-Santa Paula Road, P.O. Box 850, Ojai, CA 93023
Tel. 805-646-4343; Admissions Ext. 422; [Toll-free] 800-900-0487;
* Fax 805-646-4371*
Web Site www.besanthillschool.org
E-mail admissions@besanthillschool.org

BESANT HILL SCHOOL OF HAPPY VALLEY

Founded in 1946 by Aldous Huxley, J. Krishnamurti, Guido Ferrand, and Rosalind Rajagopal on 520 acres in the resort town of Ojai, California, this residential school community offers a vigorous college preparatory curriculum with a cornerstone on creative expression and divergent thinking. Besant Hill offers 33 art electives, competitive athletics, travel and

experiential education programs, small classes, and a 4:1 student-teacher ratio. An English as a Second Language program is offered at all levels. Instructional Support is provided through the School's learning center at an extra fee. Boarding Tuition: $39,990; Day Tuition: $19,900. Need-based financial aid is available. Randy R. Bertin is Assistant Head for Advancement; Terra Furguiel is Associate Director of Admissions; Paul Amadio was appointed Head of School in 2006. *Western Association.*

Bishop Montgomery High School   1957

5430 Torrance Boulevard, Torrance, CA 90503
Tel. 310-540-2021, Admissions Ext. 226; Fax 310-543-5102
Web Site www.bmhs-la.org; E-mail cdunn@bmhs-la.org

BISHOP MONTGOMERY HIGH SCHOOL is a Roman Catholic, college preparatory day school enrolling boys and girls in Grades 9 through 12. It is located a mile from the Pacific Ocean in Torrance, a city of about 140,000 people.

The School was established by the Archdiocese of Los Angeles in 1957 and was named for Bishop George Thomas Montgomery, the first American-born bishop of Los Angeles and a staunch church leader in the late 19th and early 20th centuries. The aim of the School is to provide quality Catholic education to college-bound students of varied levels of ability and to help them become mature adults who integrate their knowledge of the world with Catholic beliefs and values. This aim is advanced in a community that sustains the life of faith through prayer, worship, and service to others. Courses in Religious Studies are required through all four years.

BISHOP MONTGOMERY HIGH SCHOOL

Bishop Montgomery is accredited by the Western Association of Colleges and Schools. A Development Advisory Board, which includes alumni and parents as members, organizes financial support for school improvements.

THE CAMPUS. Bishop Montgomery High School is situated on a 24-acre campus with three primary academic buildings housing 43 classrooms, three computer laboratories, and a library. A newly constructed 14,000-square-foot Student Activities Center, theater, gymnasium, weight room, team room, faculty center, chapel, administrative building, and stadium complete the facilities. Athletic fields are laid out on the campus outside the main cluster of school buildings.

THE FACULTY. Rosemary Libbon is Principal of the School, and

Yvette Vigon is Vice Principal. Two Assistant Principals and two Deans share the administrative responsibilities.

The men and women who teach serve in eight academic departments. They hold bachelor's and graduate degrees from Arizona State, California Polytechnic Institute (Pomona), California State University (Chico, Dominguez, Fullerton, Los Angeles), Dominican University, Long Beach State, Long Island University, Loyola Marymount, Occidental, Pepperdine, Rhode Island State, San Diego State, San Jose State, Siena Heights Michigan, Washington State, and the Universities of California (Berkeley, Los Angeles, Santa Barbara), Manila, Nevada, Notre Dame, San Juan, South Dakota, Texas, Wisconsin, and New Mexico.

BISHOP MONTGOMERY HIGH SCHOOL

First aid and supervision of student-required medications are handled by the Attendance Office. Emergency medical services are available nearby.

STUDENT BODY. The School enrolls 1200 boys and girls in Grades 9 through 12. They come from 17 parishes in the South Bay area. The School does not discriminate on the basis of race, color, national or ethnic origin in admissions, financial aid, or any of its educational policies. Approximately one third of the students are Caucasian, 16 percent are African-American, 11 percent Asian/Pacific Islander, 16 percent Filipino, and 24 percent Latino. Seventy-six percent of those currently enrolled are Catholic; non-Catholic students are admitted according to clearly stated priorities pertaining to their schooling.

ACADEMIC PROGRAM. The academic year, divided into semesters, begins in late August and extends to early June with vacations of two weeks at Christmas and ten days at Easter. The year is subdivided into six grading periods that provide two progress reports in each semester and final grades at the end of each term. Classes are held five days a week and are normally scheduled in six 50-minute sessions between 8:00 A.M. and 2:10 P.M. with a short mid-morning break and a half-hour for lunch. Variations on the schedule are made to adjust for designated Lab Days, which begin with a 95-minute laboratory session, or to accommodate special events.

To graduate from Bishop Montgomery High School, a student must complete a total of 240 credits, with 5 credits being awarded for each successfully completed semester course. Ordinarily, students carry a six-course load, and they take one course in English and one in Religious Studies in each semester. The distribution of the required credits is as follows: 40 in English; 20 in World Language, all of which must be in a single language; 30 in Social Studies; 40 in Religious Studies; 30 in Mathematics; 20 in Science; 5 in Computer Science; 10 in Fine Arts; 15 in Physical Education; and 30 in electives, which may include advanced studies in various disciplines. The electives are chosen with the help of the guidance department in accordance with the student's educational aims. Programs are tai-

lored to meet the admission requirements of the University of California or the California State Universities.

Some of the courses offered are English 1–2 (language and literature), American Literature, British Literature, Literature and Composition, Shakespeare, The Short Story; French 1–4, German 1–4, Italian 1–3, Latin 1–4, Spanish 1–4, Spanish Literature; Geography and Cultures, World History and Cultures, U.S. History to 1900, U.S. History-20th Century, Current Events and American Government, Economics, Introduction to Anthropology, Psychology, The U.S. After 1945; Introduction to Catholicism, Old Testament, New Testament, Church History, Morality, Social Justice, Christian Vocations, Campus Ministry, Religions of the World, Search for Truth, Spirituality; Pre-Algebra, Algebra 1–2, Geometry, Math Analysis, Introduction to Calculus, Calculus; Biology, Chemistry, Physics, Anatomy and Physiology, Biomedical Practicum; Computer Applications 1–2; Art 1–4, Art Design 1–2, Ceramics 1–2, Computer Design, Dance Performance, Theater Arts 1–2, Mixed Chorus 1–2, Wind Ensemble 1–2; Physical Education (conditioning, fitness), Introduction to Dance, Ethical Health, Aerobics and Nutrition, Weight Training, and coeducational team sports. Honors courses are offered in most departments, and 12 Advanced Placement courses are available in English, French, German, Latin, Spanish, U.S. History, American Government, Calculus, Biology, and Physics.

BISHOP MONTGOMERY HIGH SCHOOL

Of the 336 graduates of 2009, 335 are enrolled in institutions of higher learning, including 250 at four-year colleges, 75 at two-year colleges, and 2 in vocational schools. Of these, 49 matriculated at branches of the University of California and 122 at branches of the State University. Among other institutions where graduates enrolled are Abilene Christian, Arizona State, Boston University, Chapman, Cornell, Gonzaga, Harvard, Harvey Mudd College, Howard, Johns Hopkins, Loyola Marymount, New York University, Pepperdine, Pitzer, Purdue, Santa Clara, Stanford, and the Universities of Arizona, Colorado, Southern California, and Virginia.

The School offers remedial, review, and enrichment courses as well as athletic training and conditioning programs in a summer session from June 23 to August 1.

STUDENT ACTIVITIES. Each class chooses its own officers, and students also elect representatives to the Student Government, which organizes and directs a variety of activities including the newspaper and yearbook, Speech and Debate Club, Scholastic Federation, Key Club, Concordia, and a number of clubs organized to accommodate the expressed interests of students. Instrumental ensembles, the Chorus, and theater productions add to the list of activities.

BISHOP MONTGOMERY HIGH SCHOOL

Bishop Montgomery High School is a member of the Del Rey League and fields varsity, junior varsity, and freshman teams in football, cross-country, basketball, soccer, baseball, golf, volleyball, swimming, tennis, and track and field for boys; girls compete in golf, tennis, volleyball, cross-country, basketball, soccer, softball, swimming, and track. Cheerleading and dance teams lead support for Knights teams athletes.

The School encourages students to participate in community service, and some channel their energies into the Habitat Club, which has helped to build a home and a school in Tijuana, Mexico; contributed to library renovations at inner-city schools in East Los Angeles; and collected books to help the schools sustain their programs.

Two parents' committees, the Athletic Booster Club and the Mothers' Club, provide support for many school activities. Special events on the calendar include Homecoming Weekend, School Musical, class retreats, Christmas Mass, Charity Ball, Sports Banquet, and Teacher Appreciation Day.

ADMISSION AND COSTS. Bishop Montgomery High School seeks students who have the ability and the desire to benefit from its rigorous academic programs. Candidates should also indicate by their behavior and commitments that they are in harmony with the philosophy and goals of the School. The School gives preference to applicants from Catholic feeder schools in the region but accepts non-Catholic students and observes nondiscriminatory standards in admissions and other programs.

The admissions process begins with a family open house in early December when applications become available. The completed application with recommendations must be returned by a specific date in late January. A high school placement test, which requires a $75 testing fee, is given at the end of that month, and decisions are rendered in the first week in March. The registration fee is $500.

In 2009–10, tuition is $6750 for the first child in a family and $5450 for any others. The fees are $300 higher for non-Catholic applicants. Tuition is billed in ten payments from August to May. Parents must sign an agreement to give 10 hours of service to the School each semester and make a deposit of $150 as part of the commitment. The money is credited to their account when the service is completed.

A limited amount of financial aid is offered through the Archdiocesan Education Foundation and through the School. Applications are available through the School.

Principal: Rosemary Libbon
Vice Principal: Yvette Ligon
Dean of Men: Lee Flores
Assistant Principal/Athletics: Steve Miller
Dean of Student Life: Milana McDermott
Director of Admissions: Casey Dunn
Director of Development: Andy Marafino
Director of Campus Ministry: Dorothy Morski
Co-Directors of Athletics: Alexa Johnson & Kareem Mutire

The Bishop's School   1909

7607 La Jolla Boulevard, La Jolla, CA 92037-4799
Tel. 858-459-4021; Fax 858-459-3914
Web Site www.bishops.com; E-mail admissions@bishops.com

The Bishop's School is a college preparatory day school, affiliated with the Episcopal Church, enrolling 780 boys and girls in Grades 6–12. In the fall of 2009, Bishop's welcomed its first sixth-grade class. The 11-acre campus includes a 32,000-square-foot science center, five tennis courts, an aquatic center, two athletic fields, gymnasium, a health and fitness center, library, resource and learning center, five computer laboratories and 350 computers, performing and visual arts facilities, and a parking structure. More than half of the faculty hold advanced degrees. The average class size is 14. The curriculum includes Advanced Placement courses for college credit. Summer programs are scheduled. Tuition: $26,500. Extras: $1350. Financial Aid: $2,500,000. Josie Alvarez is Director of Admissions; Aime-claire Roche (Harvard, B.A.; Columbia, M.A.) is Head of School. *Western Association.*

Brentwood School   1972

100 South Barrington Place, Los Angeles, CA 90049
Tel. 310-476-9633; Fax 310-476-4087
Web Site www.bwscampus.com

Brentwood School, enrolling 993 boys and girls from diverse racial, ethnic, and cultural backgrounds as day students in Kindergarten through Grade 12, is committed to providing an "exceptional liberal arts education" that nurtures each child intellectually, ethically, aesthetically, and athletically. Students in all grades live by an honor code that promotes respect, trust, responsibility, caring, honesty, and community. Set on two campuses four blocks apart, Brentwood School emphasizes a strong foundation of understanding in reading, mathematics, social studies, and science in the early grades in readiness for the challenges of the Upper School. The curriculum features traditional college preparatory subjects, Advanced Placement courses, electives in the arts, and four-day wilderness retreats at national parks. Computer technology is integrated as a learning and research tool throughout the disciplines. Among the extracurricular activities are School Senate and other leadership groups, five publications, plays, musicals, community service, and 77 interscholastic teams schoolwide. Tuition: $24,575–$28,500. Financial Aid: $3,500,000. Mary Beth Barry (K–6) and Keith Sarkisian (7–12) are Directors of Admission; Dr. Michael Pratt is Head of School. *Western Association.*

Calmont School   1977

1666 Las Virgenes Canyon Road, Calabasas, CA 91302
Tel. 818-880-8820; Fax 818-880-8860
Web Site www.calmontschool.org; E-mail calmontschool@earthlink.net

Enrolling 150 boys and girls in 3-year-old Preschool through Grade 9, Calmont School provides "a personalized education in a magnificent natural setting." The School's mission is to establish a strong foundation in the arts and sciences and instill in the students a lifelong commitment to sustainability and environmental stewardship. An extensive community service pro-

California

gram prepares students to make positive contributions to their world. Computer technology, Spanish, library, physical education, art, drama, and music enrich the core curriculum and are integrated into the program, which is carried out on a spacious 22-acre campus. Tuition: $10,800–$19,500. Financial Aid: $300,000. Judith Chamberlain was appointed Head of School in 2001.

Campbell Hall   1944

4533 Laurel Canyon Boulevard, North Hollywood, CA 91607
Mailing Address: P.O. Box 4036, North Hollywood, CA 91617-0036
Tel. 818-980-7280; Fax 818-505-5319
Web Site www.campbellhall.org; E-mail admissions@campbellhall.org

CAMPBELL HALL

Campbell Hall, a coeducational, college preparatory day school affiliated with the Episcopal Diocese of Los Angeles, provides rigorous academic training within the context of the Judeo-Christian heritage. Campbell Hall's philosophy is that students are persons of both faith and reason. In that conviction, it strives to nurture in each child a quest for knowledge that leads to ethical, productive daily living. The curriculum is grounded in the traditional liberal arts, sciences, and humanities, complemented by modern languages, Advanced Placement courses, outdoor education, varied electives, and, for qualified seniors, participation in the UCLA Scholars Program. Classroom learning is enriched by field trips to art museums, the Los Angeles Music Center, and other destinations of educational and aesthetic interest. Students participate in service groups, school government, honor societies, academic teams, drama, chapel aides, and interscholastic sports, among other extracurricular options. A six-week summer session involves academic enrichment, preparation, and review. Tuition: $21,970–$27,285. Financial aid is available. Alice Fleming is Director of Admissions; Julian Bull was appointed Headmaster in 2003. *Western Association.*

The Carey School   1928

One Carey School Lane, San Mateo, CA 94403
Tel. 650-345-8205; Admissions 650-345-4410; Fax 650-345-2528
Web Site www.careyschool.com; E-mail dgoldberg@careyschool.com

The Carey School is a coeducational, independent school enrolling 224 children in Pre-Kindergarten (age 4)–Grade 5. The Carey School seeks to maximize each child's intellectual,

social, creative, emotional, and physical potential. The student-centered curriculum provides a strong educational foundation and is designed to instill a deep, lifelong love of learning. The academic program centers on reading, language arts, math, and social studies, enriched by science, technology, French, Spanish, library studies, music, physical education, and art. Teaching and learning are paced according to the individual student's capabilities in keeping with the differentiated instruction philosophy. After-school programs are offered. Tuition: $13,500–$18,800. Financial aid is available. Dana Goldberg is Director of Admissions; Eric Temple (Columbia, M.Ed.; University of Massachusetts, M.A.) is Head of School.

Cathedral School for Boys   1957

1275 Sacramento Street, San Francisco, CA 94108
Tel. 415-614-5113; Fax 415-771-2547
Web Site www.cathedralschool.net
E-mail madison@cathedralschool.net

CATHEDRAL SCHOOL FOR BOYS

Located adjacent to Grace Cathedral (Episcopal), Cathedral School for Boys enrolls 266 day students in Kindergarten–Grade 8. The School offers a rigorous academic curriculum for boys of all religious and ethnic backgrounds. Each child is encouraged to do his best, and the value of the individual and the development of mutual respect are emphasized. In Grade 2, students may audition for the world-famous Grace Cathedral Choir of Men and Boys. Latin, Mandarin, Spanish, music, art, drama, sports, science and computer labs, and extended care are offered. Environmental education and community service are part of the program. Tuition: $22,500. Adjustable tuition is available. Catherine Madison is Director of Admission; Michael Ferreboeuf is Canon Headmaster.

The Center for Early Education   1939

563 North Alfred Street, West Hollywood, CA 90048-2512
Tel. 323-651-0707; Fax 323-651-0860
Web Site www.centerforearlyeducation.org
E-mail hudnutd@cee-school.org

The Center for Early Education was founded by a group of parents who believed that children's emotional and social development were as important as their educational and academic growth. Enrolling 536 boys and girls in Preschool–Grade 6, The Center seeks to provide a stimulating, contemporary education and emphasizes a student body of different ethnic and socioeconomic backgrounds in a challenging, supportive setting. Team-taught curricular programs are designed to encourage students to become lifelong learners and to instill in them self-esteem, respect for each other, and commitment to the community beyond the school. The Preschool focuses on motor skills, self-mastery, creativity, communication, socialization, and logical and sequential thinking. The Elementary School offers classes and activities on literature, writing, math, science, social studies, art, music, physical education, computers, and library. Community service and service learning are also integrated into the academic curriculum. Day-care, after-school, and summer programs are offered. Financial aid is available. Tuition: $14,370–$21,125. Deedie Hudnut is Director of Admission; Reveta Bowers is Head of School. *Western Association.*

Chadwick School   1935

26800 South Academy Drive, Palos Verdes Peninsula, CA 90274
Tel. 310-377-1543; Admission Ext. 4025; Fax 310-377-0380
Web Site www.chadwickschool.org
E-mail judy.wolstan@chadwickschool.org

Chadwick, a nonprofit, nondenominational, coeducational day school, serves 830 culturally and economically diverse students in Kindergarten–Grade 12. Its mission encourages personal excellence; the mastery of academic, artistic, and athletic skills; and the development of social and individual responsibility. The curriculum emphasizes strong reading, writing, critical thinking, and problem-solving skills as well as effective use of technology in all disciplines. Field trips, international study and service, community service, outdoor education, and Advanced Placement courses enrich the core program. Activities include athletics, drama, music, art, school government, and publications. Tuition: $20,400–$25,100. Financial aid and transportation are available. Judith S. Wolstan is Director of Admission; Frederick T. Hill is Headmaster. *Western Association.*

Chandler School   1950

1005 Armada Drive, Pasadena, CA 91103
Tel. 626-795-9314; Admissions Ext. 177; Fax 626-795-6508
Web Site www.chandlerschool.org; E-mail info@chandlerschool.org

CHANDLER SCHOOL

Thomas and Catherine Chandler founded this coeducational day school to provide children with "innovative, inspired academic programs taught by caring, dedicated faculty." The 4.5-acre campus in the foothills above the Rose Bowl offers sweeping views of the Arroyo Sego. Enrolling 420 students in Kindergarten–Grade 8, the mission of Chandler School is to provide each student with the highest quality and most academically challenging education in a nurturing, balanced, and diverse environment. Academic excellence shares equal empha-

sis with the development of character and values. In the Lower School, language arts, math, science, social studies, and Spanish are enhanced by information technology, library, art, music, and physical education. The Middle School includes diverse electives, a laptop program, community service, personal development classes, competitive sports, and musical and dramatic presentations. After school care and summer programs are available. Tuition: $15,830–$18,350. Financial Aid; $790,490. Gretchen Lurie is Director of Admissions; John Finch was appointed Head of School in 2001. *Western Association.*

Chatsworth Hills Academy   1977

21523 Rinaldi Street, Chatsworth, CA 91311
Mailing Address: P.O. Box 5077, Chatsworth, CA 91313
Tel. 818-998-4037; Fax 818-998-4062
Web Site www.chaschool.org; E-mail info@chaschool.org

Enrolling 225 day boys and girls in Early Childhood–Grade 8, Chatsworth Hills Academy's mission is to fulfill each child's intellectual, artistic, social, and physical potential in a positive, ethical, and supportive environment. Focusing on the "whole child," this college preparatory school in the liberal arts tradition is committed to selective enrollment to permit the involvement of each student in all school programs. Pursuing a spiral curriculum that continually introduces new materials while simultaneously reinforcing previous skills and content, the Early Childhood through Grade 4 programs focus on integrating all subjects, creating a comprehensive and expansive educational experience. Students in Grades 5–8 focus on both skills and content presented throughout the major departments of liberal arts in a college preparatory program that includes English, mathematics, history, science, modern language, and the visual and performing arts. Based on the school's character education program, core values and principles of action have been identified and are practiced throughout the close-knit and supportive community. Tuition: $10,870–$16,520. Ann Gillinger is Head of School. *Western Association.*

Children's Day School   1983

333 Dolores Street, San Francisco, CA 94110
Tel. 415-861-5432; Admission Ext. 337; Fax 415-861-5419
Web Site www.cds-sf.org; E-mail amandar@cds-sf.org

Children's Day School enrolls 315 students in Preschool (3 years)–Grade 8. The School's curriculum promotes academic excellence, encourages creative exploration and critical thinking, and creates an enduring love of learning. Interdisciplinary projects involve students in problem-solving investigations that foster collaborative learning skills. Course work centers on language arts, mathematics, science, and social studies. Spanish, art and environmental education, physical education, and service learning round out the program. The School nurtures the development of the whole child—intellectually, personally, and socially—and measures success by the success of each individual student. Tuition: $2119–$21,190. Aimee Giles is Director of Admission; Rick Ackerly is Head of School.

Chinese American International School   1981
中美國際學校

150 Oak Street, San Francisco, CA 94102
Tel. 415-865-6000; Admission 415-865-6084; Fax 415-865-6087
Web Site www.cais.org; E-mail lv_adibe@cais.org

This coeducational day school, enrolling 445 students in PreKindergarten–Grade 8, provides academic programs through immersion in American and Chinese language and culture. Written and spoken fluency in English and Mandarin are emphasized in all major subjects. A Chinese-speaking background is not required for admittance to PreKindergarten and Kindergarten. Multicultural experiences, creative thinking, and developing confidence in interaction with people from around the world are major themes. Art, music, movement, sports, Chinese calligraphy, and a student exchange program with China are offered. Extended care is available. Tuition & Fees: $20,300. Financial aid is available. Linda Vann-Adibe is Director of Admission; Betty Shon is Head of School. *Western Association.*

Clairbourn School   1926

8400 Huntington Drive, San Gabriel, CA 91775
Tel. 626-286-3108; Admissions Ext. 139; Fax 626-286-1528
Web Site www.clairbourn.org; E-mail admissions@clairbourn.org

CLAIRBOURN SCHOOL

Clairbourn School, an independent day school enrolling 375 boys and girls in Preschool–Grade 8, seeks to attain educational excellence in harmony with the teachings of Christian Science. Its basic elementary program is supplemented by the study of science, art, music, drama, and computers. League sports, Student Council, and scouting are scheduled after school. An academic summer program is also offered. Tuition: $10,250–$17,000. Financial Aid: $150,000. Janna Windsor is Director of Admissions; Robert W. Nafie (University of Minnesota, B.S. 1970; University of Wisconsin, M.A.; The Claremont Graduate School, Ph.D. 1988) was appointed Headmaster in 1979.

The College Preparatory School   1960

6100 Broadway, Oakland, CA 94618
Tel. 510-652-0111; Admissions 510-652-4364; Fax 510-652-7467
Web Site www.college-prep.org
E-mail jonathan@college-prep.org

The College Preparatory School is a coeducational day school enrolling 355 students in Grades 9–12. The School strives to prepare students for productive, ethical lives in college and beyond through a challenging and stimulating education in an atmosphere of consideration, trust, and mutual responsibility. The rigorous academic program prepares students for the most selective colleges, and the student-teacher ratio is low. There are specialized facilities for music, art, dance, drama, and sports. Debate, class retreats, an Intraterm program, and community service are integral features. Tuition: $29,950. Extras: $1000. Financial Aid: $1,700,000. Jonathan Zucker is Director of Admission and Financial Aid; Murray Cohen (Johns Hopkins, Ph.D.) is Head of School. *Western Association.*

Convent of the Sacred Heart Elementary School   1887

2222 Broadway, San Francisco, CA 94115
Tel. 415-563-2900; Admissions 415-292-3113; Fax 415-929-6928
Web Site www.sacredsf.org; E-mail thorp@sacredsf.org

An independent, Catholic day school enrolling 324 girls in Kindergarten–Grade 8, Convent Elementary School, one of the Schools of the Sacred Heart, is part of a four-school complex including Stuart Hall for Boys, Stuart Hall High School, and Convent High School. The School seeks to prepare students for entrance into college preparatory high schools and to develop spiritual and social responsibility. Foreign languages, chorus, art, music, computer science, community service, and interscholastic sports are offered. A coeducational summer school program is also available. Tuition: $22,550. Financial aid is available. Pamela Thorp is Director of Admissions; Anne Wachter, RSCJ (St. Mary's College [Indiana], B.B.A.; University of San Francisco, M.A.), is Head. *Western Association.*

Convent of the Sacred Heart High School   1887

2222 Broadway, San Francisco, CA 94115
Tel. 415-563-2900; Admissions 415-292-3125; Fax 415-929-0553
Web Site www.sacredsf.org; E-mail ccurran@sacredsf.org

Convent of the Sacred Heart High School is part of a four-school complex including Convent Elementary School, Stuart Hall for Boys, and Stuart Hall High School. Convent enjoys a strong partnership with Stuart Hall High School. Students from Convent and Stuart Hall participate together in performing arts, extracurricular programs, student leadership activities, service projects, and social events. This unique opportunity at Schools of the Sacred Heart allows a serious focus on academics for young women and young men along with the benefits of a coeducational campus experience. Computer science, math, languages, science, art, music, sports, and community service are integral to the curriculum; 22 Advanced Placement courses are offered. Tuition: $30,575. Financial aid is available. Caitlin Curran is Admissions Director; Andrea Shurley (University of Texas [Austin], B.A.; Texas State University [San Marcos], M.A.) is Head. *Western Association.*

Cornelia Connelly School   1961

2323 West Broadway, Anaheim, CA 92804
Tel. 714-776-1717; Admissions Ext. 234; Fax 714-776-2534
Web Site www.connellyhs.org; E-mail admissions@connellyhs.org

Cornelia Connelly School is a Catholic, independent, fully accredited, college preparatory high school for girls with an enrollment of 270 young women. Guided by trust, reverence, and respect, girls develop into self-confident, poised, and articulate women, empowered to transform our global society. Honors and Advanced Placement courses are available in all core subjects. Cocurricular activities include an award-winning theater arts program, varsity sports, and numerous clubs and organizations. In addition to rigorous academics, students are encouraged to participate in community service and faith-building activities. Tuition: $11,950. Abby Vanausdoll is Director of Admissions; Sr. Francine Gunther, SHCJ, is Head of School. *Western Association.*

The Country School   1948

5243 Laurel Canyon Boulevard, Valley Village, CA 91607
Tel. 818-769-2473; Fax 818-752-1554
Web Site www.country-school.org; E-mail mgerrard@country-school.org

The Country School, an independent, coeducational, Preschool–Grade 8 school in Los Angeles, ignites the minds and inspires the lives of its students through a multidimensional learning experience. The School creates expansive opportunities that empower students to define and maximize their individual potential. With two credentialed teachers in each classroom, faculty tailor the curriculum to the unique learning styles of individual students. The rigorous academic curriculum is designed to build a strong foundation in language arts, mathematics, and science. Teachers seek to engage the full intellectual capacity of each student through additional studies in music, physical education and sports, the arts, environmental studies, student government, and through learning environments beyond the classroom. The School's highly regarded antibullying program is interwoven throughout the campus to produce a pleasant and respectful learning environment. Its diversity philosophy produces a student population that fully represents the broader community of Los Angeles, to better prepare each student for today's world. Tuition: $20,980–$21,550. Myra Gerrard is Director of Admissions; Joseph Perez is Head of School.

Crane Country Day School 1928

1795 San Leandro Lane, Santa Barbara, CA 93108-9986
Tel. 805-969-7732; Admission Ext. 105; Fax 805-969-3635
Web Site www.craneschool.org; E-mail dwilliams@craneschool.org

Crane Country Day School provides a traditional curriculum in which a thorough foundation in the fundamentals of English, mathematics, science, social studies, and Spanish is approached in an innovative manner. Visual arts, drama, music, athletics, and community service are essential parts of the program. Enrolling 250 boys and girls in Kindergarten through Grade 8, Crane seeks to provide a nurturing environment in which children may grow intellectually, realize personal creativity, develop self-assurance, and gain an appreciation of and respect for the diversity of the world around them. Tuition: $20,635–$21,695. Financial Aid: $800,000. Debbie Williams is Director of Admission; Joel Weiss (Harvard Graduate School of Education, M.Ed. 1983) was appointed Head of School in 2000.

Crespi Carmelite High School 1959

5031 Alonzo Avenue, Encino, CA 91316-3699
Tel. 818-345-1672; Fax 818-705-0209
Web Site www.crespi.org

CRESPI CARMELITE HIGH SCHOOL

Crespi Carmelite High School is a Catholic, college preparatory day school for approximately 600 young men in Grades 9–12. The School seeks to provide a holistic model of education emphasizing the spiritual, intellectual, moral, and social development of students. English, mathematics, science, social studies, religion, foreign language, and fine arts courses are required each year. Nineteen honors courses, 19 Advanced Placement classes, and electives such as Film, International Relations, Web Design, Becoming a Man, World Music, and Law are also offered. The average class size is 22 students. School government, Campus Ministry, National Honor Society, California Scholarship Federation, Mock Trial, *The Celt*, the school newspaper, ethnic dinners, and cultural awareness, classics, debate, fishing, and biking clubs are among the extracurricular activities. Sports available include cross-country, water polo, soccer, tennis, swimming, golf, football, basketball, lacrosse, and wrestling. All students perform 100 hours of community service before graduation. All graduates are qualified for colleges and universities. Tuition: $11,500 + Fees. Financial aid is available. Robert Kodama is Admissions Director; Fr. Paul Henson is Principal; Fr. Tom Schrader is President. *Western Association.*

Crestview Preparatory School 1986

140 Foothill Boulevard, La Cañada, CA 91011
Tel. 818-952-0925; Fax 818-952-8470
Web Site www.crestviewprep.org; E-mail mkidd@crestviewprep.org

CRESTVIEW PREPARATORY SCHOOL

Enrolling 240 boys and girls in Kindergarten–Grade 6, Crestview Preparatory School seeks to provide a balanced and healthy learning environment where students can thrive intellectually, creatively, physically, and socially. The School emphasizes self-esteem and social awareness while instilling values of responsibility, integrity, and respect. The curriculum centers on building strong skills in reading, creative writing, spelling, language arts, social science, math, science, and critical thinking. Music, Spanish, art, computer technology, and physical education complete the program. Parental involvement demonstrates to children their commitment to education while providing important support of the School's mission. Extended day care and a summer program are optional. Tuition: $12,866. Michele Poteet is Director of Admissions; Marie Kidd is Head of School.

Curtis School 1925

15871 Mulholland Drive, Los Angeles, CA 90049
Tel. 310-476-1251; Fax 310-476-1542
Web Site www.curtisschool.org

Curtis school in Los Angeles, California, is an independent day school enrolling boys and girls in Developmental Kindergarten through Grade 6. The campus is situated in suburban Los Angeles, adjacent to the San Diego Freeway and the top of the Sepulveda Pass. The School takes advantage of the opportunities afforded in the Los Angeles area for field trips to sites of historical, cultural, and environmental interest. Students travel to and from school on buses provided by an independent company or in car pools arranged by parents.

Curtis School was founded in 1925 as a proprietary school by Carl Curtis and was continued after a 1937 reorganization by his nephew, Carl F. Curtis. In 1964, the School was purchased by Willard E. Badham, who had been the athletic director for 18 years, and two partners. Over the next 10 years, enrollment grew from 100 to 400 under his leadership. The School was reorganized as a nonprofit corporation in 1975, and Mr. Badham continued as Headmaster. Curtis School moved to the Mulholland site in 1981.

Since its founding, the goal of Curtis School has been to provide sound academic training and to develop young people who are thoughtful, creative, and responsible citizens. A standard dress or uniform is worn in all grades. Morals and values are emphasized in daily teaching. Students also organize service projects to help the needy or handicapped. Because of the value the School places on a sound body, physical education and athletics are vital to the program, and all students engage in physical education daily.

Curtis School is governed by a self-perpetuating Board of Trustees, which meets six times a year. The School holds membership in the National Association of Independent Schools and The California Association of Independent Schools, among other affiliations. The Parents' Association and the Alumni Association, which represents 3300 living graduates, assist the School in social, cultural, and fund-raising activities.

THE CAMPUS. The 27-acre campus, shaded by mature trees, is located in the Santa Monica Mountains and is normally cooled by breezes off the ocean. Athletic fields and grassy malls surround low-rise, Spanish mission-style buildings with red tile roofs and functional design.

CURTIS SCHOOL

In addition to regular classroom buildings, the main features are the Ahmanson Building, a multipurpose structure housing the auditorium and art, music, and science rooms; the library/administration facility; and the Pavilion, a performing arts/gymnasium complex. The library contains more than 16,000 volumes. In addition to fields for football, baseball, soccer, and track, athletic facilities include a 25-yard heated swimming pool, a volleyball court, a tennis court, a handball/racquetball court, and three basketball courts.

The School-owned plant is valued at $20,000,000.

THE FACULTY. In 2009, Peter W. Smailes was named the sixth Headmaster of Curtis School. During his 13-year tenure at Curtis, he has held many titles including English teacher, Dean of Upper School, Head of Middle School, and Outplacement Advisor. Long respected as an educational leader in West Los Angeles and widely credited for many of the struc-

tural and programmatic improvements made at Curtis over the last decade, Peter Smailes is committed to leading the School in a manner that is both forward-looking and honors its traditions and mission.

Faculty members are graduates of such institutions as Brigham Young, Bucknell, Connecticut College, Emory, Illinois State, Ohio State, Pennsylvania State, Scripps College, United States International, and the Universities of California, Colorado, and North Carolina.

CURTIS SCHOOL

Faculty benefits include health insurance, a retirement plan, Social Security, educational and personal development grants, and leaves of absence.

A health officer is on duty full-time at the School, and emergency facilities are available nearby at the UCLA Hospital.

STUDENT BODY. In 2008–09, Curtis School enrolled 498 day boys and girls in Developmental Kindergarten–Grade 6. Students represented Bel Air, Malibu, Marina del Rey, Pacific Palisades, Santa Monica, and other communities in the Los Angeles area.

ACADEMIC PROGRAM. Curtis School offers a well-balanced academic program, with necessary skills taught in lively and creative ways designed to teach students to read, write, speak, compute, and reason.

Most students enter Curtis in Developmental Kindergarten or Kindergarten. The Lower Elementary Division (DK–Grade 2) aims to foster the natural curiosity and love of learning in young children. Reading is taught balancing elements of both phonics and whole language, and literature is a part of every classroom. The language arts curriculum stresses written and oral expression as well as the fundamental skills of grammar and spelling. The mathematics program also seeks a balance between conceptual understanding, problem solving, and the acquisition of basic skills. Social studies, a lab-based, hands-on science program, computers, and library round out the academic program.

The Upper Elementary Division (Grades 3–6) focuses on the skills and attitudes needed for secondary school success. Writing, reasoning, and experiential and cooperative learning are emphasized. The English program continues to utilize literature with focus on comprehension and fluency. Writing remains at the core of the program, and students explore poetry and a variety of other genres. The formal written report is also a key part of the Upper Elementary experience. The structure of language—grammar, syntax, and usage—increases in importance at these grade levels. Mathematics embraces a broad range of concepts and skills, incorporating the use of calculators and computers. The social studies and science programs become more project-oriented and are integrated with other subjects whenever possible. Students learn computer and technology skills appropriate to the age group. Many students go on to leading secondary schools at the conclusion of Grade 6.

The arts form an essential part of the Curtis curriculum. Holiday and Spring Concerts are annual events, and drama performances, poetry recitals, and dramatic readings are organized on a regular basis by individual teachers or through the after-school Curtis Extension Program.

STUDENT ACTIVITIES. Representatives from Grades 1 through 6 are elected to the Student Council, which organizes school activities, assists at various functions, and acts as a liaison among students, faculty, and administration.

Athletics are a major component of the Curtis program. Every Curtis student has a sports class each day, and more than 95 percent of students in Grades 4–6 participate in the extensive interscholastic sports program, which emphasizes sportsmanship and fair play. Girls' team sports include volleyball, basketball, soccer, and track, while boys' teams compete in flag football, soccer, baseball, basketball, and track. Students in all age groups swim and learn water safety skills in the Curtis pool. Middle School students may participate on the swim and debate teams as well as the award-winning orchestra and choir.

Field trips, many of them subject-related, are planned for all grades to take advantage of the cultural, historical, and community activities in the Los Angeles area. A wide range of performing arts events are scheduled for the entire School. Grades 5 and 6 take field trips to eastern cities, including Washington, D.C., during the spring break.

CURTIS SCHOOL

Special events on the school calendar include the Back to School Picnic, Curtis Fair, Holiday Program, Spring Event, Dad's Day, and Grandparent's Day.

ADMISSION AND COSTS. Curtis School seeks all-around students who will be good citizens. Students are accepted in all grades on the basis of entrance examinations and standardized test results, personal and teacher recommendations, and an interview at the School. A $150 fee is required with the application.

Tuition is $20,950 for Developmental Kindergarten–Grade 6. Uniforms, transportation, and field trip charges are extra. There is a one-time New Family Fee of $1500. Tuition insurance and payment plans are offered. The School awards more than $500,000 annually in financial aid on the basis of need.

Chief Financial Officer: Daniel Rothbauer
Director of Admissions: Mimi Petrie
Accounting Manager: Kate Fox
Director of Athletics: Mark Nott

Ecole Bilingue de Berkeley   1977

1009 Heinz Avenue, Berkeley, CA 94710
Tel. 510-549-3867; Fax 510-845-3209
Web Site www.eb.org

In an environment where "multiculturalism is a fundamental way of life," Ecole Bilingue de Berkeley enrolls 530 boys and girls from 46 nationalities in Preschool–Grade 8; over 30 percent are students of color, and 63 percent of teachers are native speakers of French. The carefully structured curriculum, taught in French and English, is designed to develop and educate the whole child intellectually, physically, and socially. Basic skills are imparted through hands-on projects; reading and writing begin in Grade 1; Spanish and Chinese are introduced in the Middle School. The core program is enriched through technology, field trips, and extracurricular activities. EB is accredited by the French Ministry of Education and the California Independent School Association. Tuition: $17,930–$20,550. Brigitte Bastrenta is Director of Admissions; Frédéric Canadas is Head of School. *Western Association.*

Foothill Country Day School   1954

1035 West Harrison Avenue, Claremont, CA 91711
Tel. 909-626-5681; Admissions Ext. 120; Fax 909-625-4251
Web Site www.foothillcds.org; E-mail dzondervan@foothillcds.org

Foothill Country Day School, founded in 1954 by Howell and Betty Webb, aims to provide an exciting environment in which children can reach their full academic potential and develop character and values. The School is expanding to include up to 360 students in Kindergarten–Grade 8 and children ages 3–5 in an associated preschool, The Seedling School. The challenging curriculum emphasizes mastery of skills in core subjects, with enrichment in Spanish, Latin, technology, drama, music, art, library skills, and physical education. Students participate in community service projects, field trips, international travel, and daily chapel programs. After-school and summer programs are available. Tuition: $15,718–$16,318. Denise Zondervan is Admissions Director; Clint Taylor, Ed.D., is Headmaster.

Francis Parker School   1912

6501 Linda Vista Road, San Diego, CA 92111
Tel. 858-569-7900; Admission 858-874-3380; Fax 858-569-0621
Web Site www.francisparker.org; E-mail admission@francisparker.org

Francis Parker School seeks to offer a superior college preparatory education in a diverse, family-oriented environment to 1230 boys and girls enrolled as day students in Junior Kindergarten through Grade 12. The School provides a challenging curriculum that fosters independence, responsibility, and character education. Along with 25 Advanced Placement courses and an innovative curriculum, Francis Parker School provides its students with an extensive athletic program, a comprehensive arts program, and opportunities to grow through service, leadership, and community involvement. Tuition: $16,860–$22,390. Financial Aid: $2,000,000. Judy Conner is Director of Admission; Dr. Richard M. Blumenthal (Harvard University, M.A., Ph.D.) is Head of School. *Western Association.*

Gateway School   1970

126 Eucalyptus Avenue, Santa Cruz, CA 95060
Tel. 831-423-0341; Admissions Ext. 302; Fax 831-454-0843
Web Site www.gatewaysc.org; E-mail admissions@gatewaysc.org

Gateway School is an independent, coeducational day school enrolling 275 students in Kindergarten through Grade 8. With its focus on active learning, small classes, and self-discovery, Gateway aims to develop confident, compassionate, articulate, and engaging students. In a theme-based curriculum, traditional core subjects are complemented by the visual and performing arts, music, physical education, and field trips. Spanish begins in Grade 1. Two hands-on science programs, Life Lab and MARE (marine science), teach environmental stewardship. Grades 6–8 engage in service projects for the greater community. Before- and after-care programs are available. Gateway is a member of the National Association of Independent Schools and California Association of Independent Schools. Tuition: $12,760–$13,970. There is need-based financial aid. Colleen Sullivan is Director of Admissions; Percy L. Abram, Ph.D., is Head of School. *Western Association.*

The Gillispie School 1952

7380 Girard Avenue, La Jolla, CA 92037-5139
Tel. 858-459-3773; Fax 858-459-3834
Web Site www.gillispie.org

The Gillispie School arose from a commitment shared by Ada Gillispie and her husband, Samuel, a local pediatrician and prominent citizen, to care for and educate children in need. Today, the School has evolved into a dynamic community of teachers and learners who seek to grow intellectually, creatively, physically, and socially. Enrolling 305 boys and girls in Early Childhood–Grade 6, Gillispie's preparatory curriculum imparts the skills, comprehension, and knowledge students will need for success in middle school. Grade 3–6 use laptops for research and discovery. Reading, language arts, math, science, and social studies are enhanced by specialty classes in Spanish, art, writing, science, library skills, and physical education. Youngsters are introduced to musical concepts through singing, playing instruments, and movement, while older grades learn digital music recording, podcasting, and composition. Summer camps are offered. Tuition: $12,280–$17,130. Financial aid is available. Margie Edwards is Director of Admissions; Alison Fleming is Head of School. *Western Association.*

The Hamlin School 1863

2120 Broadway, San Francisco, CA 94115
Tel. 415-922-0300; Admission 415-674-5400; Fax 415-674-5445
Web Site www.hamlin.org; E-mail aquino@hamlin.org

The oldest nonsectarian day school for girls in the West, Hamlin enrolls 400 girls in Kindergarten–Grade 8. The School seeks to educate talented young women to meet the challenges of their times. It provides a balanced curriculum of humanities, science, mathematics, and fine arts in facilities that include the 13,000-volume Corinne Ruiz Hester Library, three science laboratories, a computer center, art studios, a theater, and an outdoor play area. Extended-day care and after-school activities are offered, and intramural sports are scheduled after classes. Summer and vacation camps are available. Tuition: $23,475. Financial Assistance: $1,200,000. Lisa Lau Aquino '81 is Director of Admission; Wanda M. Holland Greene (Columbia University, B.A., M.A.) is Head of School.

Harbor Day School 1952

3443 Pacific View Drive, Corona del Mar, CA 92625
Tel. 949-640-1410; Fax 949-640-0908
Web Site www.harborday.org; E-mail dphelps@harborday.org

Harbor Day School, an elementary school enrolling over 400 boys and girls in Kindergarten–Grade 8, is located on a 6-acre site overlooking the Pacific Ocean. The School has a challenging academic program, competitive athletics, and an outstanding visual and performing arts program. Harbor Day School is

committed to providing a warm environment conducive to the development of character and good citizenship. Facilities include a library of more than 14,000 volumes, three fully equipped science laboratories, four computer science centers,

HARBOR DAY SCHOOL

three art studios complete with ten pottery wheels and two kilns, a woodshop, a 400-seat performing arts center, a gymnasium, a greenhouse, and athletic fields. Tuition: $16,315. Financial aid is available. Kristin H. Rowe is Director of Admissions; Douglas E. Phelps (Pepperdine University, B.A., M.S.) is Head of School. *Western Association.*

The Harker School 1893

Lower School (K–5): 4300 Bucknall Road, San Jose, CA 95130
Middle School (6–8): 3800 Blackford Avenue, San Jose, CA 95117
Upper School (9–12): 500 Saratoga Avenue, San Jose, CA 95129
Tel. 408-249-2510; Fax 408-984-2325
Web Site www.harker.org; E-mail admissions@harker.org

THE HARKER SCHOOL

Harker provides a strong college preparatory curriculum for more than 1700 day students in Kindergarten–Grade 12. The core philosophy of the program is to develop intellectual curiosity, personal accountability, and a love of learning in all students. The curriculum includes state-of-the-art computer technology, AP courses, and challenging electives. Students participate in school government, athletics, award-winning performing arts, and numerous clubs. The diverse environment resulted in multiple college offers for 99 percent of the Class of 2009 and National Merit Recognition for 54 percent. Summer offerings are available. Tuition: $22,874–$33,927. Nan Nielsen is Director of Admissions & Financial Aid; Christopher Nikoloff is Head of School. *Western Association.*

Harvard-Westlake School   1989

Grades 7–9: 700 North Faring Road, Los Angeles, CA 90077
  Tel. 310-274-7281; Admission 310-288-3200;
  Fax 310-288-3212
Grades 10–12: 3700 Coldwater Canyon, North Hollywood, CA 91604
  Tel. 818-980-6692; Fax 818-487-6631
  Web Site www.hw.com

Harvard-Westlake is a college preparatory day school enrolling 1580 boys and girls in Grades 7–12. The School seeks able, interested students who reflect the diversity of Greater Los Angeles. It aims to provide an education that enables students to appreciate and develop their spiritual, intellectual, and emotional gifts. Music, arts, and publications are offered; Advanced Placement courses are available in all disciplines. Community service and sports are extracurricular activities. There are student exchanges with schools abroad and a summer program. Tuition: $27,825. Elizabeth Gregory is Director of Admission; Thomas C. Hudnut (Princeton, A.B. 1969; Tufts, A.M. 1970) is President; Jeanne Huybrechts (University of Detroit, B.A. 1972; California State [Northridge], B.S. 1986; University of California [Los Angeles], Ed.D. 1999) is Head. *Western Association.*

Head-Royce School   1887

4315 Lincoln Avenue, Oakland, CA 94602
Tel. 510-531-1300; Admissions Ext. 2113; Fax 510-530-8329
Web Site www.headroyce.org; E-mail cepstein@headroyce.org

Head-Royce School is an independent, coeducational day school enrolling 800 students in Kindergarten–Grade 12. Founded in 1887, the School seeks students committed to scholarship, diversity, and citizenship. Head-Royce offers a challenging program in the liberal arts and sciences in a supportive environment. Honors and Advanced Placement courses and accelerated programs are available in the Upper School. Tuition: $20,100–$28,000. Financial Aid: $2,800,000. Catherine Epstein is Director of Admissions and Financial Aid; Paul D. Chapman (Yale, B.A.; Stanford, M.A., Ph.D.) was appointed Head of the School in 1984. *Western Association.*

The John Thomas Dye School   1929

11414 Chalon Road, Los Angeles, CA 90049
Tel. 310-476-2811; Fax 310-476-8675
Web Site jtdschool.com; E-mail jhirsch@jtdschool.com

THE JOHN THOMAS DYE SCHOOL in Los Angeles, California, is an independent, coeducational day school enrolling approximately 320 students from Kindergarten through Grade 6. The campus occupies 11 hilltop acres in Bel Air overlooking Santa Monica, Palos Verdes, and the Pacific Ocean. The homelike and inviting campus provides a country environment in the midst of the Greater Los Angeles urban area. Students enjoy easy access to the city's parks, zoo, museums, libraries, and performing arts centers. They are within reach of nearby beaches, mountains, and national parks.

In 1929, founders Cathryn Robberts Dye and her husband, John Thomas Dye II, started the Brentwood Town and Country School in their home for their only son, John Thomas Dye III, and his friends. Known to their students as Aunty Cathryn and Uncle John, the Dyes sought to nurture children in a loving atmosphere.

The School's reputation for academic excellence, strong ethics, and its unique learning environment attracted many new students. By 1949, the School had outgrown its home. A new, larger facility called The Bel Air Town and Country School was built on the present site. In 1959, the School was renamed in honor of John Thomas Dye III, who was killed in action during World War II. Mr. and Mrs. Dye served as Headmaster and Headmistress until they retired in 1963.

THE JOHN THOMAS DYE SCHOOL.

The vision of the founders is being carried into the 21st century by a new generation of leadership. Building on the history and core strength of the School, the present Headmaster, Raymond R. Michaud, Jr., and his elected 18-member Board of Trustees, strive to prepare children for a rapidly changing world. The basics—reading, writing, mathematics, science, history, the arts, athletics, problem solving, self-esteem, social skills, and respect for individuality—are still at the heart of the program. Because technology skills and the ability to gather and process information are vital to today's children, the entire School is linked by a state-of-the-art computer network to the Internet and the Worldwide Web.

The John Thomas Dye School, a nonprofit corporation, is accredited by the Western Association of Schools and Colleges and the California Association of Independent Schools. It is a member of the National Association of Independent Schools. One hundred percent of the School's endowment fund is actively invested. There are 2000 living alumni, many of whom continue their relationship with the School through a variety of supportive activities, including Development.

THE CAMPUS. At the center of the campus is John Dye Hall, which houses administrative offices, an assembly hall, a music room, and computer and science labs. Classrooms are located in two identical wings extending east and west from the main building. The Lower School (three Kindergarten classrooms and a K–3 Science Center) is located in a separate adjoining building. A multipurpose facility on the lower field furnishes a spacious gymnasium, an art studio, and a library with more than 13,000 volumes. Also on the grounds are two large outdoor play areas for the younger children, an athletic field for physical education and after-school sports program, and a 5-acre hiking canyon used as a living science classroom. The plant is owned by the School.

THE FACULTY. Raymond R. Michaud, Jr., has been affiliated with The John Thomas Dye School for 32 years and has been its Headmaster since 1980. He holds a bachelor's degree in History from the University of San Francisco, where he was also Assistant Director of Admissions. He received his M.A. in Educational Psychology from California Lutheran University and has held teaching and administrative positions at Harvard-Westlake School in Los Angeles.

All 46 men and women on the full-time faculty hold baccalaureates, and nearly half have earned advanced degrees. Faculty benefits include medical/dental/vision plans, life insurance, a retirement and flexible spending plan, Social Security, and long-term disability. All faculty and staff are trained in first aid and CPR by the Red Cross, and medical emergencies are handled at the nearby UCLA Medical Center.

STUDENT BODY. Students come primarily from West Los Angeles, but also from many different areas of the city and its suburbs. They are about evenly divided between boys and girls. There are three classes in Kindergarten and two each in Grades 1–6. Each classroom has two full-time teachers. One of the School's goals is to have its student body represent the cultural, economic, and ethnic diversity of the community.

ACADEMIC PROGRAM. The school year, from September to June, includes Thanksgiving, winter, and spring vacations and observances of several national and religious holidays. A typical day, including seven class periods, morning recess, and lunch, begins at 8:05 A.M. and ends at 3:05 P.M. for all students. Families may drop students off at school as early as 7:15 A.M. For an extra charge, an After-School Program lasting until 5:30 P.M. is also available.

THE JOHN THOMAS DYE SCHOOL

Classes are small, with a 7:1 student-faculty ratio. Homework is part of the school program beginning in Kindergarten. Grades are sent to parents three times a year, and parent-teacher conferences are held at least twice a year. School-

developed tests and Educational Records Bureau tests are conducted every spring to assess student progress.

The integrated curriculum focuses on the interrelationships among various disciplines. Problem solving and effective reading, writing, and oral communication skills are emphasized. Students are grouped heterogeneously to encourage them to learn from one another. In Kindergarten through Grade 4, classes are self-contained; fifth and sixth grades are departmentalized. Core subjects include reading, writing, and verbal skills; mathematics; social studies; and science. All students are taught by specialists in art, computers, library, music, and physical education.

THE JOHN THOMAS DYE SCHOOL

After graduation, 100 percent of the Class of 2009 entered leading independent secondary schools in Los Angeles.

STUDENT ACTIVITIES. Boys and girls in Grades 4–6 may develop leadership and initiative by serving on the elected student government. Officers and four representatives from each of these grades are chosen by their peers. Assisted by a faculty advisor, the group plans student activities, including community outreach projects. In recent years, John Dye students have held Thanksgiving drives for the needy, adopted Head Start families, and raised money for victims of Hurricane Katrina.

After-school athletics for Grades 4-6 include flag football, basketball, baseball, soccer, and track for boys. Girls compete in basketball, volleyball, soccer, and track. There are teams for every ability level, and everyone is encouraged to participate.

Students in Grades 4–6 also publish a school newspaper and a creative writing magazine. Older students mentor younger students; as an example, sixth graders act as Big Brothers and Sisters to first graders. Students may also serve on the Green Team, which takes responsibility for the school recycling program, and the Community Service Club. Frequent informal student variety shows, called Music for Lunch Bunch, entertain the school community. The sixth-grade play is an annual success.

Guest artists and lecturers visit the School; the Parents' Association plans field trips to enrich the classroom experience. The Cultural Resource Project invites families to share their culture, traditions, and resources with the school community. The celebration of holidays and special events is a constant cycle in the life of the School. Back to School Night, Open House, Halloween, Thanksgiving, Hanukkah, Christmas, the Candle

Lighting Ceremony, Grandparents' Day, the School Birthday, the fair, numerous festivals and feasts, and graduation provide lasting memories.

ADMISSION AND COSTS. John Thomas Dye welcomes bright, capable boys and girls who show promise of becoming strongly motivated, intellectually curious students capable of benefiting from the growth opportunities the School offers.

Acceptance of a candidate is based upon available space and upon an assessment of the child's readiness and academic ability. A study of his or her previous school record and of the results of School-administered testing helps determine readiness. Both standardized and teacher-developed tests are used. Children of alumni and siblings of current students are given priority once they have met the admissions requirements. Application, with a $125 fee, should be made one year prior to desired enrollment. The new Admissions cycle begins on August 1 and ends the third week in March, when notification of acceptance status is mailed out.

Tuition for the 2009–10 school year is $21,500 for Kindergarten–Grade 6. Required uniforms are extra. A $2000 one-time New Student Fee helps support the School's Financial Aid Program, which awards funds based on financial need. In 2009–10, the School distributed more than $500,000 in financial aid.

Assistant Heads: Josie Bahedry (K–3) & Nat Damon (4–6)
Director of Admissions: Judy Hirsch
Director of Development: Lisa Doherty
Business Manager: Robert E. Suppelsa

La Jolla Country Day School   1926

9490 Genesee Avenue, La Jolla, CA 92037
Tel. 858-453-3440; Admission Ext. 132; Fax 858-453-8210
Web Site www.ljcds.org; E-mail kjohnson@ljcds.org

LA JOLLA COUNTRY DAY SCHOOL

La Jolla Country Day School is a coeducational, college preparatory school committed to high standards. Enrolling approximately 1050 students in Nursery–Grade 12, Country Day has been developing scholars, artists, and athletes of character for more than 80 years. The 24-acre campus is nearing completion of a comprehensive multimillion-dollar campus redevelopment. New buildings include a state-of-the-art Grades 5–8 middle school, a library/academic center, an arts and science complex, and a new Kindergarten/Lower School complex. The School educates the whole child—intellectually, physically, creatively, socially, and emotionally. A low student-teacher ratio enables faculty to enhance each student's innate talents and abilities within a dynamic educational environment. The dedicated faculty has an average tenure of 16 years. Tuition assistance, extended-day care, and transportation are available. Tuition:

$16,353–$24,828. Vincent Travaglione is Director of Admission; Christopher Schuck (Princeton, B.A.; University of Pennsylvania, M.A.) is Head of School. *Western Association.*

Laurence School   1953

13639 Victory Boulevard, Valley Glen, CA 91401
Tel. 818-782-4001; Fax 818-782-4004
Web Site www.laurenceschool.com
E-mail admissions@laurenceschool.com

Over the past five decades, Laurence School has provided an "outstanding learning environment" for children in Kindergarten–Grade 6 that focuses on their total development—social, emotional, physical, and the ever-important academic. Laurence's rich, well-balanced curriculum and state-of-the-art facilities motivate its 300 students to understand important concepts, refine higher-level thinking skills, explore their special interests and talents, engage in real-world discovery, and connect learning to their everyday environment. Laurence's nationally recognized character education and community service programs instill timeless values of good character and exemplary citizenship in each student. The integrated curriculum is enriched by Spanish, music, drama, art, physical education, computer technology, library, and science lab. Activities engage students in gardening, cooking, school governance, Kids' Court, Mandarin, and interscholastic sports. Laurence is a member of the California Association of Independent Schools. Tuition: $19,900. Marvin Jacobson is Founder and Head of School; Associate Head Lauren Wolke is Director of Admissions. *Western Association.*

Live Oak School   1971

1555 Mariposa Street, San Francisco, CA 94107
Tel. 415-861-8840; Admissions Ext. 220; Fax 415-861-7153
Web Site www.liveoaksf.org; E-mail admissions@liveoaksf.org

Live Oak, a day school enrolling 257 boys and girls in Kindergarten–Grade 8, supports the potential and promise in every child. Live Oak aims to provide an exemplary education in traditional disciplines while developing classical thinking skills, confidence, integrity, and compassion. Art, music, drama, Spanish, Advanced Spanish, physical education, intramural athletics, and frequent field trips support the core curriculum. Extended care and a summer program are also available. Located in the sunny Potrero Hill neighborhood of San Francisco, the School enjoys strong neighborhood relationships in its urban setting. Parent participation is an integral component of the school community. Live Oak admits a section of students in Kindergarten and Grade 6. Tuition: $21,150–$21,600. Need-based tuition assistance is available. Tracey Gersten is Director of Admissions; Holly Horton (Briarcliff, B.S.; Wheelock, M.S.) is Head of School.

Lycée Français La Pérouse   1967

PS–Grade 5: 755 Ashbury Street, San Francisco, CA 94117
Tel. 415-661-5232, Ext. 2100; Fax 415-661-0945
Web Site www.lelycee.org; E-mail admissions@lelycee.org
PS–Grade 5: 330 Golden Hind Passage, San Francisco, CA 94925
Tel. 415-661-5232, Ext. 3100; Fax 415-924-2849
Web Site www.lelycee.org; E-mail admissions@lelycee.org
Grades 6–12: 1201 Ortega Street, San Francisco, CA 94122
Tel. 415-661-5232, Ext. 1100; Fax 415-661-0246

The Lycée Français La Pérouse, the only immersion school in San Francisco, celebrated its 40th anniversary in 2007. The college preparatory school welcomes more than 908 children from pre-Kindergarten to Grade 12 on three campuses where all students follow the authentic French program of the National Education. Students from many nationalities evolve in a truly multicultural environment. The rigorous curriculum teaches students to think, opens their minds to other cultures, and prepares them for college. The Lycée Français La Pérouse is accredited by the California Association of Independent Schools and provides students with an American high school diploma, SATs, and Advanced Placement courses in addition to the French Baccalaureate. Tuition: $11,350–$22,285. Isabelle Desmole is Director of Admissions; Frédérick Arzelier is Headmaster.

Marin Academy   1971

1600 Mission Avenue, San Rafael, CA 94901-1859
Tel. 415-453-4550; Admissions 415-453-2808; Fax 415-453-8905
Web Site www.ma.org; E-mail admissions@ma.org

Marin Academy, a college preparatory day school enrolling 400 students in Grades 9–12, asks students to think, question, and create as well as to accept the responsibilities posed by education in a democratic society. The Academy has one real goal: to foster an environment in which every student can take on the greatest possible challenges and succeed at them. An inspiring curriculum, a full interscholastic program, a celebrated fine and performing arts program, and a week-long experiential mini-course program await enrollees for 2010. Tuition: $32,100. Financial Aid: $2,300,000+. Dan Babior is Director of Admissions and Financial Aid; Travis Brownley (University of Virginia, B.A.; Dartmouth College, M.A.L.S.) is Head of School.

Marin Country Day School   1956

5221 Paradise Drive, Corte Madera, CA 94925-2107
Tel. 415-927-5900; Admission 415-927-5919; Fax 415-924-2224
Web Site www.mcds.org; E-mail admission@mcds.org

Marin Country Day enrolls 550 boys and girls in Kindergarten–Grade 8 on its 35-acre waterfront campus bordered by Ring Mountain nature preserve. The curriculum, with an interdisciplinary, hands-on approach, includes English, Spanish, Mandarin, math, physical science, and social science. The arts, athletics, and outdoor education are integral to the program. After-school care and a multicultural summer program are offered. Dedicated faculty, a low student-teacher ratio, and enrichment and extracurricular activities are designed to instill confidence, a joy for learning, and support of the core values of respect, responsibility, and compassion. The School's mission is to be a community that inspires, nurtures, and challenges children to be skilled learners and ethical individuals, motivated to make a difference in the world. Tuition: $22,395–$25,935. Financial aid is available. Jeffrey Escabar is Director of Admission; Dr. Lucinda Lee Katz is Head of School.

Marin Horizon School   1977

305 Montford Avenue, Mill Valley, CA 94941
Tel. 415-388-8408; Fax 415-388-7831
Web Site www.marinhorizon.org
E-mail admissions@marinhorizon.org

Marin Horizon School offers a challenging academic program for 300 students, toddlers to Grade 8. Inspired by Montessori's philosophy, the program nurtures children's innate curiosity and love of learning through an integrated curriculum, small classes, a devoted faculty, and multiage classrooms. Mastery of the fundamentals in core subjects, emphasis on independent critical thinking, leadership, and strong communication and social skills are expected in graduates. Spanish, music, art, phys-

ical education, and library sciences are integrated into the multicultural and interdisciplinary academic program at all levels, enhanced by field trips and an outstanding outdoor education program. Enrichment classes and a summer camp are offered. Tuition: $13,860–$23,255. Tuition assistance is available. Rosalind Hamar is Head of School; Sharman M. Bonus is Director of Admissions.

Marin Primary & Middle School   1975

20 Magnolia Avenue, Larkspur, CA 94939
Tel. 415-924-2608; Admission Ext. 215; Fax 415-924-9351
Web Site www.mpms.org; E-mail info@mpms.org

Founded to encourage children and adults to work together to enjoy a lifelong pursuit of learning, Marin Primary & Middle School enrolls 340 boys and girls in Preschool–Grade 8. Project-based learning and team teaching support a nurturing environment that includes a Library Media Center and an Outdoor Education Center. The core curriculum is enriched by woodworking, music, art, drama, and life skills. Students begin Spanish in Preschool and may continue through eighth grade. Before- and after-school care are offered. Tuition (K–8): $19,650–$23,050. Financial aid is available. Donna Fanfelle and Erin Murphy are Co-Directors of Admission; Julie Elam is Head of School. *Western Association.*

Marlborough School   1889

250 South Rossmore Avenue, Los Angeles, CA 90004
Tel. 323-935-1147; Admissions 323-964-8450; Fax 323-933-0542
Web Site www.marlboroughschool.org
E-mail jeanette.woochitjian@marlboroughschool.org

The oldest independent school for girls in Southern California, Marlborough enrolls 530 students in Grades 7–12. The School is committed to providing a superior college preparatory education in an environment imbued with high ethical values. The curriculum offers 328 classes and 148 courses including 21 Advanced Placement and 15 Honors courses. Average SAT-I scores are 674 Critical Reasoning and 670 Math; graduates enroll in selective colleges nationwide. The campus offers state-of-the-art classroom facilities, performing arts space, and expanded athletic facilities for teams in nine interscholastic sports. Tuition: $28,950. Financial Aid: $1,900,000+. Jeanette Woo Chitjian is Director of Admissions; Barbara E. Wagner (University of Colorado, M.M.E.) is Head of School. *Western Association.*

Marymount High School   1923

10643 Sunset Boulevard, Los Angeles, CA 90077
Tel. 310-472-1205; Admissions Ext. 220; Fax 310-440-4316
Web Site www.mhs-la.org; E-mail ehuebner@mhs-la.org

Marymount High School, established in 1923 by the Religious of the Sacred Heart of Mary, is a Catholic, independent, college preparatory school for girls in Grades 9–12. Hallmarks of the highly personalized and student-centered program include extensive service outreach, a rigorous curriculum that offers 17 Advanced Placement and 9 Honors-level courses, comprehensive cocurricular opportunities, 23 sports teams, and numerous leadership opportunities. All Marymount seniors go on to attend college or university, and each year, students are admitted to some of the most selective academic institutions in the world. Tuition & Fees: $24,600. Mrs. Erica Huebner is Director of Admission; Ms. Jacqueline Landry (Eastern Mennonite College, B.A.; Weston Theological Seminary, M.Div.) is Head of School. *Western Association.*

Marymount of Santa Barbara   1938

2130 Mission Ridge Road, Santa Barbara, CA 93103
Tel. 805-569-1811; Admissions Ext. 131; Fax 805-569-0573
Web Site www.marymountsb.org
E-mail rwilcox@marymountsb.org

Marymount of Santa Barbara is an independent, nondenominational K–8 school enrolling 210 boys and girls. For more than 70 years, the Marymount tradition of excellence has sought to instill a thirst for knowledge, develop core values, and create an intellectually engaging, supportive community. A 9:1 student-faculty ratio, commitment to diversity, accomplished teachers, and state-of-the-art facilities are enhanced by a picturesque 10-acre campus along the Riviera. The rigorous curriculum encourages a love of learning while arts, athletics, and service prepare students to become global citizens possessing leadership skills and diverse talents. Academics include world-class language arts and math curricula, the option of the Kaleidoscope program on world religions or reinforced Catholic studies, and beginning in Kindergarten, technology and foreign language. Facilities include portable wireless computer labs, auditorium and stage, a swimming pool, athletic fields, rock-climbing wall, and basketball and tennis courts. Activities include moviemaking, drama, music, student ambassadors, study skills, scuba diving, basketball, soccer, volleyball, and track. Tuition: $16,210–$18,730. Financial Aid: $700,000. Deborah David is Head of School; Molly Rapp-Seguel is Director of Admission.

Mayfield Junior School   1931

405 South Euclid Avenue, Pasadena, CA 91101
Tel. 626-796-2774; Fax 626-796-5753
Web Site www.mayfieldjs.org

Mayfield Junior School is a Catholic, coeducational independent day school founded and sponsored by the Sisters of the Holy Child Jesus, enrolling 486 students in Kindergarten through Grade 8. The mission of the School is to provide rich educational and cultural opportunities, nurture individual potential, and encourage responsible choices. The core curriculum, consisting of language arts, science, mathematics, religion, foreign language, social studies, the arts, and physical education, is designed to promote a love of learning and a lifelong pursuit of knowledge. Tuition: $15,850; New Student Fee: $2500. Averyl Thielen is Director of Admissions; Joseph J. Gill is Headmaster. *Western Association.*

Mayfield Senior School of the Holy Child   1931

500 Bellefontaine Street, Pasadena, CA 91105-2439
Tel. 626-799-9121; Admissions Exts. 210/287; Fax 626-799-8576
Web Site www.mayfieldsenior.org
E-mail clemmie.phillips@mayfieldsenior.org

Mayfield Senior School, a college preparatory, Catholic, independent school founded by the Sisters of the Holy Child Jesus, enrolls 300 young women in Grades 9–12. Mayfield's curriculum has been carefully constructed to develop each student's full intellectual, spiritual, artistic, physical, emotional, and social potential. Catholic values and tradition guide the daily conduct of the School, which welcomes girls from all religious and cultural backgrounds. In addition to the liberal arts and sciences, Mayfield offers 20 Honors and Advanced Placement courses as well as in-depth training in dance, music, and other special areas through its Conservatory of the Arts. Community service, Student Council, athletics, publications, and plays and concerts are among the activities. Tuition: $19,995. Financial Aid/Merit Awards: $660,000. Rita Curasi McBride is Head of School; Clemmie Phillips is Director of Admissions.

Menlo School   1915

50 Valparaiso Avenue, Atherton, CA 94027
Tel. 650-330-2000; Admissions Ext. 2600; Fax 650-330-2012
Web Site www.menloschool.org
E-mail lisa.schiavenza or cathy.shelburne@menloschool.org

Located 25 miles south of San Francisco, Menlo is a coeducational, college preparatory day school enrolling 750 students in Grades 6–12. Its environment fosters self-reliance while striving to promote growth of mind, body, and spirit. The curriculum features Honors and Advanced Placement courses in all subjects, small class size, and individual attention that engages students in the life of the mind. More than 46 athletic teams provide opportunities for physical development. Visual arts, drama, music, dance, and extracurriculars, including community service, round out student growth. Tuition: $32,000. Financial Aid: $3,700,000. Cathy Shelburne (Upper School) and Lisa Schiavenza (Middle School) are Directors of Admissions; Norman Colb (Brandeis, B.A. 1964; Harvard, M.A.T. 1965) is Head of School.

Mid-Peninsula High School   1979

1340 Willow Road, Menlo Park, CA 94025
Tel. 650-321-1991; Fax 650-321-9921
Web Site www.mid-pen.com; E-mail info@mid-pen.com

MID-PENINSULA HIGH SCHOOL

Set on a state-of-the-art campus, Mid-Peninsula enrolls 145 young men and women in a college preparatory program designed to "help students find individual paths to their personal best." Individual academic programs provide maximum opportunities for youngsters to discover and expand their talents while understanding and overcoming impediments to success. The "Stages of Development" system enables faculty to assess and monitor students' progress based on their unique abilities. Technology-based learning is integrated throughout the curriculum. Graduates typically go on to four-year colleges and universities. Sports, music, drama, and clubs are among the activities. Tuition: $25,462. Barbara Brown is Director of Admissions; Douglas C. Thompson, Ph.D., is Head of School.

The Mirman School for Gifted Children   1962

16180 Mulholland Drive, Los Angeles, CA 90049
Tel. 310-476-2868; Admissions 310-775-8411; Fax 310-775-8433
Web Site www.mirman.org; E-mail bfisher@mirman.org

One of the few schools in the country specifically dedicated to meeting the needs of highly gifted children with IQs of 145 or above, Mirman is a coeducational, ungraded school serving 330 students, ages 5–14. The School provides an educational setting in which children are encouraged to develop physically, socially, and emotionally. Located a short distance from UCLA, the campus includes two computer labs, two science labs, and specialized curricular programs in Spanish, Latin, French, choral and instrumental music, dramatic and visual arts, and athletics. The

THE MIRMAN SCHOOL FOR GIFTED CHILDREN

School was founded by Dr. and Mrs. Norman J. Mirman. Tuition: $21,250–$22,810. Need-based financial aid is available. Mrs. Becky Riley Fisher is Director of Admissions; John Thomas West III is Headmaster.

Mount Tamalpais School   1976

100 Harvard Avenue, Mill Valley, CA 94941
Tel. 415-383-9434; Fax 415-383-7519
Web Site www.mttam.org

MOUNT TAMALPAIS SCHOOL in Mill Valley, California, is a coeducational day school enrolling children in Kindergarten through Grade 8. The suburban community of Mill Valley (population 15,000) is 12 miles north of San Francisco in Marin County. Students have access to the museums, theater, opera, symphony, and ballet of the city as well as the Pacific Ocean (6 miles from the campus) and Mount Tamalpais for hiking and nature study. Private bus service is available between the School and local communities; public bus stops are within walking distance of the campus.

MOUNT TAMALPAIS SCHOOL

Founder and Director Kathleen M. Mecca, Ph.D., Ed.D., established the School in 1976. From its original enrollment of 60 students in Kindergarten–Grade 6, the School has grown to an enrollment of 240 students in Kindergarten–Grade 8.

Mount Tamalpais School seeks to provide students with a solid academic foundation and to foster a genuine enthusiasm for learning. The departmentalized, integrated curriculum focuses on concepts and research skills and permits each teacher to use a variety of methods and materials to strengthen individual skills. In addition, small-group instruction maximizes the inherent potential of each child and fosters respect for each student's interests and abilities.

MOUNT TAMALPAIS SCHOOL

A nonprofit organization, Mount Tamalpais School is governed by a Board of Trustees that includes parents, past parents, alumni, and community members. The Parent Council holds social and fund-raising events and coordinates family volunteer assistance to the School. The School holds membership in the National Association of Independent Schools, the California Association of Independent Schools, the Educational Records Bureau, the Secondary School Admission Test Board, the Educational Testing Service, and the Western Association of Schools and Colleges.

THE CAMPUS. The 12+-acre campus includes a large grass playing field and a playground with a variety of recreational structures. A 1.5-acre cypress grove is used for nature study. The four school buildings, which total more than 32,000 square feet, provide classrooms, a computer lab, an art studio, a faculty workroom, administrative offices, and the Rappaport Library Learning Center. Other facilities include a gymnasium-theater complex, tutorial rooms for individual instrumental instruction and learning assistance, two science laboratories, an art room, and a music room, and the MTSO, an observatory with a retractable roof and large-scale telescopes on adjustable piers. The value of the School-owned plant is more than $10,000,000.

THE FACULTY. Kathleen M. Mecca, Ph.D., Ed.D., has been Director of the School since its founding in 1976. A native of New Jersey, Dr. Mecca is a graduate of the University of California at Los Angeles (B.A. 1965, M.A. 1968, M.S.Ed. 1969), the University of California at Irvine (M.A. 1966), Stanford University (Ed.D. 1971), and the University of California at San Francisco (Ph.D. 1973). She has held teaching and administrative positions in public and private schools in California and has also worked as a reading specialist and child/adolescent psychologist. She was a mentor teacher and master teacher for the California State Department of Education. In addition, she has taught psychology and education courses at the college and graduate school levels.

The 32 full-time faculty hold baccalaureate and graduate degrees representing study at Brown, Bucknell, Columbia, Dartmouth, Dominican, Earlham, Harvard, Middlebury, Oberlin, Ohio State, Oregon State, Princeton, San Diego State, San Francisco State, Stanford, Trinity, Wellesley, and the Universities of California, Chicago, Michigan, Oregon, Pennsylvania, and Wisconsin. There are also part-time instructors who provide additional curricular support.

First aid is available on campus at all times. Paramedics are within 5 minutes of the School, and a hospital emergency room is 15 minutes away by vehicle.

STUDENT BODY. The School enrolls 240 boys and girls in Kindergarten–Grade 8. The students reside in communities throughout Marin County and San Francisco.

ACADEMIC PROGRAM. The 180-day school year, from late August to mid-June, is divided into trimesters and includes a Thanksgiving recess, winter and spring vacations, a mid-winter recess, and all legal holidays. The daily schedule for Kindergarten–Grade 8, from 8:00 A.M. to 3:00 P.M. Monday–Thursday, includes morning and afternoon homeroom periods, eight 40- to 45-minute class periods, a morning recess, and a 40-minute lunch period. After-school care until 6:00 P.M. daily is available to students for an additional hourly fee. On Fridays, the schedule is adjusted to permit 2:15 P.M. dismissal for all students. In order to allow time for parent-teacher conferences in the fall, there is one week of noon dismissals.

An average grade-level homeroom, for which there are at least two teachers, enrolls two classes of 12–14 students, a total of 24–28 students. There is a supervised study hall on Mondays, Wednesdays, and Thursdays from 3:15 to 4:15 P.M.; teachers are available to provide extra help during this time.

Students in Grades 4–8 receive letter grades each trimester in addition to narrative evaluations, and students in Kindergarten–Grade 3 receive narrative evaluations using a qualitative system. Written reports with teacher comments are sent to the parents of all students at the end of each trimester. The School encourages open communication between parents and teachers, and formal parent/teacher/student conferences are scheduled at the end of the first trimester. Throughout the year, parents are urged to consult with the homeroom teachers, who act as the child's counselors, to discuss general progress or concerns.

Homework, ranging from 20 minutes four times a week for the youngest children to approximately an hour a day for students in Grades 6–8, is assigned to provide follow-up, reinforcement, and continuity.

MOUNT TAMALPAIS SCHOOL

The Kindergarten program is developmental and is designed to provide an introduction to the School's curriculum of departmentalized, experiential learning. Learning tasks offer opportunities for enjoyment and success as well as skill development. Students are placed according to developmental criteria that take into account each child's academic, social, and emotional maturation.

For Grades 1–8, the curriculum includes Language Arts/English (reading, literature, language, grammar, spelling, and writing), Geography, Spanish, French, social studies, mathematics, computer science, science, study skills, music, chorus, drama, art, art history, health, physical education, ceramics,

woodworking, dance, movement, and sewing. An Enrichment program during the regular school day for Grades 6–8 provides elective opportunities for students to increase their skills in creative writing, music, drama, computers, dance, fine arts, current events, and film making. For Grades 4–8, values and family life are also offered. Students in Grades 6–8 study Latin in addition to French and Spanish as well as special classes in Shakespeare, Current Events, and Public Speaking. Mandarin and Japanese are electives in Grades 7 and 8. All students receive basic instruction in special etiquette classes during their elementary years.

MOUNT TAMALPAIS SCHOOL

Outdoor Education experiences for Grades 4–8 complement the program of environmental study that begins in Kindergarten. Fourth and fifth graders spend a week at various California historic sites correlated with their social science curriculum. Sixth-grade students have a week at the Point Reyes National Seashore, followed by an all-day sea kayaking trip. Seventh graders spend a week rafting and camping in the American River wilderness. The eighth graders spend a week backpacking in Yosemite National Park.

Mount Tamalpais graduates have entered leading independent secondary schools in California and throughout the United States and have been accepted at such colleges and universities as Arizona State, Boston College, Boston University, Brown, Bucknell, Cornell, Dartmouth, Denison, Dominican, Duke, Georgetown, Harvard, Ithaca, Lewis & Clark, Loyola, Northeastern, Occidental, Pepperdine, Princeton, Reed, Smith, Stanford, Tufts, Tulane, Wellesley, Williams, and the Universities of Arizona, California, Chicago, Colorado, Michigan, Notre Dame, Oregon, Pennsylvania, Southern California, Virginia, and Washington, among others.

STUDENT ACTIVITIES. The Student Council is composed of two representatives, one boy and one girl each, from Grades 3–8. With parent volunteers who help coordinate activities, the Council arranges spirit days, dances, and community service projects. Extracurricular activities include Computer and the Literary Magazine and Yearbook Committees. After-school classes in sewing, woodworking, chess, ceramics, art, dance, drama, voice, yoga, cooking, science adventures, and instrumental music are available for a small fee.

Upper-grade students compete in basketball, soccer, volleyball, cross-country, and track and field with teams from other schools in San Francisco and Marin County. Soccer teams for Kindergarten–Grade 6 play in the Mill Valley Soccer League. Intramural sports include basketball, field hockey, gymnastics, lacrosse, softball, and volleyball.

School spirit days include Halloween, Teddy Bear Day, Gratitude Day, Hat Day, Hawaiian Day, Olympic Day, Field Day, International Day, and Angel Island Day. Traditional events include Grandparents' Day, Founder's Day Picnic, and the Gala Spring Auction.

ADMISSION AND COSTS. Mount Tamalpais School seeks to enroll a diverse group of students who are responsible, willing to learn, and who can reach their full potential in a challenging academic environment. New students are admitted to all grades on the basis of very competitive enrollment criteria: three recommendations (including one from a current teacher), a school visit with an interview, standardized testing, a transcript of grades, and, for Grades 3–8, a writing sample. Parents are encouraged to observe classes in session before submitting an application for the student. Application must be made prior to January 15, 2010. The nonrefundable application fee is $150. The Director and an Admissions Committee handle admissions.

In 2009–10, tuition is $21,500 for Kindergarten–Grade 8. Mount Tamalpais School subscribes to the School and Student Service for Financial Aid. The School offers financial assistance to approximately 18 percent of the students; in 2008–09, approximately $425,000 was awarded on the basis of need.

The Oaks School   1986

6817 Franklin Avenue, Hollywood, CA 90028
Tel. 323-850-3755; Fax 323-850-3758
Web Site www.oaksschool.org; E-mail info@oaksschool.org

THE OAKS SCHOOL

Founded in 1986, The Oaks is a vibrant, creative community where mutual respect and compassion for one another are as important as stimulating intellectual pursuits. Enrolling 148 boys and girls in Kindergarten–Grade 6, the school program is founded on the belief that the best learning opportunities are created when children are able to share in the responsibility for their own learning and where they feel both physically and emotionally safe to take risks, make mistakes, and master skills. Learning at The Oaks is a partnership between a strong academic program designed for deep learning and a rich integration of the arts, physical education, technology, library arts, and personal development. Annual events include a creative athletics Circus, Medieval Pageant, Shakespeare play, and All-School Camp Out. After-school enrichment programs are offered. Tuition: $16,500; New Student Fee: $1000. Financial aid is available. Joan Beauregard is Interim Head of School; Garret Tyau is Admissions Director. *Western Association.*

Ojai Valley School   1911

Lower School: 723 El Paseo Road, Ojai, CA 93023
Tel. 805-646-1423; [Toll-free] 800-433-4687
Fax 805-646-0362
Web Site www.ovs.org; E-mail admission@ovs.org
Upper School: 10820 Reeves Road, Ojai, CA 93023
Tel. 805-646-5593

Ojai Valley School was founded by Edward Yeomans, Sr., who believed that the beautiful surroundings and temperate climate of the region would "stimulate the interests of children in a natural, spontaneous way" and would prepare them for "intelligent, benevolent, and joyous participation" in their communities and the larger world. The coeducational college preparatory school enrolls 325 students in Pre-Kindergarten (age 3)–Grade 12, with 130 five- and seven-day boarders from Grade 3 upward. The liberal arts "curriculum for life" emphasizes the mastery of those skills students need to achieve their maximum

OJAI VALLEY SCHOOL

potential in college, careers, and throughout adulthood. Qualified scholars may take AP and Honors courses in English, English Literature, Computer Science, Biology, Chemistry, French, Spanish, United States History, Government, Environmental Studies, and Studio Art. International students ages 8–18 benefit from an extensive program in ESL intended to develop their reading, speaking, and writing skills. Activities include outdoor programs, student government, community service, publications, drama, music, and sports. Boarding Tuition: $42,900; Day Tuition: $19,520. Tracy Wilson is Director of Admissions; Michael Hall-Mounsey is President/CEO. *Western Association.*

The Pegasus School   1984

19692 Lexington Lane, Huntington Beach, CA 92646
Tel. 714-964-1224; Fax 714-962-6047
Web Site www.thepegasusschool.org
E-mail nconklin@thepegasusschool.org

The Pegasus School, a coeducational day school enrolling 565 students in Preschool–Grade 8, offers a strong, challenging academic curriculum, taught by fully certified faculty. Small classes are limited to 18 students, each with a teacher and a teacher's assistant. In Kindergarten–Grade 8, the program is enriched with technology, science, Spanish, music, art, drama, and physical education. The campus features two state-of-the-art Technology Centers, Lower and Middle School science labs, an 18,000-volume library, and an Activities Center, which includes a gym, theater, and art studio. Camp Pegasus provides six weeks of summer enrichment. Tuition: $7855–$15,292. Financial aid is available. Nancy Conklin is Director of Admission; Jacqueline Smethurst, Ed.D., is Interim Head of School.

Polytechnic School   1907

1030 East California Boulevard, Pasadena, CA 91106
Tel. 626-792-2147; Fax 626-449-5727
Web Site www.polytechnic.org; E-mail admissions@polytechnic.org

Polytechnic School enrolls 859 students in Kindergarten–Grade 12 on a 15-acre campus with a state-of-the-art performing and fine arts center, professionally staffed libraries, computer labs, and media centers. Students are encouraged to excel in academic, athletic, and artistic endeavors in an atmosphere that celebrates diversity and promotes community. The School emphasizes sound thinking and effective communication while fostering personal development, integrity, responsibility, and concern for others. Community service is integral to the curriculum. An extensive outdoor education program in Grades 6–12 enhances the Poly experience. Tuition: $19,700–$26,600. Financial Aid: $3,300,000. Sally Jeanne McKenna is Director of Admissions; Deborah Reed is Head of School. *Western Association.*

Ring Mountain Day School   1976

K–Grade 8: 70 Lomita Drive, Mill Valley, CA 94941
Tel. 415-381-8183; Fax 415-381-8484
Preschool: 445 Greenwood Beach Road, Tiburon, CA 94920
Tel. 415-381-8181; Admissions 415-381-8183, Ext. 35
Fax 415-381-7508
Web Site www.ringmountain.org
E-mail admissions@ringmountain.org

RING MOUNTAIN DAY SCHOOL enrolls boys and girls in an academic program encompassing age 2¹/₂ in Preschool through Grade 8. The School occupies two campuses in Marin County north of San Francisco. Mill Valley is located at the foot of Mount Tamalpais, while Tiburon is a short ferry ride from San Francisco's Fisherman's Wharf. Both are charming residential communities that afford easy access to natural wonders such as Muir Woods as well as to the rich historic, cultural, aesthetic, and recreational attractions of the City by the Bay.

Ring Mountain Day School was established in 1976 by Gudrun Hoy, a leading educator who developed and implemented a progressive curriculum for early childhood and elementary education. At Ring Mountain, teachers are dedicated to enabling children to grow and mature in the creative, social, and emotional aspects of their young lives. The School actively seeks to achieve ethnic, racial, geographic, and socioeconomic diversity and to maintain gender balance. Ring Mountain's first class of eighth graders graduated in June of 2004.

Ring Mountain Day School Elementary/Middle School is currently in the process of accreditation by the California Association of Independent Schools.

RING MOUNTAIN DAY SCHOOL

In support of the school community, the Parent Association sponsors informational seminars, conducts the walkathon and other fund-raisers, and organizes numerous spirit-building activities.

THE CAMPUSES. The Mill Valley Campus, a former public school site leased from the Mill Valley Board of Education, is home to Kindergarten to Grade 8. Renovations to the existing

building include a new science center, an expanded technology laboratory, library, darkroom, student publication center, a multipurpose room, an art studio with a low-fire kiln, and multimedia, science, and Spanish language labs. The facility is surrounded by grassy playing fields and will accommodate 155 elementary and middle school students. The campus also features a soccer field, basketball courts, a volleyball/badminton court, outdoor playground and play structure, and space for a community garden and courtyard amphitheater.

RING MOUNTAIN DAY SCHOOL

The Tiburon Campus accommodates the Preschool Program (age 2¹/₂) and Pre-Kindergarten (ages 4–5), offering classrooms, space for art, music, and movement, and play areas.

THE FACULTY. Dr. Nancy Diamonti was appointed Head of School in 1999. She holds a B.A. degree from Caldwell College in New Jersey, an M.A. from the University of Wisconsin at Madison, and a Ph.D. in Child and Adolescent Psychology and Educational Leadership from Boston College. She has also completed doctoral course work in Curriculum and Instruction and Educational Policy Studies at the University of Wisconsin. Dr. Diamonti has more than 40 years of experience in the field of education, including 22 years as Principal/Head of School in private and public schools.

The 31 men and women on the Ring Mountain faculty hold undergraduate degrees or specialized certification as well as 12 advanced degrees. Among their representative colleges and universities are American Graduate School of International Management, Arizona State, Bank Street, Bowdoin, Brigham Young (Hawaii), Brooklyn College, California State, Chico State, Cornell, DePauw, Dominican, Gettysburg, Harvard, Lewis and Clark, Mills College, New College of California, North Park, Ohio State, Palm Beach Atlantic, St. Michael's, San Francisco State, Smith, Stanford, and the Universities of Arkansas, Birmingham (England), California (Berkeley, Irvine, Santa Barbara), Florida, Minnesota, Oregon, Toledo, and Western Ontario.

STUDENT BODY. In 2009–10, Ring Mountain Day School enrolled 50 children at the Preschool campus and 105 at the K–8 campus. They come from throughout the Bay Area and reflect the broad racial, ethnic, and cultural diversity of the region. Ring Mountain provides bus transportation between San Francisco and the Elementary/Middle School campus. Over one-third of the lower school children are San Francisco residents.

ACADEMIC PROGRAM. The school year begins the Tuesday after Labor Day and runs through the first week of June. Vacations are held at Thanksgiving and in December, February, and April, with days off for the observance of certain national and religious celebrations. Parent-teacher conferences are held in the fall and spring. The student-teacher ratio is 8:1 in Preschool and 12:1 in Grades 1–8. Student-to-student mentoring benefits those who need extra support in a specific area; specialized small-group learning centers provide a similar function. Before- and after-school care is available.

Ring Mountain Day School's progressive educational program is marked by structure and balance to provide each child with a strong foundation for future learning. The student-centered curriculum, from 2½-year-old Preschool through eighth-grade graduation, places equal emphasis on the sciences, humanities, and arts. Core subjects focus on reading and language arts, mathematics, science, Spanish, and social studies. Course work is designed to provide continuity and consistency as students progress from mastery of basic concepts in the early grades to more complex materials in the middle school.

Preschoolers' first experiences with learning revolve around play as a means of encouraging cognitive, social, and emotional growth. Students construct, design, build, choose, discuss, listen, question, experiment, and observe as they are introduced to central themes that expand as they move through the grades.

The elementary and middle schools extend the continuum of learning begun in Preschool. The language arts component focuses on reading, writing, and speaking, and children have many opportunities for self-expression, discussion, and the sharing of ideas. Students also read a wide range of age-appropriate fiction, nonfiction, and poetry as well as write daily in a variety of genres.

Math studies, including Algebra and Geometry in Grades 5–8, focus on the development of critical thinking, logic, and problem-solving skills and on the application of mathematical principles to everyday living.

RING MOUNTAIN DAY SCHOOL

In science, hands-on activities, lab experiments, and group and independent research provide lively demonstrations of key scientific processes in biology, physics, and physical and earth sciences. Environmental education is emphasized through activities such as composting, gardening, recycling, and caring for plant life.

The social studies curriculum makes use of children's experiences in their own families and communities as a means of understanding both the larger world around them and the people who make a difference in history.

Spanish language begins in Preschool and, by Kindergarten, is taught three or four times a week. The youngest children learn basic words and phrases through songs, games, and drama, while older students have more in-depth instruction in vocabulary, grammar, and conversation.

The use of technology is integrated into the teaching of core subjects beginning in Grade 1, while students in the upper grades use computers or laptops for Internet research, word processing, and data organization. The computer-student ratio is 1:2. Fifth- through eighth-grade students take part in the Just Think Foundation, a media literacy program that teaches them how to analyze media messages and become independent, critical thinkers.

In the middle school, students prepare for the Secondary School Admission Test as a core curricular component; they also attend workshops on such topics as the art of debate, conflict resolution, and appreciation for diversity.

Art, music, dance, drama, library skills, and physical education, taught by specialist instructors, enrich the program at all levels. Children from Kindergarten upward have the opportunity to take three classes a week in music, drama, and dance. At the conclusion of the classes, students participate in a dramatic presentation, sharing center stage with professional actors and musicians. Martin Charnin's *Annie* and a musical adaptation of William Goldman's *The Princess Bride* are representative productions.

Frequent field trips enliven the academic program for all students and extend the learning process beyond the classroom. Depending on age, children take nature walks, attend Marin County Farm Day at the Civic Center, and enjoy week-long excursions to Washington, D.C., Mexico, and the Shakespeare conference in Ashland, Oregon.

Eighth graders from Ring Mountain were accepted to The Bay School, The Branson School, Hawaii Preparatory Academy, Marin Academy, Marin Catholic, The Marin School, Redwood High School, San Domenico School, San Francisco University High School, Sierra Lutheran High School (Nevada), and Tamalpais High.

In the summer, students in Preschool may enroll in a series of two-week specialty camps structured for fun and learning. Students entering Grade 8 may attend Phillips Exeter Academy for a five-week summer residential program, "Access Exeter."

STUDENT ACTIVITIES. Community service involves all Ring Mountain students in learning while helping others. They take part in Earth Day clean-up projects, support a local battered women's shelter, and help raise funds for worthy causes. Specific projects are determined by the wishes of the students and their teachers. Other activities include recycling and the "greening" of the campus.

Among the traditional events on the Ring Mountain calendar are Back to School Night, Open Houses, class Halloween parties, Walk-a-Thon, Book Fair, Holiday Sing, Spirit Week, the school play, the annual spring auction and dinner dance, the Step Up ceremony, and graduation.

ADMISSION AND COSTS. Ring Mountain Day School welcomes children from all racial, ethnic, religious, and socioeconomic backgrounds who have the interest and ability to succeed in its academic, artistic, athletic, and social programs. Admission is determined by the completed application, teacher recommendations, and previous school transcripts.

In 2009–10, tuition in the Preschool ranges from $5660 for two days a week to $14,420 for five days a week. Annual tuition is $20,000 in Kindergarten through Grade 4, $20,550 in Grades 5–6, and $20,810 in Grades 7–8.

Head of School: Nancy Diamonti, Ph.D.
Director of Development: Suzanne Alpert
Business Manager: Rita Voss

Rolling Hills Preparatory School 1981

1 Rolling Hills Prep Way, San Pedro, CA 90732
Tel. 310-791-1101; Admissions Ext. 101; Fax 310-373-4931
Web Site www.rollinghillsprep.org

Rolling Hills Prep School provides an educational environment conducive to the development of disciplined minds, sound character, healthy bodies, and creative spirits. Enrolling 230 boys and girls in Grades 6–12, the School features small classes, proven teaching methods, and up-to-date technology to carry out its traditional college preparatory program. Among the activities are outdoor education, community service, robotics, clubs, and athletics. English as a Second Language and a recreational summer program are optional. Tuition: $21,200. Financial Aid: $875,000. Peter McCormack (York University, B.A. 1975; Exeter, P.G.C.E. 1976; Oxford, M.Sc. 1987) was appointed Head of School in 1993.

Sacred Heart Schools, Atherton 1898

150 Valparaiso Avenue, Atherton, CA 94027
Tel. 650-322-1866; Admission 650-473-4006; Fax 650-326-2761
Web Site www.shschools.org; E-mail admission@shschools.org

These fully accredited, Roman Catholic, college preparatory day schools enroll 550 students in Grades 9–12 at Sacred Heart Preparatory High and 520 students in Preschool–Grade 8 at St. Joseph's School of the Sacred Heart. Located on a 62-acre campus, the Schools emphasize academic excellence, Christian values, and social awareness. Programs include required religious studies, challenging curricula, and competitive athletics as well as a wide range of cocurricular activities and summer camps. Sacred Heart Prep offers Advanced Placement in 20 subjects and exchange programs with Sacred Heart Schools worldwide. Tuition: $18,550–$29,755. Financial aid is available. Wendy Quattlebaum is Director of Admission; Richard A. Dioli is Director of the Schools. *Western Association.*

Sage Hill School 2000

20402 Newport Coast Drive, Newport Coast, CA 92657
Tel. 949-219-0100; Admissions 949-219-1337; Fax 949-219-1399
Web Site www.sagehillschool.org; E-mail admission@sagehillschool.org

Parents and educators established Sage Hill School to provide Orange County families a choice in coeducational, independent, secondary day schools. Its mission is to inspire in young people a love of knowledge and the motivation to use their knowledge "creatively, compassionately, and courageously throughout their lives." Enrolling 450 students from diverse backgrounds in Grades 9–12, Sage Hill's challenging college preparatory program is grounded in the traditional liberal arts, sciences, and humanities. The core curriculum is enriched by state-of-the-art computer and information technology, modern and classical languages, the visual and performing arts, and service learning. AP courses and Advanced Art Workshops are also available to qualified students. Small classes ensure that all students receive individual attention and support. The 30-acre campus features academic buildings, a library, gym, playing fields, and a 30,000-square-foot, state-of-the-art performing and visual arts studio. More than 30 organizations include Model UN, drama, music, school government, publications, and varsity sports. All Sage Hill graduates are accepted into four-year colleges nationwide. Tuition: $27,000. Financial Aid: $1,742,000. Elaine J. Mijalis-Kahn is Director of Admission and Financial Aid; Gordon McNeill is Head of School. *Western Association.*

St. James' Episcopal School 1968

625 South St. Andrews Place, Los Angeles, CA 90005
Tel. 213-382-2315; Fax 213-382-2436
Web Site www.sjsla.org; E-mail admissions@sjsla.org

St. James' Episcopal School enrolls 344 girls and boys from diverse faiths and cultures in Preschool–Grade 6. The academic program is designed to provide a strong foundation for further education and daily life. Comprehensive reading and math programs form the basis of the core curriculum, complemented by science, music, art, physical education, religion, Spanish, computing, and library. Worship and religion are integral to the program. Children take part in school choir, bell choir, and athletics. An after-school program, including enrichment classes, study hall, and child care, is available. Tuition: $15,600. Tuition assistance is available. Stephen L. Bowers is Head of School. *Western Association.*

Saint Mark's School 1980

39 Trellis Drive, San Rafael, CA 94903
Tel. 415-472-8000; Admissions 415-472-8007; Fax 415-472-0722
Web Site www.saintmarksschool.org
E-mail nlyons@saintmarksschool.org

Saint Mark's is a nonsectarian day school enrolling 380 boys and girls in Kindergarten–Grade 8. It seeks to promote a love of learning in children of academic promise, to develop strong academic skills, and to promote character and self-confidence. Music, art, drama, technology, world languages, and physical education are required along with traditional subjects. Field trips, team sports, theater productions, the Headmaster's Reading Program, a national champion chess team, Computer Club, Science Fiction Club, and after-school enrichment classes are among the activities. Tuition: $20,777. Extras: $250–$1500. Financial Aid: $1,025,000. Norm Lyons is Director of Admissions; Damon H. Kerby (Kenyon, A.B. 1971; Stanford, M.A. 1999) was appointed Headmaster in 1987.

St. Mary and All Angels School 1994

7 Pursuit, Aliso Viejo, CA 92656
Tel. 949-448-9027; Admission Ext. 305; Fax 949-448-0605
Web Site www.smaa.org

Dedicated to excellence in an atmosphere of cultural respect and global interaction, St. Mary and All Angels is a nondenominational Christian day school spanning Preschool–Grade 8. Founded by Father Ernest D. Sillers, the School promotes lifelong learning, leading, and serving to prepare students for the world. Being an authorized IB World School ensures rigorous academics as well as physical, emotional, social, and spiritual development. Enrolling 600 boys and girls who reflect southern California's rich diversity, St. Mary's community of families is committed to the School through its Parent Teacher Fellowship. Chapel services, leadership/character development, and electives such as multimedia technology enrich course work in the arts, sciences, and humanities. Service learning and outreach programs help students give back to the community. Field studies in Grades 4–8 include California, Colorado, Chicago, and Italy. The athletic program promotes sportsmanship, school pride, leadership, and teamwork. Extended care, after-school, and summer programs are available. Tuition: $10,800–$11,050. Jennifer Risner is Director of Admission; John O'Brien is Headmaster.

St. Matthew's Episcopal Day School   1953

16 Baldwin Avenue, San Mateo, CA 94401
Tel. 650-342-5436; Fax 650-342-4019
Web Site www.stmatthewsday.org
E-mail rmalouf@stmatthewsday.org

St. Matthew's is a coeducational, independent, Episcopal school enrolling 230 students in Preschool–Grade 8. The School offers a challenging academic education and strives to help students become compassionate members of the community. The curriculum reflects an approach designed to enable children to understand the interconnectedness and interdependence of the disciplines they study. Students receive individual attention in an enriched, supportive environment that emphasizes the essential skills of reading, writing, mathematics, and critical thinking necessary for communication and problem solving. The program includes Spanish, state-of-the-art technology, music, drama, physical education, and after-school sports. Field study, community service, and student leadership are important elements of the school program. The average class size ranges from 15 to 22. St. Matthew's is fully accredited by the California Association of Independent Schools and the National Association of Episcopal Schools. Tuition: $9200–$21,375. Rosemary Malouf is Director of Admission; Mark McKee is Head of School.

St. Matthew's Parish School   1949

1031 Bienvenida Avenue, Pacific Palisades, CA 90272
Tel. 310-454-1350; Admission Ext. 150; Fax 310-573-7423
Web Site www.stmatthewsschool.com
E-mail lquiring@stmatthewsschool.com

Set near the ocean on a pastoral 30-acre campus, St. Matthew's is an Episcopal day school enrolling 325 boys and girls in Preschool–Grade 8. The School encourages each child's positive self-concept, sensitivity toward others, intellectual curiosity, and mastery of basic learning skills. In all grades, the curriculum includes laboratory science in two science centers and computer science in seven computer labs, plus art, music, drama, and foreign languages. A sports/performing arts complex houses the drama, physical education, and interscholastic athletic programs. A summer program is offered. Tuition: $12,600–$25,500. Financial Aid: $500,000. A. Lee Quiring is Director of Admission; Les W. Frost (University of California [San Francisco], D.Phar. 1968) is Head of School.

St. Paul's Episcopal School   1975

116 Montecito Avenue, Oakland, CA 94610-4556
Tel. 510-285-9600; Admissions 510-285-9617; Fax 510-899-7297
Web Site www.spes.org; E-mail info@spes.org

St. Paul's Episcopal School offers a rigorous academic program that nurtures the whole child. Located in downtown Oakland near Lake Merritt, St. Paul's serves 353 boys and girls in Kindergarten through Grade 8; the middle school is in a renovated and expanded building that includes an all-new library. St. Paul's mission is twofold: the creation of future scholars and leaders and the inculcation of values of empathy, tolerance, and service to others. Children are encouraged to explore, to take risks, to solve problems, and to search out opportunities to indulge their loves of learning. The School's award-winning Service Learning Program, now in its 22nd year, is a nationally recognized model of how to integrate community service into the academic program so that each serves as a complement to the other. Students and their families come from a wide variety of racial, ethnic, religious, and socioeconomic backgrounds, and the School prides itself in having one of the most comprehensive financial aid programs in the Bay Area. Tuition: $19,300–

$20,800. Financial aid is available. Khadija Fredericks is Director of Admissions; Karan A. Merry is Head of School. *Western Association.*

St. Timothy's Preparatory School   1967

15757 St. Timothy's Road, Apple Valley, CA 92307
Tel. 760-242-4256; Fax 760-242-2825
Web Site www.sttimsprep.com; E-mail office@sttimsprep.com

St. Timothy's Preparatory School, whose motto is "Scholarship, Character, Community," serves children from various religious, racial, and ethnic backgrounds in Preschool (age 2½)–Grade 8. In a nurturing Christian community, St. Tim's offers a classical curriculum in an environment designed to instill mastery of basic skills as well as values and ethics as understood by the Episcopal Church. Religion classes, daily chapel, and Christian principles and practices develop spiritual awareness in all aspects of school and family life. Classes enroll 10–15 children, with an 11:1 student-teacher ratio. The Preschool program focuses on math, language arts, science, large- and small-motor development, Spanish, library, art, and music. Students progress to more complex subjects in which hands-on activities and analytical thinking are emphasized as critical tools. At all levels, teachers stress globalism, service learning, writing across the curriculum, and inquiry and critical thinking skills. The natural resources of the High Desert around the campus serve as a living lab for scientific exploration. The program is enriched by musical performances, field trips, guest speakers, before- and after-school care, and summer programs. Tuition: $2500–$6100. H. John Walter III is Head of School.

Saklan Valley School   1978

1678 School Street, Moraga, CA 94556
Tel. 925-376-7900; Fax 925-376-1156
Web Site www.saklan.org; E-mail admissions@saklan.org

After merging with two earlier educational programs, Saklan Valley School was formed and moved to its present campus in Moraga. Of the approximately 155 children from the East Bay Area in Preschool–Grade 8, between 20–25 percent are of color, creating a dynamic and diverse learning environment. The School offers a well-rounded curriculum designed to provide excellence and nurture the whole child. Rigorous academics are combined with interdisciplinary and experiential learning opportunities. Core subjects emphasize language arts, math, and social studies. Special teachers provide instruction in French, art, physical education and movement, music, computer/technology, science, and library. Small classes enroll a maximum of 16 children, and the student-teacher ratio is 7:1 to ensure individual attention and support. Saklan maintains a strong focus on community and the development of respect, responsibility, and integrity among its students, faculty, and families. Extended care and summer camp are optional. Tuition: $12,900–$19,500. Tuition assistance is available. David Hague (New England College, B.A.; Castleton State, M.Ed.; Harvard University, M.Ed.; Vanderbilt University, Ed.D. [ABD]) is Interim Head of School. *Western Association.*

San Francisco Friends School   2002

250 Valencia Street, San Francisco, CA 94103
Tel. 415-565-0400; Admissions Ext. 136; Fax 415-565-0401
Web Site www.sffriendsschool.org
E-mail admissions@sffriendsschool.org

San Francisco Friends School combines "outstanding academics" with Quaker values of simplicity, mutual respect, nonviolence, and service to others. Civic volunteers, educators, and business leaders founded this coeducational K–8 school, which currently serves 365 students in Kindergarten–Grade 7. The curriculum emphasizes mastery of foundational skills while fostering independence and critical thinking. Foreign language, the arts, and physical education are integrated into the core subjects of science and stewardship, language arts, math, and humanities. A welcoming, inclusive environment for families of all faiths and backgrounds is a touchstone of Quaker education. Tuition: $22,665. Financial aid is available. Catherine Hunter is Founding Head of School; Yvette Bonaparte is Director of Admissions.

San Francisco University High School   1973

3065 Jackson Street, San Francisco, CA 94115
Tel. 415-447-3100; Admission 415-447-3104; Fax 415-447-5801
Web Site www.sfuhs.org; E-mail karen.kindler@sfuhs.org

San Francisco University High School is a coeducational, college preparatory school enrolling 389 students in Grades 9–12. Created to serve young men and women of above-average intellectual ability, the School encourages in its students a love of learning so that graduates may enjoy full, meaningful lives and the community may benefit from the development of creative, capable leaders. The college preparatory curriculum emphasizes the acquisition of essential academic skills. At the same time, the School is committed to the students' total emotional, moral, physical, and intellectual growth. Tuition: $31,500. Financial Aid: $1,600,000. Karen N. Kindler is Director of Admission & Financial Aid; Dr. Michael Diamonti is Head of School. *Western Association.*

The Seven Hills School   1962

975 North San Carlos Drive, Walnut Creek, CA 94598
Tel. 925-933-0666; Admissions Ext. 4984; Fax 925-933-6271
Web Site www.sevenhillsschool.org
E-mail sgoldman@sevenhillsschool.org

THE SEVEN HILLS SCHOOL

Accredited by the Western Association of Schools and Colleges and the California Association of Independent Schools, Seven Hills is a coeducational day school enrolling 375 students in Preschool through Grade 8. The School provides a developmentally appropriate, integrated curriculum in a small-class setting. The program emphasizes the acquisition and application of academic skills in the liberal and fine arts, supplemented by Spanish, French, music, art, physical education, computers, and electives. Summer day camp, Middle School intramural sports, clubs, an Extended Day Program, and hot lunch are available. Tuition: $7700–$19,990. Financial Aid: $560,000. Susanne Goldman is Director of Admissions and Tuition Assistance; William H. Miller (University of Notre Dame, B.A. 1970; University of San Francisco, M.A. 1980) was appointed Headmaster in 1992. *Western Association.*

Sierra Canyon School   1977

Lower School (EK–6): 11052 Independence Avenue, Chatsworth, CA 91311; Fax 818-882-8218
Upper School (7–12): 20801 West Rinaldi Street, Chatsworth, CA 91311
Tel. 818-882-8121; Fax 818-700-8642
Web Site www.sierracanyonschool.org
E-mail jskrumbis@sierracanyonschool.org

SIERRA CANYON SCHOOL

Set on two campuses totaling 35 acres in the San Fernando Valley, Sierra Canyon is a college preparatory, coeducational day school that provides students in Early Kindergarten–Grade 12 with an environment that embraces personal excellence, wherein each student has the opportunity to attain his or her best. Enrolling more than 900 students, Sierra Canyon emphasizes mastery of strong skills in core academic subjects along with a varied arts and athletics program. The Lower School lays the foundation and places strong emphasis on the development of basic skills within small classes. As they progress, the skills acquired earlier provide students with the tools necessary to excel within the rigorous curricula of the Middle and Upper School. Within this setting, students embrace the social and academic challenges set forth and thrive in an atmosphere where intellectual discourse, individual growth, and free thought are encouraged and celebrated. A pioneering service learning program and academic travel options are integrated into the curriculum. Before- and after-school care and summer programs are offered. Tuition: $13,000–$25,000. Financial Aid: $1,700,000. Steve Burnett (7–12) and Kendall Pillsbury (EK–6) are Directors of Admissions; Jim Skrumbis is Head of School.

Sinai Akiba Academy   1968

10400 Wilshire Boulevard, Los Angeles, CA 90024
Tel. 310-475-6401; Admissions Ext. 3251; Fax 310-234-9184
Web Site www.sinaiakiba.org; E-mail info@sinaiakiba.org

Sinai Akiba Academy, a Solomon Schechter Jewish day school, enrolls up to 605 boys and girls in Pre-Kindergarten–Grade 8. The school is committed to nurturing the curiosity of children, joy in the adventure of learning, and confidence in their abilities while developing disciplined study habits. In both general and Judaic studies, Sinai Akiba strives for academic excellence as it promotes a strong sense of both personal worth and Jewish identity. A challenging curriculum in core academics complements an innovative Judaic studies program, music, art, orchestra, physical education, library, technology, and an after-school enrichment program. Tuition: $17,712–$19,239. Rabbi Laurence Scheindlin is Headmaster; Barbara Goodhill is Admissions Director.

Sonoma Academy   2001

2500 Farmers Lane, Santa Rosa, CA 95404
Tel. 707-545-1770; Fax 707-636-2474
Web Site www.sonomaacademy.org; E-mail info@sonomaacademy.org

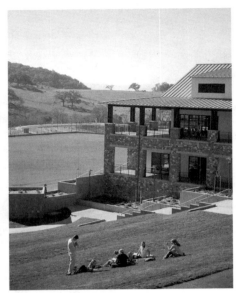

SONOMA ACADEMY

Founded by 12 community and business leaders, Sonoma Academy is a nondenominational, college preparatory day school enrolling 220 students in Grades 9–12. Its mission is to inspire, challenge, and nurture students, instilling a lifelong love of learning and motivating them to achieve their potential as scholars and citizens. The curriculum emphasizes the humanities, math-science, world languages, and the arts, with technology integrated in every discipline. Each student uses a MacBook in the classroom and at home and is linked through SA's wireless network to the Internet and to all students and teachers at the school. Small classes and dedicated teachers facilitate lively discussion and individual participation in the educational process. School-wide meetings and conferences with faculty advisors take place weekly. CONNECTIONS encompasses community service programs and travel abroad, while a January "intersession" provides in-depth immersion in a subject of special interest. Individualized college counseling begins in the sophomore year, and historically, all graduates go on to higher education. Tuition: Individualized families pay from $0 to $30,700. Scholarship funds enable SA to set costs at what each family can afford. Sandy Stack is Director of Admission; Janet Durgin is Head of School.

Stuart Hall for Boys   1956

2222 Broadway, San Francisco, CA 94115
Tel. 415-563-2900; Admissions 415-292-3113; Fax 415-929-6928
Web Site www.sacredsf.org; E-mail thorp@sacredsf.org

An independent, Catholic day school enrolling 324 boys in Kindergarten–Grade 8, Stuart Hall for Boys, one of the Schools of the Sacred Heart, is part of a four-school complex including Stuart Hall High School, Convent Elementary School, and Convent High School. Stuart Hall seeks to prepare students for entrance into college preparatory high schools and to develop spiritual and social responsibility. Foreign languages, art, music, computer science, outdoor education, community service, and interscholastic sports are integral to the curriculum. A coeducational summer school program is also offered. Tuition: $22,550.

Financial aid is available. Pamela Thorp is Director of Admissions; Jaime Dominguez (Princeton, B.A.; Michigan State, M.A.Ed.Admin.) is Head. *Western Association.*

Stuart Hall High School   2000

1715 Octavia Street, San Francisco, CA 94109
Tel. 415-345-5812; Fax 415-931-9161
Web Site www.sacredsf.org

Stuart Hall High School is a boys' school and member of Schools of the Sacred Heart San Francisco. Located in the heart of the city, "The Hall" partners with Convent of the Sacred Heart High School to offer a unique educational experience: a coeducational environment with single-sex classes. Through its student-focused teachers, rigorous college prep program, and classrooms steeped in the educational practices that help boys learn, Stuart Hall High School maximizes the intellectual and leadership potential of young men, producing confident graduates who thrive in college and life. Enrolling 170 students in Grades 9–12, Stuart Hall High emphasizes serious study, sportsmanship, artistic discovery, social responsibility, and faith development in a small, close-knit community. In addition to a challenging core curriculum, the School offers Advanced Placement and Honor courses in all subject areas. Tuition: $30,575. Financial aid is available. Shuja Khan is Admissions Director; Anthony Farrell is Head.

Town School for Boys   1939

2750 Jackson Street, San Francisco, CA 94115
Tel. 415-921-3747; Admission Ext. 125; Fax 415-921-2968
Web Site www.townschool.com; E-mail mckannay@townschool.com

Town School for Boys is an independent day school enrolling 400 students in Kindergarten–Grade 8. The academic program is complemented by a state-of-the-art science center, a laptop learning program in Grades 5–8, a PC lab, classroom computers, and a media theater. A wide range of activities includes outdoor education, intramural sports, music, drama, publications, student government, special-interest clubs, and a strong commitment to community service. Tuition: $23,710–$24,650. Tuition Assistance: $1,033,000. Lynn McKannay is Director of Admission; W. Brewster Ely IV (Ithaca, B.A. 1970; Middlebury, M.A. 1975) was appointed Headmaster in 1989. *Western Association.*

The Urban School of San Francisco   1966

1563 Page Street, San Francisco, CA 94117
Tel. 415-626-2919; Fax 415-626-1125
Web Site www.urbanschool.org; E-mail info@urbanschool.org

The Urban School of San Francisco seeks to ignite a passion for learning. Urban's teachers challenge students with a highly acclaimed academic program that combines a college preparatory curriculum with community service, fieldwork, and internships. Urban students are prepared for higher education and beyond through a mastery of subject matter and academic skills. The most enduring aspect of an Urban education is the ability for students to become self-motivated, enthusiastic participants in their education. With 352 day boys and girls in Grades 9–12, Urban sponsors many championship athletic teams and provides numerous extracurricular opportunities, including an outdoor education program and wide range of student-led clubs. A 1:1 laptop school since 2000, Urban shares its teaching expertise and curriculum development through its summer Center for Innovative Teaching professional workshop series. Tuition: $30,800. Financial Aid: $2,000,000. Bobby Ramos is Director of Admissions; Mark Salkind (Yale, B.A. 1974) is Head of School. *Western Association.*

Viewpoint School   1961

23620 Mulholland Highway, Calabasas, CA 91302
Tel. 818-340-2901; Admission 818-591-6560; Fax 818-591-0834
Web Site www.viewpoint.org; E-mail info@viewpoint.org

Viewpoint provides a dynamic college preparatory education in an environment that fosters academic excellence and good values and character. Enrolling 1210 boys and girls in Kindergarten–Grade 12, Viewpoint welcomes racial, ethnic, religious, and economic diversity. A member of The Cum Laude Society, Viewpoint offers a traditional liberal arts curriculum enhanced by 26 AP and 14 Honors courses in the Upper School, four world languages including Mandarin Chinese, advanced computer science courses, and electives such as creative writing, psychology, neuroscience, and music composition. A modern theater is home to Viewpoint's award-winning performing arts programs. Upper School students have a community service requirement and may undertake an Independent Senior Project. Educational field trips, foreign travel, a tour of historic East Coast sites, and college tours enrich the program. Graduates attend the nation's most selective colleges. Age-appropriate extracurricular activities include more than 60 clubs and organizations and 110 athletic teams. Tuition: $21,650–$25,550. Financial aid is available. Laurel Baker Tew is Director of Admissions; Dr. Robert J. Dworkoski is Headmaster. *Western Association.*

Village Christian Schools   1949

8930 Village Avenue, La Tuna Canyon, CA 91352
Tel. 818-767-8382; Admissions Ext. 209
Web Site www.villagechristian.org
E-mail camillem@villagechristian.org

VILLAGE CHRISTIAN SCHOOLS

This K–12 Blue Ribbon college preparatory school was founded in 1949 to provide an education that embodies the highest standards of academic excellence and spiritual development within a nondenominational Christian environment. Graduates currently attend challenging universities across the nation. The Elementary, Middle, and High School divisions have their own principal and facilities on a secluded, 110-acre campus in the Verdugo Hills. Village Christian provides academic, athletic, and artistic resources for all grades as well as AP and Honor classes in high school. The School encourages students and families to develop a relationship with Jesus Christ and teaches discipleship through example and application. Bible studies, chapel, and community outreach develop moral and ethical maturity. The 1100 students take part in activities such as leadership groups, publications, theater, musical groups, and a full range of varsity sports. Within the past five years, the School has won CIF division championships in football, volleyball, and softball and league championships in all other major sports. Tuition: $9500–$10,500. Financial aid is available. Ronald G. Sipus, Ph.D., is Superintendent; Camille Martinelli is Admissions Director. *Western Association.*

Village School   1977

780 Swarthmore Avenue, Pacific Palisades, CA 90272-4355
Tel. 310-459-8411; Admission Exts. 102, 117; Fax 310-459-3285
Web Site www.village-school.org; E-mail bwilliams@village-school.com

Village School in Pacific Palisades, California, is a coeducational elementary school enrolling children in Transitional Kindergarten–Grade 6. Set in a beautiful suburban community, Village School's location enables children to enjoy the quiet neighborhood setting of Pacific Palisades and the clean air of the Pacific coast. Students use the School's bus service, carpool with other families, or walk to school.

VILLAGE SCHOOL

Village School was established in 1977 by a group of parents who sought to provide a nurturing, academically strong program within the atmosphere of a neighborhood school. Village has remained faithful to its founding mission, which aims to support and celebrate families who place a high priority on educational excellence. The broad, balanced curriculum is taught in small classes in which each child is assured of receiving individual attention, nurturing, and challenge.

A nonprofit, nondenominational institution, Village School is governed by a 13-member Board of Trustees. Jointly accredited by the Western Association of Colleges and Schools and the California Association of Independent Schools, Village School is a member of the National Association of Independent Schools. The Village School Parent Association provides essential support through fund-raising, volunteering in the classrooms, and planning special events.

THE CAMPUS. The main campus is designed in a Spanish style, constructed around a large court that includes a playground, covered lunch area, and a "village green." There are separate classrooms for a Transitional Kindergarten and three sections of Kindergarten. Grades 1 through 6 occupy two classrooms each. Additional facilities include a 6000-volume library, a technology center, a science lab, and two classrooms for Spanish language instruction.

The Center for the Arts and Athletics has a gymnasium adjacent to a grassy playing field. The space also becomes an auditorium with multiple stages and balconies. A performing arts and music room and recording, art, and dance studios round out the creative spaces of this facility.

THE FACULTY. Nora Malone was named Head of School in July 1999, after serving two years as Village School's Assistant Head/Director of Admissions. A 20-year teaching veteran, Ms. Malone received a Bachelor of Arts degree in English, a Master's degree in Educational Administration, and her California teaching credential from California State University at Northridge.

VILLAGE SCHOOL

The full-time faculty includes 17 women and 7 men, all of whom have earned college degrees. Most have teaching credentials, and many hold advanced degrees from institutions across the country. Professional development is encouraged through workshops and in-service seminars. In addition to the teaching staff, 19 assistant teachers provide support in the classroom as well as outside supervision of the students. Faculty receive health insurance, a retirement plan, and additional benefits.

STUDENT BODY. In 2009–10, Village School enrolled 290 students, 151 girls and 139 boys, ages 4½ to 12 years. There are 8 students in Transitional Kindergarten, 40 in Kindergarten, 42 in Grade 1, 44 in Grade 2, 38 in Grade 3, 44 in Grade 4, 38 in Grade 5, and 36 in Grade 6. Students come from Brentwood, Los Angeles, Malibu, Pacific Palisades, Santa Monica, and other communities.

ACADEMIC PROGRAM. The school year, divided into trimesters, begins in early September and ends in early June, with vacation breaks at Thanksgiving, in the winter, and in the spring as well as the observance of several national holidays. Grades are issued three times a year, and parent-teacher conferences are held at the end of the first two trimesters. Classes, enrolling between 12 and 22 children, meet five days a week, from 8:00 A.M. to 3:00 P.M.

VILLAGE SCHOOL

The Village School curriculum combines traditional and progressive approaches, with an emphasis on providing a strong foundation in basic reading, language, and mathematical skills. Spanish begins in Transitional Kindergarten and continues through all grade levels. Science, social studies, information technology, art, music, and physical education are also integral to the core program. At the same time, emphasis is given to the development of values, responsibility, and good citizenship as members of the school and larger community.

After graduation, a majority of sixth graders enter independent secondary schools such as Brentwood, Crossroads School for Arts and Sciences, Harvard-Westlake, Marlborough, and Windward.

STUDENT ACTIVITIES. Children have the opportunity to serve their school and develop leadership qualities through membership on the Student Council, which consists of representatives in Kindergarten–Grade 6. The Council meets on alternate weeks.

The after-school enrichment program features journalism, yearbook, music, arts and crafts, science, and other areas of interest. Students stage two musical performances a year and take part in community service projects such as beach cleanup.

Village Viking teams compete in a sports league with six other schools. Athletes in Grades 4–6 play on teams in flag football, soccer, basketball, and volleyball. Students also receive training in track and field events.

VILLAGE SCHOOL

Special events are the all-school picnic, Open House, School fund-raisers, Grandparents Day/Science Fair, and Art Show. Students who graduated in June are invited to return to the School for a day in the fall.

ADMISSION AND COSTS. Village School welcomes students of average to superior ability from all racial, ethnic, and religious backgrounds who demonstrate the potential to thrive in the School's nurturing environment and to benefit from its academic and extracurricular programs. Most students enter in the Transitional Kindergarten or Kindergarten levels, although admission is offered in any grade where vacancies exist. Students are accepted based on a school visit, recommendations, and the previous school record, as applicable. Application should be made a year in advance of the desired enrollment date. The deadline for submission of applications is December 1 for all grades. Occasionally, midyear enrollment is possible. The nonrefundable application fee is $125.

In 2009–10, the tuition is $21,945, plus a one-time New Student Fee of $1500. Financial aid is awarded on the basis of need. A tuition payment plan is available.

Assistant Head of School/Director of Admissions: Barbara Ruth-Williams
Director of Finance & Operations: Manuel Pardo
Director of Advancement: Sue Slotnick

The Walden School 1970

74 South San Gabriel Boulevard, Pasadena, CA 91107
Tel. 626-792-6166; Admission Ext. 12; Fax 626-792-1335
Web Site www.waldenschool.net
E-mail admissions@waldenschool.net

Walden School, accredited by the California Association of Independent Schools and the Western Association of Colleges and Schools, enrolls 250 boys and girls as day students in Pre-Kindergarten through Grade 6. Walden teaches children to think critically, to discover the interrelatedness of what they learn, and to develop the skills of traditional scholarship. The developmentally appropriate curriculum encourages responsibility, initiative, child-led inquiry, ethical behavior, and personal excellence. Before- and after-school child-care is offered. Tuition: $15,150; New Student Fee: $500. Financial aid is available. Christena Barnes is Assistant Director/Admission Director; Matt Allio is Director. *Western Association.*

Westridge School 1913

324 Madeline Drive, Pasadena, CA 91105
Tel. 626-799-1153; Fax 626-799-9236
Web Site www.westridge.org; E-mail hhopper@westridge.org

Founded in 1913, Westridge School is an independent day school for college-bound girls in Grades 4 through 12. Designed to promote independence and self-reliance in a cooperative and interdependent community, the School's intellecutally challenging program is enhanced by offerings in art, music, drama, and computer science. Extracurricular activities include clubs, sports, and student government. There is a community service requirement for all Upper School students. Tuition: $23,000–$26,550. Financial Aid: $2,000,000. Helen V. Hopper is Admissions Director; Elizabeth J. McGregor (University of London, B.A.; Columbia University, M.Ed.) is Head of School. *Western Association.*

Westside Neighborhood School 1980

5401 Beethoven Street, Los Angeles, CA 90066
Tel. 310-574-8650; Fax 310-574-8657
Web Site www.wnsk8.com; E-mail admissions@wnsk8.com

Parents and interested citizens established Westside Neighborhood School to provide quality education in a safe, respectful, and stimulating environment. From its initial enrollment of 56 students, the School has grown to serve 315 boys and girls from diverse racial, cultural, and economic backgrounds as day students in Pre-Kindergarten–Grade 8. The challenging preparatory curriculum, which is accredited by the California Association of Independent Schools, is designed to develop each student's intellectual, social, emotional, and physical potential. A strong foundation in reading, writing, and math is at the core of the program, integrated with social studies, science, Spanish, visual and performing arts, music, and physical education. Electives may include outdoor adventure, film making, robotics, and acting. Computer technology is used as a learning and research tool across the disciplines, while field trips to destinations in the Greater Los Angeles area enhance classroom instruction. Among the activities is an elected student council with representatives from Grades 2 through 8. Students also take part in after-school sports and an optional summer program. Tuition: $17,300–$18,300. Robin Sills is Director of Admissions; Bradley Zacuto was appointed Head of School in 2008.

Wildwood School 1971

Elementary Campus (Kindergarten–Grade 5): 12201 Washington
Place, Los Angeles, CA 90066
Tel. 310-397-3134; Fax 310-397-5134
Middle/Upper Campus (Grades 6–12): 11811 Olympic Boulevard,
Los Angeles, CA 90064
Tel. 310-478-7189; Fax 310-478-6875
Web Site www.wildwood.org; E-mail wwadmission@wildwood.org

Wildwood School is a college preparatory day school for more than 700 students in Kindergarten through Grade 12. Wildwood's challenging academic program helps students develop as critical thinkers, problem solvers, and collaborators. At the elementary school, multiage classes foster social and emotional skills as well as development in foundational curriculum. The middle and upper school program focues on project-based learning and includes advisory programs, honors classes, and internships. Students take part in performing arts productions, art exhibitions, athletics, and science competitions. Tuition: $23,000–$28,000. Chantelle Pierre is Director of Admission; Landis Green is Head of School. *Western Association.*

Windrush School 1976

1800 Elm Street, El Cerrito, CA 94530
Tel. 510-970-7580; Admission Ext. 203; Fax 510-215-2326
Web Site www.windrush.org; E-mail dbond@windrush.org

WINDRUSH SCHOOL

Windrush enrolls more than 250 students from diverse backgrounds in Kindergarten–Grade 8 on a 4-acre campus in the San Francisco/East Bay area. The progressive curriculum enables graduates to navigate life in all its varied complexity with humor, optimism, and determination. A learning-by-doing approach instills a lifelong love of learning in students. The faculty consistently assesses teaching methods and student abilities to ensure success academically and personally. Students master academic and intellectual skills and develop a sense of who they are as learners and individuals. They are taught to use information critically and creatively. They also respect themselves and others while having compassion for their community, humanity, and the world. Spanish, art, and physical education are taught in all grades. Computer, music, drama, and service learning also enrich the curriculum. Tuition: $17,500–$20,000. Tuition assistance, after-school care, and summer programs are available. David Bond is Admissions Director; Ilana Kaufman is Head of School. *Western Association.*

Windward School 1971

11350 Palms Boulevard, Los Angeles, CA 90066
Tel. 310-391-7127; Admissions Ext. 224; Fax 310-397-5655
Web Site www.windwardschool.org

Educator, consultant, and visionary Shirley Windward founded the school that bears her name to provide a quality education that developed responsible, caring, ethical, well-informed, prepared students. Windward School challenges every student to achieve his or her maximum potential throgh a college preparatory program that emphasizes academic excellence as well as character and values. Enrolling 475 day stueents from diverse backgrounds in grades 7–12, Windward offers rigorous course work in the traditional liberal arts, sciences, and humanities, complemented by modern languages and information technology. Honors classes in most areas and AP courses in all disciplines are designed to enable students to matriculate in selective colleges and universities nationwide. Community service is required at all grade levels. The visual and performing arts are integral to the overall program. Among the activities are Prefects, publications, chess, debate, robotics, drama, music, and varsity and junior varsity sports. Tuition: $30,141. Financial aid is available. Sharon Pearline is Director of Admissions; Thomas W. Gilder is Headmaster. *Western Association.*

Woodland School 1981

360 La Cuesta Drive, Portola Valley, CA 94028
Tel. 650-854-9065
Web Site www.woodland-school.org
E-mail info@woodland-school.org

WOODLAND SCHOOL

Woodland School provides an educational program designed to develop "the good student and the good person in each child." A nonsectarian day school enrolling 250 boys and girls in Preschool through Grade 8, Woodland holds students to high academic and behavioral standards through a curriculum that places equal emphasis on scholastic achievement and ethical values. Core subjects promote mastery of skills and comprehension in language arts, mathematics, science, and social studies. Building on the foundation acquired in the early grades, students progress to topics in literature, algebra, human anatomy, poetry, essays, and other course work in anticipation of the challenges of college preparatory secondary schools. The 10-acre campus permits outdoor educational activities, while field trips to the San Francisco Symphony, Monterey Bay Aquarium, museums, and Yosemite extend learning beyond the classroom. After-school programs provide music lessons, chess, drawing, pastels, drama, computer labs, and other pursuits. Woodland athletes may compete in volleyball, flag football, cross-country, basketball, tennis, swimming, and golf. Tuition: $15,900–$16,900. Louise B. Douglas is Director of Admissions; John Ora is Head of School.

COLORADO

Alexander Dawson School   1970

10455 Dawson Drive, Lafayette, CO 80026
Tel. 303-665-6679; Fax 303-381-0415
Web Site www.dawsonschool.org; E-mail jmitchell@dawsonschool.org

Dawson, a coeducational college preparatory day school enrolling 420 students in Kindergarten–Grade 12, is accredited by the National Association of Independent Schools and the Association of Colorado Independent Schools. With small classes, committed teachers, and high standards, Dawson aims to develop potential, build character, and prepare students for robust, intellectual, physical, and ethical lives. A traditional program includes Honors and Advanced Placement courses, 15 sports, theater, outdoor education, and 15 arts electives. Dawson's average SAT scores are the highest in the area, and the graduating Class of 2009 earned more than $2,000,000 in scholarships. Tuition: $18,650. Financial Aid: $850,000. James Irwin Mitchell is Director of Admissions; Brian Johnson is Headmaster. *North Central Association.*

Colorado Academy   1906

3800 South Pierce Street, Denver, CO 80235
Tel. 303-986-1501; Admissions 303-914-2513; Fax 303-914-2589
Web Site www.coloradoacademy.org
E-mail info@coloradoacademy.org

Colorado Academy is a coeducational day school enrolling 890 students in Pre-Kindergarten–Grade 12. Located on a 95-acre campus in southwest Denver, the Academy provides a 9:1 student-faculty ratio and a program emphasizing a well-rounded college preparatory program. Each division (Lower, Middle, and Upper) has its own principal, faculty, and facility. Fine arts and athletics are offered at all levels. Publications, sports, drama, community service, and clubs are among the activities. A summer recreational camp with academic enrichment, arts, and sports is available. Tuition: $14,750–$19,470. Financial Aid: $2,100,000. Catherine Laskey is Director of Admission; Dr. Mike Davis (College of Wooster, B.A.; Vanderbilt University, Ph.D.) is Head of School.

The Colorado Springs School   1962

21 Broadmoor Avenue, Colorado Springs, CO 80906
Tel. 719-475-9747; Fax 719-475-9864
Web Site www.css.org; E-mail twilliamson@css.org

The Colorado Springs School offers an experiential coeducational environment for 360 students in Pre-Kindergarten–Grade 12. Through quality academics and mentoring, CSS prepares students to think independently and to meet the needs of a dynamic world with leadership, ingenuity, problem-solving skills, and personal integrity. The School values strong academics, builds character and authentic relationships, and maintains a global perspective within an inspirational environment. The rigorous curriculum includes small classes, Advanced Placement courses, speech, world languages, hands-on discovery, and in-depth college counseling and guidance. Experience-centered seminars, Mount Caravan, Walkabout, service learning, and other special programs enhance the core academic program. Students take part in numerous extracurricular programs such as interscholastic sports, school government, music, art, drama, academic clubs, and publications. Tuition: $7850–$16,900. Financial aid is available. Tiffany Williamson is Director of Admission; Kevin Reel (Stanford, B.A., M.S.) is Head of School.

The Lowell Whiteman School   1957

42605 County Road 36, Steamboat Springs, CO 80487
Tel. 970-879-1350; Admissions Ext. 12; Fax 970-879-0506
Web Site www.lws.edu; E-mail admissions@lws.edu

THE LOWELL WHITEMAN SCHOOL

The Lowell Whiteman School, located in the heart of the Rocky Mountains, serves boarding and day students in Grades 9–12. The School fosters students' personal and academic growth with a challenging, traditional liberal arts curriculum and unique opportunities beyond the classroom. An average class size of 8, small-group experience abroad and in the wilderness, and personal relationships between students and faculty provide the foundation for that growth. Of the 95 students, about one-third are competitive skiers and riders, and two-thirds study abroad. Competitive skiers and riders train with the world-renowned Steamboat Winter Sports Club. Study-abroad students immerse themselves in another culture for a month, traveling to countries such as Bhutan, Bolivia, Chile, Mongolia, Senegal, Vietnam, and Zimbabwe. The Lowell Whiteman School has graduated 16 Olympians and a Pulitzer Prize winner. All students participate in an outdoor program that offers ice climbing, kayaking, horseback riding, canoeing, skiing/riding, and mountain biking. Boarding Tuition: $32,900; Day Tuition: $17,700. Financial aid is available. Walt Daub is Headmaster.

St. Anne's Episcopal School   1950

2701 South York Street, Denver, CO 80210-6098
Tel. 303-756-9481; Fax 303-756-5512
Web Site www.st-annes.org; E-mail rkelly@st-annes.org

ST. ANNE'S EPISCOPAL SCHOOL

St. Anne's seeks to guide children toward personal development and fosters social responsibility and involvement. The School instills a genuine love of learning through a broad, challenging academic program in a supportive, nurturing environment. Committed to Judeo-Christian values, St. Anne's is a family school that embraces students of varied talents, abilities, and backgrounds. The 422 students in Preschool–Grade 8 are taught language arts, literature, math, computer, science, fine arts, and foreign language at all levels. Summer programs and extended day are available. Tuition: $8722–$16,444. Financial Aid: $895,000. Rose Kelly is Director of Admission; Alan Smiley (Middlebury College, B.A. 1987; University of Virginia, M.Ed. 1988) was appointed Head of School in 2006.

Telluride Mountain School   1998

200 San Miguel River Drive, Telluride, CO 81435-8924
Tel. 970-728-1969; Fax 970-369-4412
Web Site www.telluridemtnschool.org
E-mail info@telluridemtnschool.org

Telluride Mountain School, accredited by the Association of Colorado Independent Schools and a member of the National Association of Independent Schools, was founded to provide a challenging academic program that combines college preparation with outdoor education and community service. From an initial enrollment of 6, the School today serves over 100 day boys and girls in Preschool to Grade 12. A newly renovated 14,000-square-foot building (2006) houses all grades. The values-based curriculum develops well-rounded young citizens of their global society. The Montessori preschool phases into a more traditional approach for the upper grades. The core curriculum centers on reading/writing, language arts, math, science, and social studies, with technology across the disciplines. Spanish, music, visual and dramatic arts, and physical education are also emphasized. The Winter Sports Program includes instruction for all ability levels, from recreational skier/snowboarders to aspiring Olympic competitors. Experiential learning trips are conducted locally, regionally, nationally, and internationally. Tuition: $5140–$18,670. Financial aid is available. Karen Walker is Admissions Director; James Loan is Head of School.

THE LOWELL WHITEMAN SCHOOL

CONNECTICUT

Academy of Our Lady of Mercy, Lauralton Hall 1905

200 High Street, Milford, CT 06460
Tel. 203-877-2786; Admissions Ext. 125; Fax 203-876-9760
Web Site www.lauraltonhall.org
E-mail kshine@lauraltonhall.org

Connecticut's oldest Catholic college preparatory school for young women, known familiarly as Lauralton Hall, enrolls more than 400 students in Grades 9–12. Sponsored by the Sisters of Mercy, the school offers a rigorous, values-centered liberal arts curriculum designed to nurture the mind, heart, and spirit within a community of faith. Advanced Placement and honors courses are available, and religious studies and community service are required. Girls may participate in numerous activities, including a mentoring program, academic honor societies, publications, Youth and Government, school government, clubs, and more than 14 sports. One hundred percent of graduates enter college. Tuition: $13,315. Financial aid is available. Kathleen Shine is Director of Admissions; Antoinette Iadarola, Ph.D., is President. *New England Association.*

Brunswick School 1902

100 Maher Avenue, Greenwich, CT 06830
Tel. 203-625-5800; Admissions 203-625-5842; Fax 203-625-5889
Web Site www.brunswickschool.org
E-mail jharris@brunswickschool.org

A college preparatory day school enrolling 896 boys in Pre-Kindergarten–Grade 12, Brunswick provides an integrated program of academics, arts, community service, and athletics. Advanced Placement and honors courses are offered. Students in Grades 9–12 have coordinate classes and activities with Greenwich Academy, a neighboring girls' school. Brunswick continues to expand its technology and laptop programs. A state-of-the-art campus for the lower and middle schools, located on the 104-acre King Street site, includes extensive athletic facilities and fields. Tuition: $24,700–$32,100. Financial Aid: $4,247,600. Jeffry Harris is Director of Admission; Thomas W. Philip is Headmaster. *New England Association.*

Choate Rosemary Hall 1890

333 Christian Street, Wallingford, CT 06492
Tel. 203-697-2000; Admission 203-697-2239; Fax 203-697-2629
Web Site www.choate.edu; E-mail admission@choate.edu

Choate Rosemary Hall in Wallingford, Connecticut, is a coeducational, boarding and day, college preparatory school enrolling students in Grades 9–12 and a postgraduate year. Wallingford (population 46,000) is located off Interstate 91, 15 miles north of New Haven. New York and Boston are about two hours away; Bradley International Airport is 45 miles to the north.

Rosemary Hall (1890) was founded by Mary Atwater Choate and The Choate School (1896) by her husband, Judge William Gardner Choate, on the same site. Rosemary Hall moved from Wallingford to Greenwich in 1900 and returned to the Wallingford campus in 1971 as a coordinate school, completing the merger to coeducation in 1974.

Choate Rosemary Hall provides a rigorous academic curriculum and emphasizes the formation of character. The school encourages students to think critically and communicate clearly, understand various methods of intellectual inquiry, and develop global perspectives. Community service is mandatory.

Choate Rosemary Hall is a nonprofit corporation governed by a self-perpetuating Board of Trustees. The school is accredited by the New England Association of Schools and Colleges and holds membership in the National Association of Independent Schools, among other associations.

THE CAMPUS. The school is situated on 458 acres in a residential setting. More than 121 houses, dormitories, and classroom buildings are on campus, along with 13 athletic fields, 22 tennis courts, and the state-of-the-art Bruce '45 and Lueza Gelb Track.

CHOATE ROSEMARY HALL

The Carl C. Icahn Center for Science (1989), designed by I.M. Pei, houses classrooms, laboratories, and an auditorium. The Paul Mellon Arts Center (1972), also designed by Pei, houses two theaters, a recital hall, art galleries, studios, practice rooms, and a music production studio. The Paul Mellon Humanities Center contains the English and History, Philosophy, Religion and Social Sciences Departments, photography and digital video studios, and a computer center. The Andrew Mellon Library houses 68,000 titles, including special collections and a wide range of electronic services. The Language Media Lab with a 32-station computer laboratory is located in Steele Hall. Students can access the campus computer network from dormitory rooms. All classroom buildings and student rooms are wired for Internet access.

The Johnson Athletic Center holds basketball courts, squash courts, weight rooms, a wrestling room, a suspended $1/10$-mile indoor track, and an addition with a fitness center (2002). Other athletic facilities include the 25-meter Larry Hart Pool, Remsen Arena and Hockey Rink, Macquire Gym with climbing wall, Torrence Hunt Tennis Center, and Sylvester Boat House.

THE FACULTY. Edward J. Shanahan, a graduate of St. Joseph's

College (B.A. 1965), Fordham University (M.A. 1968), and the University of Wisconsin (Ph.D. 1982), was appointed Headmaster in 1991. Dr. Shanahan was Dean of the College at Dartmouth for eight years and was previously Dean of Students at Wesleyan University.

Ninety-three men and 73 women, including 47 administrators, comprise the faculty. Most reside on campus and act as advisers to students who live with them. In addition to bachelor's degrees, they hold 121 advanced degrees, including 7 doctorates, from such institutions as Boston University 2, Columbia 7, Cornell 2, Dartmouth 2, Harvard 2, Middlebury 17, New York University 2, Southern Connecticut State University 5, Wesleyan 11, Yale 13, and the Universities of Chicago 2, Connecticut 8, and Michigan 6.

CHOATE ROSEMARY HALL

A full-time physician and staff nurses provide round-the-clock medical care in the Pratt Health Center. Full-service hospitals are nearby.

STUDENT BODY. In 2009–10, the school enrolled 630 boarders and 220 day students in Forms 3–6 (Grades 9–12). The male-female ratio is about 50:50. Students come from 41 states and 39 foreign countries; 33 percent receive financial aid.

ACADEMIC PROGRAM. The academic year, divided into trimesters, begins in early September and ends in early June, with vacations in the winter and spring. Classes are held five days a week and on seven Saturdays, scheduled in seven 45- or 50-minute periods between 8:00 A.M. and 2:55 P.M. on Monday, Tuesday, Thursday, and Friday and between 8:00 A.M. and 12:30 P.M. on Wednesday and Saturday. Study hours are 7:30 to 9:00 P.M. and 9:45 to 10:30 P.M. on academic evenings. Parents receive reports at the end of each term three times a year.

Graduation requirements include 12 terms of English; completion of the third-year level in Chinese, French, Latin, or Spanish languages; one year of U.S. History and World History (for 3- and 4-year students); Algebra I & II and Geometry; 14 terms of quantitative courses; one year each of physical science and biological science; one term of philosophy or religion; one term of contemporary global studies; and three terms of arts, including two areas of the arts. Honors and Advanced Placement courses are offered in all areas.

Course offerings in English include American Studies, British Literature, Comparative Literature, Classical Traditions,

Latin American Literature, Irish Literature, The Graphic Novel, and writing workshops in fiction, nonfiction, poetry, and creative writing. Interdisciplinary courses include Public Speaking, Romanticism, Modernism, Post-Modernism, and Debate. Language courses include Intensive Beginning Arabic, Greek, and Italian as well as full-year courses in Chinese, French, Latin, and Spanish through the sixth year. History and social science offerings include Contemporary Issues, World History, U.S. History, British History, Modern Middle East, 20th Century Social History, War and Warfare, The Holocaust, European History, Philosophy, Moral Reasoning, World Religions, Modern Japan, Modern China, and Constitutional Law as well as several courses in political science, psychology, religion, and economics. Mathematics courses range from Algebra I through Linear Algebra and Multivariable Calculus with additional opportunities for the most advanced math students, as well as Statistics, Probability, Dynamical Modeling, and Computer Science. Science courses include Physics, Astronomy, Electronics, Astrophsics, Chemistry, Organic Chemistry, Chemistry of Food and Drugs, Environmental Science, Marine Science, Biology, Human Anatomy and Physiology, Cell Biology, and Microbiology. Music courses include a variety of ensembles, music history, theory, and production courses; visual art courses feature Art History, Drawing, Oil Painting, Sculpture, Ceramics, Weaving, Photography, Digital Video, and theater courses in Acting, Directing, and Dance as well as performance opportunities outside the curriculum.

The school offers study abroad language-immersion programs in China, France, and Spain as well as cultural-immersion programs in Germany and Rome, Italy. Seniors may take an independent study project in the spring under faculty direction. Signature academic programs include the Capstone Program, Science Research Program, and Arts Concentration.

Virtually all graduates go to college. Popular choices for the Class of 2009 include Georgetown University 10; Yale 8; Columbia, Wesleyan, and the University of Pennsylvania, 7 each; and Dartmouth, George Washington, Harvard, Johns Hopkins, and Princeton, 5 each.

Summer Programs include the Writing Project, the John F. Kennedy Institute of Government, English Language Institute, and programs for students of middle school age including Math/Science Institute for Girls and the Writing Workshop.

STUDENT ACTIVITIES. The Student Council provides a forum for student views. Students are also elected to the Judicial Committee, which aids the Dean of Students in cases of school rule violations.

CHOATE ROSEMARY HALL

Activities include the yearbook, newspaper, literary magazine, sports weekly, and campus radio station; language clubs, math team, tutoring society; and computer, science, and theater clubs. Community service programs allow students to volunteer locally. Choral groups, student orchestra, string ensembles, and the jazz ensemble provide performance opportunities. Six student theater productions are staged each year. Interest groups include Amnesty International, Gold Key (campus tour guides), International Club, and Movie Appreciation Club, among others.

All students participate in athletics, and the school fields varsity and junior varsity teams to compete in football, cross-country, field hockey, soccer, water polo, basketball, ice hockey, squash, swimming, volleyball, wrestling, archery, baseball, softball, crew, golf, lacrosse, tennis, and track. Intramural and non-competitive sports include basketball, swimming, rock climbing, volleyball, tennis, weight training, dance, and others.

Theater productions, films, concerts, and dances are offered on campus, while field trips take students to museums and theaters in New York, Boston, and New Haven. Special events include Parents and Reunion weekends and programs sponsored by the Spears Endowment for Spiritual and Moral Education.

ADMISSION AND COSTS. Choate Rosemary Hall seeks to enroll students from diverse ethnic and social backgrounds who are highly motivated and passionate about learning. Applicants are admitted in all grades on the basis of previous academic performance and their ability to contribute to the community. Transcripts, standardized test results, and letters of recommendation are required along with a personal interview. The application fee is $50 for U.S. applicants and $100 for international students.

CHOATE ROSEMARY HALL

Boarding tuition for 2009–10 is $43,380; day tuition is $33,030. Tuition insurance is included in the tuition; payment plans are available. Choate Rosemary Hall subscribes to the School & Student Services by NAIS and offers financial aid amounting to about $8,500,000 annually. The Icahn Scholars Program, an initiative made possible by the Icahn Charitable Foundation of New York City, identifies bright, motivated, and talented middle schoolers from disadvantaged backgrounds and provides them with a fully funded Choate Rosemary Hall education.

Associate Headmaster & Dean of Academic Affairs: Kathleen Lyons Wallace
Assistant Headmaster & Dean of Faculty: Stephen C. Farrell
Assistant Headmaster & Dean of Students: John H. Ford
Director of Admission: Ray Diffley III

Executive Director of Development & Alumni Relations: Daniel J. Courcey III '86
Director of College Counseling: Tina Segalla Grant
Chief Financial Officer: Richard Saltz
Director of Athletics: Ned Gallagher

Cold Spring School   1982

263 Chapel Street, New Haven, CT 06513
Tel. 203-787-1584; Admissions Ext. 216; Fax 203-787-9444
Web Site www.coldspringschool.org
E-mail sarmstrong@coldspringschool.org

COLD SPRING SCHOOL

Cold Spring School enrolls 135 children from Preschool through Grade 6 in a richly diverse urban neighborhood adjacent to a city park. Multiage classrooms, each with a master teacher and an associate teacher, are designed to foster the intellectual and emotional needs of students and provide them with a strong sense of community. The project-based curriculum, enriched by art, music, Spanish, and physical education, develops strong academic skills, a positive self-image, and a sense of civic responsibility. An optional extended day program from 3:00 to 5:30 P.M. is $2400. Tuition: $12,450–$18,100. Financial aid is available. Sara Armstrong is Director of Admissions; Jeff Jonathan (Middlebury College, B.A.; Columbia University, M.A.) is Head of School.

Convent of the Sacred Heart   1848

1177 King Street, Greenwich, CT 06831
Tel. 203-531-6500; Admissions 203-532-3534; Fax 203-531-5206
Web Site www.cshgreenwich.org; E-mail admission@cshgreenwich.org

Convent of the Sacred Heart is an independent, Catholic, college preparatory day school enrolling 770 girls in Preschool–Grade 12. Part of the international Network of 200 Sacred Heart Schools, including 21 in the U.S., Sacred Heart provides a strong academic foundation appropriate to each student's individual talents and abilities within an environment that fosters spirituality and establishes a strong sense of personal values. Approximately 94 percent of the Class of 2009 earned admission to at least one college ranked "most competitive" or "highly competitive." The 110-acre campus includes a new Middle School and Library/Media Center, technology centers, including a new broadcast journalism suite, theater and expanded space for the arts, and two new synthetic-turf fields. The laptop program is in use in Grades 7–12. Girls take part in varsity and junior varsity sports, Student Council, publications, music groups, Model UN, and community service programs. Tuition: $28,500–$31,300. Financial aid is available. Catherine Machir is Director of Admission and Financial Aid; Pamela Juan Hayes '64 (Briarcliff College, B.A.; Manhattanville College, M.A.) is Head of School.

The Country School   1955

341 Opening Hill Road, Madison, CT 06443
Tel. 203-421-3113; Fax 203-421-4390
Web Site www.thecountryschool.org

The Country School in Madison, Connecticut, is a coeducational day school offering a traditional education for students in Preschool through Grade 8. With an enrollment of 250 students, The Country School offers spirited teaching, hands-on learning, and a balanced program of academic, artistic, and athletic challenges. The newly completed low ropes course and the children's garden enhance the School's hallmark program in Outdoor Education. Faculty and staff recognize their responsibility to meet not only academic challenges but personal and ethical ones as well. The School encourages its students to look beyond themselves, to work cooperatively with others, and to serve their communities and the larger world. The Country School expects much of its students in the belief that they have much to give. Tuition: $9900–$22,785. Financial Aid: $437,000. Christine Aulicino is Director of Admission; William E. Powers (Fairfield University, B.A.; Wesleyan University, M.A.) was appointed Head of School in 2005.

Eagle Hill School   1975

45 Glenville Road, Greenwich, CT 06831-5392
Tel. 203-622-9240
Web Site www.eaglehillschool.org

The mission of Eagle Hill School is to educate bright children with learning disabilities. The individualized, interdisciplinary, and trasitional curriculum is structured to meet the needs of young people with language-based learning disabilities in a structured and nurturing environment. Serving the tristate area of Connecticut, New York, and New Jersey, Eagle Hill enrolls 250 boys and girls from diverse backgrounds, ages 6–16, as five-day residential and day students. The School aims to instill the academic skills and self-confidence that enable students to reach maximum potential and return to mainstream educational settings as quickly as possible. The core academic program emphasizes reading and writing, oral language, history, math, science, social studies, and study skills. Daily tutorial classes provide in-depth remedial instruction in language arts as a basis for all learning, with exercises in note taking, time management, and other study skills essential to academic success as well as speech and motor training. The fine arts, technology, and athletics round out the experience. Summer programs are available. Boarding Tuition: $67,200; Day Tuition: $52,650. Tom Cone is Director of Admissions; Dr. Marjorie Castro is Head of School.

The Ethel Walker School   1911

230 Bushy Hill Road, Simsbury, CT 06070
Tel. 860-658-4467; Fax 860-658-6763
Web Site www.ethelwalker.org
E-mail admission@ethelwalker.org

The Ethel Walker School is a college preparatory day and boarding school enrolling nearly 300 young women in Grades 6–12. A dedicated and academically gifted faculty strives to foster creativity, respect, confidence, responsibility, and compassion. A traditional liberal arts curriculum offers over 100 courses, including AP courses, off-campus and independent study, exchange programs, and internships. An average class size of 11 and a 5:1 student-faculty ratio ensure individualized attention. Extracurricular options include school government, athletics, equestrian programs, dance, choir, drama, arts, and clubs. Service learning and environmental stewardship are key elements in curriculum and campus life. The 300-acre campus features a performing arts center, dormitories, extensive athletic

THE ETHEL WALKER SCHOOL

fields and facilities, tennis courts, observatory, library, and a nondenominational chapel. Adjacent conservation acreage includes wetlands, meadows, streams, and hiking trails and offers experiential learning and outdoor education. Boarding Tuition: $43,350; Day Tuition: $31,785. Financial aid is available. Erin Corbett is Director of Admission; Elizabeth Speers (Middlebury, B.A.; Johns Hopkins, M.L.A.) is Head of School. *New England Association.*

Fairfield Country Day School   1936

2970 Bronson Road, Fairfield, CT 06824
Tel. 203-259-2723; Fax 203-259-3249
Web Site www.fairfieldcountryday.org
E-mail richard.runkel@fcdsmail.org

Fairfield Country Day is an independent school for 270 boys in Kindergarten through Grade 9. All aspects of a Country Day education are designed to help each student expand his desire and ability to acquire knowledge, stimulate his curiosity and creativity, and enhance his self-esteem and respect for others. At every grade level, Country Day boys work in a curriculum constantly evolving to meet their needs. Emphasis and attention is devoted to the core subjects and fundamental skills integral to fostering the enjoyment of learning within each child and laying the foundation for academic success: reading, writing, and mathematics. Every student also has specialized instruction in science, foreign language, and technology. These curricular offerings prepare students to succeed in the most demanding secondary schools while identifying their personal passions and academic interests. Tuition: $28,200–$30,200. Financial aid is available. Richard Runkel is Director of Admissions; Robert Kaufmann is Headmaster.

The Foote School   1916

50 Loomis Place, New Haven, CT 06511
Tel. 203-777-3464; Fax 203-777-2809
Web Site www.footeschool.org; E-mail laltshul@footeschool.org

The Foote School, enrolling 470 day boys and girls in Kindergarten–Grade 9, seeks to provide educational excellence in a child-centered environment by a grounding in basic skills with emphasis on the aesthetic and intellectual development of each student. Foote is committed to a multicultural curriculum, designed to foster an appreciation of human differences. Art, music, drama, French or Spanish, community service, and gym are taught in all grades. Computer literacy programs begin in Grade 1, Latin in Grade 7. Special activities and sports teams are offered in upper grades. A summer program serves ages 3–15. Tuition: $18,370–$21,370. Financial Aid: $1,300,000. Laura O. Altshul is Director of Admissions; Carol Maoz (University of Massachusetts, B.A.; Harvard, M.Ed.) is Head of School.

Glenholme School   1969

81 Sabbaday Lane, Washington, CT 06793
Tel. 860-868-7377; Fax 860-868-7894
Web Site www.theglenholmeschool.org
E-mail admissions@theglenholmeschool.org

GLENHOLME SCHOOL

An exceptional boarding school for students with special needs, The Glenholme School offers an individually prescribed learning environment with a steadfast academic curriculum. Using effective individualized services, the School applies a positive behavior support model focused on development of social skills and lifelong strategies for success. Glenholme's milieu therapy addresses varying levels of academic, social, and special-needs development in boys and girls ages 10 through postgraduates, preparing them for continued education in traditional day and boarding schools, colleges, and universities. The School specializes in Asperger's/ADHD, emotional, behavioral, and learning disabilities, motivational management, self-discipline strategies, character development, relationship mentoring, social coaching, multimedia curriculum, and career exploration. A summer program includes academics and camp. Boarding Tuition: $117,000; Day Tuition: $43,000. Kathi L. Fitzherbert is Director of Admissions; Maryann Campbell is Executive Director.

Greens Farms Academy   1925

P.O. Box 998, 35 Beachside Avenue, Greens Farms, CT 06838-0998
Tel. 203-256-0717; Admission 203-256-7514; Fax 203-256-7591
Web Site www.gfacademy.org; E-mail admission@gfacademy.org

Greens Farms Academy, a K–12, coeducational day school located in the Greens Farms section of Westport, enrolls 650 students of diverse backgrounds from more than 30 communities in Connecticut. The school is known for its culture of achievement, sense of community, and attention to character. In addition to academic excellence, GFA offers a broad arts program, competitive athletics, and substantial community service at all levels. Student life hinges on trust and close faculty-student relationships. Two new Middle and Upper School science and performing arts wings have expanded the program offerings. The Upper School offers Advanced Placement and Honors courses in all major disciplines, and students take advantage of independent studies, science research, and off-campus study both nationally and internationally. Students of color represent 17 percent of the enrollment. Summer programs are available. Tuition: $29,560–$32,450. Need-based Financial Aid: $1,800,000. Stephanie B. Whitney is Director of Admission; Janet M. Hartwell (University of Leeds, B.A.; Columbia, M.A.) was appointed Head of School in 2003. *New England Association.*

Greenwich Academy   1827

200 North Maple Avenue, Greenwich, CT 06830
Tel. 203-625-8900; Admission 203-625-8990; Fax 203-625-8912
Web Site www.greenwichacademy.org
E-mail akatz@greenwichacademy.org
E-mail nhoffmann@greenwichacademy.org

Greenwich Academy, enrolling 795 girls in Pre-Kindergarten–Grade 12, emphasizes rigorous academics, active community service, and extensive programs in athletics and the arts. Lower School encourages a love of learning and mastery of basic skills. Middle School develops literary analysis, creative writing and research methods, and an understanding of math, world history, current events, and scientific principles. Upper School, coordinated with Brunswick School for boys, includes Honors and Advanced Placement courses in most disciplines. Laptop computers are required in all classes in Grades 7–12. Tuition: $29,900–$32,100. Financial Aid: $4,359,850. Abby S. Katz is Dean of Admission and Financial Aid; Molly H. King is Head of School. *New England Association.*

Hamden Hall Country Day School   1912

1108 Whitney Avenue, Hamden, CT 06517
Tel. 203-752-2600; Admissions Ext. 610; Fax 203-752-2651
Web Site www.hamdenhall.org

HAMDEN HALL COUNTRY DAY SCHOOL in Hamden, Connecticut, is a coeducational college preparatory school enrolling 555 students in Pre-School through Grade 12. Hamden (population approximately 55,000) is situated in south-central Connecticut, 3 miles north of New Haven.

Hamden Hall was founded in 1912 as a day school for boys by Dr. John P. Cushing, its first Headmaster. Coeducation was introduced in 1927 and, within seven years, the School was expanded to encompass Grades 9–12.

Hamden Hall's mission is to challenge students to develop a strong sense of personal integrity and social responsibility while preparing them for demanding academic programs at the collegiate level. Faculty serve as role models and mentors in the classroom, on the playing field, and in other areas of school life. With an 8:1 student-teacher ratio, the School aims to offer a nurturing environment in which young people can reach their full potential intellectually, physically, and socially.

A nonprofit institution, Hamden Hall is governed by a 20-

member Board of Trustees. It is accredited by the New England Association of Schools and Colleges and holds membership in the National Association of Independent Schools and the Connecticut Association of Independent Schools.

THE CAMPUS. Hamden Hall is set on 12 acres overlooking Lake Whitney. The Dolven Admissions Center contains administrative and college counseling offices, a large art studio, and a computerized video production center. In front of Dolven, a colorful display of the flags of 35 nations represents the nationalities and ethnic backgrounds of the School's diverse student body. The three-story Joseph and Esther Schiavone Science Center houses classrooms, state-of-the-art facilities for science and the arts, Middle and Upper School computer labs, and the dining room. The Taylor Fine Arts Center features a fully equipped theater, music studios, and practice rooms. The Taylor Gymnasium includes basketball, wrestling, and weight-training facilities. Classrooms for the primary grades (Pre-School–Grade 3) are located in the Ethyle R. Alpert Building, while the upper Elementary (Grades 4–6), Middle School (Grades 7–8), and Upper School (Grades 9–12) are housed in Whitson Hall. The Ellen and Charles Swain Library, with separate library facilities for the Lower and Middle/Upper Schools, houses a collection of more than 25,000 volumes, 60 periodicals, and extensive reference resources. Swain is linked electronically to computer networks via the Internet.

HAMDEN HALL COUNTRY DAY SCHOOL

The campus has an athletic field, a challenging outdoors program, and a play area for younger children. An additional 30-acre sports facility is located 1.5 miles away, and students use golf and swimming facilities at Yale University and other local colleges.

THE FACULTY. Robert J. Izzo is Head of School. He earned a B.A. in Education from the University of Rhode Island in 1983 and an M.B.A. from Bryant University in 1987. Since joining Hamden Hall in 1989, Mr. Izzo has served as chief financial officer, mathematics teacher, and coach. Previously, he taught at the elementary-school level and served as a school administrator.

The faculty include 13 administrators and 83 teachers. They have earned 94 baccalaureate and 60 advanced degrees, including 6 doctorates, representing study at such institutions as Adelphi, Albertus Magnus, Amherst, Bates, Beirut College for Women, Boston College, Bowdoin, Brandeis, Brown, Bryant, Central Connecticut State, Clark, Colby, Colgate, College of William and Mary, Colorado State, Columbia, Dartmouth, Denison, Eastern Connecticut State, Fairfield, Franklin and Marshall, Franklin College, George Mason, Glassboro State, Hamilton/Kirkland, Hartt College of Music, Hartwick, Harvard, Hobart and William Smith, Indiana University, Indiana University of Pennsylvania, Kings College (England), Knox, Lehigh, Loyola, Manhattanville, Mary Washington, Miami University, Middlebury, New York University, Northeastern, Northern Michigan, Oxford (England), Pennsylvania State, Princeton, Providence, Quinnipiac, Rensselaer, Rutgers, Sacred Heart, St. Lawrence, Simmons, Skidmore, Southern Connecticut State, Springfield, Temple, Thiel, Union, Vassar, Villanova, Wake Forest, Walden University, Washington and Lee, Weber State, Wesleyan, Western Connecticut State, Wheaton, Wheelock, Williams, Yale, Yeshiva, and the Universities of Bridgeport, Connecticut, Delaware, Guelph (Canada), Havana, Illinois, Kentucky, London, Miami, New Mexico, New Orleans, Paris IV and X, Rhode Island, Vermont, and Wisconsin.

The staff also includes two librarians, reading and learning consultants, three computer resource specialists, a consulting psychologist, and an athletic trainer.

STUDENT BODY. In 2009–10, Hamden Hall enrolled 555 boys and girls, including 277 in the Upper School. They come from diverse racial, ethnic, and religious backgrounds and represent 38 towns within a 30-mile radius of the School.

ACADEMIC PROGRAM. The school year, from early September to early June, is divided into two semesters, with Thanksgiving, winter, and spring recesses and observances of several national and religious holidays. Parent-teacher conferences are held in November and April, or more often if needed. Written progress reports are issued four times a year, with interim reports sent home in the middle of each marking period.

Classes, enrolling an average of 15 students, are held five days a week from 8:10 A.M. to 3:00 P.M. Periods are 45 minutes long, and extra-help sessions are incorporated into the schedule.

The Lower School curriculum emphasizes reading and writing, comprehension, and critical thinking as well as the mastery of problem-solving and computational skills in mathematics. The introduction of laboratory sciences enables children to observe, experiment, research, and discuss scientific theories and concepts. Understanding other cultures from a global perspective is the focus of the social studies program, which utilizes regular field trips, guest lecturers, and group projects to reinforce classroom instruction. Specialists teach music, fine arts, computer activities, and physical education. Students in Grades 1–4 take Spanish and French for two years, followed by Latin in Grades 5–6. An Extended-Day program provides after-school enrichment for students in Pre-School–Grade 6.

The Middle School program curriculum builds on the skills acquired in the early grades, combined with new challenges and techniques designed to maximize learning. English classes emphasize classical authors while providing students with opportunities to produce their own creative and expository essays. In mathematics, basic computational skills lead to the mastery of problem solving and a preview of algebraic concepts. Life science and physical science studies offer an overview of scientific vocabulary, concepts, and methods of investigation. French, Spanish, or Latin and participation in studio arts, music, and theater are required. Beginning in Grade 7, students work with a faculty advisor who meets with them regularly.

Students in the Upper School carry five courses each semester. To graduate, they must complete 19 credits as follows: four years of English; two and one-half years of history, including U.S. History; through the third level of a foreign language; mathematics through the junior year, including Geometry and Algebra II; two years of science, including Biology and a physical science; one year of fine arts; and four years of physical education, including participation in fall sports and winter or spring sports. Students must also demonstrate proficiency in computers.

Among the required and elective courses in the Upper School are English 9–12, British Fiction, Creative Writing, Modern American Fiction, American Literature, Shakespeare, Modern Poetry; African American History, Ethics, Constitutional Law, U.S. History, Vietnam; Meteorology and Oceanography, Geology, Astronomy, Zoology, Anatomy and Physiology, Physics, Electronics, Chemistry; Latin I–IV, Spanish I–V, French I–V; Algebra I–II, Trigonometry, Pre-Calculus, and Calculus AB/BC. Advanced Placement and honors courses are offered in most major disciplines. With the approval of the Director of Studies, students may undertake independent study projects.

In 2009, 69 graduating seniors entered such institutions as Arizona State, Auburn, Bates, Boston College, Boston University, Brown, Clarkson, Colgate, College of the Holy Cross, Culinary Institute of America, Dickinson, Eastern Connecticut State University, Embry-Riddle Aeronautical, Emory, Fairfield University, Franklin and Marshall, George Washington, Gettysburg, Howard, Lafayette, Lake Forest College, Maine Maritime, Middlebury, New York University, Nichols College, Oberlin, Pennsylvania State, Princeton, Providence, Rensselaer, Rochester Institute of Technology, Saint John's, Skidmore, Stonehill, Susquehanna, Syracuse, Villanova, Western New England College, West Virginia University, Worcester Polytechnic, and the Universities of Alabama, Colorado, Connecticut, Hartford, Kentucky, Massachusetts, Michigan, Mississippi, New Haven, and Pennsylvania.

Hamden Hall conducts a nine-week summer program of academics, arts, and sports.

STUDENT ACTIVITIES. Hamden Hall participates in The Princeton Peer Leadership Program, through which selected seniors undertake training to help their fellow students solve problems, seek alternatives, and improve communications on social and ethical issues. An elected Student Government provides further opportunities to develop leadership qualities and share responsibility for the quality of life at the School.

HAMDEN HALL COUNTRY DAY SCHOOL

Middle and Upper School students publish their own literary magazines and newspapers, and the Upper School issues the yearbook. Among the groups organized to meet diverse interests are Thespians, debate clubs, tour guides, peer tutoring, environmental clubs, and Academic Decathlon. Students perform community service through the Jewish Home for the Aged and inner-city tutoring.

Interscholastic teams are formed in football, soccer, wrestling, basketball, baseball, lacrosse, and tennis for boys; and field hockey, soccer, basketball, lacrosse, tennis, softball, and volleyball for girls. Golf, ice hockey, and cross-country squads are coeducational.

ADMISSION AND COSTS. Hamden Hall seeks motivated students who are academically strong and eager to participate fully in the life of the School. Acceptance is based on the candidate's potential, previous record, math and English teacher recommendations, and the results of standardized testing. A campus tour is recommended; a personal interview is required.

HAMDEN HALL COUNTRY DAY SCHOOL

In 2009–10, tuition, including lunch, ranges from $13,000 in Pre-School to $27,750 in Grades 9–12. Hamden Hall awards financial aid to approximately 30 percent of its student body, based on need.

Head of School: Robert J. Izzo
Head of Lower School: Andrew Niblock
Head of Middle/Upper School: Robert H. Schroeder
Director of Admission: Janet B. Izzo
Director of Development & Alumni Relations: Jodi Amatulli
Director of College Counseling: Frederick B. Richter, Jr.
Director of Athletics: Bernard J. Kohler

Hopkins School   1660

986 Forest Road, New Haven, CT 06515
Tel. 203-397-1001; Admissions Ext. 211; Fax 203-389-2249
Web Site www.hopkins.edu; E-mail admissions@hopkins.edu

Hopkins school, in New Haven, Connecticut, is a coeducational, college preparatory day school enrolling 685 students in Grades 7–12. The campus offers a country setting with access to all that Yale University and New Haven offer, including museums, historical sites, theaters, orchestras, and dance companies.

Founded in 1660 with a bequest from Edward Hopkins, the first governor of Connecticut Colony, Hopkins Grammar School began as a one-room schoolhouse on the New Haven Green. Then a boys' school, Hopkins moved to the current site in 1925. The Day School (1938) and Prospect Hill School (1930) were prominent girls' schools that merged in 1960. Cooperative ventures between Hopkins Grammar and Day Prospect Hill led to the 1972 merger that formed the institution known today as Hopkins School.

Celebrating its 350th anniversary in 2010, Hopkins defines itself as a community of civility and learning, educating students from diverse backgrounds to a full measure of their talents and humanity. Hopkins seeks to instill a love of learning; the courage to live and think as responsible individuals; the creative vitality of the artist and competitive spirit of the athlete; the wisdom and goodwill necessary to gain confident self-reliance; and the character essential to a rich and purposeful life.

HOPKINS SCHOOL

A nonprofit organization, Hopkins is governed by a self-perpetuating Committee of Trustees, which includes parents and alumni. Endowment totals more than $51,000,000. The Alumni Association, representing approximately 6000 living alumni, promotes participation in school events; *Views from the Hill* is published twice yearly, and an Annual Report of Giving is published annually. Hopkins is accredited by the New England Association of Schools and Colleges and holds membership in the National Association of Independent Schools and the Educational Records Bureau.

THE CAMPUS. The 108-acre campus offers 7 athletic fields, 11 tennis courts, and an outdoor adventure course.

Thompson Hall, a $17,000,000, 34,000-square-foot Junior School and Arts Building, opened in the fall of 2009. In 2008, Hopkins completed a $5,500,000 renovation of its library, expanding the area to 16,000 square feet, with 25,000 volumes and wireless technology throughout, and staffed by four full-time faculty. Baldwin Hall provides classrooms, a technology laboratory, a language lab, and offices; there are also classrooms in Hopkins House as well as the admissions, business, and college counseling offices. Also on campus are Lowell Hall, home to the Drama Department; the Alumni House; the Walter Camp Athletic Center with basketball courts, wrestling room, trainer's room, lockers, and swimming pool; and the 25,000-square-foot Malone Science Center with ten laboratories, a student-faculty project room, and prep rooms. Heath Commons provides a 308-seat dining hall and commons space, a café, and two outdoor terraces. It also houses offices for the high school Head Advisers, the Director of Diversity, the Director of Academic Support, and Breakthrough-New Haven.

THE FACULTY. Barbara Masters Riley became Head of School in 2002. A 1973 graduate of Yale College, Ms. Riley earned M.A. and M.Phil. degrees in American Studies from Yale University in 1976. She joined the Hopkins faculty in 1996 after teaching history and English for five years at The Foote School in New Haven. Ms. Riley is the parent of three Hopkins graduates.

The full-time faculty numbers 114. There are also 7 part-time teachers. All hold undergraduate degrees; more than two-thirds have advanced degrees. Representative colleges and universities include Bowdoin, Colgate, Columbia, Cornell, Dartmouth, Georgetown, Harvard, Kenyon, Middlebury, Princeton, St. Lawrence, Wellesley, Williams, Yale, and the Universities of Michigan and Pennsylvania.

The support staff includes a full-time consulting psychologist and the Director of Academic Support. Three full-time athletic trainers provide first aid, and emergency facilities are nearby.

STUDENT BODY. In 2009–10, the School enrolled 685 students from 49 Connecticut towns.

ACADEMIC PROGRAM. The school year, from early September to early June, is divided into semesters with Thanksgiving and midwinter recesses and December and March vacations. A typical day for Grades 7–12 is divided into six 55-minute periods, one of which is dedicated to athletics, from 8:20 A.M. to 3:30 P.M. The schedule is adjusted to permit early dismissal on Wednesday for athletic contests and club activities and, on Mondays and Fridays, for all-school assemblies.

The average class size is 12 students. There are supervised study halls for students in Grades 7–10; juniors and seniors may study in the Library or Heath Commons during free periods. Grades and comments are sent to parents four times a year; interim reports may be issued for students experiencing academic difficulties. Parent-teacher conferences are held once a year or as appropriate.

The prescribed curriculum for Grades 7–8 consists of English, Latin, History, Pre-Algebra (Grade 7), Elementary Algebra (Grade 8), Life Science (Grade 7), Physical Science (Grade 8), and art, drama, music, and woodworking. French or Spanish may be elected as a second language.

To graduate, students in Grades 9–12 must earn a total of 18 credits including 4 credits of English, 3 of a foreign language, 2 of history, 3 of mathematics, 2 credits of lab science, and 1 credit of arts. They must also fulfill athletics and community service requirements.

HOPKINS SCHOOL

Among the courses offered are English courses such as The Writing Semester, Heroic Figures in Literature, Dante, Political Shakespeare, Love in Shakespeare's Plays, About Poetry, Great Novels, Creative Writing, Russian Literature, and Philosophy, Wit and Wisdom. Other courses include French 1–6, Greek 1–3, Chinese 1–3, Italian 1–3, Latin 1–5, Spanish 1–6; Civics, Atlantic Communities I–III, African-American History, Asian Studies, Islam and the West, Urban Studies, Military History, The Holocaust and the Individual, Twenty-first Century Democracy; Algebra, Accelerated Algebra, Geometry, Accelerated Geometry, Advanced Algebra, Functions, Statistics and Trigonometry, Precalculus, Calculus AB, Calculus BC, Multivariable Calculus, Finite Mathematics, Introduction to Computers and Programming, HTML, Fractals and Chaos, Linear Algebra; Biology, Chemistry, Development & Applications of Technology, Physics, Contemporary Issues in Biology, Ecology, Physiology, Introduction to Organic Chemistry, Astronomy; and Studio Art 1–2, Photography 1–3, Pottery, History of Film, Classical Ensemble, Jazz/Rock Ensemble, Mixed Chorus, Music Theory, Performance Workshop, Video Production, Acting, and Graphic Design. Advanced Placement and honors-level courses are offered in 20 subject areas.

HOPKINS SCHOOL

Colleges attended by Hopkins graduates in the past four years include Yale 32; University of Connecticut 21; Boston College 16; Columbia 15; Tufts and the University of Pennsylvania, 14 each; Johns Hopkins 13; and Bates, Connecticut College, Emory, and Georgetown, 10 each.

Entering its 109th year, the Hopkins Summer School offers two concurrent six-week programs, one academic, the other sports, for boys and girls in Grades 3–12. Breakthrough-New Haven provides a comprehensive academic enrichment program for public and parochial school students in Grades 7–8. Hopkins is also home to the Adam Kreiger Adventure Program, a state-of-the-art challenge course available to the Hopkins and Greater New Haven communities.

STUDENT ACTIVITIES. The Student Council, composed of elected representatives from Grades 9–12 and the President, elected by Grades 8–12, organizes school service and recreational activities. Council representatives and other students serve on faculty committees devoted to the examination of various school issues.

Students publish a newspaper, literary magazine, and a yearbook. Among the many other organizations and activities available are a Debate Team, Varsity and Junior Varsity Math teams, the Concert Choir, Model UN, the Hopkins Drama Association, three a cappella singing groups, Environmental Club, Amnesty International, GASP (Gay and Straight People), and SURE (Students United for Racial Equality). Hopkins has a thriving community service program. The majority of students become involved through programs sponsored by the Community Service office and the Maroon Key umbrella of student organization. Beginning with the class of 2007, seniors are required to participate in all four days of a School-sponsored community service project.

Hopkins teams compete with those of public and independent schools in Connecticut, Massachusetts, and New York. Boys' teams are organized in baseball, basketball, cross-country, football, golf, lacrosse, soccer, swimming and diving, squash, crew, tennis, track, fencing, water polo, and wrestling. Girls compete in basketball, cross-country, lacrosse, field hockey, golf, soccer, softball, swimming and diving, tennis, track, squash, crew, fencing, water polo, and volleyball. Junior School teams include baseball, basketball, field hockey, lacrosse, football, soccer, swimming and diving, tennis, and wrestling.

Dances and drama productions are held throughout the year. Traditional events for the school community include Pumpkin Bowl, Homecoming, Reunion Weekend, and various functions sponsored by the Student Council and the Parent Council.

ADMISSION AND COSTS. Hopkins seeks to enroll a diverse group of students who are eager to learn and willing to work hard. New students are admitted to all grades, although most often to Grades 7 and 9, on the basis of an application, a personal interview, results of the Secondary School Admission Test or the Independent School Entrance Examination, a writing sample, the transcript from the applicant's previous school, and two teacher references. Application should be made in the fall; the application deadline is January 20. There is a $50 application fee.

HOPKINS SCHOOL

In 2009–10, tuition is $29,400. Tuition covers all costs except books ($300–$600), an activities fee ($350), student accident insurance, and trip and store charges. In the current year, Hopkins awarded more than $2,250,000 in financial aid to 115 students. Tuition payment plans and tuition insurance are available.

Chief Financial & Operating Officer: David E. Baxter
Assistant Head of School: R. John Roberts
Director of Admissions: Pamela McKenna
Dean of Academics: David Harpin
Dean of Faculty: Carla J. MacMullen
Dean of Students: Eric W. Mueller
Director of Athletics: Thomas A. Parr, Jr.
Director of Development: Barbara Price Monahan
Director of Development for Alumni & Parent Affairs: Deena Mack
Director of College Counseling: Susan Moriarty Paton
Director of Community Service: Daniel Kops '98
Director of Diversity: Veronica Guinazu
Director of Summer School: Thomas A. Parr, Jr.
Director of Academic Support: Matthew Treat
Alumni Association President: Bethany Schowalter Appleby '85

The Hotchkiss School 1891

11 Interlaken Road, P.O. Box 800, Lakeville, CT 06039
Tel. 860-435-2591; Admission 860-435-3102; Fax 860-435-0042
Web Site www.hotchkiss.org; E-mail admission@hotchkiss.org

THE HOTCHKISS SCHOOL

Hotchkiss, set on an 880-acre campus in northwest Connecticut, is a coeducational college preparatory school enrolling 587 students from 38 states and 35 nations in Grade 9–Postgraduate. About 92 percent are boarding students. Hotchkiss sees itself as a national school on a global stage. A diverse student group is encouraged especially to develop global-mindedness and environmental stewardship. The Hotchkiss curriculum is distinguished by three Rs: rigorous, restless, and reflective. The new Humanities Program incorporates the best of traditional learning with new methods of inquiry. This integrated two-year curriculum spans four disciplines—the arts, English, history, and philosophy and religion. With 245 courses in 16 departments as well as Advanced Placement in 21 subjects and independent and international study options, Hotchkiss students enjoy an array of exciting choices. Boarding Tuition: $41,885; Day Tuition: $35,700. Financial Aid: $7,200,000+. Rachael N. Beare is Dean of Admission and Financial Aid; Malcolm H. McKenzie is Head of School. *New England Association.*

The Independent Day School 1961

115 Laurel Brook Road, P.O. Box 451, Middlefield, CT 06455
Tel. 860-347-7235; Fax 860-347-8852
Web Site www.independentdayschool.org
E-mail ids@independentdayschool.org

THE INDEPENDENT DAY SCHOOL

The Independent Day School, enrolling 190 boys and girls from Beginners (age 3) to Grade 8, offers an academically challenging program in a family-like environment. The School draws students from more than 30 towns. Balanced programs of academics, physical fitness, and studio and performing arts

provide students with a well-rounded educational experience. Spanish is taught throughout the grades beginning in Pre-K. Community service is also an integral part of the IDS program, promoting an awareness of and empathy toward others in the world at large. Academically driven field trips, interscholastic sports, and class plays broaden students' experiences. After-school care programs, both after-school and summer theater and dance programs, and a summer camp are available. Tuition: $8550–$21,810. Mary Lou Stewart is Director of Admission; John Barrengos is Head of School.

King Low Heywood Thomas 1865

1450 Newfield Avenue, Stamford, CT 06905
Tel. 203-322-3496; Admission Ext. 350; Fax 203-504-6288
Web Site www.klht.org; E-mail admission@klht.org

KING LOW HEYWOOD THOMAS, familiarly known as King in Stamford, Connecticut, is a coeducational, college preparatory day school enrolling students in Pre-Kindergarten through Grade 12. Students are drawn from Stamford and several surrounding towns in Fairfield and Westchester Counties, areas that provide numerous opportunities for discovery and learning and allow students to experience the culture of both urban and suburban environments.

KING LOW HEYWOOD THOMAS

The School's origins date back to Mrs. Richardson's School, an all-girls school founded in 1865. In 1883, Miss Louisa Low and Miss Edith Heywood purchased and renamed the School. Low-Heywood merged with Miss Thomas's School in 1973, and, in 1988, Low-Heywood Thomas merged with the all-boys King School, which was founded in 1875, also in Stamford.

The School seeks to develop each individual's talents and character by offering intellectual, creative, athletic, leadership, and service opportunities, thereby preparing its students for lives of learning in college and adulthood. Acquisition of communication skills, cultivation of intellectual ability, evolution of individual character, and attainment of personal growth are also emphasized.

Accredited by the New England Association of Schools and Colleges, the School is governed by a Board of Trustees. The Board appoints the Head of School and creates policies that enhance and underline the School's mission statement.

THE CAMPUS. The 36-acre campus is near both the Merritt Parkway and I-95, so parents can reach the School easily during visits, and field trip locations in surrounding areas are accessible.

A new state-of-the-art Middle School opened in September 2004. As students and faculty moved into that facility, renovations to the Lower School further enhanced the expanded space available for those students. The Upper School boasts updated library facilities, new science labs, expanded lounge areas for students, and state-of-the-art technology.

KING LOW HEYWOOD THOMAS

The Head of School's Office, Admission Office, and the Lower and Middle Schools are on the South Campus, while the Upper School and the College Counseling Office are on the North Campus.

THE FACULTY. Thomas B. Main was appointed Head of School in 2002. He matriculated at Bates College with a Bachelor of Arts in English and received a Master of Arts in Liberal Studies degree from Wesleyan University. Prior to moving to King Low Heywood Thomas, he was a Middle School English teacher, coach, and advisor at King School, served in a variety of teaching and administrative positions at Rye Country Day School, and was Head of the Upper School at Cincinnati Country Day School.

King's faculty is comprised of 104 teachers and administrators, with 80 holding master's degrees and 7 holding doctoral degrees. The faculty attended such colleges and universities as Bates College, Berklee College of Music, Boston College, Boston University, Bowdoin College, Columbia University, Cornell University, Dartmouth College, Duke University, Fairfield University, George Washington University, Harvard, Ithaca College, Johns Hopkins University, Lafayette College, New York University, Southern Connecticut State University, Trinity College, Wesleyan University, Williams College, Yale University, and the University of Pennsylvania.

STUDENT BODY. The School enrolls 190 students in the Lower School, 189 students in the Middle School, and 290 students in the Upper School. Students come from approximately 30 towns in Fairfield and Westchester Counties and encompass a wide range of ethnic and racial backgrounds. Approximately 25 percent enrolled in the Upper School are students of color.

ACADEMIC PROGRAM. The school year is divided into semesters in the Upper School and trimesters in the Lower and Middle Schools. Multiple-day vacations occur at Thanksgiving, in December and in March. Day vacations include Rosh Hashanah, Columbus Day, Martin Luther King Day, and Presidents' Weekend. The academic day begins at 8:00 A.M. and ends at 3:15 P.M.

Lower School teachers endeavor to build a foundation that serves students in Pre-Kindergarten through Grade 5 for the remainder of their schooling and throughout their adult lives. The Lower School has a maximum class size of 15 and focuses on exploration and growth. Classes revolving around math,

social studies, science, and language arts help students develop more abstract and complex thinking and problem-solving skills. Students in Grades 4 and 5 can begin instrumental instruction, and all students are introduced to Spanish culture, language, and history.

Because Grades 6–8 are a transition period, King seeks to create a supportive yet challenging environment in which students can develop successfully and move on to the Upper School as thoughtful, perceptive, and sensitive young adults. With an average class size of 14, individual attention is guaranteed both academically and emotionally. Students take classes in English, mathematics, history, science, and French or Spanish along with various sports and arts programs. Teachers in the Middle School aim to hone the basic skills learned in the Lower School and encourage social responsibility and self-awareness.

The Upper School runs from Grade 9 to Grade 12. Although average class size is 15, many classes are smaller, particularly at advanced levels. All courses are college preparatory, with Honors, Advanced Placement, and Independent Study options also available. Advanced Placement courses are offered in 19 subjects.

Students must take a minimum of five credits of courses each year, and participation in two theater productions and four athletic seasons is also required. Upper School graduation requirements are as follows: four credits in English; three credits in history, science, and mathematics; modern languages through level 3; a half-credit in performing arts; a half-credit in visual art; and a half-credit in life skills.

Classes available include, among others, Fundamentals of Composition and Literary Study, Writing about Literature, American Literature, Literature of Social Reflection, Poetry Writing, Fiction Writing, Literary Analysis; Algebra 1, Geometry, Algebra 2 and Trigonometry, Discrete Mathematics, Statistics, Pre-Calculus, Calculus, Multivariable Calculus; World History, America, Vietnam, and the Sixties, United States History, European History, Micro/Macro Economics, Philosophy; Biology, Chemistry, Physical Anthropology, Physics, Meteorology, Oceanography, Forensics, Archaeology; Painting, Drawing, Clay Workshop, Printmaking, 2-D Graphic Design, 3-D Animation, Web Development; French, Spanish, and Mandarin Chinese. Choir and a jazz ensemble are also provided.

KING LOW HEYWOOD THOMAS

College counseling begins in Grade 9 and becomes more involved as students progress through the Upper School. In Grades 9 and 10, students are urged to do their best academically and are introduced to the college application process, while sophomores are coached through all the steps of the PSAT. Students in Grade 11 visit several colleges during a class trip. The Office of College Counseling guides seniors through the process of applying to college and assists them with deadlines, transcripts, and recommendations.

Members of the Class of 2009 enrolled in schools such as Boston College, Bucknell, Cornell, Dartmouth, Dickinson,

Duke, Elon, Johns Hopkins, Lehigh, McGill, New York University, Oberlin, Roanoke, Skidmore, Syracuse, Tufts, Tulane, and the Universities of Colorado, Michigan, Pennsylvania, Richmond, and Vermont.

STUDENT ACTIVITIES. Sports available to Lower, Middle, and Upper School students include soccer, football, cross-country, field hockey, volleyball, cheerleading, ice hockey, basketball, lacrosse, baseball, softball, and tennis. Varsity teams belong to the Fairchester Athletic Association and compete against schools in the Western New England Prep School Athletic Association and the New England Prep School Athletic Council. Students in Grades 5 and 6 and in Grades 7 and 8 play on separate sports teams that foster skill building, sportsmanship, and teamwork.

KING LOW HEYWOOD THOMAS

Students also take part in cocurricular activities that enhance the academic, artistic, and athletic program. All students participate in community service and school government, and Upper School students form special-interest groups such as the A cafellas and A capella (singing groups), Amnesty International, Building with Books, United Cultures Club, Student Council, Film Making Club, Creative Writing Club, Cooking Club, Debate Club, Math Team, and Model UN. Students in Grades 9–12 publish *Kaleidoscope*, a yearbook, and *The Standard*, the school newspaper. Both Middle and Lower School students also publish magazines of their literary work. Middle School students can participate in drama, chorus, band, and art as extracurricular activities outside of athletics.

Special events include Homecoming, Upper and Middle School drama productions, holiday concerts, field trips and dances.

ADMISSION AND COSTS. King seeks students who are academically motivated and who wish to become citizens who are involved in their communities. The application fee is $75; deadline is January 1. Candidates must visit the campus, complete the application and a Student Questionnaire, meet with a member of the admission committee, submit a transcript and teacher recommendations, and take an age-suitable standardized admission test.

Tuition ranges between $27,750 for Pre-K and $31,400 for Upper School students; activity fees are from $200 to $625, depending on the student's grade. Other expenses include lunch, snacks, tuition refund insurance, and student accident insurance. All parents are asked to contribute to the Annual Fund to improve the School and its ability to educate students well. Need-based financial aid is available.

Director of Admission and Financial Aid: Carrie Salvatore
Associate Head of School, Advancement: Bill Ennist
Assistant Head, Finance & Operations: Kimberly Leeker
Director of College Counseling: David Bonner
Director of Athletics: Tom Decker

Kingswood-Oxford School   1969

170 Kingswood Road, West Hartford, CT 06119
Tel. 860-727-5001; Fax 860-236-3651
Web Site www.kingswood-oxford.org; E-mail admission@k-o.org

This coeducational, college preparatory day school, one of the oldest independent day schools in the United States, was formed by the 1969 merger of the Oxford School (1909) and the Kingswood School (1916). The founders of those two schools sought to provide an academic program that enabled talented students to excel intellectually, athletically, and artistically in a challenging and dynamic environment. Kingswood-Oxford School today serves a diverse student body of 505 young people with a liberal arts curriculum that focuses on teaching essential 21st century skills through a rigorous curriculum and Signature Programs that bring students to the world and the world to the students. Virtually all graduates enter four-year colleges and universities nationwide. Students participate in a wide range of extracurricular offerings that promote leadership and self-awareness. June Term programs are optional. Tuition: $29,750. Financial aid is available. James E. O'Donnell is Director of Enrollment Management; Dennis Bisgaard was named Head of School in 2006. *New England Association.*

The Loomis Chaffee School   1914

4 Batchelder Road, Windsor, CT 06095
Tel. 860-687-6000; Admissions 860-687-6400; Fax 860-298-8756
Web Site www.loomis.org; E-mail admissions@loomis.org

The Loomis Chaffee School offers an outstanding educational experience to young men and women of all ethnic, religious, and racial backgrounds on its 300-acre campus in north-central Connecticut. The 690 students in Grades 9–12 include 400 boarders from around the country and worldwide, providing a wealth of diversity that enriches the entire community. The grounds feature a 60,000-volume library, science center, and extensive facilities for information technology, the performing arts, and athletics. The School's mission is to nurture the intellectual, moral, and personal development of each student through a challenging college preparatory curriculum. The academic program features nearly 200 courses, including AP and advanced classes, modern and classical languages, off-campus internships, and independent study options. Among the activities are student government, debate, math team, music groups, robotics, SADD, community service, various interest clubs, and 55 teams in 18 sports. All graduates gain entrance to four-year colleges and universities nationwide. Boarding Tuition: $43,000; Day Tuition: $32,600. Financial Aid: $6,500,000+. Erby Mitchell is Assistant Head of School for Enrollment; Sheila Culbert is Head of School. *New England Association.*

The Mead School   1969

1095 Riverbank Road, Stamford, CT 06903
Tel. 203-595-9500; Admissions Ext. 46; Fax 203-595-0735
Web Site www.meadschool.org; E-mail admissions@meadschool.org

The Mead School is a progressive learning environment committed to the development of the whole child. Enrolling approximately 150 boys and girls as day students in Nursery–Grade 8, the School combines developmentally appropriate academic programs with equal emphasis on the expressive arts and personal development. Honest and affectionate relationships, individualized programs, and the development of autonomous learners are priorities. Special-interest activities are incorporated into the regular curriculum. A summer program

THE MEAD SCHOOL

is available for children, ages 2–14. Tuition: $10,300–$30,350. Financial Aid: $640,600. Brooke Wachtel is Director of Admissions; Karen Biddulph is Director.

Mooreland Hill School   1930

166 Lincoln Road, Kensington, CT 06037
Tel. 860-223-6428; Fax 860-223-3318
Web Site www.mooreland.org; E-mail admissions@mooreland.org

Mooreland Hill is an independent, coeducational day school serving 50 Central Connecticut students in Grades 5 through 9. For 80 years, Mooreland Hill School's primary mission has been to enable each child to excel academically and to master the skills essential for success in college and in life. In an environment that is both challenging and nurturing, students undertake a traditional liberal arts curriculum that emphasizes core subjects as well as critical thinking and self-discipline. English, literature, social studies, math, science, French, Spanish, Latin, health and human development, art, and chorus are at the center of the academic program. A burgeoning outdoor education program complements the traditional academic pursuits. A variety of extracurricular activities is available. All students participate in the athletic program, which includes soccer, field hockey, basketball, hiking, baseball, softball, and tennis. Teams compete against other independent schools at the varsity and junior varsity level. Inclusive Tuition (books, athletic fees, lunch): $19,900. Financial aid is available. Michael D. Dooman (Trinity College, M.A.) was appointed Headmaster in 2006.

Notre Dame of West Haven   1946

24 Ricardo Street, West Haven, CT 06516-2499
Tel. 203-933-1673; Admission Ext. 501; Fax 203-933-2474
Web Site www.notredamehs.com
E-mail admissions@notredamehs.com

Founded and operated by the Brothers of Holy Cross, Notre Dame of West Haven is a Roman Catholic, college preparatory day school enrolling 700 young men in Grades 9–12. The school's mission is to assist parents in educating their sons, working to develop respect, dedication, and excellence in each student. The curriculum, which includes honors and Advanced Placement courses, accommodates a variety of learning abilities, and a 12:1 student-faculty ratio permits close, individualized attention. A strong athletic program, the fine arts, student government, publications, and interest clubs are among the activities. Tuition: $9450. Financial aid is available. Pasquale G. Izzo is Director of Admissions; Br. James Branigan, CSC, is President. *New England Association.*

Pear Tree Point School   1996

90 Pear Tree Point Road, Darien, CT 06820-0682
Tel. 203-655-0030; Fax 203-655-3164
Web Site www.ptpschool.org; E-mail info@ptpschool.org

PEAR TREE POINT SCHOOL

Pear Tree Point School is a small, close-knit learning community enrolling over 200 boys and girls as day students in Pre-Kindergarten through Grade 5. As an official Core Knowledge School, Pear Tree Point School focuses on the development of cultural literacy through in-depth studies in history, geography, language arts, math, and science. Children learn in classrooms of 15 or fewer students, each staffed by a head teacher and an assistant; the overall faculty-student ratio is 1:4. Spanish, Mandarin, drama, technology, music, art, and physical education enrich the program at all levels. Students take part in after-school activities such as chess, crafts, cooking, photography, and team sports. Tuition: $26,500–$30,650. Financial aid is available. Janice Hawes is Director of Admissions; David Trigaux is Headmaster.

Rumsey Hall School   1900

201 Romford Road, Washington Depot, CT 06794
Tel. 860-868-0535; Fax 860-868-7907
Web Site www.rumseyhall.org; E-mail admiss@rumseyhall.org

Rumsey hall school in Washington Depot, Connecticut, is a coeducational boarding and country day school for students in Kindergarten through Grade 9. The boarding program begins in Grade 5. Situated in the southern range of the Berkshire Hills, Washington (population 4000) is 42 miles west of Hartford and 80 miles northeast of New York City. The region, which offers wooded countryside and access to several ski areas, is the site of numerous other independent schools and colleges.

Founded by Mrs. Lillias Rumsey Sanford in Seneca Falls, New York, in 1900, the School moved to larger quarters in Cornwall, Connecticut, in 1907, and to the present campus in 1948. Mrs. Sanford has been succeeded as Director by John F. Schereschewsky, Sr. (1941–1969), John F. Schereschewsky, Jr. (1969–1977), Louis G. Magnoli (1969–1985), and Thomas W. Farmen, the present Headmaster.

Since its inception in 1900, Rumsey Hall School has retained its original philosophy: to help each child develop "to his or her maximum stature as an individual, as a member of a family, and as a contributing member of society." The School aims to provide the support, nurture, and care that children need while presenting appropriate academic challenge and rigor. The basic curriculum is designed to teach students to read, write, and calculate proficiently and to establish the educational foundations that prepare them for success in secondary school and college. Rumsey Hall embraces the ideal of "honor through effort" and emphasizes effort more than grades as the criterion for achievement.

RUMSEY HALL SCHOOL

A nonprofit institution, Rumsey Hall School is directed by a 22-member Board of Trustees, which meets quarterly. The School holds membership in the National Association of Independent Schools, the Connecticut Association of Independent Schools, Junior Boarding Schools Association, the Educational Records Bureau, the Secondary School Admissions Test Board, and Western Connecticut Boarding Schools Association.

THE CAMPUS. The 147-acre campus on the Bantam River provides landscaped and wooded areas, nine athletic fields, two skating ponds, and three outdoor tennis courts. The John F. Schereschewsky Center contains indoor athletic facilities, including three tennis courts.

The School is housed in 29 buildings, most of which have been constructed since 1950. Five structures provide a total of 27 classrooms, including the new Dicke Family Math and Science Centers. Other buildings house the study hall, three computer labs, and seven language skills classrooms.

The recently built Maxwell Sarofim '05 Performing Arts Center enhances the drama and music programs. The newest additions to the School include two girls' dormitories and the Lufkin Hockey Rink.

THE FACULTY. Thomas W. Farmen, appointed Headmaster in 1985, is a graduate of New England College (B.A.) and Western Connecticut State University (M.S.A.). He has also served at Rumsey Hall as a teacher, Director of Athletics, and Director of Secondary School Placement.

There are 57 full- and part-time teachers, 28 men and 29 women. Thirty, including 11 with families, reside on campus. They hold 57 baccalaureate and 15 master's degrees, representing study at such institutions as Allegheny, Barnard, Bates, Bethany, Bowdoin, Colby, Columbia, Connecticut College, Dartmouth, Elmira, Harvard, Lafayette College, Long Island University, Lynchburg, Middlebury, New England College, Northern Kentucky, Pennsylvania State, Randolph-Macon, Rollins, St. Lawrence, Springfield, Syracuse, Trinity, Tulane, Wesleyan, Western Connecticut State, Wheaton, Williams, Yale, and the Universities of Connecticut, Massachusetts, Michigan, New Hampshire, and Vermont.

Three nurses staff the school infirmary, and a local doctor is on call. Emergency facilities are located in New Milford, 10 miles distant.

STUDENT BODY. In 2009–10, the School enrolled 303 students including 83 boarding boys, 50 boarding girls, 90 day boys, and 80 day girls in Kindergarten–Grade 9. There are 221 students in the Upper School and 82 in the Lower School. In addition to Connecticut, resident students come from 17 other states and 11 countries.

ACADEMIC PROGRAM. The school year, from September to early June, provides 32 weeks of instruction, a Thanksgiving recess, and extended vacations at Christmas and in the spring. Classes, which have an average enrollment of 12, meet six days a week for the upper school and five days a week for the lower school. The daily schedule, from 8:00 A.M. to 4:30 P.M., includes a school meeting each morning, eight 40-minute class periods, lunch, extra-help sessions, and athletics in the afternoon. A supervised study hall is conducted from 7:00 to 8:30 P.M. each evening for boarding students. Clubs and activities meet each Monday.

All faculty members are available to provide special assistance during the afternoon extra-help period. Individualized language skills programs, administered by reading specialists, and English as a Second Language are offered at an additional cost.

Students have appropriate homework assignments, to be completed during study halls. Class assignments for the week are issued on Monday and graded each day. Faculty members meet once a week to review the work of each student and prepare reports, based on homework and class quizzes, that are issued biweekly to parents and students. Faculty members also compile a weekly effort list of students who the instructors feel have put forth maximum effort during that period. Both art and music are required in all grades.

In 2009, the School's graduates entered such independent secondary schools as Avon Old Farms, Cheshire Academy, Choate Rosemary Hall, Deerfield, The Hill School, Proctor Academy, St. Paul's, Salisbury, Suffield, and Taft.

RUMSEY HALL SCHOOL

Rumsey's five-week academic summer session enrolls approximately 75 boarding and day students in Grades 3–9. The program offers courses in English, elementary mathematics, algebra, and study skills. Classes are held five days a week.

STUDENT ACTIVITIES. Students in the Upper School may join such interest groups as community service, computer keyboarding, biking, fly fishing, school newspaper, chorus, rocketry, weight lifting, ceramics, yearbook, Ultimate Frisbee, golf, street hockey, a cappella, and drama clubs. In the Lower School, students can be involved in the creation of an original opera, either composing, writing, designing, set building, lighting, or performing. Student government organizations exist for students of all ages.

Interscholastic teams for students are organized in football, soccer, cross-country, hockey, skiing, wrestling, baseball, tennis, crew, and lacrosse for boys, and in field hockey, soccer, hockey, basketball, cross-country, volleyball, skiing, softball, tennis, and crew for girls. The student body is divided into Red and Blue teams, with intramural competition culminating in a Red and Blue Track Meet on Memorial Day. An equestrian program and recreational sports such as sledding, skiing, hiking, mountain biking, and fishing are also available.

Although boarding students have free time on weekends, they also participate in organized on-campus activities. Off-campus trips and various activities are planned each weekend, and day students are welcome to attend. Rumsey's location allows students to enjoy numerous cultural and entertainment activities in New Haven, Hartford, Boston, and New York City. Traditional annual events for the school community include Parents' Days, the Holiday Concert, a winter ski trip in Bromley, Vermont, Grandparents' Day, and Commencement.

ADMISSION AND COSTS. Rumsey Hall seeks to enroll students of good character and ability without regard to race, creed, or color. Students are admitted to Grades K–9 on the basis of an application form, a personal interview, recommendations from previous teachers, and an official school transcript.

RUMSEY HALL SCHOOL

In 2009–10, tuition is $41,300 for boarding students and between $15,550 and $19,600 for day students, depending on grade. In the current year, students received $812,450 in financial aid.

Associate Headmaster/Director of Residential Life: Rick S. Spooner
Dean of Students: Clayton Ketchum
Assistant Headmaster/Director of Admissions: Matthew S. Hoeniger
Director of Studies: Brooke Giese
Director of Development: Kim Pugh
Assistant Headmaster for Academic Affairs/Secondary School
   Placement: Francis M. Ryan
Business Manager: Dorota Habib
Director of Athletics: Jay Przygocki
Director of Lower School: Rob Brenner
Coordinator of Girls' & Women's Issues: Allison Spooner-Linley

St. Thomas's Day School   1956

830 Whitney Avenue, New Haven, CT 06511
Tel. 203-776-2123; Fax 203-776-3467
Web Site www.stthomasday.org; E-mail info@stthomasday.org

St. Thomas's is an Episcopal day school serving 150 children in Junior Kindergarten–Grade 6. As a mission of St. Thomas's Church, the School strives to educate students of all backgrounds by cultivating intelligence while engaging heart and spirit. It fosters academic excellence through a challenging, integrated curriculum with attention to each child's potential and learning style. St. Thomas's is characterized by a strong sense of community, a genuine commitment to children, and active parent participation. An extended-day program is available. Tuition: $17,300. Financial Aid: $318,000. Roxanne Turekian coordinates admissions; Fred Acquavita (Kansas State, B.S. 1968; Bank Street, M.S. 1981) was appointed School Head in 1981.

The Stanwich School, Inc.   1998

257 Stanwich Road, Greenwich, CT 06830
Tel. 203-542-0000; Admissions 203-542-0035; Fax 203-542-0025
Web Site www.stanwichschool.org
E-mail info@stanwichschool.org

THE STANWICH SCHOOL, INC.

Stanwich, a day school enrolling 425 boys and girls in Pre-Kindergarten–Grade 8, offers a rigorous and challenging college preparatory curriculum presented in a supportive way that encourages students to take increasingly greater responsibility for achieving their highest potential. It is balanced with creative fine and performing arts instruction and an athletic program that promotes healthy growth and teamwork. All faculty members hold advanced degrees and work closely with students in every aspect of school life, enriching, challenging, and encouraging them to be their best. A character culture is established through actively taught values and ethics classes founded on Judeo-Christian principles and tradition, meaningful community service, and a wide variety of enrichment activities. Small class sizes reinforce classroom lessons. Tuition: $19,500–$26,750. Financial Aid: $897,000. Kay Wall (Pre-K–Grade 3) and Ann Croll (Grades 4–9) are Directors of Admission; Pat Young is Founding Headmistress.

The Taft School   1890

110 Woodbury Road, Watertown, CT 06795
Tel. 860-945-7777; Admissions 860-945-7700; Fax 860-945-7808
Web Site www.taftschool.org; E-mail admissions@taftschool.org

Taft is an independent, coeducational, college preparatory school enrolling 468 boarding and 108 day students in Grade 9–Postgraduate. The School fosters individual development by emphasizing moral responsibility and academic excellence while providing the finest of liberal arts education through its 220-course curriculum. Importance is also placed on diversity, as students come from 32 states and 34 countries. Advanced Placement courses are offered in every discipline, and electives may include Literary Journalism, Human Rights & Global Realities, and Linear Algebra. Sixty-nine percent of the faculty hold advanced degrees, and the student-teacher ratio is 6:1. Students enjoy such extracurricular activities as 30 sports teams, the visual and performing arts, school government, and community service. The 220-acre campus holds a 58,500-volume library, science center, two hockey rinks, and a golf course. A variety of summer enrichment courses is available. Boarding Tuition: $43,775; Day Tuition: $32,500. Financial Aid: $6,500,000. Peter A. Frew '75 is Director of Admission; William R. MacMullen (Taft '78; Yale, B.A. 1982; Middlebury, M.A. 1989) was appointed Headmaster in 2001. *New England Association.*

Westover School   1909

1237 Whittemore Road, P.O. Box 847, Middlebury, CT 06762
Tel. 203-758-2423; Admission 203-577-4521; Fax 203-577-4588
Website: www.westoverschool.org
E-mail admission@westoverschool.org

WESTOVER SCHOOL

Enrolling 200 college-bound students, primarily boarders, Westover School challenges young women in Grades 9 to 12 to participate in all areas of academic, community, and athletic life. The School is diverse, with students from 16 countries and 19 states. Traditional liberal arts classes teach girls how to reason, make good decisions, and ask meaningful questions. Students also take advantage of numerous electives such as Poetics and The Iliad, Chemistry of Art, Alternative Energy Engineering, and Walls and Bridges: American Foreign Policy, 1945–2009. Nineteen AP courses, 1:1 student-teacher conferences, and a student-faculty ratio of 7:1 enhance the curriculum. Extracurricular activities offered include ten sports teams, the arts, and student council. Four special programs are available: Women In

Science and Engineering, a co-collaborative program with Rensselaer Polytechnic Institute; a joint program with the Manhattan School of Music Precollege Division; a co-curricular program with the Brass City Ballet; and international exchanges with schools in South Africa, Jordan, Australia, France, Spain, and England. Summer camp programs are available. Boarding Tuition: $42,400; Day Tuition: $29,200. Financial Aid: $2,500,000. Laura Volovski '83 is Director of Admission; Ann S. Pollina is Head of School.

The Williams School   1891

182 Mohegan Avenue, New London, CT 06320
Tel. 860-443-5333; Fax 860-439-2796
Web Site www.williamsschool.org
E-mail admissions@williamsschool.org

Founded in 1891, The Williams School is a coeducational, col-preparatory school enrolling 295 day students in Grades 7–12. The Williams School aims to foster the intellectual, moral, and aesthetic growth of young people as they develop into thoughtful, responsible citizens in an ever-changing global community. The Classics curriculum is dedicated to the liberal arts, sciences, and humanities, with honors courses beginning in Grade 10, Advanced Placement in the major disciplines, and, for students needing additional attention and support, the SMART program. Twelfth graders are encouraged to undertake a Senior Project, and qualified students may take independent study courses at Connecticut College, which shares its campus with Williams, and at the U.S. Coast Guard Academy. The School hosts international students, and Williams students may elect travel and study programs abroad. Among the extracurricular choices are Student Council, Ambassadors, yearbook, instrumental and vocal ensembles, drama, visual arts, community service, and varsity sports. Tuition: $23,935. Financial aid is available. Gayle Holt is Director of Admission; Mark Fader is Head of School.

The Woodhall School   1983

58 Harrison Lane, P.O. Box 550, Bethlehem, CT 06751
Tel. 203-266-7788; Fax 203-266-5896
Web Site www.woodhallschool.org
E-mail woodhallschool@woodhallschool.org

The Woodhall School is a small, family-owned learning community for young men of average to superior ability who have not met their potential in traditional mainstream settings. Founded by Jonathan and Sally Campbell Woodhall, this boarding and day school enrolls 40 boys in Grade 9–Postgraduate. The curriculum, which is primarily college preparatory with some general secondary courses, is individualized to help each young man reverse patterns of failure, reach his potential, and achieve success in higher education and life. Boys proceed according to their own ability and pace. Teachers work closely with each student providing encouragement and support at every level, and interim grades and evaluations are given on a regular basis. Communications Groups for Self-Expression with Accountability provide opportunities for reflection, discussion of feelings, and examination of personal responses to life situations. Clubs, publications, coordinate events with area girls' schools, and athletics are among the activities. Boarding Tuition: $57,200; Day Tuition: $43,680. Matthew Campbell Woodhall is Head of School. *New England Association.*

DELAWARE

Archmere Academy   1932

3600 Philadelphia Pike, Claymont, DE 19703
Tel. 302-798-6632/610-485-0373
Admissions 302-798-6632, Ext. 703; Fax 302-798-7290
Web Site www.archmereacademy.org
E-mail jjordan@archmereacademy.org

Archmere Academy was founded by Norbertine priests on the site of a former country estate. Today, the 48-acre property is home to this Roman Catholic, coeducational, college preparatory day school that enrolls 580 students from diverse religious heritages in Grades 9 through 12. Archmere focuses on the whole student, promoting academic excellence, social growth, faith reflection, and service to others. Staffed by Norbertine clergy and lay faculty, the Academy maintains a student-teacher ratio of 15:1. Curriculum requirements include math, science, modern language, religion, history, and English. Varied electives offer courses in music, art, computer, and speech. Students may also choose from 19 Advanced Placement options in major disciplines. School-wide liturgies and community outreach help students deepen spiritual values. Among the activities are Student Council, National Honor Society, 17 varsity sports, language clubs, Mastersingers, jazz band, publications, robotics, forensics, and stage crew. Tuition: $19,375. Financial aid is available. John J. Jordan is Director of Admissions; William Doyle, Ed.D., is Principal; the Rev. Joseph McLaughlin, O.Praem. (University of Wisconsin, M.A.; Villanova, M.A.), is Headmaster. *Middle States Association.*

Centreville School   1974

6201 Kennett Pike, Centreville, DE 19807
Tel. 302-571-0230; Fax 302-571-0270
Web Site www.centrevilleschool.org
E-mail admissions@centrevilleschool.org

Now in its 37th year of educating learning-different students, Centreville enrolls approximately 145 children, ages 4–14, of average or above-average ability and equips them with the skills they need to flourish academically and socially. The School's primary mission is to maximize students' strengths and overcome areas of weakness through a carefully structured, personalized course of study predicated on the unique way each individual student learns. After thorough diagnostic testing, specialist teachers create an Individualized Educational Program, which encompasses traditional subjects such as reading and language arts, math, science, and social studies. Small classes, committed teachers, and a nurturing environment provide students the self-esteem and strategies they need to rise above their challenges. Reading, speech/language, and occupational therapists on staff further aid in the learning experience. Students are placed in developmentally based, ungraded classrooms and progress at their own pace. A summer program is offered, and financial aid is available. Tuition: $24,230. Rich Taubar is Director of Admissions; Denise G. Orenstein was appointed Head of School in 2008. *Middle States Association.*

Saint Mark's High School   1969

2501 Pike Creek Road, Wilmington, DE 19808
Tel. 302-738-3300; Fax 302-738-5132
Web Site www.stmarkshs.net; E-mail communications@stmarkshs.net

Saint Mark's High School is a Roman Catholic, college preparatory, coeducational day school enrolling 1451 students in Grades 9–12. A Saint Mark's education provides students not only with the tools needed to succeed intellectually in college and beyond, but with the tools to build a life around the values of faith, humility, integrity, and excellence that are grounded in the Catholic faith. Five academic levels reflect the School's unique ability to meet student needs in a variety of learning areas. In addition, Saint Mark's offers the most comprehensive Advanced Placement program in the state. With the guidance of the college counseling staff, more than 97 percent of all graduates go to college. More than 48 different athletic teams in 26 sports and 45 cocurricular clubs and activities provide students many opportunities to explore their interests, gain confidence in their abilities, and provide service to the community. Tuition: $9196. Financial Aid: $950,000. Thomas Lemon is Admissions Director; Mark John Freund (Towson University, B.A.; Loyola College [Maryland], M.Ed.) was appointed Principal in 1998. *Middle States Association.*

Salesianum School   1903

1801 North Broom Street, Wilmington, DE 19802-2891
Tel. 302-654-2495; Fax 302-654-7767
Web Site www.salesianum.org; E-mail mwinchell@salesianum.org

SALESIANUM SCHOOL in Wilmington, Delaware, is a Roman Catholic, college preparatory day school enrolling boys in Grades 9 through 12. It is located at the intersection of Broom and 18th Streets, a few blocks from where Interstate 95 and Route 202 cross, and is easily accessible for those traveling by car. Many students commute to and from school by buses, some operated by companies contracted by Salesianum and other private schools, and some on public lines. The regularly scheduled buses cover routes in Delaware, Maryland, and parts of Pennsylvania and southwestern New Jersey.

SALESIANUM SCHOOL

Salesianum School was founded by the Oblate Fathers and Brothers of Saint Francis de Sales, the 17th-century teacher and spiritual writer who became known as "the Gentleman Saint." Three members of the Oblate order were the first faculty members, and 12 boys were enrolled when Salesianum opened in 1903. By 1957, when the School began a new era by relocating to its present site, 2312 young men had been graduated. Another era opened as the School approached its 2003 centennial celebration with major building and renovation projects that are still being implemented.

Salesianum continues to educate its students following the model of Saint Francis de Sales, who counseled that one should submit to the guidance of God-given reason, live with a mind open to learning and growth, serve the community, value brotherhood, and contribute positively to society. The love of learning is central to the School's aims, and the key to learning is study.

Salesianum School is governed by a Board of Trustees that includes members of the Oblate order, alumni, and parents. The School now has more than 13,000 alumni living in 48 states and around the world, and they provide financial and other support for the School.

Salesianum is fully accredited by the Middle States Association of Colleges and Schools.

THE CAMPUS. The School is situated on a 22-acre campus directly across North Broom Street from Wilmington's Brandywine Park.

A 34,000-foot science center is the most significant addition to the main academic building since 1999. Eight science laboratories occupy the top two floors, and the first floor contains seven "smart" classrooms for social studies. The spaces vacated by other science departments have been re-formed as the Fine Arts Center. The first floor is devoted to the music program, including classrooms and an auditorium for performances. The top floors were renovated for art and drafting. A technology corridor with 45 computer workstations and other equipment was established for training both students and faculty. The School also renovated the gymnasium and the faculty residence and built a conference center and memorial chapel. A new dining center was completed in 2007.

The campus includes six tennis courts, two baseball diamonds, two soccer fields, a lacrosse field, a football practice area, and facilities for jumping and weight events in track and field. Some varsity athletic contests are played across 18th Street at Wilmington's Baynard Stadium.

SALESIANUM SCHOOL

Secure parking is provided on the campus for students, faculty, staff, and visitors.

THE FACULTY. The faculty includes 13 priests and brothers of the Oblate order, 78 lay teachers, and a professional staff of 28. Approximately two-thirds of the faculty members hold master's degrees, and the average length of teaching experience is 23 years.

STUDENT BODY. Salesianum School enrolls 1033 boys of all faiths in Grades 9 through 12. The students come from four states, with the majority from Delaware and others from Maryland, Pennsylvania, and New Jersey.

ACADEMIC PROGRAM. The academic year begins at the end of August and extends to the first of June. Vacations are scheduled at Christmas and Easter with several individual holidays occurring through the year. Classes are scheduled on a rotating basis to provide depth in all subjects and are held in six 53-minute periods between 8:17 A.M. and 2:40 P.M., five days a week. Students are grouped by ability in each subject, based on their classroom performance. Grades are issued quarterly. A Director of Educational Support Services monitors the progress of students who have a diagnosed medical condition, learning

disability, or Attention Deficit Disorder, and these needs are addressed as far as possible. Teachers are available to provide extra help during the day and up to an hour after the end of the school day.

SALESIANUM SCHOOL

To graduate from Salesianum School, a student must complete the following credits: 4 each in Religious Studies, English, mathematics, and social studies; 3 credits in science; 3 in one foreign language; $1\frac{1}{2}$ in physical education and health; $\frac{1}{2}$ in fine arts; $\frac{1}{2}$ in technology skills; $\frac{1}{4}$ in driver education; $\frac{1}{4}$ for Junior Advisory; and 3 electives.

Some of the courses offered include Composition and Literature, American Literature, British Literature, The Novel and Drama, Western Literature, Shakespeare Theater, Journalism; French 1–5, Spanish 1–5, Latin 1–5; World History, U.S. History, Foreign Policy, Modern European History, Anthropology and Archaeology, Economics, Psychology; Catholic and Salesian Identity, Sacred Scripture, Morality and Social Justice, Christian Lifestyles, Senior Religion Seminar, Christian Service; Algebra, Geometry, Trigonometry, Probability/Statistics, Pre-Calculus, Introduction to Programming, Computer Science, Web Page Design; Biology, Macrobiology, Microbiology, Cell Biology, Chemistry, Physics, Advanced Physics, Biotechnology and Forensic Science, Human Anatomy/Physiology, Ecology, Environmental Science; Physical Education, Health, Sports Psychology; Concert Band, Wind Ensemble, Mixed Chorus, Music Appreciation, Music Technology, Art, Medium Exploration, Drafting, TV Production, Acting; and Accounting, Marketing, Business Law, and Personal Finance. Advanced Placement courses are available in 23 subjects. Salesianum students participate in exchange courses with Ursuline and Padua Academies and have opportunities for independent study as well.

Virtually all graduates of Salesianum go on to further education. Some of the institutions where the most recent graduates are enrolled are Albright, American University, Boston College, Boston University, Bucknell, Carnegie Mellon, Colorado State, Cornell, Delaware College of Art and Design, De Sales, Dickinson, Drexel, Duquesne, Gettysburg, Goucher, Hamilton, Hofstra, Holy Family, Iona, James Madison, Johns Hopkins, La Salle, Lafayette, Lehigh, Loyola, Marist, Niagara, North Carolina State, Ohio State, Pennsylvania State University, Princeton, Purdue, Randolph-Macon, Rensselaer Polytechnic Institute, Rider, Saint Joseph's, Saint Vincent, Seton Hall, Vanderbilt, Villanova, and the Universities of Alabama, Colorado, Connecticut, Delaware, Indiana, Maryland, Michigan, North Carolina, Notre Dame, Pennsylvania, Richmond, Southern California, Vermont, Virginia, and Washington.

STUDENT ACTIVITIES. Students elect representatives to the Student Council, which plans and organizes social events and other activities and also serves as a forum for student views. More than 80 percent of the student body are involved in an activity.

Service activities are central to student life and are required in the Religious Studies program. Some of the regular service activities are the Key Club, Minutemen, Peer Counselors, and SADD/Yell, which acts to curb destructive behavior both among their peers and in community groups. Many boys work through the Campus Ministry to become involved in peer counseling, tutoring at nearby grammar schools, and working with peace and justice groups such as Amnesty International. They also assist the Campus Minister in daily and special liturgies and morning prayer.

The National Honor Society, foreign language honor societies, Academic Challenge, Mathletes, Science Olympiad, and Model United Nations are academic activities that complement and enhance the classroom experience. Artistic outlets are found in five bands, chorus, theater programs, the student newspaper, and a literary and arts magazine. Students use Salesianum's television production facilities for news and special programs on a channel within the School.

The School's athletic programs are well known and have a strong history of success. Salesianum athletes have earned more State Championships than any other school in Delaware. The School fields varsity teams in football, cross-country, soccer, basketball, ice hockey, indoor track, wrestling, swimming, tennis, golf, baseball, outdoor track and field, volleyball, and lacrosse. A strong intramural program draws participation by more than 300 students each year.

ADMISSION AND COSTS. Salesianum School is open to any young man who has the ability to take advantage of the academic opportunities it offers and the willingness to join in following the educational model of Saint Francis de Sales. The School administers its Entrance, Placement and Scholarship Examination to eighth graders in early December. Candidates should submit a completed application at least one week prior to the date of the exam to preregister for it. Seventh graders can take the exam as a practice test in the spring. The fee for the test is $55. Applicants are also invited to schedule visits to the School where they can attend classes. Admissions decisions are rendered in early February, based on exam results, elementary school record, and recommendations from teachers and principals.

SALESIANUM SCHOOL

Tuition for 2009–10 is $10,975. Bus costs range from $1300 to $1600, and these are offset by state subsidies for residents of Delaware and Pennsylvania. Academic scholarships, based on merit, total $315,000 annually, and financial aid, based on need, totals $475,000.

President: Rev. James E. Dalton, OSFS
Principal: Rev. William T. McCandless, OSFS
Assistant Principal/Academic Dean: Mr. Jude M. Szczerba '96
Assistant Principal/Dean of Students: Mr. Michael Gallagher '69
Assistant Principal/Director of Activities: Mr. Robert McConaghy

Director of Educational Support Services: Mrs. Susan Gardner
Director of Admissions: Mr. Mark Winchell '98
Director of Development: Mr. Daniel Sarkissian '97
Associate Director of Development/Alumni Affairs: Mr. Jon Allison '97
Director of Communications: Mr. Peter Castagna

Sanford School   1930

6900 Lancaster Pike, P.O. Box 888, Hockessin, DE 19707-0888
Tel. 302-239-5263; Fax 302-239-5389
Web Site www.sanfordschool.org
E-mail admissions@sanfordschool.org

Sanford is an independent day school enrolling 600 boys and girls in Junior Kindergarten–Grade 12. The college preparatory curriculum offers performing and studio arts, foreign languages, humanities, reading programs, literature, writing, history, mathematics, sciences, computer studies, and physical education, with Advanced Placement courses in 14 subjects. Sports include soccer, field hockey, indoor track, cross-country, volleyball, basketball, wrestling, baseball, tennis, lacrosse, and golf. A summer program offers enrichment and review courses. Tuition: $13,625–$21,250. Financial Aid: $1,600,000. Andrew R.N. Walpole is Director of Admissions and Financial Aid; Douglas MacKelcan, Jr. (Hobart, B.A. 1971; Wesleyan, M.A.L.S. 1979), was appointed Head of School in 1998. *Middle States Association.*

The Tatnall School   1930

1501 Barley Mill Road, Wilmington, DE 19807
Tel. 302-998-2292; Admissions 302-892-4285; Fax 302-998-7051
Web Site www.tatnall.org; E-mail admissions@tatnall.org

THE TATNALL SCHOOL

Tatnall, a college preparatory day school enrolling 650 boys and girls age 3–Grade 12, strives to provide the highest-level academic curriculum in a nurturing environment in which each student can grow in self-esteem and meet success. Art, music, drama, and athletics complement the academic program. Numerous Advanced Placement and college-credit courses are available. Situated on a beautiful 110-acre campus, Tatnall offers its students 23 sports and more than 30 clubs and activities. A year-round Extended Day Program provides care up to 6:00 P.M. Summer programs are offered. The School is accredited by the National Association for the Education of Young Children. Tuition: $10,320–$22,100. Financial aid is available. Leon Spencer is Director of Enrollment and Financial Aid; Eric G. Ruoss (University of Virginia, Ed.D. 1992) is Headmaster. *Middle States Association.*

Ursuline Academy 1893

1106 Pennsylvania Avenue, Wilmington, DE 19806
Tel. 302-658-7158; Fax 302-658-4297
Web Site www.ursuline.org

Ursuline Academy is a Catholic, college preparatory day school, serving girls age 3–Grade 12 and boys age 3–Grade 3. Ursuline has preserved its tradition, established 474 years ago by foundress St. Angela Merici, of motivating students toward academic excellence. Embedded in that tradition is the school motto, *Serviam,* or "I will serve"; all Upper School students perform a minimum of 80 hours of service by the end of Grade 10, and National Honor Society students in Grades 11–12 perform 50 hours a year. All students and teachers in Grades 7–12 use a personal laptop as part of a networked community that integrates technology throughout the curriculum. Classes in liberal arts, sciences, and humanities are offered at college preparatory and honors levels; qualified scholars can earn college credits in 16 AP courses. Class size is no larger than 18 but often smaller. Ursuline offers Montessori and traditional Pre-Kindergarten and Kindergarten. Extended care and a summer camp are offered. Tuition: $5200–$15,330. Jamie Jones and Jennifer Callahan are Directors of Admission; Cathie Field Lloyd is President. *Middle States Association.*

Wilmington Friends School 1748

101 School Road, Wilmington, DE 19803
Tel. 302-576-2900; Admissions 302-576-2930; Fax 302-576-2939
Web Site www.wilmingtonfriends.org
E-mail admissions@wilmingtonfriends.org

This college preparatory, coeducational day school enrolls 780 students in Preschool–Grade 12. In the Quaker tradition of strong academics grounded in active learning and ethical discussion, students accept challenges, opportunities, and responsibilities as they prepare for those that lie ahead. The International Baccalaureate Diploma Programme is offered. Service is required in all divisions. Activities include athletics, cultural arts, and publications. After-school and summer camp programs are available. Tuition: $8350–$20,875. Financial Aid: $2,000,000. Kathleen Hopkins is Director of Admissions and Financial Aid; Dr. Bryan Garman (Bucknell University, B.A.; Emory University, M.A., Ph.D.) is Head of School. *Middle States Association.*

SALESIANUM SCHOOL

DISTRICT OF COLUMBIA

Beauvoir, The National Cathedral Elementary School   1933

3500 Woodley Road, NW, Washington, DC 20016
Tel. 202-537-6485
Web Site www.beauvoirschool.org

BEAUVOIR, THE NATIONAL CATHEDRAL ELEMENTARY SCHOOL in Washington, D.C., is an Episcopal, elementary day school enrolling boys and girls from Pre-Kindergarten through Grade 3. Beauvoir is situated within the 60-acre Close of the Washington National Cathedral, a magnificent Gothic structure begun in 1907 that has been the focal point of numerous significant events throughout its history. Students and faculty make frequent use of the many cultural and educational resources of the nation's capital. There is limited bus service to the School; however, most families use car pools or make their own transportation arrangements.

The Protestant Episcopal Cathedral Foundation established Beauvoir in 1933 as the elementary division of National Cathedral School; in 1939, it was recognized as an independent institution.

BEAUVOIR, THE NATIONAL CATHEDRAL ELEMENTARY SCHOOL

The School aims to provide an educational environment that will foster a lifetime enthusiasm for learning and growth while nurturing the spiritual, ethical, intellectual, emotional, physical, and social development of each child. Faculty teach basic skills through a broad-based, integrated curriculum enriched by offerings in science, the arts, technology, physical education, and Spanish. Developing students' understanding of themselves in relation to the larger community and establishing a diverse faculty and student body are integral to the program. The School also supports a strong relationship among parents,

students, and faculty as a means of implementing its guiding mission and philosophy.

Beauvoir is guided by a self-sustaining Governing Board and is accredited by the Middle States Association of Colleges and Schools and the Association of Independent Maryland Schools. It holds membership in the National Association of Independent Schools, the Mid-Atlantic Episcopal School Association, and the Association of Independent Schools of Greater Washington. Beauvoir parents, as members of the Beauvoir Parents Association, participate actively in all aspects of school life such as raising significant funds for scholarships and other needs, sponsoring book fairs, organizing community service projects, and supporting the educational programs in many ways.

THE CAMPUS. Beauvoir is located within the Close of the Cathedral of St. Peter and St. Paul, known familiarly as Washington National Cathedral, and shares the grounds with the National Cathedral School for Girls and St. Albans School. In addition to the completely renovated main academic building, which houses classrooms for each grade level, there is an interior courtyard, landscaped playground, and fields for outdoor play.

THE FACULTY. Paula J. Carreiro was appointed Head of School in 1992. She holds a B.S. degree from Northeastern Oklahoma State University and a master's degree from Oklahoma State University.

BEAUVOIR, THE NATIONAL CATHEDRAL ELEMENTARY SCHOOL

There are 58 faculty members, including 22 classroom instructors and 16 associate teachers as well as 19 resource teachers and a school nurse. All faculty are trained and experienced in Early Childhood and Elementary Development and Curriculum, and a strong emphasis is placed on professional development.

STUDENT BODY. In 2009–10, Beauvoir enrolled 390 boys and girls. Students come from throughout the Greater Washington metropolitan area and represent a wide diversity of ethnic, racial, and religious backgrounds. The Governing Board has a proactive Outreach Committee charged with increasing the diversity of the applicant pool.

ACADEMIC PROGRAM. The school year, from early September to early June, includes a Thanksgiving recess, vacations in the winter and spring, and observance of national holidays. The full-day program extends from 8:15 A.M. to 3:00 P.M. Monday through Thursday, with dismissal at 2:30 P.M. on Fridays. An Extended Day option until 6:00 P.M. provides activities, snacks, a rest period, and time reserved for homework and outdoor play.

Recognizing that there are individual learning styles and paces, the School evaluates each child's progress in terms of individual development based on his or her potential as well as on specific academic accomplishments. Parent conferences are held in the early fall, the late spring, and at other times as needed. Parents receive written reports twice a year. There are three classes in Pre-Kindergarten and four each in Kindergarten through Grade 3. Classes range in size from 18 to 21, with an overall student-teacher ratio of 10:1.

BEAUVOIR, THE NATIONAL CATHEDRAL ELEMENTARY SCHOOL

Following completion of Grade 3 at Beauvoir, students enter the fourth grade at other private and public schools including St. Albans and National Cathedral School.

Summer Program sessions for children ages four to nine are conducted on campus from mid-June through early August. The summer program includes art, music, drama, sports, movement, crafts, science, and swimming.

ADMISSION AND COSTS. Beauvoir seeks students, ages four to eight, of varying backgrounds, personalities, and talents, regardless of race, creed, color, or national or ethnic origin. Applicants for Pre-Kindergarten must be four years old by September 1 of the desired year of enrollment. Tours of the School are scheduled for prospective parents from October through the middle of January. Individual testing and school visits are required. Parents are notified of admissions decisions in mid-March.

In 2009–10, tuition is $27,320. Financial aid is awarded on the basis of demonstrated need.

Capitol Hill Day School   1968

210 South Carolina Avenue, SE, Washington, DC 20003
Tel. 202-547-2244; Admissions Ext. 120; Fax 202-547-0510
Web Site www.chds.org; E-mail priscillal@chds.org

Located in a historic District of Columbia school building, Capitol Hill Day serves approximately 230 students in Pre-Kindergarten–Grade 8. The School offers a strong academic program in a creative environment. An extensive Field Education Program, intricately linked to the curriculum, enables faculty to make use of the resources in the metropolitan area. The art program is integrated into other subjects—math, literature, science, and social studies. French and Spanish are introduced at the early-childhood level, followed by a choice of French or Spanish in Grade 1. The selected language is continued through Grade 8. The After School Program and Summer Camps are

optional and provide a balance of structure and play essential in creating engaged learners. Tuition: $20,450–$24,290. Financial aid is available. Priscilla Lund is Admissions Director; Michael Eanes is Head of School.

Edmund Burke School   1968

4101 Connecticut Avenue, NW, Washington, DC 20008
Tel. 202-362-8882; Admissions Ext. 670; Fax 202-362-1914
Web Site www.eburke.org; E-mail admissions@eburke.org

Edmund Burke School, a coeducational, college preparatory day school, serves 320 students in Grades 6–12. Located conveniently near the Van Ness Metro stop, the School offers a rigorous curriculum in an informal environment. The student-teacher ratio of 7:1 and the small classes allow individual attention. Edmund Burke has a complete sports program and encourages participation in drama, music, and the arts. Advanced Placement and independent study courses are available. The Summer Programs feature academic courses, sports and arts programs, and a musical theater. Tuition: $29,510. Kai-Anasa George is Director of Admissions; David Shapiro (Oberlin, B.A.; Columbia, M.A.; Baruch College, M.S.) is Head of School.

The Field School   1972

2301 Foxhall Road, NW, Washington, DC 20007
Tel. 202-295-5800; Fax 202-295-5850
Web Site www.fieldschool.org; E-mail admissions@fieldschool.org

Enrolling 320 day boys and girls in Grades 7–12, The Field School offers a college preparatory program designed to provide a strong grounding in the liberal arts and sciences and to prepare students for responsible citizenship. The curriculum emphasizes the interrelationships among the diverse fields of knowledge, blending both traditional and innovative methods of teaching to accommodate various learning styles. An average class size of 11 ensures individualized attention; instruction is primarily through dialogue among students and teachers. The core academic program is enriched by an extensive studio arts program for all students and an annual two-week Winter Internship experience. Activities include varsity athletics and clubs. Tuition: $32,100. Will Layman is Director of Admission; Dale T. Johnson is Head of School. *Middle States Association.*

Georgetown Day School   1945

Lower/Middle School: 4530 MacArthur Boulevard, NW,
  Washington, DC 20007
Tel. 202-295-6200; Admissions 202-295-6210; Fax 202-295-6211
High School: 4200 Davenport Street, NW, Washington, DC 20016
  Tel. 202-274-3200; Admissions 202-274-3210
  Fax 202-274-3211
  Web Site www.gds.org; E-mail info@gds.org

Georgetown Day, a coeducational, college preparatory school enrolling 1060 students in Pre-K–Grade 12, honors the integrity and worth of each individual within a diverse school community. It aims to provide a supportive atmosphere in which teachers challenge the abilities of its students and foster strength of character and concern for others. The High School offers 19 Advanced Placement courses. Each year, approximately 35 percent of seniors earn recognition in the National Merit and National Achievement Scholarship programs. Activities include athletics, performing arts, publications, clubs, and required community service. Tuition: $26,713–$30,571. Financial Aid: $3,900,000. Vincent Rowe is Director of Enrollment Management & Financial Aid; Peter M. Branch is Head of School.

Georgetown Visitation Preparatory School 1799

1524 35th Street, NW, Washington, DC 20007
Tel. 202-337-3350; Fax 202-342-5733
Web Site www.visi.org; E-mail jkeller@visi.org

Throughout its history, Georgetown Visitation Prep has provided an educational experience that combines academic excellence with spirituality, common sense, and kindness for girls from many faiths and cultures. Visitation currently enrolls 475 day students in Grades 9–12 on a 20-acre wooded campus in Georgetown. The facilities include both historic and modern structures such as Founders Hall, the main academic building dating to 1873 (renovated 1995), the Nolan Performing Arts Center (1998) and the Fisher Athletic Center (1998). The college preparatory curriculum features Advanced Placement and honors courses in all disciplines and requires students to perform a minimum of 80 hours of Christian service prior to graduation. Girls compete in 13 varsity and junior varsity sports. The performing arts, with chorus, drama, and dance, and more than 30 clubs and leadership groups provide opportunities for students to develop new interests and skills and enjoy social interaction with peers. Tuition: $21,500. Financial Aid: $1,500,000. Sr. Mary Berchmans Hannan, VHM, is President Emerita; Daniel M. Kerns is Head of School; Janet D. Keller is Director of Admissions. *Middle States Association.*

The Lab School of Washington 1967

4759 Reservoir, NW, Washington, DC 20007
Tel. 202-965-6600; Fax 202-944-3078
Web Site www.labschool.org
E-mail alexandra.freeman@labschool.org

This nonprofit day school enrolls 348 learning-disabled children ages 6–18 with average to superior intelligence. The individualized Lower School program is enriched by skills taught in history clubs, music, dance, drama, film making, art, and woodwork. Sciences, Humanities, Student Council, the yearbook, and team sports augment the Junior High and High School programs. Summer School includes remediation and an arts program. There is a postsecondary night school, diagnostic and tutoring service, career counseling, college guidance, and a monthly lecture series for parents and professionals. The new Baltimore campus at 2220 St. Paul Street enrolls students ages 6–18. Tuition: $30,810–$33,150. Susan F. Feeley is Admission Director; Katherine Schantz is Director.

Lowell School 1965

1640 Kalmia Road, NW, Washington, DC 20012
Tel. 202-577-2000; Admissions 202-577-2004; Fax 202-577-2001
Web Site www.lowellschool.org; E-mail mbelton@lowellschool.org

Lowell School is a progressive school serving approximately 300 students, age 3–Grade 6. The program reflects a philosophy that emphasizes the student's responsibility and expectation for attaining strong communication, collaborative, and academic skills, within a nurturing environment. Lowell's stimulating, thematic, integrated, project-oriented curriculum is enhanced by the arts, Spanish, physical education, field trips, and service learning. After-school and summer programs are offered. Tuition: $14,990–$25,997. Financial aid is available. Michelle Belton is Director of Admission; Debbie Gibbs (Pomona College, B.A.; University of Minnesota, B.S.; University of San Francisco, M.A.) is Head of School.

Maret School 1911

3000 Cathedral Avenue, NW, Washington, DC 20008
Tel. 202-939-8800; Admissions 202-939-8814; Fax 202-939-8845
Web Site www.maret.org; E-mail admissions@maret.org

This coeducational, college preparatory day school, founded by educator Louise Maret, enrolls 635 students in Kindergarten–Grade 12. Located on the Woodley Estate, Maret uses the nation's capital as an extension of classroom instruction. Small classes, an advisor system, and a learning skills program provide strong student support. The humanities, math, science, computer studies, and foreign languages form the basis of the demanding curriculum. Advanced Placement and independent study opportunities are offered as well as summer study on campus or in Florida, Costa Rica, or France. Tuition: $25,685–$29,565. Financial aid is available. Annie M. Farquhar is Admission Director; Marjo Talbott (Williams, B.A.; Harvard, M.Ed.) was named Head of School in 1994. *Middle States Association.*

National Cathedral School 1899

Mount St. Alban, Washington, DC 20016-5000
Tel. 202-537-6300; Admission 202-537-6374; Fax 202-537-2382
Web Site www.ncs.cathedral.org; E-mail ncs.admissions@cathedral.org

National Cathedral School is a college preparatory, Episcopal day school enrolling approximately 580 girls in Grades 4–12. The School aspires to excellence in education for girls, values the spiritual life of its students, and strongly supports a multicultural environment. A coordinate academic and social relationship is maintained with St. Albans School for boys. Extracurricular activities include sports, clubs, and the arts. Tuition: $32,220. Financial Aid: $2,000,000. Susan Mantilla-Goin is Director of Admission and Financial Aid; Kathleen O. Jamieson (University of Maryland, B.A. 1977; Columbia, M.Ed. 1997) was appointed Head of School in 2003. *Middle States Association.*

St. Albans School 1909

Mount St. Alban, Washington, DC 20016
Tel. 202-537-6435; Admissions 202-537-6440; Fax 202-537-2225
Web Site www.stalbansschool.org
E-mail sta_admission@cathedral.org

This Episcopal, college preparatory school for boys enrolls 570 students in Grades 4–12, including 30 boarders in Grades 9–12. Set on the Close of the National Cathedral, St. Albans seeks to develop the spiritual, intellectual, and physical well-being of its students and to encourage participation in their School, church, and community. The School aims to teach students to think creatively and develop skills of analysis and expression through the core curriculum of the arts, sciences, and humanities. Students in the Lower School study the fundamentals of reading, writing, and math with an emphasis on logical thinking and powers of observation, while Upper School students take more focused higher-level classes. The program is enriched by six languages, Advanced Placement and Honors courses, and the resources of the nation's capital. Student Council, drama, publications, music, community service, 17 sports, and academic and special-interest clubs are among the activities. Many boys are acolytes and choir members at the Cathedral. A summer program is also available. Boarding Tuition: $46,667; Day Tuition: $32,990. Financial Aid: $3,000,000. Hart Roper is Director of Admissions and Financial Aid; Vance Wilson is Headmaster.

District of Columbia

St. Patrick's Episcopal Day School   1956

4700 Whitehaven Parkway, NW, Washington, DC 20007-1554
Tel. 202-342-2805; Admission 202-342-2807; Fax 202-342-2839
Web Site www.stpatsdc.org; E-mail admission@stpatsdc.org

A coeducational parish school serving 507 students in Nursery–Grade 8, St. Patrick's Episcopal Day balances tradition and innovation in an educational program emphasizing acquisition of essential skills, integration of disciplines, and active learning. It seeks to educate young people who will grow in intellectual and academic competence, personal integrity, openness to change, commitment to service, and confident and ethical involvement in the world. On two campuses, facilities include science labs, libraries, art studios, music rooms, a gymnasium, three play parks, and a playing field. After-school, sports, extended day, and summer programs are offered. Tuition: $14,347–$27,496. Financial Aid: $1,400,000. Jennifer S. Danish is Director of Admission and Financial Aid; Peter A. Barrett was appointed Head of School in 1994. *Middle States Association.*

ST. PATRICK'S EPISCOPAL DAY SCHOOL

ST. PATRICK'S EPISCOPAL DAY SCHOOL

FLORIDA

Academy of the Holy Names   1881

3319 Bayshore Boulevard, Tampa, FL 33629
Tel. 813-839-5371; Admission Ext. 307; Fax 813-839-1486
Web Site www.holynamestpa.org
E-mail jwilson@holynamestpa.org

The Academy of the Holy Names is a Catholic, independent, coeducational elementary school (PK–Grade 8) and a college preparatory high school for young women, sponsored by the Sisters of the Holy Names of Jesus and Mary. Its mission is to develop the spiritual, academic, personal, and physical growth of each student; provide quality educational opportunities for students of diverse ethnic, economic, and religious backgrounds; and encourage each student to realize his/her full potential as an intelligent, cultured, spiritual, and socially aware individual. Students are involved in more than 30 clubs and 10 team sports. Tuition: $11,480–$14,270. Jacqueline D. Wilson is Enrollment Manager; Dr. Harry Purpur is President/CEO.

All Saints' Academy   1966

5001 State Road 540 W, Winter Haven, FL 33880-8009
Tel. 863-293-5980; Admission Ext. 2252; Fax 863-329-8489
Web Site www.allsaintsacademy.com
E-mail gbonnichsen@allsaintsacademy.com

ALL SAINTS' ACADEMY

All Saints' Academy enrolls 625 boys and girls from diverse backgrounds as day students in PreK–3 through Grade 12. Set on a scenic, 60-acre campus in Central Florida, ASA is committed to developing the mind, heart, and spirit of each student in an environment of academic challenge and Judeo-Christian values. At All Saints', the educational program emphasizes the mastery of skills and knowledge designed to promote effective writing and speaking, independent problem solving, Socratic dialogue, and the ability to work cooperatively with others. The core curriculum centers on English, mathematics, science, and social studies and is enriched by classes in world languages, technology, film, and the visual and performing arts. Honors and Advanced Placement courses are offered in the major departments. The quality of this curriculum results in a consistent, 100 percent college acceptance rate. Chapel services and religious education promote spiritual growth and understanding among students from all faiths. School government, academic honor societies, orchestra, dance team, publications, community service, and interscholastic sports are among the activities. Tuition: $6929–$10,660. Tony Jordan is Headmaster; Gail Bonnichsen is Director of Admission.

The Benjamin School   1960

PK3–Grade 8: 11000 Ellison Wilson Road, North Palm Beach,
* FL 33408*
* Tel. 561-472-3451; Fax 561-472-3410*
Grades 9–12: 4875 Grandiflora Road, Palm Beach Gardens,
* FL 33418*
* Tel. 561-472-5998; Fax 561-691-8823*
* Web Site www.thebenjaminschool.org*

This coeducational day school provides a diverse student body a challenging college preparatory education. Enrolling 1175 students in PK3–Grade 12, The Benjamin School combines academic excellence with a structured, nurturing community environment. Character education, world languages, and the arts are integral to the curriculum. State-of-the-art computer technology, including a laptop program, enhances the acquisition of knowledge. Middle and Upper School students benefit from an advisor system as they further their development as independent and collaborative learners. Graduates enter leading colleges and universities throughout the country and worldwide. Student government, honor societies, dance, drama, chorus, band, visual arts, debate, SADD, RACE (Respecting All Cultures Equally), Political issues, Model UN, and 47 Buccaneer athletic teams are among the cocurricular opportunities. Benjamin is a member of the Florida Council of Independent Schools and the Florida Kindergarten Council. Tuition: $7500–$21,525. Financial Aid: $2,000,000+. Mary Lou Primm is Director of Admission; Robert S. Goldberg is Head of School.

Berkeley Preparatory School   1960

4811 Kelly Road, Tampa, FL 33615
Tel. 813-885-1673; Fax 813-886-6933
Web Site www.berkeleyprep.org; E-mail mcilvjan@berkeleyprep.org

BERKELEY PREPARATORY SCHOOL in Tampa, Florida, is a coeducational day school enrolling students in Pre-Kindergarten through Grade 12. The School's location allows convenient access for residents of the Tampa Bay and neighboring areas.

BERKELEY PREPARATORY SCHOOL

The Latin words *Disciplina, Diligentia,* and *Integritas* in the School's motto state the values underlying the rigorous college preparatory curriculum of Berkeley, founded in 1960 and opened for Grades 7–12 the next year. Kindergarten through

Grade 6 were added in 1967 and Pre-Kindergarten, in 1988. The School's purpose is to enable students to achieve academic excellence in preparation for higher education and to instill in them a strong sense of morality, ethics, and social responsibility.

Incorporated as a nonprofit institution, Berkeley Preparatory School is directed by a Board of Trustees. The School is accredited by the Southern Association of Colleges and Schools and the Florida Council of Independent Schools and is a member of the National Association of Independent Schools, among other affiliations. In 1995 and again in 2000, Berkeley was designated a Blue Ribbon School by the U.S. Department of Education.

THE CAMPUS. The 77-acre campus in the Town 'n' Country suburb of Tampa features classrooms, a fine arts center, a science wing, two libraries, general convocation rooms, physical education fields, a Pre-Kindergarten and Kindergarten wing, a 19,000-square-foot student center, and administrative offices for Lower, Middle, and Upper Divisions.

BERKELEY PREPARATORY SCHOOL

Berkeley athletes participate in two gymnasiums, a junior Olympic swimming pool, a wrestling/gymnastics room, a weight-lifting room, a rock-climbing wall, tennis courts, baseball and softball diamonds, and a stadium for football, track, and soccer.

The arts program is enhanced by a 634-seat performing arts center, which also includes a gallery for visual arts displays, a flex studio for dance and small drama productions, dressing rooms, and an orchestra pit.

THE FACULTY. Joseph A. Merluzzi, appointed Headmaster in 1987, is a graduate of Western Connecticut State College and holds a master's degree in mathematics from Fairfield University. Previously, Mr. Merluzzi served as Head of the Upper School, Assistant Headmaster, and Dean of the Upper School at Cranbrook-Kingswood School in Michigan.

There are 175 teachers and administrators. They hold 78 graduate and 6 doctoral degrees from such colleges and universities as Amherst, Duke, Florida State, Furman, Indiana University, James Madison, Michigan State, Middlebury, Ohio State, Ohio University, Parsons School of Design, Pennsylvania State, Princeton, State University of New York, Vanderbilt, West Virginia University, Williams, Yale, and the Universities of Alabama, California, Florida, Illinois, Maryland, Miami, Missouri, New Brunswick, North Carolina, Notre Dame, Oregon, Tampa, Texas, and Wisconsin.

STUDENT BODY. In 2009–10, the School enrolled approximately 1200 students in Pre-Kindergarten–Grade 12 as follows: 400 in the Lower Division (Pre-Kindergarten–Grade 5), 300 in the Middle Division (Grades 6–8), and 500 in the Upper Division (Grades 9–12).

ACADEMIC PROGRAM. The school year, from late August to early June, includes Thanksgiving, Christmas, and spring vacations.

The average class size in the Middle and Upper Divisions is 15–20. The day begins at 8:00 A.M. and ends at 3:15 P.M. An activity period and divisional convocations are scheduled into each class day. All Middle Division students, ninth graders, and other students who do not qualify for study hall exemptions attend supervised study halls when they do not have a scheduled class. Teachers are available for extra help during the activity period and at other times during the day. Grades are sent to parents four times a year.

In the Lower Division, students attend school from 8:00 A.M. to 3:10 P.M. Curricular emphasis is on the core subjects of reading and mathematics. Students receive a firm foundation in grammar and vocabulary development. Math skills are developed and used in problem-solving. Social studies and science curricula are designed to aid children in mastering the skills they need in a rapidly changing, technological society. An interdisciplinary approach is used in foreign language and social studies. Daily Spanish instruction exists at all Lower Division grade levels. Manipulatives are used extensively in both the science and mathematics programs. Music, art, drama, and physical education are integral parts of the Lower Division curriculum. Each student also receives instruction in library skills and computers.

Academic requirements in the Middle Division are English, English expression, mathematics, history, world languages, science, computers, physical education, art, drama, and music. All students in Grades 6 and 7 take Latin in addition to Spanish, French, or Chinese. Continuing students in Grade 8 choose from Spanish, French, Chinese, or Latin.

In the Upper Division, students take four or five credit courses each year in addition to the fine arts and physical education requirements. To graduate, students must complete a total of 22 credits. Specific requirements are 4 credits in English; 3 each in mathematics, history, science, and foreign language; 2 academic electives; one year of personal fitness/health and an additional year of physical education; and two years of fine arts. In addition, Berkeley students are required to complete 76 hours of community service. Advanced Placement courses are offered including English, Chinese, Spanish, Latin, French, European History, Government (U.S. and Comparative), U.S. History, Calculus (AB and BC), Computer Science, Biology, Chemistry, Physics (B and C), Statistics, Environmental Science, Economics (Macro and Micro), and Psychology. Advanced topics seminar courses are also available in English: literature; English: writing; history; and science.

BERKELEY PREPARATORY SCHOOL

Grades 4–12 use laptop computers to enhance their learning experience.

Traditionally, 100 percent of Berkeley graduates attend college. Members of the Class of 2009 were accepted at more than

130 colleges and universities throughout the United States including Boston College, Brown, Columbia, Cornell, Dartmouth, Duke, Emory, Georgetown, Harvard, Johns Hopkins, New York University, Northwestern, Princeton, Stanford, Vanderbilt, Villanova, Yale, and the Universities of Florida, Miami, Michigan, North Carolina, Pennsylvania, and Virginia. Scholarship offers totaling over $6,700,000 were made to 90 percent of the graduates.

BERKELEY PREPARATORY SCHOOL.

There is a six-week academic summer program for students in Pre-Kindergarten–Grade 12. Tuition ranges from $725 to $1500. Fine arts and sports camps are also offered in the summer.

STUDENT ACTIVITIES. The Student Forum is responsible for presenting student views to the Upper Division administration and the Headmaster for discussion, and for recommending new ideas to the administration. Other student leadership roles are given to 20 senior prefects who are selected each year by a faculty committee. The Student Guide organization assists the Director of Admissions in acquainting prospective families with Berkeley's campus and programs.

Students publish the *Fanfare*, the student newspaper; *Small Voices*, a literary magazine for Kindergarten–Grade 5; *Soundings*, a literary magazine for Grades 6–8; *Phoenix*, a literary magazine for Grades 9–12; and the *Buccaneer*, the student yearbook for Pre-Kindergarten–Grade 12. Qualified students may be invited to join The Cum Laude Society, the National Honor Society, or honor societies in French, Latin, Spanish, math, and drama. Opportunities are available for students to participate in the Latin Forum, and the Art, Photography, Social Services, Cheerleading, Drama, French, Mathematics, Music, Forensics, Science and Environmental, Model United Nations, and Spanish clubs. Berkeley sponsors its own all-School philanthropy, Project Berkeley, which benefits a local food bank; students, faculty, administration, staff, and parents participate on a monthly basis.

Varsity sports for boys are baseball, basketball, cross-country, diving, football, golf, soccer, swimming, tennis, volleyball, weight lifting, wrestling, track, lacrosse, and crew; sports for girls are basketball, cross-country, diving, soccer, softball, tennis, track, swimming, cheerleading, lacrosse, weight lifting, volleyball, and crew. Berkeley competes in the Upper Division with schools of the Bay Conference and in the Middle and Lower Divisions with schools in the Florida West Coast League or the Youth Sports League.

Seasonal sports award banquets, a homecoming football game, a spring field day, alumni day, grandparents' day, student retreats, Middle and Upper Division dances, and honors convocations are among the yearly events. The Berkeley Parents' Club and the Buccaneer Club hold fund-raising events for the School.

ADMISSION AND COSTS. Berkeley Preparatory School is committed to enrolling a talented and diverse student body that is able to thrive in a college preparatory program. The School has a policy of nondiscrimination regarding students on the basis of race, color, and national or ethnic origin or any other class protected by law.

The School uses the Secondary School Admission Test and its own testing program. Recommendations and transcripts from the previous school are required. Application should be made as early in the year as possible; most grades are on a wait-list basis by late spring. There is an application fee of $50.

Tuition is $15,260 for Pre-Kindergarten–Grade 5, $17,070 for Grades 6–8, and $18,360 for Grades 9–12. Books and uniforms are extra. Lower and Middle Division students wear a uniform daily. Upper Division students must comply with the school dress code Monday through Thursday and must wear a uniform on Friday. A required tuition payment plan with eight monthly payments is in effect. Scholarship funding and financial aid are available.

Headmaster: Joseph A. Merluzzi
Director of Admissions: Janie McIlvaine
Assistant Headmaster/Upper Division Director: Hugh Jebson
Middle Division Director: Cynthia Boss
Lower Division Director: M. Joanne Moore
College Counselor: Kemp Hoversten
Business Manager: Charlie Simpson
Director of Development: Laura Grams
Director of Athletics: Bobby Reinhart
Physical Plant Director: Hal Schaeffer
Technology Director: Mike Speer

The Canterbury School   1964

8141 College Parkway, Fort Myers, FL 33919
Tel. 239-481-4323; Admissions 239-415-8945; Fax 239-481-8339
Web Site www.canterburyfortmyers.org
E-mail jpeters@canterburyfortmyers.org

THE CANTERBURY SCHOOL

The Canterbury School, located on 33 acres, is a coeducational, college preparatory day school committed to high standards. Enrolling 655 students in Pre-K through Grade 12, Canterbury balances academics with competitive athletics and the visual and performing arts; activities include drama, sports, publications, and service groups. More than half of the faculty hold advanced degrees. With rigorous academic standards, the School strives to educate the whole child for a lifetime of intellectual exploration, personal growth, and social responsibility. Honors courses are offered in the Middle and Upper School. Advanced Placement courses are available for qualified upper-level students, and elective options are offered in all major disciplines and the arts. College counseling is provided. Tuition: $13,445–$17,285. Financial Aid: $1,150,000. Julie Peters is Director of Admission; John Anthony Paulus II (Stanford, B.A.; Boston University, M.Ed.) is Head of School.

Carrollton School of the Sacred Heart   1962

3747 Main Highway, Miami, FL 33133
Tel. 305-446-5673; Fax 305-446-4160
Web Site www.carrollton.org; E-mail admissions@carrollton.org

Carrollton, established by the Society of the Sacred Heart, is a Roman Catholic college preparatory school enrolling 790 girls as day students in a Montessori three-year-old program to Grade 12. It aims to educate its students to a personal and active faith in God, respect for intellectual values, social consciousness, the building of community, and personal growth. A member of the Network of Sacred Heart Schools in 21 cities, all sharing the same traditions, the School conducts annual reviews of its programs and sets new directions accordingly. Carrollton offers the International Baccalaureate Program, which is a demanding pre-university course of study for juniors and seniors. Tuition: $14,266–$21,836. Financial Aid: $1,800,000. Ana J. Roye is Director of Admissions and Financial Aid; Sr. Suzanne Cooke, RSCJ (Manhattanville, B.A.; University of Chicago, M.A.), is Headmistress.

Episcopal High School of Jacksonville   1966

4455 Atlantic Boulevard, Jacksonville, FL 32207
Tel. 904-396-5751; Admissions Ext. 1220; Fax 904-396-7209
Web Site www.episcopalhigh.org
E-mail admissions@episcopalhigh.org

EPISCOPAL HIGH SCHOOL OF JACKSONVILLE

Set on an 88-acre campus on the St. Johns River, Episcopal High School is a church-affiliated, coeducational day school enrolling 850 socially and culturally diverse students in Grades 6–12. Its mission is to offer educational excellence from a Christian perspective, developing the intellectual, spiritual, social, and leadership potential of every student. In addition to core college preparatory subjects, students have courses in theology, foreign languages, information technology, and the arts. Community service, student leadership programs, publications, drama, music groups, and interscholastic athletics are among the extracurricular activities. A summer session and financial aid are available. Tuition: $16,600–$17,400. Peggy Fox is Director of Admissions; Dale Regan is Head of School. *Southern Association.*

Independent Day School–Corbett Campus   1968

12015 Orange Grove Drive, Tampa, FL 33618
Tel. 813-961-3087; Admissions Ext. 306; Fax 813-963-0846
Web Site www.idsyes.com; E-mail pbarfield@idsyes.com

Independent Day School—Corbett Campus provides a dynamic educational environment that uses innovative, proven strategies to incorporate joy and challenge in learning. Faculty, who are chosen for their lifelong learning focus, use interactive techniques to allow students to take an active role in their education. Implementation of M.O.R.E. (Multiple Options for Results in Education) promotes involvement in all aspects of student life through cooperative learning, high-level critical thinking skills,

independent day school Corbett Campus

INDEPENDENT DAY SCHOOL–CORBETT CAMPUS

multiple intelligences, integrated curriculum, global perspectives, and an emphasis on character and community service. *It's All About Kids: Every Child Deserves a Teacher of the Year* describes how the School combines the best in academics with social, emotional, and physical well-being. This Blue Ribbon School, serving 550 boys and girls in PreK3–Grade 8, offers superior academic programs, International Baccalaureate Middle Years Program (MYP), state-of-the-art technology, competitive sports, an accomplished fine arts program, a community school of the arts, and a summer camp with academic and recreational programs. Tuition: $8930–$11,195. Dr. Joyce Burick Swarzman is Headmaster; Pam Barfield is Director of Admissions.

Maclay School   1968

3737 North Meridian Road, Tallahassee, FL 32312
Tel. 850-893-2138; Admission 850-893-7857; Fax 850-893-7434
Web Site www.maclay.org

Maclay is a college preparatory day school enrolling 970 girls and boys in Preschool–Grade 12. It seeks to teach the liberal arts creatively and to help students realize their full potential through self-discipline and persistence. Computer studies, creative writing, music, and drama complement the traditional curriculum. Sports, student government, honor societies, publications, theater, and service clubs are among the activities. A summer session offers remedial and enrichment courses. Tuition: $9425. Financial Aid: $480,000. Michael Obrecht is Director of Admission; William W. Jablon (Boston College, B.A. 1968; Florida State, M.A. 1972) was appointed President/Headmaster in 1976. *Southern Association.*

Miami Country Day School   1938

601 NE 107 Street, P.O. Box 380608, Miami, FL 33161
Tel. 305-759-2843; Admission 305-779-7230; Fax 305-758-5107
Web Site www.miamicountryday.org
E-mail lakej@miamicountryday.org

Miami Country Day is an independent college preparatory school founded in 1938, dedicated to the development of the whole child through a uniquely diverse and enriching educational experience. The School, enrolling 1000 students in Pre-Kindergarten (age 3)–Grade 12, provides a caring learning community focused on unleashing the potential of every student, every day. A multifaceted curriculum encourages the development of a child's six potentials. Challenging academics, state-of-the-art technology, and extensive enrichment programs find balance with an emphasis on values, character development, and the rewards and responsibilities of global citizenship. The result is a student with the consciousness, capacity, and confidence for success in college and life. Miami Country Day is affiliated with the Florida Council of Independent Schools, the Florida Kindergarten Council, and the National Association of Independent Schools. Tuition: $13,850–$22,169. John P. Davies, Ed.D., is Head of School; Jasmine Lake is Director of Admission. *Southern Association.*

Oak Hall School   1970

8009 SW 14th Avenue, Gainesville, FL 32607
Tel. 352-332-3609; Fax 352-332-4975
Web Site oakhall.org; E-mail agarwood@oakhall.org

Oak Hall School is a coeducational, college preparatory day school enrolling approximately 760 students in PreKindergarten–Grade 12. The School aims to challenge college-bound students to reach the limits of their academic ability as they prepare for college and future responsibilities. Facilities include a new performing arts center, a state-of-the-art Media Center, a Fine Arts Center, a theater, and a new Middle School Science Center. Community service, clubs, and athletics are principal cocurricular activities. Tuition: $7700–$11,390. Alice Garwood is Director of Admissions; Richard H. Gehman (Princeton University, B.A. 1975; University of Massachusetts, M.Ed. 1980) was appointed Headmaster in 1993.

The Out-of-Door Academy   1924

PK–Grade 6: 444 Reid Street, Sarasota, FL 34242
Tel. 941-349-3223; Admission 941-554-3400
Fax 941-349-8133
Web Site www.oda.edu; E-mail admissions@oda.edu
Grades 7–12: 5950 Deer Drive, Sarasota, FL 34240
Tel. 941-349-3223; Admissions 941-554-5954; Fax 941-907-1251

THE OUT-OF-DOOR ACADEMY

The Out-of-Door Academy is an independent, coeducational, college preparatory day school enrolling 620 students from Sarasota, Manatee, and Charlotte Counties in PreKindergarten–Grade 12. The school's mission is to provide an environment in which students strive to achieve their highest academic goals and to build character through a balanced program of academics, athletics, and the arts. The traditional curriculum is designed to prepare graduates for the most rigorous colleges

and universities. The average class size is 16, with a 10:1 student-faculty ratio. Tuition: $13,000–$17,000. Financial aid is available. David V. Mahler is Head of School; Laura Murphy is Director of Admissions.

PACE-Brantley Hall School   1972

3221 Sand Lake Road, Longwood, FL 32779-5898
Tel. 407-869-8882; Admissions Ext. 221; Fax 407-869-8717
Web Site www.mypbhs.org; Admissions doneal@mypbhs.org
E-mail kshatlock@mypbhs.org

PACE-Brantley Hall School was founded in 1972 with the mission of providing an atmosphere where all students can learn and advance in a safe and nurturing environment. Serving a student population with diagnosed learning disabilities in Grades 1 through 12, the School offers a multisensory program designed to remediate and accommodate while teaching compensation skills. The focus of the program is to rebuild student confidence and self-esteem. The student-teacher ratio is 10:1. Tuition: $13,385–$13,855. Barbara Winter is Admissions Director; Donna A. O'Neal is Admissions Assistant; Kathleen Shatlock is Executive Director.

Palm Beach Day Academy   2006

PK–3: 1901 South Flagler Drive, West Palm Beach, FL 33401
Tel. 561-832-8815; Fax 561-832-3343
Web Site www.palmbeachdayacademy.org
E-mail malbanese@palmbeachdayacademy.org
4–9: 241 Seaview Avenue, Palm Beach, FL 33480
Tel. 561-655-8349; Fax 561-665-5794

Palm Beach Day Academy was formed by the 2006 merger of two successful and respected elementary day schools: Palm Beach Day School (1921) and The Academy of the Palm Beaches (1981). The union of these two institutions maximizes the resources, programs, and opportunities available to 520 boys and girls age 2 through Grade 9. The cornerstone of the school program is educating the minds and spirits of its students in a challenging, vibrant community that prizes academic excellence. Palm Beach Day Academy prepares students for appropriate secondary school studies and endeavors to provide a foundation for a lifetime of enthusiastic learning. Course work centers on language arts, math, foreign language, history, and science, enriched by library, computer technology, art, music, drama, and physical education. Among the activities are Student Council, athletics, and community service. Tuition: $12,250–$21,950. Meghan Albanese is Director of Admission; Dr. Rebecca van der Bogert is Head of School.

Pine Crest School   1934

Pre-K–Grade 12: 1501 Northeast 62nd Street, Fort Lauderdale, FL 33334
Tel. 954-492-4100; Admission 954-492-4103
Fax 954-492-4188
Pre-K–Grade 8: 2700 St. Andrews Boulevard, Boca Raton, FL 33434
Tel. 561-852-2800; Admission 561-852-2801
Fax 561-852-2832
Web Site www.pinecrest.edu; E-mail pcadmit@pinecrest.edu

Pine Crest is an all-faith, coeducational, college preparatory day school enrolling 2576 students on two campuses. The 20-acre

Boca Raton site features a 750-seat performing arts center, athletic complex, state-of-the-art middle school, science lab building, professional TV studio, and a newly planned LEED-certified Lower School with contemporary classrooms and amenities. Eighth-grade graduates join their counterparts on the 49-acre Fort Lauderdale campus to continue their Upper School education. Along with an accelerated curriculum, the Fort Lauderdale program features numerous offerings in fine arts and athletics such as band, chorus, orchestra, dance, drama, and more than 60 sports teams. Pine Crest encourages commitment to community service, and the Upper School offers a unique program of political participation through the Institute for Civic Involvement. College placement is consistently successful, and, in 2008, Pine Crest students took 1368 AP exams. After-school programs on both campuses include enrichment, extended care, private music lessons, and summer camps and academics. Tuition: $17,985–$21,990. Elena Del Alamo is Vice President for Admission; Dale M. Smith is Head of School; Lourdes M. Cowgill, Ph.D., is President.

Ransom Everglades School   1903

Upper School: 3575 Main Highway, Coconut Grove, FL 33133
 Tel. 305-460-8800; Admission 305-250-6875
 Fax 305-854-1846
 Web Site www.ransomeverglades.org
 E-mail asayfie@ransomeverglades.org
Middle School: 2045 South Bayshore Drive, Coconut Grove,
 FL 33133
 Tel. 305-250-6850

RANSOM EVERGLADES SCHOOL

The Adirondack-Florida School, founded in 1903, later became the Ransom School for Boys and merged with Everglades School for Girls in 1974 to form Ransom Everglades School, enrolling 1056 boys and girls in Grades 6–12. The School believes the pursuit of academic excellence should be complemented by a concern for each student's moral, physical, emotional, and aesthetic development. The curriculum encompasses visual and performing arts; activities include drama, sports, publications, and service groups. A summer academic program is offered. Ransom Everglades is a member of the National Association of Independent Schools. Tuition: $25,200. Financial Aid: $3,312,627. Amy Sayfie is Director of Admission and Financial Aid; Ellen Y. Moceri (Washington University, B.A., M.A.; Columbia University Teachers College, A.B.D.) is Head of School. *Southern Association.*

Riverside Presbyterian Day School   1948

830 Oak Street, Jacksonville, FL 32204
Tel. 904-353-5511; Admission 904-353-3459; Fax 904-634-1739
Web Site www.rpds.com; E-mail sfrancis@rpds.com

Riverside Presbyterian, founded by the church bearing the same name, enrolls 500 boys and girls in Pre-Kindergarten through Grade 6. The School's primary goals are to "educate the mind, nurture the spirit, and foster the development of the whole child while affirming the teachings of the Christian faith." Art, music, Bible, computer, library, Spanish, physical education, and weekly chapel services enrich a strong curriculum of reading, language arts, math, science, and social studies. An extended-day program is available on a year-round basis and includes creative activities and field trips. Riverside Presbyterian Day School is accredited by the Florida Council of Independent Schools and the Florida Kindergarten Council. Tuition: $4959–$9600. Tuition Assistance Program: $173,754. Shirley W. Francis is Director of Admission and Head of Lower School; H. Palmer Bell (Denison University, B.S.; Rutgers University, M.Ed.) is Headmaster. *Southern Association.*

Saint Edward's School   1965

Lower School/North Campus: 2225 Club Drive, Vero Beach, FL 32963
 Tel. 772-231-5357
Middle & Upper Schools/South Campus: 1895 Saint Edward's Drive,
 Vero Beach, FL 32963
 Tel. (Middle School) 772-231-1677
 Tel. (Upper School) 772-231-4136; Admissions Ext. 2360
 Fax 772-231-2427
 Web Site www.steds.org

SAINT EDWARD'S SCHOOL in Vero Beach, Florida, is a coeducational, college preparatory day school enrolling 735 students in Pre-Kindergarten through Grade 12 on two campuses. Vero Beach, with a population of 23,900, is on Florida's mid-Atlantic coast, known as the Treasure Coast. Vero Beach is equidistant from Melbourne to the north and Stuart to the south and is located in Indian River Country, known for its pleasant climate, beautiful beaches, and abundant natural resources.

An independent school in the Episcopal tradition, Saint Edward's was founded in 1965 to empower students of many faiths and cultures to reach their full potential. In a community of advocacy, the School aims to challenge the whole child, cultivate moral courage and spiritual growth, and instill a lifelong passion for learning. Students adhere to an Honor Code designed to encourage responsible citizenship, ethical behavior, and an appreciation for diversity. Chapel services are attended by all students and led by the school chaplain.

A not-for-profit institution guided by a Board of 18 Trustees, Saint Edward's is accredited by the Florida Council of Independent Schools and holds membership in the National Association of Independent Schools, National Association of Episcopal Schools, Educational Records Bureau, Council for Religion in Independent Schools, and the Council for Advancement and Support of Education. The Parents Association and the Alumni Council support Saint Edward's in carrying out its mission.

THE CAMPUS. The Lower School campus was the original Riomar Country Club (1929), one of the first structures built on the barrier island. Bought by Saint Edward's in 1965, the 6-acre site was renovated in 1988, preserving the Old Florida, Mediterranean-influenced architecture still evident today.

A pre-kindergarten and kindergarten complex, fine arts center, and two state-of-the-art computer labs were added in 1996.

SAINT EDWARD'S SCHOOL

The 27-acre Upper and Middle School campus was opened in 1972 and occupies a unique location along the Indian River. The School has expanded, doubling the size of its south campus, to include a separate Middle School, an Activities Center, a fine arts center, the 880-seat Waxlax Center for the Performing Arts, and Oglethorpe Hall, which houses administrative services. The $20,000,000 expansion project includes a retrofit of Upper School classrooms, state-of-the-art lab spaces, computer labs, writing center, and athletic program enhancements.

THE FACULTY. Mr. Michael J. Mersky became Saint Edward's seventh Head of School in 2009. A graduate of Friends' Central School, Mr. Mersky earned a B.S. in Education from Lock Haven University and an M.S. in Education from St. Joseph's University, both in Pennsylvania. Before assuming his present position, he held administrative and teaching posts at McDonogh School, Sewickley Academy, The Haverford School, Friends' Central School, and Lancaster Country Day School. He also served as Chief of Staff at ESF Camps, Inc.

The cornerstone of Saint Edward's is its 85-member faculty, with 52 percent holding advanced degrees. Their degrees represent colleges and universities such as Assumption, Ball State, Boston University, Bowling Green State, Brown, Central Michigan, Colgate, Columbia, Cornell, Duke, Fairleigh Dickinson, Florida Atlantic, Florida State, Harvard, Lehigh, Loyola, Middlebury, New York University, Nova, Ohio State, Quinnipiac College, Rollins, Southwest Texas State, Springfield College, Stanford, Susquehanna, Temple, Tufts, Vassar, Wesleyan, Wilkes, and the Universities of Florida, London, Maryland, Massachusetts, Michigan, North Carolina, Pennsylvania, Pittsburgh, San Francisco, Vermont, Virginia, Washington, and Wisconsin.

The Richardson Wellness Program offers physical, emotional, and spiritual support programs and services, including student health education programs, faculty training programs, leadership workshops, and a student-led Spiritual Life Commit-

tee. The Wellness Team includes two guidance counselors, a chaplain, and two registered nurses. Emergency medical service for both campuses is readily accessible.

STUDENT BODY. In 2009–10, Saint Edward's enrolled 735 students in its Lower (Pre-Kindergarten–Grade 5), Middle (Grades 6–8), and Upper School (Grades 9–12) divisions. Students commute via carpool or by bus service provided by the School from Vero Beach and the tricounty area. They represent a wide cross-section of racial, ethnic, religious, and socioeconomic backgrounds.

ACADEMIC PROGRAM. The 175-day school year, from late August to early June, is divided into four marking periods, with a Thanksgiving recess, vacations in December and in the spring, and observances of several national and school holidays. Teachers provide the individual attention each student needs in classrooms with a class size average of 17. Courses are offered in Advanced Placement, college preparatory, and honors tracks, with special accommodations for students with learning differences.

Students attend classes daily from 8:15 A.M. to 3:15 P.M. in the Lower School and from 8:00 A.M. to 3:30 P.M. in the Middle and Upper Schools. All students are required to select six academic classes, and many concentrate their efforts in Advanced Placement courses. The Advanced Studies Program at Saint Edward's is a comprehensive program specifically designed for highly motivated students in Grades 9–12.

The Lower School academic program provides a strong foundation in the traditional disciplines, beginning with reading and mathematics readiness in pre-kindergarten and building on mastery of those skills as students progress through the primary and intermediate grades. The schedule is departmentalized from Grade 4 on, with a major emphasis on language arts and math. The core academics are enhanced by mini courses in fine arts, music, computer science, ethics, foreign language, and physical education.

In the Middle School, the curriculum is designed to provide age-appropriate challenges in core subjects in readiness for the college preparatory course work of the Upper School. Students take full-year courses in English, history, mathematics, science, foreign language, and physical education/health, with one semester each year in the arts, research, writing, and technology. The Middle and Upper Schools enjoy a 1:1 tablet computer program.

SAINT EDWARD'S SCHOOL

To graduate from the Upper School, students must complete a minimum of 23 credits as follows: 4 each in English, mathematics, and history; 3 or 4 in science and foreign language; and 1 each in religion, personal fitness, and life management, plus 4 credits of electives from any department. Saint Edward's does not provide class rank until graduation, and grades shown on transcripts are unweighted, although extra weight is awarded for Honors or Advanced Placement courses.

Among the academic offerings are English 9–12, Writing Lab, Photo Journalism; French 1–4, Spanish 1–5, Chinese 1–4; American Government, United States History, Globalization, Contemporary Issues, World History, Economics, Sociology, Psychology; Algebra 1–2, College Algebra, Geometry, Pre-Calculus; Biology, Chemistry, Physics, Anatomy and Physiology, Integrated Science, Environmental Science, Marine Biology; Ethics; and Art History, Concert Choir, Studio Art, and Theatre Arts. Honors and/or Advanced Placement courses are available in all major departments.

College counseling begins in Grade 8 and continues throughout the entire planning, application, and admission process. Historically, all graduates pursue advanced education. Members of the Class of 2009 were accepted at such institutions as American University, Auburn, Bryn Mawr, Bucknell, College of Charleston, DePaul, Elon, Florida State, George Washington, Lehigh, Pratt Institute, Rutgers, Sarah Lawrence, Savannah College of Art and Design, Vanderbilt, Wake Forest, Wellesley College, Worcester Polytechnic Institute, and the Universities of Colorado, Denver, Florida, Notre Dame, and Virginia.

Saint Edward's offers extensive summer programs and after-school programs through the External Studies Division, including EXCEL, the Educational Center for Exceptional Learners, which enrolls academically gifted students in Grades 2–6 in a three-week session. A six-week program offers remediation and enrichment to approximately 200 students; a seven-week water-oriented summer camp program and various sports camps are also available.

STUDENT ACTIVITIES. A diverse extracurricular program engages students in leadership roles, special-interest clubs, and athletics.

More than 30 Class 2A and 1A interscholastic teams are organized in football, baseball, crew, lacrosse, golf, volleyball, soccer, cross-country, swimming, basketball, tennis, and cheerleading.

As members of a greater community, students are encouraged to become active volunteers on and off campus. Two of the most successful student outreach programs are the Pals in Partnership for special-needs children and the Care to Share program for the elderly.

SAINT EDWARD'S SCHOOL

Among the special events on the school calendar are the Fun Run, poetry readings, Living Museum, Science Fair, annual speech presentations, fall and spring dramas, spring musical, Christmas Concerts, Homecoming Weekend, Alumni Holiday Reception, and the Lower School class plays.

ADMISSION AND COSTS. Saint Edward's welcomes students who are good citizens with a desire for a first-rate education. Acceptance is based on standardized test results, current tran-

scripts, evaluations by the student's mathematics and English teachers, recommendations from the principal or guidance counselor, writing samples, and a personal interview. For first-round consideration at the Middle and Upper School level, applications are due by February 15. Subsequent applications will be considered on a space-available basis. Applications are acted on by the Admission Committee on March 1 of the year of intended enrollment. The nonrefundable application fee is $50.

SAINT EDWARD'S SCHOOL

For 2009–10, tuition ranges from $8300 to $22,100 and includes bus transportation. Uniforms, books, lunch, class trips, and tablet computers are additional. Tuition insurance is required for all new students. Annually, the School awards financial aid to students who have demonstrated need and academic ability.

Associate Head of School/Head of Upper School: Mr. Bruce R. Wachter
Head of Middle School: Dr. Kristine Alber
Head of Lower School: Mrs. Barbara Mohler
Director of Admission: Mr. Andy Sheffer
Dean of Students/Upper School: Mr. Richard Hartley
Dean of Students/Middle School: Ms. Kristine Fojtik
Dean of Students/Lower School: Mrs. Ginger Topp
Director of College Counseling: Mrs. Michele Sternberg
Athletic Director: Mr. Jeff Lamscha

St. John's Episcopal Parish Day School   1951

Grades 5–8: 240 South Plant Avenue, Tampa, FL 33606
  Tel. 813-849-4200; Fax 813-849-1026
  Web Site www.stjohnseagles.org; E-mail scox@stjohnseagles.org
Grades 1–4: 906 South Orleans Avenue, Tampa, FL 33606
  Tel. 813-849-5200; Fax 813-258-2548
PreK–K: 1002 Rome Avenue, Tampa, FL 33606
  Tel. 813-849-6200

Now in its 59th year, St. John's enrolls 530 boys and girls from diverse religious and cultural backgrounds in pre-kindergarten (4-year-olds) through eighth grade. St. John's Episcopal Parish

Day School offers an academically rigorous program in a Christian and nurturing environment. Every day begins with a chapel service designed to inspire spiritual awareness and moral character. The curriculum centers on English, literature, writing, mathematics, science, and social studies and is enhanced by courses in Spanish, Latin, studio art, music, physical education, and a divinity program. Technology is woven throughout the

ST. JOHN'S EPISCOPAL PARISH DAY SCHOOL

curriculum with two computer labs, computers in all classrooms, SMART boards, and a high-speed Internet service providing a 21st-century education. Extracurriculars include clubs, National Junior Honor Society, drama productions, math team, Science Olympiad team, and, from Grade 5, competition in seven sports. Tuition: $8570–$8810. Financial aid is available. Cindy Fenlon is Director of Admissions; Gordon R. Rode is Headmaster.

Saint Joseph's Episcopal School 1958

3300 South Seacrest Boulevard, Boynton Beach, FL 33435
Tel. 561-732-2045; Fax 561-732-1315
Web Site www.sjsonline.org; E-mail maperavich@sjsonline.org

This independent, Episcopal, coeducational day school welcomes approximately 200 students from diverse faith backgrounds in Pre-Kindergarten through Grade 8 on its main campus and at its nearby Early Childhood Academy, which serves children ages 1–3. Saint Joseph's provides a rigorous education in mind, body, and spirit in a safe, Christian climate. The college preparatory curriculum emphasizes the mastery of skills and content and directs students toward lifelong learning. Spanish, integrated technology, and the Academy of the Arts enhance the School's academic program. Students participate in community service and a variety of team sports, including flag football, volleyball, soccer, basketball, baseball, and lacrosse. Tuition: $10,475–$13,325; Financial aid is available. Mary Aperavich is Admission Director; Tami Pleasanton is Head of School.

St. Mark's Episcopal Day School 1970

4114 Oxford Avenue, Jacksonville, FL 32210
Tel. 904-388-2632; Admission Ext. 21; Fax 904-387-5647
Web Site www.stmarksdayschool.org
E-mail smeds@stmarksdayschool.org

St. Mark's Episcopal Day School, enrolling approximately 440 students, is a parish school that instills Christian values, builds a strong academic foundation, encourages personal achievement, stimulates creative expression, and fosters a heart of giving in a nurturing environment in children age 1 year through Grade 6. Enrichment resources include Spanish, computer, physical education, science, library, music, art, and Christian education. St.

Mark's also offers an Extended Day Program, after-school enrichment, and a summer day camp. Tuition: $2035–$9600. Financial aid is available. Susan Kwartler is Director of Admissions; Cathy Hardage is Head of School.

St. Mark's Episcopal School 1959

1750 East Oakland Park Boulevard, Fort Lauderdale, FL 33334
Tel. 954-563-4508; Admissions 954-563-1241; Fax 954-563-0504
Web Site www.saintmarks.com; E-mail admissions@saintmarks.com

St. Mark's is a coeducational, Episcopal day school enrolling 580 students in PK1 through Grade 8. In a unique learning environment within a solid Episcopal tradition, the School seeks to offer a superior academic program complemented by regionally recognized offerings in the arts, including band, chorus, drama, and studio art. The athletic program features teams for boys and girls at both varsity and intramural levels. Emphasizing a strong foundation in core subjects, the academic program includes Spanish language, technology, physical education, art, music, and guidance. Daily chapel services and the religion curriculum emphasize the Episcopal values of inclusion, open inquiry, and respect for all faiths. More than 40 percent of fourth and seventh graders qualify for the Duke Talent Identification Program. Afterschool enrichment and summer programs are also offered on St. Mark's 10-acre campus. The challenging preparatory program ensures that graduates are accepted into the independent secondary schools of their choice. Tuition: $4800–$14,550. Financial aid is available. Ms. Alice Hendrickson is Director of Admission; Fr. Dub Brooks is Head of School.

St. Mary's Episcopal Day School 1953

2101 South Hubert Avenue, Tampa, FL 33629-5648
Tel. 813-258-5508; Fax 813-258-5603
Web Site www.smeds.org; E-mail kathleen.lopez@smeds.org

St. Mary's Episcopal Day School, enrolling 420 girls and boys in Pre-Kindergarten–Grade 8, offers a well-balanced and challenging curriculum delivered by talented, enthusiastic teachers in a caring, Christian community. Early grades emphasize comprehensive skills, including computer use and Spanish, leading to advanced levels in writing, algebra, and lab sciences by Grade 8. Grade 6 studies Latin; Grades 7–8 study Latin or Spanish. Religion, public speaking, music, and art are taught. Activities include competitive athletics, choir, publications, community service, student council, and drama. Before- and after-school care are offered. Tuition: $10,700. Financial aid is available. Kathleen Lopez is Director of Admissions; Scott D. Laird (West Chester, B.S. 1978; Florida Atlantic, M.Ed. 1987, M.A. 1993) is Headmaster.

Saint Paul's School 1968

1600 Saint Paul's Drive, Clearwater, FL 33764
Tel. 727-536-2756; Admissions Ext. 238; Fax 727-531-2276
Web Site www.st.pauls.edu; E-mail hleiser@st.pauls.edu

Saint Paul's, enrolling 402 boys and girls in Pre-Kindergarten 3–Grade 8, is affiliated with the Episcopal Church and celebrates the rich diversity of its school community. Its mission is to provide an excellent education in a nurturing environment, laying the foundation for successful academic progress, and to create a desire for lifelong learning. Intellectual, spiritual, and physical development are stressed through a challenging curriculum, hands-on science, fine arts, interscholastic athletics, intramurals, foreign languages, a state-of-the-art technology center, summer programs, extracurriculars, and community service. Tuition: $7625–$14,825. Financial Aid: $330,201. Holly Leiser is Director of Admissions; Dr. Angél Kytle is Head of School.

St. Stephen's Episcopal Day School 1958

3439 Main Highway, Miami, FL 33133
Tel. 305-445-2606; Fax 305-445-7320
Web Site www.sseds.org; E-mail cdarcy@sseds.org

St. Stephen's Episcopal Day School enrolls nearly 300 boys and girls from diverse racial, ethnic, economic, and religious backgrounds in a dynamic, coeducational program encompassing Pre-Kindergarten through Grade 6. The School's mission is to provide a solid intellectual, moral, and spiritual foundation within a nurturing environment. The core curriculum is designed to instill in children the skills they need to succeed in a rapidly changing society. Centered on reading, math, science, language arts, and technology, the program is complemented by Spanish language instruction, physical education, speech and drama, library, sacred studies, and the visual arts. Classes are small to allow individual attention and ensure proficiency in all subject areas. Judeo-Christian values govern the daily conduct of school life, and regular chapel services and sacred studies deepen spiritual formation. Students may take part in educational assemblies, school government, and community service as well as special events such as the Book Fair, Blessing of the Animals, Carnival and Picnic, and Grandparents' Day. Tuition: $13,860. Financial aid is available. Cathie D'Arcy is Director of Admission; Silvia Larrauri is Head of School.

Saint Stephen's Episcopal School 1970

315 41st Street West, Bradenton, FL 34209
Tel. 941-746-2121; Admissions Ext. 568; Fax 941-746-5699
Web Site www.saintstephens.org
E-mail saintstephen@saintstephens.org

A college preparatory day school, Saint Stephen's Episcopal School enrolls 650 boys and girls in Pre-Kindergarten 3–Grade 12. In a family-like environment, Saint Stephen's strives to encourage learning beyond the classroom walls. Chapel services help students of all religions understand the importance of spirituality in their lives. Fundamentals and theme-based units characterize the curriculum through Grade 8. Upper School students follow a traditional liberal arts course of studies with Advanced Placement classes in all disciplines. Academics are complemented by fine arts, clubs and activities, interscholastic sports, and the Service Learning Program. Tuition: $11,000–$15,800. Financial Aid: $390,000. Linda Lutz is Director of Admissions; Janet S. Pullen is Head of School.

Seacrest Country Day School 1983

7100 Davis Boulevard, Naples, FL 34104-5314
Tel. 239-793-1986; Fax 239-793-1460
Web Site www.seacrest.org; E-mail seacrest@seacrest.org

SEACREST COUNTRY DAY SCHOOL in Naples, Florida, is a coeducational, college preparatory school enrolling students from 3 years old through Grade 12. Naples (population 38,879) is on Florida's Gulf Coast between Fort Myers and Marco Island. A favorite destination for tourists because of its sunny climate and beautiful beaches, Naples offers a wealth of nature preserves, cultural and historic attractions, shopping, and outdoor recreation.

Seacrest Country Day School opened its doors in 1983 with 18 students. Today, this Outstanding Model School of America enrolls nearly 600 children. A $30,000,000 capital campaign has added 30 acres to the existing 10-acre campus and provides state-of-the-art facilities to accommodate the Upper School campus.

The mission of Seacrest Country Day is to nurture the social, cognitive, and emotional development of every student. In the belief that learning has no boundaries, the School offers a challenging, well-rounded curriculum designed to unleash the unlimited potential that is in each child, balancing academic, aesthetic, and athletic opportunities with life skills, character development, and values education.

SEACREST COUNTRY DAY SCHOOL

Guided by a 20-member Board of Trustees, Seacrest is accredited by the Florida Council of Independent Schools, the Southern Association of Colleges and Schools, the Southern Association of Independent Schools, and the Florida Kindergarten Council. Seacrest is one of only a few schools in Florida to be accredited by all four organizations. It holds membership in numerous professional organizations including the National Association of Independent Schools, among other affiliations.

THE CAMPUS. The Seacrest Country Day School campus is graced by mature trees, flowering shrubs, and gardens as well as a wetland preserve, outdoor learning laboratory, and playing fields. Grouped around the center courtyard are several buildings. The Lynne Marz Powell Student Services Center houses administrative and departmental offices, while the Resource Center provides a 20,000-volume library, a media center, TV production equipment, six classrooms, and two computer labs. Networked computers are also located in every classroom. A Math and Science Challenge Lab provides Lego building blocks, gears, pulleys, levers, and other instruments to solve advanced math and physics problems. The Lower School regulation-sized Gymnasium and Performing Arts Center is the setting for indoor sports and a wide range of programs and plays using the latest sound, lighting, and projection systems.

The high school campus boasts a new, 26,000-square-foot Gymnasium/Science Center. The gym features a maple floor and has the capacity to host tournament play. Biology, chemistry, and physics labs are the centerpiece of the second floor. The high school also includes a modular village, a baseball stadium, soccer field, and track as well as a beach volleyball venue.

THE FACULTY. Lynne M. Powell, Ed.D., was appointed Head of School in 1993, having served as Seacrest's Academic Dean since 1987. She holds baccalaureate and master's degrees in Elementary Education and earned her doctorate in Educational Leadership from Nova University. Dr. Powell has also done postgraduate work at Boston University and the University of New Hampshire and taught in New Hampshire public schools for 20 years.

All 70 men and women on the teaching faculty hold bachelor's degrees from colleges and universities nationwide, and more than 70 percent have earned or are working toward advanced degrees; 7 hold doctorates.

STUDENT BODY. In 2009–10, Seacrest Country Day School enrolled nearly 600 boys and girls in Preschool through Grade 12. The students come from communities in Collier and Lee Counties, including Marco Island, and represent a wide diversity of racial, ethnic, religious, and socioeconomic backgrounds.

ACADEMIC PROGRAM. The school year, from late August to early June, is divided into quarters, with a Thanksgiving recess and longer vacations in the winter and spring. Grades are issued at the midpoint and end of each quarter, and parent conferences are scheduled in November and April. Younger students receive evaluations ranging from Outstanding to Unsatisfactory; letter grades are issued beginning in Grade 4. Homework is assigned and checked on a regular basis and varies in amount according to grade.

A typical day begins at 8:30 A.M., with dismissal at 2:45 P.M. in the elementary division and 8:15 A.M. with 3:30 P.M. dismissal in the middle and high schools. Classes, with an 8:1 student-teacher ratio, are 30 to 70 minutes in length, depending on grade. Both the middle and high schools use a 10-day schedule rotation that includes time for club meetings and activities. Extended care, open to all Seacrest students, begins at 7:15 A.M. and ends at 5:30 P.M. There is no charge for before-school care; families can use the after-school program on a regular or as-needed basis for a fee. Seacrest also offers Learning Labs for all its students.

SEACREST COUNTRY DAY SCHOOL

The fully integrated, multisensory curriculum emphasizes the acquisition and mastery of strong skills in core subjects as the foundation for success in higher education and in life. In Prekindergarten through Grade 2, age-appropriate content and hands-on activities introduce children to key concepts in language arts, mathematics, science, social studies, Spanish, art, and the fine arts and music. The program is enriched by life skills, computer technology, media and learning strategies, and health and physical education.

As students progress through the grades, the curriculum increases in breadth and depth. In fourth grade, children create, plant, and maintain a garden that provides opportunities for the application of lessons in math and natural science. Fifth graders visit Mote Marine Lab in Sarasota to delve into marine life indigenous to Florida Waters. Grades 6–7 engage in biology research at Marinelab in Key Largo; and eighth graders may take part in outdoor education or travel to Washington, Philadelphia, or New York. Qualified Middle School students may take high school-level and advanced courses in math and Spanish, and each year, students in Grades 4 through 7 qualify for Duke University's Talent Identification Program.

The high school program features traditional college preparatory courses in the liberal arts and sciences. To earn a Seacrest diploma, students must complete 28 credits as follows: 4 each in language arts and history/social studies; 3 each in math, science, and foreign language; 1 each in humanities, technology, physical education/health; 1 elective each in math or science, studio arts, and music; and 5 additional electives.

SEACREST COUNTRY DAY SCHOOL

Among the specific offerings are World Mythologies, World Literature, Writing Seminar/American Literature; Spanish I–IV, Latin, French I–IV; World History, U.S. History, Modern Government/Economics; Algebra I–II, Geometry, Pre-calculus, Calculus, Statistics; Biology, Forensic Science, Chemistry I, Applied Chemistry, Physics, Genetics, Introduction to Environmental Science; and Fundamentals of Computer Science, and Web Design. Honors courses are open to qualified scholars in all major departments. Advanced Placement opportunities are provided in Statistics, Psychology, Calculus AB and BC, Music Theory, and Computer Programming. Private instruction in art and musical instruments is available.

High school students participate in Seacrest Seminars related to topics in Ethics and Attributes of a Leader, Opposition and Solution, Leadership in a Global Context, and Effective Communication.

Seacrest graduated its first high school class in May 2008. Students have been admitted to Agnes Scott, Ave Maria, Bard, Bates, Belmont Abbey, Bennington, Denison, Eckerd, Edison, Emerson, Emory, Florida Gulf Coast, Florida State, Furman, Hampshire, Mount Holyoke, New York University, Rensselaer, Rice, Samford, Sarah Lawrence, Sewanee, Southern Methodist, Tulane, Union, Valparaiso, Vanderbilt, Wake Forest, Worchester, and the Universities of Central Florida, Florida, Miami, Oxford (England), Richmond, Rochester, South Carolina, and Tampa.

STUDENT ACTIVITIES. Seacrest's extracurricular program provides opportunities to develop leadership and social skills, form new friendships, and engage in wholesome, fun activities. School teams compete in Scholar Bowl and the National Geography Bee and, in 2003, 2006, 2007, and 2008, reached the World Finals in Odyssey of the Mind. In 2005, the high school robotics team took first place in a national competition. Students publish a newspaper, yearbook, and literary magazine as well as present plays and musicals for the public.

Service learning is valued as a means of reaching out to help others in the local community and well beyond. Students have sent shoes to Haiti, linen supplies to flood victims in North Dakota, and toys to be distributed by local firefighters. Middle Schoolers perform on-campus service in the form of visiting and working with younger students. High Schoolers host an annual event and donate to the charity of their choice. Seniors spend a week in service to the people of Immokalee, Florida.

The athletic program at Seacrest emphasizes fitness, fun, and sportsmanship, and the middle school's "no cut" policy ensures that each student can try any sport. Boys' and girls' interscholastic teams are organized at varsity and junior varsity levels in basketball, soccer, volleyball, tennis, golf, cross-country, track and field, baseball, softball, and swimming.

SEACREST COUNTRY DAY SCHOOL

Among the special traditions and events on the school calendar are Flag Ceremony, High School Morning Meeting (a contemplative time for both students and faculty), Red Ribbon Week, Halloween Costume Parade, Heritage Luncheon, Breakfast with a Buddy, Book Fair, Grandparents' and Special Friends' Day, Young Authors' and Young Artists' Week, Awards Evening, monthly seminars for parents and the community, and Graduation.

ADMISSION AND COSTS. Seacrest Country Day School welcomes students from all racial, ethnic, religious, cultural, and socioeconomic backgrounds who are willing and able to participate enthusiastically in its programs. Admission is based on prior school records, the results of standardized tests, teacher recommendations, and an interview. The application fee is $75; an initial payment fee of $1500, which includes a one-time $500 enrollment fee, is due when the enrollment agreement is submitted.

In 2009–10, tuition is $13,246 in Prekindergarten–Grade 5, $13,976 in Grades 6–8, and $16,375 in Grades 9–12. Annual fees are $1300 per child. Payment plans and tuition insurance are available.

According to statistics from the National Association of Independent Schools, Seacrest awards 30 percent more in need-based financial aid than the national average for elementary day schools. In 2009–10, the School provided more than $1,000,000 in need-based financial aid to nearly one-third of its students.

Head of School: Dr. Lynne M. Powell
Lower School Head: Dr. Jennifer Amico
Upper School Head: Erin Duffy
Academic Dean: Howard Schott
Dean of Student Life: Dr. Deb Merwin
Admission Officer: Caroline Randall
Chief Financial Officer: Helen Ruisi
Athletic Director: Mark Marsala

Trinity Preparatory School   1968

5700 Trinity Prep Lane, Winter Park, FL 32792
Tel. 407-671-4140; Admission 321-282-2523; Fax 407-671-6935
Web Site www.trinityprep.org; E-mail inquire@trinityprep.org

TRINITY PREPARATORY SCHOOL

An Episcopal day school enrolling 820 students in Grades 6–12, Trinity Prep has a rich tradition of excellence, and students are guided by dedicated professionals in a safe, caring, and challenging environment. Its mission is to develop students who are able to excel in college and beyond, contribute to their communities, lead in a changing society, and grow spiritually. Trinity Prep fosters spiritual growth while respecting cultural and religious diversity. The program offers AP courses, extensive fine arts and community service opportunities, and athletics at the JH, JV, and varsity levels in 14 sports. Tuition: $15,700. Malone Scholars Program and financial aid are available. Sherryn M. Hay (Rollins College, B.A.) is Director of Admission; Craig S. Maughan (Washington University, B.A.; University of North Carolina [Chapel Hill], M.S.P.H.; University of Kansas, M.B.A.) is Headmaster.

GEORGIA

Atlanta International School 1984

2890 North Fulton Drive, Atlanta, GA 30305
Tel. 404-841-3840; Admission 404-841-3891; Fax 404-841-3873
Web Site www.aischool.org; E-mail info@aischool.org

Parents, educators, and business and civic leaders founded Atlanta International School to prepare young people for leadership in the global society of the 21st century. The coeducational day school enrolls 931 students from over 50 nations in Pre-Kindergarten (age 4)–Grade 12. The school population is about evenly divided between American and international students. The rigorous college preparatory curriculum leads to the International Baccalaureate, which qualifies graduates for admission to universities worldwide. Instruction in core subjects is in two languages, with time divided equally between English and the student's choice of French, German, or Spanish. Course work focuses on traditional offerings in the liberal arts, sciences, and humanities, enhanced by challenging electives. Reflecting the School's international outlook, many students take part in Model United Nations, examining critical world issues and formulating research papers that are shared with the UN. Students also participate in yearbook, drama, music, clubs, and sports. Tuition: $16,409–$18,721. Financial aid is available. Reid Mizell is Director of Admission; Kevin Glass is Head of School. *Southern Association.*

Brandon Hall School 1959

1701 Brandon Hall Drive, Atlanta, GA 30350-3706
Tel. 770-394-8177; Admissions Ext. 215; Fax 770-804-8821
Web Site www.brandonhall.org; E-mail admissions@brandonhall.org

"The intensive care of education," Brandon Hall School offers a challenging but supportive college preparatory curriculum for students in Grade 4–PG who benefit from a 3:1 student-teacher ratio and an emphasis on organization, structure, applied study skills, multisensory instruction, and accountability. The School serves three distinct groups: underachievers, students with diagnosed learning disabilities, and international students seeking ESL classes. Enrolling approximately 120 students, Brandon Hall offers nine athletic teams, 14 clubs, a state-acclaimed drama program, music, and art classes. Annually, there is a 100 percent college acceptance rate. Weekly, detailed emails as well as newsletters keep parents apprised of student progress and opportunities. Located in the Sandy Springs suburb of Atlanta, the School incorporates the cultural, athletic, and recreational opportunities in the metropolitan area. The proximity to the Hartsfield-Jackson International Airport and the interstate highway system benefits students' transportation needs. Boarding Tuition/Fees: $44,300–$51,300; Day Tuition/Fees: $28,400–$31,200. One-to-one classes are available at an additional charge. Paul R. Stockhammer (Mercer University, B.A., M.Ed.) is President. *Southern Association.*

Brookstone School 1951

440 Bradley Park Drive, Columbus, GA 31904-2989
Tel. 706-324-1392; Fax 706-571-0178
Web Site www.brookstoneschool.org
E-mail msnyder@brookstoneschool.org

As the only Pre-K–12, independent college preparatory program in Columbus, Brookstone School provides its 800+ coeducational day students with a challenging academic program. In addition, the school community welcomes dramatic expression as much as athletic prowess, making it easy for students to explore their multifaceted interests. Academically, students can excel in honors and 15 Advanced Placement classes and take courses not offered in many secondary programs. Foreign language is introduced in Pre-K and continues through Upper School. Realizing that tomorrow's leaders will need to think independently, work collaboratively, and reach past differences to find common ground, Brookstone has shaped its program to encourage students to think beyond the confines of the campus. Through state-of-the-art technology and a dynamic servant leadership program, students are involved in both the local and global communities. Extracurricular opportunities are numerous, with 17 varsity sports teams, fine and performing arts, and academic teams and clubs. There is also a licensed extended day program. Tuition: $6795–$12,870. Financial Aid: $827,400. Mary S. Snyder is Enrollment Director; Frank D. Brown is Headmaster. *Southern Association.*

Cliff Valley School 1966

2426 Clairmont Road, Atlanta, GA 30329
Tel. 678-302-1302; Fax 678-302-1300
Web Site www.cliffvalleyschool.org
E-mail info@cliffvalleyschool.org

For more than 40 years, Cliff Valley School has been providing an environment where children can develop to their fullest potential academically, socially, emotionally, and physically. By supporting each child's creativity, imagination, and individual needs, the School's programs promote high academic standards. From preschool through fifth grade, Cliff Valley offers small classes with two teachers each. Student-teacher ratios are low, ranging from 6:1 to 12:1. Music, art, physical education, and Spanish are staples, as is Cliff Valley's "Outdoor Classroom," where students learn about the environment from the environment. The School teaches students to think critically, preparing them to be responsible decision-makers and to manage their lives successfully in a complex and diverse world. The new campus features facilities for both indoor and outdoor environmental education, earth-friendly building materials, state-of-the-art security, computers in each elementary classroom, a library/media center, meeting facilities, and much more. Tuition: $13,350. Megan Vitale is Admissions Manager; Michael Edwards, Ed.D., is Head of School.

The Galloway School 1969

215 West Wieuca Road, NW, Atlanta, GA 30342
Tel. 404-252-8389; Admission Ext. 106; Fax 404-252-7770
Web Site www.gallowayschool.org

Founded by Headmaster Emeritus Elliott Galloway, this coeducational day school enrolls approximately 715 students in Preschool through Grade 12. The student-teacher ratio is 10:1. The goals of Galloway's student-centered college preparatory program are to develop in each student a value for learning as a lifelong process, to encourage engaged and active learning, and to teach all members of the community to respect the dignity of the individual. A range of successful athletic options and clubs joins a nationally known theater program to provide a wide variety of experiences for students. Galloway also offers extensive after-school and summer programs. Tuition: $10,650–$18,430. Rosetta Gooden is Director of Admission; Thomas G. Brereton is Headmaster. *Southern Association.*

The Heritage School 1970

2093 Highway 29 North, Newnan, GA 30263
Tel. 770-253-9898; Admissions 678-423-5393; Fax 770-253-4850
Web Site www.heritagehawks.org
E-mail ariley@heritagehawks.org

THE HERITAGE SCHOOL

Accredited by the Southern Association of Independent Schools, Heritage was founded in 1970 to create an outstanding educational opportunity for the families of Coweta, Fayette, and surrounding counties. As an independent, coeducational, college preparatory, nonsectarian day school, Heritage serves a student population of approximately 400, age 3–Grade 12. The mission of The Heritage School is to develop the mind in preparation for college and later life, to develop the body through competition and teamwork, to develop the spirit through self-awareness and growth, and to develop camaraderie through shared experience. The School recognizes the unique strengths and needs of every child and works with those assets to create enthusiasm for learning and a path for each child's personal growth and development. As stewards of human potential proud of the ethos of its graduates, Heritage values family, an intimate learning environment, and self-respect. Tuition: $6710–$12,705. Need-based financial aid is available. Amy Riley is Director of Admissions; Judith Griffith is Head of School. *Southern Association.*

The Lovett School 1926

4075 Paces Ferry Road, NW, Atlanta, GA 30327
Tel. 404-262-3032; Fax 404-479-8463
Web Site www.lovett.org; E-mail dlange@lovett.org

Lovett is a coeducational, college preparatory day school committed to developing the whole child. Enrolling 1550 students in Kindergarten–Grade 12, the curriculum includes a full range of honors and Advanced Placement courses as well as an Academic Resource Center for academic support. Programs in all the fine arts are available at every level, and a full athletic pro-

gram provides an opportunity to experience teamwork and sportsmanship. Lovett operates within the Judeo-Christian tradition, with regular chapel services. The School seeks students from all ethnic, cultural, racial, and religious backgrounds who

THE LOVETT SCHOOL

can benefit from a challenging academic program. Tuition: $16,365–$19,515. Financial aid is available. Debbie Lange is Director of Admission and Financial Aid; William S. Peebles IV is Headmaster. *Southern Association.*

Marist School 1901

3790 Ashford-Dunwoody Road NE, Atlanta, GA 30319-1899
Tel. 770-457-7201; Fax 770-457-8402
Web Site www.marist.com; E-mail admissions@marist.com

Founded and operated by the Society of Mary, this coeducational, Roman Catholic day school enrolls 1070 students in Grades 7–12. Marist School's mission is to provide spiritual and ethical guidance within a challenging college preparatory program. Religious studies, campus ministry, and retreats involve students from many faiths. The curriculum includes 20 Advanced Placement courses, and all graduates enter four-year colleges and universities. Activities include peer support and leadership programs, honor societies, award-winning student publications, Habitat for Humanity, a comprehensive music program, dramatic and visual arts, and 18 sports. Tuition: $15,225; Registration Fee: $500. Need-based Financial Aid: $1,500,000. James G. Byrne is Director of Admissions; Rev. Joel Konzen, S.M., is Principal; Rev. John Harhager, S.M., is President. *Southern Association.*

Pace Academy 1958

966 West Paces Ferry Road, NW, Atlanta, GA 30327
Tel. 404-262-1345; Admissions 404-240-9109; Fax 404-240-9124
Web Site www.paceacademy.org; E-mail cstrowd@paceacademy.org

Enrolling 995 boys and girls in Pre-First–Grade 12, Pace Academy is a college preparatory day school committed to academic excellence within a framework of Judeo-Christian values. Pace is accredited by both the Southern Association of Colleges and Schools and the Southern Association of Independent Schools. The school offers a strong foundation in liberal arts, math, science, and technology. A demanding curriculum includes honors and Advanced Placement courses and a wide variety of electives. Students participate in service learning and peer leadership programs. Activities include athletics, drama,

PACE ACADEMY

debate, art, and leadership programs. Pace's ideal size creates opportunities for involvement and a sense of belonging. Tuition: $17,550–$20,200. Financial Aid: $1,000,000. Claire Strowd (Middle/Upper) and Susan Gruber (Lower) are Directors of Admissions; Frederick G. Assaf is Headmaster. *Southern Association.*

St. Martin's Episcopal School   1959

3110-A Ashford Dunwoody Road, Atlanta, GA 30319
Tel. 404-237-4260; Admissions Ext. 709; Fax 404-237-9311
Web Site www.stmartinschool.org
E-mail bmarsau@stmartinschool.org

St. Martin's Episcopal School is a parish day school enrolling 585 boys and girls in PreKindergarten–Grade 8. The School seeks to offer a quality academic program based on a traditional curriculum within a Christian environment. Core instruction is supplemented by art, music, foreign language, drama, public speaking, physical and health education, computer, and religion. Small class size and individualized instruction characterize the three divisions within the School—Early Childhood, Elementary, and Middle School. There is a variety of extracurricular activities. Tuition: $9660–$14,890. Financial Aid: $300,000. Blythe Marsau is Director of Admissions; The Reverend Dr. James E. Hamner IV (University of the South, M.Div.; University of Oxford, M.Phil., D. Phil.) is Headmaster. *Southern Association.*

Savannah Country Day School   1905

824 Stillwood Drive, Savannah, GA 31419
Tel. 912-925-8800; Fax 912-920-7800
Web Site www.savcds.org; E-mail barfield@savcds.org

Savannah Country Day School is an independent, Pre-Kindergarten through Grade 12 school that seeks to prepare 910 students of academic and personal promise to meet with confi-

dence, imagination, and integrity the challenges of college and life. In partnership with supportive families, Country Day strives to cultivate in each student the desire and the discipline to grow wise, to lead lives of personal honor, to appreciate beauty, to pursue physical well being, and to serve others with a generous and

SAVANNAH COUNTRY DAY SCHOOL

compassionate spirit. Tuition: $7708–$16,160. Financial aid is available. Terri Barfield is Director of Admissions; Marcia Hull is Head of School. *Southern Association.*

Trinity School   1951

4301 Northside Parkway, NW, Atlanta, GA 30327
Tel. 404-231-8100; Admissions 404-231-8118; Fax 404-231-8111
Web Site www.trinityatl.org; E-mail kbaty@trinityatl.org

Trinity School is a nondenominational day school enrolling 589 children from age 3 through Grade 6. Established by Trinity Presbyterian, the School operates in the Judeo-Christian tradition. The challenging, developmentally appropriate program includes an integrated curriculum and cooperative learning methods. The child-centered atmosphere nurtures each student's positive self-image. Spanish, art, music, technology, and physical and outdoor education are vital parts of the curriculum. Every student in Grade 6 has a tablet PC for use at home and school. Forty-seven percent of the School's well-qualified faculty members hold advanced degrees. There is an after-school enrichment program. Tuition: $12,250–$17,600. Financial aid is available. Kristin Baty is Director of Admissions; Stephen Kennedy (University of Tulsa, M.A.) is Head of School. *Southern Association.*

The Walker School   1957

700 Cobb Parkway North, Marietta, GA 30062
Tel. 770-427-2689; Admission 678-581-6921; Fax 770-514-8122
Web Site www.thewalkerschool.org
E-mail mozleyp@thewalkerschool.org

The Walker School is a coeducational day school enrolling 1100 students in Pre-Kindergarten–Grade 12. The School seeks to provide quality education through the efforts of a caring faculty with the ability to motivate children to achieve. The major emphasis is a traditional college preparatory academic program that includes the visual and performing arts, publications, computer technology, and physical education. A variety of Advanced

Placement and honors courses is offered. The Dean of College Counseling and Guidance works individually with each student. Historically, 100 percent of graduates are accepted to colleges or universities. Extracurricular activities include sports, clubs,

THE WALKER SCHOOL

music, and drama. Tuition: $9230–$16,510. Financial Aid: $800,000. Patricia H. Mozley is Director of Admission and School Relations; Donald B. Robertson (College of William and Mary, B.S. 1968; Rider University, M.A. 1974) was named Headmaster in 1985. *Southern Association.*

The Westminster Schools   1951

1424 West Paces Ferry Road, NW, Atlanta, GA 30327-2486
Tel. 404-355-8673; Admission 404-609-6202; Fax 404-367-7894
Web Site www.westminster.net; E-mail admissions@westminster.net

THE WESTMINSTER SCHOOLS

A Christian, college preparatory day school for 1848 boys and girls of various backgrounds in Pre-First–Grade 12, Westminster .seeks to develop each student's potential for sound values, continuing education, and community service. The academic program includes Advanced Placement courses in 28 subjects. Extracurricular activities include athletics, fine arts, performing arts, and an experiential education program. Graduates have attended 432 colleges and universities in 40 states and 8 countries. The 180-acre campus is valued at $79,000,000, and the endowment is $229,000,000. Tuition: $17,030–$19,750. Financial Aid: $2,600,000. Marjorie Mitchell is Director of Admission; William Clarkson IV (A.B., M.Div., D.Min.) is President. *Southern Association.*

Woodward Academy   1900

1662 Rugby Avenue, College Park, GA 30337
Tel. 404-765-4000; Admissions 404-765-4001; Fax 404-765-4009
Web Site www.woodward.edu; E-mail admissions@woodward.edu

WOODWARD ACADEMY in College Park, Georgia, is a coeducational college preparatory school enrolling 2780 day students in Pre-Kindergarten through Grade 12. Woodward Academy is comprised of five divisions. The Primary School (Kindergarten–Grade 3), Lower School (Grades 4–6), Middle School (Grades 7–8), and Upper School (Grades 9–12) are located on the main campus in College Park, a suburban community 7 miles south of downtown Atlanta, and convenient to the Hartsfield-Jackson International Airport. Woodward North (Pre-Kindergarten–Grade 6), is located in North Fulton County along the Chattahoochee River.

WOODWARD ACADEMY

Founded in 1900 as Georgia Military Academy by Col. John C. Woodward, the school was originally a secondary military academy for boys; an elementary division was subsequently added. In 1964, the Academy became coeducational, and in 1966, the Academy's charter was amended to discontinue the military program and to rename the school in honor of its founder. Colonel Woodward was succeeded by his son-in-law, Col. William R. Brewster, Sr.; Capt. William R. Brewster, Jr., served as President from 1961 until December 1978. Dr. Gary M. Jones was installed as Woodward's fourth President in January 1979 and retired in July of 1990. Mr. A. Thomas Jackson served as the fifth President of the Academy from 1990 to 1999. Dr. Harry C. Payne was named the sixth Academy President in 2000 and was succeeded in 2009 by Dr. Stuart Gulley.

The Academy is incorporated as a nonprofit institution under a self-perpetuating Governing Board comprised of alumni and patrons of the school. Woodward Academy's productive endowments are valued at more than $100,000,000. Woodward is accredited by the Southern Association of Colleges and Schools; it holds membership in the National Association of Independent Schools, the Southern Association of Independent Schools, the Georgia Independent Schools Association, and the Atlanta Area Association of Independent Schools. The 7000 living graduates are served by an Alumni Association.

THE CAMPUS. The 80-acre College Park campus contains more than 50 buildings, practice fields, a football stadium, and a nine-court tennis center. Carlos Hall contains the administrative and business offices. West Hall contains Upper School offices and the infirmary, with Upper School classrooms located in the adjacent Brewster Hall. A new 45,000-square-foot Math/Science Building, completed in 2008, features new laboratories, a planetarium, an electron microscope, and an auditorium. The Colquitt Student Center houses a snack bar, student lockers, and a recreation area. The George C. Carlos Library houses

25,000 volumes and includes an Academy archive, conference rooms, reading areas, and study carrels for both Middle and Upper School students. The 92,000-square-foot Richardson Fine Arts Center contains classrooms, offices, studios, a gallery, a 400-seat auditorium, and a closed-circuit television station. The Alumni Center houses the alumni and development offices. A $32,000,000 athletic complex, comprised of new gymnasiums, a fitness center, and physical education offices, is currently under construction. Adjacent to the new athletic complex is the Kennedy Natatorium, housing an eight-lane pool. More than 5000 spectators can be seated in the lighted Colquitt Stadium. Upper School meals are served in Robert W. Woodruff Hall. The 600-seat Richard C. Gresham Chapel also contains a multipurpose conference room. Middle School offices, classrooms, laboratories, dining and art spaces, and study areas are located in Jordan Carlos Middle School Complex, constructed in 2003. Lower School offices, classrooms, a 15,000-volume library, computer lab, gymnasium, and cafetorium are located in Thomas Hall.

A new Primary School Building was completed in 2007. The $9,000,000 Primary School campus features a central complex containing administrative offices, classrooms, a library, and a cafetorium. The grounds also include an athletic field. The 36-acre Woodward North campus includes a facility containing administrative offices, a cafetorium, a library, adjacent athletic fields, nature trails, and a performing and visual arts center.

THE FACULTY. Dr. Stuart Gulley, President, is a graduate of Vanderbilt University (B.A.), Emory University (M.Div.), and Georgia State University (Ph.D.).

The faculty include 350 full-time instructors and 110 academic support staff. Faculty and staff hold more than 225 master's or higher educational degrees, including 6 doctorates. Two or more degrees were earned at Agnes Scott, Auburn, Brenau, Cleveland State, Emory, Georgia Institute of Technology, Georgia Southern, Georgia State, Jacksonville State, LaGrange, Louisiana State, Mercer, Miami of Ohio, Michigan State, Milligan, Millsaps, Notre Dame College, Oglethorpe, Ohio State, Peabody, Purdue, Shorter, Wake Forest, West Chester State, West Georgia, West Virginia, William and Mary, and the Universities of Alabama, Arkansas, Central Florida, Georgia, Mississippi, North Alabama, North Carolina, South Carolina, South Florida, and Tennessee.

WOODWARD ACADEMY

The Academy provides a salary schedule, supplements for extracurricular activities, merit pay, comprehensive major medical insurance, and a retirement program.

STUDENT BODY. Woodward Academy enrolls 2780 students, of whom 51 percent are boys and 49 percent girls. Students come from communities throughout the metropolitan Atlanta area.

ACADEMIC PROGRAM. The academic year, from mid-August

to late May, is divided into two semesters and includes Thanksgiving, Winter Break, and Spring vacations. Classes begin at 8:30 A.M. and end at 3:05 P.M., depending on individual schedules.

A college preparatory curriculum is offered to all Upper School students; available electives include computer programming, television production, science fiction, astronomy, oceanography, satire, Shakespeare, and dance. Honors courses and Advanced Placement courses include English, European history, American history, mathematics, computer science, biology, chemistry, physics, French, Japanese, Spanish, music, and art. Report cards are provided to parents at six-week intervals, and interim reports are sent to parents in cases of deficient or unsatisfactory work.

WOODWARD ACADEMY

Middle School students are required to take Computer Science, Foreign Language, and Life Skills in addition to English, reading, mathematics, science, social studies, fine arts, and physical education. Honors and regular sections are offered in most departments; tutorials and study halls are available.

The Lower Schools offer a competitive program of instruction. The upper elementary grades are departmentalized, and reading and mathematics receive primary emphasis along with computer science, social studies, science, art, music, drama, and physical education. The main campus Lower School and Woodward North offer a Student Transition Education Program for above-average students with slight learning differences. Tutorials, interim reports, and parent-teacher conferences chart a student's progress.

The 270 members of the Class of 2009 attend such institutions as Agnes Scott, Appalachian State, Auburn, Boston University, Clemson, Cornell, Dartmouth, Duke, Florida State, Georgia Institute of Technology, Georgia Southern, Harvard, Louisiana State, Mercer, Miami (Ohio), Southern Methodist, Stanford, U.S. Air Force Academy, U.S. Military Academy, U.S. Naval Academy, Vanderbilt, Wellesley, Williams, and the Universities of Alabama, Colorado, Michigan, Mississippi, Pennsylvania, South Carolina, and Virginia.

STUDENT ACTIVITIES. The Academy offers a wide variety of activities to students. Lower School activities include Cub Scouts, chorus, band, patrols, intramural sports, cultural programs, and educational trips. Middle School activities include a Student Government, class activities, a Camera Club, an Art Club, and Honor Council. Dances are held periodically. Upper School activities include Student Government, Honor Council, the National Honor Society, French and Spanish honor societies, debate, newspaper, yearbook, Camera Club, cheerleaders, flag corps, Art Club, choruses, Drama Club, band, a dance ensemble, ten service clubs, and the WATV crew. Upper School students are required to fulfill a 20-hour work contract during the year by working on campus. All Upper School students are involved in small group sessions through the Peer Leadership and Teacher Advisory programs. These programs assist students in dealing with peer pressure, academic stress, and other pertinent issues.

Interscholastic and intramural sports include football, baseball, basketball, soccer, swimming and diving, tennis, track, wrestling, cross-country, volleyball, fast-pitch softball, lacrosse, ultimate frisbee, and golf. Social activities include formal and informal dances and weekend outings.

Frequent assemblies provide a forum for various speakers and school groups.

ADMISSION AND COSTS. It is Woodward Academy's policy to admit students from a variety of racial, ethnic, and economic backgrounds who desire to attend the Academy and who provide evidence of good character, conduct, and academic achievement. New students are accepted at all grade levels except Grade 12. An entrance examination, an interview, school records, teacher/principal evaluations, and evidence of extracurricular interests are required, especially for older students.

In 2009–10, tuition is $12,300 for Pre-Kindergarten, $16,985 for Kindergarten–Grade 6, and $19,950 for Grades 7–12. Additional charges for all students include textbooks ($300–$500) and uniforms (approximately $700). Additional fees may be levied for private lessons, private tutoring, developmental reading, the yearbook, and the diploma. An additional $8600 is required for students in the Transition Program to provide the small classes and individual tutoring such children require. More than $2,200,000 in financial aid is awarded annually to approximately 12 percent of the students in the Middle and Upper Schools.

President: Dr. Stuart Gulley
Dean of Faculty: Mr. David R. McCollum
Dean of Students: Mrs. Elaine T. Carroll
Dean of Admission: Mr. Russell L. Slider
Director of Development: Mr. Robert F. Hawks
College Counselor: Mrs. Missy Sanchez
Business Manager: Ms. Barbara Egan
Director of Athletics: Mr. David H. Chandler

WOODWARD ACADEMY

HAWAII

Hanahau'oli School 1918

1922 Makiki Street, Honolulu, HI 96822
Tel. 808-949-6461; Admission Ext. 107; Fax 808-941-2216
Web Site www.hanahauoli.org
E-mail ctakamine@hanahauoli.org

A coeducational, nonsectarian elementary school enrolling 200 children in Junior Kindergarten–Grade 6, Hanahau'oli's philosophy of "learning by doing" informs its curriculum while creating an environment in which students share experiences and cooperate as a large family. A multiage classroom system recognizes that children of the same age learn at different paces and allows team teaching and flexibility in instruction to support individual progress toward academic excellence. Specialists in music, visual arts, physical education, technology, physical world lab, and French integrate curricula with classroom programs. Tuition: $16,420. Beverly Crum is Director of Admission; Robert G. Peters (University of Massachusetts, B.A., M.A., Ed.D.) is Headmaster. *Western Association.*

Holy Nativity School 1949

5286 Kalanianaole Highway, Honolulu, HI 96821
Tel. 808-373-3232; Admissions Ext. 113; Fax 808-377-9618
Web Site www.holynativityschool.org
E-mail admissions@holynativity-hi.org

Holy Nativity School, an independent, coeducational, Episcopal day school, enrolls 170 students in a co-op for three-year-olds and in Pre-Kindergarten–Grade 6. Holy Nativity provides students with an integrated, research-based curriculum, which is developmentally appropriate and aligned with national standards. Small group and individualized instruction in a nurturing environment contributes to the quality of the program. In addition to classroom teachers who provide a solid foundation in the core subject areas, students attend music, art, religion, computer technology, and physical education classes with specialist teachers weekly. Teachers work collaboratively, ensuring a seamless transition between grades, maximizing the cumulative effect of instruction, and thus preparing students for a successful trasition to seventh grade at Hawai'i's fine secondary schools. A summer program offers various subjects, activities, and field trips. Tuition: $7300–$11,900. Financial aid is available. Kelly Goheen is Director of Admission; Dr. Robert H. Whiting (University of Colorado [Boulder], Ph.D.) is Head of School. *Western Association.*

Le Jardin Academy 1961

917 Kalanianaole Highway, Kailua, HI 96734
Tel. 808-261-0707; Fax 808-262-9339
Web Site www.lejardinacademy.com
E-mail staylor@lejardinacademy.com

Le Jardin Academy is a coeducational, college preparatory day school enrolling 800 youngsters in Prekindergarten–Grade 12.

Le Jardin seeks to enable students to develop in mind, body, and character. The curriculum provides a strong foundation in academic subjects while encouraging creative and critical thinking and effective decision making. The core program is enriched by Japanese, after-school sports, drama, band, and orchestra. Exchanges with schools in Japan and China and outdoor educational programs promote cultural understanding

LE JARDIN ACADEMY

and appreciation for the environment. Le Jardin's state-of-the-art campus includes classroom buildings for Kindergarten–Grade 12, an auditorium, swimming pool, and playing fields. Extended-day care and a summer program are optional. Tuition: $9250–$14,500. Ms. Susan L. Taylor is Director of Admission; Mr. Adrian Allan (Leeds University, B.S.; University of Alabama, M.A.) is Headmaster. *Western Association.*

St. Andrew's Priory School for Girls 1867

224 Queen Emma Square, Honolulu, HI 96813
Tel. 808-536-6102; Admissions 808-532-2418; Fax 808-531-8426
Web Site www.priory.net; E-mail sawargo@priory.net

St. Andrew's Priory is an Episcopal day school enrolling 550 young women from many ethnic, cultural, and religious backgrounds in Kindergarten–Grade 12. It also has a coeducational preschool enrolling 150 children ages 2 to 5. Following traditions set by its founder, Hawaii's Queen Emma, the School offers a well-balanced college preparatory education that is designed to prepare young women to meet the challenges and opportunities of college and adult life. Extensive technology, athletics, and visual and performing arts complement the curriculum. Tuition: $12,910–$13,610. Sue Ann Wargo is Admissions Director; Sandra J. Theunick (Newton College, B.A.; Washington Theological Union, M.Div.) was appointed Head of School in 2008. *Western Association.*

ILLINOIS

The Avery Coonley School   1906

1400 Maple Avenue, Downers Grove, IL 60515-4897
Tel. 630-969-0800; Fax 630-969-0131
Web Site www.averycoonley.org; E-mail minicar@averycoonley.org

The Avery Coonley School, enrolling 374 day students in Early Childhood (age 3)–Grade 8, offers a challenging program designed to meet the needs of academically bright and gifted students. A student-teacher ratio of 11:1 allows each child to receive a high level of individual attention and to progress at an accelerated rate. The enriched curriculum is designed to nurture the development of students so that they will become critical thinkers and independent learners. The program also includes French, art, music, drama, physical education, technology, and character education. Student Council, fine arts, athletics, and many interest clubs are among the activities. Tuition: $4700–$16,100. Andy Gilla is Director of Admission and Marketing; Mr. Paul Barton (Loras College, B.A.; St. John's College, M.A.) is Head of School.

Bernard Zell Anshe Emet Day School   1946

3751 North Broadway Street, Chicago, IL 60613
Tel. 773-281-1858; Admissions 773-572-1236; Fax 773-281-4709
Web Site www.bzaeds.org; E-mail admissions@bzaeds.org
E-mail info@bzaeds.org

The Bernard Zell Anshe Emet Day School is a fully accredited, independent, coeducational, Jewish day school with 500 students in nursery through eighth grade. Day School families represent a microcosm of Chicago's diverse Jewish community. Students share a common Jewish experience in school and develop a connection to universally respected values. The Day School's commitment to academic excellence is evident in both general and Jewish studies with small classes and innovative teaching methods creating an ideal learning environment. Students have many opportunities for enrichment and enjoyment in and out of the classroom. A 45,000-square-foot athletic field is used by classes and teams. After-school activities support various interests such as chess, band, science, Chinese and Spanish language, performance and studio art, and more. Faculty, committed parents, and seasoned administrators work together, creating a vibrant, caring, student-centered community. Students graduate well prepared for high school and for the world beyond. Tuition: $15,590–$23,130. Alyson K. Horwitz, Ed.D., is Head of School; Pamela Popeil is Director of Admissions and Financial Aid.

Brehm Preparatory School   1982

1245 East Grand Avenue, Carbondale, IL 62901-3600
Tel. 618-457-0371; Fax 618-529-1248
Web Site www.brehm.org; E-mail admissionsinfo@brehm.org

Carol Brehm founded Brehm Preparatory School to provide an appropriate educational setting for her son and other students with learning differences. Today, Brehm Prep is the Midwest's only boarding school specifically designed to help youngsters with complex learning disabilities and disorders such as ADD and ADHD. Enrolling 98 boys and girls ages 11–21, the School provides a full range of services to meet individual academic, social, and emotional needs. In a family environment, students undertake a college preparatory curriculum that implements Orton-Gillingham and other methodologies related to personalized education. Using a team approach, faculty address each student's areas of academic strength and weakness with the goal of empowering him or her to become an independent learner

BREHM PREPARATORY SCHOOL

and self-advocate. In addition to academic course work, Brehm also focuses on the development of life skills such as time management and problem solving. Among the activities are Student Council, weekend field trips, physical fitness, outdoor pursuits, basketball, indoor soccer, and community service. Boarding Tuition: $59,000; Day Tuition: $36,000. Donna Collins is Director of Admissions; Richard G. Collins, Ph.D., is Executive Director.

The Catherine Cook School   1975

226 West Schiller Street, Chicago, IL 60610
Tel. 312-266-3381; Admissions Ext. 146; Fax 312-266-3616
Web Site www.catherinecookschool.org
E-mail admissions@catherinecookschool.org

The Catherine Cook School is an urban, coeducational, nondenominational day school that enrolls 480 children from Preschool through Grade 8. The liberal arts educational program includes core curriculum, math, science, literacy, and humanities as well as fine arts, music, physical education, foreign language, and character development. The School's approach incorporates hands-on, experiential learning designed to instill critical thinking and problem-solving strategies. Small classes and careful attention to individual learning patterns ensure that all students have the ability to reach their full potential. Student Government, interest clubs, and athletic programs enrich the core program. Extended day is optional. Tuition: $11,100–$15,990. Need-based financial aid is available. Jill Due is Director of Admission; Dr. Michael Roberts is Head of School.

Elgin Academy   1839

350 Park Street, Elgin, IL 60120
Tel. 847-695-0300; Admissions 847-695-0303; Fax 847-695-5017
Web Site www.elginacademy.org; E-mail info@elginacademy.org

Elgin Academy, the oldest nonsectarian, coeducational college preparatory school west of the Allegheny Mountains, enrolls

450 students from diverse backgrounds in Preschool–Grade 12. The educational program gives students sound knowledge in the arts and sciences and the skills necessary to acquire and use that knowledge as lifelong learners. Students are active in the arts, athletics, and community service. World language study begins in Preschool; Advanced Placement-level courses and independent study are available in the Upper School. All

ELGIN ACADEMY

seniors are college bound and attend universities throughout the United States. Tuition: $10,800–$17,000. Financial Aid: $1,300,000. Mr. Shannon Howell is Director of Admission; Dr. John W. Cooper (Syracuse, Ph.D.) is Head of School. *North Central Association.*

Fenwick High School 1929

505 Washington Boulevard, Oak Park, IL 60302
Tel. 708-386-0127; Admissions Ext. 115; Fax 708-386-3052
Web Site www.fenwickfriars.com
E-mail fcasaccio@fenwickfriars.com

FENWICK HIGH SCHOOL

Fenwick, a Catholic, coeducational, college preparatory school founded in 1929 by the Dominican Order of Preachers, draws 1197 students from more than 60 communities and a broad spectrum of cultural and socioeconomic backgrounds. Emphasizing academic excellence and participation in athletics, activities, and community service, Fenwick prepares its students for college, with a 100 percent college acceptance rate, and for life and leadership. Motivated students, qualified faculty, and a sup-

portive community of parents and graduates result in Fenwick's recognition as an exemplary high school by the U.S. Department of Education. Tuition: $10,450. Financial aid is available. Francesca Casaccio is Director of Admissions; Rev. De Porres Durham, O.P., is President; Richard Borsch is Principal.

Lake Forest Country Day School 1888

145 South Green Bay Road, Lake Forest, IL 60045
Tel. 847-234-2350; Admissions Fax 847-234-8725
Web Site www.lfcds.org; E-mail nicoletc@lfcds.org

Lake Forest Country Day School enrolls 470 boys and girls in Preschool (age 2) to Grade 8. Education in basic skills is stressed, along with a substantial program in interdisciplinary studies and the arts to help students develop the capacity to think independently, achieve their full potential, and interact effectively with others. Included are art, music, drama, computer, outdoor education, athletics, and community service programs. French, Mandarin Chinese, and Spanish instruction begins at age 3. Summer offerings feature study skills, language arts, mathematics, and the arts, plus a computer and sports camp. Tuition: $3600–$19,645. Financial Aid: $470,000. Christine R. Nicoletta is Director of Admission; Robert Bullard is Assistant Head of School; Michael Robinson was appointed Head of School in 2005.

The University of Chicago Laboratory Schools 1896

1362 East 59th Street, Chicago, IL 60637
Tel. 773-702-9450; Admissions 773-702-9451; Fax 773-834-1520
Web Site www.ucls.uchicago.edu
E-mail admissions@ucls.uchicago.edu

THE UNIVERSITY OF CHICAGO LABORATORY SCHOOLS

Founded by John Dewey to test his educational theories, The University of Chicago Laboratory Schools enroll 1776 boys and girls in Nursery (ages 3–4)–Grade 12. The Schools offer a culturally and racially diverse community within which students actively engage in an academically rigorous, experience-centered education. The program challenges each student to think independently by encouraging the individual's natural curiosity and cultivating his or her love of learning. The college preparatory program includes Advanced Placement courses in most disciplines. Many extracurricular activities and a summer program are available. The University of Chicago Lab Schools hold membership in the Independent Schools Association of the Central States. Tuition: $12,882–$22,671. Financial Aid: $1,600,000. William J. Newman is Executive Director of Admissions and Financial Aid; David W. Magill, Ed.D., is Director. *North Central Association.*

INDIANA

Canterbury School   1977

Grades 9–12: 3210 Smith Road, Fort Wayne, IN 46804
 Tel. 260-436-0746; Fax 260-436-5137
 Web Site www.canterburyschool.org
 E-mail admissions@canterburyschool.org
EC–Grade 8: 5601 Covington Road, Fort Wayne, IN 46804
 Lower School: Tel. 260-432-7776; Fax 260-436-9069
 Middle School: Tel. 260-436-7721; Fax 260-436-6665

CANTERBURY SCHOOL

Canterbury School, set on 71 acres, offers a coeducational, college preparatory education to 910 students in Early Childhood (age 2)–Grade 12. Students come from a wide range of racial, ethnic, religious, and economic backgrounds, creating a lively diversity that promotes respect and understanding. The liberal arts academic program is designed to stimulate intellectual curiosity and creativity while developing young people of good character and ethical standards. The curriculum promotes excellence and comprehension in English and language arts, the sciences, social studies, and mathematics, with French beginning in Kindergarten and other languages, including Latin, Spanish, and Japanese, introduced in higher grades. Upper School students may sit for AP exams in 14 subject areas. Virtually all graduates go on to four-year colleges and universities across the nation. Among the activities are school government, Model UN, Amnesty International, Mock Trial, Habitat for Humanity, orchestra, band, chorus, publications, and interscholastic sports. A summer program is optional. Tuition: $12,420–$12,730. Financial aid is available. Susan Johnson (9–12) and Krista Lohmar (KPrep–8) are Directors of Admissions; Jonathan Hancock is Headmaster.

Evansville Day School   1946

3400 North Green River Road, Evansville, IN 47715
Tel. 812-476-3039; Admission Ext. 205; Fax 812-476-4061
Web Site www.evansvilledayschool.org
E-mail lcox@evansvilledayschool.org

Founded by parents, the Evansville Day School is a coeducational college preparatory school enrolling 335 students in Junior Pre-Kindergarten–Grade 12. The School provides a tra-ditional curriculum stressing personal growth, academic excellence, and character education. The educational experience is enhanced by a wide range of learning and extracurricular activities including off-campus Intersession projects and a variety of athletic teams and clubs. A personal development program and a caring faculty provide a positive learning atmosphere. A block schedule for Grades 8–12 includes numerous Advanced Placement courses. Tuition: $2110–$12,650. Financial Aid: $250,000; Merit Scholarships: $50,000. Laura Cox is Admission Director; Mr. Kendell Berry is Head of School.

The Orchard School   1922

615 West 64th Street, Indianapolis, IN 46260
Tel. 317-251-9253; Admissions 317-713-5753; Fax 317-254-8454
Web Site www.orchard.org; E-mail khein@orchard.org

Orchard, a nonsectarian, coeducational, progressive school, enrolls 615 students in Preschool–Grade 8. The curriculum integrates learning through language arts, social studies, math, fine and performing arts, science, Spanish, physical education, technology, and outdoor education. The Dignity Center, core values, problem solving, critical thinking, field trips, components of the "Responsive Classroom," and service learning are integral to the social and academic curriculum. Learning support, speech-language therapy, assessment and evaluation, and school counseling are available. Extended-day programs are offered. Tuition: $4499–$15,487. Financial Aid: $1,555,000. Kristen Hein is Admissions Director; Joseph P. Marshall (Franklin and Marshall, B.A.; Hofstra, M.Ed.) is Head of School.

The Stanley Clark School   1958

3123 Miami Street, South Bend, IN 46614-2098
Tel. 574-291-4200; Fax 574-299-4170
Web Site www.stanleyclark.org; E-mail douglass@stanleyclark.org

The Stanley Clark School, a nationally recognized private elementary school accredited by the Independent School Association of the Central States, enrolls 365 day boys and girls in Preschool through Grade 8. A multifaceted curriculum, emphasizing academics, fine arts, athletics, and technology, provides the basis for continuing success in high school, college, and the workplace. In addition to traditional academics, there are foreign languages, dramatics, and optional minicourses. The preschool is based on the Reggio philosophy with an optional all-day program. Extended day is available before and after school. Tuition: $3850–$14,100. Financial Aid: $650,000. Maria Reilly is Director of Admissions; Robert G. Douglass (University of Bridgeport, B.A., M.A.) was appointed Headmaster in 1988.

Sycamore School   1985

1750 West 64th Street, Indianapolis, IN 46260
Tel. 317-202-2500; Admissions 317-202-2519; Fax 317-202-2501
Web Site www.sycamoreschool.org
E-mail skarpicke@sycamoreschool.org

Parents and educators established this coeducational day school to provide intellectual stimulation for academically gifted children. Sycamore School enrolls 410 children from diverse racial, ethnic, and socioeconomic backgrounds in a preparatory curriculum that spans Early Childhood (2 years, 8 months) to Grade 8. Classroom instructors are either endorsed in gifted education or are candidates for endorsement. Sycamore's curriculum is broader, faster-paced, deeper, and more complex than most and helps students develop high-level thinking skills. In addition to core academics, all students receive instruction in art, music, Spanish, physical education, and computer technology. Local and long-distance field trips and guest speakers enrich classroom instruction. A low teacher-student ratio allows faculty to implement the curriculum and provide maximum personalized interaction. Students are challenged academically in a supportive environment where being smart and loving to learn are the norm. Tuition: $5030–$13,495. Financial aid is available. Diane Borgmann is Head of School.

University High School   2000

2825 West 116th Street, Carmel, IN 46032-8730
Tel. 317-733-4475; Admission Ext. 102; Fax 317-733-4484
Web Site www.universityhighschool.org
E-mail nwebster@universityhighschool.org

University High School is an independent, nonsectarian, college preparatory day school that enrolls 220 girls and boys in Grades 9–12. The School's mission is "to expand the hearts and minds of students and to nurture excellence through academic, creative, and physical achievement." The School emphasizes critical thinking, character building, and intellectual stimulation. A formal mentoring program; 100 percent college placement; an intensive, one-subject January Term; competitive, inclusive sports; and small classes provide a personal and challenging approach to learning. Extracurriculars include community service, varsity sports, academic and special-interest clubs, publications, and theater. Tuition: $14,895. Nancy Webster is Director of Admission; Chuck Webster is Head of School.

CANTERBURY SCHOOL

IOWA

Rivermont Collegiate   1884

1821 Sunset Drive, Bettendorf, IA 52722-6045
Tel. 563-359-1366; Admission Ext. 302; Fax 563-359-7576
Web Site www.rivermontcollegiate.org
E-mail info@rvmt.org

RIVERMONT COLLEGIATE

Rivermont Collegiate is dedicated to providing an environment that challenges each student to fulfill his or her maximum potential academically, creatively, and morally. This coeducational, college preparatory day school enrolls 200 students in Early School (age 3)–Grade 12 from the Greater Quad City area, consisting of Bettendorf and Davenport in Iowa, Rock Island and Moline in Illinois, and smaller surrounding communities. Academic diversity in Early and Lower School as well as discipline-specific teachers in science, foreign language, art, music, technology, and physical education allow for teaching one to two grades above grade level. Latin is required of all Middle School students who may also choose to study High School-level Spanish or French. Chinese language is an elective beginning in Grade 10. In addition, the school offers an accelerated math program in Lower School as well as AP, Honors classes, and independent study in the Upper School. Rivermont Collegiate was honored in 2008 and 2009 as #1 in the Iowa AP Index, with 30 percent of the Class of 2009 honored by the National Merit Scholarship Program. Tuition: $2360–$10,830. Financial aid is available. Cindy Murray is Director of Admission; Richard St. Laurent is Headmaster.

LOUISIANA

The Dunham School   1981

11111 Roy Emerson Street, Baton Rouge, LA 70810-1786
Tel. 225-767-7097; Fax 225-767-7056
Web Site www.dunhamschool.org
E-mail linda.spear@dunhamschool.org

The Dunham School was founded to provide "an education of the mind and the heart" for children from a wide diversity of backgrounds. Offering a challenging college preparatory program within a distinctively Christian context, Dunham's curriculum focuses on the mastery of strong skills in core academic subjects combined with chapel services, Bible studies, and

counseling. The 23-acre campus in a residential area of South Baton Rouge accommodates 795 day boys and girls in Pre-Kindergarten–Grade 12. Teachers are chosen based on their instructional skills as well as their ability to serve as Christian role models and mentors. The student-teacher ratio is 11:1, and

THE DUNHAM SCHOOL

the average class enrolls between 14 and 16 students, allowing ample opportunity for participation, discussion, and individual support. English, math, science, social studies, modern language, and religious studies are at the heart of the academic program, with elective enhancements in art, music, drama, technology, and physical education. There is 1:1 Apple laptop integration campus-wide. Field trips, school government, publications, plays, music groups, community service, and athletics are among the activities. Tuition: $7100–$10,750. Linda Spear is Director of Admission & Financial Aid; Robert W. Welch is Headmaster. *Southern Association.*

Isidore Newman School   1903

1903 Jefferson Avenue, New Orleans, LA 70115-5699
Tel. 504-899-5641; Admission 504-896-6323; Fax 504-896-8597
Web Site www.newmanschool.org; E-mail jrosen@newmanschool.org

Since 1903, Isidore Newman School has been providing top-quality college preparatory education to the children of New Orleans. Newman enrolls 965 boys and girls in Pre-Kindergarten through Grade 12 and enjoys a national reputation for excellence and achievement in academics, athletics, and the arts. The curriculum includes sophisticated science programs in the Lower School as well as multiple world language offerings. Twenty-three Advanced Placement and honors courses are currently offered. More than 60 team sports, arts, publications, debate, community service, and other student clubs are available. Newman also provides after-school enrichment, a summer camp, and summer academic offerings. Tuition: $15,582–$17,588. Need-based financial aid is available. Jennifer Rosen is Admission Director; T. J. Locke is Head of School.

Kehoe-France School   1962

720 Elise Avenue, Metairie, LA 70003
Tel. 504-733-0472; Fax 504-733-0477
Web Site www.kehoe-france.com; E-mail janet@kehoe-france.com
Northshore Campus: 25 Patricia Drive, Covington, LA 70433
Tel. 985-892-4415; Fax 985-875-7636
Web Site www.kehoe-francens.com
E-mail lori@kehoe-francens.com

Frank A. and Patricia Kehoe France founded this elementary school to provide an excellent educational experience directed toward the intellectual, spiritual, emotional, and social development of each child. Enrolling 1200 boys and girls age 18 months–Grade 8 on two campuses, Kehoe-France's curriculum emphasizes strong skills in core subjects to enable all students to realize their full personal and academic potential. A wide range of enrichment programs engages youngsters in community service, dramatic presentations, vocal and instrumental ensembles, team sports and Environmental Awareness and Wilderness Studies enrichment. Extended day care is available before and after school, and there is a summer camp program. Tuition: $6546–$6738. Janet Pananos is Admissions Director; Frank A. France and his three sons direct the School.

Ridgewood Preparatory School   1948

201 Pasadena Avenue, Metairie, LA 70001-4899
Tel. 504-835-2545; Fax 504-837-1864
Web Site www.ridgewoodprep.com
E-mail mmontgomery@ridgewoodprep.com

Ridgewood Preparatory School is a day school enrolling 300 boys and girls in Pre-Kindergarten–Grade 12. Its aim is to prepare students for college and life through development of intellectual skills, awareness of the world and its beauties, participation in society, and preparation for a vocation. Beginning in Pre-Kindergarten, the School provides a traditional curriculum including art, music, and physical education. Student government, service and activity clubs, publications, band, and interscholastic sports are among the activities. Tuition & Fees: $4000–$5750. Susan Schenken is Director of Admissions; M. J. Montgomery, Jr. (Loyola, B.S. 1959, M.Ed. 1962), was appointed Headmaster in 1972. *Southern Association.*

St. Andrew's Episcopal School   1957

8012 Oak Street, New Orleans, LA 70118
Tel. 504-861-3743; Fax 504-861-3973
Web Site www.standrews.k12.la.us
E-mail admissions@standrews.k12.la.us

St. Andrew's Episcopal School, the oldest Episcopal day school in New Orleans, enrolls 150 boys and girls in Prekindergarten–Grade 8. Small classes promote a challenging learning environment where students interact with teachers and grow spiritually, socially, and intellectually. A strong academic program, enhanced by state-of-the-art technology, includes Spanish, Chinese, music, chapel, fine arts, athletics, and library skills. Student publications, dramatics, intramurals, and community service round out the St. Andrew's experience. Tuition: $7665–$9900. Financial aid is available. Lisa Witter is Coordinator of Admission; D. Mason Lecky was appointed Head of School in 2009.

St. Mark's Cathedral School   1953

2785 Fairfield Avenue, Shreveport, LA 71104
Tel. 318-221-7454; Admission 318-226-4036; Fax 318-221-7060
Web Site www.stmarksschool.com
E-mail cwilkinson@stmarksschool.com

The Vestry of St. Mark's Cathedral founded this coeducational day school to provide quality education infused with Christian values. St. Mark's Cathedral School offers a lively, rigorous academic program designed to nurture the intellectual, spiritual, and social development of each child. Currently enrolling 325 children from diverse religious backgrounds in Preschool–Grade 8, St. Mark's emphasizes the mastery of skills in core subjects, enriched by modern and classical languages, theater, technology, and opportunities to earn high school credit in some course work. Students take part in services at the Cathedral and

enjoy activities in school government and team sports. Tuition: $2800–$7800. Charlotte Wilkinson is Director of Admission; Chris Carter is Head of School.

St. Martin's Episcopal School   1947

225 Green Acres Road, Metairie, LA 70003
Tel. 504-733-0353; Admissions 504-736-9917; Fax 504-736-8802
Web Site www.stmsaints.com; E-mail susan.pansano@stmsaints.com

St. Martin's Episcopal School is a 62-year-old coeducational, college preparatory, diocesan-sponsored day school with 650 students from diverse backgrounds age 12 months–Grade 12. Located on 18 beautiful acres, St. Martin's utilizes the Total Human Development Model, a comprehensive approach promoting core values of respect and responsibility as the basis for good character in all phases of school and life. The School is distinguished by Core Operating Principles including rigorous academics, intentional integration of faith and learning, collaborative community-based philosophy, balanced preparation for life, lifelong learning, and student-led servant leadership. St. Martin's understands that each student learns in his or her own way and offers many programs in academics, athletics, arts, and activities to help students tap their talents and discover their passion. The curriculum includes 24 honors and AP courses for qualified Upper School scholars. All students contribute to age-appropriate community service projects. Tuition: $8200–$16,800. Financial aid is available. Susan Pansano is Director of Admission; Dr. Jeffrey P. Beedy is Headmaster.

Southfield School   1934

1100 Southfield Road, Shreveport, LA 71106
Tel. 318-868-5375; Fax 318-869-0890
Web Site www.southfield-school.org;
E-mail ccoburn@southfield-school.org

Southfield was founded by a group of local residents to provide their children with the finest educational opportunity. The preparatory day school serves 435 boys and girls in Preschool through Grade 8. The School is accredited by the Independent Schools Association of the Southwest and the National Association for the Education of Young Children. The liberal arts curriculum challenges students while providing them the skills necessary to succeed. The application of technology is evident throughout the program. After-school care and summer programs are offered. Tuition: $2940–$9100. Financial aid is available. Jeffrey Stokes (State University of New York, B.A.; University of North Carolina, M.A.T.) is Headmaster; Clare Coburn is Admissions Director.

Trinity Episcopal School   1960

1315 Jackson Avenue, New Orleans, LA 70130
Tel. 504-525-8661; Admission 504-670-2506; Fax 504-523-4837
Web Site www.trinitynola.com; E-mail sderussy@trinitynola.com

Trinity Episcopal School was established by Trinity Church in 1960 as an elementary school for approximately 335 boys and girls from Prekindergarten through Eighth Grade. The School is dedicated to fostering the academic, emotional, social, and spiritual growth of its students through a skills-based curriculum. Trinity students, faculty, and staff begin each day with Chapel, which establishes and reinforces the tone of the school community. Art, music, drama, foreign language, and physical education enhance the core subjects at each grade level. Child care is offered before and after school. Tuition: $10,500–$14,800. Tuition assistance is available. Susie DeRussy is Director of Admission; the Reverend Dr. Michael C. Kuhn is Headmaster.

MAINE

Foxcroft Academy 1823

975 West Main Street, Dover-Foxcroft, ME 04426
Tel. 207-564-8351; Fax 207-564-8394
Web Site www.foxcroftacademy.org
E-mail jay.brennan@foxcroftacademy.org

FOXCROFT ACADEMY

One of the oldest private schools in the U.S., Foxcroft serves a diverse coeducational population of 410 day and boarding students in Grades 9–12. The challenging college preparatory curriculum offers 135 courses including 32 Honors and 21 AP courses. The math and science program exceeds national standards and utilizes state-of-the-art technology, while the humanities program explores the culture of an era through study of its history, literature, art, and music. In addition to traditional subjects, students may take courses in music composition, web design, art history, economics, computer-assisted drawing, personal finance, vocational subjects, ethics, and four levels of French, Latin, Spanish, and Chinese. For international students, there are three levels of ESL, including ESL Writing. The Academy fields 32 sports teams for boys and girls, and the school holds several regional and state titles. Foxcroft also provides more than 20 clubs and student organizations. Three new dorms opened in 2009. Boarding Tuition: $33,340; Day Tuition: $11,200. ESL: $1500. Jay Brennan is Associate Head of School for Admissions and Residential Life; Raymond Webb is Head of School.

Hebron Academy 1804

Route 119, P.O. Box 309, Hebron, ME 04238-0309
Tel. 207-966-2100; Fax 207-966-1111
Web Site www.hebronacademy.org
E-mail admissions@hebronacademy.org

Inspiring and guiding students to reach their highest potential in mind, body, and spirit, Hebron Academy enrolls 250 girls and boys in Grade 6–Postgraduate, including 144 boarders from Grade 9 upward. The school provides a challenging educational experience designed to prepare graduates for success in college. Course work in the liberal arts and sciences is complemented by honors and Advanced Placement courses, English as a Second Language, and more than 20 electives. Activities include fine arts, student government, publications, drama, music groups, and 14 interscholastic sports. Boarding Tuition: $43,995; Day Tuition: $23,995. Joseph A. Hemmings is Director of Admissions; John J. King (Williams, B.A.) is Head of School. *New England Association.*

Washington Academy 1792

High Street, P.O. Box 190, East Machias, ME 04630
Tel. 207-255-8301; Admissions Ext. 207; Fax 207-255-8303
Web Site www.washingtonacademy.org
E-mail admissions@washingtonacademy.org

Washington Academy has a rich heritage focused on success for the individual. With college preparatory, career technology, and vocational programs for 330 coeducational day students in Grade 9–Postgraduate and 80 boarding students from around the world, students may choose course work consistent with their abilities and interests. Advanced Placement and Honors courses, ESL, Culinary Arts, Health Occupations, and instruction for students with special needs enhance the core curriculum. Marine Vocational Technology emphasizes skills and knowledge related to seafaring, and Environmental Studies provides experience in research and problem solving. Located in a safe, coastal community in Maine, the Academy has small classes with offerings in art, music, math, science, digital video editing, carpentry, biodiesel, and marine mechanics. Sports include soccer, tennis, swimming, wrestling, football, basketball, golf, and others. Drama, music, and more than 50 extracurricular activities are also available. Boarding Tuition: $32,500; Day Tuition: $12,000. Kim Gardner is Director of Admissions; Judson L. McBrine III is Headmaster. *New England Association.*

MARYLAND

The Academy of the Holy Cross 1868

4920 Strathmore Avenue, Kensington, MD 20895-1299
Tel. 301-942-2100; Admissions 301-929-6442; Fax 301-929-6440
Web Site www.academyoftheholycross.org
E-mail schooloffice@academyoftheholycross.org

This Catholic college preparatory school, sponsored by the Sisters of the Holy Cross, since 1868, is dedicated to educating young women in a Christ-centered community that values diversity. The Academy is committed to developing women of courage, compassion, and scholarship who responsibly embrace the social, spiritual, and intellectual challenges of the world. The Academy offers its 600 students a challenging curriculum with opportunities for spiritual growth through religious studies, community prayer, and Christian service. Honors and Advanced Placement courses and a Senior Project internship enhance the program. The Academy is a candidate school for the International Baccalaureate Organization (IBO) Diploma Programme and has been pursuing authorization as an IB World School. Girls participate in a wide range of cocurricular activities and sports teams. Tuition: $16,050. Extras: $900. Louise Hendon is Director of Admissions; Claire Helm, Ph.D., is President. *Middle States Association.*

Barrie School 1932

13500 Layhill Road, Silver Spring, MD 20906-3299
Tel. 301-576-2800; Fax 301-576-2803
Web Site www.barrie.org; E-mail admissions@barrie.org

BARRIE SCHOOL.

Barrie School is a coeducational, independent day school serving approximately 390 students from Pre-Kindergarten through Grade 12. Barrie is one of the oldest progressive schools in the Washington area. The School is located on a beautiful, 45-acre wooded campus minutes from the nation's capital. The campus boasts athletic fields, an equestrian center, a state-of-the-art gymnasium complex, and Black Box theater. The unique Barrie experience is one that emphasizes hands-on learning and empowers students to develop confidence, independent thinking, and teamwork essential for world citizenship. Before- and after-school supervision and transportation services are offered. Tuition: $11,750–$24,080. Need-based financial aid is available. Andrea Williams is Director of Admission and Financial Aid; Michael Kennedy is Interim Head of School. *Middle States Association.*

Charles E. Smith Jewish Day School 1965

Lower School: 1901 East Jefferson Street, Rockville, MD 20852
Tel. 301-881-1400; Admissions 301-692-4870
Fax 301-984-7834
Upper School: 11710 Hunters Lane, Rockville, MD 20852
Tel. 301-881-1400; Admissions 301-692-4870
Fax 301-230-1986
Web Site www.cesjds.org; E-mail scohen@cesjds.org

Now in its fifth decade of providing Jewish families with excellence in Judaic and general studies, Charles E. Smith is the largest Jewish community day school in the United States, enrolling nearly 1500 boys and girls from diverse Jewish religious and family backgrounds in Kindergarten through Grade 12. The School is set on two distinct yet united campuses and offers at all levels a dual curriculum that combines the best elements of Judaic and general studies. The academic environment is designed to develop students' maximum potential as scholars and as responsible, dedicated Jewish-American citizens. General studies are college preparatory, centered in the liberal arts, sciences, and humanities. In the Judaic curriculum, students learn about Jewish history, culture, and tradition, study Torah, and have instruction in the Hebrew language as they acquire a deep appreciation for Jewish values, Zionism, and the Jewish nation. Seniors spend one semester in Israel to experience firsthand the rich heritage of their faith and their people. Among the activities are school government, publications, clubs, and sports. Tuition: $18,450–$23,680. Tuition assistance is available. Susan Cohen is Director of Admissions; Jonathan Cannon is Head of School. *Middle States Association.*

Connelly School of the Holy Child 1961

9029 Bradley Boulevard, Potomac, MD 20854
Tel. 301-365-0955; Fax 301-365-0981
Web Site www.holychild.org; E-mail admissions@holychild.org

Connelly School of the Holy Child is a Catholic, college preparatory day school enrolling 320 young women from diverse backgrounds in Grades 6–12. The School traces its origins to the first Holy Child school founded in 1846 by Cornelia Connelly, a nun and educational reformer. The School continues to value the philosophy of its foundress to nurture "the intellectual, spiritual, artistic, social and physical development of each student; to instill academic challenge and the joy of learning; and to educate women of faith and action for compassionate service to humanity." The curriculum, which includes honors and AP courses in most disciplines, centers on the liberal arts, sciences, and humanities. Community service, Campus Ministry, and shared liturgies deepen spiritual awareness in girls of all religious faiths. Activities designed to meet many interests include Student Council, language clubs, drama, vocal and instrumental music groups, yearbook, literary magazine, newspaper, overseas travel experiences, and interscholastic athletics. Tuition: $19,240–$20,580. Financial aid is available. Meg Mayo is Director of Admissions and Financial Aid; Maureen K. Appel (Rosemont, B.A.; Long Island University, M.S.) is Headmistress. *Middle States Association.*

Georgetown Preparatory School 1789

10900 Rockville Pike, North Bethesda, MD 20852
Tel. 301-493-5000; Fax 301-493-6128
Web Site www.gprep.org; E-mail admissions@gprep.org

Founded by Bishop John Carroll, Georgetown Preparatory School is America's first Catholic secondary school and its only Jesuit boarding school. Set on a 90-acre campus with tennis courts, a golf course, and playing fields, the School enjoys convenient access to the rich resources of the nation's capital. Prep enrolls 473 young men from diverse faiths in Grades 9–12; approximately 100 are resident students from 19 states and 27 countries. The rigorous college preparatory curriculum is infused with Christian ethics; boys of all religious beliefs adhere to a strict code of conduct, take part in liturgies, and perform social outreach. The academic program includes 24 Advanced

GEORGETOWN PREPARATORY SCHOOL.

Placement courses, English as a Second Language, and off-campus internships. The average class enrolls 17, ensuring a personalized and participatory learning environment. Among the activities are Student Government, Model UN, Dramatics Society, Forensics Club, Math Team, and competition in 16 sports. Virtually all graduates enter four-year colleges and universities. Boarding Tuition: $44,000; Day Tuition: $25,650. Financial Aid: $2,000,000. Brian J. Gilbert is Director of Admissions; Jeffrey Jones is Headmaster; Rev. William L. George, S.J., is President. *Middle States Association.*

Gibson Island Country School   1956

5191 Mountain Road, Pasadena, MD 21122
Tel. 410-255-5370; Fax 410-255-0416
Web Site www.gics.org; E-mail admissions@gics.org

GIBSON ISLAND COUNTRY SCHOOL

Gibson Island Country School is a coeducational day school enrolling more than 85 students in Pre-Kindergarten–Grade 5. The School's challenging, integrated curriculum emphasizes hands-on, experiential learning in a unique waterfront setting. The student-teacher ratio is 7:1, and the atmosphere is nurturing and attentive to individual needs. Science, foreign language, computer, library, music, art, and physical

education are taught to all grades by specialists. Activities include student government, assemblies, community service, field trips, athletics, special theme days, and numerous environmental projects. GICS is a Maryland Green School. Bus service and after-school care are available. Tuition: $7915–$12,265. Financial aid is available. Jane C. Pehlke is Director of Admission; Laura Kang (University of Kansas, B.S.Ed.; Loyola College, M.A.) is Head of School.

Gilman School   1897

5407 Roland Avenue, Baltimore, MD 21210
Tel. 410-323-3800; Fax LS 410-864-2823, US 410-864-2825
Web Site www.gilman.edu; E-mail admissions@gilman.edu

GILMAN SCHOOL

America's first country day school, Gilman offers a challenging, K–12 liberal arts curriculum to 1015 young men in Pre-K–Grade 12. Gilman seeks to produce men of character and integrity who have the skills and ability to make a positive contribution to the communities in which they live. The Upper School offers Advanced Placement in the major disciplines. All Gilman graduates go on to higher education, and 75 percent are accepted by the most competitive or highly competitive colleges and universities. Community service, Mock Trial, a radio station, publications, the arts, and athletics are among the activities. Tuition: $19,400–$22,665. Financial Aid: $3,000,000. William H. Gamper is Director of Admissions; John E. Schmick is Headmaster.

Glenelg Country School   1954

12793 Folly Quarter Road, Ellicott City, MD 21042
Tel. 410-531-8600; Admission 410-531-7347; Fax 410-531-7363
Web Site www.glenelg.org; E-mail wootton@glenelg.org

Glenelg Country School, enrolling 800 day students in Pre-K–Grade 12, emphasizes academic growth and the development of the whole child. The School balances rigorous academics, creative arts, interscholastic sports, community service, and social activities. The faculty provides personal attention in classes of 12–18 students. The Upper School features 19 Advanced Placement courses and a Director of College Counseling. The School's 87 acres offer state-of-the-art classrooms, athletic facilities, tennis courts, and a swimming pool. Summer programs include a day camp and an academy for basics and enrichment. Tuition: $10,700–$21,500. Financial Aid: $2,000,000. Karen Wootton is Director of Admission/Financial Aid; Gregory Ventre is Head of School.

Green Acres School 1934

11701 Danville Drive, Rockville, MD 20852
Tel. 301-881-4100; [Toll-free] 888-410-4152; Admissions Ext. 189
Fax 301-881-3319
Web Site www.greenacres.org; E-mail admissionoffice@greenacres.org

Green Acres is a coeducational, progressive day school enrolling 320 students in Pre-Kindergarten–Grade 8. Set on a 15-acre campus outside Washington, D.C., the School is dedicated to fostering the natural curiosity of students and engaging them actively in the joy of learning. The intellectually rigorous program is cognitively and creatively challenging. Green Acres values acceptance of a variety of viewpoints and diversity. The curriculum includes technology, visual/performing arts, and physical/outdoor education. Extended day and after-school classes are available, including interscholastic sports for Grades 5–8. A recreational summer camp is offered for ages 4–12. Tuition: $26,070. Susan Friend and Nina Chibber are Co-Directors of Admission; Neal Brown is Head of School.

Gunston Day School 1998

911 Gunston Road, P.O. Box 200, Centreville, MD 21617
Tel. 410-758-0620; [Toll-free] 800-381-0077; Admission Ext. 104
Fax 410-758-0628
Web Site www.gunstondayschool.org
E-mail dhenry@gunstondayschool.org

Founded in 1911 and located on the Corsica River, Gunston Day School today enrolls 140 motivated and capable young men and women in Grades 9–12. Students come from several counties on Maryland's Eastern Shore and from several foreign countries through international programs. Gunston's mission is to provide a supportive, challenging environment in which the art of learning is accompanied by critical thinking, creative expression, stewardship, and self-discipline. The school community adheres to high standards of academic excellence, with an equal emphasis on ethical behavior and physical well-being. Centered on the traditional liberal arts, sciences, and humanities, the challenging college preparatory curriculum includes honors and Advanced Placement courses. The School's Bay Studies program offers week-long explorations of the Chesapeake aboard ship or in a canoe. Students are involved in activities such as school government, publications, drama, choral ensembles, and interest clubs. Gunston offers 15 team sports including sailing, crew, and swimming as well as five club sports. Tuition: $21,730. Financial aid is available. David Henry is Director of Admission; Christie B. Grabis is Interim Head of School. *Middle States Association.*

Harford Day School 1957

715 Moores Mill Road, Bel Air, MD 21014
Tel. 410-838-4848; Fax 410-836-5918
Web Site www.harfordday.org; E-mail info@harfordday.org

Located 20 miles northeast of Baltimore, Harford Day School enrolls 340 boys and girls in K-Prep–Grade 8. The School seeks to offer a program of challenging academics in a dynamic, empowering atmosphere. The student-teacher ratio is 9:1. Fundamental skills, reasoning, independent thinking, and character building are emphasized, and frequent field trips to Baltimore, Washington, and Delaware enrich classroom learning. French, Spanish, Latin, computer skills, music, art, drama, and athletics are offered at all levels. An Extended Day program is optional. Tuition: $12,630. Financial Aid: $345,925. Molly Cain is Director of Admissions and Head of Lower School; Susan G. Harris (Bucknell University, B.S.) was appointed Head of the School in 1994.

The Ivymount School 1961

11614 Seven Locks Road, Rockville, MD 20854
Tel. 301-469-0223; Admissions Ext. 107; Fax 301-469-0778
Web Site www.ivymount.org; E-mail jwintrol@ivymount.org

Founded in 1961 to serve students with special needs including developmental delays, learning disabilities, speech/language deficits, health impairments, and autism/PDD, Ivymount seeks to maximize each student's educational, physical, and social potential. Ivymount enrolls over 200 students annually in a day program offering speech and language therapy, occupational and physical therapy, counseling, adaptive physical education, music and art, and technology support. Students, ages 4–21, come from throughout the Washington metropolitan area and are served in both ungraded and graded programs as follows: the Multiple Learning Needs Program, the Autism Program, and the Model Asperger Program. Tuition: $43,000–$64,000. Jan Wintrol is Director.

The Key School 1958

534 Hillsmere Drive, Annapolis, MD 21403
Tel. 410-263-9231; Fax 410-280-5516
Web Site www.keyschool.org; E-mail ilatimer@keyschool.org

Located in Annapolis, The Key School is a nonsectarian, college preparatory day school enrolling 700 boys and girls in Pre-Kindergarten–Grade 12. The School encourages intellectual rigor, independence of thought, curiosity, creativity, and openness to differing ideas and perspectives. The curriculum includes music, art, and modern and classical languages, with electives in African-American Literature, Dance, Estuarine Biology, and Music Theory. Theater, chorus, jazz and instrumental ensemble, debate, math team, and Model Congress are among the activities. Extensive field trips and outdoor education are integral to the program. Tuition: $11,385–$22,250. Financial aid is available. Jessie D. Dunleavy is Director of Admission; Marcella M. Yedid (Indiana University, B.S.; Brown, M.A.) is Head of School.

Landon School 1929

6101 Wilson Lane, Bethesda, MD 20817
Tel. 301-320-3200; Fax 301-320-1133
Web Site www.landon.net; E-mail george_mulligan@landon.net

LANDON SCHOOL

Landon, a nonsectarian, college preparatory day school enrolling 680 boys in Grades 3–12, is committed to developing students for productive lives as caring, accomplished, and responsible men in today's global community. Landon seeks to foster the values of honor, perseverance, teamwork, fair play, respect, and trust through its Code of Character, which is administered by the boys themselves. The rigorous academic program is centered in English, science, math, social studies, world languages, and computer technology, with AP courses in every department. A junior semester in the Vermont countryside and travel to China, France, Italy, and Spain expand learning and living beyond the classroom. Other programs include the Center for Teaching and Learning Resources, Ethics and Leadership Conference, Model Senate, and comprehensive college counseling. Landon adheres to the teacher-coach-mentor model in which faculty find teachable moments in all aspects of school life. All graduates are accepted by four-year institutions in the U.S. and abroad. Tuition: $27,810–$28,826. Financial Aid: $2,000,000. George Mulligan is Admissions Director; Russ Gagarin is Director of Enrollment and Financial Aid; David M. Armstrong is Headmaster. *Middle States Association.*

Loyola Blakefield   1852

500 Chestnut Avenue, Towson, MD 21204
Tel. 410-823-0601; Admissions 443-841-3680; Fax 443-841-3105
Web Site www.loyolablakefield.org
E-mail admissions@loyolablakefield.org

Loyola Blakefield, founded by the Society of Jesus, is a Roman Catholic, college preparatory day school enrolling 1000 boys in Grades 6–12. Its aim is to graduate young men who are intellectually competent, open to growth, religious, loving, and committed to justice. Core requirements include 20 course units in English, mathematics, modern language, science, and social studies. Fine arts, computer science, physical education, and religious studies are also required. Loyola Blakefield offers a variety of cocurricular activities. Tuition: $14,630; Fees: $715. Michael Breschi is Director of Admissions; Rev. Thomas A. Pesci, S.J. (Weston School of Theology [Cambridge, Massachusetts], M.Div.), is President.

The Maddux School   2008

11614 Seven Locks Road, Rockville, MD 20854
Tel. 301-469-0223; Fax 301-469-0778
Web Site www.madduxschool.org; E-mail amullins@madduxschool.org

The Maddux School offers half-day pre-school and pre-kindergarten classes as well as full-day kindergarten and first-grade classes. Its mission is to enable students to follow their dreams with confidence as they grow and learn. The Maddux School celebrates the different learning styles, personalities, and interests of young children. It is committed to establishing strong academic, communication, and social skill foundations through innovative activities that complement the strengths, meet the needs, and promote the self-esteem of each student. The School provides individualized, supportive programming; small classes (generally with a 4–6:1 student-teacher ratio); and highly trained, certified, and experienced teachers. Speech pathologists and occupational therapists deliver small-group integrated services to all students and provide consultation to staff. Informal assessments; enrichment activities including art, music, library, and gym; ongoing dialogue with parents; referrals to, and collaboration with, private therapists as needed; and school transition advice and support are available to all families. Interested parents should schedule an orientation visit and/or request an application. Tuition: $17,200–$23,300. Andrea A. Mullins, M.Ed., is Director.

Maryvale Preparatory School   1945

11300 Falls Road, Brooklandville, MD 21022
Tel. 410-252-3366; Admissions 410-560-3243; Fax 410-308-1497
Web Site www.maryvale.com; E-mail info@maryvale.com

Maryvale, an independent, Catholic, girls' school founded by the Sisters of Notre Dame de Namur, provides an atmosphere in which each student can reach her academic, spiritual, physical, and civic potential. Enrolling 375 young women from many faiths as day students in Grades 6–12, Maryvale seeks to inspire excellence in all aspects of life in an environment of mutual respect. The student-teacher ratio is 9:1. Middle School girls focus on active learning and problem solving while studying such topics as world geography, algebra, French, Spanish, and American history. The Upper School academic program centers on the liberal arts and sciences, supplemented by Advanced Placement and honors courses, religious studies, and arts, and computer technology throughout the disciplines. Electives such as Latin, Web Design, Sociology, and Biological Anthropology are available. All girls complete at least 100 hours of community service before graduation. Other extracurricular activities include Student Council, Mock Trial, National Honor Society, four publications, drama, chorus, band, and nine interscholastic sports. Tuition: $15,150. Monica C. Graham is Director of Admissions; Sr. Shawn Marie Maguire, SND, is Headmistress. *Middle States Association.*

McDonogh School   1873

8600 McDonogh Road, Owings Mills, MD 21117-0380
Tel. 410-363-0600; Admissions 410-581-4719; Fax 410-998-3507
Web Site www.mcdonogh.org; E-mail admissions@mcdonogh.org

McDonogh School enrolls 1312 boys and girls in Kindergarten–Grade 12, including 80 five-day boarding students in Grades 9–12. Emphasizing academic excellence, moral character, responsibility, and leadership, McDonogh "offers students the opportunities of a large school plus the advantages of a smaller one." Class size averages 15, and 16 Advanced Placement courses are offered. Upper School students choose from 27 interscholastic sports and 50 clubs and activities. The campus is set on 800 acres northwest of Baltimore. Bus transportation and lunches are included in tuition. Boarding Tuition: $30,280; Day Tuition: $20,230–$22,520. Financial Aid: $3,000,000. Anita Hilson is Director of Admissions; Charles Britton is Headmaster.

The Montessori School   1962

10807 Tony Drive, Lutherville, MD 21093
Tel. 410-321-8555; Fax 410-321-8566
Web Site www.montessorischool.net
E-mail admissions@montessorischool.net

This coeducational day school seeks to provide a progressive, child-centered program in which students joyfully and actively engage in the learning process. The Montessori School enrolls 300 youngsters from diverse backgrounds in Pre-Kindergarten–Grade 8. Multiaged classes are grouped heterogeneously to encourage peer teaching, sharing, and natural social development. The core program focuses on language arts, math, science, and social studies, enhanced by art, music,

French, physical education, outdoor education, and library skills. Before- and after-school care and a summer program are

THE MONTESSORI SCHOOL

available. Tuition: $7100–$14,900. Financial Aid: $95,000. Beth Callahan is Admissions Director; Albert J. Swartz (St. John's, B.A.; Long Island University, M.Ed.) is Head of School. *Middle States Association.*

The Nora School 1964

955 Sligo Avenue, Silver Spring, MD 20910
Tel. 301-495-NORA; Fax 301-495-7829
Web Site www.nora-school.org; E-mail janette@nora-school.org

The Nora School is a progressive, coeducational, college preparatory day school serving 60 students in Grades 9–12. Its mission is to nurture and empower bright students who have not realized their potential in larger, more traditional school settings. The School offers a challenging curriculum in an environment designed to develop and maintain a just community, communal decision-making, a high level of discourse, and attention to individual needs and concerns. At all levels, students study the traditional disciplines—English, social studies, mathematics, science, and foreign language—via thematic, engaging approaches. Tuition: $21,450. Janette Patterson is Director of Admissions; David Mullen (University of Maryland, M.S.Ed.) is Headmaster. *Middle States Association.*

Norwood School 1952

8821 River Road, Bethesda, MD 20817
Tel. 301-365-2595; Admission 301-841-2130; Fax 301-841-4636
Web Site www.norwoodschool.org

Norwood, a coeducational day school for more than 520 students in Kindergarten–Grade 8, seeks to offer individual attention and superior instruction. The School's mission is to help each child grow intellectually, morally, physically, and socially. Norwood provides training in fundamental skills, logical and analytical thinking, and independence of mind and self-expression. The curriculum emphasizes facility in both language and math. Art, music, French, Spanish, Latin, Chinese, science, social studies, technology, and physical education are integral parts of the program. Tuition: $24,430–$25,300. Financial Aid: $1,500,000. Mimi Mulligan is Director of Admission and Enrollment Management; Richard T. Ewing, Jr., is Head of School.

The Primary Day School 1944

7300 River Road, Bethesda, MD 20817
Tel. 301-365-4355; Fax 301-469-8611
Web Site www.theprimarydayschool.org
E-mail j.mccaffery@theprimarydayschool.org

The Primary Day School's rich and varied curriculum is designed to cultivate a love of learning and a strong academic and personal foundation in every child. Enrolling up to 155 girls and boys in Pre-Kindergarten through Second Grade, students develop strong fundamental skills, citizenship, and an appreciation for the arts. Core subjects of language arts, math, science, and social studies are enriched by music, art, technology, creative writing, physical education, and the school library. The Phonovisual Method, a multisensory phonetic system that promotes comprehension and fluency, is the basis of Primary Day's language arts. Weekly assemblies and class performances provide experience and poise in public speaking. Tuition: $15,500–$17,300. Financial aid is available. Julie A. McCaffery is Director of Admission; Louise K. Plumb is Head of School.

Queen Anne School 1964

14111 Oak Grove Road, Upper Marlboro, MD 20774
Tel. 301-249-5000; Admissions Ext. 305; Fax 301-249-3838
Web Site www.queenanne.org; E-mail cpochet@queenanne.org

QUEEN ANNE SCHOOL

A college preparatory, coeducational day school enrolling 156 students in Grades 6–12, Queen Anne is located on 60 acres between Washington and Annapolis. Affiliated with St. Barnabas' Episcopal Church, the School offers a demanding, comprehensive program, including Advanced Placement courses in all disciplines, community outreach, and a biology of the Chesapeake Bay program. Fine arts, a full athletic program, and other electives enhance the curriculum. Classes are small, and students are prepared to be critical thinkers and mature individuals. Tuition: $17,500–$18,500. Before- and after-care, transportation, and need-based financial aid are available. Courtney Pochet is Director of Admissions; Christiana Holyer is Acting Head of School. *Middle States Association.*

Radcliffe Creek School 1995

201 Talbot Boulevard, Chestertown, MD 21620
Tel. 410-778-8150; Fax 410-778-8176
Web Site www.radcliffecreekschool.org
E-mail ezierfuss@radcliffecreekschool.org

Radcliffe Creek School provides an ungraded, alternative education for learning-disabled youngsters of average to above-average intelligence. Enrolling 103 boys and girls from age 3 to 14, the School seeks to remediate weaknesses in reading, writing, spelling, and math while building on individual strengths to promote success. Quality, rather than quantity, of work is emphasized in a stimulating environment free of time constraints and competition. Certified teachers, innovative instruction, small classes, and multisensory, hands-on methods of learning benefit students and facilitate the return to traditional classrooms. Daily job teams and a unique program of behavior management encourage children to assume personal responsibility and integrity. Tuition: $6500–$24,000. Molly Judge is Head of School.

Roland Park Country School   1901

5204 Roland Avenue, Baltimore, MD 21210
Tel. 410-323-5500; Fax 410-323-2164
Web Site www.rpcs.org; E-mail admissions@rpcs.org

A college preparatory day school for 710 girls in K–12, RPCS offers comprehensive academic, arts, and athletic programs. The School seeks to aid the intellectual, aesthetic, physical, and moral development of its students. The Lower School academic program is designed to develop strong skills and foster a genuine love of learning. Middle School provides transition from concrete to abstract thinking and time to understand one's own learning style. Upper School offers core subjects as well as electives in art, music, theater, computer science, and public speaking. It also features AP courses in all disciplines and eight languages including Russian, Chinese, and Arabic. Strong college counseling, foreign exchanges, and numerous clubs are available. Upper School coordination with Gilman School offers the option of coeducational classes. RPCS has its own squash courts and a state-of-the-art Athletic Complex with a vegetative roof, indoor rowing tanks, and two synthetic turf fields. After-school activities and a summer camp are available. Tuition: $21,890. Financial Aid: $2,000,000. Peggy K. Wolf is Director of Admissions; Jean Waller Brune is Head of School.

St. Andrew's Episcopal School   1978

Potomac Village Campus (Preschool–Grade 3): 10033 River Road,
* Potomac, MD 20854*
Postoak Campus (Grades 4–12): 8804 Postoak Road, Potomac,
* MD 20854*
Tel. 301-983-5200; Admission Ext. 236; Fax 301-983-4620
Web Site www.saes.org; E-mail admission@saes.org

St. Andrew's Episcopal School provides a comprehensive coeducational college preparatory program for day students in Preschool–Grade 12 in an inclusive environment that embodies the faith and perspective of the Episcopal Church. The School seeks a broadly diverse community to promote educational excellence. St. Andrew's programs are designed to serve students of varied interests and abilities capable of achievement in a challenging academic environment. To create such an environment, St. Andrew's supports a dedicated faculty and administration who respect and appreciate students. St. Andrew's challenges and supports all students in a balanced program to nurture their academic, artistic, athletic, and spiritual growth. Because it values the benefits of community, the School encourages students to lead lives of responsibility to each other and to the larger community.

St. Andrew's is a nonprofit institution governed by a 25-member Board of Trustees, including a representative of the Bishop of Washington. It is accredited by the Middle States

Association of Colleges and Schools and holds membership in the National Association of Independent Schools and other organizations. The Parents Association promotes, supports, and enhances the total program.

THE CAMPUS. The Lower School campus, nestled in the heart of Potomac Village, features newly renovated classrooms, a science lab, art studio, library, assembly room, extended day classroom, two playgrounds, an athletic field, and blacktop.

ST. ANDREW'S EPISCOPAL SCHOOL

Situated in a residential neighborhood, the 19.2-acre Postoak Road campus features state-of-the-art classrooms, science and technology laboratories, a two-story library, a media center, a darkroom, and theater/assembly hall. The sports program is supported by two synthetic turf athletic fields, baseball and softball diamonds, four tennis courts, a weight-training room, girls' and boys' locker rooms, dance studio and wrestling room, a gymnasium, and an athletic medicine training room.

THE FACULTY. Robert Kosasky (Yale, B.A.; Columbia, M.A.) was appointed the fourth Head of School of St. Andrew's in 2002.

ST. ANDREW'S EPISCOPAL SCHOOL

The 82 faculty and administrators who teach hold 77 baccalaureate degrees and 47 advanced degrees, including 5 doctorates, from such colleges and universities as Brown, Colgate, College of Wooster, Columbia, Cornell, Dartmouth, Dickinson, Duke, Northwestern, Princeton, Rhode Island School of

Design, Vanderbilt, Wesleyan, Yale, and the Universities of Maryland, Michigan, North Carolina (Chapel Hill), and Virginia.

A nurse and a certified athletic trainer are on duty full-time during school hours. Hospital facilities are approximately 6 miles from both campuses.

STUDENT BODY. In 2009–10, St. Andrew's enrolled 525 students in Preschool–Grade 12. The first fourth-grade class started in the fall of 2009; Grade 5 will begin in the fall of 2010. Students come from diverse racial, ethnic, religious, and socioeconomic backgrounds.

ACADEMIC PROGRAM. The School's calendar, from early September to early June, is divided into 12-week trimesters, with Thanksgiving, Christmas, and spring vacations and observances of national holidays. The school day begins between 8:25 and 8:45 A.M., with dismissal between 3:05 and 3:30 P.M., depending upon the age of the student. For 6th through 12th graders, the school day includes a morning meeting, followed by either seven 40-minute class periods or a modified block schedule and a lunch break.

ST. ANDREW'S EPISCOPAL SCHOOL

The Lower School (Preschool I–Grade 3) curriculum is developmentally appropriate, with attention to the differing needs and interests of individual children. Students benefit from a challenging, integrative approach to language arts, reading and phonics, creative writing, mathematics, science, social studies, and religion.

Language arts, reading, and mathematics meet daily each morning. Daily morning and lunchtime recesses provide ample time for play and socialization. Morning and closing meetings are part of the daily schedule, with Drop Everything and Read (D.E.A.R.) time incorporated several times a week, depending on grade level. Chapel is held in St. Francis Episcopal Church weekly for elementary students and biweekly for preschoolers. Religion classes are taught weekly in all grades. Art, music, science, computer education, language, library, and physical education classes meet one to three times a week. Students in Preschool I–Grade 3 study either French or Spanish each year.

The normal course load in Grades 6–12 is five academic courses in English, history, math, science, and languages. Parents receive written evaluations of their child's progress in each course at the midpoint and end of each trimester. Exceptional achievement is recognized on the Academic and Effort Honor Rolls.

To graduate, high school students must complete four years each of English, history, and physical education; three years of science and mathematics, including Algebra I–II or Algebra II/Trigonometry and Geometry, Geometry, and Trigonometry; two consecutive years of a language; eight trimesters of art; three trimesters of religion; and two trimesters of health. A senior research paper and 120 hours of community service are also required.

High school courses include English 9–12, Creative Writing, Critical, Media, and Cyber Literature in the 21st Century, Journalism; Art History, Economics; French I–IV, Latin I–IV, Spanish I–IV; Algebra I–II, Calculus, Geometry, Multivariable Calculus, Trigonometry; Service Learning 9, World Religions, Ethics, Philosophy of Religion; Biology, Chemistry, Physics I–II, Robotics; Ceramics, Drawing, Painting, Photography I–III, Photo-Journalism, 3-D Art, Video I–III, Guitar I–II, Musical Theater, Technical Theater I–II, Traveling Chorus, Orchestra I–III, Public Speaking, and Computer Graphics.

Advanced Placement courses are offered in all academic disciplines. Consortium courses are provided for juniors and seniors from St. Andrew's and other independent schools. Each seminar meets three times a week from 7:15 to 8:00 A.M.

All students in Grades 6–12 are assigned a faculty advisor with whom they meet several times a week. For students who experience academic difficulties, the School offers tutoring space and a "clearing house" service to connect parents and tutors. There are four academic deans in the Upper School who monitor course selection and academic progress for an entire grade through graduation.

In 2009, all 82 seniors entered college; 15 percent were admitted by early decision. Students are attending such institutions as Boston University, Bucknell, College of Charleston, Cornell, Dartmouth, Dickinson, Gettysburg, Hamilton, New York University, Northwestern, Rice, Tufts, Tulane, United States Naval Academy, Wake Forest, and the Universities of Maryland (College Park), Rochester, and St. Andrews (Scotland).

STUDENT ACTIVITIES. After-school activities in Preschool II–Grade 3 include tae kwon do, yoga, and golf, which are available for an additional fee. Students in the sixth through eighth grades have an activity period generally once a week during the school day. High school students participate in activities such as band, Black Student Alliance, Book Club, Bridge Club, chorus, dance, Debate Club, Diversity Club, drama, Gay-Straight Alliance, Improv Club, Jazz Band, Jewish Culture Club, Model UN, orchestra, Recycling Club, and Student Vestry. Clubs focusing on religion, women's issues, and service organizations are also offered, along with student-published literary magazines, newspapers, and an annual yearbook. The Student Council and Student Government Association enable students to participate in school government and policies.

ST. ANDREW'S EPISCOPAL SCHOOL

Athletics offered for girls and boys in Grades 7–12 include aikido, basketball, cross-country, dance, equestrian team, fitness, golf, lacrosse, soccer, tennis, track, volleyball, and wrestling. Boys may also participate in baseball, and girls play softball. St. Andrew's is a member of the Independent School League and the Mid-Atlantic Conference.

Lower School group community service activities are planned for students in Kindergarten–Grade 3. Middle School activities occur periodically throughout the year in small groups organized by grade level. Ninth graders participate in service learning during the school day as part of their trimester religion course. All students in Grades 10–11 must complete 20 hours of community service a year. During the senior year, students must select an approved project of at least 60 hours in which to participate during the final two weeks of school.

Field trips include visits to places in and around Washington and Baltimore, and athletic, recreational, class, and curricular-related trips are planned during the school year and summer. The Upper School also sponsors service learning opportunities and international and exchange trips to Dominica, Egypt, Honduras, and South Africa, among other countries.

ADMISSION AND COSTS. St. Andrew's seeks students who have demonstrated academic ability, intellectual curiosity, motivation, and a desire to contribute to the community. Admission decisions are based on the candidate's individual strengths and talents and his or her potential to be successful at St. Andrew's. The application and all supporting materials must be received by February 1. After that deadline, admission is granted as space is available.

In 2009–10, tuition is $5,750–$19,190 for Preschool–Grade 3, $22,900 for Grade 4, $29,975 for Grades 6–8, and $31,130 for Grades 9–12. Textbooks for students at the Postoak Road Campus are purchased online and cost approximately $400–$700 per year. Financial aid is based solely upon demonstrated financial need, and tuition insurance and payment plans are offered. Financial aid applications and other materials must be submitted to the School by December 15 for current financial aid recipients and by February 1 for new applicants.

Head of School: Robert Kosasky
Assistant Head of School: John Holden
Head of the Upper School: Joanne Beach
Head of the Middle School: Mark Segal
Upper School Dean of Students: Virginia Cobb
Middle School Dean of Students: Amanda Macomber
Head of the Lower School & Assistant Head of School: Patricia
 Talbert Smith
Director of Admission & Financial Aid: Julie Jameson
Director of Lower School Admission & Assistant Head of Lower School:
 Spring Swinehart
Director of College Counseling: Randy Tajan
Director of Development: Linda Kiser
Chief Financial Officer: Walter Manning
Chaplain: The Reverend Luther Zeigler
Director of Summer Programs: Christine Polyak
Director of Athletics: Al Hightower & Joan Kowalik

Saint James School 1842

17641 College Road, St. James, MD 21781
Tel. 301-733-9330; Fax 301-739-1310
Web Site www.stjames.edu; E-mail admissions@stjames.edu

Saint James, the oldest Episcopal boarding school in the United States based on the English model, was founded by Bishop William Whittingham in 1842. The School offers a challenging college preparatory curriculum to 235 young men and women in Grades 8–12, including 150 resident students from 16 states, 9 countries, and diverse religious, racial, ethnic, and socioeconomic backgrounds. Students of all faiths take part in the spiritual life of the community including theology and scripture studies, daily worship, and shared prayer. The academic program emphasizes the liberal arts, sciences, and humanities, with

Advanced Placement courses in the major disciplines. With an average enrollment of 12, students have personalized attention and support. Typically, all graduates go on to four year-colleges. Prefect and Honor Councils and Disciplinary Committee provide leadership experience, while required community service

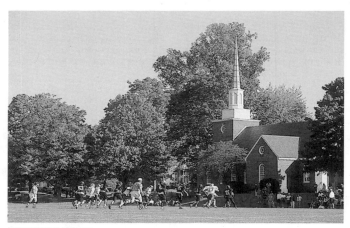

SAINT JAMES SCHOOL

develops responsibility and sensitivity to others. Drama, music, publications, tour guides, interscholastic sports, and a variety of interest clubs are among the extracurricular activities. Boarding Tuition: $34,600; Day Tuition: $22,900. Lawrence Jensen is Director of Admissions; the Reverend Dr. D. Stuart Dunnan is Headmaster. *Middle States Association.*

St. John's Parish Day School 1965

9130 Frederick Road, Ellicott City, MD 21042
Tel. 410-465-7644; Fax 410-465-7748
Web Site www.stjohnspds.org; E-mail jtolen@stjohnsec.org

Founded by St. John's Episcopal Church, this coeducational school provides a rigorous education in a spiritual environment for 375 boys and girls from many ethnic, religious, and cultural backgrounds in Early Childhood through Grade 5. The curriculum is designed to prepare children for success in middle and secondary school and beyond while instilling high standards of personal ethics. Core subjects are complemented by science, music, art, media, technology, Spanish, and physical education, taught by specialist teachers. All students take part in regular chapel services. St. John's has been recognized for its innovative environmental, diversity, and community service programs. It has also been designated a Maryland Green School for its recycling program as well as for the development of a schoolyard habitat that features a meadow, a bluebird trail, and an alphabet garden. Parental involvement is valued as a means of bringing the school community together in various celebrations and spirit-building activities. After-school enrichment includes garden club, chess, sports, Spanish, and tae kwon do. Tuition: $9000–$10,500. Financial Aid: $270,000. Jane Tolen is Admissions Coordinator; Stephen Harrison (Anderson University, B.A.; Princeton Seminary, M.Div.) is Headmaster.

St. Paul's School for Girls 1959

Falls Road & Seminary Avenue, Brooklandville, MD 21022
Tel. 410-823-6323; Admission 443-632-1046; Fax 410-828-7238
Web Site www.spsfg.org; E-mail shasler@spsfg.org

A college preparatory school in the Episcopal tradition, St. Paul's School for Girls enrolls 442 day students in Grades 5–12. The program combines academics, athletics, the arts, and the spiritual, with opportunities for coed studies with young men at adjoining St. Paul's School. Faculty teach girls "the way girls learn best." The Middle School curriculum centers on a team approach. The Upper School includes Advanced Placement and honors courses and a unique leadership program for young women. Technology is state-of-the-art, and technology tools such as laptops and tablets are routinely used in classrooms. Numerous clubs, community service outreach, and travel/study to Europe, Mexico, Australia, and Japan enhance the program. The School seeks to provide a secure, diverse community that challenges each student to strive for excellence. Tuition: $22,300. Financial Aid: $1,427,445. Susan Hasler is Director of Admission; Dr. Monica Gillespie is Head of School.

St. Timothy's School   1882

8400 Greenspring Avenue, Stevenson, MD 21153
Tel. 410-486-7400; Admission 410-486-7401; Fax 410-486-1167
Web Site www.stt.org; E-mail admis@stt.org

ST. TIMOTHY'S SCHOOL in Stevenson, Maryland, is a boarding and day school, affiliated with the Episcopal Church, enrolling young women in Grades 9–12. The School's rural setting is 15 minutes from downtown Baltimore and an hour north of Washington, D.C. It is easily reached by Interstate 95 and from the Thurgood Marshall Baltimore-Washington International Airport. Students and faculty make excellent use of the rich cultural, historical, and recreational resources of the two cities and their environment as an extension of classroom learning.

St. Timothy's School was founded in 1882 by sisters Sally and Polly Carter, who shared a vision of a rigorous educational environment in which bright young women could stretch and expand their intellectual capabilities, without limitations, for their own enrichment and the betterment of their world. During the 1970s, the School consolidated with Hannah More Academy, the first Episcopal school for girls in the country.

ST. TIMOTHY'S SCHOOL

St. Timothy's School seeks girls with energy, character, and high potential. Its mission is to build in its students the capability, confidence, and integrity they need to compete and contribute effectively and ethically throughout their lives. Challenging academics, based on the International Baccalaureate Diploma Program, are integrated with broad exposure to the arts, athletics, and service to the community. Girls live according to an Honor Code that has been developed and administered by students throughout the years.

Governed by a 25-member Board of Trustees, St. Timothy's School is accredited by the Middle States Association of Colleges and Schools and the Association of Independent Mary-

land Schools, and holds membership in the National Association of Independent Schools, the Association of Independent Maryland Schools, National Coalition of Girls' Schools, and the National Association of Episcopal Schools, among other organizations. An IB World School, St. Timothy's is also a member of the Council of International Schools.

THE CAMPUS. St. Timothy's 22 buildings include the Hannah More Arts Center, which houses a 350-seat theater, scenery and costume shops, a spacious dance studio, music practice rooms, and a gallery. The Art Barn holds facilities for two- and three-dimensional studies including design, photography, and ceramics. Fowler House, the academic building, has science and computer laboratories and the 22,000-volume Ella R. Watkins Library containing computerized catalog search capabilities. Each classroom is equipped with an on-line computer. Girls live two or three to a room in a stately 1930s mansion and a more contemporary residence, each containing living rooms, faculty apartments, study areas, and computer labs. A health center, chapel, and new Student Life Center featuring the school bookstore, additional food options, a study area, and a student lounge, are also on campus.

ST. TIMOTHY'S SCHOOL

Athletic facilities include six all-weather tennis courts, an outdoor swimming pool, a gymnasium, and cross-country, hiking, and running trails. A state-of-the-art athletic complex (2003) houses basketball courts, locker rooms, a fitness center, and a training room. The School's extensive riding program, which involves students in interschool horse shows, is facilitated by indoor and outdoor riding rings, five fenced fields, and a 24-stall barn.

THE FACULTY. Randy S. Stevens, appointed Head of School in 2003, earned a B.A. from the University of South Carolina and a Master of Public Administration from Cornell University.

There are 38 full-time and 7 part-time members of the faculty and administration. Twenty faculty members have ten or more years' teaching experience; 47 percent of the faculty and administration hold advanced degrees; and 66 percent live on campus. They have graduated from colleges and universities such as Bowdoin, Brown, Colby, Columbia, Cornell, Dartmouth, Drake University, George Washington, Goucher, Harvard, Hobart and William Smith, Johns Hopkins, Lafayette, Maryland Institute College of Art, Middlebury, Princeton, Towson, Vassar, Washington College, Washington University in St. Louis, Williams, Yale, and the Universities of California, Maryland, Massachusetts, North Carolina, Pennsylvania, South Carolina, Virginia, and Wisconsin.

STUDENT BODY. In 2009–10, St. Timothy's School enrolled 160 young women, 75 percent boarding and 25 percent day students, in Grades 9–12. They come from throughout the United States and from 17 countries, representing a wide diversity of religious, ethnic, and racial heritages.

ACADEMIC PROGRAM. St. Timothy's curriculum is based on the International Baccalaureate Program, which is one of the most rigorous and advanced curricula for preparing students for the varied challenges they will confront throughout their lives. St. Timothy's offers a rich and highly individualized program with extensive resources in athletics, the arts, clubs, world affairs, and community service that capitalize on the talents and strengths of each student.

Each girl has an advisor who keeps track of her academic progress and personal growth and maintains a liaison with her parents. With a 5:1 student-teacher ratio, classes enroll, on average, 12 girls, ensuring each student individual attention and encouraging full participation in the learning process.

Juniors and seniors spend two years studying the IB curriculum, culminating in both internal and external exams for the IB diploma. IB course work in English draws on American and European literature, focusing on the different genres of fiction, non-fiction, poetry, and drama, including Shakespeare. In science, students may undertake comprehensive studies in their choice of biology, chemistry, or physics over a two-year period. Mathematics are offered at three ability levels ranging from practical applications to advanced college-level courses. World and European History provides a survey of world events in the 20th century with an emphasis on historiography and analysis of contemporary issues. The Foreign Language component intensifies French, Latin, Mandarin, or Spanish language studies in the context of history, culture, and daily living. IB Options enable students to round out their schedule with a choice of courses in visual arts, theater arts, economics, geography, or a second foreign language or science. The Theory of Knowledge course involves girls in the pursuit of knowledge and truth utilizing their critical thinking and research skills.

ST. TIMOTHY'S SCHOOL

College advising begins early and involves both the student and her parents. One hundred percent of St. Timothy's School girls attend college. In the last three years, graduates have been accepted at American University, Bates, Bennington, Boston University, Bowdoin, Brown, Carnegie Mellon, Columbia, Connecticut College, Cornell, Drexel, Duke, Fashion Institute of Technology, Georgetown, Goucher, Hamilton, Johns Hopkins, Lafayette, New York University, Peabody Conservatory, Pennsylvania State, Princeton, Rutgers, Roanoke, Skidmore, Smith, Stanford, Swarthmore, Syracuse, Tufts, Vanderbilt, Washington and Lee, Washington University in St. Louis, Wellesley, Wesleyan, Williams, and the Universities of Chicago, Massachusetts, Pennsylvania, and Virginia, and various other institutions.

STUDENT ACTIVITIES. St. Timothy's School provides a wide range of extracurricular opportunities that meet a variety of interests and abilities, involving students in leadership, community service, and social and athletic activities.

Varsity and junior varsity teams are formed in basketball, ice hockey, volleyball, squash, field hockey, lacrosse, indoor soccer, softball, and tennis; badminton, golf, and dance are also available. The riding program, headed by a professional horsewoman, is an integral component of the School's athletic offerings. Girls take part in competitive horse shows, fox hunting, combined training events, dressage, and trail and recreational riding.

On-campus organizations include Amnesty International, Challenge 20/20, Choir, Bell Choir, two a cappella singing groups, literary magazine, yearbook, Tour Guides, Chapel Club, Current Events, Model UN, Environmental Awareness, International Club, Equestrian, Shalom, and Social Services Clubs.

St. Timothy's School enjoys many time-honored traditions, among them the hard-fought Brownie-Spider basketball game that has been played just before Thanksgiving for over 100 years.

ADMISSION AND COSTS. St. Timothy's School welcomes girls who have high personal standards, leadership potential, and a good academic record. Candidates submit an application along with an essay. Acceptance is based on a personal interview, results of either the Secondary School Admissions Test or the Independent School Entrance Examination, personal recommendations from the student's math and English teachers and principal or advisor, a parent's statement, the student's transcript, a graded essay, and the completed application. The application fee is $50.

In 2009–10, boarding tuition is $43,000; day tuition is $25,000; the ESL program is $44,500. Additional expenses include transportation, a $675 social activities fee, $400–$600 for books and academic supplies, approximately $250 for the required school uniform and $900–$2600 for the optional Riding Program. Financial aid is awarded to more than 40 percent of the student body.

Head of School: Randy S. Stevens
Academic Dean: John Bradfield
Dean of Students: Jackie Geter-Hunter
Associate Head for Enrollment Management: Deborah Haskins
Associate Director of Admission: Gina B. Finn
Assistant Director of Admission: Tracy Olsen '05
Director of College Counseling: Anne R. Mickle
Director of Development & Alumnae Relations: Jennifer A. Summers
CFO & Business Manager: Anne Esposito
Director of Athletics: Kara Carlin

Severn School   1914

Water Street, Severna Park, MD 21146
Tel. 410-647-7700; Admissions 410-647-7701, Ext. 267
Fax 410-544-9451
Web Site www.severnschool.com; E-mail admissions@severnschool.com

Severn School, founded in 1914, is a coeducational day school for Grades 6–12, located 6 miles from Annapolis. Severn believes in educating the whole person in a student-centered school community and challenges its students to pursue excellence in character, conduct, and scholarship. The current enrollment is 601 students. Severn offers foreign languages, mathematics, science, English, history, fine and performing arts, Advanced Placement and honors courses, and independent study. Severn also has a Learning Resource Center available for all grades and has introduced a Fellows Program for rising seniors. There are over 25 sports teams, including a National Championship sailing team, and 35 clubs and activities for student participation. Severn's summer program includes academic study, computer training, SAT prep, a day camp, and chess and sports camps. Tuition: $21,100. Financial Aid: $1,000,000. Molly M. Green '83 is Director of Advancement; Douglas H. Lagarde (College of William and Mary, A.B.; Harvard University, M.Ed.) was named Headmaster in 2006. *Middle States Association.*

Stone Ridge School of the Sacred Heart   1923

9101 Rockville Pike, Bethesda, MD 20814
Tel. 301-657-4322; Admissions Ext. 321; Fax 301-657-4393
Web Site www.stoneridgeschool.org
E-mail admissions@stoneridgeschool.org

As one of the worldwide Network of Sacred Heart Schools, Stone Ridge commits itself to the mutual goals shared by its members: to educate toward an active faith, to respect intellectual values, to acquire social awareness, and to build community and personal growth. The School enrolls 650 girls in Pre-Kindergarten–Grade 12, with boys in Pre-Kindergarten and Kindergarten only. Stone Ridge offers a challenging, college preparatory curriculum grounded in the liberal arts, sciences, and humanities. State-of-the-art technology is integrated across the disciplines. Religious studies are required of students of all faiths, while service out-reach and inclusive liturgies develop spirituality and ethical values. In addition to core subjects, there are AP classes in all departments. Girls take part in a four-year social action program that assists the needy. Students also participate in exchange programs with other Sacred Heart schools in the U.S., Europe, and Australia. Leadership groups, publications, the arts, and sports are among the activities. A coed summer program offers academics and sports. Tuition: $11,305–$22,420. Financial aid is available. Lori D. Backlund is Director of Admission; Catherine Ronan Karrels '86 is Head of School.

Washington Waldorf School   1969

4800 Sangamore Road, Bethesda, MD 20816
Tel. 301-229-6107; Admissions Ext. 154; Fax 301-229-9379
Web Site www.washingtonwaldorf.org
E-mail llawson@washingtonwaldorf.org

One of more than 900 Waldorf (Rudolf Steiner) schools worldwide, this coeducational, nonsectarian school enrolls 261 students in Preschool–Grade 12. Students of various social, religious, and economic backgrounds comprise Washington Waldorf's diverse makeup. The rich curriculum and innovative instructional methods provide an education that addresses the needs of the whole child, working to develop clarity of thought, balance in feeling, and initiative in action. This academic, artistic, and practical program provides a continuum of education, in preparation for college, from the earliest grades through high school graduation. Interscholastic sports are offered for boys and girls. Tuition: $6800–$21,300. Lezlie Lawson is Enrollment Director; Natalie R. Adams is Faculty Chair. *Middle States Association.*

The Woods Academy   1975

6801 Greentree Road, Bethesda, MD 20817
Tel. 301-365-3080; Admissions Ext. 130; Fax 301-469-6439
Web Site www.woodsacademy.org
E-mail admissions@woodsacademy.org

A Catholic, coeducational day school enrolling 300 students from many faiths and nationalities, The Woods Academy has celebrated the education of mind, body, and spirit for over two decades. A Woods education begins in Montessori Preschool and concludes as graduating eighth-graders choose from a wide range of selective secondary schools. The academic program is enhanced by daily French or Spanish, technology, Chicago Math, hands-on laboratory science, computer labs, and a 15,000-volume library. Activities include student government, sports, publications, theater arts, and community service. Extended care is offered. Tuition: $11,500–$18,100. Financial Aid: $80,000. Barbara B. Snyder is Director of Admission; Mary C. Worch (Trinity, B.A., M.A.) is Head of School. *Middle States Association.*

ST. TIMOTHY'S SCHOOL.

MASSACHUSETTS

Austin Preparatory School   1961

101 Willow Street, Reading, MA 01867
Tel. 781-944-4900; Admissions Ext. 17; Fax 781-942-0918
Web Site www.austinprepschool.org
E-mail kdriscoll@austinprepschool.org

Founded by the Augustinian Friars, Austin Prep is a coed, Catholic, independent day school, serving 725 students in Grades 6–12 from 55 communities. Austin offers a rigorous academic program, designed to equip students for success in higher education and in all aspects of life. The daily academic schedule consists of three 90-minute classes. In the Augustinian tradition of "one mind, one heart, intent upon God," the Campus Ministry program seeks to inspire spiritual growth in students of all faiths. The curriculum, though challenging, accommodates students' varied academic and skill levels, at both college prep and honors levels, including 17 Advanced Placement offerings. There are 50 student clubs and organizations. The Fr. Smith Library has a current circulation of 50,000 volumes and periodicals, as well as 30 desktop computers for research use. The science division was renovated completely in 2007. There are 40 sports teams at middle school, sub-varsity, and varsity levels. Tuition: $13,700. Scholarships, financial aid, and sibling discounts are available. Kevin J. Driscoll is Director of Admission and Financial Aid; Paul J. Moran is Head of School. *New England Association.*

Bancroft School   1900

110 Shore Drive, Worcester, MA 01605
Tel. 508-853-2640; Admission Ext. 206; Fax 508-853-7824
Web Site www.bancroftschool.org; E-mail scranford@bancroftschool.org

Bancroft School is a coeducational, college preparatory day school enrolling 575 students in Kindergarten–Grade 12. Attracting families from nearly 60 Worcester-area cities and towns, Bancroft's mission is to provide a comprehensive, caring, and creative curricular and extracurricular program that fosters an experience of excellence for each student. Inspired students, a dedicated faculty, and engaged families thrive in Bancroft's diverse, safe, and supportive environment. Students have the opportunity to learn to embrace confidently and responsibly the moral and ethical challenges of being lifelong learners, teachers of others, and citizens of an increasingly complex global community. Tuition & Books: $13,000–$23,800. Financial Aid: $1,500,000. Susan Cranford is Director of Admission and Financial Aid; Scott R. Reisinger was appointed Headmaster in 1999. *New England Association.*

Belmont Day School   1927

55 Day School Lane, Belmont, MA 02478
Tel. 617-484-3078; Admissions Ext. 226; Fax 617-489-1942
Web Site www.belmontday.org; E-mail dbrissenden@belmontday.org

From its beginnings in 1927, Belmont Day School has been a place where faculty and parents work together to provide a rich and challenging educational program based on the core values of respect, responsibility, honesty, caring, joy, and excellence. Located just a few minutes from Boston, Belmont Day School is a coeducational middle and elementary school on 11 acres of land encompassing woods, fields, and a state-of-the-art facility. The School offers a strong academic program balanced with arts, athletics, technology, and social competency skills instruction to 275 students in Pre-Kindergarten to Grade 8. After-school, extended-day, vacation, and summer session programs are offered. Financial aid is available to qualified candidates.

Tuition: $18,100–$28,790. Deborah Brissenden is Director of Admissions; Lenesa Leana (Oberlin College, A.B.; University of Missouri, M.A.) is Head.

Belmont Hill School   1923

350 Prospect Street, Belmont, MA 02478-2662
Tel. 617-484-4410; Admissions Ext. 220; Fax 617-484-4688
Web Site www.belmonthill.org; E-mail grant@belmonthill.org

Belmont Hill School is a day and five-day boarding school enrolling 425 boys in Grades 7–12. In its effort to develop young men of character, the School seeks to combine a rigorous curriculum featuring traditional subjects taught by innovative faculty, with an outstanding art department and an extensive athletic program. Activities, many of which are coordinated with The Winsor School for Girls, include glee club, drama, debate, Student Council, and literary publications. A six-week, coeducational summer program is offered. Five-day Boarding Tuition: $38,850; Day Tuition: $32,700. Financial Aid: $2,800,000. Michael R. Grant is Director of Admission; Richard I. Melvoin (Harvard, A.B.; University of Michigan, M.A., Ph.D.) is Head of School. *New England Association.*

Boston University Academy   1993

One University Road, Boston, MA 02215
Tel. 617-353-9000; Fax 617-353-8999
Web Site www.buacademy.org; E-mail admissions@buacademy.org

Boston University Academy seeks to provide an exceptional education for students with genuine intellectual curiosity, strong academic abilities, and diverse interests. A coeducational day school of 150 students, the Academy is located on the Boston University campus and offers highly motivated students in Grades 9–12 an "unparalleled preparation for the college experience." Engaging with dedicated teachers in a caring community, students first immerse themselves in a classically based core curriculum and then continue their intellectual interests through course work at Boston University. Students take as many as two University classes a semester in Grade 11 and up to four in Grade 12. To graduate, all students much complete an independently researched senior thesis under the guidance of a university professor as well as 20 hours of community service each year. Activities include Art Club, competitive athletic teams, Chamber Orchestra, Environment Club, Jazz Band, Literary Magazine, Model UN, robotics and science teams, and Student Council. Tuition & Fees: $30,123. Financial aid is awarded to 33 percent of families. Paige Brewster is Director of Admission and Financial Aid; James Berkman (Harvard, A.B., J.D.; Oxford, M.A.) is Head of School.

Brimmer and May School   1939

69 Middlesex Road, Chestnut Hill, MA 02467
Tel. 617-566-7462; Admissions 617-738-8695; Fax 617-734-5147
Web Site www.brimmer.org; E-mail admissions@brimmer.org

Brimmer and May School, founded in 1880, is a coeducational, independent day school serving students from 50 communities in the Greater Boston area and from 10 world nations. With an enrollment of 395 students in Pre-Kindergarten–Grade 12, the School is celebrating its 130th year. Located 3 miles west of Boston, the School is an inclusive, caring community of learners committed to maintaining rigorous academic standards while implementing innovative educational ideas. The objective is to prepare students to be committed participants in a diverse and changing world; therefore, Brimmer and May challenges them to use their talents and abilities within and beyond the school community. Strong academic programs, including 11 AP courses, an Honors Program, and Mandarin in the Upper School, computer technology, creative arts, and Middle and

Upper school sports teams, are emphasized. Extended care is offered for Lower School students. Bus service is available from Boston. Tuition: $20,100–$33,200. Financial Aid: $2,110,000. Barbara Shoolman is Director of Admissions; Anne C. Reenstierna is Headmistress. *New England Association.*

Brooks School   1926

1160 Great Pond Road, North Andover, MA 01845-1298
Tel. 978-686-6101; Admission 978-725-6272; Fax 978-725-6298
Web Site www.brooksschool.org; E-mail admission@brooksschool.org

Brooks School provides a coeducational, college preparatory program for 360 students on a 250-acre campus overlooking Lake Cochichewick. Small classes allow students to work closely with teachers, fostering a relationship that is at the core of the warm, close-knit community. With a challenging academic curriculum that includes 19 Advanced Placement courses, Brooks also offers opportunities to study abroad in Europe and Africa. A unique summer science program places juniors in labs at MIT and Harvard and on the coast of Canada in Labrador. On the stage and in the gallery, visual and performing arts are an integral part of school life, while in the athletic fields, numerous teams have won New England or league championships in recent years. Boarding Tuition: $44,370; Day Tuition: $33,060. Financial Aid: $2,640,000. Judy Beams is Director of Admission; John Packard is Headmaster. *New England Association.*

Brookwood School   1956

Brookwood Road, Manchester, MA 01944
Tel. 978-526-4500; Admissions Ext. 6203; Fax 978-526-9303
Web Site www.brookwood.edu; E-mail admissions@brookwood.edu

Brookwood, a coeducational day school enrolling 395 students in Prekindergarten–Grade 8, stands on two foundation stones: a demanding program of academics, athletics, and arts and a commitment to sociomoral and affective education designed to foster self-esteem, self-discipline, respect for others, and an appreciation of both competition and cooperation. Team sports, community service, student publications, field trips, multicultural assembly programs, and student government supplement the curriculum. There are before-school and after-school REACH programs. Tuition: $15,345–$24,895. Financial Aid: $1,148,000. Barbara W. DiGuiseppe is Admissions Director; John C. Peterman (Wittenberg, B.A.; Loyola University [Chicago], M.Ed.) was appointed Headmaster in 1992.

Cambridge Friends School   1961

5 Cadbury Road, Cambridge, MA 02140
Tel. 617-354-3880; Admission Ext. 144; Fax 617-876-1815
Web Site www.cfsmass.org

Cambridge Friends is a Quaker coeducational day school serving 215 students in Pre-Kindergarten–Grade 8. Established by the Friends Meeting at Cambridge, it has a socioeconomically, racially, and culturally diverse student body with a range of family structures. Guided by Quaker principles, Cambridge Friends School engages students in meaningful academic learning within a caring community strongly committed to social justice. The curriculum is designed to develop comprehensive literacy and to stimulate intellectual integrity and love of learning in all students. Cambridge Friends School provides a nurturing setting for academic, social, and spiritual development. The rigorous learning environment teaches children how to think critically with competency and confidence. Teachers help students develop a commitment to truthfulness and personal integrity, with the skills to solve problems and do so as members of a global community. Tuition: $17,500–$23,900. Tuition Assistance: $905,050. Sarah M. Turner is Admission Director; Peter Sommer is Head of School.

Cape Cod Academy   1976

50 Osterville-West Barnstable Road, Osterville, MA 02655
Tel. 508-428-5400; Admissions Ext. 216; Fax 508-428-0701
Web Site www.capecodacademy.org
E-mail admissions@capecodacademy.org

Cape Cod Academy, a coeducational college preparatory school serving 335 day students in Kindergarten–Grade 12, offers a challenging education that emphasizes the liberal arts and sciences, underscored by the values of honesty, respect, and compassion. Small classes and an 8:1 student-teacher ratio provide personal support and encouragement from faculty. Interscholastic athletics, drama, chorus, music, and outdoor club are among the activities. A new Science Building houses six classroom/labs, project and conference rooms, a 65-seat auditorium, and an atrium with a Foucault pendulum. Tuition: $18,320–$22,020. Financial aid is available. Steve DiPaolo is Director of Admissions; Clark Daggett (Johns Hopkins, B.A.; Drew University, M.Litt.) is Head of School. *New England Association.*

The Carroll School   1967

25 Baker Bridge Road, Lincoln, MA 01773
Tel. 781-259-8342; Admissions Ext. 3023; Fax 781-259-8852
Web Site www.carrollschool.org; E-mail admissions@carrollschool.org

Encompassing Grades 1–8, The Carroll School provides education for 300 bright boys and girls with language-based learning differences. With only 6–8 children per class, qualified specialist instructors and tutors use proven teaching methods, specific strategies, and remedial support services to develop students' maximum potential and equip them for success in mainstream schools. Guest speakers and diverse enrichment activities, including Bounders, Carroll's modified version of Outward Bound, enhance classroom instruction. Extended-day activities and a summer program are offered. Tuition: $36,285. Lesley Nesbitt is Director of Admission and Transition; Stephen Wilkins is Head of School. *New England Association.*

Charles River School   1911

6 Old Meadow Road, Box 339, Dover, MA 02030
Tel. 508-785-0068; Admissions 508-785-8213; Fax 508-785-8290
Web Site www.charlesriverschool.org
E-mail mearley@charlesriverschool.org

Charles River School, enrolling 216 children in Pre-Kindergarten–Grade 8, has a strong commitment to a balance of academic, creative, physical, and social growth within a progressive school environment that celebrates differences. The program engages children in active learning and encourages them to explore, assume responsibility, and gain self-awareness and respect for others. The interdisciplinary curriculum emphasizes critical thinking, writing, reading, and math skills as well as science, social studies, computer, world language and culture, art, music, and physical education. After-school sports and extended-day programs are offered. Tuition: $19,635–$28,875. Financial Aid: $787,500. Marion L. Earley is Director of Admissions; Catherine H. Gately (Boston University, B.A., M.Ed.) is Head.

The Chestnut Hill School   1860

428 Hammond Street, Chestnut Hill, MA 02467
Tel. 617-566-4394; Fax 617-738-6602
Web Site www.tchs.org; E-mail admissions@tchs.org

The Chestnut Hill School, a coeducational day school located in a residential section of Newton, encompasses a preschool program for ages 3–4, an all-day Kindergarten, and Grades 1 to 6. Two hundred seventy-five children are enrolled, with two sections at each grade level. Because of the comparatively small size and the favorable student-teacher ratio, Chestnut Hill is able to offer a rigorous academic program that embraces diversity and promotes community. Special subjects are art, computers, library, music, physical education, science, Spanish, and woodworking. Before- and after-school programs are optional. Tuition: $19,500–$27,500. Financial aid is available. Wendy W. Borosavage is Director of Admission; Steven Tobolsky (Princeton, A.B.; Columbia University Teachers College, M.A., Ph.D.) is Head.

Commonwealth School   1957

151 Commonwealth Avenue, Boston, MA 02116
Tel. 617-266-7525; Fax 617-266-5769
Web Site www.commschool.org; E-mail admissions@commschool.org

COMMONWEALTH SCHOOL in Boston, Massachusetts, is a day school enrolling boys and girls in Grades 9–12. The School is in the Back Bay area of Boston and is served by city and commuter buses and trains.

The School was founded in 1957 by Charles Merrill, who was Headmaster until his retirement in 1981. Commonwealth aims to give its students the ability to write forceful and effective English; a historical perspective on human nature and human affairs; well-grounded proficiency in mathematics and science; wide experience in literature and the art of reading; mastery of at least one foreign language; a rich field for creativity in the arts; and vigorous training in and enthusiasm for athletic endeavor.

COMMONWEALTH SCHOOL

The School is a nonprofit organization whose 31-member Board of Trustees includes faculty and alumni/ae members and nonvoting student and faculty representatives. The endowment includes approximately $10,500,000 in productive funds.

Commonwealth is accredited by the New England Association of Schools and Colleges and is a member of the National Association of Independent Schools and other organizations.

THE CAMPUS. Commonwealth's location in the heart of Boston, two blocks from the Boston Public Library and a short distance from the Museum of Fine Arts, encourages students to take advantage of the city's resources. Two adjoining 19th-century townhouses accommodate classrooms; library; laboratories; art, photography, and ceramics studios; a darkroom; lunchroom/gymnasium; student lounge; and offices. The School uses nearby athletic facilities for squash, basketball, fencing, sailing, yoga, and dance.

THE FACULTY. William D. Wharton (Brown, B.A., M.A.) was appointed Headmaster in 2000. Since joining the Commonwealth faculty in 1985, Mr. Wharton has taught history, Latin, Greek, ancient philosophy, and world religions; he has also served as Faculty Trustee, College Advisor, Acting Head, and Director of Admissions. He has received grants from the Council for Basic Education and was a recipient of a Teacher-Scholar Grant from the National Endowment for the Humanities.

COMMONWEALTH SCHOOL

There are 30 full-time teachers and administrators who teach, 13 men and 17 women. They hold 33 baccalaureate, 22 master's degrees, and 15 doctorates from Barnard, Boston College, Boston University, Brown, Federal Institute of Technology (Switzerland), Harvard, Johns Hopkins, Massachusetts Institute of Technology, McGill, Mount Holyoke, New York University, Oklahoma State, Pitzer, Princeton, Radcliffe, Stanford, Swarthmore, Tufts, Wesleyan, Williams, Yale, and the Universities of California (Berkeley), Cambridge (England), Kentucky, Massachusetts, Minnesota, Oxford (England), Paris, and Washington. There are also 6 part-time instructors who teach history, theater, ceramics, dance, jazz music, English, health, and photography and printmaking. Four of the 6 hold master's degrees; 2 hold doctorates.

Among the benefits for full-time faculty are health, dental, disability, and life insurance; a retirement plan; sabbaticals; professional development grants; tuition remission at Commonwealth for faculty children; and partial reimbursement for study undertaken to improve professional skills.

There are always several faculty members at Commonwealth who are trained in first aid; several hospitals are nearby.

STUDENT BODY. In 2009–10, Commonwealth enrolled 151 boys and girls as follows: 35 in Grade 9, 41 in Grade 10, 38 in Grade 11, and 37 in Grade 12. Most students come from Boston and surrounding communities.

ACADEMIC PROGRAM. The school year runs from early September to early June. There are two-week vacations in December and March and several long weekends. The average class size is 12 students. Grades, teachers' comments, and advisers' letters are sent to parents three times per year; for freshmen and for students in academic difficulty, a fourth grading period is observed.

The school day is divided into seven 40-minute periods. Full-credit courses meet four times a week and half-credit courses two to three times a week. On average, students carry five academic credits and two art credits. Free periods are intended for study. One-on-one conferences with teachers are a regular part of every student's experience. Additional tutorial help is available for an extra fee.

Students must complete a minimum of 16 academic credits for graduation, including four years of English, three of mathematics, three of science, three of foreign language, and three of history, one of which must be American history. Additional requirements each year include one course in the arts and participation in two of the three sports seasons. Freshmen and seniors also take half-credit courses with the Headmaster in Language and Ethics. Ninth-graders enroll in a City of Boston course for one term and health and community workshops for another. All students must perform 70 hours of community service before the beginning of the junior year.

Once a week, the entire School meets for an assembly, often with public figures. Each grade holds its own weekly meeting, and there is an all-school meeting each Tuesday.

Among the full-credit courses offered are English 9–12, English 12: Reasons for Writing; Ancient History, Medieval World History, United States History, Economics; Biology I–II, Chemistry I–II, Physics I–III; and Intermediate Algebra, Algebra II, Geometry, Calculus, Advanced Calculus, Applied Calculus, and Theoretical Calculus.

Courses that receive half credit include Short Story, Fiction Writing, Latin American History, Intellectual History, Empires and Nationalism, Art History; Film Analysis, Jazz Theory I–II, Music Theory I–III; Multivariable Calculus, Statistics; and Environmental Science, Introduction to Programming, Software Engineering, Advanced Topics in Computer Science, and Conceptual Foundations of Quantum Mechanics.

For art credits, students may choose from Acting I–IV, Advanced Dance, Chorus, Chorale, Orchestra, Jazz Ensemble, Beginning and Advanced Photography, Beginning and Advanced Printmaking, Ceramics, Drawing and Painting I, Advanced Drawing and Painting, Life Drawing I, Advanced Life Drawing, and Artists' Books.

City of Boston, Reading in Ethics, and Language and Ethics carry a quarter-credit each.

Twice a year, the entire School adjourns to a camp in southern Maine for four days. Students and teachers take hikes, prepare meals, perform skits, play games and sports, and hold activities and discussion sections on subjects ranging from maskmaking to mushroom identification to foreign policy.

During Project Week, younger students can become involved in activities outside the scope of regular schoolwork. Students participate in projects ranging from hospital work to teaching to working in a senator's Washington office. In the spring, seniors engage in similar projects that last for a whole month.

COMMONWEALTH SCHOOL

Commonwealth participates in three-week exchange programs with schools in France and Spain. Financial aid is provided for all students demonstrating need.

The 41 graduates of the Class of 2009 are attending such institutions as Amherst, Bard, Barnard, Brown, Carleton, Haverford, Johns Hopkins, Mount Holyoke, New York University, Pennsylvania State, Pratt Institute, Reed College, Rice, Smith, Stanford, and the University of Chicago.

STUDENT ACTIVITIES. All students help clean up after lunch and recycle trash as part of the jobs program. Two nonvoting student representatives are elected to the Board of Trustees each year. Students tutor other students, give assemblies, publish the yearbook and literary magazine, and plan dances and the prom. They join the debate team, science team, chess club, Improv Club, environmental club, and Model UN.

COMMONWEALTH SCHOOL

Commonwealth teams compete interscholastically in soccer, basketball, squash, sailing, fencing, and Ultimate Frisbee. All sports are open to all grades and to both boys and girls.

Traditional events include the Senior-Freshman Lunch, Ninth-Grade Cookout, New Parents' Evening, Parent-Teacher evenings for each grade, fall and spring Parents' Association meetings, Alumni/ae Reunions in various cities, Impromptu Day, Skate into Vacation, Fall Open House, Beach Day, two choral concerts, dance and jazz concerts, two theater productions, and a spring art show.

ADMISSION AND COSTS. Commonwealth seeks boys and girls of character and intelligence, without regard to race, color, religion, or national or ethnic origin, who are willing to work hard for a good education. Applicants are asked to submit recommendations, transcripts, and Secondary School Admission Test scores. An interview with the applicant and parents and a full-day visit by the applicant are also required. Applications for fall admission must be completed by January 1. The School accepts new students later in the year if places remain.

In 2009–10, tuition is $30,465, including lunches, with additional expenses of $1925. Scholarship aid of $1,100,000 was given to approximately 33 percent of the student body. A Technology Grant Program for students receiving financial aid helps in purchasing a computer. All grants are made on the basis of financial need.

Headmaster: William D. Wharton
Director of Admissions: Helene Carter
Director of Studies: Rebecca Jackman
Director of Student Life: Mary Kate Bluestein
College Counselor: Fern Nesson

Consulting Psychologist: Debbi Offner
Director of Athletics: Meagan Kane
Business Manager: Diane Morris
Director of Development: Janetta Stringfellow
Director of Communications: Tristan Davies

Dana Hall School   1881

45 Dana Road, Wellesley, MA 02482
Tel. 781-235-3010; Admission Ext. 2531; Fax 781-239-1383
Web Site www.danahall.org; E-mail admission@danahall.org

Dana Hall School, an all-girls college preparatory school, enrolls 487 students in Grades 6–12, including 134 boarders beginning in Grade 9. In addition to maintaining its traditional focus on academic preparation for college, Dana Hall encourages young women to develop intellectual curiosity, self-knowledge, and a sense of community in an atmosphere enriched by diversity among its students and faculty. Situated on 52 acres 12 miles west of Boston, Dana Hall's location offers the cultural advantages of the city as well as the benefits of a suburban campus. AP classes are offered in all core disciplines in addition to numerous electives and honors courses. Dynamic visual and performing arts supplement the core curriculum. The Writing Center, Math Lab, and Language Lab provide support for students outside the classroom. Students have several extracurricular options including athletics, musical ensembles, publications, student government, awareness clubs, and service clubs. In addition, The Dana Hall School of Music and the Riding Center enrich the program. Boarding Tuition: $46,700; Day Tuition: $35,340. Financial Aid: $2,800,000. Wendy Sibert Secor is Director of Admission; Caroline Erisman was appointed Head of School in 2008. *New England Association.*

Dedham Country Day School   1903

90 Sandy Valley Road, Dedham, MA 02026
Tel. 781-329-0850; Fax 781-329-0551
Web Site www.dedhamcountryday.org; E-mail etretter@dcds.net

Dedham Country Day School enrolls 245 boys and girls in Pre-Kindergarten–Grade 8. With close teacher-student rapport and an emphasis on excellence in traditional academics, the School seeks to develop independent thinking and personal responsibility. Art, music, drama, shop, and physical education, including team sports for upper grades, are offered at all levels. Spanish begins in Grade 4, Latin in Grade 6. Computer instruction is offered in all grades. Extended Day and summer camp are available. All-inclusive Fees: $19,620–$29,625. Financial aid is available. Ellen Tretter is Director of Admissions; Nicholas S. Thacher (Yale University, A.B.; Balliol College [Oxford], M.Phil.) was appointed Head in 2005.

Derby Academy   1784

56 Burditt Avenue, Hingham, MA 02043
Tel. 781-749-0746; Admission Ext. 46; Fax 781-740-2542
Web Site www.derbyacademy.org; E-mail admissions@derbyacademy.org

Founded in 1784 to provide equal education for girls and boys, Derby Academy enrolls 336 students, ages 4–14, in Prekindergarten–Grade 8. The school's mission is to bring together motivated students, talented faculty, and a challenging program for a well-balanced education. The curriculum is designed to prepare students for the rigors of competitive secondary schools and allow them to develop individual strengths in the arts and

athletics. Summer offerings include The Young Explorers Club for ages 4–6, a creative arts camp for ages 7–14, and several sports camps. Tuition: $17,750–$25,610 (all-inclusive). Financial Aid: $830,000. Jay K. Sadlon is Director of Admission; Andrea Archer (Warwick University, M.Sc.; Oxford University, M.A.) was appointed Head of School in 2007.

Dexter School   1926

20 Newton Street, Brookline, MA 02445-7498
Tel. 617-522-5544; Fax 617-522-8166
Web Site www.dexter.org; E-mail admissions@dexter.org

DEXTER SCHOOL

Enrolling 439 boys in Pre-Kindergarten through Grade 12, Dexter develops students' mental and physical abilities and helps them form good social, moral, and spiritual attitudes and habits. The School emphasizes academic skills and traditional subjects, including Latin in Grades 6–12, with additional classes in art, woodworking, and music. Outstanding science opportunities are offered in the Clay Center for Science and Technology, with advanced astronomy programs using research-grade telescopes and at the School's Briarwood Marine Science Center on Cape Cod. All students participate in athletics using the gym, an indoor pool, two indoor ice rinks, five playing fields, and a rowing facility on the Charles River. Interscholastic sports begin in Grade 7. There is a weekly chapel assembly, and community service is required in the upper school. All boys are taught public speaking in Kindergarten–Grade 12. Summer programs include academic enrichment, sci-tech, hockey, and day camps at Dexter and marine science and sailing at Briarwood. A sister school, Southfield, enrolls 370 girls on the same 36-acre campus. Tuition: $22,995–$35,695. Financial Aid: $4,153,000. William H. Southwick is Director of Admissions; William F. Phinney is Headmaster.

Eaglebrook School   1922

271 Pine Nook Road, Deerfield, MA 01342
Tel. 413-774-7411; Admissions 413-774-9111; Fax 413-774-9119
Web Site www.eaglebrook.org; E-mail admissions@eaglebrook.org

Eaglebrook School, enrolling 281 boarding and day boys from 28 states and 18 countries in Grades 6–9, aims to help each boy develop his innate talents, to improve the skills needed for the challenges of secondary school, and to establish values that will allow him to become a thoughtful, compassionate person. The core curriculum places equal emphasis on academic excellence and character. English, math, science, history, and foreign languages are enhanced by technology, music, drama, and visual arts. Boys take part in athletics, Student Council, Mountain Club, publications, and community service. English as a Second Language and a coeducational summer session are available. Boarding Tuition: $43,700; Day Tuition: $28,000. Theodore J. Low is Director of Admissions; Andrew C. Chase is Headmaster. *New England Association.*

The Eliot Montessori School   1971

Six Auburn Street, South Natick, MA 01760
Tel. 508-655-7333; Fax 508-655-3867
Web Site www.eliotmontessori.org
E-mail shiggins@eliotmontessori.org

The Eliot Montessori School enrolls 100 boys and girls as day students in Kindergarten–Grade 8 (ages 4.10–14). Montessori philosophy is the foundation of the School's approach and program. Specially trained teachers discern and nurture each child's strengths and talents. Eliot combines a child-centered approach and a personalized multidisciplinary curriculum to create an interactive learning environment that fosters independence, initiative, innovation, interaction, and individuality. Tuition: $18,050–$19,000. Susan Higgins is Director of Admissions; Denny Grubbs is Head of School.

Falmouth Academy   1977

7 Highfield Drive, Falmouth, MA 02540
Tel. 508-457-9696; Fax 508-457-4112
Web Site www.falmouthacademy.org
E-mail mearley@falmouthacademy.org

Falmouth Academy is a coeducational college preparatory school enrolling 210 day students in Grades 7–12. The rigorous core curriculum focuses on traditional liberal arts and sciences, with a strong emphasis on reading and writing in all subjects. Science classes utilize the resources of the nearby Woods Hole oceanographic and marine biology facilities, while the art-in-humanities program integrates the fine arts with course work across the disciplines. Students perform in drama and musical productions and engage in a wide range of activities from publications and landscaping to academic clubs and athletics. Tuition: $22,070. Financial Aid: $985,000. Michael Earley is Director of Admissions; David C. Faus was appointed Headmaster in 2005. *New England Association.*

Fayerweather Street School   1967

765 Concord Avenue, Cambridge, MA 02138
Tel. 617-876-4746; Admission Ext. 703; Fax 617-520-6700
Web Site www.fayerweather.org; E-mail info@fayerweather.org

Fayerweather Street School was founded in 1967 by parents and educators interested in exploring alternatives in schooling. They set out to provide child-centered education that respected each student's thinking while also valuing the role that families and communities play in their education. The School celebrates and promotes diversity in its student body of 205 boys and girls in Pre-Kindergarten–Grade 8. Mixed-age classes allow for a wider range of companions and learning partners. The curriculum is enriched by music, drama, library, Spanish, woodshop, art, resource room, physical education, field trips, and a weekly All-School Meeting. Extended care and vacation programs are optional. Tuition: $14,995–$24,000. Financial aid is available. Cynthia Bohrer is Admission Director; Edward Kuh is Head of School.

The Fenn School   1929

516 Monument Street, Concord, MA 01742-1894
Tel. 978-369-5800; Admission 978-318-3606; Fax 978-371-7520
Web Site www.fenn.org; E-mail ajolly@fenn.org

The Fenn School is a day school enrolling 308 boys in Grades 4–9. It seeks to offer sound academic training in an intellectually stimulating atmosphere tempered with an understanding of the emotional needs of the early adolescent. Students develop basic skills at the fourth- and fifth-grade levels and enter a fully departmentalized program in Grade 6. Spanish and Latin begin in Grade 6. The School has a long tradition of supporting its challenging academic program with extensive art courses and a competitive athletic program. Graduates are accepted at leading secondary schools nationwide. Tuition: $25,950–$30,975. Financial Aid: $800,000. Amy Jolly is Director of Admissions and Financial Aid; Gerard J.G. Ward (Boston University, B.A.; Harvard, Ed.M.) is Headmaster.

Glen Urquhart School   1977

74 Hart Street, Beverly Farms, MA 01915
Tel. 978-927-1064; Admission Ext. 15; Fax 978-921-0060
Web Site www.gus.org; E-mail rnance@gus.org

Glen Urquhart School, enrolling 235 boys and girls as day students in Kindergarten–Grade 8, creates an environment where each student is encouraged to fully develop his or her knowledge, imagination, and character. The School believes that a combination of all three is essential in developing intelligent, creative people who are emotionally mature, socially involved, and well prepared for their future. Field trips, special events, and visiting artists are part of the program. Spanish is taught in all grades, and Latin is taught in Grades 7 and 8. Team sports begin in Grade 6. An extended-care program is available, and a summer camp emphasizing creative arts runs for six weeks. Tuition: $14,475–$21,650. Financial aid is available. Leslie Marchesseault is Director of Admission; Raymond Nance is Head.

Hillside School   1901

Robin Hill Road, Marlborough, MA 01752-1099
Tel. 508-485-2824; Admissions 508-303-5731; Fax 508-485-4420
Web Site www.hillsideschool.net; E-mail admissions@hillsideschool.net

HILLSIDE SCHOOL in Marlborough, Massachusetts, an independent, nonsectarian school, has been enrolling boys as boarding and day students in Grades 5 through 9 for more than 100 years. Marlborough (population 37,444) is 30 miles west of Boston and 17 miles east of Worcester. The rural, wooded areas surrounding the School provide opportunities for many outdoor pursuits, while the nearby cities offer ample cultural, recreational, and historic attractions.

Hillside School offers a strong, fundamental education within a nurturing family environment. Caring, qualified faculty aim to instill core values of honesty, respect for others, compassion, and determination with the goal of developing each boy's academic strengths, civic and social awareness, and personal standards. Beginning in 1925, Hillside has been the recipient of generous assistance from the Daughters of the American Revolution, one of only six schools in the nation to be endowed by this organization.

A nonprofit institution since 1907, Hillside is guided by a 24-member, self-perpetuating Board of Trustees. It holds membership in the National Association of Independent Schools, the Independent School Association of Massachusetts, and other professional organizations. The Hillside Parents Association is instrumental in organizing special events and financial support for the School.

THE CAMPUS. The Assabet River flows through the Hillside School's 200-acre wooded campus, which has its own spring-fed pond, a working farm, and 6 acres of athletic fields. The academic hub of the School is centered in the Stevens Wing of the Academic and Health Center, opened in March 2008. The Stevens Wing contains 14 classrooms, WiFi computer access, and the science laboratory. Linked to the wing is the Tracy gymnasium/auditorium. The Student Center houses the dining room, school offices, and the state-of-the-art Wick Tutorial Center. The Academic and Health Center features fitness rooms, a health center, a wrestling/multipurpose room, offices for health and wellness and counseling programs, and 9 classrooms, 3 of which are science labs. Hillside has also constructed an all-weather, six-lane, professional-grade running track (2008), and a new baseball diamond is scheduled for completion in the spring of 2009.

THE FACULTY. David Z. Beecher was appointed Headmaster in 1998. An honors graduate of The Choate School, Mr. Beecher earned a B.A. degree in American Studies and Education from Lake Forest College, where he was named a Lila B. Frank Scholar. Prior to coming to Hillside, he served as Director of Admission & Financial Aid at Fay School and Wilbraham & Monson Academy, both in Massachusetts. Mr. Beecher also spent six years at Berkshire School as Dean of Students, teacher, dorm parent, coach, and member of the Admissions and Development departments. At Yale University, he served as Athletic Administrator and assistant men's varsity ice-hockey coach. Mr. Beecher and his wife, Carrie, have two daughters, Madeline and Haley.

HILLSIDE SCHOOL.

In addition to Mr. Beecher, there are 70 staff members, including 30 teachers and administrators who teach. Faculty are chosen for their ability to motivate students through their teaching strategies and their commitment to helping young people reach their full potential. In addition to teaching, they are coaches, dorm parents, study hall supervisors, and advisors to the various clubs and campus groups.

A registered nurse staffs the Drinkwater Infirmary. Complete hospital facilities are available 3 miles away in Marlborough.

STUDENT BODY. In 2009–10, Hillside School enrolls 140 boys as boarders and day students in Grades 5–9. The boys come from 15 states and 10 foreign countries.

ACADEMIC PROGRAM. The school year is divided into trimesters, beginning in September and concluding in early June, with vacations at Thanksgiving, Christmas, and in the spring. Grades are mailed to parents each trimester, and two parent-teacher conferences are scheduled each year.

Students who require extra academic support take part in the tutorial program, with small groups working under the supervision of several learning specialists. Tutorials include organizational and study skills and language, math, and social skills development. On Sunday through Thursday, boarding students attend supervised evening study halls.

HILLSIDE SCHOOL

Hillside School embraces the four core values of honesty, compassion, respect, and determination as the guiding principles for overseeing student behavior and achievement. Shades of Hillside Blue, a system based on these values, is designed to give students and families comprehensive and timely feedback about a boy's overall performance at school. During a biweekly period, boys are evaluated in all areas of school life using three shades of blue. Royal blue, the school color, signifies that a boy consistently meets established expectations. Sky blue signifies that he meets expectations with some assistance, and navy blue indicates that he needs frequent guidance in attempting to meet expectations. Each student has an advisor who reviews this feedback with the boy and his family. The advisor works in conjunction with the Dean of Students and other faculty in helping boys to set and meet appropriate individual goals on an ongoing basis.

A typical school day begins at 6:30 A.M., with breakfast served for boarders at 7:15. Day students arrive on campus by 8:00 A.M. Classes are held five days a week, with seven 50-minute periods scheduled from 8:00 A.M. to 3:30 P.M., followed by athletic practices and the Outdoor Program. After dinner and evening study hall, students enjoy free time with open gym time, board games, an Open House with the Headmaster in his home, and other recreational activities. "Lights out" is between 9:00 and 10:00 P.M., depending on age and dorm "shade" level.

Hillside School recognizes the importance of committed faculty, small classes, and a highly structured program as factors in developing the student's self-confidence, self-esteem, individual thinking, and decision-making ability. Students in Grades 5 and 6 learn in self-contained classrooms, with a core curriculum consisting of mathematics, language arts, social studies, and reading, and specialized instruction in art, science, and music.

In Grades 7–9, the curriculum includes English, history, science, math, studio art, music, farming, and French, Latin, or Spanish.

The Honors Seminar Program at Hillside is for eighth and ninth graders. The boys are selected by faculty to challenge top students and to better prepare them for competitive secondary schools. In 2006, seminars were The Writing in Mathematics and The Myths of the Settling of the American West, for Grades 8 and 9 respectively.

The Leadership Training Program is required of all grades to learn teamwork and leadership skills. With the new low-ropes course, students are able to incorporate skills they have acquired, both by leading and listening to their peers.

Responding to concerns about school violence in America, a Peace Initiatives course allows students to review essays and ideas about how to promote peace within our society. Also, Hillside has incorporated a special health and wellness focus across the entire curriculum to enhance students' well-being and development.

Excellence in academics, athletics, citizenship, and self-improvement is recognized by several awards and named scholarships. Among these are the E. Sherwin Kavanaugh Memorial Sportsmanship Award, Mentor of the Year, the Moody Robinson Award for excellence in English, the Dorothy Willard Award for improvement in math, and the Warren I. and Marion F. Higgins Award for outstanding contributions to the farm program by a returning student.

Among past secondary school choices were Bancroft, Brewster Academy, Cambridge School of Weston, Concord Academy, Cushing, Dublin, Eagle Hill, Hebron, The Hill School, Holderness, Lawrence Academy, Marvelwood, Middlesex, New Hampton, Noble and Greenough, Pomfret, Portsmouth Abbey, St. Andrew's, St. Mark's, St. Thomas More, Tabor, Tilton, Vermont Academy, and Wilbraham & Monson.

STUDENT ACTIVITIES. All students must take part in a sport or athletic activity in each trimester. Boys compete interscholastically in soccer, cross-country, basketball, hockey, wrestling, track and field, baseball, and lacrosse.

HILLSIDE SCHOOL

Boys selected to participate in the Farm Program live in their own dorm and take responsibility for rising early each morning to feed and water the animals.

The Outdoor Program features downhill skiing, snowboarding, hiking, canoeing, mountain biking, and sailing. On the weekends, students enjoy faculty-supervised activities including swimming, fishing, ice- and roller-skating, and sledding. The School also arranges trips throughout New England to high school and college sporting events, movies, museums, and bowling. Other groups include the newspaper, the Drama Club, the yearbook, Sudoku, and Chess Society.

ADMISSION AND COSTS. Hillside School welcomes boys of average to above-average intelligence who will benefit from a supportive, structured environment. Many applicants have not performed to their potential, either academically or socially. Candidates are admitted on the basis of past school transcripts, standardized test results, psychological/educational evaluations, and three teacher recommendations. The application fee is $50.

In 2009–10, boarding tuition is $43,150 for five days and $47,100 for seven days; tuition for day students is $27,700.

Head of School: David Z. Beecher
Associate Head & Dean for Parents: Arthur Goodearl
Dean of Academics: Rich Meyer
Dean of Student Life: Dan Marchetti
Director of Development: Emily Kent
School Counselors: Abby Pettee & Alf Wilson
Associate Dean of Student Life: Nathan Boston
Dean of Athletics: Mike Foster
Dean of Faculty: Harry Worrall
Director for Admission & Financial Aid: Kristen Naspo
Associate Dean of Faculty & Technology: Matthew Laliberte

Landmark School   1971

429 Hale Street, P.O. Box 227, Prides Crossing, MA 01965-0227
Tel. 978-236-3000
Web Site www.landmarkschool.org
E-mail admission@landmarkschool.org

Landmark School, offering customized programs for students in Grades 2–12, with a residential program for Grades 9–12, is one of the most comprehensive schools serving students with language-based learning disabilities in the U.S. It accepts bright, emotionally healthy, motivated students who need remedial help with reading, writing, spelling, listening, speaking, and math. With a 1:3 teacher-student ratio, the key to Landmark's successful model is the daily 1:1 tutorial. A customized tutorial curriculum remediates specific language needs such as decoding, fluency, phonological awareness, written composition, and organizational skills. A summer program for Grades 1–12 combines intensive, academic skill development with recreational activities. The program includes a daily 1:1 tutorial designed to improve overall language skills. This program accepts students of average to superior intelligence and a history of healthy emotional development who have a language-based learning disability. Set on two campuses 25 miles north of Boston, students enjoy the many cultural opportunities of the area. Tuition: $43,900–$58,500. Carolyn Orsini Nelson is Director of Admission; Robert J. Broudo, M.Ed., is Head of School.

Lexington Christian Academy   1946

48 Bartlett Avenue, Lexington, MA 02420
Tel. 781-862-7850; Admissions Ext. 185; Fax 781-863-8503
Web Site www.lca.edu; E-mail admissions@lca.edu

LEXINGTON CHRISTIAN ACADEMY

Founded by leaders of Boston's business and professional community, Lexington Christian Academy is a college preparatory day school enrolling 315 boys and girls in Grades 6–12. A rigorous academic program is taught from the perspective of a Christian worldview, encouraging students to ask the hard questions. The curriculum includes Advanced Placement and Honors courses and incorporates state-of-the-art technology with individual and group inquiry. The Academy conducts an Interim Program in March when students take week-long courses or trips that allow for concentrated study and experiential learning. Tuition: $19,400–$21,250. Financial Aid: $950,000. Cynthia Torjesen is Director of Admission; Mark Davis is Head of School. *New England Association.*

The Meadowbrook School of Weston   1923

10 Farm Road, Weston, MA 02493
Tel. 781-894-1193; Admissions Ext. 227; Fax 781-894-0557
Web Site www.meadowbrook-ma.org
E-mail salpert@meadowbrook-ma.org

THE MEADOWBROOK SCHOOL OF WESTON

Meadowbrook, a nationally recognized School of Excellence, enrolls 306 boys and girls in Junior Kindergarten–Grade 8. A mission-driven school, it seeks to help students achieve excellence in academics and to develop honesty, courtesy, and respect for others. The curriculum is challenging, innovative, and integrated. A second language begins in Junior Kindergarten, with added language choices starting in Grade 5. A wide range of arts and computer studies are offered at all levels. Leadership training, field trips, and an athletic program are among the activities. After-school and summer programs are available. Detailed information is offered on the web site. Tuition: $18,885–$27,660. Financial Aid: $788,737. Barbara T. Vincent is Director of Admissions; Stephen T. Hinds was appointed Headmaster in 1986.

Milton Academy   1798

170 Centre Street, Milton, MA 02186
Tel. 617-898-1798; Admission 617-898-2227; Fax 617-898-1701
Web Site www.milton.edu; E-mail admissions@milton.edu

Milton Academy was established under the Massachusetts land-grant policy, which called for a school that would "open the way for all the people to a higher order of education than the com-

mon schools can supply." Now in its 212th year of academic excellence within a highly diverse community of teachers and learners, Milton Academy enrolls 965 students in Kindergarten–Grade 12, with approximately 335 boarders in Grades 9–12. The Academy's challenging college preparatory curriculum includes AP and honors courses, world languages, and state-of-the-art computer technology. All graduates are accepted to four-year colleges and universities around the world. The extracurricular program offers 11 publications, glee club, orchestra, environmental groups, peer counseling, speech team, school government, social outreach projects, drama, and 15 interscholastic boys' teams, 15 interscholastic girls' teams, and 8 intramural teams. Boarding Tuition: $41,960; Day Tuition: $20,050–$34,470. Financial Aid: $7,100,000. Paul Rebuck is Dean of Admission; Todd B. Bland is Head of School. *New England Association.*

Montrose School   1979

29 North Street, Medfield, MA 02050
Tel. 508-359-2423; Admissions Ext. 315; Fax 508-359-2597
Web Site www.montroseschool.org
E-mail dconvery@montroseschool.org

Parents and educators founded Montrose School to provide a challenging academic program integrated with the Christian values that develop sound character and prepare students for life. Enrolling 153 day girls in Grades 6–12, the School offers a classical liberal arts curriculum, including selected Advanced Placement courses, options in Spanish and French, and Catholic theology and philosophy courses. Classes in the fine arts are also offered. Cocurricular activities include newspaper, yearbook, drama, chorus, speech team, Student Council, the National Honor Society, athletics, and other clubs. Tuition: $16,900 (Domestic)–$21,500 (International). Financial aid is available. Deborah Convery is Director of Admissions; Hadley Pennington is Associate Director of Admissions; Dr. Karen E. Bohlin (Boston College, B.A.; Boston University, Ed.D.) is Head.

Nashoba Brooks School   1980

200 Strawberry Hill Road, Concord, MA 01742
Tel. 978-369-4591; Admission Ext. 129; Fax 978-287-6038
Web Site www.nashobabrooks.org

Nashoba Country Day School (founded 1958) and The Brooks School of Concord (1928) merged in 1980 as an elementary day school. Enrolled are 157 boys and girls in Preschool–Grade 3 and 150 girls in Grades 4–8. The School strives to recognize each student's contributions to the community, whether they be academic, artistic, dramatic, or athletic. Art, music, physical education, Spanish, and Latin are included in the curriculum. Tuition: $18,110–$28,700. Jean Stahl Heaton is Director of Admission; E. Kay Cowan (Manhattanville College, M.A.) is Head of School.

The Newman School 1945

247 Marlborough Street, Boston, MA 02116
Tel. 617-267-4530; Fax 617-267-7070
Web Site www.newmanboston.org; E-mail plynch@newmanboston.org

THE NEWMAN SCHOOL in Boston, Massachusetts, is a college preparatory day school enrolling boys and girls in Grades 9–12. The School is situated in the city's Back Bay, within a few blocks of significant cultural and historic institutions, where students and faculty find special resources to enrich their academic work. With its downtown location, the School is easily accessible by subway, bus, or car.

Founded in 1945 as The Newman School for Boys and since transformed into a coeducational institution, the School shapes its program in harmony with the vision of Cardinal John Henry Newman, the 19th-century British cleric who emphasized the relationship between faith and reason and whose writings set standards for liberal education. The Newman School strives to provide a rigorous educational experience that encourages students to be open-minded, to grow intellectually, and to take an active role in their own cultural and moral development. The aim is to prepare students with a solid academic background and the confidence, flexibility, and integrity to succeed in a complex world.

The Newman School is governed by a Board of nine Trustees, including alumni and parents. It is accredited by the New England Association of Schools and Colleges and holds membership in the Association of Independent Schools of New England and other professional organizations.

THE CAMPUS. The main school building at 245–247 Marlborough Street houses classrooms, science labs, and some special facilities including a computer lab and a 2000-volume school library. The library collection consists mainly of reference materials and nonfiction carefully selected to support the curriculum. In addition, all students must hold a Boston Public Library card, and they are introduced as freshmen to the main library three blocks away. The School librarian teaches a course in Library Research Skills in which students learn to access databases provided through the Boston Public Library web site. Adjacent to the School's library is the Newman Computer Lab with 16 workstations. All classrooms are equipped with wireless capability to enable teachers to use the computers without going to the Computer Lab. Twelve wireless laptops are available for student use on a daily basis. There are two Macintosh labs dedicated respectively to art and science classes.

THE NEWMAN SCHOOL

Art classes and individual students take advantage of the nearby Gardner Museum and the Museum of Fine Arts as well as the Newbury Street art galleries to enrich their studies; The Newman School also maintains an affiliation with the Copley Society of Art. Classes attend professional theater and musical performances on a frequent basis.

The School rents athletic fields and tennis and basketball courts from the city and private organizations for home games and practices.

THE FACULTY. J. Harry Lynch, a graduate of College of the Holy Cross (B.A.) and Northeastern (M.B.A.), is President and Headmaster.

THE NEWMAN SCHOOL

The full-time teaching faculty includes 21 men and women. They all hold bachelor's degrees, and 11 hold advanced degrees from Berklee College of Music, Boston College 2, Boston State, Boston University 2, College of Charleston, College of the Holy Cross, Dartmouth, Gordon, McDaniel, Northeastern, Politecnico of Milan, St. Anselm, Simmons, State University of New York (Binghamton), and the Universities of Massachusetts 2, New Hampshire 2, Seville (Spain), and Virginia. Faculty members serve as mentors, coaches, and advisors to students and to their activity groups. Professional guidance counselors help students with a variety of issues.

STUDENT BODY. The Newman School enrolls approximately 240 boys and girls from all parts of Metropolitan Boston as well as students from 27 foreign countries such as Brazil, China, Germany, Indonesia, Italy, Morocco, Russia, Spain, and Vietnam. The School admits students of any race, color, religion, and national or ethnic origin.

ACADEMIC PROGRAM. Newman is recognized by the International Baccalaureate Organization as a "World School," offering the International Baccalaureate Diploma Programme in the 11th and 12th grades. Freshmen and sophomores pursue a course of pre-IB studies in language, mathematics, English literature and composition, and lab science leading to IB studies in the junior and senior years. The academic year is divided into semesters, and each semester includes four marking periods. At the end of each quarter, grade reports are mailed home. Academic alert reports are mailed at any time when faculty observe poor performance by the student. Classes meet on a five-day rotating schedule. Most classes are 45 minutes in length, but some are double periods lasting 90 minutes. The day begins at 8:15 A.M. and ends at 2:40 P.M. A mandatory school meeting takes place at 9:50 A.M. when daily announcements are made and individual students, teachers, and staff members may address the community. Additional studies, athletics, activities, and extra help begin at 2:45 P.M. Freshmen and other new students have a monitored homework session available daily from 2:45 to 3:30 P.M. to help them with the transition to Newman.

All students must complete a total of 22 credits, taking a

six-course load in all semesters. These must include 4 in English, 4 in mathematics, 2 in foreign language, 3 in social studies, 3 in laboratory science, 1 in visual arts, and 5 electives. A demonstrated proficiency in computer science and completion of a technology portfolio are also necessary. International students take English as a Second Language at intermediate and advanced levels.

Among the courses are English 9–12, Writing Workshop, Basic Literature, Creative Writing, The Bible as Literature; French 1–4, Spanish 1–4, Latin 1–4; World Cultures, American History, U.S. History, Twentieth Century America, U.S. Government and Politics, Moral Reasoning/Ethics, Psychology, The History of Boston, The World's Religions; Algebra 1–2, Geometry, Trigonometry, Calculus; Biology, Chemistry, Physics, Anatomy and Physiology, Computer Science; and Art and Music Integration. Honors courses are available in most subjects, and Advanced Placement courses are offered in English, Government and Politics, Calculus, and Biology. Qualified students may enroll in courses at nearby colleges and earn credit for both high school and college records.

Guidance seminars are conducted to help students with academic planning. In the junior and senior years, these seminars focus on the college application process and the transition to college. Nearly all students at Newman go on to further education. Members of the Classes of 2008 and 2009 are currently enrolled at Boston University, Brandeis, Bryant, Clark, College of the Holy Cross, Eckerd, Emmanuel, Ithaca, Manhattan, Massachusetts College of Art, New York University, Northeastern, Providence, Rochester, Roger Williams, St. Anselm, Salem State, Simmons, Suffolk, Tufts, Wentworth, Wheelock, Worcester Polytechnic Institute, and the Universities of Connecticut, Massachusetts, New Hampshire, Maine, and Vermont.

STUDENT ACTIVITIES. Students elect eight of their peers to the Student Council, which organizes activities throughout the year and works to enhance the quality of student life.

THE NEWMAN SCHOOL

Other activities include National Honor Society, Literary Journal, Yearbook, Peer Tutoring, Prom Committee, International/American Friends Club, Chess Club, Drama Society, Choral Society, Recycling, Mock Trial, and Math Club.

The Newman School is a member of the Mass Bay Independent League and the Girls Independent League and fields teams for interscholastic competition in soccer, tennis, crew, cross-country, boys' and girls' basketball, baseball, tennis, and girls' lacrosse.

ADMISSION AND COSTS. The Newman School seeks to enroll young men and women in Grades 9–12 who have the ability and motivation to be active participants in a rigorous educational program. Applicants are evaluated on the basis of prior school records, a personal essay, entrance examination or SSAT or PREP scores, and a teacher recommendation. A full-day visit to the school, with a parent, is recommended. A $40 fee payment should accompany the application.

THE NEWMAN SCHOOL

Tuition for the 2009–10 school year is $13,600: scholarships and financial aid are available. International student tuition is $23,500.

Dean of Administration: Karen Briggs
Dean of Studies: Daniel Ohman
Dean of Students/Director of Guidance: Tamara Walsh
Director of Admissions: Patricia Lynch
International Admissions Coordinator: Patricia Ridge
Director of Development: Louise Merrigan
Buildings Supervisor: Frank Hartigan

Noble and Greenough School   1866

10 Campus Drive, Dedham, MA 02026-4099
Tel. 781-326-3700; Admission 781-320-7100; Fax 781-320-1329
Web Site www.nobles.edu; E-mail admission@nobles.edu

Noble and Greenough is a coeducational college preparatory school enrolling 570 five-day boarding and day students in Grades 7–12. It aims to provide a rigorous program to stretch academic abilities and foster curiosity, involvement, self-reliance, honesty, and a commitment to others. Intellectual skills and the use of language and technology in effective communication are emphasized. All students participate in an afternoon program including athletics, performing arts, or community service. Boarding Tuition: $38,900; Day Tuition: $33,900. Financial Aid: $3,000,000. Jennifer Hines is Dean of Enrollment Management; Robert P. Henderson, Jr. (Dartmouth, B.A. 1980, M.A.L.S. 1989), was appointed Head of School in 2000. *New England Association.*

The Park School   1888

171 Goddard Avenue, Brookline, MA 02445
Tel. 617-277-2456; Fax 617-232-1261
Web Site www.parkschool.org

Park School is a coeducational day school serving a diverse student body from the Boston metropolitan area. Located on a 26-

acre wooded campus, Park enrolls 550 students in Pre-Kindergarten–Grade IX. Small classes, rigorous academics, and close contact with parents are emphasized. Four sections of 15–16 children at each grade level ensure individual attention. Music, art, and physical education are integral to the program. Activities include interscholastic athletics, drama, and service learning. Park offers afterschool care and a wide range of summer programs. Tuition: $19,440–$31,470. Financial Aid: $2,253,000. Merle Jacobs is Director of Admission; Dr. Jerrold I. Katz (Harvard, Ed.D.) was appointed Head of School in 1993.

Pine Cobble School   1937

163 Gale Road, Williamstown, MA 01267
Tel. 413-458-4680; Admission Ext. 15; Fax 413-458-8174
Web Site www.pinecobble.org; E-mail ljl.becker@pinecobble.org

Pine Cobble School, enrolling 165 boys and girls as day students in Nursery–Grade 9, provides a rigorous liberal arts curriculum designed to instill in each child a lifelong passion for learning. Within a caring environment, students of varying academic abilities acquire a firm foundation in core subjects in readiness for the challenges of higher education. Small classes, dedicated teachers, and enrichment activities such as community service, math and science fairs, and Latin and French studies are cornerstones of the program. Students participate in drama and sports, including skiing. A summer session is optional. Tuition: $12,425–$16,775. Financial Aid: $275,000. Linda J. L. Becker is Director of Admissions and Placement; Nicholas M. Edgerton (Brown, A.B.; Columbia, M.A.) is Headmaster.

Pingree School   1961

537 Highland Street, South Hamilton, MA 01982-1316
Tel. 978-468-4415; Fax 978-468-3758
Web Site www.pingree.org; E-mail estacey@pingree.org

Pingree School was founded through the generosity of Mr. and Mrs. Sumner Pingree, who donated their home and 50 acres of land to create a girls school. Today Pingree is coeducational and enrolls 335 day students from a wide diversity of ethnic, racial, and religious backgrounds in Grades 9–12. Pingree is committed to providing a college preparatory program marked by academic excellence and high personal standards that are emphasized equally in an honors-level curriculum. Small classes, an 8:1 student-teacher ratio, and personalized college counseling result in the admission of virtually all graduates to four-year colleges. Students choose from more than 100 courses in the eight major departments. Now comprised of 105 acres, the campus is enhanced by a 25,000-square-foot Academic Center with state-of-the-art technology. Among the activities are student government, publications, drama, music ensembles, 44 teams in 24 sports, and required community service. Tuition: $32,000. Financial Aid: $1,500,000. Eric Stacey '81 is Director of Admission; Dr. Timothy M. Johnson was appointed Head of School in 2009. *New England Association.*

St. Sebastian's School   1941

1191 Greendale Avenue, Needham, MA 02492
Tel. 781-449-5200; Admissions 781-247-0125; Fax 781-449-5630
Web Site www.stsebastiansschool.org; E-mail admissions@stsebs.org

St. Sebastian's School is a Roman Catholic, independent day school enrolling 350 boys in Grades 7–12. Students participate in a structured and rigorous liberal arts curriculum, with carefully sequenced courses in English, mathematics, classical and modern foreign languages, science, and social studies. The School places heavy emphasis on verbal skills enrichment, and all freshmen take a required writing course. Upper School courses are taught on standard, honors, and Advanced Placement levels. The extracurricular program features 11 inter-

scholastic sports and 22 nonathletic clubs. Tuition: $31,550. Financial Aid: $1,600,000. Gregory W. Wishart is Director of Admission and Financial Aid; William L. Burke III (Middlebury College, B.A.; Boston College, M.A.) is Headmaster. *New England Association.*

School Year Abroad   1964

439 South Union Street, Lawrence, MA 01843
Tel. 978-725-6828; Fax 978-725-6833
Web Site www.sya.org; E-mail mail@sya.org

School Year Abroad is a nonprofit organization with schools in China, France, Italy, Spain, and Vietnam whose mission is to teach self-reliance, responsibility, resourcefulness, and respect for other cultures. SYA's central elements — the 9-month home stay and an academic program emphasizing foreign language acquisition — ensure that students return home with a real mastery of the language and a deep understanding of the host country's culture. Approximately 60 students spend their junior or senior year in each school. The schools in France and Spain have a two-year language requirement, while the other three are open to beginners. Students live with selected local families while earning U.S. graduation credits and preparing for entrance to selective colleges and universities nationwide. SYA offers a traditional liberal arts program, AP courses, and college counseling, and all required standardized testing is administered in its schools. English and math are taught in English by American faculty. Extracurricular activities and extensive educational and independent travel enhance the academic experience. While each academic program is similar in rigor and excellence, cultural practices and traditions vary from nation to nation. For more details, refer to additional listings under the specific countries. Tuition: $41,000. Extensive financial aid is available, with over 40 percent of students receiving assistance. Roland Lemay is Director of Admissions; Nelson Chase is Executive Director.

Southfield School   1992

10 Newton Street, Brookline, MA 02445-7498
Tel. 617-522-6980; Admissions 617-454-2721; Fax 617-522-8166
Web Site www.southfield.org; E-mail admissions@southfield.org

SOUTHFIELD SCHOOL

Serving 370 girls in Pre-Kindergarten–Grade 12, Southfield is located on a 36-acre estate. The School provides a classical curriculum, which emphasizes academic fundamentals. Along with skills in reading, writing, and math, major subjects include history, geography, science, and Latin. All students participate in Southfield's public speaking program from Kindergarten through Grade 12. Opportunities for advanced study are offered in the Clay Center for Science and Technology, which houses research-grade telescopes, and at Briarwood Marine Science Center on Cape Cod. Other facilities include five fields; two indoor hockey rinks; an indoor pool; a gym; studios for art, woodworking, and music; and a boathouse on the Charles River. All girls take part in athletics, and interscholastic sports begin in Grade 7. There is a weekly chapel assembly, and community service is required in Grades 10–12. Summer programs include sci-tech, academic enrichment, hockey, and day camps on the Brookline campus and marine science and sailing at Briarwood. Southfield's brother school, Dexter, enrolls 439 boys on the same grounds. Tuition: $19,990–$35,695. Financial Aid: $3,380,000. William H. Southwick is Director of Admissions; William F. Phinney is Head.

Stoneleigh-Burnham School   1869

574 Bernardston Road, Greenfield, MA 01301
Tel. 413-774-2711; Fax 413-772-2602
Web Site www.sbschool.org; E-mail admissions@sbschool.org

STONELEIGH-BURNHAM SCHOOL in Greenfield, Massachusetts, is a college preparatory boarding and day school for girls in Grades 7 through 12 and a postgraduate year. The School is 3 hours from New York, 2 hours from Boston, and an hour from Bradley International Airport in Hartford, Connecticut. Students have access to academic symposiums and cultural events at nearby Smith, Mount Holyoke, Williams, Hampshire, and the University of Massachusetts; the ski areas of Vermont and New Hampshire are nearby.

STONELEIGH-BURNHAM SCHOOL

Stoneleigh-Burnham was formed in 1968 by the merger of the Mary A. Burnham School (1877) and the Stoneleigh-Prospect Hill School (1869). The School continues its 140-year tradition of encouraging girls to develop their interests to the best of their abilities, to enjoy the challenge and rewards of learning, and to gain self-confidence and independence. Stoneleigh-Burnham seeks to achieve these goals through programs and personnel who respect young women's voices and intellects and who understand how girls learn best.

The School is a nonprofit corporation directed by a Board of Trustees composed of alumnae, parents, and friends. There is an active Alumnae Association. Accredited by the New England Association of Schools and Colleges, Stoneleigh-Burnham holds membership in the National Association of Independent Schools, among other organizations.

THE CAMPUS. The School occupies more than 100 wooded acres. The entire campus is connected through a wireless technology network. The Main Building, with the addition of Mary Burnham Hall, houses classrooms, the technology center, the

library, the infirmary, dorm rooms, student lounges and common rooms, and dining facilities. There are faculty apartments on the second floor as well as in Ferdon House. The Jesser Science Center for chemistry, biology, and physical science houses laboratories, lecture and discussion space, and a reading resource room for the Upper School. The Jesser Science Center also houses the Middle School program. Emerson Hall has a gymnasium, a dance studio, and an auditorium. The Student Arts Center and The Geissler Gallery contain teaching and studio facilities for drawing, painting, digital photography, desktop publishing, computer graphics, film editing, other arts, and a renovated fitness area.

On campus are five tennis courts, an outdoor swimming pool, three playing fields, and cross-country ski trails. The School's state-of-the-art riding facilities include stabling for 60 horses, two indoor riding arenas, two outdoor riding rings, the McDonald Jumper Derby course, a cross-country riding course, and a hunt course.

THE FACULTY. On July 1, 2008, Sally Mixsell officially began her role as Head of School. An alumna of Stoneleigh-Burnham's Class of 1969, Ms. Mixsell holds a Bachelor of Arts degree in Comparative French and American Literature from Wells College and a Master's Degree in Education Administration with a focus in private school leaderships from Teachers College, Columbia University, where she was also a Klingenstein Fellow. Ms. Mixsell was also project director at the Klingenstein Center for Independent School Education, which included overseeing and instructing in the Leadership Academy's master's degree program. Her academic career has included teaching French, English, ESL, and leadership in day and boarding schools in Connecticut and Pennsylvania. Her work in independent school administration has included service as academic dean and director of curriculum instruction.

The faculty and administrators hold baccalaureate and 32 advanced degrees from such institutions as Aberdeen, Aichi, Amherst, Bates, Boston University, Brown, Bryn Mawr, Colgate, Columbia, Hamilton, Harvard, Juilliard, Macalester, McGill, Middlebury, Mount Holyoke, Princeton, Providence, Smith, Stanford, and the Universities of Massachusetts and Michigan.

The Health Care Center staff includes three registered nurses in addition to an athletic trainer who works directly with student-athletes. Students have the opportunity to visit outside physicians, a gynecological nurse practitioner, and an orthopedic/sports physician. Hospital facilities are located in Greenfield at the Bay State Franklin Medical Center less than a mile away.

STUDENT BODY. In 2009–10, the School enrolled 125 girls in Grades 7–12. The majority of the population are boarding students.

ACADEMIC PROGRAM. The school year is divided into trimesters from early September to early June, with Thanksgiving, winter, and spring vacations. Stoneleigh-Burnham's course offerings are designed to place each girl in classes most commensurate with her scholastic ability, and each discipline offers college preparatory, honors, and Advanced Placement courses. The Academic Skills Program supports students who need additional help in reading, writing, mathematics, and organizational skills. Faculty advisors monitor academic progress and assist with issues relating to general life at school. The student-faculty ratio is approximately 6:1. Evening study hall for boarding students is required for two hours five nights a week in addition to one daily 40-minute study hall. Progress reports and written teachers' comments are issued every three weeks to students; grades are mailed to parents at the end of each trimester.

In Grades 7–8 (Middle School), classes include humanities, math, science, foreign language, visual and performing arts, physical education, and health. All students may participate in the Upper School's athletic, riding, music, and dance programs.

To graduate, students must earn a minimum of 18 credits in Grades 9–12, including four years of English; two years of the same foreign language; three years each of mathematics and laboratory science; and three years of social studies, including one of United States History; two trimesters each year in the arts; and four years of physical education.

English courses in Grades 9–12 focus on vocabulary, grammar, writing, and literature. English electives are required of juniors and seniors in the spring semester. Stoneleigh-Burnham is recognized nationally for its science program for girls. Courses include Advanced Placement Environmental Science and Biology, plus Conceptual Physics, Biology, Chemistry, Physics, Equine Studies, Health, and several science electives. Other full-term and elective courses include French, Chinese, Spanish; Algebra I–II, Geometry, PreCalculus, Discrete Math, Calculus, Advanced Placement and Multivariable Calculus; World History, U.S. History, Advanced Placement U.S. History, Advanced Placement European History, Political Science, Gender Studies; Drawing I–II, Painting, Design and Color, Watercolor and Painting, Computer Art, Advanced Placement Studio Art, Desktop Publishing, Photography I–III, Papier Maché Sculpture, Ceramics I–III; and Music Theory, Music History, Chorus, Octet, and Acting. Honors classes are offered in each discipline. Private music lessons are available. There are several instrumental ensemble groups, a big band, a chamber group, a rock band, and a jazz combo, and instruction is offered in ballet, jazz, and modern dance at all levels.

English as a Second Language, available in English and history, provides help in basic English skills at three levels.

The Senior Project allows students to work in a yearlong project with regional colleges and other organizations to study or research a topic of their choice.

STONELEIGH-BURNHAM SCHOOL

Graduates from the last three years are attending such colleges and universities as Bates, Boston University, Bowdoin, Carnegie Mellon, Colby, College of the Holy Cross, College of William and Mary, Columbia, Cornell, Davidson, Dickinson, Georgetown, George Washington, Massachusetts Institute of Technology, Middlebury, Mount Holyoke, Providence, Reed, Rhode Island School of Design, Skidmore, Smith, Syracuse, Texas A&M, Trinity, Tufts, Union, Wellesley, Wesleyan, Wheaton, Williams, William Smith, and the Universities of Colorado, Illinois, New Hampshire, North Carolina, Vermont, and Virginia.

STUDENT ACTIVITIES. Each year, students have the opportunity to participate in Student Council, Blue Key Society, Riding Club, Community Service Club, and Yearbook. In the past, other clubs and activities have included the Literary Society, Peer Mediation, Student Activities, GSA, Pangea, and MECCA. Students may create new clubs, and clubs and activities change yearly based on student interests.

STONELEIGH-BURNHAM SCHOOL

The Stoneleigh-Burnham Debate Team competes nationally and is one of the top-ranked teams in New England.

Stoneleigh-Burnham athletes compete in the Western New England Prep School Association in soccer, cross-country, basketball, volleyball, softball, lacrosse, and tennis. Recreational skiing is also offered.

With one of the country's most extensive riding programs, Stoneleigh-Burnham has been national champion in the hunters interscholastic riding category. The School hosts numerous horse events each year for Stoneleigh-Burnham riders and the outside community.

Stoneleigh-Burnham offers three two-week sessions of the Bonnie Castle Summer Riding Camp for girls ages 9–17. Residential camps for girls in softball, debate, dance, math/English, and ESL are also held on campus.

ADMISSION AND COSTS. Stoneleigh-Burnham seeks girls with above-average to superior academic abilities who demonstrate a respect for learning and who will contribute positively to the school community. Candidates must submit academic transcripts, standardized test scores, a personal reference, references from the school counselor and English and math teachers, and the parent-guardian and student questionnaires. The application fee for 2009–10 is $50 for domestic students and $100 for international students. The application deadline is February 15.

In 2009–10, tuition for boarding students is $44,405 and $27,776 for day students. There are additional fees for the academic skills, ESL, and horseback riding programs.

Financial aid is available on the basis of need as determined by the School and Student Service for Financial Aid. In 2008, $920,000 was awarded to 56 students. There is an Honor Scholarship Program, and the Alumnae Association funds a scholarship to be awarded each year to the daughter of an alumna.

Head of School: Sally Mixsell '69
Academic Dean: Natalie Demers
Dean of Students: John Larson
Director of Admission: Eric Swartzentruber
Director of Development: Regina Moody, Ph.D.
Director of Communications: Holly Mott
Director of College Counseling: Lauren Cuniffe
Business Manager: Leslie Brown
Director of International Programs: Andrea Patt
Director of Athletics: Jeremy Deason

Thayer Academy   1877

745 Washington Street, Braintree, MA 02184
Tel. 781-843-3580; Admission 781-664-2221; Fax 781-843-2916
Web Site www.thayer.org; E-mail admissions@thayer.org

Tʜᴀʏᴇʀ ᴀᴄᴀᴅᴇᴍʏ in Braintree, Massachusetts, is a coeducational, college preparatory day school enrolling 693 students in Grades 6 through 12. First colonized in 1625, historic Braintree (population 33,828) is a residential community 13 miles southeast of Boston in an area accessible to a myriad of educational, cultural, and recreational resources.

The School was founded in 1877 by Gen. Sylvanus Thayer, a distinguished soldier, engineer, and educator who is widely known as "The Father of the United States Military Academy." General Thayer established high standards of scholarship and instituted a performance evaluation process for each student with the goal of producing "worthy leaders of high character."

Today's Thayer Academy holds true to its founder's ideals by providing a rigorous learning environment designed to inspire in students "moral, intellectual, aesthetic, and physical excellence so that each may rise to honorable achievement and contribute to the common good." Faculty are chosen for their devotion to scholarship and their sincere interest in the development of their students.

THAYER ACADEMY

Thayer Academy is accredited by the New England Association of Schools and Colleges and the Massachusetts Department of Education; it holds membership in the National Association of Independent Schools, The Cum Laude Society, Association of Independent Schools of New England, and the Secondary School Admission Test Board, among other professional affiliations.

THE CAMPUS. At the heart of the 25-acre suburban campus is the historic Main Building, constructed in 1877. A new Center for the Arts (2008) features a 550-seat theater, dance studios, and expanded visual arts studios in Frothingham Hall. The Glover Laboratory contains math, science, and computer science classrooms and two recently completed, state-of-the-art biology labs. Southworth Library resources support the Upper School curriculum and include 22,000 volumes, 21 database subscriptions, 19 computers, wireless laptops, digital still and video cameras, and 58 periodicals. Cahall Observatory houses a 12-inch Schmidt Cassagrain telescope and three Newtoniuns for viewing the cosmos. Cahall Campus Center (1998) contains dining facilities for all students and faculty. The Sawyer Gymnasium houses three gyms and a two-story fitness center. Athletic resources include four new synthetic-grass playing fields, a running track, cross-country trails, tennis and basketball courts, and a ropes course. Thayer also utilizes seven additional off-site facilities.

The Hale Learning Center supports a learning resource lab in each division.

An IT department of four professionals supports 13 computer labs and 53 Audio-Visual Presentation systems, and a campus-wide network featuring individual electronics files and e-mail. The student-to-computer ratio is 2:1.

THAYER ACADEMY

The Thayer Academy Middle School, accommodating 220 students in Grades 6–8, was expanded and upgraded to include a new satellite library, two state-of-the-art technology labs, a newly renovated studio art space, and a new learning resource center.

THE FACULTY. W. Theodore "Ted" Koskores, a 1970 graduate of Thayer Academy, was appointed the school's ninth Headmaster in 2006. Mr. Koskores received a baccalaureate degree from Boston University and holds advanced degrees from Columbia University.

Of Thayer's 107 faculty members, 67 percent hold master's or doctoral degrees, and 17 teachers have been at the school for 25 or more years. Faculty have graduated from four-year colleges and universities such as Amherst, Ball State, Bates, Bowdoin, Brown, California Lutheran, Colby, College of Wooster, Connecticut College, Dartmouth, Hamilton, Harvard, Johns Hopkins, Kenyon, Laval, Marymount, Massachusetts College of Art, Massachusetts Institute of Technology, Middlebury, New England School of Law, New School for Social Research, Ohio State, Pepperdine, Purdue, Rhode Island School of Design, Simmons, Skidmore, State University of New York, Suffolk University, Tufts, Wesleyan, Wheaton, Williams, Worcester Polytechnic, Yale, and the Universities of Colorado, Massachusetts (Lowell), New Hampshire, North Carolina, Pennsylvania, Rhode Island, Rochester, Vermont, and Virginia.

STUDENT BODY. In 2009–10, Thayer Academy enrolled 693 young men and women—220 in Grades 6 through 8 and 473 in Grades 9–12. They come from widely diverse ethnic, racial, religious, and socioeconomic backgrounds.

ACADEMIC PROGRAM. The school year extends from September to June, with vacations at Thanksgiving, in December, and in the spring, along with observances of several national holidays. The student-teacher ratio is approximately 6.4:1, and the average class enrolls between 13 and 16 students.

Overall, Thayer offers 135 courses in addition to nearly 80 electives. The curriculum in the Middle School centers on English, history, math, modern languages plus required Latin in Grade 6, computer science/technology, the arts, and health. Students can receive additional academic support from teachers upon request.

To graduate, Thayer students must successfully complete 4 years of English; 3 years each of math and science; 2 years of a foreign language (Chinese, French, Latin, Spanish); 3 years of history (World, United States, and Modern European);

11 terms of physical education or interscholastic sports; $\frac{1}{2}$ credit in an arts elective plus Foundation in the Arts; and a Senior Project.

Among the specific course offerings are English Language and Literature, English Language and Composition, American Masterworks, World Literature, Scene to Screen, Crossing Borders: Journeys and Transformations, African History and the African-American Experience, Sports Literature, Memoir and Biography: The Stories of Our Lives, Rag and Bone Poetry Workshop, Modern American Culture, Imaginative Literature, Philosophy and Literature; French I–V, Latin I–II, Spanish I–V, Hispanic History and Culture, Chinese I–II, Chinese Culture; World History, Australian Studies, Modern European History, United States History, Vietnam and the '60s, Contemporary Issues, Psychology, Hiroshima and the Holocaust, Sports and Society; Algebra I–II, Geometry, Precalculus; Physics, Biology, Chemistry, Chemistry in Community; Environmental Science, Earth Science; Architectural Design, Photography, Pottery, Graphic Design, Acting, Choreography Workshop; and Health.

Thirty-seven honors and Advanced Placement courses for qualified students include Biology II, Chemistry II, Physics II, Calculus AB/BC, English Literature and Composition, French, Latin, Spanish, U.S. History, and Environmental Science. Thayer students consistently qualify as AP scholars, and over 90 percent earn scores of 3 or higher on their respective exams.

Thayer strongly believes that international travel and study abroad are important elements in a student's education and has developed rich cultural exchange programs with sister schools in France, England, and China.

THAYER ACADEMY

Traditionally, 100 percent of Thayer graduates enter four-year colleges and universities. Members of the Class of 2008 have been accepted at such institutions as Boston Architectural Center, Boston College, Boston University, Brown, College of the Holy Cross, Cornell, Connecticut College, Dartmouth, Dickinson, Fairfield, Goucher, Hamilton, Harvard, Hobart and William Smith, Hofstra, Lafayette, Lake Forest, Macalester, Massachusetts Maritime Academy, McGill, New York University, Northeastern, Northwestern, Ohio Wesleyan, Providence College, Quinnipiac, St. Lawrence, Salve Regina, Stonehill, Trinity College (Dublin), Trinity (Connecticut), Wake Forest, Worcester Polytechnic Institute, and the Universities of Arizona, Chicago, Massachusetts, North Carolina, Pennsylvania, Richmond, South Carolina, Southern California, and Vermont.

Thayer Academy conducts a summer school program of enrichment, remediation, and advanced course work as well as sports camps and other recreational pursuits.

STUDENT ACTIVITIES. Thayer's extracurricular program is structured to meet the many diverse interests and abilities of its student body. Community Council offers students a voice in school decisions and policies and the opportunity to plan spirit-building activities.

Thirty-seven organizations include Mathletes, cultural enrichment, three yearly drama productions, seven jazz ensembles, three choirs, yearbook, and *Voice,* Thayer's award-winning student magazine.

THAYER ACADEMY

Community service learning comprises a vital component of a Thayer education. Students, faculty, and staff tutor children as part of the local Head Start program; conduct food drives for the homeless and hungry; walk to raise money for cancer and AIDS research; advocate for human rights as members of Amnesty International; and visit residents of the Braintree Manor Nursing Home. Through these and many other outreach activities, the Thayer community experiences first-hand its potential to have a significant impact on the lives of others.

The athletic program is open to students at all levels, with 90 teams in 28 sports. Some sports are offered to both Middle and Upper School athletes. Among the offerings are baseball, basketball, cross-country, football, skiing, field hockey, softball, swimming, lacrosse, wrestling, tennis, golf, and ice hockey.

ADMISSION AND COSTS. Thayer Academy admits students of good character and academic potential as determined by past school transcripts, personal and teacher recommendations, standardized testing (ISEE or SSAT), a campus visit, and the completed application. Candidates are notified of admission decisions on or about March 10. Application due date is February 1.

In 2009–10, tuition is $31,650. The school provides more than $4,500,000 in need-based financial aid to approximately one-third of its student body.

Headmaster: W. Theodore Koskores '70
Upper School Director: Michael Clarke
Middle School Director: Carson Smith
Director of Admissions: Jonathan White
Director of Development: Mark Gutierrez
Director of Communications: David Casanave
Business Manager: William Stephenson
Director of Athletics: Matthew McGuirk '92

The Williston Northampton School   1841

19 Payson Avenue, Easthampton, MA 01027
Tel. 413-529-3000; Admissions 413-529-3241; Fax 413-527-9494
Web Site www.williston.com; E-mail admissions@williston.com

Williston Northampton offers a rigorous academic curriculum for 550 day (Grade 7–Postgraduate) and boarding (Grade

9–Postgraduate) students in an educational setting designed to foster respect, independence, and responsibility. The beautiful 125-acre campus features a state-of-the-art Science Tech Lab

THE WILLISTON NORTHAMPTON SCHOOL

and Technology Center, a 45,000-volume library, a theater, art studios, lighted turf field, and athletic complex. Enrichment offerings include college-level courses, advanced Photojournal-

ism, and visiting Writers' Workshops. Students take part in leadership activities such as community and campus work service, travel abroad, tutoring, and clubs. Boarding Tuition: $44,500; Day Tuition: $26,000–$31,000. Financial Aid: $3,000,000. Ann C. Pickrell is Director of Admission; Brian Wright, Ph.D., is Headmaster. *New England Association.*

The Winsor School   1886

Pilgrim Road, Boston, MA 02215
Tel. 617-735-9500; Fax 617-912-1381
Web Site www.winsor.edu; E-mail admissions@winsor.edu

Founded by Mary Pickard Winsor, The Winsor School is a college preparatory day school enrolling 425 girls in Grades 5–12. The School offers an academically challenging curriculum, features small classes, uses the cultural and scientific resources of Boston, and shares some activities with nearby boys' schools. Physical education and fine arts are integral parts of the program. Facilities include a renovated library with 27,000 volumes plus access to 850 periodicals, a multimedia language lab, 3 computer labs, 3 art studios, 8 science labs, a new turf athletic field, tennis courts, and a gymnasium. Tuition: $32,250. Financial Aid: $2,100,000. Pamela Parks McLaurin is Director of Admission and Financial Aid; Rachel Friis Stettler was appointed Director in 2004. *New England Association.*

THAYER ACADEMY

MICHIGAN

Academy of the Sacred Heart   1851

1250 Kensington Road, Bloomfield Hills, MI 48304
Tel. 248-646-8900; Admissions Ext. 129; Fax 248-646-4143
Web Site www.ashmi.org; E-mail blopiccolo@ashmi.org

The Academy of the Sacred Heart, a member of the Network of Sacred Heart Schools, is Michigan's oldest independent school, founded in 1851. It is a Catholic, college preparatory day school enrolling approximately 500 girls, infant to Grade 12, and boys, infant to Grade 8. Students reflect many cultures and faiths from the Detroit area. Coeducational classes in the Early Childhood Program through Grade 4 focus on the wide span of developmental needs in these formative years. The Academy offers a Middle School for boys, Kensington Hall, and Middle (Grades 5–8) and Upper (Grades 9–12) Schools for Girls. Each program adapts curriculum, student activities, retreats, and extracurricular programs to challenge and maximize the potential of each student. The goals and criteria of Sacred Heart education enable students to live lives of faith, intellectual excellence, responsibility to self and community, and personal integrity. Tuition: $12,700–$19,900. Financial aid is available. Barbara Lopiccolo is Director of Admissions; Bridget Bearss, RSCJ (Maryville University, B.A.; Washington University, M.A.), was appointed Head of School in 2000.

The Grosse Pointe Academy   1885

171 Lake Shore Road, Grosse Pointe Farms, MI 48236
Tel. 313-886-1221; Admissions Ext. 146; Fax 313-886-4615
Web Site www.gpacademy.org; E-mail mmcdermott@gpacademy.org

THE GROSSE POINTE ACADEMY in Grosse Pointe Farms, Michigan, is an independent day school enrolling boys and girls in a Montessori Early School (ages 2¹/₂–5), a Lower School (Grades 1–5), and a Middle School (Grades 6–8). Grosse Pointe Farms is a suburb located six miles northeast of downtown Detroit and is the central community of the five Grosse Pointes. The school makes extensive use of the museums and other cultural resources of southeastern Michigan.

The Grosse Pointe Academy was founded as the Academy of the Sacred Heart in 1885. It was operated by the Religious of the Sacred Heart as a day and boarding primary, middle, and upper school for girls. The Academy's coeducational Montessori Early School was built in 1887. In 1969, the school was reincorporated under the original charter as The Grosse Pointe Academy and ownership was transferred to the Academy Board of Trustees. In September of that year, The Grosse Pointe Academy opened as an independent, coeducational day school with 270 students from metropolitan Detroit enrolled in Pre-Kindergarten through Grade 8.

The Grosse Pointe Academy holds that learning is a continuous and highly personalized process extending throughout life and requires a strong intellectual, moral, and physical foundation. Moral values and Montessori principles, emphasizing

attention to individual needs, govern the Early School and are sustained throughout the grades. Founded on Christian principles, the school has as its mission to respect all religious beliefs and cultures while honoring the value and growth of each individual child. It is within this framework that all life at the Academy is conducted.

The Academy is a nonprofit organization governed by a self-perpetuating Board of 25 Trustees, which meets eight times a year. There are 727 living alumnae of the Academy of the Sacred Heart and 1341 alumni of The Grosse Pointe Academy. The Academy, through its Parent Coordinating Council, operates an active parent volunteer program. Parents, alumni, and friends assist the school financially through Annual Fund and "Action Auction," a yearly fund-raiser involving the entire community.

The Grosse Pointe Academy is a member of the Independent Schools Association of the Central States, the National Association of Independent Schools, the Association of Independent Michigan Schools, the American Montessori Society, and the Educational Records Bureau.

THE CAMPUS. The Academy is situated on a stately, 20-acre campus overlooking Lake St. Clair. The historic facilities, which include a half-mile double row of maples known as the Nun's Walk, appear in local, state, and national registers of historic sites. Six tennis courts, two playgrounds, and fields for lacrosse and soccer are also located on campus.

THE GROSSE POINTE ACADEMY

The Lakeshore Building, completed in 1885 as the Academy and Convent of the Sacred Heart, now houses business, alumni, and advancement offices. It is also used for meetings and social functions. The Montessori Early School (circa 1887) has spacious classrooms. An additional classroom and a new gymnasium were added in 1987. The main school building, which houses Grades 1–8, was completely renovated for the start of school in 2007–08. The renovations brought a modern learning environment to the Academy while maintaining the traditional look and feel of the historic building. Classrooms are now 200 to 250 square feet larger with new computers and plasma televisions. Renovations also include improved lighting and acoustics, a centerpiece library/media center, state-of-the-art science and computer labs, dedicated Lower and Middle School wings, a new performing arts wing, and a spacious third-floor loft for visual arts, foreign language, and Christian life classes. The Tracy Fieldhouse gymnasium/auditorium was dedicated in 1990. The Grosse Pointe Academy Chapel (circa 1899) is the site of many weddings and school chapel assemblies. The school-owned plant is valued at more than $30,000,000.

THE FACULTY. Phil Demartini (Columbia University, B.A.; Fordham University, M.Ed.) is the Head of School. He is the former Headmaster of St. Francis School in Goshen, Kentucky. Prior to that, Mr. Demartini was Lower School Principal at Metairie Park Country Day School in New Orleans, Louisiana, and Principal of the Upper School at Elisabeth Morrow School in Englewood, New Jersey.

The full-time faculty consist of 5 men and 39 women. They hold baccalaureate degrees from Albion, Baldwin-Wallace, Central Michigan, Chatham, College of St. Catherine, Columbia, Cortland State, Curry, Denison, Eastern Michigan, Hillsdale, Kalamazoo, Marygrove, Mercy, Michigan State, Nazareth, Northern Illinois, Oakland, Ohio State, Purdue, St. Joseph's, St. Lawrence, St. Mary's of Notre Dame, Sweet Briar, Trent, Wayne State, Western Michigan, and the Universities of Akron, Denver, Maryland, Michigan, and Windsor. They hold advanced degrees from Eastern Michigan, Fordham, Long Island University, Marygrove, Michigan State, Oakland, Ohio State, Wayne State, Xavier, and the Universities of Michigan and Toronto.

THE GROSSE POINTE ACADEMY

Faculty benefits include health and dental insurance, life insurance, long-term disability, a retirement plan, and Social Security. Leaves of absence are granted on approval of the Board of Trustees.

A school nurse is on duty at the Academy and three hospitals are located nearby.

STUDENT BODY. In 2008–09, the Academy enrolled 321 boys and girls, with 105 students in the Early School and 216 in Grades 1–8. Students came from the Grosse Pointes and 32 metropolitan Detroit communities and reflected a wide range of socioeconomic backgrounds.

ACADEMIC PROGRAM. The academic year, divided into semesters, begins in early September and ends in mid-June. Major vacations are scheduled in December and March. Classes are held five days a week between 8:30 A.M. and 3:20 P.M. In the Early School, students are taught on an individualized basis, using Montessori methods of education. No more than ten children are in the charge of each adult. Grades 1–3 are in self-contained classrooms and Grades 4 and 5 provide a transition to the fully departmentalized programs of Grades 6–8. The emphasis on individual attention is maintained throughout the Middle School years. Academy teachers pride themselves on enabling students to achieve in all areas and are available to assist students as necessary. Grades are sent to parents three times a year supplemented by regular conferences scheduled in October and February.

All students in Grades 1–5 take reading, language arts (including spelling, vocabulary, writing, grammar, and literature), French, Spanish, Chinese, social studies, mathematics, computers, science, religion, music, art, library/reference skills,

and physical education. The emphasis is on mastery of basic skills. Multitexts and teacher-designed programs for reinforcement and enrichment are used so that each student can progress at his or her level. Computers, videotapes, and video disks are employed. Electives in music, art, the social sciences, and science supplement the regular program. Instruction in environmental education is also offered. A formalized leadership program is a hallmark of the eighth-grade year.

Before- and After-School Care programs are available, at an extra charge, for children ages 3 to 14 on a daily or occasional basis.

Students graduating from The Grosse Pointe Academy enroll at private, parochial, and public high schools. In recent years, graduates have attended the Academy of the Sacred Heart, Andrews School, Brother Rice, Cranbrook, DeLaSalle Collegiate, Detroit Country Day, Fay School, Grosse Pointe North, Grosse Pointe South, The Gunnery, Holderness, Hotchkiss, The Hun School of Princeton, Kingswood, Lake Forest Academy, Lawrenceville, The Leelanau School, Marian High School, Mercy, Miss Porter's, Pomfret, Portsmouth Abbey, Proctor, St. George's School, St. Mark's, University Liggett School, University of Detroit High School, and Woodberry Forest.

Academy Adventures, a summer program for boys and girls ages 10 to 15, offers a variety of learning opportunities.

STUDENT ACTIVITIES. Middle School students are elected to the Student Council. The Council operates a number of extracurricular programs.

Students are involved in school activities through the yearbook, crafts, and cooking. Grades 4–8 participate in volunteer services and Student Council activities. Grades 7 and 8 perform 20 hours of community service each year.

Middle School teams compete with other private schools in lacrosse, soccer, basketball, and tennis for boys; and tennis, basketball, volleyball, and soccer for girls. Both boys and girls participate in the cross-country team. Teams from Grades 4 and 5 play limited interscholastic schedules.

An intramural sports program for Grades 1–5 includes soccer, floor hockey, basketball, softball, and lacrosse.

THE GROSSE POINTE ACADEMY

Special events include the Back to School Picnic, Parents' Orientation Nights, Fall and Winter/Spring Sports Awards Assemblies, Spirit Nights, Alumni Reunions, Book Fair, a tree-lighting ceremony, Alumni Scholarship Benefit, Dads' Day, Grandparents' Day, the Eighth Grade Play, and the William Charles McMillan III Lecture Series.

ADMISSION AND COSTS. The Grosse Pointe Academy seeks academically strong and motivated students. Students are admitted in all grades with available spaces on the basis of standardized tests, recommendations, and personal interviews. Applications, with a fee of $50, should be submitted before

July 1. Students may be admitted during the school year under special conditions.

THE GROSSE POINTE ACADEMY

In 2009–10, tuition for half-day Early School is $9600; for full-day Early School, $13,800; the fees for Grades 1 through 8 range from $14,800 to $17,100, depending on grade. Tuition insurance and payment plans are available. The Grosse Pointe Academy subscribes to FACTS for Financial Aid and offers approximately $500,000 in financial aid annually to 13 percent of the students on the basis of need and academic standing.

Principal, Early School and Grades 1–3: Jennifer Kendall
Principal, Middle School: Scott Tily
Director of Admissions: Molly McDermott
Director of Finance & Operations: Angela Boyle
Director of Advancement: Jennifer H. Parke

Kalamazoo Country Day School   1979

4221 East Milham Road, Kalamazoo, MI 49002
Tel. 269-329-0116; Fax 269-329-1850
Web Site www.kalamazoocountryday.org
E-mail sbridenstine@kalamazoocountryday.org

Kalamazoo Country Day School, founded by a group of families interested in providing quality education in the area, enrolls 200 boys and girls in Pre-School–Grade 8. It provides a supportive environment that emphasizes active learning, enhancement of self-esteem, and promotion of individual talents and community responsibility. Spanish, computers, music, art, and drama complement the traditional subjects. Students with learning differences are accommodated. Science fair, speech festival, Student Council, ski club, and sports are among the activities. Tuition: $8194–$8324. Financial aid is available. Sheila Bridenstine (Saint Louis University, A.B.) is Director.

The Leelanau School   1929

One Old Homestead Road, Glen Arbor, MI 49636
Tel. 231-334-5800; Admissions 231-334-5824
[Toll-free] 800-533-5262; Fax 231-334-5898
Web Site www.leelanau.org; E-mail admissions@leelanau.org

Teachers Cora and William "Skipper" Beals founded The Leelanau School in 1929 to provide an "experience based, five-senses education" in a caring, family-like environment. A co-

educational, college preparatory school enrolling 50 boarding and day students in Grades 9–12, Leelanau encourages students to pursue high moral standards, practice self-discipline, and make wise decisions throughout their lives. The 42-acre campus on Lake Michigan's Sleeping Bear Bay provides a living classroom for environmental and scientific studies. The curriculum emphasizes effective instruction in language usage, humanities, math, and science. Advanced Placement courses, the Learning Resource Center, and English as a Second Language are also integral to Leelanau's program. Student government, publications, music and fine arts, community service, wilderness trips, and interscholastic sports are also emphasized. A summer academic program is available. Boarding Tuition: $49,853. Day Tuition: $24,368. Five-day boarding is an option. Todd A. Holt is Director of Admissions; Matthew Ralston was appointed President and Head of School in 2009.

Notre Dame Preparatory School and Marist Academy   1994

1300 Giddings Road, Pontiac, MI 48340-2108
Tel. 248-373-5300; Fax 248-373-8024
Web Site www.ndpma.org; E-mail ndp@ndpma.org

NOTRE DAME PREPARATORY SCHOOL AND MARIST ACADEMY in Pontiac, Michigan, is a Roman Catholic, college preparatory day school enrolling young women and men in Grades 9 through 12. Marist Academy, Notre Dame Prep's middle school counterpart, enrolls students in Grades 6 through 8. A second campus housing Junior Kindergarten–Grade 5 is located in Waterford. Pontiac, an industrial city of 72,800 residents, is located 30 miles northwest of Detroit. Many students take private car pools to the campus, and the School maintains a fleet of eight buses.

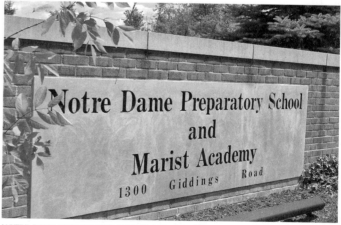

NOTRE DAME PREPARATORY SCHOOL AND MARIST ACADEMY

At the request of the Archbishop of Detroit, the Marist Fathers and Brothers of the Boston Province founded Notre Dame Preparatory to provide an excellent college preparatory program with a strong Catholic identity. The School opened in 1994 with 183 high school students and 18 staff members and met with immediate success. The middle school was added a few years later, and today Notre Dame Prep and Marist Academy enroll 1021 young people with the support of 125 faculty and staff.

Notre Dame Prep's mission derives from the philosophy of Fr. Jean-Claude Colin, founder of the Marist Fathers and Brothers. The School seeks to train students as faithful and active disciples of Christ, to instruct them in "all virtues," and to teach them "letters and various branches of knowledge." Intended to develop "Christian people, upright citizens, and academic scholars," the rigorous curriculum encompasses a wide range of liberal arts and sciences while placing equal emphasis on moral conduct and the formation of spiritual values.

NOTRE DAME PREPARATORY SCHOOL AND MARIST ACADEMY

A not-for-profit institution, Notre Dame is operated by the Marist Fathers and Brothers, USA Province. It is governed by a Board of Directors whose members are provincial councilors of the sponsoring congregation; the 26-member Board of Trustees is chosen from a slate presented to the Directors. The School is accredited by the North Central Association of Colleges and Schools and the Independent Schools Association of the Central States. Notre Dame holds membership in the National Catholic Educational Association and is also an International Baccalaureate World School.

THE CAMPUS. Notre Dame Prep and Marist Academy occupy nearly 100 wooded acres on the outskirts of Pontiac. The 150,000-square-foot main building contains all the School's classrooms, science and computer labs, and art and music studios as well as a chapel, guidance and counseling center, bookstore, cafeteria, gymnasium, and the 10,000-square-foot St. Pete.

Notre Dame Prep's rapid growth has necessitated a vigorous expansion of its facilities. The School plans to continue an equally aggressive expansion program over the course of the next several years. A ProGrass artificial turf surface and six new, state-of-the-art tennis courts are among the improvements to the athletic facilities. A new, 22,000-square-foot gym/band building opened in the spring of 2008.

The School proper is owned by the Marist congregation; the building is leased from the Archdiocese of Detroit.

THE FACULTY. In 1993, Rev. Leon M. Olszamowski, s.m., was appointed to organize the founding of Notre Dame Preparatory School. He serves as President of both Notre Dame and Marist Academy. A native of Detroit, Father Leon graduated from Notre Dame High School in Harper Woods, Michigan, where he was later Principal. He holds a B.A. from Boston College, an M.A. from the University of Notre Dame, an M.Div. from Weston School of Theology, and M.A. and Ph.D. degrees from The Catholic University of America. Rev. Joseph C. Hindelang, s.m. (Assumption College, B.A.; Weston School of Theology, M.Div.), became Principal in 2002. Mrs. Sandra Favrow (Wayne State University, B.A.; Saginaw Valley State University, M.A.) has headed Marist Academy for 13 years.

Notre Dame Prep and Marist Academy have a combined faculty and staff of 125, all but 6 of whom are full-time. In the Upper School, 75 percent hold advanced degrees, including 3 doctorates. Among their representative colleges and universities are Alma, Assumption, Central Michigan, Ferris State, Marygrove, Michigan State, Northern Illinois, Northern Michigan, Oakland University, Ohio University, Olivet College, Pennsylvania State, Rutgers, Saginaw Valley State, St. Mary's College, Temple, Trinity, Wayne State, Western Michigan, Siena, and the Universities of Arizona, Dayton, Detroit, Maryland, Massachusetts, Michigan, Notre Dame, and Washington.

STUDENT BODY. In 2009–10, 680 boys and girls are enrolled at Notre Dame and 195 at Marist Academy. While 82 percent are Roman Catholic, students from all faiths are welcome.

ACADEMIC PROGRAM. The school year, from late August to early June, is divided into semesters, with Thanksgiving, Christmas, Winter Break, and Easter vacations and several religious and national holidays. Grades are posted six times a year.

All students wear the school uniform throughout the day. The school day consists of nine periods between 7:30 A.M. and 2:45 P.M. Some students have a study hall. The average enrollment is 22–24 in core courses or as few as 5 in specialized courses. Members of the National Honor Society provide tutoring three days a week.

At Marist Academy, students follow the curriculum set by the IB North America Middle Years Programme. Authorization for this program arrived July 13, 2009.

To graduate, Upper School students must earn 28 credits including 4 each in religion and English; 3 each in mathematics, science, and social science; 2 in a modern language; 1 in health/physical education; and .5 each in fine and performing arts and computer applications. Ten hours of community service are required each year. These requirements meet or exceed the admission criteria of Michigan's state universities. The ACT composite is 26. The Upper School has the highest Michigan Merit Exam score among Michigan Catholic schools.

NOTRE DAME PREPARATORY SCHOOL AND MARIST ACADEMY

Among the Upper School courses are Old Testament, New Testament Studies 1–2, Foundations of Catholic Morality, Moral Issues and Lifestyles, History of the Church 1–2; Composition 1–2, Research and Speech, Introduction to the Classics, American and English Authors 1–2, World Literature 1–2, Theater, Public Speaking, Lincoln-Douglas Debate, Forensics; Algebra 1–2, Geometry 1–2, Trigonometry and Pre-Calculus, Probability and Statistics; five-year programs in French, German, Mandarin Chinese, Spanish; Biology 1–2, Chemistry 1–2, Astronomy 1–2, Human Anatomy and Physiology; World History and Cultures 1–2, United States History 1–2, American Government, The

Modern World Since 1945, Economics, Current Issues, Law, Psychology, Sociology; Computer Applications, Computer Science Topics, JAVA and C++ Programming; Accounting 1–2, Business Law; Exploration in Art, Drawing, Painting, Pottery, Commercial Art, Portfolio 1–2; Marching/Symphonic Band, Jazz Band 1–2, Concert Choir, Honors Choir; and Health/Physical Education 1–2, Weight Training, and Officiating.

NOTRE DAME PREPARATORY SCHOOL AND MARIST ACADEMY

Advanced Placement courses are available in Computer Science, Literature, Composition, Calculus, French, Spanish, German, American History, European History, Chemistry, Biology, Physics, Environmental Science, Psychology, and Art. A complete range of International Baccalaureate courses is also offered.

All 193 seniors in the Class of 2009 were accepted to college; 99 percent were accepted to four-year colleges and universities, and nearly all were admitted by "early decision." They were offered nearly $11,000,000 in scholarships. Michigan State, Oakland University, and the University of Michigan (Ann Arbor) were the graduates' three most popular choices; other schools included Art Institute of Chicago, Boston College, Bowling Green State, DePaul, George Washington University, Loyola, Purdue, School of Visual Arts, Syracuse, Western Michigan University, Xavier, and the Universities of Colorado, Nevada, Notre Dame, Pittsburgh, Tennessee, and Wisconsin.

A summer program offers enrichment in language arts, mathematics, and computer science.

STUDENT ACTIVITIES. Extracurricular activities are designed to meet diverse student interests, provide leadership opportunities, and maintain school spirit and morale. Grades 9–12 elect eight representatives per class to the Student Council, which is responsible for overseeing the "life-giving" events of the School, such as dances, fund-raisers, games, and interaction with other schools.

Interscholastic sports are played at all grade levels and involve more than three-quarters of the student body. Marist Academy is a member of the Catholic Youth Organization; Notre Dame holds membership in the Detroit Catholic High School League and the Michigan High School Athletic Association.

Fighting Irish teams compete in football, soccer, golf, cross-country, basketball, ice hockey, wrestling, baseball, lacrosse, tennis, and track for boys, while girls' teams are organized in basketball, cross-country, tennis, swimming, volleyball, soccer, softball, pompon, lacrosse, and track. Notre Dame's cheerleading squads are an important addition to many varsity contests.

Among the various groups in which students are involved are a statewide Student Congress discussion tournament, the National Honor Society, forensics and debate, a drama and theater program, and the Optimist (community outreach), Computer, Modern Language, Students Against Drunk Driving, F.I.R.S.T. Robotics, and Chess Clubs. Students publish *The Legend* (yearbook) and *The Leprechaun* (newspaper). Other popular activities are musical performances in the fall and spring, band and chorus concerts, and a visual arts exhibit.

Throughout the year, the Campus Ministry plans Kairos and other retreats and special liturgies and provides pastoral counseling as a means of furthering spiritual development. Homecoming, a three-day celebration of school spirit enjoyed by students, parents, and alumni, features a pep rally, football game, and dance. The calendar also includes traditions such as Halloween Party, Thanksgiving Liturgy, Irish Week, Walk-a-Thon, sports banquets, Mothers' Mass and Brunch, Awards Night, senior prom, and graduation.

ADMISSION AND COSTS. Notre Dame Prep and Marist Academy welcome capable students of good character and ability, regardless of racial, ethnic, religious, or socioeconomic backgrounds. Students are accepted in Junior Kindergarten–Grade 12. Admission is offered on the basis of the entrance exam, previous academic transcripts and testing, teacher and principal recommendations, and a personal interview. Acceptance letters are mailed on the fourth Friday in January. The application fee is $40.

In 2009–10, tuition is $10,470, plus uniforms, books, and parking and retreat fees. Merit-based scholarships are awarded in the amount of $375,000, and need-based financial aid of about $200,000 is available. Students may earn money for some on-campus jobs.

President: Rev. Leon M. Olszamowski, s.m., Ph.D.
Vice-President: Andrew A. Guest
Principal: Rev. Joseph C. Hindelang, s.m.
Middle School Principal: Sandra J. Favrow
Lower School Principal: Diana Atkins
Vice-Principal & Dean of Faculty: Donna A. Kotzan
Assistant Principal: Rev. James J. Strasz, s.m.
Assistant Principal: Kimberly Anderson
Assistant Principal: Jill Mistretta
Campus Ministers: Deacon Anthony Morici, Rev. Brian Cidlevich & Ms. Grace Seroka
Directors of Admissions: Gregory P. Simon, Barbara Hall & Kathleen Offer
Vice President for Advancement: Andrew Guest
College Counselor: Justine Sciriha
Business Manager: Anthony Block
Directors of Athletics: Betty Wroubel, Marty Simmons & Megan Thayer

The Roeper School   1941

41190 Woodward Avenue, Bloomfield Hills, MI 48304
Tel. 248-203-7300; Admissions 248-203-7317; Fax 248-203-7350
Web Site www.roeper.org; E-mail admissions@roeper.org

The Roeper School is a coeducational day school for gifted children enrolling approximately 620 students in Pre-Kindergarten–Grade 12. Founded by George and Annemarie Roeper, it seeks to "provide an environment that fosters intellectual stimulation, independence, breadth of view, and compassion." The Lower School is in Bloomfield Hills; the Middle/Upper School is in Birmingham. A strong core curriculum is enhanced

THE ROEPER SCHOOL

by a broad selection of classes and activities to meet the interests of students. Tuition: $4500–$21,250. Financial Aid: $500,000. Lori Zinser is Admissions Director; Randall Dunn (Brown University, A.B.; Harvard University, M.Ed.) was appointed Head of School in 2004.

University Liggett School   1878

Main Campus: 1045 Cook Road, Grosse Pointe Woods, MI 48236
Tel. 313-884-4444; Fax 313-884-1775
Middle School: 850 Briarcliff Drive, Grosse Pointe Woods, MI 48236
Tel. 313-886-4220; Fax 313-417-8002
Web Site www.uls.org; E-mail kbreen@uls.org

University Liggett School is a coeducational learning community enrolling 545 students as day students in Pre-Kindergarten–Grade 12. The two campuses, totaling more than 50 acres, provide three libraries, two swimming pools, language and science labs, and an outdoor ice arena. The college preparatory curriculum is designed to create a lifelong quest for knowledge through challenging courses in the liberal arts, sciences, and humanities. The School's goals support growth of self-reliance, self-respect, concern for others, and commitment to community service. Character development and leadership skills share equal emphasis with academic achievement. In the Upper School, honors and AP courses are available in every discipline, and students may choose from Latin, Ancient Greek, Chinese, French, and Latin. All ULS graduates go on to college. Middle and Upper School teams compete in ten sports. Other extracurricular activities including yearbook, dance, drama, art guild, singing groups, academic club, and summer programs. Tuition: $5180–$19,580. Financial aid is available. Kevin Breen is Director of Enrollment; Joseph P. Healey, Ph.D., is Head of School.

UNIVERSITY LIGGETT SCHOOL

MINNESOTA

The Blake School   1900

Northrop Campus (Upper School): 511 Kenwood Parkway,
Minneapolis, MN 55403
Blake Campus (Lower/Middle School): 110 Blake Road South,
Hopkins, MN 55343
Highcroft Campus (Lower School): 301 Peavey Lane, Wayzata,
MN 55391
Tel. 952-988-3400; Admissions 952-988-3420; Fax 952-988-3455
Web Site www.blakeschool.org

THE BLAKE SCHOOL

Founded in 1900, The Blake School is an independent, coeducational, nonsectarian, college preparatory day school serving Pre-Kindergarten–Grade 12. Coming from more than 56 Twin Cities' communities, over 1375 students attend Blake on one of three campuses in Minneapolis, Hopkins, and Wayzata. The challenging liberal arts curriculum integrates academics, arts, and athletics. All graduates go on to four-year colleges. Blake is dedicated to creating a safe and inclusive environment that encourages risk-taking, recognizes effort, and provides opportunity for success for everyone. The School is committed to diversity, and community involvement is expected of every student. Tuition: $13,000–$21,600. Financial Aid: $3,800,000. Adaline Shinkle is Director of Admissions; John C. Gulla is Head of School.

Breck School   1886

123 Ottawa Avenue North, Minneapolis, MN 55422
Tel. 763-381-8100; Admissions 763-381-8200; Fax 763-381-8288
Web Site www.breckschool.org; E-mail info@breckschool.org

Enrolling 1200 students in Preschool–Grade 12, Breck is a coeducational, college preparatory day school in the Episcopal tradition. Founded in 1886, Breck is a welcoming community with a long-standing commitment to offering its diverse student body an experience rich in academic rigor, arts, athletics, and service. Breck's mission is to provide a supportive and caring environment in which young people from all faiths and backgrounds can develop self-worth and acquire the knowledge and skills essential to a productive life. Chapel attendance and religion courses are required. Emphasis on mastery of fundamental concepts in reading and language arts, math, science, and social studies in the Lower School prepares students for the challenges and opportunities in the higher grades. The arts, modern languages, and technology are integrated throughout the curriculum at all levels. AP courses, independent study, international travel, and off-campus internships enhance the program in Grades 9–12. Student Councils, Mock Trial, Quiz Bowl, music, drama, publications, interest clubs, and intramural, coed, and interscholastic sports are among the activities. Tuition & Fees: $15,470–$22,825. Financial aid is available. Jim James is Director of Admissions; Edward Kim is Head of School.

Convent of the Visitation School   1873

2455 Visitation Drive, Mendota Heights, MN 55120-1696
Tel. 651-683-1700; Admissions 651-683-1707; Fax 651-454-7144
Web Site www.visitation.net; E-mail vischool@vischool.org

CONVENT OF THE VISITATION SCHOOL

Visitation enrolls 575 day students, with boys and girls in Preschool–Grade 6 and girls only in Grades 7–12. The School provides a challenging college preparatory program within a sound religious environment. The curriculum emphasizes the liberal arts and sciences, enhanced by theology, computers, and Advanced Placement courses in the Upper School. The School takes an individualized approach to educating young people, recognizing each one's unique gifts and talents. Seniors undertake a two-week service project, and service learning is incorporated into the curriculum at all levels. The School's philosophy is rooted in joyful optimism and the infinite worth of each individual. The athletic program begins in Kindergarten, with 13 varsity sports options in Grades 7–12. Students in Grades 7–12 collaborate with young men from Saint Thomas Academy, Visitation's brother school, in many areas. Visitation fine arts program is nationally renowned. Leadership skills development is incorporated into the program, recognizing each young person's leadership potential. Tuition: $6500–$16,600. Financial aid is available (K–12). Katie Owens is Director of Admissions; Dawn Nichols, Ed.D., is Head of School.

MISSISSIPPI

Jackson Academy   1959

4908 Ridgewood Road, P.O. Box 14978, Jackson, MS 39236-4978
Tel. 601-362-9676; Fax 601-364-5722
Web Site www.jacksonacademy.org
E-mail lpurviance@jacksonacademy.org

JACKSON ACADEMY in Jackson, Mississippi, is the state's largest independent school, enrolling approximately 1300 boys and girls as day students in K3 through Grade 12. Located 180 miles north of New Orleans, the state capital (population 350,000) is home to five colleges, the Mississippi Arts Festival, Civil War battlefield sites, museums, and civic opera, theater, and the International Ballet Competition. Students and faculty enjoy frequent enrichment excursions to such attractions as a means of enlivening and reinforcing classroom learning.

Jackson Academy was established in 1959 to teach children to read by phonics. Today, the school continues its emphasis on reading and writing across the disciplines as it renews its commitment to provide a "superior academic program in every subject." Preparation for success in four-year colleges is a primary focus, and 100 percent of Jackson Academy graduates go on to higher education. In a nurturing, family-like environment, students are respected and challenged to become responsible citizens capable of achieving their highest intellectual, spiritual, social, emotional, and physical potential. The nonsectarian school, which promotes values and ethical conduct, welcomes students from diverse racial, ethnic, religious, and socioeconomic backgrounds.

JACKSON ACADEMY

Governed by a 12-member Board of Trustees, Jackson Academy is accredited by the Southern Association of Colleges and Schools and the Southern Association of Independent Schools. The Academy holds membership in the National Association of Independent Schools, among other organizations. In 2005, The Cum Laude Society installed a chapter at Jackson Academy. The school is aided in its mission by parent groups and the Alumni Association, which represents more than 2500 graduates.

THE CAMPUS. Jackson Academy's spacious campus is on the corner of Ridgewood Road and Sheffield Drive in the northeast area of the city. The 48 acres contain nine major academic buildings housing preschool, elementary, and junior and senior high divisions, each with its own library. In the Learning Center are upper school language, art, and social studies classrooms and the networked secondary library, equipped with an online database and computer labs to provide access to information. The entire campus is completely networked with Internet connections in every classroom and additional access through three labs, a multimedia training and presentation theater, and a teacher-training lab. Other academic facilities are science labs, art and music rooms for all grade levels, a multipurpose building, two fully equipped gymnasiums, and a band hall. Recently, Jackson Academy opened a new Performing Arts Center that houses an 800-seat theater. Athletic resources include a lighted football stadium, and Raider Park, with lighted baseball and softball diamonds, a soccer field, and a dedicated track and field facility. Play areas for younger children are also on campus.

THE FACULTY. James Peter Jernberg, Jr., was appointed President and Head of School in 2005. He has earned bachelor's and master's degrees from Delta State University and completed additional graduate work at Mississippi State University and the Universities of Mississippi and South Carolina. Previously, Mr. Jernberg held administrative positions at Indianola Academy and is past president of the Southern Association of Independent Schools and a member of the Board of Trustees of the Southern Association of Colleges and Schools.

JACKSON ACADEMY

Dr. Pat Taylor took office as Headmaster in 2007. Previously, he spent 34 years at St. Paul's Episcopal School in Mobile, Alabama, where he served in several administrative and teaching positions. Dr. Taylor has also held leadership positions with SACS and SAIS.

The 150 faculty members hold baccalaureate degrees, and over 60 percent have earned advanced degrees. They are graduates of colleges and universities throughout the United States who participate regularly in opportunities for continued growth and professional development.

STUDENT BODY. In 2009–10, Jackson Academy enrolled 1268 students in K3 (age 3) to Grade 12.

ACADEMIC PROGRAM. The school year, from mid-August to late May, is divided into four nine-week grading periods, with Thanksgiving, Christmas, and spring recesses and several national holidays. A typical day, from 8:00 A.M. to 3:00 P.M., includes seven classes, lunch, and an activity break. Preschoolers are dismissed at 11:30 A.M. unless they are enrolled in the optional Lunch Bunch program.

Jackson Academy's preschool program is designed to promote a nurturing and loving learning environment where children acquire self-esteem and a positive approach to the educational experience. Basic concepts in core disciplines are introduced through reading, phonics, handwriting, story time, and library activities. Students work and play in small groups and rotate their activities every 20 minutes. Art, music, perceptual motor skills, and character/values are also integrated into the program. A highlight of the preschool program is an annual weeklong visit to the "World of Beatrix Potter" where children enjoy exploring the author's art and stories in an English-garden setting and then develop their own story-telling abilities.

Grades 1–6 feature a traditional curriculum centered on reading, writing, mathematics, science, social studies, and technology. Hands-on learning and age-appropriate materials provide students with a strong foundation on which to build academic competence. Music, Spanish, French, art, community service, and physical education, including Little Dribblers Basketball, round out the program.

The Secondary School (Grades 7–12) offers a curriculum of more than 80 required and elective courses, including English 7–12, English Literature, World Literature, Forensics, Creative Writing, Speech; World History, American History, American Government/Politics, American Government/Economics; Biology, Chemistry, Physics, Anatomy and Physiology, Computer Programming, Computer Applications; Algebra I–III, Pre-Calculus, Calculus, Geometry; French I–V, Spanish I–V, Latin I–IV; and Art I–IV, Band, Film History, Select Choir, and Foundations of Music.

JACKSON ACADEMY

An Honors program in math, science, and English begins in Grade 7, and Advanced Placement courses for Grades 11–12 are available in English Language, English Literature, American History, American Government/Politics, Biology, Chemistry, Physics, Calculus, and Art. About 40 percent of juniors and seniors take these courses, which are weighted according to the subject's degree of difficulty. Of those sitting for AP exams, 80 percent score "3" or higher. In addition, over the last four years, approximately 10 percent of the senior class has been recognized as National Merit Semifinalists. The school has also graduated a Rhodes Scholar.

To receive a Jackson Academy diploma, students must earn at least 22 credits and successfully complete four years of English, math, science, and history/social studies; two years of a foreign language (Latin, French, or Spanish); four electives; and one-half unit of computer application.

JACKSON ACADEMY

All 98 graduates in the Class of 2009 went on to higher education. Seniors chose to attend colleges and universities around the country including such Mississippi schools as Belhaven, Delta State, Millsaps, Mississippi College, Mississippi State, and the University of Mississippi. Other institutions attended by 2009 graduates included Columbia, Duke, Samford, Southern Methodist, Vanderbilt, Vassar, Virginia Military Institute, and the Universities of Alabama, California (Berkeley), and Notre Dame.

Jackson Academy's summer enrichment program provides courses for academic credit, leadership, reading and study strategies, art, cheerleading, and sports camps.

STUDENT ACTIVITIES. The extracurricular program is designed to develop new interests, promote leadership and service, and provide fun, socialization, and athletic and artistic opportunities. Qualified scholars may be invited to membership in the Junior and Senior National Honor Societies and Mu Alpha and Chi Alpha (math) Honor Societies. Jackson Academy is a chapter member of The Cum Laude Society. Academic clubs are organized in science, Latin, Spanish, French, math, forensics, pre-med, chess, and other areas. Students regularly achieve distinction in state and national tournaments and arts and music festivals.

In the fine arts, students perform in color guard, three bands, Encore show choir, and other vocal groups. They also stage music and dramatic productions and publish a yearbook, newspaper, and award-winning literary magazine. Leadership opportunities are found through such organizations as Junior and Senior High Student Councils, Earth Team, Students Against Destructive Decisions, Relay for Life (fund-raising for cancer research), Student Traffic Aides, Big Brothers/Sisters, Fellowship of Christian Athletes, scouting, and Key Club.

In all grades, students reach out to others through a variety of age-appropriate, service-oriented activities such as working for Habitat for Humanity and Toys for Tots, tutoring inner-city children, visiting the elderly, organizing food drives, and undertaking environmental improvement projects.

Jackson Academy athletics help develop sportsmanship, camaraderie, and physical fitness. Raider teams compete in the Mississippi Private School Association and at the AAA state level.

Boys and girls compete in basketball, track, tennis, swimming, golf, soccer, and cross-country. Boys also play football and base-ball, and girls play fast-pitch and slow-pitch softball. Junior High and varsity cheerleaders as well as the Accents and Silver Steppers, all-girl dance groups, provide lively entertainment and spirit-building at games throughout the season. Jackson Academy athletes have a long history of championship teams and currently hold a number of local, state, and regional titles. There are also elementary interscholastic teams in many sports.

Among the traditional events are preschool and first-grade tea parties, All-Sports Night, Homecoming, open houses, Fall Carnival, Winter Festival, Career Day, Features Pageant, awards days, and graduation. Other activities include canoe trips, the junior-senior prom, and national and overseas travel.

ADMISSION AND COSTS. Jackson Academy seeks to enroll stu-dents of good character and academic ability who are eager to excel and participate in the life of the school. It places strong emphasis on personal integrity, achievement, and growth and does not discriminate on the basis of race, color, or national or ethnic origin. Admission is based on standardized test scores, previous academic records, letters of recommendation from teachers and counselors, and a personal interview with the Aca-demic Dean.

In 2009–10, tuition ranges from $4980 in Preschool to $10,380 in Grades 9–12, plus registration fees of $400 to $700, depending on grade. Families of first-time students entering Grades 1–6 pay an Elementary Fund fee of $50 to $300. Dis-counts for siblings, tuition payment plans, and need-based financial aid are available.

President and Head of School: Peter Jernberg
Headmaster: Dr. Pat Taylor
Associate Headmaster: Keith Branning

Director of Alumni Relations: Becky Greer
Director of Admissions & Financial Aid: Linda Purviance
Director of Development: Tim McWilliams
College Admissions Counselor: Amy Bush
Dean of Financial & Legal Affairs: Clifton Kling
Athletic Director: Bobby West

Jackson Preparatory School   1970

3100 Lakeland Drive, Jackson, MS 39232-8834
Tel. 601-939-8611; Fax 601-936-4068
Web Site www.jacksonprep.net

Jackson Preparatory School is a coeducational, college prepara-tory day school that enrolls 764 students in Grades 6 through 12. The School inspires and challenges students toward aca-demic, athletic, and artistic excellence, instills personal integrity through biblical values, and equips students to pursue lives of distinction in service to society. Prep is home to a dedicated fac-ulty, 58 percent of whom hold advanced degrees. Prep offers 13 Advanced Placement courses and electives such as Greek and Mandarin Chinese. The student-teacher ratio is 16:1. Extracur-ricular options include athletics, fine arts, and community ser-vice. The Junior High and Senior High buildings each have computer centers with Internet-connected workstations. The Guyton Science Center houses six state-of-the-art classrooms and a 200-seat Lyceum. The McRae Fine Arts and Media Cen-ter is comprised of three art rooms, a pottery studio, an art gallery, a band hall, and a choral music room. Patriot Avenue features a central plaza and amphitheater seating. The multi-purpose Dining Commons offers alfresco dining and perform-ing space. Tuition & Registration Fee: $9840–$10,840. Tuition assistance is available. Lesley Morton is Director of Admission; Susan Lindsay is Head of School. *Southern Association.*

JACKSON ACADEMY

MISSOURI

Andrews Academy—Lake Saint Louis   2005

170 Feise Road, Lake Saint Louis, MO 63368
Tel. 636-561-7709
Web Site www.andrewsacademy.com
E-mail rciampoli@andrewsacademy.com

Based on progressive educational principles, Andrews Academy at Lake Saint Louis is a traditional, elementary day school enrolling boys and girls in Kindergarten–Grade 5. The school is affiliated with Andrews Academy in St. Louis, founded in 1979. A grade will be added in each of the next four years up to Grade 8. At the state-of-the-art Lake Saint Louis campus, children undertake the time-proven curriculum and program that has been the cornerstone of the original Academy for nearly 30 years. The new school is committed to the highest standards of intellectual, physical, and personal development of each child through an individualized approach to teaching and learning. The campus provides spacious, airy classrooms, digital technology, computer and science labs, art and music studios, and a gym. The curriculum focuses on the acquisition and mastery of skills in language arts, writing, spelling, grammar, science, math, and social studies. Core subjects are enhanced by computer technology, Spanish, library, physical education, and the visual and performing arts. Age-appropriate after-school activities are offered. Tuition: $9110. Robert Ciampoli (Webster University, M.Ed.) is Head of School.

Andrews Academy   1979

888 North Mason Road, St. Louis, MO 63141
Tel. 314-878-1883; Fax 314-878-0759
Web Site www.hope-andrews.com/academy.htm

Andrews Academy is a coeducational day school enrolling 250 students in Junior Kindergarten–Grade 6. The philosophy of Andrews Academy is committed to the highest intellectual, physical, and social development of each child. The curriculum places emphasis on basic skills and individualized instruction. Computer instruction, Spanish, physical education, art, music, science laboratory, and library are offered at all levels. A summer camp, located on the Academy's 20-acre campus, offers numerous activities to nearly 300 campers. Extended-day care for working parents is offered at no extra fee. Tuition: $13,580–$14,220. Joseph C. Patterson (Washington University, B.S., M.Ed.) was appointed Headmaster in 1983.

The Barstow School   1884

11511 State Line Road, Kansas City, MO 64114
Tel. 816-942-3255; Admission 816-277-0307; Fax 816-942-3227
Web Site www.barstowschool.org

The Barstow School offers its 650 students a challenging, creative, and supportive environment where learning is constant, immersive, active, and exciting. The close-knit Preschool–Grade 12 community promotes independence and investigation to help develop forceful, compassionate thinkers, writers, and citizens. Classes stress individual attention and invite self-expression. A Barstow education encourages students and teachers to gather knowledge, seek inspiration, and articulate understanding while growing intellectually, ethically, and emotionally in an atmosphere as rigorous as it is nurturing. The curriculum includes 16 AP courses, a variety of offerings in the visual and performing arts, and an emphasis on technology. Athletics, student government, honor council, clubs, and service learning all teach leadership and the importance of commitment to the greater community. Tuition: $11,125–$16,480. Elizabeth Bartow is Director of Admission; Shane Foster is Head of School.

The College School   1963

1 Newport Place, Webster Groves, MO 63119
Tel. 314-962-9355; Admissions Ext. 111; Fax 314-962-5078
Web Site www.thecollegeschool.org
E-mail admissions@thecollegeschool.org

The College School engages 260 children, age 3–Grade 8, in joyful, meaningful, and creative learning through an adventurous, theme-based, experiential curriculum. The diverse community works as a partnership, cultivating excellence in academics, character, and collaboration as it prepares students for lifelong learning, service, and citizenship. In addition to core subject classes, students have specialist classes in drama, art, music, physical education, and Spanish. Students also engage in theme studies throughout the grades. Themes are focused studies on a science or social studies topic that is examined through a multidisciplinary approach. The School owns three buses, and 60 percent of the faculty have commercial driver's licenses. As a result, transportation is readily available for field trips that connect to areas of study. Outdoor experiences also enrich the School's curriculum. A new greenhouse, gardens, and a teaching kitchen enhance the physical facilities. The early childhood program incorporates the Reggio philosophy. An extensive summer program is available. Tuition: $6370–$12,990. Adrienne Rusbarsky is Director of Admissions; Sheila Gurley is Head of School.

Community School   1914

900 Lay Road, St. Louis, MO 63124
Tel. 314-991-0005; Admission Ext. 315; Fax 314-991-1512
Web Site www.communityschool.com
E-mail admissions@communityschool.com

COMMUNITY SCHOOL

Community School, located on a 16-acre campus in suburban St. Louis, is a coeducational day school enrolling 335 students age 3–Grade 6. The School provides a setting in which each individual can develop and emerge with positive attitudes and values and strong academic achievement. Basic skills are emphasized; French, linguistics, science, social studies, art, shop, band, drama, computer, and physical education are included in the curriculum. The After School Program includes Extended Day, Homework Club, and "mini" classes. A summer program for ages 3–5 is also offered. Tuition: $15,030. Financial aid is available. Dana Scott Saulsberry is Admission Director; Dr. Matthew A. Gould (Earlham College, B.A. 1990; University of Chicago, Ph.D. 1997) is Head of School.

Forsyth School   1961

6235 Wydown Boulevard, St. Louis, MO 63105
Tel. 314-726-4542; Fax 314-726-0112
Web Site ForsythOnline.com
E-mail admission@forsythonline.com

FORSYTH SCHOOL

Forsyth, with 386 day boys and girls age 3–Grade 6, offers a challenging, engaging academic program with support from exceptional teachers on a unique campus located near Washington University. Forsyth stresses individual attention by maintaining a low student-teacher ratio and two teachers per class. With a strong academic foundation that includes the visual and performing arts, sports, and challenge education, graduates are well prepared for excellent secondary schools. Forsyth offers summer programs, a commitment to diversity, a comprehensive extended-day program, year-round league sports, and tuition assistance. A health office, a farm-to-school lunch program, nutrition education, and a strong commitment to daily physical education focus on children's health and well-being. The School employs specialist faculty in science, pre-primary science, library/technology, art, music, drama, Spanish, French, Latin, physical education, and challenge/outdoor education. Recent improvements include a Visual and Performing Arts Center; professional-grade turf field and track, playgrounds, and the Forsyth Adventure Center with a climbing wall, high ropes course, and high beam. Tuition: $15,090. Erica Axelbaum is Director of Admission; Michael J. Vachow is Head of School.

John Burroughs School   1923

755 South Price Road, St. Louis, MO 63124
Tel. 314-993-4040; Admission Ext. 242; Fax 314-567-2896
Web Site www.jburroughs.org; E-mail clavigne@jburroughs.org

Burroughs, a coeducational, college preparatory day school, enrolls 600 students in Grades 7–12 in a curriculum balancing academics, arts, athletics, and activities. Students are actively engaged in learning, and small classes promote respect among faculty and students. Community service and environmental awareness, objectives set by the founders, are integral to the mission. Burroughs emphasizes ethics, diversity, student government, and activities such as American Field Service and International Model UN. The 47.5-acre campus is enhanced by an outdoor facility in Missouri's Ozarks. Informality, challenging academics, and community spirit distinguish a Burroughs education. Tuition: $20,400. Tuition Aid: $1,707,000. Caroline LaVigne is Admission Director; Andy Abbott is Head of School.

Mary Institute and Saint Louis Country Day School   1859

101 North Warson Road, St. Louis, MO 63124
Tel. 314-993-5100; Admission 314-995-7367; Fax 314-872-3257
Web Site www.micds.org; E-mail admissions@micds.org

MARY INSTITUTE AND SAINT LOUIS COUNTRY DAY SCHOOL

Mary Institute and Saint Louis Country Day School, enrolling 1210 students in Junior Kindergarten–Grade 12, is a community where people strive to think critically, live virtuously and compassionately, and act responsibly. The rigorous college preparatory program is designed to foster academic excellence, leadership, and self-confidence; the coordinate Middle School (Grades 5–8) balances single-gender classes in the core curriculum with coed classes and activities. MICDS offers fine arts activities, service learning opportunities, and athletics. Cutting-edge technology, including a 1:1 computer initiative, enhances teaching and learning. A summer program is offered. Tuition: $16,575–$20,040. Financial Aid: $3,400,000. Peggy B. Laramie is Director of Admission; Lisa Lyle is Head of School.

The Pembroke Hill School   1910

400 West 51st Street, Kansas City, MO 64112
Tel. 816-936-1200; Admissions 816-936-1231; Fax 816-936-1218
Web Site www.pembrokehill.org; E-mail csullivan@pembrokehill.org

This coeducational day school enrolls 1180 students in Early Years (age 2)–Grade 12 in a college preparatory program designed to develop the unique intellectual, physical, and creative abilities of each youngster to full potential. In small classes taught by committed, qualified faculty, students undertake an academic curriculum that includes Advanced Placement classes in all departments. Among the activities are student government, publications, community service, and interscholastic teams in 20 sports. Extended care and a summer program of academics, recreation, and athletics are available. Tuition: $7070–$18,335. Carolyn Sullivan is Assistant Head for Admissions and Financial Aid; Steven J. Bellis (Kansas State, B.A.; University of Texas [Austin], M.B.A.; University of Kansas, Ed.D.) is Head.

Rohan Woods School   1937

1515 Bennett Avenue, St. Louis, MO 63122
Tel. 314-821-6270; Fax 314-821-6878
Web Site www.rohanwoods.org; E-mail spage@rohanwoods.org

Rohan Woods School is a private school educating 120 children age 3 through Grade 6. This established St. Louis institution has been educating tomorrow's leaders since 1937 with an accelerated curriculum that emphasizes personal responsibility and respect for all individuals. Rohan Woods offers a learning environment where every child is cherished, encouraged, and prepared for continued success as a lifelong learner. Known for its award-winning leadership and service learning programs, which begin with its youngest students, Rohan Woods is purposely small as a result of more than 40 years of national educational research showing that small schools get results. Children are a part of small-group and multiage-group activities that together create a strongly meshed community reflective of the family feeling that is integral to the fabric of Rohan Woods. To ensure small-group learning and personalized attention, enrollment is limited to an overall 8:1 student-teacher ratio. Tuition: $15,450 (including before-school care, lunches, textbooks, & supplies). Financial aid is available. Sam Templin-Page is Admission Director; Kelly R. Horn is Headmaster.

Rossman School   1917

12660 Conway Road, St. Louis, MO 63141-8625
Tel. 314-434-5877; Fax 314-434-1668
Web Site www.rossmanschool.org; E-mail kmartin@rossmanschool.org

Rossman is an elementary day school featuring a challenging academic program for 230 boys and girls in Junior Kindergarten (age 4)–Grade 6. Seeking to maximize each child's potential, the School holds to a student-teacher ratio of 8:1. The curriculum focuses on the basics of mathematics and language arts and integrates computers, science, social studies, Spanish, Latin, music, art, library, and physical education. A cultural enrichment program, field trips, and athletics supplement the curriculum. After-school Enrichment and Extended Day are available. Tuition (including lunch): $15,125. Applications for financial aid are welcome. Katharine Martin is Director of Admission; Patricia A. Shipley (Webster University, B.A.) is Head of School.

The Wilson School   1913

400 DeMun Avenue, St. Louis, MO 63105
Tel. 314-725-4999; Fax 314-725-5242
Web Site www.wilsonschool.com; E-mail lchartung@wilsonschool.com

Wilson, located in a beautiful, tree-lined neighborhood in historic Clayton, is a coeducational, elementary day school seeking to inspire students to be "confident, passionate, and smart." The nurturing community is small, enrolling approximately 190 children age 3 through Grade 6. Students have the benefit of two teachers per classroom, one class per grade, and specialists who provide instruction in French, Latin, science, music, art, physical education, technology, and library. In the core programs of reading and writing, math, and science, Wilson students often rank nationally in the 90th to 99th percentile on standardized tests. Students are also recognized in regional, state, and nationwide competitions. A new, state-of-the-art gymnasium and a pro-turf soccer field enhance the curriculum. Tuition: $14,490. Laura C. Hartung is Director of Admission; Thad M. Falkner is Head of School.

FORSYTH SCHOOL

NEVADA

The Meadows School 1984

8601 Scholar Lane, Las Vegas, NV 89128
Tel. 702-254-1610; Fax 702-254-2452
Web Site www.themeadowsschool.org
E-mail cgoodman@themeadowsschool.org

THE MEADOWS SCHOOL.

The Meadows is a nonprofit, nonsectarian, coeducational, college preparatory day school serving 910 students in Preschool–Grade 12. Located on a 40-acre campus, the School offers accelerated academics and broad extracurricular, technology, arts, and athletic programs. It seeks to develop in students a love of learning and the desire to become knowledgeable, productive, and compassionate members of society. Standards of high academic achievement are supported by up to 28 AP and 52 Honors courses in all disciplines. The School offers 100 percent four-year college and university acceptance. The Spanish immersion program is mandatory in Kindergarten–Grade 8; Latin is required in Grades 6–8. Tuition & Fees: $8950–$20,420. Financial Aid: $1,100,000. Henry L. Chanin is Headmaster; Carolyn G. Goodman is Founder and President. *Pacific Northwest Association.*

Sage Ridge School 1998

2515 Crossbow Court, Reno, NV 89511
Tel. 775-852-6222; Admissions Ext. 503; Fax 775-852-6228
Web Site www.sageridge.org; E-mail cmurphy@sageridge.org

SAGE RIDGE SCHOOL.

Sage Ridge School is a traditional, core-centered, college preparatory day school serving 234 boys and girls in Grades 5 through 12. The School provides an innovative educational experience that generates excitement for learning and discovery. The dynamic curriculum emphasizes a traditional approach in all grades, integrating technology with a variety of disciplines. Sage Ridge stresses the arts and challenges students to mature as excellent scholars, compassionate citizens, and self-confident adults. Small class sizes ensure individual attention and adequate time for the mastery of core skills and concepts. The School offers a wide range of performing arts and interscholastic athletics. Tuition: $17,000–$17,500 (laptop required). Financial aid is available to qualified families. Carol Murphy is Director of Admission; William Heim III is Headmaster.

NEW HAMPSHIRE

Hampshire Country School   1948

28 Patey Circle, Rindge, NH 03461
Tel. 603-899-3325; Fax 603-899-6521
Web Site www.hampshirecountryschool.org
E-mail admissions@hampshirecountryschool.net

HAMPSHIRE COUNTRY SCHOOL in Rindge, New Hampshire, is a seven-day boarding school enrolling 20–25 high-ability boys who want and need a family-like school community and highly personalized learning environment in order to thrive. Most students are ages 9–15, but boys as young as 8 may be accepted, and a few students may remain through high school graduation. Rindge (population 5200) is situated in the southwestern part of the state, about 35 miles west of Nashua and 60 miles northwest of Boston, Massachusetts. The town is in the Monadnock Region, a predominantly rural area of historic small towns and a wealth of outdoor activities.

Hampshire Country School was founded at its present location in 1948, after being developed gradually by Henry and Adelaide Patey, a psychologist and teacher, respectively. In 1936, the Pateys had welcomed into their home a bright, sensitive young boy who was severely overreacting to the stresses of his own home and community. As other children and young adults joined the Pateys, their home expanded into a small school.

The emphasis of the School has always been on nurturing and developing the abilities and interests of highly intelligent students whose sensitivities and, perhaps, idiosyncrasies, have made adapting to the more aggressive and competitive social climate of larger schools a major challenge. While these students are often labeled with such diagnoses as Asperger's Syndrome, nonverbal learning disabilities (NLD), or ADHD, it is the students' interests, abilities, and natural goodness that are the focus of the School, rather than their disabilities, which can usually be accommodated without undue concern in the small-school setting. Students benefit particularly from the personal attention they receive from approximately 15 faculty members who reside on campus as teachers, dorm parents, and activity instructors, and who work with students in classes of 4–6, dorm groups of 6–7, and activity groups of about 2–15.

HAMPSHIRE COUNTRY SCHOOL

Hampshire Country School is governed by a Board of Trustees, accredited by the New England Association of Schools and Colleges, and approved by the State Department of Educa-

tion. It holds membership in the National Association of Independent Schools, The Association of Boarding Schools, the Small Boarding School Association, and the Independent Schools Association of Northern New England, among other affiliations.

THE CAMPUS. The School is set on the site of historic Cheshire Place, an experimental town established in the late 19th century. The rural area is removed from major traffic arteries and offers a quiet setting far from the distractions of city and suburbia. The School's 1700 acres are intersected by historic stone walls and foundations and feature meadows, woodlands, lakes, streams, beaver ponds, and abundant wildlife. The Wapack Trail crosses the School's wooded ridge, providing 50-mile views in all directions.

HAMPSHIRE COUNTRY SCHOOL

Students reside in four small dorms, each containing single and double rooms, a common living and play room, and a full kitchen for snacks or special occasions. Nutritious meals are served in the School dining room, where students and faculty join together for three family-style meals daily.

Three buildings house the academic facilities, which include six classrooms, a music room, science lab, theater, and a 3000-volume library. Several computers are available exclusively for school work.

THE FACULTY. Bernd Foecking was appointed Headmaster in 2009, after five years at Hampshire Country School as German teacher, dorm parent, and academic coordinator. He holds a B.A. degree from Ruhr Universitat Bochum and an M.Ed. in Experiential Education from Plymouth State University. Mr. Foecking works closely with William Dickerman, the former headmaster, who continues full-time at the School as a faculty member and admissions director.

The 15 men and women of the faculty interact with students both in and out of class. Most have served in various roles during their years at the School. At any one time, 6 have classroom teaching as their primary responsibility; 5 have dorm life and extracurricular activities as their primary responsibility; and 4 carry administrative and supervisory responsibilities. All are involved in teaching or leading afternoon and weekend activities. All have been chosen not only for their scholastic and extracurricular expertise but also for their ability to enjoy and support boys who require an unusual amount of adult energy, personal interest, and accommodation.

Faculty and administrators hold bachelor's and advanced degrees from such institutions as Boston University, California State, Dickinson, Elmira College, Grove City College, Houghton, New England Conservatory of Music, and the Universities of New Hampshire, the South, and Wisconsin.

A registered nurse is on campus four days a week and on

call at other times. Four pediatricians affiliated with a nearby hospital are available as needed.

STUDENT BODY. Small by design, Hampshire Country School enrolls 20–25 boys, primarily ages 9–15, in Grades 3–12. They typically come from about 15 states, well distributed throughout the continental United States, plus an occasional student from abroad.

ACADEMIC PROGRAM. The daily pace at Hampshire Country School is relaxed but purposeful. The 35-week academic year, divided into trimesters, runs from early September to the second week in June. Courses are taught in a traditional manner but with the extra support, attention, and personal interest that is possible in a class of 3–6 students.

On a typical day, students rise at 7:30 A.M., eat breakfast, and take six 55-minute classes beginning at 9:00 A.M. Course work focuses on the core subjects of English, mathematics, science, social studies, and a foreign language. Music, art, and physical education are scheduled as noncredit courses and activities after the school day and on weekends. Letter grades are issued every trimester and at the end of the year, along with written teacher comments. A student's participation in class, test and quiz results, special projects, completion of assignments, and effort determine his overall evaluation. Students are identified with a specific grade level, but youngsters from different grades are regularly grouped together in their courses.

Classes end at 3:30 P.M., followed by snack, afternoon activities, supper, a one-hour study period, and bedtime between 9:00 and 10:00 P.M., depending on age.

Courses in Grades 3–6 are designed to instill strong basic skills in English, reading, writing, history and geography, science, and math. Younger students are taught in a mostly self-contained, mixed-grade class that allows flexibility in both schedule and curriculum in order to take full advantage of the group's interests, needs, and teachable moments. As an example, a lesson that has the students fully engaged can easily be extended, while a period in which they are unduly restless can be modified to adapt to the mood of the class.

HAMPSHIRE COUNTRY SCHOOL

Seventh- and eighth-grade courses include English; U.S. History, World Geography; General Math, Pre-algebra, Algebra; Earth Science, Life Science, and General Science. Students in Grades 7 and 8 are in classes together, and the selection of courses taught each year depends on the educational needs of the particular group.

Among the courses for Grades 9–12 are English (literature, grammar, reading, writing); American History, World History, Civics; General math, Algebra 1–2, Geometry, Pre-calculus; biology, Environmental Science, Physical Science, Anatomy and Physiology, Chemistry; and a foreign language.

While classwork and courses provide the formal portion of the Hampshire Country School educational program, the learning process continues throughout the afternoons, evenings, and weekends, as students rehearse for theater productions; take music lessons; explore the School's ponds, streams, and natural environment; read for pleasure; play trivia games; listen to concerts or lectures; and engage in dinner-table discussions with teachers.

Students in all grades take the Stanford Achievement Test in the spring. They are also encouraged to take the SSAT, PSAT, and SAT at appropriate times. Students generally gain the most by spending three to five years at Hampshire Country School and transferring elsewhere during their early high school years. Many find that a medium-size boarding school is the best next step, and high school choices in recent years have included Buxton, Dublin, Gould, Holderness, Marvelwood, Putney, Rectory, and Sandy Spring.

STUDENT ACTIVITIES. Extracurricular activities and interests grow out of the School's rustic setting and the students' fertile imaginations, combined with the absence of television and video games. Active, spontaneous play is a major part of student life, and care is taken not to impose so much formal structure that natural playfulness is lost. Outdoors, students explore beaver ponds, build snow forts, play hide-and-seek, and chase imaginary dragons. Indoors, they build with Legos, race toy cars, paint miniature figures, and play a wide variety of strategy board games.

HAMPSHIRE COUNTRY SCHOOL

More formal activities include drama, beginning and intermediate music lessons, canoeing, and sports such as soccer, softball, flag football, tennis, and floor hockey played for fun and recreation. Hiking, exploring, and camping are regular weekend activities. Occasional trips may include museums, classical concerts, live theater, skiing, and hiking. Each weekend ends with a jacket-and-tie dinner and Sunday Forum, a special lecture, concert, or presentation.

Family weekends in October and February bring families together to enjoy the School's outdoor resources, attend student performances, and meet formally with teachers and administrators. The last Sunday afternoon of each month is also open for casual visits by families who live close enough to attend.

ADMISSION AND COSTS. Hampshire Country School students are typically bright, sensitive boys who have had serious difficulty adapting to the complexities and social stresses of larger schools. They seek a school that can provide a solid education, interesting activities, and a peer group that shares their interests and abilities. Applicants are evaluated on the basis of educational and personal histories, a personal interview, and, when appropriate, medical and psychological evaluations.

For 2009–10, the fee for room, board, and most other expenses is $44,500. Clothing and personal supplies, ski rentals, and vacation transportation are additional.

Kimball Union Academy   1813

57 Main Street, Meriden, NH 03770
Tel. 603-469-2000; Admissions 603-469-2100; Fax 603-469-2041
Web Site www.kua.org; E-mail admissions@kua.org

KIMBALL UNION ACADEMY

Kimball Union Academy, founded in 1813, is a coeducational boarding and day school serving 324 students in Grades 9 through 12 and a postgraduate year. Kimball Union Academy's location in the heart of the Upper Connecticut River Valley and its proximity to Dartmouth College have long made it the choice for students seeking an educational experience that develops the whole person as scholar, athlete, artist, and global citizen. The scenic 800-acre campus includes state-of-the-art facilities and many opportunities to enjoy its rural village setting. Boarding Tuition: $43,800; Day Tuition: $28,500. Financial Aid: $2,400,000. Rich Ryerson is Director of Admissions & Financial Aid; Michael J. Schafer (Colby, B.A.; Harvard, M.Ed.) is Head of School. *New England Association.*

Seacoast Academy   2006

356 Exeter Road, Hampton Falls, NH 03844
Tel. 603-772-9093
Web Site www.seacoastacademy.org

Seacoast Academy, a day school in the Episcopal tradition, enrolls 60 boys and girls in Grades 6–8 in a learning environment designed to meet the academic, social, and emotional needs of pre-adolescent and young adolescent students. A passion for learning, academic excellence, creative exploration, physical challenge, and spiritual curiosity are valued principles at the school. Guided by the core values of honesty, respect, diligence, celebration, and caring, Seacoast Academy offers a curriculum based in the traditional arts, sciences, and humanities. English and reading, math, social studies, and science are enriched with offerings in technology, Spanish, music, art, and drama. Classroom teachers emphasize study skills such as note taking, organization of materials, questioning, and critical thinking in preparation for the rigors of secondary school and beyond. Frequent visits from scientists, doctors, authors, and other professionals provide students with hands-on opportunities to understand and experience "real world" concepts. A chapel program for students of all faiths promotes ethical conduct. Summer SAT prep courses and various fun camps are optional. Tuition: $15,000. Martha Shepardson-Killam is Head of School.

NEW JERSEY

Collegiate School   1896

Kent Court, Passaic Park, NJ 07055
Tel. 973-777-1714; Fax 973-777-3255
Web Site www.collegiateschoolnj.com

Collegiate School is a coeducational, college preparatory day school enrolling 164 students in Pre-Kindergarten through Grade 12. The School aims to provide a traditional and classical academic program in a nurturing climate that will motivate students to think independently and to meet the future with industry and challenge. Faculty seek to help students embrace both tradition and innovation by providing a well-rounded education across the disciplines. Diversity also plays a large role at Collegiate School; 39 percent of the student body are students of color. Younger children focus on language arts, mathematics, science, and social studies; art, music, Spanish, physical education, and computers begin in Pre-Kindergarten. Upper School students enroll in sequential, higher-level courses that develop problem-solving, communication, observation, and abstract-thinking skills. All classes have a maximum size of 15 students in order to foster a sense of community and to individualize attention. Recreational and interscholastic athletic teams, the fine and performing arts, special-interest clubs, and scholastic competitions are the principal extracurricular activities. Tuition: $4700–$7200. Paula G. Steele was appointed Headmaster in 2006. *Middle States Association.*

The Craig School   1980

10 Tower Hill Road, Mountain Lakes, NJ 07046
Tel. 973-334-1295; Fax 973-334-1299
Web Site www.craigschool.org; E-mail spark@craigschool.org

THE CRAIG SCHOOL

Enrolling approximately 160 day students in Grades 3–12, Craig is committed to meeting the educational needs of youngsters of average to above-average ability whose progress has been impeded by difficulties in speech and language, reading comprehension, information processing, and other key areas. In a structured environment, certified specialist teachers and professionals provide individualized instruction in classes of 8 or fewer. The college preparatory program focuses on developing strong written language skills, strategies for critical thinking, content acquisition and retention, and the social, behavioral, and self-advocacy skills that are vital to success in the extended community. After-school and summer programs are available. Tuition: $29,213–$32,390. Suzanne Park is Director of Marketing and Admission; Janet M. Cozine is Lower School Director; Eric Caparulo is Upper School Director; David Dennen Blanchard is Headmaster. *Middle States Association.*

The Elisabeth Morrow School   1930

435 Lydecker Street, Englewood, NJ 07631
Tel. 201-568-5566; Admissions Ext. 7212; Fax 201-568-2065
Web Site www.elisabethmorrow.org
E-mail admissions@elisabethmorrow.org

A day school for 500 boys and girls age 3–Grade 8, The Elisabeth Morrow School pursues the highest educational standards in a supportive, creative environment. The program emphasizes strong values, hard work, creative problem-solving, and the attitude that learning is a lifelong experience. In an atmosphere of intellectual challenge, the School seeks to meet the individual needs of its students through a comprehensive educational program and close contact between home and school. Summer, after-school, and child-care programs are offered. Tuition: $12,050–$25,800. Blair Talcott Orloff is Director of Admissions and Financial Aid; David M. Lowry (Haverford College, B.A. 1967; Teachers College Columbia University, M.S. 1972, Ph.D. 1981) is Head of School.

The Hudson School   1978

601 Park Avenue, Hoboken, NJ 07030
Tel. 201-659-8335; Admissions Ext. 107; Fax 201-222-3669
Web Site www.thehudsonschool.org
E-mail hudson@thehudsonschool.org

Founded to provide challenging academic and arts programs for gifted and talented students, The Hudson School enrolls more than 200 urban students from diverse racial, economic, and cultural backgrounds in Grades 5–12. The college preparatory curriculum, which emphasizes the creative and performing arts, classical and modern languages, science, and math, is enriched by Advanced Placement and honors courses, retreats, field trips, and student exchanges abroad. Electives include chess, chorus, instrumental music instruction, yoga, video production, dance, sports, theater, and community service. Tuition: $14,070–$15,270. Financial aid is available. Suellen Newman (Oberlin, B.A.; University of Chicago, M.Ed.) is Founding Director. *Middle States Association.*

Kent Place School   1894

42 Norwood Avenue, Summit, NJ 07902-0308
Tel. 908-273-0900; Admission Ext. 254; Fax 908-273-9390
Web Site www.kentplace.org
E-mail admission@kentplace.org

Founded in 1894, Kent Place School is New Jersey's largest independent nonsectarian, college preparatory day school for girls, enrolling more than 600 students in Nursery–Grade 12, with boys admitted only in Nursery–Preschool. Kent Place is committed to an overall program of excellence that allows each girl to achieve her maximum academic, physical, and creative potential. Small classes, a Women's Life Studies Program, individualized college counseling, state-of-the-art technology, and diverse options in the fine arts are hallmarks of a Kent Place education. Students live by an Honor Code and participate in community service, interscholastic athletics, and other activities. Tuition: $12,000–$29,516. Nancy Humick is Director of Admission and Financial Aid; Susan C. Bosland is Head of School. *Middle States Association.*

Moorestown Friends School   1785

110 East Main Street, Moorestown, NJ 08057
Tel. 856-235-2900; Admissions Exts. 226–228; Fax 856-235-6684
Web Site www.mfriends.org; E-mail admiss@mfriends.org

Moorestown Friends School (MFS) is New Jersey's only three-division Friends School. At MFS, more than two centuries of academic excellence combine with Quaker values to create an empowering learning environment. The School welcomes boys and girls of all faiths; only a minority of the enrollment are Quaker. MFS, like other Friends schools, views ethical development as the foundation of the curriculum. The college preparatory day school serves 725 girls and boys in Preschool–Grade 12 and provides a challenging liberal arts education. Instrumental music, chorus, drama, athletics, fine arts, clubs, and service opportunities are offered as extracurricular activities. Tuition: $15,100–$21,100. Financial Aid: $1,800,000. Karin B. Miller is Director of Admissions & Financial Aid; Laurence R. Van Meter (Hamilton, B.A.; Dartmouth, M.B.A.) was appointed Head of School in 2001.

Morristown-Beard School   1971

70 Whippany Road, Morristown, NJ 07960
Tel. 973-539-3032; Fax 973-539-1590
Web Site www.mobeard.org; E-mail admissions@mobeard.org

This day school was formed by the merger of two single-sex schools to provide a coeducational program for 543 college-bound students in Grades 6–12. Morristown-Beard School aims to nurture each young person's intellectual, social, creative, and athletic potential, instilling the skills and knowledge needed to sustain them throughout life. Sharing equal emphasis with the academic and cocurricular programs are character development and the Core Values of Respect, Responsibility, Integrity, Courage, and Compassion. Course work is tailored to each student's unique aptitudes and interests, with small classes and a 7:1 student-teacher ratio. Classes are available at standard, honors, and AP levels, and required service learning is integral to the Morristown-Beard experience. The Learning Center provides assistance from teaching specialists, and qualified students can earn credit from self-directed independent study. School government, publications, Quiz Bowl, Math League, language clubs, interest groups, and varsity sports for boys and girls are among the activities. Tuition: $27,675–$28,930. Financial Aid: $1,800,000. Hillary Hayes is Director of Admissions; Dr. Alex C. Curtis is Head of School. *Middle States Association.*

Mount Saint Mary Academy   1908

1645 U.S. Highway 22 at Terrill Road, Watchung, NJ 07069
Tel. 908-757-0108; Admissions Ext. 4506; Fax 908-756-8085
Web Site www.mountsaintmary.org
E-mail dtoryak@mountsaintmary.org

Mount Saint Mary Academy, founded by the Sisters of Mercy, is a Roman Catholic, college preparatory day school enrolling 350 young women in Grades 9–12. The Academy features a rigorous curriculum for the average to above-average student in a nurturing, supportive environment. Honors and Advanced Placement courses, varied technology offerings, and in-depth college guidance are additional highlights. Student government, clubs, drama, music, and varsity sports are among the activities. Tuition & Fees: $17,100. Financial Aid: $100,000. Donna Venezia Toryak is Director of Admissions; Sr. Lisa Gambacorto, RSM (Georgian Court, B.A.; Seton Hall, M.A., Ed.S.), was appointed Directress in 2000. *Middle States Association.*

Newark Academy   1774

91 South Orange Avenue, Livingston, NJ 07039
Tel. 973-992-7000; Admission Ext. 323; Fax 973-992-8962
Web Site www.newarka.edu; E-mail admissions@newarka.edu

Newark Academy offers a college preparatory education to 565 young men and women from diverse backgrounds in Grades 6–12. In a dynamic community of learners and teachers, the curriculum is designed to provide a strong base of knowledge

and understanding in the liberal arts and sciences. Advanced Placement courses are available in all disciplines, and selected scholars may earn the International Baccalaureate diploma. From middle school through graduation, students enjoy a wide range of opportunities in the visual and performing arts, leadership groups, more than 40 interest clubs, an award-winning newspaper, and interscholastic athletics. Tuition: $27,600. Financial aid is available. Willard L. Taylor, Jr., is Director of Admission; Donald M. Austin is Head of School. *Middle States Association.*

Oak Hill Academy   1981

347 Middletown-Lincroft Road, Lincroft, NJ 07738
Tel. 732-530-1343; Fax 732-530-0045
Web Site www.oakhillacademy.com
E-mail clarkins@oakhillacademy.com

Oak Hill Academy combines "the strongest possible academic atmosphere with a supportive caring environment" in which children can develop into confident, motivated students who have a love of learning. Enrolling 400 boys and girls in Pre-Kindergarten–Grade 8, Oak Hill emphasizes the mastery of basic skills in a curriculum that provides both standard and accelerated classes to accommodate different learning styles. In addition to traditional subjects in the liberal arts and sciences, students benefit from participation in school government, publications, music and band, drama, team sports, and interest clubs. Selective summer sessions are offered. Tuition: $14,400. Financial Aid: $120,000. Christina Larkins is Director of Development; Joseph A. Pacelli is founding Headmaster. *Middle States Association.*

Oak Knoll School of the Holy Child   1924

44 Blackburn Road, Summit, NJ 07901-2408
Tel. 908-522-8100
Web Site www.oakknoll.org

A premier independent school, Catholic in the tradition of the Society of the Holy Child Jesus, Oak Knoll School of the Holy Child enrolls 550 students in Kindergarten–Grade 12. Dedicated to the education of the whole child, the atmosphere is known for a spirit of joy, mutual respect, and trust. The School welcomes religious, racial, and ethnic diversity. A Lower School serves boys and girls in K–6 while the Upper School enrolls young women in Grades 7–12. Lower School boys attend the area's finest independent and Catholic schools; Upper School alumnae enroll at the most competitive colleges and universities. Oak Knoll's courses and activities stress academic, athletic, social, creative, and moral development. The rigorous Upper School curriculum includes 14 AP and honors classes; courses range from Italian to "The Infinity Project," a national award-winning pre-engineering initiative. Oak Knoll offers extensive technology resources, including a laptop program, fully networked wireless campus, and the latest interactive teaching tools. After-school and summer camp programs are also available. Tuition: $23,600–$29,300. Financial Aid: $1,200,000. Suzanne Kimm Lewis is Admissions Director; Timothy J. Saburn is Head of School.

The Peck School   1893

247 South Street, Morristown, NJ 07960
Tel. 973-539-8660; Admissions Ext. 117; Fax 973-539-6894
Web Site www.peckschool.org; E-mail egordon@peckschool.org

The Peck School, an independent, coeducational day school of approximately 325 students in Kindergarten–Grade 8, strives to prepare each child to succeed in secondary school and, ultimately, to lead a productive and healthy life. Since its founding, Peck has remained devoted to excellence in both teaching and learning. It offers an academically challenging curriculum focusing on the development of academic skills, 21st-century life skills, character, and consideration of others. With a caring faculty and a supportive school environment, Peck provides a rigorous and well-balanced curriculum designed to develop students' curiosity, talents, and critical thinking skills. In addition to its academic reputation, the School's character development (InDeCoRe) and athletic programs and use of laptop technology are widely recognized. Peck embraces a variety of perspectives and ethnic and cultural backgrounds. A strong academic and moral foundation with a positive attitude toward learning make Peck graduates successful candidates for secondary school placement. Tuition: $24,400–$27,700. Erin K. Gordon is Director of Admissions & Financial Aid; John J. Kowalik (Williams, B.S.; Columbia, M.A.Ed.Adm.) was appointed Headmaster in 2003. *Middle States Association.*

Peddie School   1864

South Main Street, Hightstown, NJ 08520
Tel. 609-490-7500; Admission 609-490-7501; Fax 609-944-7901
Web Site www.peddie.org; E-mail admission@peddie.org

With a 230-acre campus and a history dating from 1864, Peddie enrolls 530 boys and girls as boarding and day students in Grade 9–Postgraduate. Mixing tradition and innovation, the School provides rigorous academics including 20 Advanced Placement courses. Students have opportunities in the arts, interscholastic sports, and Study Abroad. They must participate in the campus Work Program and the Community Service Program. In a friendly and supportive environment, faculty encourage students to reach for new levels of achievement. Tuition fees include a laptop computer. Boarding Tuition: $41,000; Day Tuition: $31,100. Raymond H. Cabot is Director of Admission; John F. Green (Wesleyan University, B.A.; Harvard, M.Ed.) was appointed Head of School in 2001. *Middle States Association.*

The Pennington School   1838

112 West Delaware Avenue, Pennington, NJ 08534
Tel. 609-737-1838; Admissions 609-737-6128; Fax 609-730-1405
Web Site www.pennington.org; E-mail admiss@pennington.org

Pennington is an independent, coeducational school for 476 boarding and day students in Grades 6–12. The college preparatory curriculum emphasizes the development of the whole student through academics athletics, community service, and the creative and performing arts. Within the curriculum, there are also small programs for international students and students with learning differences. Founded in 1838, Pennington values both tradition and innovation, applying the values gleaned from centuries of learning, along with the most up-to-date knowledge, to a rapidly changing world. Faculty members focus not only on what they can teach students but also on what the varied perspectives of the student body can impart to the overall educational experience. The academic program centers on the liberal arts, sciences, and humanities, with honors and AP courses in 20 subject areas. ESL and support for language-based learning differences are also available. More than 30 activities include Student Council, drama, Mock Trial, Model UN, publications, dance, art, language clubs, and community service. Boys' and girls' teams compete interscholastically in 16 sports. Boarding Tuition: $40,600; Day Tuition: $27,300. Financial Aid: $1,400,000. Mark Saunders is Director of Admissions; Stephanie G. Townsend is Head of School. *Middle States Association.*

The Pingry School   1861

Kindergarten–Grade 5: Country Day Drive, Short Hills, NJ 07078
Tel. 973-379-4550; Fax 973-379-1861
Web Site www.pingry.org
Grades 6–12: Box 366, Martinsville Road, Martinsville, NJ 08836
Tel. 908-647-5555; Fax 908-647-3703

Pingry is a coeducational, college preparatory, country day school on two campuses enrolling approximately 1050 students in Kindergarten–Grade 12. Since its founding by Dr. John F. Pingry in 1861, the School has earned a reputation for excellence in teaching, high moral standards, a student-driven Honor Code, and the development of integrity and character among its students by an enthusiastic and committed faculty. The School offers extracurricular opportunities including athletics, music, drama, art, special-interest activities, and community service. Specialized and general summer camps are offered. Tuition: $24,195–$28,745. Financial aid is available. Sara Boisvert is Interim Director of Admission; Nathaniel Conard is Headmaster. *Middle States Association.*

Princeton Day School   1965

The Great Road, P.O. Box 75, Princeton, NJ 08542
Tel. 609-924-6700; Admissions Ext. 1200; Fax 609-279-2703
Web Site www.pds.org; E-mail admissions@pds.org

The 1965 merger of two older, single-sex schools formed Princeton Day, a coeducational, college preparatory school enrolling approximately 900 students in Pre-Kindergarten–Grade 12. Lower, Middle, and Upper Schools share common values of integrity, independence of thought, respect and compassion for others, and a love of learning. Princeton Day offers opportunity for intellectual growth and character development through high standards of academic excellence and caring, individualized teaching. PDS students consistently exceed national standards. Nearly 20 percent of seniors in the past five years have earned National Merit Scholarship recognition, and virtually all graduates are accepted by highly selective four-year colleges and universities. The core curriculum is enhanced by study/travel exchanges in the U.S. and abroad. The 105-acre campus features an art gallery, three libraries, a 400-seat theater, a 100-seat amphitheater, science and computer labs, and art, music, photography, and ceramics studios. Summer academic, sports, and adventure camps are optional. Tuition: $23,140–$28,340. Financial Aid: $2,600,000. Kelly Dun is Director of Admission; Paul J. Stellato was appointed Head of School in 2008. *Middle States Association.*

Princeton Montessori School   1968

487 Cherry Valley Road, Princeton, NJ 08540
Tel. 609-924-4594; Fax 609-924-2216
Web Site www.princetonmontessori.org; E-mail pmonts@pmonts.org

This coeducational day school enrolls nearly 300 children in five divisions: Infant (to 18 months), Toddler (to 3 years), Primary (to Kindergarten), Elementary (to Grade 5), and Middle School (to Grade 8). Princeton Montessori is dedicated to the highest-quality education of children, parents, and teachers, according to the values and principles of the Montessori philosophy. American Montessori Society-certified teachers nurture each child's innate abilities and self-exploration that provide the skills and foundation for leading full lives. The recruitment, training, and continued mentorship of faculty, along with the integrated curriculum and environments tailored to meet individual developmental needs, are the School's priorities. The curriculum centers on language arts, math, social studies, and science, enriched by Spanish, music, art, and fitness. Students learn in multiaged classrooms to enable older children to role-model and teach younger children as well as receive personalized instruction. Clubs and other activities include technology, cooking, chorus, ceramics, ecology and photography. Extended care and summer sessions are offered. Tuition: $5275–$25,300. Mary Beth Evans is Director of Admission; Marsha Stencel is Head of School. *Middle States Association.*

Ranney School   1960

235 Hope Road, Tinton Falls, NJ 07724
Tel. 732-542-4777; Admissions Ext. 109; Fax 732-460-1078
Web Site www.ranneyschool.org
E-mail admissions@ranneyschool.org

RANNEY SCHOOL

Ranney School, enrolling 817 day students age 3–Grade 12, offers a college preparatory curriculum that nurtures intellectual inquiry, creative expression, and diversity. The School emphasizes basic and traditional learning skills, refined by the fine and performing arts, foreign languages, computer science, and athletic and extracurricular programs. Small classes allow students to become fully involved in their learning. All graduates attend college, with the majority enrolling at the most prestigious universities. The Middle and Upper School complex provides state-of-the-art technology and a college-style dining facility. Tuition: $10,550–$24,410. Heather Rudisi is Associate Head for Admissions & Marketing; Lawrence S. Sykoff (University of San Diego, M.Ed., Ed.D.) is Head of School. *Middle States Association.*

The Red Oaks School   1965

21 Cutler Street, Morristown, NJ 07960
Tel. 973-539-7853; Admissions Ext. 20; Fax 973-539-5182
Web Site www.redoaksschool.org
E-mail admissions@redoaksschool.org

A coeducational early childhood and elementary day school for 160 students ages 3–12, The Red Oaks School promotes a love of learning, self-confidence, and development of 21st century skills such as global awareness, critical thinking, problem solving, and creativity. The educational approach is informed by leading thinkers and the latest validated research in education,

psychology, and related disciplines, including the time-tested insights and methods of Dr. Maria Montessori. With mixed-age classes and a 9:1 student-teacher ratio, Red Oaks embraces a child-centered curriculum that allows students to learn deeply and at their own pace. Core values of respect, dignity, and social awareness are thoroughly imbedded into the culture of the School. Artist- and scientist-in-residence programs, environmental projects, music, drama, foreign language, and technology enhance the program. The School benefits greatly from strong parental involvement and a gifted and caring faculty. Red Oaks is accredited by the American Montessori Society. Tuition: $11,075–$17,500. Rebecca Spence is Director of Admission; Marilyn E. Stewart is Head of School. *Middle States Association.*

The Rumson Country Day School   1926

35 Bellevue Avenue, Rumson, NJ 07760
Tel. 732-842-0527; Admissions Ext. 112; Fax 732-758-6528
Web Site www.rcds.org; E-mail spost@rcds.org

THE RUMSON COUNTRY DAY SCHOOL

Parents seeking challenging, independent education for their children founded The Rumson Country Day School, opening in 1926 with 23 students and five teachers. Today, the School serves 450 boys and girls in a preparatory program that encompasses Nursery (age 3) through Grade 8. Students come from a wide range of racial, ethnic, religious, and economic backgrounds, providing a diverse and dynamic learning environment where respect and understanding for all is a universal concept. The core curriculum emphasizes strong skills and clear comprehension of English literature, language arts, math, science, and history, enhanced by French or Spanish, the visual and performing arts, information technology, and health and physical education. Classes are small, ranging from 9 to 14 students, depending on grade, and the student-teacher ratio is 7:1. RCDS also provides a unique "school within a school" program for students with language-based learning differences. Among the activities are community service, school government, drama, minicourses, overnight class trips, and interscholastic sports. Tuition: $9325–$19,400. Financial Aid: $500,000. Suzanne R. Post is Director of Admissions; Chad B. Small is Headmaster. *Middle States Association.*

Rutgers Preparatory School   1766

1345 Easton Avenue, Somerset, NJ 08873
Tel. 732-545-5600; Fax 732-214-1819
Web Site www.rutgersprep.org; E-mail forte@rutgersprep.org

The oldest independent school in New Jersey, Rutgers Prep is a coeducational day school enrolling 700 students from diverse backgrounds in Pre-Kindergarten–Grade 12. Rutgers Prep nurtures intellectual curiosity, personal integrity, aesthetic appreciation, and healthy emotional and physical development. From the foundation skills taught in the Lower School, students progress to the departmentalized Middle School before transitioning into Grades 9–12. The Upper School emphasizes the traditional liberal arts, sciences, and humanities, with honors sections in most disciplines and AP courses in 12 subject areas. Classes are small with a student-teacher ratio of 8:1 to ensure individual attention. All students take part in community service, and there are numerous extracurricular activities. Upper School opportunities include Math League, Model UN, publications, dramatic and musical productions, academic clubs, and, beginning in Grade 7, interscholastic sports. Tuition: $12,000–$24,900. Financial aid is available. Diane Glace (PK–6) and Tara Klipstein (7–12) are Co-Directors of Admission; Steven A. Loy, Ed.D., is Headmaster. *Middle States Association.*

Saddle River Day School   1957

147 Chestnut Ridge Road, Saddle River, NJ 07458
Tel. 201-327-4050; Admission Ext. 1105; Fax 201-327-6161
Web Site www.saddleriverday.org
E-mail glee@saddleriverday.org

SADDLE RIVER DAY SCHOOL in Saddle River, New Jersey, is a coeducational, college preparatory day school enrolling students in Kindergarten through Grade 12. The suburban town of Saddle River (population 7198) is located in the northeastern corner of the state. The School is 18 miles from New York City and benefits from the cultural opportunities available in the metropolitan area.

In 1957, founding Headmaster Douglas S. Ogilvie leased a site, formerly the Denison Estate, owned by John C. and Diane Alford. Together, they created Saddle River Day School to provide families with school choice and to create lasting educational value for the community. The School had its first graduate in 1959.

SADDLE RIVER DAY SCHOOL.

Saddle River Day School seeks to provide a safe, intellectually challenging environment where children are encouraged to learn, to question, and to grow as individuals while being part of a community. With its goal of helping students become caring, competent adults able to succeed in and contribute to society, the School best serves those who have the ability to thrive in a traditional, college preparatory curriculum. All students subscribe to the School's Honor Code.

A nonprofit institution, the School is governed by a 20-member Board of Trustees. An Alumni Association and a Parents' Guild sponsor programs and special events. The School is currently involved in a Long Range Plan designed to strengthen its mission in curriculum, faculty, admissions, marketing, funding, and a campus master plan. Accredited by the Middle States Association of Colleges and Schools, Saddle River Day holds membership in the National Association of Independent Schools, the Educational Records Bureau, and the Council for Advancement and Support of Education, among other organizations.

THE CAMPUS. The 26-acre campus provides a view of the Ramapo Mountains and includes two full-size soccer fields, a softball field, a baseball diamond, six all-weather tennis courts, an outdoor climbing wall, two playgrounds, and the Headmaster's House as well as formal gardens, lawns, and woods. The original estate mansion, now Main Hall, contains the Lower School and administrative offices. Alford Hall (1963) houses science and mathematics classrooms, the Athansia M. Tsoukas Biology Laboratory, the Performing Arts Center, two art studios, and the office of the Middle School Dean. The Connell Science Wing was added in 1986. North Hall (1971) holds classrooms, the Computer Center, an amphitheater, reading lab, dining rooms and kitchen, gymnasium and fitness room, the music room, the library-media center, and the Minton Library Wing (1986). The offices of the Upper School Dean, Dean of Students, and the Director of College Placement are also located here.

THE FACULTY. Eileen Lambert, appointed Head of School in 2009, graduated with a B.A. *[magna cum laude]* from Bowdoin College and an M.A. in Classical Languages and Archaeology from the University of Cincinnati.

The 29 women and 18 men on the faculty hold baccalaureate degrees and 29 master's degrees. Each of the three school divisions has its own dean; each academic department has its own chairperson. Saddle River's teachers also coach, counsel, and conduct the extracurricular program. The School's registered nurse is trained in first-aid procedures.

STUDENT BODY. The School serves a diverse population of students, ages 5–18, drawn from 64 nearby communities in New Jersey and New York State. In the 2009–10 school year, 275 students are enrolled, including 146 boys and 129 girls, as follows: 68 in the Lower School (Kindergarten–Grade 5); 64 in the Middle School (Grades 6–8); and 143 in the Upper School (Grades 9–12).

ACADEMIC PROGRAM. The school year, which begins in early September and ends in early June, includes Thanksgiving, winter, and spring breaks. The Upper School year is divided into semesters of two marking periods each. In Grades 6–12, a midyear exam is given in January and a final exam in June.

The Lower School combines classroom learning with hands-on experiences in an integrated curriculum. Students are engaged in reading/language arts, mathematics, science, and social studies. Art, music, world language, physical education, and computer lab supplement the core curriculum. Extracurricular activities include field trips, special events, and a performance orchestra and chorus that is open to Grade 4 and higher. Students in Kindergarten–Grade 3 are instructed in self-contained classrooms, while Grades 4–5 take advantage of increasing departmentalization. Throughout the Lower School, there is only one section per grade level with an average of 16 per grade.

Middle School students follow a fully departmentalized curriculum. Core courses include literature, composition, research skills, mathematics, calculator skills, laboratory science, history and world cultures, and foreign language including Latin, French, and Spanish. Minor courses include art, computer, family life, and geography. Qualified students may move into Upper School courses in math and world language. Extracurricular opportunities include music, theater, orchestra, student government, publications, sports skills, art, computer, and community service.

Upper School courses include English I–IV, World Literature; Algebra I–III, Geometry, College Algebra, PreCalculus; Physical Science, Biology, Chemistry, Physics, Ecology; World History, Foundations of the 21st Century, U.S. History I–II; Latin I–III, French I–III, Spanish I–III; Theater Arts, Drama, Tech Theater, Experiencing Art, Independent Art, Portfolio Art; and Experiencing Music, Advanced Music Literature, Music Theory, Concert Choir, and Concert Orchestra. All students write a research paper each year as part of their social science course. Most courses have Honors sections. Advanced Placement courses are offered in English, Calculus AB and BC, Biology, Chemistry, Physics, Computer Science, U.S. History, European History, Latin, French, and Spanish. Class size is small, with a teacher-student ratio of 1:7.

To graduate, students must complete four years of social sciences and English; three years each of mathematics and laboratory science; three levels of a world language; and six credits of visual or performing arts. Graduates must be proficient in word processing and computers and are required to have completed four years of physical education. Independent study courses are offered for capable students wishing to pursue an area of interest not offered in the course catalog.

Qualified seniors may participate in a special project starting in May. The project, consisting of community service work, is designed to provide meaningful educational experience outside the classroom.

The academic day contains nine periods lasting from 8:18 A.M. to 3:20 P.M.

The advisor program, designed to provide academic guidance as well as social and community awareness, assigns each Middle and Upper School student to a faculty member. Each advisor has 7–10 students in the same grade. Advisors and students are expected to keep in individual contact throughout the year. The Peer Leadership Program offers qualified students a chance to act as an "advisor" to younger students.

SADDLE RIVER DAY SCHOOL

College counseling is a four-year process involving the student, family, and counselor. More than 75 college representatives visit the School each year. Typically, 100 percent of the senior class matriculates at college. Graduates of the Class of 2008 and 2009 were accepted at such institutions as American University, Boston College, Brown, Colgate, Columbia University, Cornell, Dickinson, Drew, Emory, Fairfield, Franklin and Marshall, Georgetown, George Washington, Indiana University, Johns Hopkins, Lafayette, Lehigh, Muhlenberg, New York University, Princeton, Quinnipiac, Rensselaer Polytechnic Institute, School of the Museum of Fine Arts (Boston), Skidmore, State University of New York (Binghamton), Swarthmore, Trinity (Connecticut), Tufts, Union, Villanova, Washington University, Wheaton (Massachusetts), and the Universities of Colorado, Delaware, and Michigan.

STUDENT ACTIVITIES. Students may participate in a variety of activities: student government, judiciary committee, yearbook, newspaper, literary magazine, peer leadership, concert choir, orchestra, theatrical productions, student-sponsored dances, field days, and junior varsity and varsity sports. The School has chapters of Interact, SADD, the Spanish National Honor Society, the French National Honor Society, and The Cum Laude Society.

SADDLE RIVER DAY SCHOOL

Middle and Upper School interscholastic teams in baseball, basketball, cross-country, golf, soccer, softball, tennis, track, and volleyball practice from 3:30 to 5:30 P.M. Student art exhibitions, three major theater productions, two levels of chorus, three orchestras, and individual instrument lessons highlight the arts program.

Students who maintain a 3.0 or higher grade-point average and who exhibit exemplary character and leadership ability may be nominated to the Zeta Chi fraternity to serve as in-house tutors and admissions ambassadors.

ADMISSION AND COSTS. Saddle River Day School admits students who show evidence of creative, analytical, and critical thinking and reasoning skills as well as those students who will make positive and meaningful contributions to the School. New students are accepted at all grade levels as space permits. Along with a $50 application fee, candidates must submit transcripts from the past two years, any standardized test scores, two teacher recommendations, and results of the Independent School Entrance Examination. An interview with parents and student is required. While admission is made on a rolling basis, families are encouraged to apply early.

In 2009–10, tuition is $16,000 for Kindergarten, $19,681 for Grades 1–5, $22,435 for Grade 6, $25,276 for Grades 7–8, and $26,328 for Grades 9–12. There is a technology fee of $450. Financial aid is available based upon need. In 2009–10, approximately $800,000 in financial aid was awarded. The School offers a tuition payment plan and tuition insurance.

Head of School: Eileen Lambert
Director of Admission & Financial Aid: Gretchen Lee
Head of the Upper Division: Andrew J. Rork
Head of the Middle Division: Kirk Effinger
Head of the Lower Division: Eileen Lambert
Dean of Academic Affairs: Evan C. Strager
Director of Development: Matthew Honeycutt
Financial Officer: Judith Kuhlman
Director of College Placement: Mary Ellen Zittel
Director of Technology: Lucian Micu
Athletic Director: Joseph S. Augienello

St. Benedict's Preparatory School   1868

520 Dr. Martin Luther King, Jr., Boulevard, Newark, NJ 07102
Tel. 973-792-5800; Fax 973-643-6922
Web Site www.sbp.org; E-mail graybee@sbp.org

St. Benedict's is a Roman Catholic, college preparatory day school with a 75-student boarding program enrolling 550 boys in Grades 7–12. Founded by monks of the Order of St. Benedict at Newark Abbey, the School aims for academic and personal excellence in a student body that reflects the racial and cultural diversity of the city. A rigorous curriculum is supplemented by special projects, elective programs, and short-term exchanges with other schools. A full athletic program, publications, drama, choir, and clubs are among the activities. A six-week summer session is mandatory. Tuition: $8000; Boarding Fee: $5000. Financial aid is available. Mario Gallo is Director of Admissions; Rev. Edwin D. Leahy, OSB (Seton Hall, A.B.; Woodstock College, M.Div.), is Headmaster. *Middle States Association.*

The Wardlaw-Hartridge School   1882

1295 Inman Avenue, Edison, NJ 08820
Tel. 908-754-1882; Admission Ext. 110; Fax 908-754-9678
Web Site www.whschool.org; E-mail cdavis@whschool.org

THE WARDLAW-HARTRIDGE SCHOOL

Formed by the merger of two schools founded more than a century ago, The Wardlaw-Hartridge School is a coeducational, college preparatory day school enrolling 420 students in Pre-Kindergarten 3–Grade 12. The Wardlaw-Hartridge School prepares students to lead and succeed in a world of global interconnection. It provides an educational atmosphere characterized by academic challenge, support for individual excellence, diversity, and a familial sense of community. Small classes, academically challenging Advanced Placement and honors courses, varied extracurricular activities, and a vigorous athletic program help each individual develop according to his or her potential. Tuition: $14,800–$26,900. Charlotte Vigeant is Director of Admission and Financial Aid; Andrew Webster (Brown University, B.A.; University of Virginia, M.A.) is Head of School.

The Willow School   2000

1150 Pottersville Road, Gladstone, NJ 07934
Tel. 908-470-9500; Admissions Ext. 1015; Fax 908-470-9545
Web Site www.willowschool.org
E-mail aworthington@willowschool.org

The Willow School is a coeducational day school for Kindergarten–Grade 8, located on 34 wooded acres. The School's buildings have earned gold and platinum certifications from the U.S. Green Building Association's Leadership in Energy and Environmental Design (LEED) rating system. The School is built on the belief that children thrive in a setting that embraces the joy of learning and the wonder of the natural environment. The curriculum maintains a deliberate balance of rigorous academics and creative projects and emphasizes the School's unique commitment to environmental sustainability. This program, in the hands of talented teachers, fans the flame of each child's natural curiosity and desire to learn. Small classes create

THE WILLOW SCHOOL

an atmosphere of trust and allow teachers to focus on children's individual strengths and needs. Through the virtues program, children become knowledgeable and wise, curious and creative, responsible and confident. Tuition: $20,453–$22,822. Annette Worthington is Director of Admissions; Kate Burke Walsh (American University, B.A.; Antioch University, M.A.) is Head of School.

The Wilson School   1909

271 Boulevard, Mountain Lakes, NJ 07046
Tel. 973-334-0181; Fax 973-334-1852
Web Site www.thewilsonschool.com; E-mail info@thewilsonschool.com

Wilson serves 80 boys and girls as day students in Pre-Kindergarten–Grade 8. Its mission is to create a nurturing environment in which children become independent, thoughtful, and confident learners. The curriculum emphasizes strong skills in key concepts. In the lower grades, subjects are presented thematically, while older students learn through interdisciplinary units that emphasize the relationships among the liberal arts, sciences, and humanities. French begins in Pre-Kindergarten, and computer technology is integrated throughout all disciplines. Activities include drama, music, community service, field trips, weekly swim lessons, and a variety of sports. An after-school program is optional. Tuition: $16,100–$20,700. Christopher Vakulchik is Admissions Director; Carolyn Borlo is Head of School. *Middle States Association.*

The Winston School   1981

100 East Lane, Short Hills, NJ 07078
Tel. 973-379-4114; Fax 973-379-3984
Web Site winstonschool.org; E-mail plewis@winstonschool.org

Accredited by the New Jersey Association of Independent Schools, The Winston School was established to meet the needs of intellectually capable boys and girls who were encountering problems in school due to language-based learning disabilities. Enrolling 62 day students ages 7–14, the School seeks to provide students with the strategies needed to achieve academic success. Each student's program is designed based on his/her academic profile. Classes, taught by certified specialists, are limited in size to ensure personalized attention and support. The program includes art, music, physical education, computers, and speech-language and occupational therapy. Tuition: $29,000–$36,000. Financial aid is available. Paula Lordy is Director of Admissions; Peter S. Lewis (Middlebury College, B.A.; Stanford University, M.A., Ph.D.) was appointed Head of School in 2009. *Middle States Association.*

THE RUMSON COUNTRY DAY SCHOOL

NEW MEXICO

Albuquerque Academy 1955

6400 Wyoming Boulevard, NE, Albuquerque, NM 87109
Tel. 505-828-3200; Admission 505-828-3208; Fax 505-828-3128
Web Site www.aa.edu; E-mail hudenko@aa.edu

Dedicated to attracting some of the finest students and teachers in the country, Albuquerque Academy is a college preparatory day school enrolling 1100 young men and women in Grades 6–12. The Academy serves the greater Albuquerque area and commits its resources to a mission comprising accessibility, affordability, excellence, caring, and outreach. This mission, along with the Academy's generous financial aid program, has fostered one of the strongest student bodies in the nation, with 95 National Merit Semifinalists over the past three years. Emphasizing mastery of fundamentals and independent judgment, the Academy seeks the full academic, creative, moral, and physical development of each student, offering a challenging curriculum with more than 20 Advanced Placement courses and required participation in experiential education and community service programs. Tuition: $17,468. Financial Aid: $4,600,000+ to approximately one-third of the student body. Judy Hudenko is Director of Admission; Andrew T. Watson is Head of School.

Manzano Day School 1938

1801 Central Avenue, NW, Albuquerque, NM 87104-1197
Tel. 505-243-6659; Admission Ext. 401; Fax 505-243-4711
Web Site www.manzanodayschool.org
E-mail mprokopiak@manzanodayschool.org

Manzano Day School is an independent, nonsectarian elementary school enrolling students in Pre-Kindergarten through Grade 5. The School offers a strong core curriculum as well as six cocurricular areas of Spanish, art, music, physical education, technology, and library skills. Manzano is a member of the National Association of Independent Schools, a Blue Ribbon School, and a member of Exemplary Schools Attuned Network. It is one of only a few schools nationwide that offers a separate campus for environmental studies at the elementary level. Founded in 1938 in historic Old Town Albuquerque, Manzano remains true to its mission—*Joy in Learning®*. The student-teacher ratio is 10:1. An extended day program and summer school are offered. Tuition: $9630–$12,295. Madonna Prokopiak is Director of Admission; Neal Piltch is Head of School.

Rio Grande School 1978

715 Camino Cabra, Santa Fe, NM 87505
Tel. 505-983-1621; Admission Ext. 2002; Fax 505-986-0012
Web Site www.riograndeschool.org
E-mail jay_underwood@riograndeschool.org;
* maureen_devlin@riograndeschool.org*

Rio Grande is an independent coeducational day school enrolling approximately 160 students in Pre-Kindergarten–Grade 6. The School offers an integrated curriculum that includes traditional academics, fine and performing arts, and outdoor activities. Small classes and personalized attention for each student are features of the program. Class activities are enlivened by field trips to study local cultures, overnight stays, and service learning projects. An extended-day program is available as well as a summer program. Tuition: $11,500–$16,375. Extras: $300. Tuition assistance is available. Barbara Bentree is Director of Admission; Jay Underwood is Head of School.

Sandia Preparatory School 1966

532 Osuna Road, NE, Albuquerque, NM 87113
Tel. 505-338-3000; Fax 505-338-3099
Web Site www.sandiaprep.org; E-mail info@sandiaprep.org

Founded by Mrs. Albert G. Simms II, Sandia Prep is a college preparatory day school enrolling 670 students in Grades 6–12. The joy of learning and living is at the center of its college preparatory curriculum. Sandia Prep provides a well-balanced program based on the five A's: academics, arts, athletics, activities, and atmosphere. Sandia Prep has been recognized nationally for its rigorous academic program and has received awards for its advisory, community service, drama, and no-cut sports programs. Tuition: $15,500. Financial Aid: $988,150. Ester Tomelloso is Director of Admission; Richard L. Heath (Cornell, A.B. 1969; Colgate, M.A.T. 1972) was appointed Headmaster in 1986.

ALBUQUERQUE ACADEMY

NEW YORK

Allendale Columbia School 1890

519 Allens Creek Road, Rochester, NY 14618-3497
Tel. 585-381-4560; Fax 585-249-0230
Web Site www.allendalecolumbia.org
E-mail acarroll@allendalecolumbia.org

Allendale Columbia, a coeducational day school accredited by the New York State Association of Independent Schools (NYSAIS), enrolls 450 students in a challenging college preparatory day program spanning Nursery to Grade 12. The academic program is designed to enable students to fulfill their intellectual potential and to develop as well-rounded citizens. Set on a 30-acre campus, the School offers a curriculum that includes Advanced Placement courses in 16 disciplines, extensive offerings in the arts, computer technology, and foreign languages. Students take part in school leadership groups, community service, drama, vocal and instrumental ensembles, interest clubs, and competitive sports. Tuition: $6300–$18,125. Alan Carroll is Director of Admission; Charles F. Hertrick is Head of School.

The Allen-Stevenson School 1883

132 East 78th Street, New York, NY 10075
Tel. 212-288-6710; Fax 212-288-6802
Web Site www.allen-stevenson.org

Founded in 1883 to teach young men "intelligent habits of study and to develop straightforward, manly characters," Allen-Stevenson enrolls 409 day boys in Kindergarten–Grade 9. The traditional curriculum prepares students for entrance to challenging secondary schools. Courses include French, Spanish, language fundamentals, computers, shop, music, and art. Extracurricular activities include orchestra, Student Council, publications, and arts and drama groups. Facilities include a gymnasium, shop, art, and multipurpose room. Tuition: $35,500. Financial Aid: $1,500,000. Ronnie R. Jankoff is Director of Admissions; David R. Trower (Brown University, B.A. 1968; Union Theological Seminary, M.Div. 1973) was appointed Headmaster in 1990.

Bank Street School for Children 1915

610 West 112th Street, New York, NY 10025
Tel. 212-875-4420; Admissions 212-875-4433; Fax 212-875-4733
Web Site www.bankstreet.edu/sfc
E-mail schoolforchildrenadmissions@bankstreet.edu

Bank Street School for Children, enrolling 425 day boys and girls ages 3–13, is the demonstration school for the Bank Street College of Education. The School sees social, emotional, and intellectual growth as equally important and inseparable. Reading and writing skills are developed in the core social studies and language arts program. Science and mathematics are presented as methods of inquiry with skill acquisition related to concepts. Curricular activities include social studies trips, creative arts, music, and physical education. After-school and summer recreational programs are available. Tuition: $32,000. Financial Aid: $2,000,000. Marcia Roesch is Director of Admissions; Alexis Wright (Rutgers University, B.S.; University of Miami, M.A.) is Dean of Children's Programs.

The Birch Wathen Lenox School 1916

210 East 77th Street, New York, NY 10075
Tel. 212-861-0404; Fax 212-879-3388
Web Site www.bwl.org; E-mail admissions@bwl.org

THE BIRCH WATHEN LENOX SCHOOL in New York, New York, is a college preparatory day school for students in Kindergarten through Grade 12. The School was founded in 1991 by the consolidation of The Birch Wathen School (founded 1921) and The Lenox School (founded 1916).

The School seeks to provide a challenging academic curriculum with a balance among traditional education, student achievement, and social development. Birch Wathen Lenox implements its curricular commitments with small classes, a student-faculty ratio of 6:1, and an emphasis on individual attention to students.

THE BIRCH WATHEN LENOX SCHOOL

The Birch Wathen Lenox School is a nonprofit corporation directed by a self-perpetuating Board of Trustees, which includes alumni and parents. An active Alumni Association represents more than 4000 graduates. The School's program is accredited by the State University of New York and the Middle States Association of Colleges and Schools, and it is registered by the New York State Board of Regents. Birch Wathen Lenox is a member of the New York Guild of Independent Schools, the New York State Association of Independent Schools, the National Association of Independent Schools, the Association of College Admissions Counselors, The College Board, and the Educational Records Bureau.

THE CAMPUS. The entire School—Lower (Kindergarten–Grade 5), Middle (Grades 6–8), and Upper (Grades 9–12)—is housed in a traditional, spacious building on Manhattan's Upper East Side. Facilities include a gymnasium, library, computer center, science laboratories, auditorium, music and art studios, cafeteria/commons area, and a rooftop play area. A $19,000,000 renovation of the School's facility was completed in 2006.

THE FACULTY. Frank J. Carnabuci III, formerly Assistant Headmaster of The Dalton School, was appointed Headmaster in 1992. He holds a B.A. degree from Drew University and master's degrees in education from Columbia and Harvard.

There are 30 men and 85 women on the faculty. All faculty members hold baccalaureate degrees; 95 percent hold master's degrees or higher. The staff includes instructors of music and art, reading specialists, science and mathematics coordinators, a full-time nurse, a librarian, two computer specialists, a college guidance counselor, and two school psychologists.

STUDENT BODY. The Birch Wathen Lenox School enrolls 550

boys and girls, 5 to 18 years of age, from Kindergarten through Grade 12. The diverse student population is drawn from all parts of New York City.

ACADEMIC PROGRAM. The school year, from mid-September to mid-June, includes Thanksgiving recess, four religious and patriotic holidays, and two-and-one-half-week vacations at Christmas and in the spring. Classes meet on a five-day schedule. School begins at 8:15 A.M., with dismissal at 3:00 P.M. A typical school day includes five class periods, activity and athletics periods, lunch, and time for independent study and teacher conferences. Homework, assigned in all grades, ranges up to one hour per day in the Lower School and 20 to 30 minutes per subject per day in the Middle and Upper schools. There is standardized testing throughout the year in all three divisions.

The curriculum provides a program in English, composition, mathematics, science, and history. Foreign languages begin in Grade 4. Computer science, word processing, art, drama, speech, instrumental and vocal music, and woodworking are taught from Kindergarten through Grade 12. Advanced Placement course work is offered in all major curricular areas to eligible Upper School students.

A full, extended-day after-school program is available for Lower School students. There is a comprehensive physical education program. The full interschool athletic sports program includes soccer, softball, volleyball, tennis, basketball, swimming, modern dance, ice hockey, golf, and lacrosse.

THE BIRCH WATHEN LENOX SCHOOL

Birch Wathen Lenox graduates have enrolled at such colleges and universities as Brown, Colgate, Columbia, Cornell, Duke, Harvard, Northwestern, Princeton, Tufts, Yale, and the University of Pennsylvania.

STUDENT ACTIVITIES. The Student Forum, headed by an elected speaker, meets periodically and plans assembly programs. The Student Council, composed of a president and class representatives, brings questions to the attention of the Forum and has responsibility for the annual Student Activity Budget. There is also a Student-Faculty Judiciary Committee.

The traditional academic curriculum is complemented by extensive cocurricular activities such as the School newspaper, the literary journal, and the yearbook; the Community Services Program and the Model U.N.; chorus; and Business, Foreign Language, Overseas Study Program, Photography, and Drama clubs.

ADMISSION AND COSTS. Birch Wathen Lenox has a policy of accepting students "without regard to race, creed, or nationality of applicants." Students are accepted in Kindergarten–Grade 12 on the basis of entrance examination results, previous school records, teacher recommendations, and an interview. Applicants may take either the Educational Records Bureau tests or the Secondary School Admission Test. Application should be made 9 to 12 months in advance of entrance. Applications should be received no later than November 30. The application fee is $50.

THE BIRCH WATHEN LENOX SCHOOL

In 2009–10, tuition is $30,410 in Kindergarten, $32,451 in Grades 1–4, $32,436 in Grades 5–7, $32,615 in Grades 8–9, and $32,912 in Grades 10–12. Lunch and additional fees are approximately $2000. A tuition payment plan is available. The Harrison W. Moore Merit Scholarship Award is presented annually in the Upper School, and scholarship aid is available at all grade levels based on need, ability, and character.

Director of Admissions: Julianne Kaplan
Assistant Directors of Admissions: Danielle Tormey & Barbara B. Kaplan
Director of Development: Janine Hopley
College Counselor: Brad Battaglia
Business Manager: Ann Glickman
Director of Athletics: Todd DiVittorio

The Brearley School   1884

610 East 83rd Street, New York, NY 10028
Tel. 212-744-8582; Admission 212-570-8600; Fax 212-472-8020
Web Site www.brearley.org; E-mail sborbay@brearley.org

Founded in 1884, The Brearley School challenges girls of adventurous intellect to think critically and creatively and prepares them for active, responsible citizenship in a democratic society. A Brearley education is designed to provide every student with the competence and confidence to succeed in whatever pursuit she may choose, while promoting growth in kindness and conscience. Brearley's broad liberal arts curriculum combines tradition and innovation, giving students the foundational knowledge and versatility to excel in college and to become leaders and agents of progress in an increasingly borderless world. A college preparatory day school, Brearley enrolls 690 girls in Kindergarten through Grade 12. Tuition & Fees: $34,000–$34,350. Financial Assistance: $4,000,000. Joan Kaplan and Winifred Mabley are Directors of Admission and

Financial Aid; Dr. Stephanie J. Hull (Wellesley College, B.A.; Harvard University, A.M., Ph.D.) was appointed Head of the School in 2003.

The Brick Church School   1940

62 East 92nd Street, New York, NY 10128
Tel. 212-289-5683; Fax 212-289-5372
Web Site www.brickchurch.org/dayschool
E-mail lspinelli@brickchurch.org

Founded by and affiliated with The Brick Presbyterian Church, this coeducational day school offers a developmentally appropriate early childhood program for 160 children in Nursery/Kindergarten (ages 3–6). In an environment marked by warmth and mutual respect, students are introduced to literacy, mathematics, science, social studies, cooking, dramatic play, art, and music. Teachers, all of whom are certified in Early Childhood Education, use various activities and materials designed to inspire self-confidence, curiosity, and joy in learning and play. A weekly nondenominational chapel service involves the entire School. Tuition: $14,900–$19,500. Holly Burke and Kathy Flintoft are Admissions Directors; Lydia Spinelli (Tufts, B.A.; Teachers College, Columbia University, M.A., M.Ed., Ed.D.) is Director.

Brooklyn Friends School   1867

375 Pearl Street, Brooklyn, NY 11201
Tel. 718-852-1029; Fax 718-643-4868
Web Site www.brooklynfriends.org
E-mail jknies@brooklynfriends.org

Serving a diverse community of 645 boys and girls in Preschool through Grade 12, Brooklyn Friends School offers a challenging educational experience. The Upper School offers the International Baccalaureate Diploma program for juniors and seniors. The liberal arts curriculum nurtures young people at every stage of development while instilling independence and a love of learning. Quaker ideals guide school life, and global awareness and community service enrich the program. Students develop creative expression through offerings in dance, music, art, and drama. School government, Model UN, clubs, and interscholastic sports are among the extracurricular activities. Tuition: $15,200–$29,500. Financial aid is available. Sara Soll is Preschool Admissions Director; Jennifer Knies is Director of Admissions; Dr. Michael Nill is Head of School.

Brooklyn Heights Montessori School   1965

185 Court Street, Brooklyn, NY 11201
Tel. 718-858-5100; Admissions Ext. 20; Fax 718-858-0500
Web Site www.bhmsny.org; E-mail emattia@bhmsny.org

Brooklyn Heights Montessori School seeks to develop and educate the whole child, nurturing the social, physical, emotional, and intellectual well-being of each student in an environment marked by mutual trust and respect. Set in historic Cobble Hill, Brooklyn Heights Montessori School welcomes 256 boys and girls from varied backgrounds in Preschool (age 2) through Middle School (Grades 7–8). Children work independently or in small groups, using age-appropriate materials to understand key concepts in core subjects of reading and language arts, math, science, social studies, computer technology, and the arts. Students learn according to their own pace and style as they progress through the grades. Beginning in Grade 7, students develop portfolios and have special instruction to prepare them for success in high school. Community service and outreach is practiced at all levels in and beyond the school, while field trips in New York City and to Cape May, Long Island, Boston, and Washington, D.C., enhance classroom lessons. Soccer and bas-

ketball teams are open to students from Grade 6. Tuition: $7450–$28,500. Need-based tuition assistance is available. Elise Mattia is Director of Admissions; Dane L. Peters is Head of School.

Buckley Country Day School   1923

I. U. Willets Road, North Hills, Roslyn, NY 11576
Tel. 516-627-1910; Admissions Ext. 117; Fax 516-627-8627
Web Site www.buckleycountryday.com
E-mail aduffy@buckleycountryday.com

Buckley Country Day School is an independent, coeducational day school enrolling 339 children in Toddler–Grade 8. The School provides a superior elementary education to an intellectually capable and diverse student body. Emphasis is placed on core skills in reading, writing, and mathematics, using a broad repertoire of teaching techniques and technologies. Buckley believes in fostering integrity, hard work, kindness, personal and social responsibility, and mutual respect. The School's educational philosophy is centered on intellectual, physical, and artistic development. French and Spanish begin in Pre-Kindergarten, Latin in Grade 7. Tuition: $11,300–$23,100. Financial Aid: $753,630. Ann V. Duffy is Director of Admissions; Dr. Jean-Marc Juhel (University of Paris, B.A. 1983, M.A. 1988; Columbia University, M.A. 1997; Michel de Montaigne University, Ph.D. 1995) was appointed Headmaster in 2002.

The Buckley School   1913

113 East 73rd Street, New York, NY 10021
Tel. 212-535-8787; Fax 212-472-0583
Web Site www.buckleyschool.org
E-mail jlynch@buckleyschool.org

The Buckley School is a day school that enrolls 370 boys in Kindergarten through Grade 9. The goals of a Buckley education are that every boy learn fundamental skills, gain self-confidence through disciplined thought and action, develop personal integrity and respect for others, and discover the joy of learning and the satisfaction of pursuing excellence. The traditional curriculum—math, English, science, history, and foreign languages including Latin—is supplemented by field trips to museums, special exhibitions, and events in Manhattan. Sports are mandatory as are class plays, arts, and music, all of which contribute to a well-rounded education. Tuition: $33,500. Financial Aid: $1,100,000. Jo Ann Lynch is Admissions Director; Gregory J. O'Melia (Harvard, A.B., Ed.M.) was appointed Headmaster in 2001.

Buffalo Seminary   1851

205 Bidwell Parkway, Buffalo, NY 14222-9904
Tel. 716-885-6780; Fax 716-885-6785
Web Site www.buffaloseminary.org
E-mail admissions@buffaloseminary.org

Buffalo Seminary is a college preparatory boarding and day school enrolling 160 girls in Grades 9–12. While the school has no religious affiliation, values are emphasized through the school's Honor Code. Buffalo Seminary aims to develop scholarship, leadership, sportsmanship, and a commitment to service through a rigorous academic curriculum, studio and performing arts programs, and activities including athletics, honor societies, self-government, music, and drama. Advanced Placement and honors courses are available by invitation. Boarding Tuition: $32,500; Day Tuition: $15,970. Financial aid is available. Carrie Auwarter is Director of Admissions; Jody Douglass (Bates College, B.A.; Middlebury College, M.A.) was appointed Head of School in 2007. *Middle States Association.*

The Caedmon School 1961

416 East 80th Street, New York, NY 10075
Tel. 212-879-2296; Admissions Ext. 306; Fax 212-879-0627
Web Site www.caedmonschool.org
E-mail admissions@caedmonschool.org

The Caedmon School enrolls 240 children, ages 2.9 to 10 years. At Caedmon, faculty and staff embrace their responsibility to help children develop into capable, confident, creative, and caring human beings. They furnish students with the skills they will need to achieve academic excellence and pursue a life of learning. The curriculum includes language arts, math, social studies/geography, science, Spanish, technology, music and violin, physical education and yoga, art, and library. Caedmon follows a "modified Montessori" program, which stresses socialization and thoughtfully adapts traditional Montessori practices to the needs of children today. The School provides children an opportunity for a variety of after-school activities and music lessons as well as a summer camp. Caedmon's fifth-grade graduates are admitted to a wide range of New York City's most competitive independent schools. Families are welcome to participate in the School through volunteer opportunities and as classroom visitors. Tuition: $14,040–$25,996. Financial aid is available. Erica L. Papir is Director of Admissions; Dr. Greg Blackburn (Hendrix College, B.A.; University of Arkansas, M.S.; University of Mississippi, Ph.D.) is Head of School.

The Cathedral School 1949

319 East 74th Street, New York, NY 10021
Tel. 212-249-2840; Fax 212-249-2847
Web Site www.cathedralschoolny.org

Located on Manhattan's Upper East Side, The Cathedral School provides a warm, nurturing, and family atmosphere to 130 day students in Nursery–Grade 8. With a 10:1 student-teacher ratio, an international student body, and placement of graduates in the city's best high schools, The Cathedral School continues its legacy of educating children in the tradition of The Classics. The curriculum includes Ancient Greek in Grades 7–8, mythology in Kindergarten–Grade 4, and drama in Grades 4–8. Chess is offered as part of the curriculum to K–Grade 8. In addition to the standard core classes of math, English, history, social studies, and science, The Cathedral School offers French, computer science, physical education, art, and music. Movement and exercise are taught to Early Childhood classes. After-school activities include sports, karate, music, art, writing, newspaper club, *Mad Science*, and Greek language and culture. Tuition: $10,500–$12,500. Financial aid is available. Athena Efter is Admissions Director; Sonia Celestin is Head of School.

The Cathedral School of St. John the Divine 1901

1047 Amsterdam Avenue, New York, NY 10025-1702
Tel. 212-316-7500; Admission 212-316-7510; Fax 212-316-7558
Web Site www.cathedralnyc.org; E-mail admission@cathedralnyc.org

The Cathedral School, an Episcopal day school, welcomes 270 boys and girls of all faiths in Kindergarten–Grade 8. It seeks to develop confident, open-minded students who accept responsibility as active citizens of their diverse community and the world. The School's setting, complete with outdoor playgrounds, gardens, and free-roaming peacocks, provides an oasis in Manhattan. The rigorous academic program offers a strong foundation of knowledge and skills, combining traditional and innovative teaching methods. Individualized attention and student engagement are ensured by a small class size of about 16 students. The award-winning foreign language program includes Latin studies for all seventh and eighth graders. Students participate in community service, sports, and school government and have the opportunity to sing in the choir of The Cathedral of St. John the Divine. Tuition (including lunch &

fees): $32,200. Approximately 35 percent of students receive financial aid, the level of each grant determined according to need. Kassandra Hayes is Director of Admission; Marsha K. Nelson is Head of School.

The Chapin School 1901

100 East End Avenue, New York, NY 10028
Tel. 212-744-2335; Fax 212-628-2126
Web Site www.chapin.edu

Chapin, a college preparatory day school enrolling 675 girls in Kindergarten–Grade 12, is dedicated to preparing young women to thrive and lead in an increasingly complex, competitive world through the pursuit of academic excellence, personal integrity, and community responsibility. Personal growth and community involvement are fostered through the homeroom program. The rigorous curriculum is enhanced by a commitment to the arts and athletics. Course offerings may be enriched by independent study and off-campus programs. Numerous activities are offered in the Middle and Upper Schools. Tuition: $31,500. Financial Aid: $3,600,000. Tina I. Herman is Director of Admissions; Dr. Patricia Hayot was appointed Head of School in 2003.

The Churchill School and Center 1972

301 East 29th Street, New York, NY 10016
Tel. 212-722-0610; Fax 212-722-1387
Web Site www.churchillschool.com
E-mail wfederico@churchillschool.com

THE CHURCHILL SCHOOL in New York City is a coeducational K–12 day school enrolling students of average to above-average cognitive ability whose progress in a mainstream classroom is compromised by a learning disability.

In 1972, Harry S. Valentine III founded Churchill for elementary-age children with learning disabilities. In 1986, the program expanded to include students up to age 14. Relocation in 2001 to the present site permitted the addition of a high school.

The Churchill Center was established in 1981 to build upon and disseminate the expertise of The Churchill School. The Center's educational programs and professional development in the field of learning disabilities assist students, parents, teachers, and related service providers. Ongoing programs include courses in literacy instructions and multisensory techniques for teaching reading and writing. The Center School Advisory Service is an information, resource, and referral service for parents and professionals in choosing appropriate school and/or summer programs for students. The Referral Service recommends qualified tutors and other professionals with expertise in working with students who have diverse learning styles. Additionally, the Center's Reading Initiative provides a free, 27-week after-school program of multisensory reading instruction to children in Grades 1–3 in New York City who need to improve reading skills. The Center's 10-week Enhancing Social Skills Development program helps children ages 5–14 interact effectively with peers and handle social situations.

In educating students, the School seeks to identify and use their strengths, stimulate intellectual curiosity, and expand knowledge. Their progress may have been hindered in traditional classrooms by a language or reading disability, attention problems, or perceptual and/or motor weaknesses. Churchill addresses the academic, cognitive, social, and emotional needs of its students so that they may reach their full potential. Blending instruction and application in all areas, the flexible interdisciplinary program offers structured, multisensory experiences, learning-style strategies, a low student-teacher ratio, and numerous opportunities in which to succeed. Students are encouraged to manage their learning disabilities, becoming advocates for themselves as they prepare for the future.

THE CHURCHILL SCHOOL AND CENTER

A member of the New York State Association of Independent Schools and the National Association of Independent Schools, Churchill is chartered by the Board of Regents of the State of New York. In 2004, the Board of Regents also granted The Churchill High School full registration status. Churchill has been designated as an "approved non-public school" by the New York State Commissioner of Education since 1972. A 25-member Board of Trustees governs the School, and the Parents Association publishes a newsletter and sponsors informational, social, and fund-raising activities for the Churchill community.

THE CAMPUS. The School's site on East 29th Street features a seven-story, 72,000-square-foot building containing 36 classrooms, a multimedia library, an auditorium with stage and music room, a soundproof band room and recording studio, four science labs, two state-of-the-art computer labs with school-wide Intranet and Internet access, a television/video production studio, a radio station, and three art studios. Recreational facilities include a rooftop playground and a regulation-size gymnasium with bleachers, and a fitness center. Students eat lunch in a spacious cafeteria; a garden and greenhouse are used by the Churchill community and for environmental programs.

THE FACULTY. Bob Siebert, who began his educational career in 1971, was appointed Head of The Churchill School and Center in 2008. Previously, he was Superintendent of the Lakeland School District in Northern Westchester County (1993–99) and of the Eastchester District in Southern Westchester (1999–2008). He holds New York State certification as a school district administrator and as a secondary social studies teacher. Dr. Siebert earned an Ed.D. in Educational Administration from Fordham, a Professional Diploma in Educational Administration from State University of New York (New Paltz), a master's in American Studies from Fairfield University, and a B.A. in History from the College of the Holy Cross.

All head teachers are state-certified and hold a master's degree in Special Education. High School faculty members are certified in their content area. Specialists include speech and language personnel, occupational therapists, psychologists, social workers, and a registered nurse. Among their representative institutions are Bank Street College of Education, Teachers College at Columbia University, Fordham, Hunter College, and New York University.

STUDENT BODY. The Churchill School enrolls 396 boys and girls from Kindergarten age (5½) through Grade 12. The ratio of boys to girls is 60:40. Representing a diverse range of racial, ethnic, religious, and socioeconomic backgrounds, students come from New York City's five boroughs as well as Westchester County, Long Island, and New Jersey.

ACADEMIC PROGRAM. The 180-day school year begins in early September and ends in mid-June, with breaks at Thanksgiving, winter holiday, midwinter, and spring.

The school day runs from 8:15 A.M. to 2:45 P.M. Classes, which enroll up to 12 students, are formed on the basis of both performance level and learning style. Homework is an essential complement to the curriculum, providing opportunity for review and reinforcement of skills taught in the classroom. Middle and High School students may attend a faculty-monitored study hall from 3:00 to 5:00 P.M.

The Elementary School is an ungraded program for children age 5½ through the equivalent of Grade 5. Each class is led by a head teacher and an assistant teacher. Age, gender, cognitive and language abilities, management needs, reading and math levels, and social factors are all considered in making up a class. Reading and math skills are taught in smaller groups, while social studies and science are taught in a whole-class setting. The process-based writing curriculum is designed specifically for children with language-based learning disabilities. Art, music, health, library, computer, and physical education are integral parts of the program. Some students receive speech and language services and/or occupational therapy in small groups one to three times weekly, using a pull-out model. Three parent conference days are scheduled during the year, and in-depth reports by teachers are written in January and June.

The Middle School comprises Grades 6–8. Subject departmentalization begins at this level, and students learn the necessary organization and study skills. Direct teaching in language arts and math skills continues. Science and social studies curricula are project-based. Expository writing is emphasized, and research skills are taught. Once a week, through the pull-out model, some students in Grades 6 and 7 receive speech and language therapy in groups averaging six students. Students in Grade 8 receive this therapy through the collaboration model in the classroom once weekly. All Middle School students take part in Counseling/Health groups related to issues of adolescence, health, and learning disabilities. Quarterly reports to parents from all teachers and related service providers include formal grades.

THE CHURCHILL SCHOOL AND CENTER

The High School offers a four-year college/career preparatory program in Grades 9–12. Students may obtain a Regents, a Local, or an Individual Education Plan diploma and receive both college and career counseling. The core curriculum requires four credits, or years, of both English and history, three each of science and math, two of physical education, and one each in art and health. The language-based English curriculum emphasizes mastery of basic skills in reading, writing, listening, and speaking. Courses include surveys of American and English

Literature. Other specific academic courses are Global History and Geography, U.S. History and Government; Biology, Earth Science, Chemistry, Environmental Science; Competency Math, Pre-algebra, Math A/B, Applications for Business and Science; Computer Technology, Graphics, Programming; Comparative Politics, Media Ethics, Native American Culture; and Photography, Music, Theater, and Electronics. Speech and language services continue for some students via the classroom collaboration model once weekly. Some short-term pull-out sessions are provided for those students who could benefit from more specific strategies and skills. Health and Human Relations classes meet once a week with a psychologist or social worker. Conferences with teachers, parents, and students are held three times a year.

THE CHURCHILL SCHOOL AND CENTER

A primary goal of the School is to prepare students to continue their education at appropriate mainstream schools. In the past several years, students have transferred to Birch Wathen Lenox, Brooklyn Friends, Dwight, The Ethical Culture Fieldston School, Forman, Friends Seminary, Hewitt, Kildonan, Pennington, PolyPrep, The School at Columbia University, Trinity-Pawling, and York Preparatory.

Churchill graduates have enrolled in such postsecondary schools as Adelphi, American, Clark, College of the Holy Cross, Concordia, Curry, Fordham, Guilford, Indiana University, Ithaca, Johnson and Wales, Lynn, Manhattanville, Mitchell, Marist, Savannah College of Art and Design, School of Visual Arts, State University of New York (Plattsburgh, Purchase), Suffolk, Trinity, and the Universities of New Hampshire, New Haven, and North Carolina (Greensboro).

STUDENT ACTIVITIES. On Friday afternoons, elementary-age children engage in activities such as newspaper, science, puppetry, cooking, sewing, and model building. Middle School students may participate in sketching and drawing, cooking, jewelry making, guitar, board games, and newspaper. High School students may express their interests in web design, radio broadcasting, digital art and photography, and portfolio creation. Middle and High School sports teams in cross-country, track, soccer, softball, baseball, basketball, and volleyball compete with other area independent schools. Required community service begins in the Middle School.

ADMISSION AND COSTS. Churchill accepts students with average to above-average intelligence who have specific learning disabilities and who could benefit from a small, individualized, and supportive learning environment. Along with a $75 fee, candidates must submit a completed application, a developmental history, educational and psychological testing, speech and language evaluation, and teacher questionnaires. High School applicants must also write a personal essay and submit school transcripts.

In 2009–10, tuition is $39,000. Under provisions of Section 4402 of the State Education Law, the tuition of some students classified as "learning disabled" or "speech/language impaired" may be reimbursed by New York State.

Director of Admissions: Wendy Federico
Director of the Churchill Center: Dr. Jane Gertler
Director of Annual Giving & Special Events: Michele Lugosch
Chief Financial Officer: Michael Devine
Elementary School Principal: Meryl Schwartz
Middle School Principal: Susan Jackson
High School Principal: Glenn Corwin

City & Country School   1914

146 West 13th Street, New York, NY 10011
Tel. 212-242-7802; Admissions Ext. 217; Fax 212-242-7996
Web Site www.cityandcountry.org; E-mail elisec@cityandcountry.org

City & Country School, a coeducational, progressive day school enrolling 320 students ages 2 to 13, was founded in 1914 by Caroline Pratt. Believing that education is fundamentally a social process, City & Country strives to create a vital school environment that supports each child's innate passion for learning while also expanding his or her understanding of communities and cultures that exist beyond home and school. Social Studies, the core curriculum, is enriched by science, mathematics, literature, and the arts. Extended day, after-school classes, and a summer program are available. Tuition: $15,400–$30,100. Financial Aid: $900,000. Elise Clark is Director of Admissions; Kate Turley is Principal.

Claremont Preparatory School   2005

41 Broad Street, New York, NY 10004-2513
Tel. 212-232-0266; Fax 212-232-0284
Web Site www.claremontprep.org
E-mail admissions@claremontprep.org

Claremont Prep, set in the heart of Manhattan's Financial District, is a coeducational day school enrolling 550 students, with a capacity of 850 students age 3–Grade 9. They come from New York's five boroughs and from New Jersey and represent a wide diversity of racial, ethnic, and socioeconomic backgrounds. Centered in a 125,000-square-foot, newly refurbished building, the School offers state-of-the-art facilities including wireless computer technology, a 15,500-volume library, an indoor swimming pool, an outdoor play roof, full-size gym, and an early childhood play area. Claremont's mission is to develop independent thinkers, to instill a love of the arts, and to develop each child's physical skills in a dynamic learning environment. Community service is a vital part of the curriculum and involves students in age-appropriate activities related to the environment, migrant workers, the elderly, and urban planning. The curriculum emphasizes the traditional arts, sciences, and humanities and includes studies in Mandarin Chinese, French, and Spanish. Classroom instruction is enriched by a variety of field trips to New York's many cultural and educational attractions. Tuition: $21,850–$31,500. Financial aid is available. Irwin Shlachter is Headmaster.

Collegiate School   1628

260 West 78th Street, New York, NY 10024
Tel. 212-812-8500; Admissions 212-812-8552; Fax 212-812-8547
Web Site www.collegiateschool.org
E-mail jheyman@collegiateschool.org

The oldest independent school in the nation, this college preparatory day school enrolls approximately 635 boys in Kindergarten–Grade 12. Different student talents, interests, and backgrounds add immeasurably to the academic excellence and to the spirit of Collegiate School. The academically rigorous program, while classical in nature, recognizes developmental differences and offers an impressive array of electives, including Advanced Placement in 16 fields and independent study. Teams are fielded in eight sports. Service and leadership are integral parts of the School's program. Collegiate students benefit from going to school in New York City where the boys learn about themselves and their world through the broad range and challenge of academic and extracurricular activities, opportunities in athletics and the performing arts, and participation in the community. Tuition: $33,400. Financial Aid: $3,600,000. Joanne P. Heyman is Director of Admissions & Financial Aid; Dr. Lee M. Levison (Amherst College, B.A.; Harvard University, M.A., Ed.D.) is Headmaster.

Columbia Grammar and Preparatory School 1764

5 West 93rd Street, New York, NY 10025
Tel. 212-749-6200; Fax 212-865-4278
Web Site www.cgps.org; E-mail admissions@cgpsmail.org

COLUMBIA GRAMMAR AND PREPARATORY SCHOOL in New York, New York, is a college preparatory day school for boys and girls in Pre-Kindergarten through Grade 12. The School has two divisions, each with its own director: Grammar School (Pre-Kindergarten–Grade 6); and Preparatory School (Grades 7–12). Located just off Central Park West, it allows students to take advantage of the city's many cultural and educational resources.

In 1764, Columbia Grammar School was founded by King George II as a boys' preparatory school for Kings College (now Columbia University). Closed when the British occupied the city during the Revolutionary War, the School reopened in 1784 as the Grammar School of Columbia University. It functioned under the auspices of the university until 1864, when it was transferred to private ownership. It became coeducational in 1956 and was renamed Columbia Grammar and Preparatory School in 1969.

COLUMBIA GRAMMAR AND PREPARATORY SCHOOL

The School endeavors to provide a warm yet structured environment in which the student may "grow intellectually, develop a strong sense of responsibility, and learn tolerance for the opinions of others." The Grammar School emphasizes an approach that replaces memorization with investigation and discovery in a step-by-step process designed to provide an understanding of the structure of a subject area. Learning skills and disciplined work habits are stressed throughout the School.

Columbia Grammar and Preparatory School is a nonprofit,

nonsectarian institution governed by a self-perpetuating Board of Trustees. Board members include parents and alumni representatives. The School is accredited by the New York State Association of Independent Schools and is chartered by the New York State Board of Regents. It holds membership in the National Association of Independent Schools and other educational organizations.

THE CAMPUS. The School occupies eight buildings on West 93rd and 94th streets. One of these, at 5 West 93rd, houses an art studio, a swimming pool, the grammar school gymnasium and cafeteria, a computer room, a library, a science room, and classrooms for Grades 3 and 4. Five converted brownstones, at 20–28 West 94th Street, house Pre-Kindergarten–Grade 2. In addition to classrooms, these buildings contain music studios, an art studio, and the grammar school nurse's office. They are connected to the building at 5 West 93rd Street by a covered walkway. The facility at 4 West 93rd Street houses Prep School classrooms, six science labs, a library, writing center, the prep school nurse's office, music classrooms and practice space, and two gymnasiums as well as a state-of-the-art theater seating 200. The facility at 36 West 93rd Street houses classrooms for Grades 5–6, three science labs, two computer rooms, and a library, plus five art studios, a drama practice room, a theater, and a cafeteria. Central Park is used for outdoor activities, including tennis. Another brownstone includes the admissions and development offices.

School facilities are valued at $100,000,000+.

THE FACULTY. Richard J. Soghoian is the Headmaster. He is a graduate of the University of Virginia (B.A.) and Columbia University (Ph.D.).

The full-time faculty consists of 172 teachers, 52 men and 120 women. In addition to baccalaureate degrees from such colleges and universities as Brown, Columbia, Cornell, Harvard, New York University, Oberlin, Tufts, Williams, Yale, and the University of Michigan, faculty also hold 139 master's degrees and 2 doctorates. There are 22 part-time instructors, 5 men and 17 women, including administrators who teach.

Two registered nurses are on duty during school hours, and the School has a part-time consulting psychologist.

STUDENT BODY. In 2009–10, the School enrolled 1193 students in Pre-Kindergarten–Grade 12, 607 boys and 586 girls. Grade sizes are approximately 35 in Pre-Kindergarten, 80 in Kindergarten–Grade 6, and 90 in Grades 7–12. Most students reside in Manhattan, but other boroughs, Long Island, Westchester County, and New Jersey are also represented.

ACADEMIC PROGRAM. The school calendar, with major holidays at Christmas and in the spring, provides 36 weeks of instruction divided into two terms of approximately 18 weeks each. Grammar School students attend school from 8:15 A.M. to 3:10 P.M. Monday through Thursday and to 2:20 P.M. on Friday. Preparatory school students have homeroom at 8:00 A.M., and classes meet on a six-day cycle from 8:20 A.M. to 2:55 P.M. Monday through Friday.

There are 10–15 students in an average teaching section. At designated times before, during, and after school, the faculty are available for extra help. Quarterly grades are issued, and written reports are sent to the parents at the end of each semester. Supplementary progress reports may be sent as the need arises. There are two parent-teacher conferences each year at the middle of each semester.

In Grades 1–4, the curriculum focuses on establishing proficiency in reading, writing, and mathematics. Science, social studies, physical education, art, and music supplement the basic program. Departmentalization of instruction begins in Grade 5 to ensure a well-planned, sequential curriculum in language skills, social studies, modern and traditional mathematics, computer, science, music, and fine arts. Beginning in Grade 4, ensemble classes offer orchestral instruction on string, woodwind, and brass instruments. Physical education includes indoor athletic activities, gymnastics, swimming, and outdoor play.

An arts program for students in Grades 7–12 offers special semester electives. Students choose from among such courses as photography, beginning instrumental music, orchestra, chorus, filmmaking, ceramics, painting and drawing, printmaking, and three-dimensional art.

The curriculum for Grades 7 and 8 includes English, history and social sciences, mathematics, earth and natural sciences, and creative arts. A foreign language sequence for Grade 7 provides an introduction to French, Japanese, Spanish, and Latin; Grade 8 students may select one of those languages for in-depth, daily study. A drugs/sex education course is part of the program.

To graduate, Preparatory School students must complete four years of high school English, history, and math; three years each of a foreign language and science, and two semester courses in art, music, or theater history.

Full-year courses include English 9–10, History 9–10, French, Latin, Japanese, Spanish; an integrated mathematics curriculum beginning in Grade 7; and Biology, Chemistry, and Physics. Typical of the varied semester electives are Modernist Literature, Creative Non-Fiction, Nature Writing Workshop, New York Literature; Introduction to Philosophy, Introduction to Psychology, Latin American Studies, Law and Society, Modern Middle East; Meteorology, Evolution, Human Anatomy and Physiology; Computer Graphics, Music Technology, Programming for the Worldwide Web; Acting, Playwriting, Painting and Drawing, Jewelry, Photography, Filmmaking, Ceramics, Chorus, Orchestra; and Weight Training. Opportunities are provided for Advanced Placement study in all departmental areas.

Graduates of the Class of 2009 are attending Amherst, Bard, Boston University, Bowdoin, Brandeis, Brown, Columbia, Connecticut College, Cornell, Davidson, Duke, Emory, Franklin and Marshall, Georgetown, George Washington, Guilford, Hampshire, Haverford, Indiana University, Ithaca, Lehigh, Louisiana State, McGill, Muhlenberg, New York University, Northwestern, Oberlin, Reed, Rhode Island School of Design, Skidmore, State University of New York (Binghamton), Susquehanna, Syracuse, Tufts, Tulane, Union, Vanderbilt, Washington University of St. Louis, Wesleyan, Yale, and the Universities of Chicago, Michigan, Pennsylvania, Rochester, St. Andrews (Scotland), Vermont, and Virginia.

STUDENT ACTIVITIES. Students in Grades 9–12 participate in a service program. Among the possible projects are tutoring fellow students, teaching in the Grammar School, working as hospital volunteers, and helping in political offices. One hundred hours of service must be performed during the student's high school years.

COLUMBIA GRAMMAR AND PREPARATORY SCHOOL

Student organizations vary according to expressed interest. In the upper grades, activities include student government, the yearbook, a newspaper, a literary magazine, Issues and Human Rights, Jazz Band, Prep School Chorus, Film Apprecia-

tion, Environmental Awareness, and chapters of SADD and the Coalition for the Homeless. Each year, students are chosen to attend A Presidential Classroom for Young Americans and the Model UN.

COLUMBIA GRAMMAR AND PREPARATORY SCHOOL

Varsity and junior varsity teams for boys are organized in basketball, baseball, track, golf, tennis, and soccer; girls' teams are formed in basketball, softball, volleyball, swimming, soccer, tennis, and track. There is also a coeducational cross-country team as well as an optional after-school sports program for Grades 5–8 involving both intramural and interschool games in basketball, baseball, soccer, and track.

Special activities are dances, movies, field trips, and ski trips. Annual events include a street fair, orchestra and chorus concerts, several student plays, Moving-Up Day, Field Day, and Graduation.

ADMISSION AND COSTS. The School enrolls students without discrimination "on the basis of race, color, and national or ethnic origin." Students are chosen for their emotional maturity, ability to work in a demanding program, talents, concern for others, and potential for growth. Depending upon grade level, requirements include an admission test, academic transcripts, written exercises, and a personal interview. Application for fall enrollment should be made in the preceding fall or winter. There is a $60 application fee.

In 2009–10, tuition and fees range from $33,040 (Pre-Kindergarten) to $34,990 (Grade 12), including a full lunch program. A tuition payment plan and tuition insurance are available.

Columbia Grammar and Preparatory School subscribes to the School and Student Service for Financial Aid and awards financial aid on the basis of need. In 2009–10, 20 percent of the students received aid totaling $5,000,000.

Deans of Students: Barrie Allen, Monica Markovits, David Morss, Margo Potter & Vic Puccio
Director of Admission: Simone Hristidis
Director of the Annual Fund: Sara Ziff
College Counselors: Nicolette Love and Mark Speyer
Chief Financial Officer: Sharonah Volkowitz
Director of Athletics: Stephen Rybicki

Convent of the Sacred Heart   1881

1 East 91st Street, New York, NY 10128-0689
Tel. 212-722-4745; Fax 212-996-1784
Web Site www.cshnyc.org

The oldest independent college preparatory girls' school in New York City, Convent of the Sacred Heart enrolls 670 day students in Pre-Kindergarten–Grade 12 and offers a comprehensive, rigorous curriculum that promotes academic excellence and intellectual growth within a community of respect and trust. As one of 22 Sacred Heart schools in the United States and 155 worldwide, Convent of the Sacred Heart in New York offers extensive opportunities for educational exchange throughout the world. The education focuses on the development of the "whole child," building faith and respect for intellectual values while fostering community and providing opportunities for personal growth. In addition to its broad array in the humanities, arts, and sciences, programs in sports, community service, and extracurricular activities abound. Tuition: $17,530–$33,985. Jackie Casey is Director of Admissions; Dr. Joseph Ciancaglini is Head of School.

Corlears School   1968

324 West 15th Street, New York, NY 10011
Tel. 212-741-2800; Fax 212-807-1550
Web Site www.corlearsschool.org
E-mail saphiatoun@corlearsschool.org

Corlears School specializes in the early childhood education of students ages 2½ to 10. Its commitment is to perpetuate a love of learning and to provide students with the academic, social, and emotional tools they need. Now enrolling 151 boys and girls, the School emphasizes problem solving and interdisciplinary learning in a supportive environment as the basis for mastery of skills in reading, writing, mathematics, science, and the visual and performing arts. Tuition: $17,500–$25,975. Financial Aid: $530,000. Saphiatou N'Jie is Director of Admissions and Tuition Aid; Thya Merz (Norwich University, B.A.; Johns Hopkins University, M.S.) is Head of School.

The Dalton School   1919

108 East 89th Street, New York, NY 10128-1599
Tel. 212-423-5200; Admissions 212-423-5452
Web Site www.dalton.org

A coeducational, college preparatory day school enrolling 1302 students in Kindergarten–Grade 12, Dalton is recognized as a model of progressive education based on a rigorous academic curriculum. The "Dalton Plan" provides the structural foundation of the School's program, promoting self-reliance, independence, and a strong sense of community. The School is known for extensive visual and performing arts programs and innovative use of technology in the humanities and sciences. Required community service, athletics, publications, and internships are among the activities. Tuition: $34,100. Financial Aid: $6,700,000. Elizabeth Krents, Ph.D., is Director of Admissions; Ellen C. Stein (University of Pennsylvania, B.A.; Columbia University, M.B.A.) is Head of School.

Doane Stuart School   1852

199 Washington Avenue, Rensselaer, NY 12144
Tel. 518-465-5222; Admission Ext. 209; Fax 518-465-5230
Web Site www.doanestuart.org; E-mail admissions@doanestuart.org

Doane Stuart is an interfaith day school offering a rigorous college preparatory program to 278 students of diverse faiths. Encompassing Nursery–Grade 12, Doane Stuart seeks to prepare young people for higher education and life while providing a strong moral and spiritual foundation. Small classes with an average of 14 students and a 7:1 student-faculty ratio are taught by dedicated, highly qualified teachers, 80 percent of whom hold advanced degrees. Students contribute 5000 hours of community service yearly and take part in school government, team sports, publications, music, drama, the arts, and numerous interest clubs. Tuition: $12,075–$19,795. Michael P. Green is Director of Admission; Dr. Richard D. Enemark (Columbia, Ph.D.) was appointed Headmaster in 1998.

Dutchess Day School   1955

415 Route 343, Millbrook, NY 12545
Tel. 845-677-5014; Fax 845-677-6722
Web Site www.dutchessday.org; E-mail admissions@dutchessday.org

Located on 23 acres in the middle of rural Millbrook, New York, Dutchess Day School enrolls 146 boys and girls from Dutchess, Columbia, Fairfield, and Litchfield Counties. The comprehensive program encompasses preschool through eighth grade. The School seeks to create an environment where children thrive intellectually, emotionally, and physically. There is an active athletic program for all grades, PK through 8, and interscholastic competition in Grades 5–8. A well-balanced curriculum emphasizes the mastery of skills, excites a child's natural curiosity and imagination, and encourages responsible citizenship. Small class sizes allow students to take intellectual risks and pursue individual projects and interests. Respect for the individuality of each child and for human differences is fundamental to Dutchess Day School's tradition and philosophy. A strong partnership between parents and faculty adds to the success of educating the whole child. Tuition: $14,700–$19,950. Financial Aid: $272,430. Ellen Potter is Admissions Director; John Cissel (Wesleyan University, M.A.L.S. 1986) is Head of School.

The Dwight School   1880

291 Central Park West, New York, NY 10024
Tel. 212-724-6360; Admissions 212-724-7524; Fax 212-724-2539
Web Site www.dwight.edu; E-mail admissions@dwight.edu

THE DWIGHT SCHOOL

The Dwight School is an International Baccalaureate, college preparatory day school enrolling 485 boys and girls in Pre-Kindergarten–Grade 12. Dwight formed a consortium with The Anglo-American School in 1993 and became the first in the United States to offer the International Baccalaureate program in Pre-Kindergarten–Grade 12. The School believes that every child has a "spark of genius" that will be discovered and nurtured. Spanish and Chinese beginning in Kindergarten, and 17 other languages are featured as well as state-of-the-art technology, athletics, arts, a comprehensive after-school program, and numerous study-abroad opportunities. Tuition: $31,365–$33,800. New Student Registration Fee: $750–$1500. Alicia Janiak and Marina Bernstein are Directors of Admissions; Stephen H. Spahn is Chancellor. *Middle States Association.*

East Woods School   1946

31 Yellow Cote Road, Oyster Bay, NY 11711
Tel. 516-922-4400; Admissions Ext. 114; Fax 516-922-2589
Web Site www.eastwoods.org; E-mail admissions@eastwoods.org

Interested parents founded East Woods School to provide their sons and daughters a high-quality, challenging educational program that combines exemplary academics with character development. The School, which enrolls 275 children in Pre-Nursery–Grade 9, seeks to instill a lifelong love of learning through a child-centered approach that develops each student's intellectual and personal potential. Integrity, leadership, independence, cooperation, compassion, and respect for others are at the core of the East Woods philosophy. In a warm, nurturing environment, small classes provide every student with attention and support for individual learning styles. Advanced Learning Programs in science, math, and technology complement the curriculum. Spanish begins in Kindergarten, French in Grade 5, and Latin in Grades 7–8. After graduation, ninth graders enter a wide variety of secondary schools, both boarding and day, in preparation for four-year colleges and universities across the nation. Sports, after-school enrichment, and community service are among the activities. Extended care and summer programs are available. Tuition: $4100–$21,300. Financial Aid: $750,000. Carol Rogers is Director of Admissions; Dr. Nathaniel W. Peirce is Headmaster.

The Elmwood Franklin School   1895

104 New Amsterdam Avenue, Buffalo, NY 14216
Tel. 716-877-5035; Admissions Ext. 113; Fax 716-877-9680
Web Site www.elmwoodfranklin.org
E-mail eacker@elmwoodfranklin.org

Elmwood Franklin School provides its students with the unique experience of sophisticated academics in a nurturing, child-centered environment. The School enrolls 350 students, beginning with a two-year Prep division, moving to Lower School (Grades 1 to 4), and finishing in Upper School (Grades 5 to 8). There is a balance of traditional academic work, along with physical education, foreign language, technology, music, and arts instruction offered to all students. Summer and extended-day programs are available. Tuition: $14,000–$16,000. Financial Aid: $800,000. Elaine Acker is Director of Admissions; Anthony G. Featherston IV (Boston College, B.A.; Boston University, M.A.) is Headmaster.

Ethical Culture Fieldston School   1878

33 Central Park West, New York, NY 10023
Tel. 212-712-6220
Web Site www.ecfs.org; E-mail admissions@ecfs.org
3901 Fieldston Road, Bronx, NY 10471
Tel. 718-329-7300; Admissions 718-329-7575
Lower School Admissions Fax 718-329-7337
Middle/Upper School Admissions Fax 718-329-7302

Ethical Culture Fieldston School offers coeducational instruction to 1700 students at two locations: Ethical Culture (Pre-Kindergarten–Grade 5) in Manhattan, and Fieldston Lower (Pre-Kindergarten–Grade 5), Fieldston Middle (Grades 6–8) and Fieldston (Grades 9–12) in the Riverdale section of the Bronx. The rigorous curriculum integrates arts, humanities, and sciences with ethical values. Community service is required. Activities include sports, the arts, and publications. After-school programs and a summer day camp are offered. Tuition & Fees: $34,045. Financial Aid: $8,600,000. Taisha Thompson is Director of Enrollment Management & Financial Aid; Mark J. Stanek is Head of School.

Friends Seminary   1786

222 East 16th Street, New York, NY 10003
Tel. 212-979-5030; Admissions Ext. 138; Fax 212-979-5034
Web Site www.friendsseminary.org
E-mail fsadmissions@friendsseminary.org

Friends Seminary, the oldest continuously operating coeducational school in New York City, offers a sound academic education within a Quaker environment. Steeped in history and tradition, Friends Seminary remains a progressive institution, offering course work that is timely and relevant to today's world. In 2008, the school became the first in New York City to offer an Arabic language class to a student body that is not predominantly Arabic. Guided by the school's mission, Friends Seminary prepares students not only for the world that is, but helps them "bring about the world that ought to be." Friends Seminary serves 700 college-bound day students in Kindergarten–Grade 12. The academic program includes AP opportunities, course work at New York University, and international/travel study exchanges. The arts, community service, clubs, and athletics are among the activities. Tuition: $31,940. Harriet Burnett is Director of Admissions; Robert Lauder, M.A., is the Principal.

The Gow School   1926

P.O. Box 85, South Wales, NY 14139
Tel. 716-652-3450; Fax 716-687-2003
Web Site www.gow.org; E-mail admissions@gow.org

THE GOW SCHOOL in South Wales, New York, is a college preparatory boarding school, encompassing Grades 7 through 12 and a postgraduate year, for young men who have a specific language disability often referred to as dyslexia. South Wales, a rural community in the western portion of the state, is on New York Route 16. Located a short distance from Niagara Falls, it is approximately 30 miles southeast of Buffalo, New York, and 100 miles south of Toronto, Canada.

THE GOW SCHOOL

The Gow School was founded in 1926 by Peter Gow, Jr., an educator who wanted to develop better methods for teaching young men who were experiencing academic failure. His work plus his personal and professional friendships with Dr. Samuel

T. Orton and Anna Gillingham led to the establishment of a program for students who have at least average ability but a developmental disability in one or more phases of language usage. Reconstructive Language training, reading, and other aspects of language development are stressed in a learning environment that is individualized as much as possible.

THE GOW SCHOOL.

Gow, a nonprofit school, is governed by a self-perpetuating Board of Trustees, 23 in number. The Board, composed primarily of alumni, meets three times a year. The School is registered by the New York State Board of Regents; it holds membership in the National Association of Independent Schools, the New York State Association of Independent Schools, and the International Dyslexia Association.

THE CAMPUS. The 100-acre campus, which is traversed by a trout stream, includes hilly woodland, athletic fields, tennis courts, a ski/snowboard slope, and a ropes course.

The Main Building contains the business office, development office, ten classrooms, infirmary, and the Gow Bookstore. Orton Hall provides 12 classrooms including a tutoring room, a science laboratory, two computer classrooms, the computer writing lab, and a study hall. The Green Cottage furnishes living quarters for students and two masters' apartments. Other facilities include The Admissions Building and the School House, which contains the Art Department. Students and masters reside in Cornwall House, Templeton Dormitory, Brown House, Ellis House, Whitcomb Dormitory, and Warner House. The 49,000-square-foot Gow Center provides a student union, classrooms, two indoor tennis courts, two basketball courts, three squash courts, and a fitness center. The new state-of-the-art dining hall is 10,300 square feet and features a gourmet kitchen and seating for 240. The campus also provides housing for the Headmaster and 23 teachers and their families.

The Isaac Arnold Memorial Library, with a capacity of 10,000 volumes, contains a reading room, seven classrooms, a faculty room, and the Headmaster's office. The Reid Arts Center houses three classrooms, a technology workshop, and painting, drawing, and 3-D design studios. The Simms Family Theater is also located in the arts center.

The plant is valued at approximately $14,000,000.

THE FACULTY. M. Bradley Rogers, Jr., was elected Headmaster in 2004. He holds a B.A. degree from the University of Dayton in Ohio and a master's degree from Johns Hopkins University. Prior to assuming his present position, Mr. Rogers was Headmaster at The Odyssey School in Maryland. He and his wife reside on campus with their four sons.

The faculty consists of 42 teachers and administrators who teach, 23 of whom live in the dormitories or in other campus housing. They hold 34 baccalaureate degrees, 28 master's degrees, and a doctorate from Canisius, Catholic University of

America, Cornell, Duke, East Stroudsburg University, Hamilton, Hiram College, Hobart, Indiana, Johns Hopkins, Kenyon, Macalester, Medaille College, Nazareth, St. Bonaventure, Slippery Rock, Springfield College, State University of New York (Binghamton, Brockport, Buffalo, Cortland, Fredonia, Geneseo), Syracuse, Texas A&M, Texas Tech, Towson State, Union College, and the Universities of Colorado, Minnesota, New Hampshire, Rochester, Virginia, and Washington.

A local doctor serves as the School physician, and emergency facilities are minutes away. School nurses coordinate all medical activities.

STUDENT BODY. In 2009–10, The Gow School enrolled 133 young men, 12 to 19 years of age, as boarders in Grades 7–12. They came from 23 states, Barbados, Bermuda, Brazil, Burkina Faso, Canada, Cayman Islands, Costa Rica, Dominican Republic, Hong Kong, Indonesia, Japan, Malaysia, Mexico, The Netherlands, Saudi Arabia, Sri Lanka, Sweden, and Trinidad.

ACADEMIC PROGRAM. The school year, which is divided into semesters, extends from early September to mid-May, with Thanksgiving, winter, and spring breaks. Comprehensive written reports are sent to parents at the end of each marking period. Advisor reports, summarizing student performance in academics, athletics, and residential life, are written at the midpoint of each marking period. The student-teacher ratio of 4:1 ensures that each young man receives individualized attention and support.

Classes have an average enrollment of five students and meet six days per week. The weekday schedule begins with the rising bell at 7:00 A.M., followed by breakfast and house jobs. Classes, lunch, athletics, tutorials, and supervised study hall are scheduled between 8:00 A.M. and 6:00 P.M. After dinner, all Upper School students have a brief reading period and two hours of supervised study before quiet time in the dorm from 9:00 to 10:00 P.M. or, at times, to 11:00 P.M. Faculty members are available for individual help whenever necessary. Middle School students have a 90-minute study period in the evening.

THE GOW SCHOOL.

The core of the Gow curriculum is based on Reconstructive Language, using a multisensory approach, as an effective tool in teaching dyslexic/language learning-disabled students to read and improve language skills, particularly with regard to the printed or written word. Study skills such as note taking, test preparation, and drill work are integrated into all disciplines. The School has a laptop program, and all classrooms and student rooms are wireless for Internet access.

Generally, a student takes five academic courses in addition to one Reconstructive Language course. The language course involves training in deriving meaning from reading, in vocabulary extension, and in oral and written expression. In mathematics courses, effective traditional methods are employed as well as teaching math concepts and applications with manipulative materials. Instruction begins with the most basic operations and proceeds to more advanced concepts. Daily oral and written work is assigned as a means of promoting accurate and immediate recall.

The curriculum is designed to prepare students to enter college. To graduate, each student must complete 21.5 academic credits in Grades 9–12, including English 4, mathematics 3, history 4, laboratory science 2, art/music, health, and computer 1, which includes keyboarding, word processing, and data design.

The core curriculum in Grades 7–12 includes Grammar, Literature, Composition, Shakespeare, American Literature; United States History, Global History I–II; Developmental Math, Pre-Algebra, Algebra 1–2, Plane Geometry, Pre-Calculus, Calculus; and Science 7, Earth Science, Environmental Science, Biology, Conceptual Physics, Chemistry, and Physics. Among the elective offerings are courses in music, art, drama, economics, computer, business seminar, and advanced biology.

Among the colleges at which recent graduates have been accepted are Bethany College, Boston College, Catholic University, Cornell, Elon, Embry-Riddle, Fairleigh Dickinson, George Washington, Landmark College, Loyola University (New Orleans), Marshall, Mount Allison University, Muskingum College, Northeastern, Regis University, Rochester Institute of Technology, Roger Williams, St. Lawrence, Savannah College of Art and Design, Southern Illinois, Trinity, Tulane, Virginia Institute of Technology, Western State College, Widener, Wilfred Laurier University (Canada), and the Universities of Arizona, Denver, Oregon, Toronto, Utah, Vermont, and Wisconsin.

STUDENT ACTIVITIES. Extracurricular activities vary from year to year in response to student interest. In student affairs, the young men are represented by a school council, resident assistants, and class officers. Typical groups are the newspaper and yearbook staffs, and the Photography, Instrumental Music, Golf, Roller Blading, Skiing, Mountain Biking, and Outing Clubs. All students are encouraged to participate in drama activities, which include the production of at least two major plays each year in conjunction with girls from neighboring schools.

Interscholastic teams are organized in soccer, squash, lacrosse, basketball, cross-country, tennis, rowing, and wrestling. School teams compete with nearby public and independent schools, including Nichols School and Park School of Buffalo. Weight training, winter camping, and intramural sports are among the activities offered on a noncompetitive basis.

The extracurricular program includes dances and trips to Buffalo, Toronto, and Niagara Falls. Students attend NFL and NHL games as well as concerts, theater, and visits to area museums.

ADMISSION AND COSTS. The Gow School admits young, dyslexic men capable of college preparatory work who need language-based remediation. School records, completed student and parent questionnaires, math and English teacher recommendations, educational assessment including WIAT or Woodcock-Johnson battery, WISC-IV or WAIS test results, and a personal interview are required for admission. In addition, specific skill testing to determine class placement is required. Placement testing and an interview take place on campus and are completed in one day. New students are admitted in any grade, and late enrollment is permitted if vacancies exist. There is a nonrefundable $4900 registration/deposit fee, which is applied to the first year's tuition, and a $100 application fee.

Tuition, board, lodging, technology fee, and transportation for regular school activities are $49,825 for the 2009–10 school year. Books, supplies, laundry, athletic supplies, and personal expenses are additional. Twenty-six percent of the student body receive financial aid from the School.

Director of Upper School and Assistant Headmaster: Daniel F. Kelley
Director of Middle School: Jeffrey Sweet
Director of Admission: Robert Garcia
Director of Development: Gayle Hutton

Director of College Counseling: Charles Brown
Director of Finance: Rosemary Bastian
Director of Athletics: Mark Szafnicki

Grace Day School 1955

23 Cedar Shore Drive, Massapequa, NY 11758
Tel. 516-798-1122; Fax 516-799-0711
Web Site www.gracedayschool.org

Grace Day School is a coeducational, Episcopal-affiliated school enrolling approximately 400 students in Nursery–Grade 8. Faculty and staff aim to prepare highly motivated students for the most selective and competitive secondary schools in the region. The school environment is guided by Christian principles and values. The curriculum focuses on high student expectations for achievement in the academic core subjects. Small class size, personal attention, and integrated/interdisciplinary studies are hallmarks of the school syllabus. Grace Day's program is enriched by the New York State Regents curriculum in science and math as well as substantial attention to the arts, music education including choral and instrumental opportunities, foreign languages, and computer technology. All students engage in community service and volunteer efforts with a goal toward developing a deeper sensitivity to those in need. Parents and faculty members are partners in creating exciting learning experiences at every grade level. The School's motto reflects its commitment to provide youngsters with "Roots to Stand and Wings to Soar." Tuition: $8800–$9200. Patricia Quinto is Director of Admissions; Laurance Anderson is Head of School.

The Green Vale School 1923

250 Valentine's Lane, Old Brookville, NY 11545
Tel. 516-621-2420; Fax 516-621-1317
Web Site www.greenvaleschool.org; E-mail info@greenvaleschool.org

Green Vale is proud to be celebrating its 86th year. With 485 day boys and girls in pre-Nursery (age 3)–Grade 9 on a 40-acre campus, the School promotes competence, confidence, good citizenship, character building, and high academic expectations as essential ingredients of the Green Vale program. As important, faculty and staff work to instill moral values, tolerance, and compassion for meaningful, productive engagement in an ever-changing world. The curriculum balances the liberal arts and sciences, enriched by art, music, crafts, technology, library, and physical education. Sports, a health and wellness curriculum, and service learning are integral parts of the program. A strong partnership between faculty and parents adds to the success of the program and strength of the community. Tuition: $5800–$24,200. Financial aid is available. Anne B. Watters is Director of Admission; Stephen H. Watters is Head of School.

Hackley School 1899

293 Benedict Avenue, Tarrytown, NY 10591
Tel. 914-631-0128; Admissions 914-366-2642; Fax 914-366-2636
Web Site www.hackleyschool.org; E-mail admissions@hackleyschool.org

Hackley school in Tarrytown, New York, is a nonsectarian, coeducational, college preparatory school enrolling day students in Kindergarten through Grade 12 and five-day boarding students in Grades 9 through 12. Tarrytown (population 12,000) is located in the heart of the scenic Hudson Valley, 25 miles north of Manhattan. The School is reached easily by bus, car, or train.

The School was founded in 1899 by Mrs. Caleb Brewster Hackley to provide an educational culture in which a deliberate approach to social relationships stimulates and supports the moral, intellectual, artistic, and athletic accomplishments of individuals. Hackley students encounter serious classes, demanding homework assignments, and a peer environment that respects commitment and unreserved effort. In the belief that students grow in character and responsibility through service to others, all grades commit energy, time, and imagination to assisting others beyond the spheres of home and school as they carry out Hackley's motto: "United We Help One Another."

HACKLEY SCHOOL

A nonprofit institution, Hackley is governed by a 20-member Board of Trustees. It is registered by the New York State Board of Regents and holds membership in the National Association of Independent Schools, the College Board, the Association of College Admissions Counselors, and the New York State Association of Independent Schools. The Parents Association enhances school life through volunteer activities and fund-raising. Hackley's Centennial Campaign raised $50,000,000.

THE CAMPUS. The School, situated on a hilltop overlooking the Hudson, is graced by rambling, turn-of-the-century buildings of English Tudor style. Among the facilities are a Performing Arts Center with a music conservatory, a new Lower School building, a new Middle School, a new Upper and Middle School science building, new international squash courts, an indoor swimming pool, several art studios, a photography lab, and a library. There are computer labs in each division and Internet access in every classroom.

Boarders, who spend weekends and holidays at home, are housed in single or double rooms in the main building complex. Resident faculty supervise the boarding corridors.

The 285-acre campus offers six tennis courts, numerous playing fields, four international squash courts, and a 3.2-mile cross-country trail.

THE FACULTY. Walter C. Johnson was appointed Headmaster in 1995. He graduated *summa cum laude* from Amherst (B.A. 1974) and earned master's degrees in literature and educational administration from the University of Pennsylvania and Teachers College, Columbia University, respectively. Mr. Johnson has had educational and administrative experience at Trinity School and Collegiate School in New York City and at The American School in London.

Faculty, including assistants and administrators who teach, number 149. Fifty-eight of the full-time teachers live on campus. They hold 149 baccalaureate and 125 graduate degrees representing study at more than 100 colleges and universities.

The College Counseling office is staffed by three experienced, full-time professionals. Other support services include a full-time nurse, three full-time psychologists, and a learning specialist.

STUDENT BODY. In 2009–10, the School enrolled 403 day boys, 417 day girls, 11 boarding boys, and 12 boarding girls, as follows: 218 in Kindergarten–Grade 4, 246 in Grades 5–8, and 379 in Grades 9–12. Day students come from 96 communities throughout New York, New Jersey, and Connecticut.

ACADEMIC PROGRAM. The school year, from early September to early June, is divided into semesters, with breaks for Thanksgiving, winter, and spring vacations.

Average class size is 16 students. There are supervised study halls throughout the day for students in Grades 5–12. Boarders also have supervised evening study. Teachers provide extra help as necessary; long-term tutoring is offered for an hourly fee. Grades are issued and sent to parents four times yearly, with interim reports issued as required.

The curriculum for Kindergarten–Grade 3 emphasizes reading and oral and written expression. Starting in Grade 3, students write a weekly theme and begin to work on research papers. The Singapore math program teaches the logical structure of the number system and fosters dexterity in solving word problems and in computation. Also included in the program are history, science, art, music, computers, and physical education. Spanish is introduced in Grade 3. The Interim Director of the Lower School is Anne Ewing Burns.

The curriculum for Grade 4 and the Middle School (Grades 5–8) includes English, which focuses on grammar, oral expression, expository and creative writing, and literary analysis; American history (Grade 4), ancient history and world history (Grades 5–7), and Asian civilizations (Grade 8); mathematics (emphasizing the four basic operations and probability, graphing, statistics, pre-algebra, algebra I, and geometry); science including the physical world (Grades 5–6), life science (Grade 7), and chemistry in biology (Grade 8); and art, drama, and music. All Middle School students are required to take a computer curriculum and health education. They may choose to study Latin, Chinese, Spanish, or French in Grade 6. Alona Scott is Director of the Middle School.

HACKLEY SCHOOL

To graduate, Upper School students must complete four years of English; three years of a foreign language (French, Spanish, Chinese, or Latin); three years of required history sequence; mathematics through algebra II and trigonometry; three years of science, one of which must be a laboratory course; and one year of performing or visual arts. The Upper School puts a major emphasis on writing. The Monday composition period assigns at least 20 additional essays during the academic year.

In addition to required courses, the Upper School offers Advanced Placement courses in 20 subjects across the disciplines. Other courses include Surviving the Apocalypse/New York City: Imagination and Desire, Hyphenated Americans/Satire, History of Western Theatre, Seminar in Creative Writing (print- and Web-based), Economics, Modern European History,

Government and Politics: The U.S.A. and the World, Media & Culture, Italian, Computer Science, Ecology, Biology, Organic Chemistry, Chemistry, 9th Grade Physics, Advanced Physics, Marine Biology, Environmental Science, Calculus, Finite Math, Statistics, Music Theory, Jazz Improvisation, Art History, Studio Art, Advanced Ceramics, Photography, Computer Graphics, 3-D Sculpture and Design, and Architecture & Design. The Director of the Upper School is Andrew King.

In the past four years, the following colleges and universities have enrolled the greatest number of Hackley graduates: Colgate, Columbia, Cornell, George Washington, Harvard, New York University, Princeton, Trinity, Tufts, Williams, Yale, and the University of Pennsylvania.

STUDENT ACTIVITIES. The Community Council, composed of student and faculty representatives from Grades 5–12, organizes social and service activities. Students also participate in Model Congress and a student-faculty judicial board. Students publish a yearbook, a newspaper, and a literary magazine. All Lower and Middle School students perform in grade-level dramatic and musical productions annually. Students may join chorus, orchestra, band, and jazz bands, performing major choral works, chamber music, and vocal recitals. The Hackley Music Institute provides individual instruction for preprofessional and other music students in both vocal and instrumental music. There is also a variety of student clubs and a Student Teacher program working in Lower School classrooms.

Hackley families attend the Americana Festival, Book Fair, Fall Fair, school art shows, gym & swim nights, and parent dinners. Hackley also holds dances and coffee house evenings for students.

Annual trips include sixth-grade overnight trip to nature's classroom at Club Getaway, seventh-grade visit to Philadelphia, the eighth-grade cultural exploration of New York City, and ninth-grade outdoor challenge experience. Students take trips supplementing their courses such as visits to the Metropolitan Museum and Ellis Island, zoology and marine biology studies on a research vessel in Long Island Sound, and field trips to sites in the Hudson River Valley.

In 2000, Hackley received a grant for an annual educational trip; students and faculty have visited Cuba, Vietnam, Malawi, Japan, China, the Galapagos, Italy, and Greece. The School also sponsors student exchanges with a school in France during the spring recess.

HACKLEY SCHOOL

Varsity sports for boys and girls include basketball, cross-country, fencing, indoor track, lacrosse, golf, soccer, squash, swimming, track and field, and tennis. Boys also compete in baseball, football, and wrestling, while girls play field hockey and softball. A member of the Ivy League of the metropolitan area, Hackley competes against league members and public and parochial schools. Physical education courses include noncompetitive activities such as fitness center and hiking. Swimming is required in Kindergarten–Grade 6.

ADMISSION AND COSTS. Hackley seeks students of diverse backgrounds who demonstrate quickness of intellect and resourcefulness in problem solving, tempered by curiosity and love of truth. Students are admitted on the basis of a personal interview and written essay, a campus visit, two teacher recommendations, previous transcripts and the results of the Independent School Entrance Examination or Secondary School Admission Test for Middle and Upper Schools. In the Lower School, candidates for Kindergarten and Grade 1 take Hackley's own admissions test. Candidates for Grades 2, 3, and 4 must undergo the early childhood evaluation of the Educational Records Bureau. The application deadline is December 15. There is a $55 application fee.

HACKLEY SCHOOL

In 2009–10, tuition ranges from $28,700 for Kindergarten to $31,000 for Grade 12. The boarding charge is $10,100. Tuition includes lunch but not the cost of Middle and Upper School books.

In the current year, a total of $3,000,000 in financial aid was awarded to 121 students on the basis of demonstrated need. Low-interest loans, an installment payment plan, and tuition insurance are also available.

Headmaster: Walter C. Johnson
Assistant Headmaster: Philip Variano
Director of Development: Katherine Valyi
Co-Directors of Admissions: Julie S. Core & Christopher T. McColl
Co-Directors of College Counseling: Julie D. Lillis, Peter Latson & Jean Nadell
Technology Director: Joseph E. Dioguardi
Director of Finance: Peter McAndrew
Director of Athletics: Jason Edwards

Harbor Country Day School 1958

17 Three Sisters Road, St. James, NY 11780
Tel. 631-584-5555; Fax 631-862-7664
Web Site www.harborcountrydayschool.org
E-mail cpryor@harborcountrydayschool.org

Founded by parents, Harbor Country Day School enrolls 145 boys and girls in Nursery–Grade 8. The enriched curriculum focuses on the basic academic disciplines of language arts, mathematics, social studies, and science, while fostering good work habits, self-esteem, and consideration of others. Foreign language and instruction in music, art, computer science, and physical education are offered at every level beginning in Kindergarten. Competitive sports, intramurals, and the performing arts are also part of the School's program. Summer programs are offered. Financial aid is available. Tuition: $4850–$12,300. Christine Spahr is Director of Admissions; Christopher C. Pryor (Roanoke College, B.A.; Teachers College, Columbia University, M.A.) was appointed Headmaster in 2007.

The Harley School   1917

1981 Clover Street, Rochester, NY 14618
Tel. 585-442-1770; Admissions Ext. 3010; Fax 585-442-5758
Web Site www.harleyschool.org; E-mail admissions@harleyschool.org

Housed in spacious, modern buildings on a 20-acre suburban campus, The Harley School is a coeducational, college preparatory day school enrolling 500 students in Nursery through Grade 12. Harley encourages involvement in all areas of school life: academic study, visual and performing arts, athletic competition, extracurricular activities, and community service. Harley offers a full range of Advanced Placement classes, arts and music classes, foreign languages, science laboratories, and various electives. Summer programs and extended day are also offered. Tuition: $10,400–$18,670. Financial aid is available. Valerie A. Mynnti is Director of Admissions; Dr. Timothy R. Cottrell was appointed Head of School in 2006.

The Harvey School   1916

260 Jay Street, Katonah, NY 10536
Tel. 914-232-3161; Admission Ext. 138; Fax 914-232-6034
Web Site www.harveyschool.org; E-mail admissions@harveyschool.org

The Harvey School's traditional college preparatory curriculum emphasizes the mastery of basic skills and offers opportunities to excel in both honors and AP courses. The curriculum is flexible and personalized to meet the needs of students of varying abilities, interests, and learning styles. Information technology in most disciplines provides resource materials to enhance classroom instruction. Enrolling 340 students, with five-day boarders in Grades 9–12 and day students in Grades 6–12, Harvey employs a highly qualified faculty and staff who work individually with students in a warm, supportive environment. The 100-acre campus 40 miles north of Manhattan combines a country setting with easy access to the resources in the greater metropolitan area. Students come from 65 communities in New York and Connecticut. Among the activities are a nationally recognized Model UN program, visual and performing arts, publications, community service, and interscholastic sports in all grades. Tuition: $29,800; Boarding Fee: $7000. Financial aid is available. William Porter is Director of Admissions; Barry W. Fenstermacher is Headmaster.

Horace Mann School   1887

Grades 6–12: 231 West 246th Street, Riverdale, NY 10471
Tel. 718-432-4000; Admissions 718-432-4100
Fax 718-432-3610
Web Site www.horacemann.org; E-mail admissions@horacemann.org
Kindergarten–Grade 5: 4440 Tibbett Avenue, Riverdale, NY 10471
Tel. 718-432-3300
Nursery Division: 55 East 90th Street, New York, NY 10128
Tel. 212-369-4600

Horace Mann is a day school enrolling 1750 boys and girls from diverse backgrounds in Nursery–Grade 12. The college preparatory curriculum is designed to challenge the imagination and intellect of its students while developing moral character and a

love of learning. The core program, which includes Advanced Placement in all disciplines, is enhanced by programs at the School's 265-acre nature laboratory in Connecticut. All graduates typically enroll in four-year colleges. Varsity sports, Model United Nations, instrumental and vocal groups, publications, and activity clubs meet a variety of student interests. Tuition: $24,440–$34,050. Financial Aid: $7,600,000. Lisa J. Moreira is Director of Admissions; Thomas M. Kelly, Ph.D., is Head of School. *Middle States Association.*

The Kildonan School   1969

425 Morse Hill Road, Amenia, NY 12501
Tel. 845-373-8111; Fax 845-373-9793
Web Site www.kildonan.org; E-mail admissions@kildonan.org

Kildonan, a coeducational, college preparatory school for dyslexic students of average to above-average intelligence, enrolls boarders in Grade 7–Postgraduate and day students in Grade 2–Postgraduate. In addition to regular subjects, the highly structured program features daily one-on-one language tutoring designed to help students develop the necessary level of proficiency in academic skills to allow them to return to another school or enter college. Computer and word processing are an integral part of a full curriculum that includes art, woodshop, riding, and interscholastic/intramural athletics. Boarding Tuition: $52,250–$54,500; Day Tuition: $31,500–$39,000. David J. Tuttle is Admissions Director; Benjamin N. Powers is Headmaster.

The Knox School   1904

541 Long Beach Road, St. James, NY 11780
Tel. 631-686-1600; Admissions Ext. 414; Fax 631-686-1650
Web Site www.knoxschool.org; E-mail dmarshall@knoxschool.org

THE KNOX SCHOOL

Set on 40+ acres overlooking Stony Brook Harbor, Knox provides the opportunity for 125 motivated students in Grades 6–12 to excel within a liberal arts program in preparation for success in selective colleges and universities. Six Core Values—scholarship, respect, responsibility, integrity, kindness, and courage—guide the School's Principles of Action. Students benefit from small classes in a familial environment that fosters character and leadership. Faculty are available for extra support during and after the school day. Clubs, a student exchange program in England, and athletic teams, including an equestrian program, are offered. Boarding Tuition: $38,700–$40,800; Day Tuition: $20,700–$22,500. George K. Allison is Headmaster; Duncan Marshall is Director of Admissions. *Middle States Association.*

Loyola School 1900

980 Park Avenue, New York, NY 10028
Tel. 212-288-3522; Admissions 646-346-8132; Fax 212-861-1021
Web Site www.loyola-nyc.org; E-mail admissions@loyola-nyc.org

LOYOLA SCHOOL

Loyola School is the only Roman Catholic, Jesuit, coeducational, secondary day school in the tristate area. The School was founded by members of the Society of Jesus to develop young people spiritually, intellectually, artistically, athletically, and socially. In concert with Jesuit schools worldwide, Loyola seeks to challenge students to become academically excellent, open to growth, loving, religious, and committed to doing justice. Loyola currently enrolls 205 boys and girls in Grades 9–12 who reflect the diversity of New York City in their faith, ethnic, racial, and economic backgrounds. All follow a curriculum based on the traditional Jesuit education designed to equip graduates for excellence in the liberal arts, sciences, and humanities. Technology, modern and classical language, theology, and Advanced Placement courses in ten subjects round out the program. In addition to retreat and service programs, Loyola students participate in Math League, art and outdoors clubs, photography, publications, drama, orchestra, chorus, and interscholastic sports for boys and girls. All graduates go on to four-year colleges. Tuition: $27,000. Lillian Díaz-Imbelli is Director of Admissions; Rev. Stephen N. Katsouros, S.J., is President. *Middle States Association.*

The Mary Louis Academy 1936

176-21 Wexford Terrace, Jamaica Estates, NY 11432
Tel. 718-297-2120; Admissions Ext. 228; Fax 718-739-0037
Web Site tmla.org

This Catholic, college preparatory day school enrolling 950 young women in Grades 9–12 aims to provide an environment of encouragement for spiritual, physical, emotional, and social growth. In addition to diploma/Regents requirements, sequences are offered in art, language, mathematics, music, and science. Religious studies and physical education are required. Honors and Advanced Placement courses, a full technology program, and state-of-the-art labs in chemistry, physics, and earth science are available. Activities include athletics, forensics, journalism, performing arts, and many cultural clubs. Tuition: $6800. Sr. Filippa Luciano is Admissions Director; Sr. Kathleen McKinney, CSJ (St. Joseph's, B.A.; Adelphi, M.S.; St. John's, Ed.D.), is Principal. *Middle States Association.*

Mary McDowell Center for Learning 1984

20 Bergen Street, Brooklyn, NY 11201
Tel. 718-625-3939; Fax 718-625-1456
Web Site www.marymcdowell.org; E-mail info@mmcl.net

The Mary McDowell Center for Learning, enrolling 225 students ages 5–14, is a Friends school for children with learning disabilities. It provides a supportive and nurturing learning environment that enables students to use their full intellectual, social, and emotional potential to become successful learners. Through a serious academic curriculum, which is experiential and language-based in presentation, each student's work is highly individualized to encourage strengths while addressing areas of need. The Center offers speech/language and occupational therapy as well as a comprehensive enrichment program. In September 2010, the Center will open a high school to further serve the needs of learning-disabled children. Tuition: $41,100. Financial aid is available. Deborah Edel is Director of Admissions; Debbie Zlotowitz is Head of School.

Marymount School 1926

1026 Fifth Avenue, New York, NY 10028
Tel. 212-744-4486; Admissions Ext. 152; Fax 212-744-0716
Web Site www.marymount.k12.ny.us
E-mail admissions@marymount.k12.ny.us

MARYMOUNT SCHOOL

Founded by the Religious of the Sacred Heart of Mary, Marymount School is an independent, college preparatory, Catholic day school enrolling 575 girls in Nursery–Class XII. Located in four turn-of-the-century mansions on Fifth Avenue, Marymount's proximity to the Metropolitan Museum of Art provides numerous opportunities for partnerships between the School and the Museum. Marymount is part of an international network, with 21 RSHM schools in such cities as Los Angeles, Rome, Paris, London, Lisbon, Fatima, Oporto, and Medellin. Central to the mission of the School is the academic enterprise—the acquisition of knowledge and the development of lifelong skills of critical thinking and clear expression. Emphasizing classic disciplines and scientific inquiry, the curriculum includes 14 Advanced Placement courses, 13 team sports including field hockey, fencing, and soccer, and a variety of aesthetic and performing arts. Tuition: $19,575–$34,000. Financial Aid: $1,800,000. Lillian Issa is Director of Admissions; Concepcion Alvar (Maryknoll College [Philippines], B.A.; Columbia Teachers College, M.A.) is Headmistress.

The Melrose School 1963

120 Federal Hill Road, Brewster, NY 10509
Tel. 845-279-2406; Admission Ext. 1; Fax 845-279-3878
Web Site www.melrose.edu; E-mail admissions@melrose.edu

THE MELROSE SCHOOL.

Melrose is a PreK–Grade 8, coeducational day school that offers a challenging academic program to bright, motivated students. The School welcomes 120 students of all faiths and backgrounds. Melrose believes that excellence begins with high expectations and relies on an active collaboration among students, family, faculty, and staff to achieve them. Dedicated to developing the full potential of all students, the curriculum, small class size, and talented faculty ensure that students grow academically, socially, spiritually, artistically, and athletically. French is taught in all grades. In Grades 5–8, accelerated and honors classes are offered in math and language arts, and Spanish is available. Melrose students consistently score in the top percentile on standardized achievement tests, and graduates attend nationally recognized secondary schools. Band, choir, drama, community service, Student Council, soccer, volleyball, and basketball help boys and girls build teamwork, self-confidence, leadership, and physical skills. Melrose is a member of the National Association of Episcopal Schools and accredited by the New York State Association of Independent Schools. Tuition: $4300–$16,500. Tom Burns is Director of Admission; Diane Cikoski is Interim Head. *Middle States Association.*

Millbrook School 1931

131 Millbrook School Road, Millbrook, NY 12545
Tel. 845-677-8261, Ext. 138; Fax 845-677-1265
Web Site www.millbrook.org; E-mail admissions@millbrook.org

Located on 800 acres 90 miles north of New York City, Millbrook is a coeducational boarding and day school that offers its 260 students in Grades 9–12 a rigorous college preparatory program integrating academics, service, athletics, arts, and leadership. Since its founding in 1931, students have been encouraged to develop as strong and healthy individuals as well as concerned citizens of their world and its environment. All participate in an on-campus community service program. A traditional liberal arts curriculum features Honors and AP courses in the major disciplines, independent study opportunities, a culminating experience for seniors, and a variety of electives including Animal Behavior, Astronomy, Constitutional Law, Anthropology, Digital Art Video, and Aesthetics. Facilities include Holbrook Arts Center, Mills Athletic Center, the AZA-accredited Trevor Zoo, and a $12,000,000 LEED-certified math and science center that opened in 2008. Boarding Tuition: $43,050; Day Tuition: $31,300. Financial Aid: $1,900,000. Cynthia S. McWilliams is Director of Admission; Drew Casertano is Headmaster. *Middle States Association.*

Mizzentop Day School 1998

64 East Main Street, Pawling, NY 12564
Tel. 845-855-7338; Fax 845-855-1239
Web Site www.mizzentop.org; E-mail cobrien@mizzentop.org

Now in its 11th year of educating young children, Mizzentop Day School was founded to meet the need in the area for a personalized, child-centered learning experience. The School opened with 50 boys and girls in Pre-Kindergarten–Grade 1 and has expanded to a state-of-the-art facility where 165 students are enrolled up to Grade 8. Mizzentop's philosophy is predicated on the belief that the curriculum must embrace all aspects of a student's development: intellectual, ethical, social, aesthetic, and physical. A Living Values Program is interwoven throughout the program, emphasizing peace, respect, simplicity, cooperation, and other universal aspirations. Reading and language arts, math, science, and social studies form the core academic offerings. Specialists teach computer/technology, French, Spanish, library, drama, health, visual arts, and music. Interest clubs involve children in concert band, rock ensemble, chess/checkers, school government, peer mentoring, newspaper, knitting, gardening, and competitive sports. Before- and after-school care and summer programs are optional. Tuition: $3150–$11,800. Carney O'Brien is Director of Admissions; Steven J. Cash (Sonoma State University, B.A., M.A.) is Head of School.

Nichols School 1892

1250 Amherst Street, Buffalo, NY 14216
Tel. 716-875-8212; Admissions 716-332-6325; Fax 716-875-2169
Web Site www.nicholsschool.org; E-mail lyusick@nicholsschool.org

Nichols, a coeducational, college preparatory day school, enrolls 586 students, from across Western New York and Southern Ontario, as well as international students. In a nurturing environment, the Middle School (Grades 5–8) provides a stimulating atmosphere and challenging curriculum vital for academic growth, personal development, and readiness for high school. In the Upper School (Grades 9–12), small classes, a rigorous curriculum, and extensive extra-curricular activities prepare students for higher education. The fine and performing arts, interscholastic athletics, and community service enhance the traditional, technology-integrated curriculum. The dedicated faculty is focused on preparing students to thrive in the global community of the 21st century. Nichols provides inclusive access to all academic, athletic, art and cultural exchange programs. A summer academic session is available. Tuition: $16,700–$18,250. Financial Aid: $1,500,000. Laura Lombardo Yusick '96 is Director of Admissions; Richard C. Bryan, Jr. (Trinity, A.B.; University of North Carolina, M.A.), is Headmaster.

The Nightingale-Bamford School 1921

20 East 92nd Street, New York, NY 10128
Tel. 212-289-5020; Admissions 212-933-6515; Fax 212-876-1045
Web Site www.nightingale.org; E-mail admissions@nightingale.org

Nightingale-Bamford, a day school serving 560 girls in Kindergarten through Class XII, provides rigorous college preparation in a community that prizes intellectual development and self-esteem. Commitment to diversity and substantial financial aid ensure a multicultural student body. A state-of-the-art Schoolhouse features advanced computer facilities. The classical curriculum, which focuses on the major disciplines and values the arts and athletics, is updated annually to meet the needs of its students. Advanced Placement in 11 disciplines, cocurricular activities, foreign study and travel, social service, publications, and clubs supplement the program. Tuition/Fees: $33,725–$34,350. Margaret Metz is Director of Admissions; Dorothy A. Hutcheson is Head of School.

Oakwood Friends School   1796

22 Spackenkill Road, Poughkeepsie, NY 12603
Tel. 845-462-4200; Admissions [Toll-free] 800-843-3341
Fax 845-462-4251
Web Site www.oakwoodfriends.org
E-mail admissions@oakwoodfriends.org

Oakwood Friends school in Poughkeepsie, New York, is a coeducational college preparatory school enrolling day students in Grades 6–8 and both day and boarding students in Grades 9–12. It is located 4 miles south of Poughkeepsie near Vassar College and historic Hudson River sites. The School is 75 miles from New York City, 80 miles from Albany, and 220 miles from Boston.

Founded in 1796 by the New York Yearly Meeting of the Religious Society of Friends, Oakwood Friends is an educational community committed to Quakers' deep respect for the worth of each person. It seeks students who demonstrate a genuine concern for their own growth—academic, spiritual, social, and physical—and who are intent on becoming complete persons—competent, creative, responsible, and sensitive to the world and its needs for a just and moral social order.

Oakwood Friends is a nonprofit corporation managed for the New York Yearly Meeting by a Board of Managers. The School holds membership in the Friends Council on Education and the National Association of Independent Schools. It is chartered by the Regents of the University of the State of New York and accredited by the New York State Association of Independent Schools.

THE CAMPUS. The 60-acre campus includes six tennis courts, three soccer fields, two baseball diamonds, and wooded areas.

Collins Library houses 11,000 volumes, microform materials, a computer laboratory, and classrooms. The Main Building, Crowley, Collins Library, and Stokes house classrooms, a ceramics studio, the meeting room, the art room, and offices. The Turner Math and Science Building contains state-of-the-art science laboratories. Lane Auditorium is used for theatrical performances, dance and music classes, and public events; Connor Gymnasium contains a basketball court, locker rooms with showers, and a weight room. Other facilities include the Dining Hall and a fully equipped photography darkroom.

OAKWOOD FRIENDS SCHOOL

Three dorms—Craig, Reagan, and Newlin—contain faculty apartments and recreation, laundry, and kitchen facilities.

THE FACULTY. Peter F. Baily, appointed Head of School in July 2000, is a graduate of Earlham College, Nasson College (B.A., M.E.), and Bryn Mawr College (M.A.). Prior to his last position as Interim Head of School of the Quaker School at Horsham,

Mr. Baily served seven years as Head of School at Oak Lane Day School in Blue Bell, Pennsylvania.

There are 30 full-time teachers, 10 part-time instructors, and 8 administrators. Of these, most live at the School. They hold 37 baccalaureate and 22 advanced degrees from such colleges and universities as Adelphi, Alvan Ikoku, Brooklyn College, Brown, Bryn Mawr, Bucknell, Central Michigan, Colgate, College of the Holy Cross, College of William and Mary, Columbia, Cornell, Drew, Dutchess Community College, Earlham, Fashion Institute of Technology, Georgetown, Harvard, Imo State, Manhattanville, Marist, Middlebury, Nasson, New York University, Ohio State, Ohio Wesleyan, Parsons, St. John's, St. Lawrence, St. Luke's School of Education at Exeter University, St. Michael's, Scarritt, Siena, Smith, State University of New York, Tufts, Universidad de Chile, Universidad de Moron Buenos Aires, Université Lumiere-Lyon, Vassar, Wesleyan, and the Universities of Alabama, Chicago, Delaware, Denver, Illinois, Michigan, New Mexico, Portsmouth (England), and Tennessee.

OAKWOOD FRIENDS SCHOOL

The infirmary is staffed by a Director of Health Services/School Nurse, and a doctor is on call.

STUDENT BODY. Oakwood Friends enrolls 175 students in Grades 6–12. The enrollment includes 53 day boys, 46 day girls, 44 male boarders, and 32 female boarders as follows: 4 in Grade 6, 5 in Grade 7, 12 in Grade 8, 28 in Grade 9, 43 in Grade 10, 45 in Grade 11, and 38 in Grade 12. Seventy-five percent come from New York State; six other states and six countries are also represented.

ACADEMIC PROGRAM. The school year consists of trimesters of 11 weeks each. Grades are posted and reported to parents at midterm and at the end of each trimester, and written course evaluations are sent at the end of each term.

The daily schedule for all Oakwood Friends students runs from 8:00 A.M. to 3:30 P.M. and includes classes, study, lunch, and a 40-minute period, which may be used for Advisory, Community Meeting, or Meeting for Worship. Between 3:30 P.M. and dinner, students participate in interscholastic and lifetime sports. From 7:30 to 9:30 P.M., boarders study in their dormitories. Students whose grade point average earns them "Independent Status" are exempt from evening study hall. As a Quaker school, Oakwood Friends does not rank students or grant academic honors.

Graduation requirements include four years of English and history; three of science; three of math; three of a foreign language; one and one-third in the arts; and one trimester each of health, Quakerism, and computer literacy. Satisfactory participation in sports/physical education and community service is required every trimester, as well as the completion of the senior program.

The curriculum emphasizes mastery of important fundamental skills in writing, both creative and analytical; reading comprehension; and applied and theoretical mathematics and science. Emphasis is placed on the ability to analyze as well as synthesize information and to recognize the interrelationships of disciplines.

Advanced Placement courses are offered in English Language, English Literature, French, Spanish, Calculus AB, Calculus BC, Chemistry, and Biology. Elective courses include Introduction to Robotics and Engineering Applications, Greek Philosophy, Asian Religion, Creative Writing, Writing for College, Chaos Theory and Fractal Geometry, Play Writing, Photography, Drama Tech, Fashion Art and Design, Music Theory, History of Jazz, and Advanced Scene Study. Students who have mild, documented learning differences receive support in a regularly scheduled 2:1 class through the Academic Support Center, where instruction is geared toward skills enhancement (reading, writing, math, study skills, and organization) and subject-matter support.

A unified senior program begins with a camping trip to start the yearlong process of personal and group goal setting, which continues through weekly advisory group meetings. The intellectual focus of the program is provided by challenging interdisciplinary courses that involve considerable writing and critical reading of a variety of texts. These courses include Cultural Anthropology, Genocide Studies, Globalization, Existentialism, and Revolutions. After completing their end-of-year final exams, seniors embark on a short trip that allows them several days to reflect on their experience at Oakwood and enjoy one another's company before they part ways. The senior year culminates in a final, weeklong community service project.

International students must meet a minimum proficiency in English to be admitted. Students may be required to take additional ESL classes to improve their proficiency in English.

OAKWOOD FRIENDS SCHOOL

One hundred percent of Oakwood's graduates continue on to colleges and universities. Graduates of the Class of 2009 are attending Alfred, Arcadia, Boston University, Champlain College, Concordia, Drexel, Dutchess Community College, Indiana University, Ithaca, Lehigh 2, Manhattanville, Middlebury, New England College, New York University 2, Pennsylvania State, Rensselaer Polytechnic Institute, Rutgers 2, St. John's College (Maryland), Sarah Lawrence, School of the Art Institute of Chicago, Skidmore, State University of New York (Oneonta), Vassar 3, Worcester Polytechnic, and the Universities of Arizona, California, Hartford, the Pacific, and Rhode Island.

STUDENT ACTIVITIES. All students and faculty attend daily Collection and weekly Community Meetings, which are chaired by an elected student clerk, and weekly Meeting for Worship. Much of daily school life is overseen by faculty-student standing committees including Judicial, Academic, and Friends Concerns Committees. The Theater Department produces three main stage productions each year: a drama, a comedy, and a musical. All students and faculty engage in two all-school Workshare

Days each year. Student organizations include No Sweat/Peace Club, an environmental club, Model United Nations, Academic Worldquest, New Orleans Renaissance, and Student Government. Students have opportunities to participate in choral and instrumental groups as well as periodic Cabaret and "Open Mic" events. Students can assist in the production of the yearbook or share their written and art work through *Lumen,* a collection of students' creative works published each term.

OAKWOOD FRIENDS SCHOOL

Interscholastic teams are fielded in boys' and girls' basketball, soccer, tennis, and cross-country; coeducational Ultimate Frisbee and swimming; boys' baseball; and girls' softball and volleyball. Life sports include table tennis, running, martial arts, fitness club, aerobics, and yoga.

Weekend activities include faculty open houses, films, sightseeing, trips to Vassar and other colleges for special events, visits to local museums, field trips to New York City, informal cooking, hiking, skiing, and snowboarding. Parents Weekend in the fall and Alumni Day in the spring are traditional events.

ADMISSION AND COSTS. Oakwood Friends welcomes applicants of all racial and religious backgrounds who are genuinely interested in participating in the life of the School and in taking responsibility for their growth and learning. Applicants must submit school records and teacher recommendations and arrange a campus interview. Secondary School Admission Test scores are recommended but not required.

Application should be made as early as possible and will be considered as long as spaces are available. New students are admitted in Grades 6–11 and occasionally in Grade 12.

In 2009–10, tuition, room, and board is $37,625 for seven-day boarding and $32,625 for five-day boarding. Day tuition is $18,750 in Grades 6–8 and $21,725 in Grades 9–12. Tuition includes an infirmary fee, accident insurance, and normal art and laboratory fees. Additional expenses—estimated at $900—include books, spending money, school trips, and transportation. Focused Instruction is an additional $775 per term. The yearly surcharges for the Learning Skills Program and the International Student Program are $5500 and $1950, respectively. In 2009–10, $750,000 in financial aid was awarded to 39 percent of the student body. Aid is awarded on the basis of need; students who wish to be considered should apply through the School and Student Service for Financial Aid.

Upper School Head: Anna Bertucci
Middle School Head: Marcy Seitel
Director of Admissions: Susan Masciale-Lynch
Upper School Dean: Jeremy Robbins
Coordinators, Academic Support Center: Pat Meade & Karen Butt
Athletic Director: Charles Butts
Director of Alumni & Development: Elaine Miles
Business Manager: Natalia Armoza
Dean of Residential Life: David Whiting

The Packer Collegiate Institute 1845

170 Joralemon Street, Brooklyn Heights, NY 11201
Tel. 718-875-6644, Admissions 718-250-0266; Fax 718-875-1363
Web Site www.packer.edu
E-mail ddebono@packer.edu/jcaldwell@packer.edu

Founded in 1845 and accredited by NYSAIS, Packer Collegiate is a coeducational, college preparatory day school enrolling 990 students in Preschool–Grade 12. A dedicated and capable faculty offers a rich and challenging curriculum that supports students' learning and nurtures their social and emotional growth. The academic program is enriched by an array of AP courses as well as a breadth of offerings in the fine and performing arts, world languages, and athletics. Extracurricular activities provide many opportunities for independent study, travel abroad, leadership, and community service. The School's historic commitment to diversity is reflected in its student body and its ongoing support for broad and inclusive programming. Packer's collection of landmark buildings have benefited from extensive renovation, which create a dramatically expanded, dynamic campus. A school-wide wireless environment and meaningful curricular integrations of technology complement a comprehensive dual-platform laptop program in Grades 5–12. Tuition: $19,485–$28,620. Financial Aid: $4,500,000. Denise DeBono (Pre & Lower School) and Jason Caldwell (Middle & Upper) are Directors of Admission; Dr. Bruce Dennis is Head of School.

The Park School of Buffalo 1912

4625 Harlem Road, Snyder, NY 14226
Tel. 716-839-1242; Admissions Ext. 107; Fax 716-839-2014
Web Site www.theparkschool.org
E-mail jbrady@theparkschool.org

The Park School of Buffalo is a college preparatory, country day school enrolling approximately 250 boys and girls in Pre-Kindergarten through Grade 12. The School offers a comprehensive and challenging liberal arts curriculum to give students the academic foundation necessary for success and to develop their sense of responsibility and commitment. Younger children focus on grammar, communication skills, critical thinking, mathematical reasoning, scientific observation, creativity, and self-awareness. The Upper School offers Advanced Placement classes in major subjects as well as electives in mythology, economics, and physics. The 8:1 student-teacher ratio allows for individualized attention. Extracurricular activities include athletic teams, orchestra, chorus, Model United Nations, philosophy club, student government and advising, and community service projects. An extended-day program and a six-week summer day camp enhance the regular school year while utilizing the School's 15 buildings on its 33-acre suburban campus. Tuition: $5350–$17,750. Financial aid is available. Jennifer Brady is Director of Admissions; Chris Lauricella (State University of New York [Oneonta], B.A.; Teachers College Columbia University, M.Ed.) was appointed Headmaster in 2008.

Poly Prep Country Day School 1854

Upper/Middle School: 9216 Seventh Avenue, Brooklyn, NY 11228
Tel. 718-663-6060; Fax 718-238-3393
Web Site www.polyprep.org; E-mail admission@polyprep.org
Lower School: 50 Prospect Park West, Brooklyn, NY 11215
Tel. 718-663-6003; Fax 718-768-1687

Poly Prep Country Day, enrolling 1003 students in Nursery–Grade 12 on two campuses, offers a rigorous, humanistic academic program that meets the needs of the whole child at every stage of development. The Lower School, located in historic Park Slope, seeks to balance intellectual development with important social and emotional growth. The Middle and Upper Schools, on a 25-acre campus, emphasize rigorous college preparation including Advanced Placement in 17 subjects, independent study, and extracurriculars such as athletics, performing and fine arts, and interest clubs. Tuition: $9050–$30,250.

POLY PREP COUNTRY DAY SCHOOL

Financial Aid: $5,100,000. Lori W. Redell is Assistant Head of School for Admissions and Financial Aid; David B. Harman (Harvard, B.A., M.Ed.; Reed, M.A.T.) is Headmaster. *Middle States Association.*

Poughkeepsie Day School 1934

260 Boardman Road, Poughkeepsie, NY 12603
Tel. 845-462-7600; Fax 845-462-7602
Web Site www.poughkeepsieday.org
E-mail admissions@poughkeepsieday.org

Founded in 1934 by members of Vassar College child study department and parents from the surrounding community, Poughkeepsie Day enrolls 300 students in Pre-Kindergarten to Grade 12. The School features a challenging and creative academic curriculum that recognizes the strengths and talents of each child. Small classes and dedicated teachers encourage students to love learning and to become independent, critical thinkers. Seniors must complete a four-week, off-campus internship program as well as four years of every academic subject. Community service is required; sports and varied cocurricular activities are offered. All graduates are admitted to college each year. Tuition: $8725–$21,245. Financial aid is available. Jill Lundquist, M.S.W., is Director of Admissions; Josie Holford (University of Wales, B.A.; New York University, ABD, Ph.D.) is Head of School.

Riverdale Country School 1907

5250 Fieldston Road, Riverdale, NY 10471-2999
Tel. 718-549-8810; Admissions 718-519-2715
Fax 718-519-2793
Web Site www.riverdale.edu

RIVERDALE COUNTRY SCHOOL in Riverdale, New York, is an independent, college preparatory day school enrolling students in Pre-Kindergarten through Grade 12. It is located on two spacious, wooded campuses one mile apart in the northwestern corner of New York City known as Riverdale. The country setting within a short distance of the vast cultural and educational resources of one of the world's great cities provides a wide range of learning and enrichment experiences that extend beyond the boundaries of the physical plant.

The present-day institution traces its origins to The Riverdale School for Boys, which was established in 1907 by Frank Sutliff Hackett. Mr. Hackett shared a deep commitment to "scholarly, intimate teaching; rigorous, uncompromising academic standards; abundant play in the open; and a care for the best influences." In 1920, the Neighborhood Elementary School was founded, followed in 1933 by the Riverdale Girls School. In 1972, the three schools combined to form a single educational community shaped by these same goals and ideals. Riverdale Country School aims to cultivate the unique talents of its students and to nurture their intellectual, creative, physical, moral, emotional, and social development.

RIVERDALE COUNTRY SCHOOL

A nonprofit, nondenominational institution, Riverdale Country School is governed by a 30-member Board of Trustees. It is chartered by the New York State Board of Regents and accredited by the New York State Association of Independent Schools. The Parents Association and the Alumni Association assist Riverdale through various activities. Riverdale Country School is a member of the National Association of Independent Schools, among other professional affiliations.

THE CAMPUS. Riverdale Country School is the largest independent school campus in New York City with a total of 27.5 acres. The 19.5-acre Middle and Upper School Hill Campus for Grades 6–12 is located between the Henry Hudson Parkway and Van Cortlandt Park at the junction of Fieldston Road and West 253rd Street. Hill Campus buildings include the William C.W. Mow Hall, with administrative offices, classrooms, and the John R. Johnson Student Center; Frank S. Hackett Hall, containing the Roger Brett Boocock Library and the Dale E. Mayo Computer Laboratory and classrooms; the Weinstein Science Center, which houses the Lisman Laboratories, each equipped for a specific scientific discipline, as well as the Jan Falk Carpenter '71 Science Technology Center; the 9/10 Building, providing classrooms and a computer laboratory; the Linda M. Lindenbaum Center for the Arts; the Jeslo Harris Theater; and Vinik

Hall, which houses the Offices of Admission and Development. The Marc A. Zambetti '80 Athletic Center contains a state-of-the-art fitness center, an athletic training room, a basketball/volleyball court, and an Olympic-size swimming pool; other athletic facilities include three playing fields and tennis courts.

The 8-acre River Campus for Pre-Kindergarten–Grade 5, bordered by the Hudson River and Independence Avenue, is adjacent to the Wave Hill public garden, which is often used as a resource for the School. The Lower School comprises four separate buildings. The Junior Building houses the Admission Office, dining room, computer laboratory, and several music rooms. The Perkins Building holds classrooms for Grades 4–5 and Pre-Kindergarten, the library, and the Hahn Theater. The Senior Building contains art studios, band and chorus rooms, a foreign language laboratory, and Support Services specialists. The K–3 Building provides classrooms and the gymnasium, with a stage used for theatrical productions. Classes use the campus itself as part of the learning process, and children can explore the beautiful wetlands and participate in ecology and gardening projects.

THE FACULTY. Dominic A. A. Randolph assumed his duties as Riverdale's sixth Head of School in 2007. Mr. Randolph holds A.B. and Ed.M. degrees from Harvard. He had previously been Assistant Head Master at The Lawrenceville School in Lawrenceville, New Jersey, and, prior to that appointment, Dean of Studies at Lawrenceville. He has also taught English literature and language and managed academic departments at several international schools, most recently at The American School of The Hague, a K–12 school in the Netherlands.

RIVERDALE COUNTRY SCHOOL

Riverdale's faculty is comprised of 185 teachers and administrators, of whom 115 hold advanced degrees, including 20 doctorates and 120 master's degrees. The average class size in the Upper School is 16, and the student-teacher ratio is less than 8:1.

STUDENT BODY. In 2009–10, Riverdale Country School enrolled 566 boys and 544 girls in Pre-Kindergarten–Grade 12. Students reside in the immediate Riverdale area as well as Manhattan, the Bronx, Queens, Westchester, and New Jersey. Approximately 23 percent of the students are of color.

ACADEMIC PROGRAM. The curriculum in the early childhood program is designed to develop basic academic concepts and social skills. Field trips, creative play, and hands-on activities in a warm, nurturing environment help the youngest students gain an early enthusiasm for learning. Math and reading readiness skills, nature study, and introduction to computers are integrated into the program, which also includes health and physical education, music, art, and library activities.

In Grades 1–5, a strong, sequential approach to skill development in reading and math is balanced with literature, writing, and math problem solving. Students are trained in textual analysis, revising and editing their writing, and research skills. All Lower School students engage in a major research project. Students are introduced to French and Spanish in Grades 3–4, after which they choose one for continued study. A Support Services team comprised of a learning specialist, a reading and mathematics specialist, and a psychologist works with teachers, students, and parents to pilot each child's progress in the Lower School. The ethics and values program (C.A.R.E.) is integral to the curriculum and the community.

RIVERDALE COUNTRY SCHOOL

The Middle School is housed in Frank S. Hackett Hall, but students use arts, science, athletic, and dining facilities in common with upper schoolers, and the schedules of the two divisions permit teachers to teach classes in both. The Grade 6 program retains some organizational features of the Lower School, but departmentalization is the rule in Grades 7 and 8. Latin, Mandarin Chinese, and Japanese join Spanish and French as language options. The arts program strives for engagement with a full range of arts experiences for every student. Several options for after-school athletics exist for Grades 7 and 8, with intramural opportunities for Grade 6. There are special programs in information literacy, study skills, community service, and health as well as a range of activities and clubs suitable for early adolescents.

To earn a high school diploma, students in Grades 9–12 must complete 4 credits in English; 3 credits in a single foreign language or 2 credits in each of two languages; 3 in history; $2\frac{1}{2}$ to $3\frac{1}{2}$ in mathematics; 2 in science; and $1\frac{1}{2}$ in the arts. Seniors must also earn 1 credit in Integrated Liberal Studies, which features social philosophy, literature, history of science, and arts components. Each grade has a Dean of Students who coordinates academic programs and serves as a liaison between parents and school. Students in Grades 6–12 also fulfill their community service requirement through service learning and various group service projects during the academic year.

The Upper School features numerous elective courses for juniors and seniors, including honors courses in language and mathematics and Advanced Placement courses in all disciplines. Other electives include Masterpieces of Western Literature, Shakespeare, Law, Statistics, Molecular Biology, Psychology, and Urban Studies. Opportunities exist for semester or yearlong study abroad.

The 100 graduates in the Class of 2009 entered four-year colleges and universities. Five matriculated at Skidmore; 4 each are attending Brown, Northwestern, and Vanderbilt; and 3 each are at Colgate, Cornell, Duke, Washington, and the University of Pennsylvania.

STUDENT ACTIVITIES. Middle and Upper School students elect representatives to the Student-Faculty Councils, which help establish principles and procedures for student life and serve as a conduit of student opinion. In the Lower School, Student Council members are elected by their peers beginning in Grade 3. Each year, the Lower School Student Council supervises a charity outreach program entitled "Children Helping Children." Field trips enrich the program at all levels. Overnight excursions ranging from one night to one week are offered in Grades 6–12.

Upper School activities include Amnesty International, Environmental Club, Model Congress, Mock Trial, the literary magazine, the school newspaper, and the yearbook. Students regularly stage plays and musicals and perform in orchestra, jazz band, chamber ensembles, several a cappella groups, and chorus. Interscholastic and intramural teams are fielded in baseball, basketball, fencing, field hockey, football, golf, gymnastics, lacrosse, soccer, softball, squash, swimming, tennis, cross-country, ultimate frisbee, volleyball, and wrestling.

ADMISSION AND COSTS. Riverdale Country School welcomes students of strong academic ability and good character. Admission is based on the applicant's academic record, teacher recommendations, an entrance examination, a writing sample, and a personal interview. The greatest number of students enter in Kindergarten, Grade 6, and Grade 9, but candidates are admitted through Grade 11 if vacancies exist.

Tuition for 2009–10 ranges from $34,400 in Pre-Kindergarten to $36,900 in Grades 6–12. The School awards financial aid grants to approximately 20 percent of the student body based on need. Tuition payment plans are available.

Director of Studies: Michael Michelson
Head of Upper School: Kent J. Kildahl
Head of Middle School: Milton J. Sipp
Head of Lower School: Sandy S. Shaller
Director of Middle & Upper School Admission: Jenna R. King
Director of Lower School Admission: Sarah M. Lafferty
Interim Director of Development: Hayden Blood
Director of College Counseling: Kristi H. Marshall
Director of Finance & Operations: Daniel Schultz

Robert Louis Stevenson School   1908

24 West 74th Street, New York, NY 10023
Tel. 212-787-6400; Fax 212-873-1872
Web Site www.stevenson-school.org
E-mail info@stevenson-school.org

Enrolling 75 boys and girls in Grade 8–Postgraduate, Robert Louis Stevenson School seeks to prepare bright, underachieving adolescents academically and personally for college. Small but challenging classes are offered in a warm, caring milieu that includes personal therapeutic assistance and any required remedial help. The academic program focuses on the mastery of solid language and study skills and the achievement of realistic goals. Classes and advising groups average fewer than ten students. An academic summer session is offered. Tuition: $42,000. Financial Aid: $75,000. B.H. Henrichsen is Headmaster.

Rudolf Steiner School 1928

Lower School: 15 East 79th Street, New York, NY 10075
Tel. 212-535-2130; Admissions 212-327-1457; Fax 212-744-4497
Upper School: 15 East 78th Street, New York, NY 10075
Tel. 212-879-1101
Web Site www.steiner.edu
E-mail lowerschooladmissions@steiner.edu
E-mail upperschooladmissions@steiner.edu

Enrolling 360 day students in Nursery–Grade 12, Rudolf Steiner School believes that "education is an art." In each elementary school subject, presentations aim to speak to the students' experience, providing vivid images and allowing them to take part in what they hear. German, Spanish, music, and handwork begin in Grade 1 and are enriched by a sports program. In addition to strong college preparation, the high school offers exchange programs in Europe and provides opportunities in art, music, practical skills, community service, and sports. The School is one of 900 Waldorf or Steiner schools worldwide. Tuition: $20,920–$30,350. Scholarships: $1,900,000. Irene Mantel is Admissions Director for Nursery–Grade 6; Julia Hays is Admissions Director for Grades 7–12.

Rye Country Day School 1869

Boston Post Road at Cedar Street, Rye, NY 10580
Tel. 914-967-1417; Admissions 914-925-4513; Fax 914-921-2147
Web Site www.ryecountryday.org
E-mail rcds_admin@rcds.ryecountryday.org

RYE COUNTRY DAY SCHOOL in Rye, New York, is a coeducational day school enrolling students in Pre-Kindergarten–Grade 12. Rye (population 18,000), a Westchester County suburb of New York City, is 45 minutes from the city by train and is easily accessible by car and public transportation from Westchester and Rockland Counties in New York and Fairfield County in Connecticut.

The School was founded in 1869 as the Rye Female Seminary by parents who wanted to provide better educational opportunities for their daughters. The 1921 merger with Rye Country School, an all-boys' institution, led to the formation of Rye Country Day School, which enrolled girls in Kindergarten–Grade 12 and boys through Grade 8 only. In 1964, the School became entirely coeducational.

Rye Country Day School seeks to provide a superior education that "should encompass cultural, athletic, and communal experiences that stress the responsibility of each individual for the life and spirit of the whole community, resulting in a graduate able to face the world with confidence, to compete effectively, and to contribute meaningfully to society."

Rye Country Day School is directed by a 27-member Board of Trustees, including parents and alumni. The Parents' Auxiliary contributes to school life through volunteer service and fund-raising activities, and the Alumni Association represents the 3500 active graduates. Rye Country Day School is accredited by the New York Association of Independent Schools. It holds membership in the National Association of Independent Schools, among other affiliations.

THE CAMPUS. The 26-acre campus includes four artificial turf athletic fields and two play areas. Indoor athletic facilities include the Gerald N. La Grange Field House, which contains an ice rink, four tennis courts, and the Scott A. Nelson Athletic Center providing a two-court gymnasium, four squash courts, four locker rooms, and a fitness center.

Pre-Kindergarten is conducted in a classroom addition to the Administration Building. The Main Building houses classrooms for Kindergarten–Grade 8, two computer labs, four sci-

ence laboratories, three art studios, a Lower School library, a Lower School dining room, and the nurse's office. A major addition for Kindergarten–Grade 6 and a 200-seat dining room for Middle and Upper Schoolers opened in 2002. The Pinkham Building contains classrooms for Grades 9–12, offices, five science laboratories, studios for art and photography, and a college counseling center. The Klingenstein Library for Grades 5–12 connects the Main and Pinkham Buildings. The 400-seat Dunn Performing Arts Center includes a dance studio and music practice rooms. Other facilities are the Administration Building, five faculty houses, and the Headmaster's residence. The School-owned plant is valued at $46,000,000.

THE FACULTY. Scott A. Nelson, appointed Headmaster in 1993, is a graduate of Brown University (A.B. 1977) and Fordham University (M.S. 1989).

RYE COUNTRY DAY SCHOOL

The full-time faculty, including administrators who teach, number 121. In addition to baccalaureate degrees, they hold 102 master's and 11 doctoral degrees, 2 or more of which were earned at Bank Street, Bowdoin, Brown, City College of the City University of New York, College of New Rochelle, College of the Holy Cross, Columbia, Dartmouth, Fordham, Harvard, Haverford, Iona, Ithaca, Johns Hopkins, Lebanon Valley, Manhattanville, Miami (Ohio), Middlebury, New York University, Northwestern, Rollins, Saint John's, Smith, State University of New York, Syracuse, Wesleyan, Yale, and the Universities of Connecticut and Wisconsin. There are two full-time school nurses and two certified athletic trainers.

STUDENT BODY. In 2009–10, the School enrolls 454 boys and 423 girls as follows: 200 in the Lower School (Pre-Kindergarten–Grade 4), 287 in the Middle School (Grades 5–8), and 390 in the Upper School (Grades 9–12). Students come principally from Westchester County, New York City, and Connecticut's Fairfield County.

ACADEMIC PROGRAM. The school year, from early September to early June, includes Thanksgiving and midwinter recesses, winter and spring vacations, and national and religious holidays. The calendar is divided into semesters for the Lower, Middle, and Upper Schools. Upper School classes, with an average enrollment of 15, generally meet five times in a six-day rotation from 8:05 A.M. to 2:50 P.M. Pre-Kindergarten is dismissed at noon; Kindergarten–Grade 4 meet from 8:15 A.M. to 3:05 P.M.; Middle School classes meet from 8:05 A.M. to 3:20 P.M.

Supervised study halls are held throughout the day in the Upper School. Teachers are available to provide extra help at all grade levels. In the Middle School, progress reports are issued after the first six weeks of school; grades are recorded at midsemester and semester end. Interim reports are sent home whenever necessary. In Kindergarten–Grade 4, parent-teacher conferences are scheduled in the fall and winter, and a written narrative report is provided in June. In the Middle and Upper Schools, letter grades are issued twice each semester, with teacher comments accompanying the grades. Progress reports are issued for new Upper School students after the first six weeks of school. Each Middle and Upper School student has a faculty adviser. All students in Grades 7–12 have their own laptop computers.

The Lower School program fosters the acquisition of basic skills while teaching children how to think logically and creatively and manipulate symbols effectively. The program for Pre-Kindergarten emphasizes reading and mathematics readiness, communication skills, and science and social studies projects. The program in Kindergarten–Grade 4 is based in self-contained classrooms and focuses on reading, writing, mathematics, and social studies. Science, Spanish or French, music, studio art, physical education, and library skills instruction are integral to the Lower School program. There are computers in all classrooms, and a computer lab is available to Lower School students. Developing effective communication skills and appropriate social behavior are important components of the Lower School experience.

RYE COUNTRY DAY SCHOOL

Classes in the Middle School are departmentalized. Latin is introduced in Grade 5. In Grade 6, students elect to study Latin, French, Spanish, or Mandarin Chinese. The equivalent of the first year of high school language study is completed by the end of Grade 8. Honors sections are available in mathematics and Grade 8 science. In Grades 7 and 8, art, vocal and instrumental music, ceramics, woodworking, drama, photography, digital photography, and computer are offered as electives.

All Middle School students have daily physical education classes. Middle School deans provide a regularly scheduled guidance program for Grades 5–8.

RYE COUNTRY DAY SCHOOL

To graduate, students in Grades 9–12 must complete four years of English, three years of a foreign language, two years of history (including United States history), three years of mathematics, two years of lab science, and two semester-length elective units or one full-year elective course. Art, music, and health are required in Grade 9 or 10, and physical education is required each year. An interdisciplinary seminar course for seniors is required.

Full-year Upper School courses include English 1–4; French 1–6, Greek 1–2, Latin 1–6, Spanish 1–5, Mandarin Chinese 1–4; World Civilization 1–2, United States History, Government, Modern European History, Senior Seminar; Algebra 1–2, Advanced Algebra and Mathematical Analysis, Geometry, Calculus, Multi-Variable Calculus, Computer Programming 1–2; Biology, Chemistry, Physics; Studio Art 1–3, History of Art, Photography; and Music History, Choir, and Wind Ensemble. Among the partial-credit and semester electives are Philosophy, Forensics, Oceanography, Psychology, Art Survey, Concert Choir, Wind Ensemble, Jazz Ensemble, and Music Theory. The Drama Department offers elective courses in History of Theater, Film and Filmmaking, Acting Workshop, and Oral Interpretation and Public Speaking.

There are honors classes in all disciplines as well as 20 Advanced Placement courses. Independent study can be arranged in any academic area. Qualified juniors and seniors may receive credit for courses at local colleges. During the two-week June Term, students in Grade 12 participate in a service project.

In 2009, 94 members of the graduating class entered four-year colleges; 24 students matriculated "early." Over the past three years, 2 or more graduates have enrolled at Babson, Barnard, Boston College, Boston University, Brown, Bucknell, Colby, Colgate, Columbia, Connecticut College, Cornell, Dartmouth, Duke, Georgetown, George Washington, Hamilton, Harvard, Indiana, Johns Hopkins, Lehigh, Loyola, Miami, Middlebury, New York University, Northwestern, Princeton,

Providence, Skidmore, Southern Methodist, Swarthmore, Syracuse, Trinity, Tufts, Vanderbilt, Wake Forest, Wesleyan, Williams, Yale, and the Universities of Miami, Notre Dame, Pennsylvania, Richmond, Vermont, and Wisconsin.

The School conducts a six-week review and enrichment summer session and offers tutorial work.

STUDENT ACTIVITIES. The Middle School Student Council, composed of elected representatives from Grades 5 through 8, provides a forum for discussions of school issues and is responsible for implementing social activities. In the Upper School, elected student-faculty Academic Affairs, Activities, Guidance, and School Life committees meet regularly and make recommendations to the administration.

Upper School students publish a yearbook (*Echo*), a newspaper (*Rye Crop*), a current-events magazine (*FORUM*), a literary magazine (*Omega*), a sports magazine (*Topcat*). Other extracurricular activities include the African-American Culture, Astronomy, Debate, Drama, Classics, Model United Nations, Community Action Organization, International, Chess, Peer Leaders, Modern Languages, Mock Trial, Spirit, Stock Market, Entrepreneurs', and Ecology Clubs. The Upper School's musical organizations participate in county and state festivals. An active Upper School community service program involves more than 100 students as volunteers in area community agencies. The Middle School has its own community service activities as well as a chorus and wind ensemble; beginning in Grade 4, private instrumental lessons are available for all students.

Rye Country Day athletic teams compete with other independent schools in the Fairchester League. Interscholastic competition begins in Grade 7 with boys' teams organized in basketball, football, ice hockey, soccer, baseball, lacrosse, tennis, and wrestling; girls compete in basketball, field hockey, softball, soccer, lacrosse, and tennis. There are boys' varsity and junior varsity teams in baseball, basketball, football, golf, hockey, lacrosse, soccer, squash, tennis, and wrestling; varsity and junior varsity girls' teams are organized in basketball, field hockey, golf, ice hockey, lacrosse, softball, soccer, and squash. There are also coeducational teams in cross-country, sailing, and fencing. Physical education classes for Upper School students not on interscholastic teams focus on fitness, lifetime sports, and dance.

RYE COUNTRY DAY SCHOOL.

Field trips complement the academic program at all grade levels; younger children visit area attractions such as the Rye Nature Center and The Bronx Zoo. Dances are scheduled for both the Middle and Upper schools. Traditional annual events include Middle School overnight trips for Grades 6–8, evening sports programs, Wildcat Weekend and Fall Fair, music festivals, and the invitational Model United Nations/Congress.

ADMISSION AND COSTS. New students are admitted to all grades, although rarely to Grade 12, on the basis of previous academic records, the results of standardized tests, and a personal interview. Application should be made in the fall or winter prior to September entrance. There is a $50 application fee.

In 2009–10, tuition ranges from $18,700 in Pre-Kindergarten to $30,300 in Grades 11–12. Extras range from $320 in Kindergarten to $1000 in the Upper School. Tuition insurance is available. In the current year, the School awarded more than $3,383,000 in financial aid to 120 students. Rye Country Day subscribes to the School and Student Service for Financial Aid.

Associate Head of School: Corinne Grandolfo
Assistant Head of School: Barbara Shea
Director of Admission: Matthew Suzuki
Director of Finance: Robert Brody
Development & Alumni Relations: Virginia B. Rowen
College Counselors: Rosita Fernandez-Rojo & Jeffrey Bates
Director of Athletics: Frank Antonelli
Director of Diversity: Meredith deChabert

Saint Ann's School 1965

129 Pierrepont Street, Brooklyn Heights, NY 11201
Tel. 718-522-1660; Fax 718-522-2599
Web Site www.saintannsny.org

Saint Ann's School is an independent, college preparatory day school enrolling 523 boys and 559 girls in Preschool–Grade 12. With an informal ambience and rigorous curriculum, Saint Ann's represents an alternative to traditional education. The School looks for students whose abilities and motivation allow them to excel in an environment of creativity, enjoyment, and affection. Placement is geared to aptitude and learning style, and the School evaluates each student on the basis of individual progress in each subject. Instead of grades, teachers write anecdotal reports twice a year. Saint Ann's is a community diverse in its backgrounds, interests, and talents, but committed equally to academics and the arts. Tuition: $21,750–$28,100. Financial aid is available. Diana Lomask is Director of Admission; Larry Weiss (Columbia College, A.B. 1971; Columbia University, M.A. 1974, Ph.D. 1981) was appointed Head of School in 2004.

St. Bernard's School 1904

4 East 98th Street, New York, NY 10029
Tel. 212-289-2878; Fax 212-410-6628
Web Site www.stbernards.org

St. Bernard's is a day school enrolling 386 boys in Kindergarten–Grade 9. It presents a traditional curriculum emphasizing English, foreign languages, mathematics, and science. Instruction is offered in music, art, carpentry, and computer technology. A literary magazine is published, and a Shakespearean play is presented annually. The School also makes ample use of the cultural resources of the city. Boys take part in interscholastic and intramural sports. All-inclusive Tuition: $33,270. Financial aid is available. Heidi Gore and Anne Nordeman are Co-Directors of Admissions; Stuart H. Johnson III (Yale, B.A.) was appointed Headmaster in 1985.

Saint David's School 1951

12 East 89th Street, New York, NY 10128
Tel. 212-369-0058; Admission Ext. 401; Fax 212-369-5788
Web Site www.saintdavids.org; E-mail admissions@saintdavids.org

Saint David's is a day school with an enrollment of 400 boys in Pre-Kindergarten–Grade 8. The School seeks to engender intellectual curiosity, spiritual and moral development, appreciation for the arts, and skill and sportsmanship in athletics. A rigorous classical curriculum is offered within a challenging environment. Art, music, and drama are an integral part of the program. Founded by a group of Catholic families, Saint David's includes boys of all religious and ethnic backgrounds. The Saint David's Sports Center is located a short distance from the School. Tuition: $22,265–$33,400. Financial Aid: $800,000. Julie B. Sykes is Admission Director; P. David O'Halloran, Ph.D., was appointed Headmaster in 2004.

Saint Francis Preparatory School   1858

6100 Francis Lewis Boulevard, Fresh Meadows, NY 11365
Tel. 718-423-8810; Admissions Ext. 229; Fax 718-423-1097
Web Site www.sfponline.org; E-mail admissions@sfponline.org

Founded by the Franciscan Brothers, this coeducational, Catholic school has been named by the U.S. Department of Education as a School of Excellence. More than 2700 students are enrolled in Grades 9–12. Although located in an urban setting, the campus borders on parkland, providing ample athletic fields. To develop critical, responsible seekers of truth, the School provides a comprehensive, Christian education within a nurturing environment. Advanced Placement, Honors, and Regents courses, combined with music, art, 35,000 circulating and noncirculating books, and computers with full-text databases containing peer review or scholarly journals, complement the religious foundation. Tuition: $7000. Theodore Jahn is Dean of Men and Assistant Principal for Admissions; Br. Leonard Conway, OSF (Pratt Institute, M.S.), is Principal. *Middle States Association.*

Saint Gregory's School   1962

121 Old Niskayuna Road, Loudonville, NY 12211
Tel. 518-785-6621; Fax 518-782-1364
Web Site www.saintgregorysschool.org
E-mail marrao@saintgregorysschool.org

Saint Gregory's School was founded by parents to prepare their children for the challenges of competitive boarding schools and to instill in them the values and principles of the Roman Catholic faith. Enrolling 150 students, the School is coeducational in Nursery–Kindergarten and boys only in Grades 1–8. In addition to traditional academic subjects, computer science, Latin, and Spanish are required. Music, drama, physical education, and interscholastic athletics are strong components of the program. Recreational camps are conducted in the summer. Tuition: $4805–$12,335. Financial Aid: $150,000. Jeffrey P. Loomis (Siena College, B.A.; La Salle University, M.S.) is Head of School.

St. Hilda's & St. Hugh's School   1950

619 West 114th Street, New York, NY 10025
Tel. 212-932-1980; Fax 212-531-0102
Web Site www.sthildas.org

St. Hilda's & St. Hugh's is a coeducational, Episcopal day school enrolling 380 students in Beginner–Grade 8. The School reflects New York City's richly diverse community and values the Judeo-Christian heritage. A strong liberal arts curriculum promotes the developmental competencies of each child and readies students for leading secondary schools in New York City and nationwide. Studio Art is introduced in Junior Kindergarten; French, Spanish, or Mandarin Chinese in Nursery; technology in Grade 2; woodworking, drama, and English brass band in Grade 4; Shakespeare in Grade 6; and Latin in Grade 7. Extended Day Program for Beginner–Grade 8 is offered until 6:30 P.M. Tuition: $8000–$33,000. Kate Symonds is Director of Admission; Virginia Connor (Wheelock, B.S.; Columbia Teachers College, M.A.) is Head of School.

Soundview Preparatory School   1989

370 Underhill Avenue, Yorktown Heights, NY 10598
Tel. 914-962-2780; Fax 914-302-2769
Web Site soundviewprep.org

Enrolling 75 day students in Grades 6–12, Soundview provides a rigorous college preparatory program while promoting self-esteem by enabling students to develop their unique talents. Small, ability-grouped classes allow dialogue and participation by all students. The School aims to establish ethical values, formulate and meet individual goals, and encourage students to be their own advocates. Students enjoy close relationships with teachers and respond to a structured, yet relaxed environment. Academics include four languages, AP and Honors courses, and many electives such as history of philosophy, psychology, forensics, economics, and others. Students develop leadership skills and explore their interests with a full range of extracurricular activities, athletics, and community service. Tuition: $30,000–$31,000. Financial Aid: $265,000. Mary Ivanyi is Dean of Admissions; W. Glyn Hearn is Headmaster.

Staten Island Academy   1884

715 Todt Hill Road, Staten Island, NY 10304
Tel. 718-987-8100; Fax 718-979-7641
Web Site www.statenislandacademy.org
E-mail LShuffman@statenislandacademy.org

STATEN ISLAND ACADEMY is an independent, coeducational, college preparatory day school for Pre-Kindergarten through Grade 12, providing an inspiring balance of challenge, exploration, and opportunity. Successful students — achieving their goals in school and in life — are at the center of Staten Island Academy.

STATEN ISLAND ACADEMY

The Academy finds its origins in the Methfessel Institute, a boys' school founded in 1862. Two years later, the name changed to Staten Island Latin School, and it became, in 1884, a nonsectarian, coeducational, college preparatory school. After a series of expansions, mergers, and separate locations, the Academy consolidated its divisions and its campus on the Todt Hill Road location in 1963.

Staten Island Academy is a community that challenges students to excel at what they do best, pursue new interests, and express themselves in a safe environment. The Academy builds upon its 125-year tradition to focus entirely on what's best for students and their futures: 100 percent of graduates are accepted to excellent colleges and universities.

The Academy is governed by an 18-member Board of Trustees, several of whom are graduates of the school and many of whom are parents of current Academy students. The Alumni Association promotes and maintains relationships between alumni and the school. The Parents' League supports the Academy with a variety of volunteer activities. Accredited by the Middle States Association of Colleges and Secondary Schools and the New York State Association of Independent Schools, Staten Island Academy is chartered and registered by the Board of Regents, University of the State of New York.

THE CAMPUS. The 12-acre campus is located in the bucolic neighborhood of Todt Hill near the highest point on the East Coast south of Maine. Of the school's seven buildings, the heart of the campus is the recently renovated Stanley Library, which has more than 16,000 volumes of print and nonprint materials and subscriptions to more than 50 magazines, newspapers, and on-line databases. It has an automated circulation and cataloguing system and 12 computers with Internet access. Other facilities include the Science and Technology Center with computer labs, science labs, and classrooms; a commons area with dining hall; an auditorium; music and art rooms; and a fitness center completed in 2003, a gymnasium, three tennis courts, two in-ground pools, ball fields, and playgrounds.

THE FACULTY. Diane J. Hulse became Head of School in July 2002. A graduate of Beloit College, Mrs. Hulse received her master's degree from New York University. Mrs. Hulse has been involved with New York City area independent schools for more than 25 years and is the author of *Brad and Corey: A Study of Middle School Boys.*

Of the 59 members of the faculty and staff, 42 hold advanced degrees. Their representative colleges include Amherst, Bank Street College, Barnard, Boston College, Boston University, Brooklyn College, College of William and Mary, Columbia University, Drew University, Haverford, Hobart, Kenyon, Middlebury College, Muhlenberg, New York University, Northwestern University, Pratt, Rutgers, St. John's University, the Sorbonne, Wesleyan University, and the Universities of California, Massachusetts (Amherst), Miami, and Pennsylvania.

STUDENT BODY. Staten Island Academy enrolls approximately 400 students in its Lower, Middle, and Upper Schools. While most live on the Island, a number of students commute from Brooklyn, Manhattan, and New Jersey and reflect the ethnic and cultural diversity of Greater New York City.

ACADEMIC PROGRAM. The academic year begins in early September and ends in early June, with Thanksgiving, winter, and spring vacations. The school day begins at 8:10 A.M. and ends at 3:20 P.M. To accommodate family schedules, the Academy has extended hours from 7:00 A.M. to 7:00 P.M., which are included in the tuition for Pre-K through Grade 8.

In a nurturing and developmentally appropriate environment, children in the Lower School (Pre-Kindergarten through Grade 4) focus on basic and advanced skills in reading, writing, social studies, science, and mathematics taught by a cooperative team of teachers. Art, music, library, computer lab, and physical education complement the academic program.

In Middle School (Grades 5–8), students receive instruction from specialized teachers in all subject areas. The core curriculum emphasizes the language arts, mathematics, social studies, science, computer skills, and physical education. Writing workshops span the grade levels, and students in Grade 8 take algebra. Students are introduced to Latin in Grade 5 and may begin French or Spanish in Grade 6. They may study both Latin and a modern foreign language. Fine arts and elective offerings range from public speaking and book club to chorus and journalism.

The Upper School encompasses Grades 9–12 with an average class size of 17 students. To graduate, students are required to take four years of English; three years each of mathematics,

science, and social science; three years of one modern foreign language; four years of physical education; and computer science, foundation of art, music history, and an additional music or art credit. All Grade 9 students travel to London for one week as part of their integrated curriculum.

STATEN ISLAND ACADEMY

Among the courses offered are English 9 and 10, American Literature, Trial Theme in Literature, Journey Theme in Literature, Political Ideas in Literature, Fantasy & Realism in Literature, Junior/Senior Writing Seminar; French I–V, Latin I–III, Spanish I–V; Western Civilization, United States History, New York: History of a City, The American Presidency, Global Debate, The Empire that was Rome, U.S./World Events in the 20th Century, Western Art History, Contemporary Religious Convictions; Algebra I, Algebra II with Trigonometry, Geometry, Precalculus, Probability & Statistics; Biology, Chemistry, Physics, Healthful Living, Chemistry of Life, Psychology, Dimensions of Human Relations; Computer Skills, Web Page Design, Visual Basic Programming; Robotics, Music History, Foundations of Art, Orchestra, Concert Choir, Drawing/Painting, Photography, Advanced Photography, Color & Design, Introduction to Dance, Introduction to Theater, and Stagecraft. Nine Honors courses as well as Advanced Placement courses in Biology, Calculus (AB and BC), Chemistry, Computer Science, English, French, Latin, Modern European History, Psychology, Spanish, and U.S. History are available for qualified students. The Power Track program, which begins in Grade 8, is designed to accommodate the needs of superior students considering pursuing math or science in college. All students in Grade 12 must participate in the Senior Internship program.

The college guidance program begins in the ninth grade when students are assigned an advisor who will assist them with academic, personal, and social matters. In junior year, students are paired with college counselors in an 8:1 ratio as they work to meet the challenges of the college application process. The Classes of 2005–09 have matriculated at such colleges and universities as American University, Amherst, Boston College, Boston University, Brandeis, Brown, Columbia, Connecticut College, Dartmouth College, Cornell, Drew, Harvard, Haverford, Johns Hopkins, Lafayette College, Muhlenberg, Oberlin,

Parsons School of Design, Princeton University, St. Andrews University, Trinity College, Vassar, Villanova, Wagner College, Wellesley, Yale, and the University of Pennsylvania.

All grades take part in The Character Education Program, which helps students develop self-reliance, initiative, responsibility, and courage through on-going discussions of ethical issues and the performance of community service projects.

A summer day camp program, from one to ten weeks, is available. The School is also a site for the Summer Institute for the Gifted program.

STUDENT ACTIVITIES. Lower School students publish an online newspaper, *Paw Prints.* They may also enroll in the After-school Adventures Club, which provides arts and crafts, mini-sports clinics, music lessons, theater and dance workshops, and karate. Students in Grades 1–4 may participate in intramural sports.

Middle School students publish their own newspaper, *The Tiger.* They also take part in community service, student government, interscholastic athletics, plays, choral groups, orchestra, and the Junior National Honor Society.

The Upper School Student Advisory Council sponsors dances and various activities and is involved in numerous school-wide initiatives. Other extracurricular activities include choral groups, orchestra, theatrical productions, community service, The Gay-Straight Alliance, Model United Nations, National Honor Society, and the Art, Asian, Environment, Film, and Spanish Clubs. Boys' and girls' varsity teams are sponsored in soccer, tennis, volleyball, and basketball. Girls also play softball and lacrosse; there are coeducational teams in golf, cross-country, and cheerleading.

STATEN ISLAND ACADEMY

Traditional events include the Welcome Back Barbecue, Auction, Poetry Recital, Grandparents and Special Friends Day, Book Fair, Academy Day, Founders Day, and Commencement.

ADMISSION AND COSTS. The Academy admits students who will benefit from the school's rigorous academic program. The application process includes an entrance examination, school visit, and interview.

In 2009–10, tuition ranges from $15,800 for half-day Pre-Kindergarten through Grade 5 to $26,075 for Grades 6 through 11. Extended Day, field trips, and most books are included. Approximately 25 percent of the student body receives financial aid totaling more than $1,400,000 annually.

Head of Lower School: Patricia Lynch
Assistant Head for Middle & Upper Schools: Eileen Corigliano
Academic Dean: Frank Crane
Director of College Guidance: Michael Acquilano
Director of Operations: Taube Import
Director of Admissions: Linda Shuffman
Director of Development: Michael Barret Jones
Director of Finance: Angela Artale
Director of Athletics: Darlene Crowe

The Storm King School   1867

314 Mountain Road, Cornwall-on-Hudson, NY 12520-1899
Tel. 845-534-7892; Admissions [Toll-free] 800-225-9144
Fax 845-534-4128
Web Site www.sks.org; E-mail admissions@sks.org

Founded in 1867, The Storm King School, an independent, coeducational school, enrolls about 105 boarding and 35 day students in Grades 8–12. The School inspires students toward academic strength and confidence with a caring faculty in a community that embraces character, wellness, and trust. The Learning Center offers additional academic support to all students. The Mountain Center is for students with college potential and established learning differences. The School's curriculum includes three Advanced Placement courses, Chinese, and electives in the arts. Activities offered include National Honor Society, Cum Laude Society, community service, drama, music, visual arts, and sports. Boarding Tuition: $28,950–$44,950; Day Tuition: $11,950–$27,450. Financial aid is available. David T. Flynn is Director of Admissions; Helen Stevens Chinitz is Head of School. *Middle States Association.*

The Town School   1913

540 East 76th Street, New York, NY 10021
Tel. 212-288-4383; Admissions 212-288-6397; Fax 212-988-5846
Web Site www.thetownschool.org; E-mail nsahadi@townschool.org

THE TOWN SCHOOL

The Town School is a coeducational, nonsectarian school enrolling 400 day students in three divisions encompassing

Nursery–Grade 8. In keeping with Hazel Hyde's founding philosophy, it encourages the joy of learning in an academic environment with creative expression through the arts and physical education. Child-centered teaching and a low faculty-to-student ratio, combined with innovative technology and community service, develop the whole child physically, emotionally, intellectually, and morally. The Town School offers extended care daily, an after-school program, and SummerSault, a summer camp. Tuition: $19,000–$32,400. Financial aid is available. Natasha Sahadi is Director of Admissions; Christopher Marblo is Head of School.

Tuxedo Park School 1900

Mountain Farm Road, Tuxedo Park, NY 10987
Tel. 845-351-4737; Fax 845-351-4219
Web Site www.tuxedoparkschool.org
E-mail kheard@tuxedoparkschool.org

Tuxedo Park School enrolls 212 day boys and girls in Pre-Kindergarten–Grade 9. The School is committed to nurturing and developing the natural joy of learning inherent in each child. Concern for traditional and modern skills is demonstrated by the inclusion of such courses as French, Spanish, Latin, and computer throughout the School. Art, music, and sports are an integral part of the curriculum at all levels. Interscholastic sports are offered in Grades 7–9. Tuition: $16,500–$26,075. Financial aid is available. Kristen J. Heard is Director of Admissions and Financial Aid; James T. Burger (Hamilton College, B.A.; Case Western Reserve, J.D.) was appointed Head of School in 1994.

United Nations International School 1947

24-50 FDR Drive, New York, NY 10010
Tel. 212-684-7400; Admissions 212-584-3071
Fax 212-685-5023
Web Site www.unis.org; E-mail admissions@unis.org
173-55 Croydon Road, Jamaica Estates, NY 11432

This international day school was founded by parents committed to the educational principles outlined in the UN Charter. Today, United Nations International School enrolls 1500 boys and girls from over 120 countries in Kindergarten–Grade 12 on two campuses. An equally diverse faculty teaches an international curriculum with a global perspective, leading to the International Baccalaureate. The Junior School emphasizes reading, writing, speaking, listening, foreign languages, experiments and observation, computers, and the arts. The Middle School, a period of growth, fosters self-discovery, peer-group identification, and intellectual adventure. Upper School students acquire appreciation of the diversity of persons and cultures while mastering key skills in English, art, computing, mathematics, music, science, humanities, and physical education. Eight languages and ESL are available. The School was the first in the U.S. to offer the IB, preparing graduates for higher education worldwide. Outreach, publications, outdoor education, field trips, theater, school government, sports, and academic, honor, and interest clubs are among the activities. Tuition: $22,900–$25,450. Amelia Rattew is Director of Admissions; Stuart Walker is Director.

The Ursuline School 1897

1354 North Avenue, New Rochelle, NY 10804
Tel. 914-636-3950; Fax 914-636-3949
Web Site www.ursulinenewrochelle.org

THE URSULINE SCHOOL in New Rochelle, New York, is a private, Catholic, college preparatory school for young women in Grades 6 through 12. The School is located at the north end of New Rochelle in lower Westchester County, affording easy access to the many educational and cultural resources of both Westchester and New York City.

THE URSULINE SCHOOL

Central to the philosophy of The Ursuline School is a concern for the student as an individual and a commitment to the education of the whole person—intellectually, emotionally, socially, and spiritually. As a young woman prepares to assume leadership in the 21st century, she needs both challenge and support to realize her potential. Ursuline recognizes these needs and, believing in the benefits of single-gender education, places its young women firmly at the center of its philosophy and its programs. The School is committed to providing an intellectually stimulating, student-centered environment in which academic and personal achievements are demanded.

Ursuline also emphasizes the value of the total school community, fostering relationships among students and their families, faculty, and administration. Parent organizations, an alumnae association, and family and alumnae events are key elements in establishing the family atmosphere of the School.

Founded in 1897 by the Sisters of the Order of St. Ursula, the School is governed by a Board of Trustees comprised of Ursuline sisters and lay women and men. Designated a National Blue Ribbon School of Excellence three times by the United States Department of Education, Ursuline is accredited by the New York State Board of Regents and the Middle States Association of Colleges and Schools. It holds membership in the New York State Association of Independent Schools, the National Coalition of Girls' Schools, the National Catholic Educational Association, and other professional organizations.

THE CAMPUS. The 13-acre campus includes two academic buildings, a gymnasium, and a performing and fine arts center. The School's library houses more than 14,000 books, 60 periodicals, and numerous CD-ROMs and other electronic resources. The library, which has earned the designation of "Electronic Doorway Library" by the State Department of Education, is linked via a multipublic access system to public and college libraries in Westchester County. There are five state-of-the-art science laboratories for the study of biology, chemistry, and physics. Technological resources include a computer center and networked computers throughout the School as well as a schoolwide wireless network that students access using their laptops. The arts center houses a 300-seat theater, orchestra and chorus practice rooms, a dance studio, four art rooms, a darkroom, and classroom space. A small chapel provides a place for prayer, meditation, and small group liturgies.

Athletic facilities include a full-size gymnasium, a playing field, and four tennis courts. Ursuline also uses additional fields, tracks, and a swimming pool in the area.

THE FACULTY. Eileen Davidson (Iona College, M.S.) became Principal in 2005. Three assistant principals and 80 faculty members, 90 percent of whom have master's or doctoral degrees, ensure a low student-faculty ratio and individual attention for students. A Catholic chaplain is a member of the staff. A registered nurse is on campus during the school day.

STUDENT BODY. In 2009–10, Ursuline enrolled 800 students in Grades 6–12. Ursuline students come from throughout Westchester County and the Bronx as well as from Manhattan and Connecticut. They represent a broad diversity of racial, ethnic, religious, and socioeconomic backgrounds. While a Catholic school, Ursuline welcomes students of all religions, and about 20 percent of students are non-Catholic.

ACADEMIC PROGRAM. Ursuline students are required to complete 24 credits for graduation, including four years of English, social studies, and religion; three years of science, mathematics, and foreign language; a year of Latin or art/music; and computer applications and health. Physical education is also required. More than 90 percent of students take four or more years of science, math, and foreign language. The traditional college preparatory program includes four modern foreign languages (French, Spanish, Chinese, and Italian), five years of Latin, a year of classical Greek, a broad range of fine arts courses, computer courses, and a variety of electives. Honors courses are available in all disciplines, and Advanced Placement courses are offered in art, French, Spanish, Italian, Latin, English, calculus, biology, physics, European and U.S. history, and U.S. government. The School also offers an Authentic Science Research program through which, in addition to their regular science courses, students engage in three years of directed independent research working with a mentor in a professional setting. Seventh- and eighth-grade students at Ursuline have the opportunity to earn high school credit in foreign language, mathematics, and science.

THE URSULINE SCHOOL

Technology is well integrated into the curriculum. In addition to the computers networked throughout the School, Ursuline implemented a "learning with laptops" program in 1997. Every student has her own laptop computer that she uses in class and homework activities for writing, accessing, analyzing and graphing data, and creating multimedia presentations.

Interactive SMART Boards, a school-wide wireless network, an electronic learning community web site, Internet access, and e-mail ensure full integration of technology into the curriculum.

Ursuline's Reading and Language Development Program assists students who are challenged by learning differences but who are otherwise able to do college preparatory work. These students are enrolled in the regular college preparatory courses and attend additional sessions with a specialist to learn the compensatory strategies they need.

THE URSULINE SCHOOL

The Social Action Program provides a variety of volunteer experiences for the entire student body, including staffing meals at a local soup kitchen, tutoring and teaching religious education in parishes, and working in nursing homes and hospitals. "Make a Difference Day" and "Project Nicaragua" afford other opportunities for volunteer work.

Ursuline students broaden their experience through a school-sponsored European trip and networking opportunities with other Ursuline schools in the United States and abroad.

Recognizing the pressures and challenges that confront today's young women, Ursuline has in place extensive guidance and counseling services. Every student has a faculty advisor who meets with her regularly, helps her plan her schedule, and reviews her academic progress.

College guidance begins in the sophomore year and includes classes and individual meetings as well as programs and individual meetings with parents. One hundred percent of Ursuline students continue their education in college. Last year's graduates won over $15,000,000 in academic scholarships and were accepted at more than 150 colleges and universities, including Boston College, Carnegie Mellon, College of William and Mary, Columbia, Cornell, Dartmouth, Fordham, Georgetown, Harvard, Iona, Marist, New York University, Providence College, Stanford, State University of New York, Syracuse, Yale, and the Universities of Massachusetts, Pennsylvania, and Scranton.

In addition to academic guidance, a staff of four provides individual counseling, organizes groups based on student need and interest, and arranges programs for parents. A Personal Development Education Program in Grades 6–9 helps students address issues such as self-esteem, relationships with peers and parents, conflict resolution, and physical, emotional, and social development. Juniors and seniors are trained as Peer Leaders and Peer Mediators to assist with the Personal Development Program and with mediation at any level.

As a Catholic school, Ursuline emphasizes the spiritual development of its students. In addition to religion classes, a retreat program at all grade levels gives students the opportunity to reflect on their relationship with God and with others. Juniors and seniors trained as Peer Ministers help direct these retreats. School liturgies are celebrated periodically throughout the year for the entire school community, and Masses and prayer services are held regularly in the chapel.

STUDENT ACTIVITIES. A broad range of activities, open to students of every grade level, provides opportunities for leadership and service. Student Council and clubs in language and culture, publications, forensics, chorus, band, drama, computer, math, and science are representative of the diverse organizations.

Ursuline belongs to the New York State Public High School Athletic Association and fields 34 interscholastic teams in swimming, tennis, field hockey, volleyball, cross-country, cheerleading, basketball, softball, soccer, golf, lacrosse, crew, and indoor and outdoor track. Competition is available at the varsity, junior varsity, freshman, modified, and sixth-grade levels.

Traditions are another important aspect of Ursuline life, bringing together students, parents, faculty and, often, alumnae. Among the most important events are Ring Day, the Father-Daughter Dance, the Mother-Daughter Communion Breakfast, the Fair, 8th Grade Moving Up Ceremony, Senior Mass, and Graduation.

ADMISSION AND COSTS. Ursuline welcomes students of above-average ability who choose the School for its philosophy, its programs, and its atmosphere. Ursuline does not discriminate on the basis of race, color, national or ethnic origin, or religion. Admission is based on the student's performance on standardized entrance examinations and her previous academic record. For admission to Grades 6–8 and for transfer students, a personal interview is required. Applicants for all grade levels are encouraged to attend Ursuline's Open House and to visit for a day.

THE URSULINE SCHOOL

Tuition in 2009–10 is $13,800. Academic scholarships are awarded to top-scoring applicants for Grade 9, and need-based student aid is available in Grades 9–12 only.

Assistant Principals: Denise Moore, Deirdre Gaughan & Terri Agliardo
Director of Advancement: Eileen Niedzwiecki
Director of Guidance: Mary Scarella
Director of Counseling: Doretha Buster
Business Manager: Sr. Joan Woodcome, OSU
Athletic Director: Maureen Kern

Village Community School   1970

272-278 West Tenth Street, New York, NY 10014
Tel. 212-691-5146; Admissions Exts. 221 & 250; Fax 212-691-9767
Web Site vcsnyc.org; E-mail jcalixto@vcs-nyc.org

Located in historic Greenwich Village, Village Community School is a coeducational, K–8 school enrolling 330 students. VCS takes a balanced approach to teaching and learning, offering a progressive education that also incorporates traditional teaching methods. VCS students gain admission to a wide variety of high schools. The five-story, recently renovated facility houses spacious, sunny classrooms, a large outdoor play area, a free-standing woodshop, naturally lit art rooms, a state-of-the-art computer lab, three science centers, a sky-lit library, a rooftop play area, gymnasium, auditorium, and a modern kitchen and lunchroom. Approximately 22–25 percent of students benefit annually from the School's strong commitment to need-based tuition assistance. Tuition: $32,000. Judy Calixto is Director of Admissions; Eve Kleger (Wellesley, B.A.; Columbia, M.A.) is Director.

The Windsor School   1968

Admin. Bldg., 136-23 Sanford Avenue, Flushing, NY 11355
Tel. 718-359-8300; Fax 718-359-1876
Web Site www.windsorschool.com
E-mail admin@thewindsorschool.com

The Windsor School is a coeducational, college preparatory day school enrolling approximately 80 boys and 75 girls in Grades 6–12. It is dedicated to providing individual guidance and a sense of identity for middle-range and gifted students. A coordinated program, including English as a Second Language, is arranged for international students. Students are programmed individually so that they can enroll in honors or accelerated programs in those subjects in which they excel. Extracurricular activities and teams and a summer school are available. Tuition (including books): $18,600–$18,900. Philip A. Stewart, Ph.D., is Director of Admissions; James L. Seery is Principal. *Middle States Association.*

Windward School   1926

Grades 1–4: 5 Windward Avenue, White Plains, NY 10605
Grades 5–9: 40 West Red Oak Lane, White Plains, NY 10604
Tel. 914-949-6968; Admissions Ext. 2225; Fax 914-949-8220
Web Site www.windwardny.org
E-mail admissionsinquiry@windwardny.org

Windward, a coeducational day school for children with language-based learning disabilities, serves 530 students of average to superior intelligence in Grades 1–9. Windward's curriculum emphasizes skills development in a multisensory, structured, language-based program. Through direct instruction in small classes, trained staff help students improve their language skills and experience academic success. Along with opportunities for social and emotional growth, scholastic achievement enables students to understand their learning styles, build confidence, and develop self-advocacy skills. Windward is committed to helping students realize their full potential in preparation for a successful return to a mainstream educational environment. To meet these goals, the School provides ongoing training to its faculty based on the most current research and shares its expertise with the parent body, other educators, and the broader community through the Windward Teacher Training Institute. Activities include after-school programs, athletics, drama, student government, yearbook, and various clubs. Tuition: $41,900. Financial aid is available. Maureen A. Sweeney is Director of Admissions; Dr. John J. Russell is Head of School.

The Winston Preparatory School   1981

126 West 17th Street, New York, NY 10011
Tel. 646-638-2705; Fax 646-638-2706
Web Site www.winstonprep.edu
E-mail admissions@winstonprep.edu

Winston Prep is a Middle and Upper School for 210 bright boys and girls with learning differences such as dyslexia, nonverbal learning disabilities, and attention deficit problems. The program offers assessment-driven, individualized instruction based on an understanding of each student's needs. Students are grouped according to learning profile and skill level and taught in small groups. "Focus," a daily 1:1 program, is taught by speech and language pathologists, reading specialists, and learning specialists who serve as primary remedial instructors, diagnosticians, and mentors. The arts, technology, sports, electives, after-school activities, a summer session, and visits to New York's cultural sites enhance the program. Tuition/Fees: $45,000. Courtney DeHoff is Admissions Director; Scott Bezsylko, M.A., is Executive Director; William DeHaven, M.A., is Head of School.

York Preparatory School   1969

40 West 68th Street, New York, NY 10023
Tel. 212-362-0400; Admissions Ext. 127; Fax 212-362-7424
Web Site www.yorkprep.org; E-mail admissions@yorkprep.org

This college preparatory day school enrolling 340 students in Grades 6–12 offers contemporary methods to enliven a challenging, traditional curriculum. York Prep's approach emphasizes independent thought, builds confidence, and equips graduates for entrance to selective colleges and universities. Facilities include a state-of-the-art computer lab, a large gym, a spacious art studio, two professionally equipped science labs, and a small

YORK PREPARATORY SCHOOL

concert hall. Numerous activities, including a winning Model UN team and championship varsity basketball and soccer teams, enhance all aspects of school life. Tuition: $33,200–$33,900. Financial Aid: $750,000. Elizabeth Norton is Director of Enrollment; Jacqueline Leber is Director of Admissions; Ronald P. Stewart (Oxford, B.A., M.A., B.C.L.) is in his 41st year as Headmaster. *Middle States Association.*

LOYOLA SCHOOL

NORTH CAROLINA

Cannon School 1969

5801 Poplar Tent Road, Concord, NC 28027
Tel. 704-786-8171; Admission 704-721-7199; Fax 704-788-7779
Web Site www.cannonschool.org; E-mail info@cannonschool.org

Cannon School's college preparatory program is designed to promote academic excellence, personal responsibility, athletic and artistic achievement, and respect for diversity. Serving over 820 day students in Junior Kindergarten–Grade 12, it is the first independent school in North Carolina to earn dual accreditation by the Southern Association of Independent Schools and the Southern Association of Colleges and Schools. Lower and Middle Schools supplement core subjects with art, music, foreign languages, and technology. The Upper School's wireless laptop learning environment offers a full range of AP courses, service learning, fine arts, and athletics. Tuition: $9500–$16,100. Financial aid is available. Matthew E. Gossage is Head of School. *Southern Association.*

Cape Fear Academy 1967

3900 South College Road, Wilmington, NC 28412
Tel. 910-791-0287; Admissions Ext. 1015; Fax 910-791-0290
Web Site www.capefearacademy.org; E-mail info@capefearacademy.org

Cape Fear Academy, a college preparatory day school serving 650 students in Pre-Kindergarten–Grade 12, emphasizes a sense of community and trust in a challenging academic program. Critical thinking, problem solving, and study skills are key elements of its strong interdisciplinary curriculum. Upper School offers numerous AP courses and a dedicated writing lab. Students perform community service at all grade levels. Participation in extracurricular activities in the Middle and Upper Schools is strongly encouraged. A summer enrichment program is offered. Tuition/Fees: $7295–$12,160. Financial aid is available. Susan Harrell is Director of Admission; John B. Meehl (Pomona College, B.A.; Stanford University, M.A.) is Headmaster. *Southern Association.*

Carolina Day School 1987

1345 Hendersonville Road, Asheville, NC 28803
Tel. 828-274-0757; Admissions Ext. 310; Fax 828-274-0756
Web Site www.cdschool.org; E-mail rgoertz@cdschool.org

Carolina Day School is a college preparatory school enrolling 650 boys and girls in Pre-Kindergarten–Grade 12. The School strives to develop within each student a strong academic foundation, personal ethics, and concern for community. The program includes 15 Advanced Placement courses, community service, athletics, outdoor education, and fine arts. Summer Quest offers enrichment in the arts, sciences, athletics, and outdoor education. The Key School, established in 1998, serves students with language-based learning disabilities. Tuition: $7690–$18,140. Robin Goertz is Director of Admissions; Beverly H. Sgro (Virginia Tech, Ph.D.) was appointed Head of School in 1999.

Charlotte Country Day School 1941

1440 Carmel Road, Charlotte, NC 28226
Tel. 704-943-4500; Admissions 704-943-4530; Fax 704-943-4536
Web Site www.charlottecountryday.org

CHARLOTTE COUNTRY DAY SCHOOL

Charlotte Country Day School was founded in 1941 as a traditional college preparatory school. Continuing to maintain excellence in academic, athletic, and personal achievement, the coeducational program enrolls approximately 1600 students in Junior Kindergarten–Grade 12. The curriculum includes Honors and Advanced Placement courses, independent study, English as a Second Language, and an International Baccalaureate program. Among the activities are publications, community service, clubs, and a wide variety of athletics. There is a summer program. Tuition: $14,250–$20,200. Financial aid is available. Nancy Ehringhaus is Director of Admissions; Mark Reed (University of Houston, B.A.; Columbia University, M.Ed.) was appointed Head of School in 2009. *Southern Association.*

Charlotte Latin School 1970

9502 Providence Road, Charlotte, NC 28277-8695
Tel. 704-846-1100; Admissions 704-846-7207; Fax 704-847-8776
Web Site www.charlottelatin.org
E-mail admissions@charlottelatin.org

CHARLOTTE LATIN SCHOOL

Charlotte Latin is an independent, coeducational, nonsectarian, college preparatory day school enrolling 1400 students in Transitional Kindergarten–Grade 12. Latin provides opportunities and challenges to nurture students' growth, leadership qualities, and lifelong love of learning. Instruction stresses academic excellence while meeting the developmental needs of the maturing child through an innovative pedagogy taught in a traditional environment. In-depth fine arts, athletics, and extra-curricular activities are offered, including age-appropriate community service and an international exchange/study-abroad program. Enrichment and summer programs are also offered. Tuition: $14,350–$18,000. Financial Aid: $1,400,000. Kathryn B. Booe is Director of Admissions; Arch N. McIntosh, Jr. (Marshall University, B.A.; University of South Alabama, M.Ed.), is Headmaster. *Southern Association*.

Christ School   1900

500 Christ School Road, Asheville, NC 28704
Tel. 828-684-6232; Admission Ext. 106; [Toll-free] 800-422-3212
Fax 828-209-2003
Web Site www.christschool.org; E-mail admission@christschool.org

A college preparatory school for boys in Grades 8–12, Christ School enrolls 170 boarding and 60 day students. Affiliated with the Episcopal Church, the School prepares young men for success in college and beyond by providing a strong academic program, numerous athletic and outdoor opportunities, extensive offerings in the arts, and leadership opportunities for all students. Honors and Advanced Placement course work is available in all disciplines. All boys participate in chapel services, the work program, and community outreach. Boarding Tuition: $37,800; Day Tuition: $19,200. Financial Aid: $1,200,000. Merit-based Scholarships: $200,000. Denis Stokes is Director of Admission; Paul Krieger is Headmaster.

Forsyth Country Day School   1970

5501 Shallowford Road, P.O. Box 549, Lewisville, NC 27023-0549
Tel. 336-945-3151; Admission Ext. 340; Fax 336-945-2907
Web Site www.fcds.org; E-mail cindykluttz@fcds.org

Forsyth Country Day School is a coeducational, college preparatory day school enrolling 1000 students in Junior Kindergarten–Grade 12. The School aims to educate students to become productive, responsible adults meeting the challenges of the future. The Lower and Middle Schools stress basic academic skills enriched with foreign languages, art, science, music, physical education, computer, and seminars. The Upper School curriculum includes advanced courses in all disciplines, a variety of electives, and athletics, fine arts, and clubs. The Johnson Academic Center provides additional support for students with a variety of learning styles. Tuition: $7600–$17,100. Financial aid is available. Cindy Kluttz is Director of Admission; Henry M. Battle, Jr., is Headmaster. *Southern Association*.

Greensboro Day School   1970

5401 Lawndale Drive, Greensboro, NC 27455
Tel. 336-288-8590; Fax 336-282-2905
Web Site www.greensboroday.org
E-mail RobinSchenck@greensboroday.org

With an enrollment of about 900 students in Transitional Kindergarten through Grade 12, Greensboro Day School is one of the largest nonsectarian independent schools in the Piedmont Triad of North Carolina and is known throughout the nation for its excellence in education. For 40 years, the School's success has been defined by its challenging academic program, its emphasis on honor and values, and its dedication to each individual child and family. Today, Greensboro Day School remains strongly committed to developing a program that prepares students for leadership and service in the 21st century. Financial aid and transportation are available. Tuition: $7795–$17,945. Robin Schenck is Director of Admission & Financial Aid; Mark Hale (University of Washington, M.Ed. 1981) is Head of School.

Guilford Day School   1987

3310 Horse Pen Creek Road, Greensboro, NC 27410
Tel. 336-282-7044; Admission Ext. 4642; Fax 336-282-2048
Web Site www.guilfordday.org; E-mail tim@guilfordday.org

GUILFORD DAY SCHOOL

Dually accredited by the Southern Association of Independent Schools and the Southern Association of Colleges and Schools, Guilford Day School is dedicated to preparing students with learning differences and/or attention deficit for academic success in traditional settings. Enrolling 150 boys and girls in Grades 1–12, Guilford Day's college preparatory curriculum is marked by small classes taught by certified special-education instructors. Individual education plans are tailored specifically to each student's abilities, goals, and learning style. The academic program emphasizes reading, English, math, history, science, and foreign language, with challenging electives, technology, and offerings in the arts. Student Council, community service, field trips, athletics, music, and a summer session are available. Tuition: $15,963–$16,677. Tim Montgomery is Assistant Head of School/Admission Director; Laura Blackburn Mlatac is Head of School. *Southern Association*.

Kerr-Vance Academy   1968

700 Vance Academy Road, Henderson, NC 27537
Tel. 252-492-0018; Fax 252-438-4652
Web Site www.kerrvance.com; E-mail rirvin@kerrvance.com

KERR-VANCE ACADEMY

Kerr-Vance Academy, a coeducational, college preparatory day school, enrolls more than 450 students in Pre-Kindergarten–Grade 12. The School also has a licensed Day Care Center with programs for 2- and 3-year-old children. The liberal arts curriculum emphasizes academic excellence as well as ethical values and concern for others. The program centers on reading and language arts, math, science, social studies, and modern languages. Computer technology is integrated throughout the disciplines. The arts are also integral components of an education at Kerr-Vance Academy. Advanced Placement courses are offered in most subjects, and high school students perform a minimum of 15 hours of community service per year. Other activities include school government, honor societies, and athletics. Tuition: $7200–$7800. Rebecca Irvin is the Admissions Coordinator; Paul Villatico is Headmaster. *Southern Association.*

New Garden Friends School   1971

1128 New Garden Road, Greensboro, NC 27410
Tel. 336-299-0964; Admission Ext. 2501; Fax 336-292-0347
Web Site www.ngfs.org; E-mail nfriendssc@aol.com

Guided by Quaker beliefs, New Garden Friends School is an inclusive, innovative educational community for 290 boys and girls in Preschool (age 3)–Grade 12. The curriculum, which emphasizes social justice and personal responsibility, includes reading, math, science, foreign language, music, art, and physical education. Faculty believe in children's ability to act responsibly and seek to develop their reliance more on inner conviction and less on opinions of others or the fashion of the day. Each person is nourished as a growing individual in his or her search for inward authority, integrity, and personal sense of rightness. Tuition & Fees: $5625–$13,615. Financial aid is available. Chris Winchester is Admission Director; David Tomlin is Head of School.

The Oakwood School   1996

4000 MacGregor Downs Road, Greenville, NC 27834
Tel. 252-931-0760; Admission Ext. 228; Fax 252-931-0964
Web Site www.theoakwoodschool.org
E-mail info@theoakwoodschool.org

THE OAKWOOD SCHOOL

This coeducational day school was founded in 1996 by a group of parents looking for a challenging college preparatory program in a culturally diverse and secure setting. The Oakwood School enrolls 342 students in Pre-Kindergarten–Grade 12. Oakwood's mission is to ensure that all students develop the strength of character, creativity, and wisdom through which they can make a difference in the world. The curriculum accommodates students of average to high ability as well as those with mild learning differences. The 41-acre campus provides facilities for classrooms, media centers, science labs, fine arts, clubs, and sports teams. Extended care and summer programs are optional. Tuition: $9265–$9949. Financial aid is available. Louise Haney is Director of Admissions; Robert R. Peterson is Head of School. *Southern Association.*

The O'Neal School   1971

Airport Road, P.O. Box 290, Southern Pines, NC 28388
Tel. 910-692-6920; Admissions Ext. 103; Fax 910-692-6930
Web Site www.onealschool.org; E-mail adroppers@onealschool.org

O'Neal is a college preparatory school dedicated to the development of academic excellence, strength of character, and physical well-being of its students in an environment where integrity, self-discipline, and consideration for others are fundamental. There are 425 students in Pre-Kindergarten–Grade 12 on a beautiful, 40-acre campus. The curriculum in Kindergarten–Grade 8 is based on the Core Knowledge Program, which emphasizes cultural literacy and content learning. Students take part in many athletic, extracurricular, and community service activities while following a comprehensive academic program that includes 15 Advanced Placement courses. There is also a specialized learning development program. Tuition: $7000–$14,500. Financial Aid: $600,000. Alice Droppers is Director of Admissions and Financial Aid; Alan Barr (Hampden-Sydney College, B.A.; Longwood University, M.S.) is Headmaster.

Providence Day School   1970

5800 Sardis Road, Charlotte, NC 28270
Tel. 704-887-6000; Admissions 704-887-7040; Fax 704-887-7520
Web Site www.providenceday.org
E-mail admission@providenceday.org

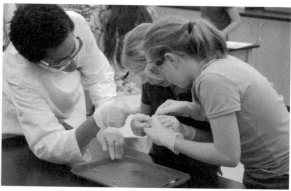

PROVIDENCE DAY SCHOOL

Providence Day, serving 1500 girls and boys in Transitional Kindergarten–Grade 12, has a reputation for high academic standards. Within a structured, yet nurturing environment, the college preparatory curriculum is designed to develop the intellectual, physical, social, and moral aspects of each student. Career exploration for seniors, a global studies program, and 26 Advanced Placement courses enrich the program. Students take part in honor societies, three publications, Student Council, clubs, and varsity athletics. An extensive summer program is available. Tuition: $14,065–$19,490. Financial Aid: $2,700,000. Scott Siegfried is Director of Admission; Dr. John E. Creeden (College of the Holy Cross, B.A. *[cum laude]* 1974; University of Wisconsin [Madison], M.A. 1976, Ph.D. 1984) is Headmaster. *Southern Association.*

Ravenscroft School   1862

7409 Falls of the Neuse Road, Raleigh, NC 27615
Tel. 919-847-0900; Admissions Ext. 2227; Fax 919-846-2371
Web Site www.ravenscroft.org; E-mail pjamison@ravenscroft.org

Ravenscroft, a Blue Ribbon School set on a spacious 125-acre campus, is a coeducational, college preparatory day school enrolling 1225 students in Pre-Kindergarten through Grade 12.

Guided by its "legacy of excellence," the Ravenscroft community nurtures individual potential and prepares students to thrive in a complex and interdependent world. School programs emphasize experiential learning activities and community service while offering a comprehensive academic program that features International Studies, Ethics and Leadership, and 27 Advanced Placement courses. A wide range of extracurricular opportunities includes an extensive Fine Arts program, competitive sports, student government, publications, and interest clubs. There is a summer program. Tuition: $10,700–$17,250. Financial aid is available. Pamela J. Jamison is Director of Admissions; Doreen C. Kelly (University of Pennsylvania, B.A. 1985, M.S. 1985) was appointed Head of School in 2003. *Southern Association.*

Saint Mary's School 1842

900 Hillsborough Street, Raleigh, NC 27603-1689
Tel. 919-424-4000; [Toll-free] 800-948-2557
Admissions 919-424-4100; Fax 919-424-4122
Web Site www.sms.edu; E-mail admission@sms.edu

Saint Mary's School is an independent, college preparatory, girls' school dedicated to academic excellence and personal achievement for Grades 9–12. Founded in 1842 in the Episcopal tradition, SMS is the seventh-largest girls' boarding and day school in the country. The historic, residential 23-acre campus is within easy driving distance of Research Triangle Park and the Raleigh-Durham International Airport. Saint Mary's School's comprehensive range of opportunities enables girls to compete in college and today's global economy. SMS offers 16 Advanced Placement and 31 honors courses, competition on 16 teams in 11 sports, a broad visual and performing arts program, and signature technology, advising, and cocurricular programs to prepare students for independence and success in college and life. Thirty-eight faculty and staff live on campus, and 75 percent of the faculty hold advanced degrees in their field. The student/faculty ratio is 8.7:1, and the average class is 12 students. The nearly 300 students represent 12 states and five countries. Boarding Tuition & Fees: $38,972; Day Tuition & Fees: $19,697. Financial aid is available. Catherine C. Leary is Director of Admission; Theo W. Coonrod is President. *Southern Association.*

St. Timothy's School 1958

4523 Six Forks Road, Raleigh, NC 27609
Tel. 919-787-3011; Admissions 919-781-0531; Fax 919-783-2399
Web Site www.sttimothys.org
E-mail cclement@sttimothys.org

St. Timothy's, an Episcopal, coeducational school, is North Carolina's oldest accredited nonpublic school and enrolls 490 students of all faiths in Kindergarten–Grade 8. The School is committed to academic excellence in an atmosphere that emphasizes traditional values, small classes, and a supportive environment.

The academic curriculum is complemented by offerings in computer, library, science lab, Spanish, music, art, and physical education. Extracurricular activities include a full interscholastic sports program for Grades 6–8, student government, clubs, journalism, and the arts. Tuition: $10,135–$12,000. Financial Aid: $450,000. Cathy Clement is Admissions Director; Michael S. Bailey (University of North Carolina, B.A.; East Carolina University, M.A.) is Headmaster. *Southern Association.*

Summit School 1933

2100 Reynolda Road, Winston-Salem, NC 27106
Tel. 336-722-2777; Admission 336-724-5811; Fax 336-724-0099
Web Site www.summitschool.com
E-mail mebeling@summitschool.com

Summit School is a day school enrolling 595 boys and girls in Pre-Kindergarten–Grade 9. The School strives to help students learn to respect their own beliefs, values, and achievements as well as those of others and encourages them to take responsibility for their own education. The traditional subjects are complemented by French (beginning in Pre-Kindergarten), Spanish, Latin, Chinese, art, music, drama, and computers. Other activities are sports and service groups. Field trips and student exchanges with other schools add variety to the program. Tuition: $10,100–$18,420. Financial Aid: $866,000. Katherine Memory is Director of Admission; Dr. Michael J. Ebeling (Lake Forest College, B.A.; University of Virginia, M.A., Ph.D.) is Head of School.

Triangle Day School 1991

4911 Neal Road, Durham, NC 27705
Tel. 919-383-8800; Fax 919-383-7157
Web Site www.TriangleDaySchool.org

Enrolling 200 boys and girls in Kindergarten through Grade 8, Triangle Day School balances challenge and support in the classroom. The School, which occupies more than 15 acres adjacent to a historic Civil War landmark, provides a rigorous interdisciplinary curriculum combined with a nurturing environment to create a unique academic setting for learning. A traditional approach to education offers students structure and establishes clear guidelines and expectations. Within this framework, students have opportunities to explore, create, and experience the excitement of learning. In addition to mastering basic skills, students learn to think critically, reason logically, and apply their knowledge in practical applications. Whether building edible cells in science class, reenacting a Civil War battle for a social studies assignment, or constructing an Egyptian Sarcophagus in art, students develop a desire to ask questions and gain the tools to discover the answers. Students take part in seasonal sports, among other activities, and a series of summer workshops is offered. Tuition: $6616–$10,920. Tuition assistance is available. Nicole A. Thompson is Director of Admission; Dr. R. Mason Goss was appointed Head of School in 2008. *Southern Association.*

OHIO

Canton Country Day School   1964

3000 Demington Avenue, NW, Canton, OH 44718
Tel. 330-453-8279; Fax 330-453-6038
Web Site www.cantoncountryday.org
E-mail pmonks@cantoncountryday.org

Canton Country Day School is a coeducational elementary and middle school enrolling 236 children in Pre-Kindergarten (age 3)–Grade 8. The School provides a solid academic foundation in a community of learners that is racially, ethnically, and economically diverse. In this environment, students are encouraged to undertake responsibility, develop a love for scholarship and knowledge, and practice respect for themselves and others. Core subjects center on English, math, science, and social studies, with classes in art, music, library, drama, creative movement, and service learning. With three computer labs, classroom Smartboards, and laptops for all teachers, CCDS students have a wide range of tools for research and information technology. Among the activities are Student Council, band, choir, yearbook, science fair, the Middle School musical, robotics, chess, and skiing, among other interests. Athletes compete in coed soccer and track and field as well as boys' and girls' basketball teams. Canton Country Day is a Nationally Recognized School of Excellence accredited by the Independent Schools Association of the Central States. Tuition: $4820–$13,517. Financial Aid: $575,000. Paul Monks is Admission Director; Pamela Shaw is Head of School.

The Columbus Academy   1911

Box 30745, 4300 Cherry Bottom Road, Gahanna, OH 43230
Tel. 614-475-2311; Admissions 614-337-4309; Fax 614-475-0396
Web Site www.columbusacademy.org
E-mail wuorinen@columbusacademy.org

The Columbus Academy is a coeducational, college preparatory day school enrolling 1055 students in Pre-Kindergarten–Grade 12. The Academy, located on a 233-acre campus, first admitted girls in 1990 and achieved full coeducation in 1992. The school is committed to providing a balanced education of academics, arts, athletics, and activities, including a significant service component. Taught by 145 full- and part-time faculty, students are provided a liberal arts foundation in the five basic disciplines. Summer enrichment and remedial courses and a day camp are conducted. Tuition: $9425–$18,750. Financial Aid: $1,500,000. John S. Wuorinen is Admissions Director; John M. MacKenzie (Bowdoin College, A.B.; Columbia University, M.A.) is Headmaster.

Gilmour Academy   1946

34001 Cedar Road, Gates Mills, OH 44040-9356
Tel. 440-442-1104; Admissions 440-473-8050; Fax 440-473-8010
Web Site www.gilmour.org; E-mail admissions@gilmour.org

Now in its 64th year of college preparatory education in the Catholic tradition of Holy Cross and the University of Notre Dame, Gilmour Academy enrolls 705 students, with day students in Preschool–Grade 12 and boarders in Grades 7–12. Students thrive in a highly personalized academic learning environment where the education of the mind and heart takes center stage. Dynamic student-teacher relationships and a vigorous advisory program combine with extensive academic offerings to help students become competent moral leaders. Boarding Tuition: $35,635; Day Tuition: $9840–$23,755. Financial Aid: $2,500,000. Steve M. Scheidt is Director of Middle and Upper

School Admissions; Megan Marrie is Director of Lower School Admissions; Br. Robert E. Lavelle, CSC, is Headmaster. *North Central Association.*

Hathaway Brown School   1876

19600 North Park Boulevard, Shaker Heights, OH 44122
Tel. 216-932-4214; Admissions 216-320-8767; Fax 216-397-0992
Web Site www.hb.edu; E-mail admissions@hb.edu

Hathaway Brown, a college preparatory day school serving 861 students in a coeducational early childhood program and all-girls Kindergarten–Grade 12, seeks to maintain a tradition of excellence through a challenging program in a creative atmosphere. The School aims to equip young women for the future with knowledge, resolve, and imagination. The curriculum offers Advanced Placement in all fields as well as the arts, computer studies, and athletics. A Science Research course enables students to work on experiments in cutting-edge labs around the city. Adventure Learning is required in Middle School; Spanish begins in Kindergarten. Tuition: $3790–$22,880. Financial Aid: $2,700,000+. Sarah L. Johnston is Director of Admission and Financial Aid; H. William Christ is Head of School.

Lake Ridge Academy   1963

37501 Center Ridge Road, North Ridgeville, OH 44039
Tel. 440-327-1175; Admissions Ext. 103; Fax 440-327-3641
Web Site www.lakeridgeacademy.org
E-mail admission@lakeridgeacademy.org

Encompassing Kindergarten–Grade 12, Lake Ridge Academy is the only independent, coeducational, college preparatory day school on the west side of Cleveland. Its mission is to develop "confident young people of integrity who think critically and creatively while embracing the joy of lifelong learning." The Academy's 359 students come from diverse backgrounds, creating a dynamic learning community in which all are respected and appreciated. The challenging curriculum, which emphasizes the liberal arts, sciences, and humanities, is carried out on an 88-acre campus of woodlands, fields, and a pond, with state-of-the-art facilities. The academic program requires English, social studies, French, Spanish, math, science, fine arts, and health and physical education, with 13 AP courses, 15 Honors courses, and 3 courses in partnership with Oberlin College. Technology is integrated throughout the disciplines. The school's Mock Trial team placed 1st in the state and 13th nationally; other activities include drama, Student Council, publications, music groups, service learning, and interscholastic teams in ten sports. Tuition: $15,750–$24,250. Financial Aid: $2,000,000. Alexa Hansen is Director of Admission; Carol Klimas is President.

The Miami Valley School   1964

5151 Denise Drive, Dayton, OH 45429
Tel. 937-434-4444; Fax 937-434-1033
Web Site www.mvschool.com; E-mail admission@mvschool.com

The Miami Valley School, the only independent, college preparatory school in the Dayton region, enrolls 440 boys and girls in Early Childhood–Grade 12. The challenging curriculum, personalized attention, and outstanding faculty provide an enriching environment for students to think critically, communicate effectively, and nurture their unique talents. All students benefit from an extensive experiential learning philosophy that culminates in a four-week intensive immersion program for Upper School students. Advanced Placement, fine and performing arts, world languages, athletics, and summer enrichment programs for all ages are offered. Tuition: $11,000–$16,723. Financial aid is available. Peter B. Benedict II is Headmaster.

The Seven Hills School   1974

5400 Red Bank Road, Cincinnati, OH 45227
Tel. 513-271-9027; Fax 513-271-2471
Web Site www.7hills.org; E-mail admissions@7hills.org

THE SEVEN HILLS SCHOOL

Formed by the 1974 merger of schools whose roots date to 1906, Seven Hills seeks to offer college preparation of superior quality in a coeducational setting for 1055 students in Prekindergarten–Grade 12. Its mission is to prepare students to be successful, contributing citizens by emphasizing academic excellence, development of individual potential, participation, and service to school and community. Wireless network connectivity in all grades and laptops for teachers enhance learning. Advanced Placement and honors courses, the fine and performing arts, athletics, an outdoor program, and summer enrichment opportunities are offered. Year-long extended care is available through Grade 5. Tuition: $9245–$19,135. Financial Aid: $2,000,000. Peter C. Egan is Director of Admissions and Financial Aid; Christopher Garten is Head of School.

The Summit Country Day School   1890

2161 Grandin Road, Hyde Park, Cincinnati, OH 45208
Tel. 513-871-4700; Fax 513-533-5373
Web Site www.summitcds.org; E-mail schiess_k@summitcds.org

THE SUMMIT COUNTRY DAY SCHOOL

Founded by the Sisters of Notre Dame de Namur, Summit is Cincinnati's only Catholic, coeducational school offering a college preparatory program in Preschool (age 2)–Grade 12. Its 1100-member student body represents many racial, ethnic, religious, and socioeconomic backgrounds. The liberal arts curriculum includes a nationally recognized Educating for Character Program. Courses in core subjects are enhanced by the School's computer technology initiative. Each year, 20 percent of seniors receive National Merit Scholarship recognition, and 100 percent go on to college. Christian outreach, social and academic clubs, drama, publications, and athletics are among the activities. Tuition: $5200–$17,500. Kelley K. Schiess is Director of Admission; Dr. Gerald M. Jellig is Head of School.

Western Reserve Academy   1826

115 College Street, Hudson, OH 44236
Tel. 330-650-4400; [Toll-free] 800-784-3776
Admissions 330-650-9717
Web Site www.wra.net; E-mail admission@wra.net

Western reserve academy in Hudson, Ohio, is a coeducational boarding and day school enrolling students in Grade 9–Postgraduate. Hudson (population 25,000) retains the flavor of an 18th-century New England village and has been cited by the National Trust for Historic Preservation as "among the top 100 historic places in the nation."

WESTERN RESERVE ACADEMY

Reserve was founded in 1826 as a college and preparatory academy by Hudson's earliest settlers. The college later moved to Cleveland and became Case Western Reserve University. After being closed for 13 years, James W. Ellsworth endowed the Academy with funding to permit its return to active operation in 1916. Mr. Ellsworth contributed an endowment that currently exceeds $92,100,000, enabling Reserve to offer substantial scholarship assistance. In 2001, Reserve was highlighted as one of the nation's 13 outstanding coeducational boarding schools by *U.S. News and World Report.*

Western Reserve Academy is a close-knit community of teachers and students fully engaged in the process of education. Academics are foremost, but they are balanced by a spirit of discovery that extends beyond the classroom. Students are challenged to ask questions and to find answers in many different ways and places, including living with young people from different countries and cultures, planning team strategy in athletics, rehearsing for performances, and extending their efforts to participate in helping the community both within and outside of Reserve.

A nonprofit institution, Western Reserve Academy is governed by 28 Trustees, 21 of whom are alumni. The Alumni Association is actively involved in all aspects of the school. Western Reserve Academy holds membership in many educational associations and foundations, including the National Association of Independent Schools and The Association of Boarding Schools, among others. It is accredited by the Independent Schools Association of the Central States.

THE CAMPUS. The 190-acre campus features outstanding examples of Greek Revival architecture along with "Brick Row" buildings modeled after Yale University. Central to Western Reserve is Seymour Hall, which is built on the Academy's cornerstone, laid in 1826. Five of the original seven buildings are still in use, including the David Hudson House, which is the oldest frame house in Ohio. The Loomis Observatory is the second-oldest structure of its kind in the nation. The 16,000-square-foot dormitory, Long House, opened in 2000 as did the 20,000-square-foot John D. Ong Library, which houses 45,000 volumes and an enlarged computer lab. In 2002, Cartwright House, a new girls' dormitory, was completed. The Knight Fine Arts Center houses studios for instruction in photography, digital imagery, the manual arts, dance, and a fine arts gallery. The fully equipped theater seats 400. The Academy's computers are connected through a fiberoptic network reaching dormitory rooms, classrooms, and offices, and students have full wireless Internet access as well as e-mail accounts. A state-of-the-art athletic complex includes a field house with a 200-meter track, varsity basketball court, and three practice courts.

Athletic facilities include a six-lane swimming pool with diving well, wrestling/multipurpose rooms, 12 tennis courts, squash courts, a state-of-the-art weight training/fitness center with new Nautilus equipment, a new 400-meter all-weather track, a new Pro-Turf all-weather field for football, soccer, lacrosse, and field hockey, a cross-country trail, a paddle tennis court, and 12 additional athletic fields. The ice-hockey team skates at Kent State University, while golf team members enjoy privileges at a local club.

More than 90 percent of Western Reserve's faculty live on campus with their families in Academy-owned homes or dormitories.

THE FACULTY. Christopher D. Burner '80 was appointed Head of School in 2008, succeeding Henry E. Flanagan, Jr., who had served in that position since 1982. Mr. Burner is a graduate of Franklin & Marshall College (B.A.), Dartmouth College, (M.A.L.S.), and Harvard University (M.Ed.). He graduated from Reserve in 1980 and most recently served as the Dean of Faculty and a Latin teacher. Mr. Burner was also Director of Admission and Financial Aid for seven years. Along with those responsibilities, he has coached football, wrestling, and lacrosse and worked in the Deans' Office.

WESTERN RESERVE ACADEMY

There are 70 full- and part-time faculty, 81 percent of whom hold advanced degrees. Most teachers continue their educational and professional growth through summer or full-year sabbaticals, writing workshops, marine biology projects, or graduate studies and seminars.

A full-time nurse heads the new Health Center and is supported by four staff members. A local doctor holds daily office hours and is on call at all times.

STUDENT BODY. In 2009–10, Reserve enrolled 146 boarding boys, 109 boarding girls, 71 day boys, and 59 day girls in Grades 9–12 and a postgraduate year. Boarding students represent 25 states and 20 countries. Day students are fully integrated into the residential experience, spending time on campus in the evenings and on weekends.

ACADEMIC PROGRAM. The school year, from September to June, is divided into four marking periods, with Thanksgiving, Christmas, and spring vacations. School begins at 8:00 A.M., with a morning meeting held three days a week, followed by academic classes, lunch, afternoon classes, activities, conferences, and athletics. "Lights out" for Grades 9–11 is 11:15 P.M.

WESTERN RESERVE ACADEMY

Reserve's academic program is designed to stretch each student to take full advantage of the Academy's offerings and to create an academic profile that builds on strengths and bolsters weaknesses. Classes are small, and teachers are available for help outside the classroom during the day and evening. The Academic Enrichment Center is also available for students who need additional support. There is a mandatory quiet study period from 7:45 to 11:00 P.M. Sunday through Friday.

To graduate, students must complete four years of English, three years each of mathematics and foreign language, three years of science, two and one-half years of history, two years of fine arts, senior seminar (an interdisciplinary course focusing on humanistic topics), and a half-year of health.

The curriculum includes such courses as English I–IV, Creative Writing; French I–V, German I–V, Latin I–IV, Spanish I–IV, Mandarin Chinese I–IV; Algebra, Geometry, Pre-Calculus, Calculus, Advanced Topics in Mathematics; Biology, Zoology, Physics, Astronomy, Chemistry; United States History, Constitutional Law, Economics; Health/Ethics; Studio Art, Photography, Dance, Choir, Music Theory, String Orchestra; Public Speaking, Dramatic Performance; and Engineering Drawing, Web Publishing, and Architectural Design.

Honors classes are offered in Latin, geometry, pre-calculus, physics, intermediate algebra, and dance. AP courses are formed in English, French, German, Latin, Spanish, U.S. History, European history, calculus, statistics, computer science, physics, chemistry, biology, and economics. Academic credit is also granted for independent study and special projects. Exchange programs are available through The English-

Speaking Union, School Year Abroad, the Ridley College Experience, and summer foreign language study abroad.

In 2009, the graduating seniors gained acceptance at 192 different colleges and universities including Amherst, Case Western Reserve University, Colgate, Columbia, Cornell, Dartmouth, Denison, Duke, George Washington University, Middlebury, Northwestern, United States Military Academy, United States Naval Academy, Vanderbilt, Wellesley, Yale, and the University of Pennsylvania.

STUDENT ACTIVITIES. The Student Council is responsible for presenting student ideas and organizing activities. All students take part in Reserve's Service Program, which may involve working in the library or dining hall or acting as a laboratory assistant or teacher aide.

WESTERN RESERVE ACADEMY

Reserve offers numerous extracurricular activities for students with a broad variety of interests including OpuS (theater), S.I.C.U. (Students for Intercultural Understanding), WWRA (student radio station), Student Affairs Committee, *The Reserve Record* (newspaper), *Hardscrabble* (yearbook), G.C.A.T. (Green Campus Action Team), R.E.A.C.H. (Reserve Ethically Advancing Community Health), and the Chess, Culinary, Debate, and Investment Clubs, among others.

Reserve's athletic program is built around a history of strong teams, dedicated coaches, and enthusiastic parent and alumni supporters. Each student is required to participate in athletics at some level in order to balance academic and extracurricular life and provide exercise and an outlet from the rigors of the classroom. All sports have varsity squads, many have junior varsity teams and "C" squads. Boys compete in the Interstate Preparatory School League in football, soccer, basketball, cross-country, wrestling, hockey, swimming, diving, baseball, precision shooting, golf, lacrosse, and tennis. Girls compete in the Private School League in field hockey, soccer, volleyball, cross-country, swimming, diving, precision shooting, basketball, ice hockey, track, softball, lacrosse, and tennis. Students may also participate in a number of intramural activities including aerobics and weightlifting.

Dances, concerts, and trips are offered on weekends, and traditional annual events include Christmas Vespers, Winter Carnival, Madrigal Feaste, and the Dads Club Family Party.

ADMISSION AND COSTS. Most students enter Reserve in Grades 9 or 10, with a few admitted to the upper grades. The Academy admits students of any race, color, or national or ethnic origin. Applicants must submit scores from either the Secondary School Admission Test or the Independent School Entrance Examination; junior or senior applicants can submit Preliminary Scholastic Aptitude or Scholastic Aptitude Test results. Applications, accompanied by a $50 fee ($150 for international students), should be submitted by February 1 for boarders and January 15 for day students; families are notified by March 10 for boarders and February 10 for day students.

Late applications will be considered as space permits.

In 2009–10, boarding tuition is $39,100; day tuition, including meals, is $27,900. Extras are approximately $500, with additional expenses for boarders of $1000. Tuition insurance and a payment plan are available.

In the current year, more than $3,315,000 was awarded in financial aid on the basis of need. Reserve uses the School and Student Service for Financial Aid to determine award amounts.

Head of School: Christopher D. Burner '80
Assistant Head of School: William A. Bugg III
Assistant Head of School for Advancement: Jay Gundy
Director of Studies: Justin Zimmerman
Dean of Faculty: Kate Mueller
Dean of Students: Brand Closen
Dean of Admission & Financial Aid: Anne Sheppard
Director of College Guidance: E. Tariq Thomas
Business Manager: Leonard Carlson
Chief Financial Officer: John Tortelli
Director of Athletics & Afternoon Programs: Herb Haller

OKLAHOMA

Casady School   1947

9500 North Pennsylvania Avenue, P.O. Box 20390, Oklahoma City, OK 73120
Tel. 405-749-3100; Admissions 405-740-3185; Fax 405-749-3214
Web Site www.casady.org; E-mail admissions@casady.org

The Episcopal Bishop of Oklahoma and dedicated laypersons founded Casady School to promote academic excellence and Christian principles. The oldest, most established independent school in the state capital, Casady enrolls 874 college-bound boys and girls in Preschool (age 3)–Grade 12 in a liberal arts program designed to develop each mind, body, and spirit. Approximately 25 percent of the students are racially and ethnically diverse. The classical curriculum emphasizes a strong foundation in core subjects, enriched by Advanced Placement courses in 18 subject areas. Historically, all Casady graduates enter four-year colleges and universities nationwide. Students enjoy a wide array of aesthetic, athletic, extracurricular opportunities, and electives. The spacious campus, clustered around a 6-acre lake, provides facilities for student-produced publications, vocal and instrumental ensembles, academic tournaments, competitive team sports, peer tutoring, and, with 10,000 volunteer hours annually, service learning projects that introduce participants to meaningful work within the larger community. Tuition: $6750–$14,850. Financial Aid: $1,000,000+. Aaron James is Director of Admission and Financial Aid; Christopher Bright is Headmaster.

Holland Hall   1922

5666 East 81st Street, Tulsa, OK 74137-2099
Tel. 918-481-1111; Fax 918-481-1145
Web Site www.hollandhall.org

Holland Hall, Tulsa's first independent school, is an Episcopal, college preparatory day school enrolling 969 boys and girls from many faiths in Preschool (age 3)–Grade 12. The school was founded to provide a quality education that enables students to succeed in the complex global society of the 21st century. Holland Hall's affiliation with the Episcopal Church is reflected in required religious studies, chapel services, and the presence of two chaplains on campus. The liberal arts curriculum emphasizes mastery of strong skills in English, math, science, and humanities. In addition to core subjects, students take classes in modern and classical languages, art, theater, music, and computer technology. AP courses in five subjects are available to qualified students, and students in Grade 12 are required to take part in a Senior Intern Program, working for local agencies or in a professional setting. Student Council, jazz and chamber ensembles, publications, the Cum Laude Society, and 62 interscholastic teams provide opportunities for enrichment and fun. Tuition: $3900–$15,400. Financial Aid: $1,600,000. Richard Hart is Director of Admission and Financial Aid: Dr. Mark D. Desjardins (University of Virginia, Ph.D.) is Headmaster.

Riverfield Country Day School   1984

2433 West 61st Street, Tulsa, OK 74132
Tel. 918-446-3553; Fax 918-446-1914
Web Site www.riverfield.org; E-mail admissions@riverfield.org

Riverfield is entering its 26th year of enriching students through innovation, small class sizes, and positive collaborative relationships. Serving 530 children from 8 weeks through Upper School, Riverfield helps students reach their full potential in a family-oriented atmosphere. Experienced faculty develop the whole person as a confident and responsible student, building a foundation for a lifetime of learning. The challenging, personalized curriculum is presented as an integrated process, blending many subjects and activities. The result is academic excellence; on standardized tests, Riverfield students score, on average, over two grade levels above their current grade. The 120-acre wireless campus includes an Upper School with Oklahoma's first Tablet PC program and a 10,000-square-foot gymnasium. A new 7,000-square-foot academic building opened in 2008. The School was re-accredited by both the Independent Schools Association of the Southwest and the National Association for the Education of Young Children during the 2008–09 school year. A dynamic summer camp program is optional. Tuition: $7310–$9320. Financial aid is available. Britton Fox is Director of Admissions; Martha S. Clark (Principia, B.S.Ed.) is Head of School.

CASADY SCHOOL.

PENNSYLVANIA

Abington Friends School   1697

575 Washington Lane, Jenkintown, PA 19046
Tel. 215-886-4350; Fax 215-886-9143
Web Site www.abingtonfriends.net
E-mail vtoomer@abingtonfriends.net

Abington Friends School is a Quaker, coeducational, college preparatory day school for approximately 640 students in Preschool–Grade 12. AFS students are inspired to excel in a challenging and vibrant curriculum and to explore their passions in depth. As leaders in Friends education for over 300 years, the School values excellence and goodness, spirit and intellect, and believes that these dynamic tensions foster hard work, commitment, and joy in learning. Students are fully engaged in academics, athletics, the arts, and the larger world. The core Quaker values of respect for individuals, equality, simplicity, integrity, and service are at the heart of all the School does in its work of educating the whole child. On its original campus in Jenkintown since 1697, AFS today is rich in racial, socioeconomic, and ideological variety. The School draws students from across the greater Philadelphia region, 100 percent of whom attend four-year colleges and universities. Tuition: $14,400–$24,900. Financial aid is available. Vikki Toomer is Director of Admissions and Financial Assistance; Richard F. Nourie (Harvard Graduate School of Education, Ed.M.) is Head of School.

Chestnut Hill Academy   1861

500 West Willow Grove Avenue, Philadelphia, PA 19118
Tel. 215-247-4700; Admissions Ext. 1133; Fax 215-247-8516
Web Site www.chestnuthillacademy.org
E-mail admissions@chestnuthillacademy.org

Chestnut Hill Academy is an independent, college preparatory day school with an enrollment of 540 boys in PreKindergarten–Grade 12. Stressing high academic standards, Chestnut Hill offers a diversity of courses and opportunities, including a coordinate program in the Upper School in which courses are shared with Springside School, a neighboring school for girls. Performing arts, community service, sports, and publications comprise the school's extracurricular activities. Tuition: $11,750–$25,500. Financial Aid: $2,100,000. Vincent H. Valenzuela is Director of Admissions; Francis P. Steel, Jr. '77 (Yale University, B.A.; University of Pennsylvania, M.A.), is Headmaster. *Middle States Association.*

The Crefeld School   1970

8836 Crefeld Street, Chestnut Hill, Philadelphia, PA 19118
Tel. 215-242-5545; Admissions Ext. 13; Fax 215-242-8869
Web Site www.crefeld.org; E-mail scunitz@crefeld.org

Crefeld, a school of new beginnings, is a coeducational, independent day school serving 100 students in Grades 7–12. Crefeld welcomes students seeking an alternative educational program—one that is progressive and college preparatory. Students seeking a safe, nurturing, and supportive environment benefit from the School's learning and emotional support, combined with a holistic, systemic approach to each young person. Students pursue high academic standards in a relaxed, intimate, and collaborative atmosphere while simultaneously promoting an appreciation for artistic creation and civic responsibility. This environment is marked by a culture that respects diversity and a staff that cares about every student. In class sizes of 8–14, students follow a hands-on, experiential curriculum designed to accommodate individual interests and learning styles. Crefeld offers weekly community service, visual and per-forming arts programs, and support for students who are gifted, sensitive, ADHD, mildly learning disabled, or who "march to the beat of a different drummer." Tuition: $21,500–$23,900. Financial aid is available. Stacey Cunitz is Director of Admissions; Dr. Mark Piechota is Head of School.

Delaware Valley Friends School   1986

19 East Central Avenue, Paoli, PA 19301
Tel. 610-640-4150; Admissions Ext. 2160; Fax 610-296-9970
Web Site www.dvfs.org; E-mail wynnk@fc.dvfs.org

DELAWARE VALLEY FRIENDS SCHOOL

Delaware Valley Friends is a coeducational day school for Grades 6–12 enrolling 187 college-bound students with learning differences and average to above-average intelligence. The School blends the Quaker mission with the mission to provide an environment that addresses individual learning needs while building upon a student's strengths. The School offers a structured program in a supportive, friendly setting. The core subjects of science, mathematics, history, and literature are enhanced by outdoor education, arts, and foreign language. All students take language arts, an individualized course designed to improve skills. Interscholastic sports are offered at the end of the day. Tuition: $34,100. Financial aid is available. Jeannie Bowman is Admissions Director; Pritchard Garrett is Head.

The Episcopal Academy   1785

1785 Bishop White Drive, Newtown Square, PA 19073
Tel. 484-424-1400; Admission 484-424-1444; Fax 484-424-1604
Web Site www.episcopalacademy.org
E-mail young@episcopalacademy.org

THE EPISCOPAL ACADEMY

Founded in 1785, The Episcopal Academy blends its heritage and tradition with a rigorous, enriching curriculum and technology. Episcopal, a PreK–Grade 12 coeducational day school with more than 1200 students from diverse religious, racial, and economic backgrounds, seeks to cultivate the mind, body, and spirit of each student. Stimulating curricula, vibrant fine and performing arts, a competitive athletic program, inclusive Chapel services, and a commitment to community outreach define the core values of the school. Class and field trips enhance learning, and AP classes are offered in 15 subjects in Upper School. One hundred percent of graduates go on to four-year colleges and universities, many at the most selective level. A large variety of extracurricular offerings is available, including publications, debate, and political and creative opportunities. In 2008, Episcopal opened on a new campus in Newtown Square and closed its Merion and Devon campuses. The new 123-acre site has state-of-the-art academic, arts, and athletic facilities including a black box theater, five basketball courts, and nine athletic fields. Tuition: $20,000–$26,500. Ellen Hay is Director of Admission; L. Hamilton Clark is Head of School. *Middle States Association.*

Friends' Central School   1845

Grades 5–12: 1101 City Avenue, Wynnewood, PA 19096
Tel. 610-649-7440; Fax 610-649-5669
Web Site www.friendscentral.org
E-mail admission@friendscentral.org
PS–Grade 4: 228 Gulph Road, Wynnewood, PA 19096
Tel. 610-642-7575; Fax 610-642-6983

For over 160 years, Friends' Central has combined the rigorous pursuit of academic excellence with the Quaker testimonies of equality, peace, integrity, and service. The School believes that each individual is valued and that each voice is important. A dedicated faculty inspires 974 boys and girls in Preschool–Grade 12 to respond to what is best in themselves, to recognize and learn from the best in others, and to have a positive impact on their world. The result is a school fueled by shared intellectual excitement, creative energy, friendship, and optimistic care for the world. A low student-teacher ratio, two campuses centrally located for both city and suburbs, and a dynamic curriculum challenge students at all stages of development. The state-of-the-art Science, Math, and Technology Center has become a model for other area schools. An all-weather track enhances the new athletic complex, which includes three gyms, seven tennis courts, an indoor pool, wrestling room, and fitness center. Typically, 20 percent of seniors earn National Merit Honors, and all students graduate prepared to excel at top colleges and universities. Tuition: $16,600–$25,400. Financial Aid: $4,800,000. Barbara Behar is Director of Admission; David M. Felsen is Headmaster.

Friends School Haverford   1885

851 Buck Lane, Haverford, PA 19041
Tel. 610-642-2334; Admission 610-642-0354; Fax 610-642-0870
Web Site www.friendshaverford.org
E-mail fsh@friendshaverford.org

This coeducational, Quaker elementary school enrolls 150 students in Pre-School (age 3)–Grade 6. Friends School Haverford derives its strength from the emphasis it places on early childhood through preadolescent education. An experienced faculty and staff present a full academic curriculum emphasizing core concepts, clear and logical thinking, and the ability to communicate ideas. The School is a caring community based on Quaker values in which children receive abundant personal attention and gain the confidence to risk, stretch, and achieve. Art, music, technology, science, health, library, Spanish, and physical education enrich the program. The School is governed by the School Committee of Friends School Haverford under the care of

Haverford Monthly Meeting of the Society of Friends. Tuition: $8600–$18,600. Financial Aid: $450,000. Beth Krick is Director of Admission; Herbert Jaques, Jr. (Harvard University, A.B.), is Interim Head of School.

Germantown Academy   1759

P.O. Box 287, Fort Washington, PA 19034
Tel. 215-646-3300; Fax 215-646-1216
Web Site www.germantownacademy.net
E-mail admission@germantownacademy.org

One of the oldest nonsectarian day schools in the United States, Germantown Academy is a college preparatory school enrolling 1120 boys and girls in Pre-Kindergarten through Grade 12. The Academy seeks to prepare students to think critically, communicate effectively, and understand the needs of others. The curriculum emphasizes a depth of analysis as Lower and Middle School students concentrate on responsibility, curiosity, organizational skills, critical thinking, leadership, and the broad application of knowledge. The Academy offers Upper School students independent study opportunities, a variety of electives, and honors and Advanced Placement courses in all subjects of the liberal arts curriculum. Extracurricular activities include 50 sports teams, the visual and performing arts, community service, and special-interest clubs. Summer programs enhance the regular school year. The 120-acre campus holds an indoor pool, tennis courts, and arts, computer, media, and science centers. Tuition: $17,905–$25,495. Financial Aid: $2,700,000. Barbara Serrill '68 is Director of Admission; James W. Connor (Eckerd College, A.B. 1972; University of Pennsylvania, M.A. 1988) is Headmaster. *Middle States Association.*

Grier School   1853

P.O. Box 308, Tyrone, PA 16686
Tel. 814-684-3000; Fax 814-684-2177
Web Site www.grier.org; E-mail admissions@grier.org

Grier School, a college preparatory boarding school, enrolls approximately 200 girls in Grade 6 through a postgraduate year. The School seeks to provide a nurturing environment in which girls can develop self-motivation, confidence, creativity, leadership skills, and respect for others. Students come from twenty-two states and fourteen countries. Classes offered include Music Theory and Composition, Chinese, Ecology, Calculus, Philosophy, Journalism, and Economics. An honors program and Advanced Placement courses in eight subjects enhance the rigorous liberal arts curriculum. Student government, a literary magazine, chorus, orchestra, jazz band, National Honor Society, and community service are among the extracurricular activities offered. All girls take part in athletics, such as club sports in skiing and ice-skating or interscholastic teams in volleyball, soccer, tennis, and horseback riding. In the past, study abroad programs have traveled to Ireland, Spain, and France. The 300-acre campus supports fine and performing arts centers, residence facilities, a library, and an indoor equestrian center. Financial aid is available. Gina Borst is Headmistress; Andrew Wilson is Headmaster and Director of Admissions. Tuition: $42,500. *Middle States Association.*

The Haverford School   1884

450 Lancaster Avenue, Haverford, PA 19041
Tel. 610-642-3020; Admission Ext. 1200; Fax 610-642-8724
Web Site www.haverford.org; E-mail kseits@haverford.org

Concerned citizens founded this all-boys day school to educate their sons and those of professors at Haverford College. The Haverford School, which opened with a 5-member faculty and

25 young men, today has 119 teachers and enrolls 971 students in Junior Kindergarten–Grade 12 in a challenging and supportive environment that emphasizes scholarship, leadership, citizenship, and high standards of character and conduct. The college preparatory academic program features five modern and classical languages, 43 advanced-level courses, and independent study for seniors. Historically, 100 percent of Haverford graduates go on to four-year colleges and universities nationwide. The 30-acre campus provides extensive facilities for extracurricular activities, which center on leadership groups, drama, the arts, three publications, choral groups, Mock Trial, Model UN, Diversity Alliance, and clubs spanning diverse interests from business and chess to rocketry and snowboarding. Boys compete in 16 sports and engage in service learning to benefit Habitat for Humanity, Special Olympics, AIDS, juvenile diabetes, and more than a dozen other causes. Tuition: $19,950–$28,475. Kevin Seits is Director of Admission; Joseph T. Cox, Ph.D., is Headmaster. *Middle States Association.*

The Hill School   1851

717 East High Street, Pottstown, PA 19464
Tel. 610-326-1000; Fax 610-705-1753
Web Site www.thehill.org; E-mail admission@thehill.org

THE HILL SCHOOL in Pottstown, Pennsylvania, is a college preparatory boarding and day school enrolling young men and women in Grades 9 through 12 (Forms Third–Sixth) and a postgraduate year. Pottstown (population 22,000) is 40 miles northwest of Philadelphia, easily accessible to New York City, Baltimore, and Washington, D.C., as well as the Pocono Mountains, the Amish country, and historic Valley Forge National Park.

Founded in 1851 by the Rev. Matthew Meigs, The Hill opened as the Family Boarding School for Boys and Young Men with an enrollment of 25 pupils. In the fall of 1998, the School became coeducational, enrolling 100 "First Girls." Although it is nondenominational, The Hill's philosophy is based on Christian principles, and all students are required to attend chapel services twice weekly.

THE HILL SCHOOL

The articles of the School's incorporation are held by the approximately 8000 alumni. There are 28 members of the Board of Trustees. The Hill School is accredited by the Middle States Association of Colleges and Schools and holds membership in the National Association of Independent

Schools, among other affiliations. The School's endowment is $125,000,000.

THE CAMPUS. The Hill School campus consists of 200 acres overlooking the Schuylkill Valley. Among the 55 buildings are Alumni Chapel, Sweeney Gymnasium, the Harry Elkins Widener Science Building, the Center For The Arts, the John P. Ryan Library, and the Music House. The 50,000-square-foot Academic Center, completed in 1998, is home to administrative offices, classrooms, a student center, and the bookstore. Boarders live in 12 residences, including Dell Dormitory (1999).

THE HILL SCHOOL

The athletic facilities include an 18-hole golf course, 15 tennis courts, an ice-hockey rink, swimming pool, 10 sports fields, a fully equipped fitness center, an all-weather Olympic track, 9 squash courts, and the David H. Mercer Field House (2001), an indoor training facility.

The campus and facilities are valued at approximately $100,000,000.

THE FACULTY. David R. Dougherty was appointed Headmaster in 1993. A graduate of Episcopal High School in Virginia, he holds a baccalaureate degree in English from Washington and Lee University and a master's degree from Georgetown. Mr. Dougherty also earned an M.Litt. degree from Middlebury College's Bread Loaf School of English at Lincoln College, Oxford. His wife, Kay, is Senior Associate–Campaign for the Faculty at The Hill.

The 57 men and 37 women on the faculty hold 93 baccalaureate, 55 master's, and 6 doctoral degrees representing study at such institutions as Amherst, Boston University, Bowdoin, Brown, Bucknell, Clemson, Colgate, College of William and Mary, Columbia, Cornell, Dartmouth, Denison, Drexel, Duke, Duke Divinity School, Earlham, Fordham, Gettysburg, Harvard, Haverford, Hollins, Ithaca, Johns Hopkins, Kenyon, Lehigh, Mary Baldwin, Middlebury, Mount Holyoke, Muhlenberg, Ohio State, Princeton, Purdue, St. John's, St. Joseph's, Swarthmore, Temple, Trinity, Ursinus, Villanova, Washington and Lee, West Chester, Yale Divinity School, and the Universities of California, Connecticut, Delaware, Massachusetts, Michigan, New Hampshire, North Carolina, Notre Dame, Pennsylvania, Texas, Virginia, and Windsor.

The school physician holds regular hours in the Health Center, and Pottstown Memorial Medical Center is available for emergencies.

STUDENT BODY. In 2009–10, The Hill enrolled 278 boys and 215 girls, approximately 80 percent of whom are boarding students. Day students are required to live on campus for at least one year, as the boarding experience is integral to a Hill education. Students come from 30 states and 21 countries and represent a wide diversity of racial, ethnic, religious, and socioeconomic backgrounds.

ACADEMIC PROGRAM. The school year begins in early September and ends in early June, with three long weekends and vacations at Thanksgiving, Christmas, and in the spring. Interim grades are sent to parents every five weeks, and term grades are sent at the end of each trimester. There are parent conferences in the fall at Parents' Weekend. Classes, with an average class size of 12 girls and boys, are held six days a week, with half-days on Wednesday and Saturday when afternoons are reserved for athletics and other activities. Faculty live on campus and are readily available for extra help.

A typical day begins with the rising bell at 7:00 A.M., followed by breakfast and classes from 7:55 A.M. to 12:05 P.M., family-style lunch, more classes until 3:10 P.M., with sports scheduled until 5:30 P.M. Supervised evening study hours are conducted from 7:45 to 9:45 P.M. except on Saturday. "Lights out" is between 11:00 P.M. and midnight, depending upon grade.

To graduate, students must complete 17 scholastic units of credit, including 4 in English; 3 each in mathematics and foreign language; 2 each in history and a laboratory science (biology, chemistry, or physics); and 1 in theology or philosophy. Honors divisions and sequences leading to Advanced Placement examinations are available in mathematics, English, the sciences, history, foreign languages, art, and computer science.

Among the courses are American Literature, World Literature, Public Speaking; Algebra I–II, Geometry; Greek 1–4, Latin 1–6, French 1–5, Spanish 1–5, German 1–4, Chinese 1–4; American Studies, Modern European History, United States History, Economics, World Civilizations, The Civil War, World War II; Biology Research, Biology 1–2, Chemistry 1–2, Concepts of Physics, Physics 1–2; Judeo-Christian Roots, Religion in Literature, Psychology; History of Art and Music, Orchestra, Jazz Ensemble, Jazz Improvisation, Glee Club, Oral Communications, Drama Workshop, Studio Art I–II, and Photography. A two-year course in the humanities may be elected in place of English 3 and 4. Independent Study projects under faculty supervision further enrich the curriculum.

In 2008, The Hill School opened a writing center with the goal of improving the writing of all students across the curriculum. It is directed by former *Washington Post* editor Tony Reid '75 and includes approximately 20 "fellows," sixth formers selected by their instructors to help coach their peers. Mr. Reid also works with faculty members in all departments to help them design writing assignments for their students, strengthening the school's culture of using writing to help students clarify their thinking.

Study-travel opportunities include both a spring break and a summer humanities program in Italy as well as year-long programs in China, Italy, France, and Spain through School Year Abroad.

All seniors in the Class of 2009 entered college immediately after graduation. Students are attending Brown, Bucknell, Colby, Connecticut College, Cornell, Davidson, Duke, Georgetown, Hamilton, Hobart, Lafayette, Lehigh, Middlebury, Trinity, United States Naval Academy, Wesleyan, Williams, and the Universities of Pennsylvania and Virginia.

STUDENT ACTIVITIES. A joint Student-Faculty Senate encourages boys and girls to develop leadership skills. In addition, select sixth formers act as dormitory prefects. Upperformers also supervise the Work Program in which all students contribute up to 30 minutes each day in school chores. Students fulfill a community service requirement and also initiate a variety of community-wide service projects.

All students participate in sports or exercise at some level. Girls' and boys' teams are fielded in cross-country, soccer, water polo, basketball, ice hockey, squash, swimming, track, golf, lacrosse, and tennis; girls also play field hockey and softball, while boys compete in football, wrestling, and baseball. Instructional-level teams are offered throughout the year in most sports and strength conditioning.

Students publish a yearbook, a newspaper, and a literary magazine. For students interested in music, there are numerous instrumental and vocal groups including the Chamber Ensem-

ble, Jazz Band, and The Hilltones and Hilltrebles, select vocal ensembles. Other groups include the Hill Athletic Association, Student Activities and Reception committees, Ellis Theatre Guild, and numerous clubs.

The Bissell Forum has sponsored programs by a number of noted guests, many of whom are Hill alumni. These have included Secretary of State James A. Baker III '48, Lamar Hunt, and Tobias Wolff '64, Penn Faulkner Award winner.

ADMISSION AND COSTS. The Hill, which maintains a nondiscriminatory policy regarding race, creed, and national or ethnic origin, seeks to enroll diverse young men and women most likely to succeed in, benefit from, and contribute to the School. Admission requirements include a student essay, transcripts from the current school, recommendations from a guidance counselor and English and mathematics teachers, an interview on campus, and the results of a standardized admission test. Application, with a $50 fee, should be made by January 31 for March 10 notification; late applications will be considered as space is available after April 10.

THE HILL SCHOOL

In 2009–10, tuition is $44,000 for boarders and $30,400 for day students. Books, transportation, lab fees, laundry, and social events are extra. Financial aid exceeding $4,700,000 is currently awarded on a need-only basis to approximately 40 percent of the enrollment. The Hill School subscribes to the School and Student Service for Financial Aid.

Director of Advancement: D. Andrew Brown
Assistant Head for Academics: Ryckman R. Walbridge
Assistant Head for Student Life: Jennifer Lagor
Dean of Students: David Allain
Director of Admission: Tom Eccleston '87
Director of College Advising: Craig Allen
Director of Business Affairs/Treasurer & CFO: Don Silverson
Director of Athletics: Karl Miran

The Hillside School 1983

2697 Brookside Road, Macungie, PA 18062
Tel. 610-967-3701; Fax 610-965-7683
Web Site www.hillsideschool.org; E-mail office@hillsideschool.org

Encompassing Kindergarten through Grade 6, Hillside is a coeducational day school that provides a carefully structured program for 128 students of average to superior ability whose learning disabilities have prevented them from achieving their potential. The School strives to promote attitudes and abilities essential to academic success through remedial, developmental, and accelerated courses designed to meet each student's specific learning needs. Full-time specialists provide support services to students, parents, and faculty, using a team approach to realize goals. Tuition: $17,300. Scholarships are available. Sue M. Straeter, Ed.D., is Head of School. *Middle States Association.*

Holy Ghost Preparatory School   1897

2429 Bristol Pike, Bensalem, PA 19020
Tel. 215-639-2102; Admissions 215-639-0811; Fax 215-639-4225
Web Site www.holyghostprep.org; E-mail rabramson@holyghostprep.org

Now in its second century of educating young men, this designated School of Excellence enrolls 505 young men in Grades 9–12 in an academic and cocurricular program formed by Catholic values and tradition. The School was founded by the Congregation of the Holy Ghost to nurture each boy's unique, God-given gifts and to develop spiritual, academic, and physical growth. Traditionally, 100 percent of graduates are accepted to college, with more than 80 percent receiving scholarships. Sports are offered at three levels; publications, bands, clubs, and a summer program are among the activities. Tuition: $14,900. Financial Aid: $700,000. Ryan T. Abramson '94 is Director of Admissions; Rev. Jeffrey T. Duaime, C.S.Sp. '76, is President; Michael O'Toole is Principal. *Middle States Association.*

Jack M. Barrack Hebrew Academy   1946

272 South Bryn Mawr Avenue, Bryn Mawr, PA 19010
Tel. 610-922-2300; Admission Ext. 2350
Web Site www.jbha.org; E-mail vyoung@jbha.org

JACK M. BARRACK HEBREW ACADEMY

Formerly Akiba Hebrew Academy, this independent, pluralistic, coeducational day school provides a dual curriculum of college preparatory and Jewish studies to 318 students in Grades 6–12. In 2008, Jack M. Barrack Academy moved to state-of-the-art facilities on a 35-acre campus in Bryn Mawr, which includes a fully equipped science wing, cutting-edge technology, a dining commons, and expanded athletic facilities. The academic program is integrated with Jewish studies, Hebrew, and classes designed to enhance understanding of Western traditions and strengthen Jewish identity. Social outreach and service programs develop young people who are spiritually and ethically aware. Activities include student government, publications, varsity sports, and an award-winning drama program. Typically, all graduates are accepted into top four-year institutions in the U.S. and Israel. Barrack alumni, including two Rhodes Scholars, play leading roles in all aspects of society. Tuition: $20,700–$23,700. Vivian Young is Director of Recruitment and Admissions; Dr. Steven M. Brown is Head of School.

The Janus School   1991

205 Lefever Road, Mount Joy, PA 17552-8843
Tel. 717-653-0025; Fax 717-653-0696
Web Site www.thejanusschool.org; E-mail info@thejanusschool.org

The Janus School, a coeducational, college preparatory day school, enrolls 80 students with learning differences in Kindergarten–Grade 12. A dedicated, trained faculty promotes self-confidence and responsibility in an environment designed to foster social, emotional, physical, and intellectual success. Because a unique learning system is devised for each new student, scholars transition easily from elementary to middle school, from middle school to high school, or from high school to college. All students study a traditional liberal arts curriculum with course work in English, math, science, social studies, foreign language, and technology. Time management, organizational, and study skills are also emphasized through 1:1 tutoring. A student-teacher ratio of 4:1 and class sizes of 4–12 allow for personalized attention as students reach their potential. Extracurricular options include the visual and performing arts, sports, and outreach projects. Six-week Summer Program classes develop academic skills and provide a head start for students in their upcoming school year. The 40-acre campus holds a greenhouse, garden, streams, science and computer labs, athletic fields, and a fine arts complex. Tuition: $24,200. Financial aid is available. Robin Payne is Director of Admission; Deborah Kost is Head of School.

La Salle College High School   1858

8605 Cheltenham Avenue, Wyndmoor, PA 19038
Tel. 215-233-2911; Fax 215-233-1418
Web Site www.lschs.org; E-mail admissions@lschs.org

LA SALLE COLLEGE HIGH SCHOOL

Inspired by three centuries of the distinctive spirituality of the Christian Brothers, La Salle College High School educates the whole person, developing young men in their unique talents and strengths. A core program balances academics, athletics, the arts, and community service. Nationally recognized technology, along with state-of-the-art facilities, enhances the School's demanding academic programs. The curriculum includes Advanced Placement courses in 19 subjects, four years of religious studies, and diverse electives. Athletic teams are formed at three levels, and students are also involved in publications, theater, speech and debate, band, chorus, and a variety of voluntary service projects. Tuition: $15,400. Br. James Rieck, FSC, is Director of Admissions; Joseph Marchese is Principal; Br. Richard Kestler, FSC, is President. *Middle States Association.*

Meadowbrook School 1919

1641 Hampton Road, Meadowbrook, PA 19046
Tel. 215-884-3238; Admission Ext. 104; Fax 215-884-9143
Web Site www.themeadowbrookschool.org
E-mail kmosteller@themeadowbrookschool.org

Meadowbrook School is a coeducational, nonsectarian day school enrolling 130 students in PreKindergarten through Grade 6. Located on a beautiful 15-acre campus, the School offers strong basics, enrichment, and tradition within an intimate, family-oriented setting. The program includes French, art, music, library, computer, science, and physical education. The science center and greenhouse afford opportunities for hands-on learning. The ice-skating and waiter programs encourage mixed-age social situations that are basic to the philosophy. Teams are fielded in soccer, softball, baseball, and field hockey. After-school care is available. Tuition: $10,250–$16,600. Fees: $1100–$1800. Kelly Mosteller is Director of Admissions; David B. Stephens (Hobart and William Smith Colleges, B.S.; Syracuse University, M.S.) was appointed Headmaster in 2008.

MMI Preparatory School 1879

154 Centre Street, Freeland, PA 18224
Tel. 570-636-1108; Fax 570-636-0742
Web Site www.mmiprep.org; E-mail mmi@mmiprep.org

MMI Preparatory School was founded in 1879 by Eckley B. Coxe as the Industrial School for Miners and Mechanics. Today, the School's mission is to provide dedicated area students with a comprehensive and inspiring college preparatory program that maximizes each individual's academic, social, and character potential in readiness for success in college and beyond. MMI's curriculum offers a challenging and rigorous framework that blends the basics of traditional education with the advanced instruction needed to equip students for the demands of future learning. The current enrollment is 251 young men and women in Grades 6–12. Student Council, special-interest clubs, and 13 interscholastic teams comprise the School's extracurricular offerings. Every student must perform annually in a public speaking Assembly and in an Open House project for public exhibition. A summer program is available. Tuition: $8895–$11,775. Financial Aid: $849,000. Kim McNulty is Director of Admissions; Thomas G. Hood (United States Military Academy, B.S.; Rensselaer Polytechnic Institute, M.S.) is President. *Middle States Association.*

Montgomery School 1915

1141 Kimberton Road, Chester Springs, PA 19425
Tel. 610-827-7222; Fax 610-827-7639
Web Site www.montgomeryschool.org
E-mail tmorrison@montgomeryschool.org

Montgomery School is an independent, coeducational day school serving 310 students in Prekindergarten through Grade 8. The School is dedicated to the development of each child in mind and body through academics, fine and performing arts, and athletics in an enriching cultural and physical environment. Montgomery School is equally committed to the development of each child's character, emphasizing integrity, respect, responsibility, and service to others. Students benefit from small classes and an atmosphere that encourages intellectual curiosity and builds self-confidence. Tuition: $9675–$21,475. Tearson W. Morrison is Director of Admission; Kevin R. Conklin is Head of School.

Moravian Academy 1742

Lower School: 422 Heckewelder Place, Bethlehem, PA 18018
Tel. 610-868-8571; Fax 610-868-9319
Middle School: 11 West Market Street, Bethlehem, PA 18018
Tel. 610-866-6677; Fax 610-866-6337
Upper School: 4313 Green Pond Road, Bethlehem, PA 18020
Tel. 610-691-1600; Fax 610-691-3354
Web Site www.moravianacademy.org

Moravian academy in Bethlehem, Pennsylvania, is a coeducational college preparatory school enrolling day students in Prekindergarten through Grade 12 on two campuses. Bethlehem and the greater Lehigh Valley (population 550,000) provide students with many educational resources including six area colleges. The community supports an art museum, a symphony orchestra, several historic museums, a repertory theater company, and community theater groups. The annual Bach Festival and Musikfest are special yearly events. Bethlehem is 50 miles from Philadelphia, 90 miles from New York, and 200 miles from Washington, D.C.

MORAVIAN ACADEMY

The Academy continues the educational commitment begun in 1742 by Countess Benigna von Zinzendorf and the early Moravian colonists. The school believes that "excellence is achieved when the needs of the whole child—body, mind, and spirit—are met." It seeks to provide a strong academic program for all students.

A nonprofit institution, the Academy is governed by a Board of Trustees, which meets quarterly.

Moravian Academy is a member of the Pennsylvania Association of Independent Schools, the National Association of Independent Schools, the Association of Delaware Valley Independent Schools, and the Council for Spiritual and Ethical Education among other organizations. It is accredited by the Middle States Association of Colleges and Schools and the Pennsylvania Association of Independent Schools.

THE CAMPUS. The buildings of the historic Lower School campus for Prekindergarten–Grade 5 form a blend of past and present. They include the Old Chapel, a simple colonial structure built in 1751; the Main Building (1857), containing administrative offices, a library, classrooms, science room, art room, and a nurse's room; the Helen de Schweinitz Building; the Gymnasium; the Devey Building, containing Kindergarten classrooms and the Lower School dining room; and the Christian Education Building, a multipurpose building with an auditorium and classrooms used cooperatively by the school and the nearby Central Moravian Church. The Middle School (Grades 6–8) is housed in two buildings, which include classrooms, two computer labs and a science laboratory, a library, a cafetorium, a gymnasium, and administrative offices.

The 120-acre Upper School (Grades 9–12) campus includes a pond, playing fields, tennis courts, and an outdoor swimming pool. Snyder House (1928) contains administrative offices, classrooms, and the music room. Art and photography studios are located in the Couch Arts Center. Walter Hall provides classrooms, administrative offices, lounges, an auditorium, a gymnasium, a library, a computer lab, and the dining room and kitchen. Science laboratories are located in the Heath House complex. A woodworking studio was completed in the spring of 2007. Benigna House and the Cottage are faculty/administrative residences.

THE FACULTY. George N. King, Jr., was appointed Headmaster in July 2007. He previously served as Head of Wooster School in Danbury, Connecticut. Mr. King received his B.A. from Murray State University in Kentucky and his Master of Science in Jazz Studies from the New England Conservatory of Music.

MORAVIAN ACADEMY

On the Academy faculty are 84 full-time teachers. All faculty members hold baccalaureate degrees and many have earned graduate degrees from such colleges and universities as Bucknell, Columbia, Dartmouth, Lehigh, Middlebury, Purdue, Temple, Villanova, and the Universities of Oxford (England) and Pennsylvania. There are also 16 part-time instructors.

A nurse is on staff for each division. Three hospitals are within a 15-minute drive of the school.

STUDENT BODY. In 2009–10, Moravian Academy enrolled 774 students, including 304 in the Lower School and 186 in the Middle School. In the Upper School, there are 284 students as follows: 70 in Grade 9, 67 in Grade 10, 70 in Grade 11, and 77 in Grade 12. The majority of the students are from Pennsylvania, but New Jersey is also represented.

ACADEMIC PROGRAM. The school year, from late August through early June, includes holiday recesses at Thanksgiving, Christmas, and Easter as well as a spring vacation. Classes are held five days a week in a schedule that varies according to grade level; the Upper School day, from 8:00 A.M. to 3:15 P.M., is divided into eight periods, with early dismissal on Thursday. A weekly chapel service is held.

The student-faculty ratio is 9:1. Generally, class sections range from 14 to 18 students. Supervised study halls are held regularly in the Middle and Upper Schools. Grades and reports are sent to parents regularly throughout the school year.

Lower School children are encouraged to develop sound work patterns and desirable social attitudes. In addition to traditional instruction, the program offers computers, French and Spanish, Rosetta Stone language offerings beginning in Grade 1, a vocal and instrumental music program using Suzuki techniques, art, a physical fitness program, and opportunities for creative play.

The Middle School curriculum includes English, French, Spanish, Latin, social studies, mathematics, science, music, instrumental music, art, drama, health, physical education, activity period, and sports program. The program is designed to reinforce basic learning and to provide opportunities for enrichment. An Advisory Program and Second Step Program are part of the Middle School experience. Some students serve on the Student Forum.

Minimum requirements for the diploma are four years of English; three years of a foreign language; Ancient History, World History, American History, World Religions; Algebra I–II, Geometry; Biology, Chemistry, and one other laboratory science; Music, Art; Physical Education; Health; and Community Service. Seniors must also participate in a post-term experience that focuses on community service and career exploration. Other Upper School courses include Twentieth Century Literature, British Literature, American Nonfiction, Drama, Film, Poetry; French I–V, Spanish I–V, Chinese I–III; Law, European History (Honors); Trigonometry, PreCalculus, Calculus, Probability and Statistics; Chemistry Honors, Physics and Advanced Physics Honors, Biology, Advanced Biology Honors, Ecology; and Introduction to Theatre, Chorale, MA Chamber Singers, Orchestra, Jazz Band, Bell Choir, Construction of Music, Photography, Portfolio Preparation, and Introduction to Woodworking. Attendance at weekly chapel services is also required.

Independent study is encouraged for superior students, and Advanced Placement study is offered in Contemporary Literature, Drama, Poetry, British Literature, French, Spanish, Advanced Chemistry, United States History, U.S. Government and Politics, and Calculus.

MORAVIAN ACADEMY

In 2009, 70 graduates were accepted at four-year colleges. Among the colleges and universities they are attending are Boston University, Bucknell, Colgate, Cornell, Drexel, Lehigh, New York University, Princeton, Stevens Institute of Technology, Swarthmore, Vassar, Wellesley, and the University of Pennsylvania.

STUDENT ACTIVITIES. The Student Council, consisting of officers, class representatives, and a faculty adviser, shares in decisions that concern student activities, privileges, and behavior. The Chorale, Instrumental Ensemble, and Drama groups present several performances each year. There is a newspaper, yearbook, and a literary magazine. Current groups include the Model United Nations, Model Congress, Pennsylvania Junior Academy of Science, Scholastic Scrimmage, Moravian Students for an Inclusive Community, and Ski, Environmental, International, and Photography Clubs. The school has a chapter of The Cum Laude Society.

Students at every level engage in community service. Many students work for local civic, church, and charitable organizations.

MORAVIAN ACADEMY

Varsity teams compete in soccer, basketball, field hockey, softball, cross-country, lacrosse, tennis, baseball, swimming, and golf.

The school sponsors dances, picnics, informal parties, and camping trips.

ADMISSION AND COSTS. Moravian Academy accepts boys and girls of high ability and potential. In the Upper School, students are admitted in Grades 9–11. A personal interview is required for all applicants. Applicants must supply a transcript from the current school and take school-administered tests. Upper School candidates also submit a formal application with four recommendations and a writing sample. Although admissions are normally completed by May, applications may be considered later if space is available.

In 2009–10, the comprehensive fee ranges from $8820 in Prekindergarten to $20,450 for students in Grades 9–12. The comprehensive fee includes all tuition, local field trips, and Kindergarten snacks. The dining room fee ranges from $670 to $1070 for lunch. Financial aid in the amount of $1,600,000 is awarded on the basis of need. Moravian Academy subscribes to the School and Student Service for Financial Aid and offers tuition insurance and a tuition payment plan.

Assistant Head: Ann S. Mindler
Director of Upper School: Carlton P. Chandler
Director of Middle School: Robert A. Bovee
Director of Lower School: Ella Jane Kunkle
Directors of Admissions: Daniel Axford (Upper School),
   Christine L. Murphy (Middle School) & Ingrid Gerber
   (Lower School)
Director of Academic Counseling: Marilyn A. Albarelli (Upper
   School)
Dean of Students: David Connors (Upper School)
Chief Financial Officer: John F. Weber
Director of Athletics: James Tiernan

Newtown Friends School   1948

1450 Newtown-Langhorne Road, Newtown, PA 18940-0848
Tel. 215-968-2225; Admissions Ext. 236; Fax 215-968-9346
Web Site www.newtownfriends.org
E-mail rniszczak@newtownfriends.org

Newtown Friends School is a day school enrolling 318 girls and boys in Pre-Kindergarten–Grade 8. Founded by the Newtown

Monthly Meeting of the Religious Society of Friends, the School strives to provide a strong academic program that emphasizes critical and intellectual inquiry while fostering each student's sense of social responsibility. Art, music, computer instruction, and sports are integral to the curriculum. Students are involved in community service and participate in an intergenerational program with nearby Pennswood Village. Camping, field trips, and activities enrich the program. Tuition: $11,400–$15,600. Financial Aid: $452,000. Rebecca A. Niszczak is Director of Admissions; Steven R. Nierenberg (Earlham College, B.A.; Temple University, M.Ed.) is Head of School.

Rosemont School of the Holy Child   1949

1344 Montgomery Avenue, Rosemont, PA 19010
Tel. 610-922-1000; Admissions 610-922-1010; Fax 610-922-1030
Web Site www.rosemontschool.org; E-mail info@rosemontschool.org

ROSEMONT SCHOOL OF THE HOLY CHILD

Founded by the Society of the Holy Child Jesus, Rosemont School of the Holy Child is an independent, coeducational day school in the Catholic tradition, enrolling 323 students in Nursery–Grade 8. RSHC seeks to develop the whole child by combining vigorous intellectual and physical growth with sound religious training. Art, computers, music, Latin, physical education, religion, Spanish, and science enhance the traditional curriculum. Early Childhood Center programs prepare children for the Lower and Middle School curricula. Spanish begins in PreKindergarten. Sports, musical recitals, clubs, and the annual school play are among the activities. From its founding, RSHC students have learned together in an environment informed by Christian values and by the high ideals of a liberal arts education. Children are taught with individual learning styles and needs taken into consideration. Students develop leadership skills early on and thrive in a family-oriented culture where Rosemont's philosophy is summarized in its vision statement: "Nurturing Excellence in a Joyful Catholic Community." Summer camp programs with various activities for all age groups are offered. Tuition: $7,215–$17,395. Financial Aid: $450,000. Sr. Mary Broderick, SHCJ, is Head of School; Jeanne Marie Blair is Director of Admissions.

Saint Basil Academy   1931

711 Fox Chase Road, Jenkintown, PA 19046
Tel. 215-885-3771; Admissions 215-885-6952; Fax 215-885-4025
Web Site www.stbasilacademy.org
E-mail admissions@stbasilacademy.org

Enrolling 410 day girls of diverse backgrounds in Grades 9–12, Saint Basil Academy, founded by the Sisters of Saint Basil the Great, is affiliated with the Byzantine Ukrainian Catholic Church and maintains its heritage through liturgies and language offerings. Within a community of faith, students undertake a college preparatory program that includes Advanced

Placement courses, business and computer studies, music, and art. Students may also take courses at Manor College. Activities include Student Council, community service, language and drama clubs, publications, and athletics. Tuition: $9300–$9600. Academic Scholarships & Financial Aid: $140,000. Mrs. Maureen McKeown Walsh is Director of Admissions; Sr. Carla Hernández, OSBM, is Principal. *Middle States Association.*

St. Joseph's Preparatory School   1851

1733 Girard Avenue, Philadelphia, PA 19130
Tel. 215-978-1950; Admission Ext. 1958; Fax 215-765-1710
Web Site www.sjprep.org; E-mail jzazyczny@sjprep.org

St. Joseph's Prep, a Catholic high school in the Jesuit tradition, serves 980 young men from many religious, racial, and ethnic backgrounds. The School is dedicated to educating "the whole man," nurturing the moral, academic, spiritual, and social growth of each student. All boys take part in liturgies, retreats, and community service as a means of developing character and commitment to others. The college preparatory curriculum includes Advanced Placement courses in 17 areas. Students are involved in school government, publications, music and drama, and 14 interscholastic sports. Summer school and financial aid are available. Tuition: $16,600. Jason Zazyczny is Director of Admission; Rev. George W. Bur, S.J., is President; Mr. Michael Gomez is Principal. *Middle States Association.*

St. Peter's School   1834

319 Lombard Street, Philadelphia, PA 19147
Tel. 215-925-3963; Fax 215-925-3351
Web Site www.st-peters-school.org
E-mail bmunsterteiger@st-peters-school.org

This multidenominational day school enrolls 219 boys and girls from diverse backgrounds in Preschool–Grade 8. Within a safe, nurturing environment, students at St. Peter's School are encouraged to experience the joys of childhood while developing positive values and expanding their knowledge. Acquisition and mastery of strong skills in reading, language, and math are emphasized along with development of children's confidence in their thinking, creativity, and decision-making abilities. French instruction begins in Preschool; computer studies begin in Kindergarten. Field trips, music, community service, physical education, and the arts enrich classroom learning. Sports, handbell chorus, and an art and literary magazine are among the activities. Thirty percent of students receive need-based financial aid. Tuition: $14,425–$19,475. Brit Munsterteiger is Director of Admissions; David J. Costello is Head of School.

Shady Side Academy   1883

423 Fox Chapel Road, Pittsburgh, PA 15238
Tel. 412-968-3000; Admission 412-968-3206; Fax 412-968-3213
Web Site www.shadysideacademy.org
E-mail admissions@shadysideacademy.org

Shady Side Academy is a coeducational, independent school serving 950 students in Pre-kindergarten through Grade 12 across three unique campuses. At all levels of the Shady Side Academy experience, students are offered academic and personal growth opportunities and supported by a committed, talented, and caring faculty. At the Junior School (PK–5), located in Point Breeze, the curriculum is guided by the philosophy of the Responsive Classroom, focusing on interdisciplinary teaching and learning through play and investigation. At the Middle School (Grades 6–8), located in Fox Chapel, students are encouraged to take on greater personal responsibility in their learning and to delve deeper into their individual strengths and abilities. At the Senior School (Grades 9–12), also in Fox Chapel,

students further develop and refine critical thinking, writing, and analytical skills that distinguish them in the college search. A five-day boarding program is also available for Grades 9–12. Shady Side Academy enjoys virtually a 100 percent college placement. Summer programs are available. Tuition: $13,850–$23,900. Boarding Fee: $9625. Katherine H. Mihm is Director of Enrollment Management; Thomas N. Southard is President. *Middle States Association.*

The Shipley School   1894

814 Yarrow Street, Bryn Mawr, PA 19010-3598
Tel. 610-525-4300; Admissions Ext. 4118; Fax 610-525-5082
Web Site www.shipleyschool.org; E-mail admit@shipleyschool.org

THE SHIPLEY SCHOOL

Now in its 116th year, Shipley is a coeducational, college preparatory school located across the street from Bryn Mawr College. With over 850 students, Shipley remains committed to educational excellence and to developing in students a "love of learning and a compassionate participation in the world." Honors courses are offered in 18 subjects. Foreign language study begins with French in Grade 2 and Spanish in Grade 5 and later includes the study of Latin and/or Mandarin, a new offering in the 2009–10 school year. Athletics are required in Middle School and strongly encouraged in Upper School. Community service is required for graduation. Graduates attend a wide variety of excellent colleges and universities. Approximately 20–25 percent of students receive financial aid. Tuition: $19,975–$27,950. Financial Aid: $3,450,000. Jennifer R. Biehn is Director of Admissions; Steven S. Piltch (Harvard, Ed.D.) is Head of School.

Springside School   1879

8000 Cherokee Street, Philadelphia, PA 19118
Tel. 215-247-7200; Admissions 215-247-7007; Fax 215-247-7308
Web Site www.springside.org; E-mail admissions@springside.org

The oldest girls' school in Philadelphia, Springside is a college preparatory school enrolling 665 students in Pre-Kindergarten–Grade 12, with a coeducational program with Chestnut Hill Academy in the Upper School. Springside offers an outstanding academic program and the advantages of small classes and individual attention. One-third of recent graduates have earned National Merit recognition. A rich extracurricular program includes 14 interscholastic sports, state-of-the-art technology, and an extensive variety of courses in the visual and performing arts, including multimedia digital production. Early Bird and After-School programs are available. Tuition: $15,900–$24,650. Financial Aid: $2,100,000. Peggy Klein Mandell '69 (Lower School) and Elizabeth Brode Harris '91 (Middle/Upper Schools) are Directors of Admissions; Dr. Priscilla G. Sands (University of Pennsylvania, Ed.D.) is Head of School.

The Swain School   1929

1100 South 24th Street, Allentown, PA 18103
Tel. 610-433-4542; Fax 610-433-8280
Web Site www.swain.org

Swain is a coeducational, independent day school enrolling 315 students ages 3 through Grade 8. The Swain School is a vibrant community that strives to inspire students to achieve academic excellence, develop a strong sense of character, and act responsibly in a changing world. Swain empowers children to build confidence, explore knowledge, and work collaboratively in a diverse and safe environment. The 11-year program includes the study of core subjects, enriched with experiences in the arts (visual, music, theater), library, technology, physical education, Latin, and Spanish. The "no-cut" athletics program begins in Grade 5, and there is a comprehensive character education program. The physical plant, housed on 20 wooded acres in the Lehigh Valley, includes a full complement of classrooms, science labs, full-size gym/performing arts center, two athletic fields, common areas, and an art gallery. Tuition: $5814–$16,130. Financial Aid: $850,000. Leah Papp is Director of Admissions; Todd P. Stansbery, M.A., was appointed Head of School in 2006.

Valley School of Ligonier   1947

Box 616, Ligonier, PA 15658
Tel. 724-238-6652; Fax 724-238-6838
Web Site www.valleyschoolofligonier.org
E-mail mkennedy@valleyschoolofligonier.org

Valley School of Ligonier, founded by Mrs. Richard King Mellon as an independent, elementary day school, enrolls 210 boys and girls in Kindergarten–Grade 9. The School aims to build the strong academic foundation necessary to future scholastic success and personal fulfillment and to maintain a disciplined but friendly atmosphere in which energy and hard work can be productive. The traditional curriculum includes art, computer, music, physical education, and science for all grades. French begins in Grade 1, and Latin and Spanish begin in Grade 6. The School sponsors a summer day camp. Tuition: $10,900. Financial Aid: $466,042. Johnette DeRose is Admission Director; Clair Ward is Head of School.

William Penn Charter School   1689

3000 West School House Lane, Philadelphia, PA 19144
Tel. 215-844-3460; Admissions Ext. 103; Fax 215-843-3939
Web Site www.penncharter.com; E-mail sbonnie@penncharter.com

This Quaker-affiliated, coeducational day school, chartered by William Penn, has an enrollment of 940 students in Pre-Kindergarten–Grade 12. The School strives to inspire students to think independently and to realize their full potential. A college preparatory curriculum is followed, and athletics, instrumental music, drama, chorus, service activities, and fine arts are offered as extracurricular activities. Summer courses are also available. Tuition: $15,000–$24,380. Extras: $1100–$3200. Financial Aid: $4,900,000. Dr. Stephen A. Bonnie is Director of Admissions; Dr. Darryl J. Ford (Villanova, B.A., B.S.; University of Chicago, M.A., Ph.D.) is Head of School. *Middle States Association.*

The Wyndcroft School   1918

1395 Wilson Street, Pottstown, PA 19464
Tel. 610-326-0544; Admission Ext. 113; Fax 610-326-9931
Web Site www.wyndcroft.org; E-mail mschmidt@wyndcroft.org

Wyndcroft School, a coeducational, independent day school with 90 years of commitment to academic excellence, enrolls 250 students in Early Childhood (age 3) through Grade 8. The mission of the School is to provide a traditional and challenging academic program emphasizing basic skills in a secure and friendly environment. The curriculum includes French in Pre-School–Grade 8, Latin in Grades 5–8, and competitive sports in Grades 6–8. Special-area classes include art, music, library, computer, health, and physical education. Extended-day and after-school care are available. Tuition: $4460–$15,960. Maureen K. Schmidt is Director of Admission; Gail L. Wolter is Assistant Head of School; Kathleen E. Wunner, Ph.D., is Head of School.

Wyoming Seminary   1844

Sprague Avenue, Kingston, PA 18704
Tel. 570-270-2100; Admissions 570-270-2160; Fax 570-270-2191
Web Site www.wyomingseminary.org
E-mail admission@wyomingseminary.org

WYOMING SEMINARY in Kingston, Pennsylvania, is a coeducational, college preparatory school enrolling day students in Preschool–Grade 12 and boarding students in Grades 9–12 and a postgraduate year. The Lower School campus is located in Forty Fort, approximately 3 miles from the Upper School campus. Kingston (population 14,500) is located in the Wyoming Valley (area population 353,000), along the banks of the Susquehanna River. Kingston is a 2.5-hour drive from New York City, 2.25 hours from Philadelphia, and 4 hours from the District of Columbia. The Wilkes-Barre/Scranton International Airport (AVP), 20 minutes from campus, is served by major airlines; bus service from Wilkes-Barre is also available. Five colleges, the Northeastern Pennsylvania Philharmonic, Steamtown National Historic Park, and the Kirby Center for the Performing Arts provide cultural opportunities. Skiing, biking, hiking, whitewater rafting in nearby state parks, and the Yankees AAA farm club baseball games are popular weekend activities.

WYOMING SEMINARY

Wyoming Seminary was founded in 1844 by leaders of the Methodist church to "prepare students for the active duties of life—for a course of professional or collegiate studies, or any degree of collegiate advancement." Today, Wyoming Seminary students and teachers challenge themselves and each other to reach their academic and personal goals. Students learn to manage their time, write and speak clearly and effectively, study efficiently, and work with others to achieve a common goal.

Wyoming Seminary is directed by a Board of Trustees elected by the Board itself, the Alumni Association, and the Wyoming Annual Conference of the United Methodist Church. Endowment for general operation and scholarships is valued at over $39,047,000. Wyoming Seminary is accredited by the Middle States Association of Colleges and Schools; it is approved by the University Senate of the United Methodist Church; and it is a member of the National Association of Independent Schools, among numerous professional affiliations.

THE CAMPUS. Wyoming Seminary Upper School occupies a 22-acre main campus including academic, athletic, performing arts, and residential facilities. Nesbitt Hall contains classrooms, state-of-the-art science laboratories, art studios, an art gallery, a darkroom, and a dance studio. Housed in the Stettler Learning Resources Center are the admission offices, a conference area, and the Kirby Library, with more than 20,000 volumes, CD-ROM towers, seminar rooms, and audiovisual facilities.

The Buckingham Performing Arts Center houses a 460-seat auditorium with high-tech stage equipment, music practice rooms and rehearsal studios, and a dramatics practice area and scenery construction shop. The Great Hall provides additional performance and classroom space.

Swetland, Fleck, and Darte Halls, erected in 1853, contain the girls' residence hall, a boys' residence hall, faculty quarters, a dining hall, and lounges. Carpenter Hall is a boys' dormitory with faculty apartments.

Carpenter Athletic Center houses a large gymnasium, a four-lane swimming pool, and exercise/weight and wrestling rooms. The adjoining Pettebone-Dickson Student Center incorporates an all-purpose gymnasium, the Antinnes Fitness Center, a climbing wall, a game room, lounge, a club room and a snack bar. Nesbitt Memorial Stadium is equipped with a grandstand, a football field, a baseball diamond, four tennis courts, and a fieldhouse. An artificial-turf field was added in 2006 for field hockey and lacrosse, and the new six-court tennis center opened in 2009.

WYOMING SEMINARY

The Lower School (Age 3–Grade 8), on 6.5 acres, consists of two buildings. A main building provides classrooms, administrative offices, a gymnasium, the Sordoni Library, containing 12,500 volumes, the Amato Auditorium, and a cafeteria. Three-year-olds meet in the smaller "Little White House." Athletic fields and a playground surround the school.

THE FACULTY. Dr. Kip P. Nygren was appointed the 11th President of Wyoming Seminary in July 2007. He holds a Ph.D. in Aerospace Engineering from Georgia Institute of Technology, a master's in Aeronautics & Astronautics from Stanford Univer-

sity, a master's in Industrial Engineering from Stanford University, and a bachelor's in General Engineering from the U.S. Military Academy. Prior to working at Sem, Dr. Nygren was Professor and Head of the Department of Civil & Mechanical Engineering at the U.S. Military Academy. He retired from the Army in 2007 and was advanced to the rank of Brigadier General.

WYOMING SEMINARY

The Upper School teaching faculty includes 25 women and 37 men; two-thirds of the faculty live on campus. There are 40 women and 8 men at the Lower School. Faculty hold baccalaureate and graduate degrees representing study at Antioch University, Bowdoin College, Brown, Bucknell, Catholic University, Columbia, Drexel, Emory University, Franklin and Marshall, Georgia Institute of Technology, Hamilton, Lehigh, Middlebury, Pennsylvania State, Purdue University, St. Joseph's, St. Lawrence, Smith, Stanford, State University of New York (Albany, Cortland), Susquehanna, Syracuse, Tulane, United States Military Academy, Villanova, Virginia Polytechnic, Washington and Lee, Wesleyan, Westminster Choir College, Williams College, Yale, and the Universities of California (San Diego), Delaware, Massachusetts, Michigan, Pennsylvania, and Virginia.

The infirmary facilities are staffed by two nurses, and a doctor is on call. Wilkes-Barre General Hospital is 5 minutes away.

STUDENT BODY. In 2009–10, Wyoming Seminary Lower School enrolled 340 day students in Pre-School–Grade 8. The Upper School enrolled 189 boarders and 251 day students.

Students came from 15 states and 20 foreign countries.

ACADEMIC PROGRAM. The school year, from September to late May, includes three terms, Thanksgiving, Christmas, and spring vacations, and long weekends at midterm. Classes meet five days per week, with an average of 12–14 students. A typical daily schedule in the Upper School (from 8:00 A.M. to 3:30 P.M.) includes four 45-minute class periods in the morning, lunch, three classes in the afternoon, and a conference period in addition to weekly school meetings and chapel. Students—with the exception of juniors, seniors, postgraduates, and honor students—are expected to attend supervised study hall during free periods. In addition, boarding students study in their rooms from 7:30 until 9:50 P.M. Sunday through Thursday. Faculty members give individual assistance as needed. Grades are distributed six times a year; advisors keep families apprised of academic progress throughout the year. All students in Grades 9–12 have individual phone and e-mail accounts, and every dorm room and classroom has Internet access.

To graduate, a student must accumulate a minimum of 19.33 credits; students earn .33 credit for a term course or 1 credit for a full-year course. Specific requirements are English 4, mathematics 3, foreign language 3, history/social science 3, laboratory science 3, physical education 4, health .33, religion

.33, music history .33, art history .33, public speaking .33, and computer science .33.

The curriculum offers a variety of one-term, two-term, and full-year courses. Typical year courses or three-term sequences are freshman and sophomore English; French I–IV, Latin I–IV, Spanish I–IV, Russian I–IV; World Civilizations, U.S. History; Algebra I–II, Geometry, Advanced Algebra/Trig, Precalculus, Calculus AB&BC; Biology, Chemistry, Physics; and Drawing and Design. Among the term courses are Shakespeare, Women and Literature, Greek Legacy, Creative and Expository Writing, Evil in Literature, Contemporary Drama, Public Speaking; 13 studio art electives; Art History, Masterpieces of Music; Contemporary American History, Problems of Democracy, World War II, Mid-East History, Asian History, Economics, Psychology, World Religions; Discrete Mathematics; Marine Biology, Ecology; Basic Computer Programming; Health; and Bible.

Twenty-six Advanced Placement courses are available in all disciplines including French, Latin, Russian, Spanish, American Seminar, European History, Government, Biology, Chemistry, Physics, Environmental Science, Calculus, Statistics, Computer Science, Art/Music History, Music Theory, and Studio Art.

Qualified students may enroll in advanced courses at nearby Wilkes University or King's College. With faculty approval, juniors and seniors may pursue independent study programs for one or more terms.

In 2009, 100 percent of the graduates entered college. Among the colleges accepting recent graduates are American University, Boston College, Brown, Carnegie Mellon, Colby, College of William and Mary, Duke, Georgetown, Hampshire, Johns Hopkins, Lafayette, Lehigh, New York University, Pennsylvania State, Smith, Syracuse, United States Military Academy, United States Naval Academy, Villanova, Wesleyan, Yale, and the Universities of California, Pennsylvania, and Pittsburgh.

STUDENT ACTIVITIES. The Seminary Upper School Government—composed of students, faculty, and administrators—is responsible for many nonacademic aspects of school life. There are four standing committees: spirit, activities, assemblies and programs, and finance.

Student activities include Peer Group, *The Wyoming* (yearbook), *The Opinator* (newspaper), *Clio's Camera* (online history journal), Chorale and Madrigal Singers, Drama, Dance, International Club, "W" Club, Blue Key, Mock Trial, Model United Nations, Rocket Club, Jazz Band, and Orchestra. Three plays are produced each year, and the chorus presents both formal and informal concerts. Involvement in community service is required.

Weekend activities take advantage of the school's proximity to major cities' sporting and cultural events as well as the hiking, skiing, and outdoor opportunities available in the Pocono Mountains.

Wyoming Seminary varsity and junior varsity athletic teams compete in the PIAA (Pennsylvania Interscholastic Athletic Association) and with independent schools in New York, New Jersey, Connecticut, and Pennsylvania. Sports for boys are football, basketball, tennis, lacrosse, baseball, wrestling, golf, ice hockey, soccer, cross-country, and swimming. Girls compete in field hockey, basketball, swimming, golf, softball, cross-country, ice hockey, lacrosse, soccer, and tennis.

ADMISSION AND COSTS. Wyoming Seminary seeks students who will challenge themselves and their peers to reach academic and personal goals. All applicants must submit school transcripts, letters of recommendation, and the application form, which includes a writing sample. Candidates should submit SSAT (Secondary School Admission Test) results; those applying for Grade 12 or the postgraduate year must submit SAT scores. An interview on campus is required. New students are accepted at all grade levels; late or midyear enrollment is sometimes possible. The application fee is $75 for domestic students and $100 for international students.

In 2009–10, Upper School tuition is $39,375 for boarding students and $19,900 for day students. Additional expenses include allowances, books, athletic clothing, a technology fee, and travel. A tuition payment plan is offered. Need-based financial aid is available. Presently, Wyoming Seminary awards about $6,000,000 in aid to 50 percent of all students.

President: Kip P. Nygren, Ph.D.
Dean: John Gordon
Dean of Admission: John R. Eidam
Director of Upper School Admission: David Damico
Vice President of Advancement: John H. Shafer
Director of Development: A. Kay Young
Director of College Guidance: Harvie Ruggles
Business Manager: John T. Morris
Director of Athletics: Karen Klassner

Wyoming Seminary 1807

Preschool–Grade 8: 1560 Wyoming Avenue, Forty Fort, PA 18704
Tel. 570-718-6600; Admissions 570-718-6610; Fax 570-718-6649
Web Site www.wyomingseminary.org
E-mail admission@wyomingseminary.org

Wyoming Seminary's Lower School is an elementary day school enrolling 337 boys and girls in Preschool–Grade 8. The school's programs are child-centered, addressing individual learning styles in an environment that focuses on developing lifelong learning skills. Art, music, computer science, and athletic programs are a vital part of the curriculum. Students are introduced to the study of French and Spanish in Kindergarten; Latin is offered in Grades 7–8. Tuition: $4800–$16,150. Dawn Leas is Director of Admission; Dr. Kip P. Nygren (U.S. Military Academy, B.S.; Stanford University, M.S.; Georgia Institute of Technology, Ph.D.) is President; Mary Kolessar (King's College, B.S.; Misericordia University, M.S.) is Middle School Dean; Dr. Claire Hornung (Smith College, B.S., M.Ed.; Lehigh University, Ed.D.) is Primary Dean.

RHODE ISLAND

The Gordon School   1910

45 Maxfield Avenue, East Providence, RI 02914
Tel. 401-434-3833; Fax 401-431-0320
Web Site www.gordonschool.org; E-mail admission@gordonschool.org

This coeducational, independent day school enrolling 409 students in Nursery to Grade 8 offers a rigorous, integrated, and multicultural curriculum. The Gordon School encourages each student to develop as an individual, to be respectful of others, to work cooperatively, to contribute to the community, and to excel academically. Students learn by exploring connections, questioning assumptions, seeking new perspectives, and creating solutions. The School aims to produce confident leaders, creative thinkers, problem solvers, and involved citizens. The arts, music, sports, and a visiting-artist program are integral to the curriculum. Tuition: $7320–$23,100. Financial Aid: $1,000,000. Emily Anderson is Director of Admission; Ralph L. Wales (Harvard, B.A., M.Ed.) is Head of School.

Overbrook Academy   1984

836 Warwick Neck Avenue, Warwick, RI 02889
Tel. 401-737-2850; Fax 401-737-2884
E-mail information@overbrookacademy.org
Web Site www.overbrookacademy.org

OVERBROOK ACADEMY in Warwick, Rhode Island, is a Roman Catholic boarding school enrolling girls from the United States, Europe, and Central and South America in Grades 6 through 9. Warwick (population 85,427), located on Narragansett Bay, is 15 minutes south of Providence and within driving distance of Boston and New York City. The school plans many activities that take advantage of the physical and cultural resources found throughout New England and other parts of the Northeast.

Overbrook Academy was established by the Legion of Christ in Orange, Connecticut, in 1984 and moved to Dallas, Texas, for two years before relocating to its present site in 1991. The school is affiliated with Oak International, a Roman Catholic organization founded in Rome, Italy, in 1969 and committed to the integral formation of young people. It operates schools in Ireland, Switzerland, and the United States, including Everest Academy in Michigan and Oaklawn Academy in Wisconsin.

The harmonious development of each girl's intellectual, human, and spiritual potential is at the core of Overbrook's academic and extracurricular activities. Religious studies, moral training, and spiritual retreats are integral to an Overbrook education, and preparation for the sacrament of Confirmation is offered.

Overbrook Academy is approved by the Rhode Island Department of Education and is a member of The Private Independent School and the official Catholic Directory.

THE CAMPUS. Overbrook Academy occupies a beautiful 90-acre campus of lawns and woodlands with sweeping views of Narragansett Bay. The focal point of the grounds is the imposing Romanesque chapel where the school community comes together for liturgies, celebrations, and other special gatherings. Two dormitory wings accommodate up to 185 girls in triple-occupancy rooms as well as 10–18 adult supervisors. The academic program is carried out in 13 classrooms; a library for student research; science, computer, and language labs; art and music rooms; a 300-seat auditorium for special events such as theater performances, cultural activities, and choir presentations; and an e-mail center.

The Academy's athletic facilities consist of a gymnasium with basketball and volleyball courts and fields for softball and hockey. Swimming, horseback riding, tennis, golf, and figure skating take place off campus.

THE FACULTY. Teachers are carefully selected as educators trained in the philosophy and methods of Oak International.

STUDENT BODY. Overbrook Academy enrolls 185 girls in an environment designed to foster friendship. To ensure personal attention, the student body is divided into sections, each with its own dean and team of assistants. Students come from the United States as well as Canada, Chile, Colombia, France, Guatemala, Italy, Mexico, Spain, and Venezuela. The presence of international students broadens the Overbrook experience with cultural enrichment.

ACADEMIC PROGRAM. The academic year, divided into three terms, begins in early September and extends to early June, with recesses at Christmas and Easter. Classes, enrolling between 15 and 25 students, meet five days a week; the student-teacher ratio is 19:1. Grades are issued five times a year, and personal progress reports are mailed to parents three times a year. Parents may also access academic and medical information through a password-secure page of the school's web site. Upon entering the Academy, each girl is assigned a guidance counselor who provides assistance in academic, spiritual, and personal matters.

On a typical weekday, girls attend classes from 9:00 A.M. to 3:30 P.M. Their classes include an extra emphasis on a foreign language. After classes, students participate in clinics and directed studies.

OVERBROOK ACADEMY

At Overbrook, a broad-based humanities program serves as the cornerstone of the academic curriculum, with an emphasis on the development of strong reading, writing, and language skills across the disciplines. Courses in English are offered to meet the needs of students at introductory, intermediate, and advanced levels of proficiency as well as for native speakers. Girls make use of the Language Laboratory to practice verbal communication skills, while reading classes foster an appreciation for American literature and British classics.

Other specific courses include Science, Physics, Biology, Health; Social Studies, History, Geography, Civics; Mathematics,

Pre-Algebra, Algebra I–II, Computers; Religion, Confirmation Preparation; Spanish for native speakers; and Physical Education.

Following an initial language evaluation, girls may choose to study English, French, or Spanish as a second language at one of three ability levels, and international students are required to take the Test of English as a Foreign Language (TOEFL).

Throughout the year, girls have the opportunity to test their skills in language and mathematics competitions. Students in all English classes are encouraged to participate in regional, state, and national competitions including the Young Author's International Literary Contest, United States National Spelling Bee, and the National Language Arts Olympiad. Academy students have received top recognition for their participation in the Rhode Island Science Fair.

STUDENT ACTIVITIES. Overbrook believes that a balanced, comprehensive extracurricular program is essential to the overall health and well-being of the student. A variety of clinics enables girls to concentrate in an athletic or artistic area of particular interest, and all students are required to participate in two clinics a semester. Among their choices are tennis, swimming, figure skating, horseback riding, ballet, jazz, musical theater, and aerobics. Additionally, there are opportunities to engage in pursuits such as oil painting, piano, photography, etiquette, culinary arts, field hockey, golf, and softball. Girls are also encouraged to volunteer time to worthwhile community service projects both on and off campus.

OVERBROOK ACADEMY

Two trips are offered to the students during Christmas and Easter break. At Christmas, girls may visit Rome, with such highlights planned as a papal audience, Mass at St. Peter's Basilica, and excursions to Assisi, Florence, Tivoli, and Castelgandolfo. The Easter trip to Canada features a stop at Niagara Falls, sightseeing in Toronto, and a visit to the Ontario Science Centre. Other outings are planned to the Providence Theater, Mystic Seaport, downtown Boston, and New York's Radio City Music Hall.

Among the highlights on the school calendar are spiritual retreats, Christmas Pageant, Parents Weekend, Holy Week Activities, and Commencement Awards Ceremony.

ADMISSION AND COSTS. Overbrook Academy welcomes girls of good character and ability whose parents seek a quality education that emphasizes the spiritual, intellectual, and human dimensions of their daughter's natural gifts. Students are admitted to Grades 6 through 9.

In 2009–10, tuition, room, and board are $32,248. Enrollment in the autumn or spring term includes a fee; the tuition, room, and board cost is based on the yearly tuition. Other expenses include a personal allowance, optional travel, and fees for supplementary uniforms and special clinics. Some scholarships are available to meet special needs on an individual basis.

Director: Kristina Piñero
Dean of Studies: Jessica Snell
Director of Admissions: Valerie McGovern
Administrator: Andrea Wisnieski
Director of Development: Marco Rivera

The Pennfield School   1971

Little Slocum Farm, 110 Sandy Point Avenue, Portsmouth, RI 02871
Tel. 401-849-4646; Fax 401-847-6720
Web Site www.pennfield.org; E-mail kburke@pennfield.org

Founded as The New School by teachers, parents, and friends to provide a superior academic education, this country day school, located on 19 acres, enrolls approximately 210 boys and girls in three-year-old Nursery–Class VIII. The sign over The Pennfield School's entry reads "Joy, Understanding, Respect." At Pennfield, children are challenged academically while having fun. Emphasizing concern for the individual, Pennfield aims to develop basic skills, resourcefulness, self-discipline, self-confidence, and responsibility in a supportive environment. Art, Spanish, music, lab science, computer, and physical education begin in Kindergarten and are required through Grade 8. Tuition: $15,345–$17,400. Extras: $260–$645. After-school care from 3:00 to 5:00 P.M. is $6.25 per hour. Financial aid is available. Kathleen M. Burke is Director of Admissions; Robert A. Kelley (Tufts University, B.A., M.A.T.) was appointed Headmaster in 2005.

The Providence Country Day School   1923

660 Waterman Avenue, East Providence, RI 02914-1714
Tel. 401-438-5170; Admissions Ext. 137; Fax 401-435-4514
Web Site www.providencecountryday.org
E-mail admissions@providencecountryday.org

The Providence Country Day School is a college preparatory, coeducational school for approximately 300 students in Grades 5–12. The School draws from over 45 towns in Southeastern New England to create a diverse student body. The School seeks to foster confidence, respect, honesty, intellectual curiosity, and hard work in each child. All students follow a traditional liberal arts curriculum, while older students enjoy AP courses, electives, senior projects, independent study, and opportunities for study abroad. Instruction in reading analytically, writing logically and persuasively, making connections across disciplines, and using technology effectively is emphasized in all grades. An average class size of 12 ensures individualized attention. An array of visual and performing arts classes, including instrumental ensemble classes at the nearby Rhode Island Philharmonic School of Music, are woven into the curriculum. Extracurricular opportunities include athletics, theater, school government, service clubs, Mock Trial, publications, and special-interest clubs. Graduates historically attend the nation's most selective colleges and universities. Tuition: $26,600. James J. Skiff is Assistant Head; Susan M. Haberlandt is Head of School.

St. Michael's Country Day School   1938

180 Rhode Island Avenue, Newport, RI 02840
Tel. 401-849-5970; Admissions Ext. 302; Fax 401-849-7890
Web Site www.stmichaelscountryday.org

Located on a 7-acre campus, St. Michael's is a nondenominational, coeducational school enrolling nearly 240 children in Pre-School–Grade 8. It aims to help students develop a strong, lifetime love of learning. Small classes, a supportive faculty, and a developmentally appropriate curriculum meet the academic needs of the youngest learners as well as those being prepared for the rigorous academic challenges beyond St. Michael's. French, Spanish, computer and science labs, a recently computerized library, a school-based publishing house, and lively music, drama, arts, and athletic programs are available to all students. Tuition: $9950–$19,490. Sally Ann Jenkins is Director of Admissions; Whitney C. Slade (Tufts, B.A.; Harvard, M.Ed.) is Head of School.

The Wheeler School   1889

216 Hope Street, Providence, RI 02906
Tel. 401-421-8100; Fax 401-751-7674
Web Site www.wheelerschool.org

Wheeler, a college preparatory day school enrolling 775 girls and boys in Nursery–Grade 12, aims to provide a diverse academic experience, develop individual talents, and encourage involvement in school and world affairs. The traditional curriculum is enriched by electives, special-interest and cocurricular activities, and various sports. The Hamilton School at Wheeler, enrolling 66 boys and girls in Grades 1–8, serves high-potential, language-disabled students through a structured, multisensory approach applied to reading, spelling, and writing skills. Tuition: Wheeler—$12,360–$25,275; Hamilton—$35,615. Financial Aid: $2,007,786. Jeanette Epstein is Director of Admission; Dan B. Miller (Amherst, B.A.; Harvard, M.A., Ph.D.) is Head of School. *New England Association.*

THE WHEELER SCHOOL

SOUTH CAROLINA

Charleston Collegiate School 1970

2024 Academy Drive, Johns Island, SC 29455-4437
Tel. 843-559-5506; Admission Ext. 224; Fax 843-559-6172
Web Site www.charlestoncollegiate.org
E-mail hburr@charlestoncollegiate.org

Set on a beautiful 30-acre campus in South Carolina's Low Country, Charleston Collegiate School serves 275 boys and girls as day students in Pre-Kindergarten through Grade 12. The enrollment is diverse, including African-Americans, Latinos, and descendants of the island's native and early white settlers. All are united in the desire to prepare for success in higher education and in adult life, able to meet the challenges of an ever-changing world. Now in its 38th year, Charleston Collegiate offers a traditional liberal arts program designed to qualify graduates for admission to four-year institutions nationwide. Advanced Placement courses are available in major subjects. Modern languages, information technology, and opportunities for enrichment in music, art, and drama enhance the core curriculum. The Learning Center provides services and resources to meet the individual needs of learning-different students. Boys and girls compete at varsity and junior varsity levels in nine team sports. Among the activities are service learning, school government, publications, vocal and instrumental music groups, and a variety of special-interest clubs. Tuition: $8300–$13,250. Hacker Burr is Admission Director; J. Robert Shirley, Ph.D., is Headmaster. *Southern Association.*

Charleston Day School 1937

15 Archdale Street, Charleston, SC 29401-1918
Tel. 843-377-0315; Admission 843-722-7791, Ext. 2
Fax 843-720-2143
Web Site www.charlestondayschool.org
E-mail caroline.moore@charlestondayschool.org

Charleston Day School serves 186 boys and girls in Grades 1–8 on an urban campus located in the heart of historic Charleston, South Carolina. Founded in 1937, Charleston Day School provides a rigorous academic experience for its students. The school environment fosters scholarship, integrity, respect, and responsibility. In all grades, a core curriculum is enhanced by French, art, music, and physical education. Students in Grades 5–8 may take Spanish, and students in Grades 7–8 advanced math courses, including Honors Algebra I. Special academic programs, team sports, community service, and fine arts productions enrich learning. After-school programs are available. Tuition: $14,250. Caroline Moore is Director of Admission; Brendan J. O'Shea is Headmaster.

Porter-Gaud School 1867

300 Albemarle Road, Charleston, SC 29407-7593
Tel. 843-556-3620; Admissions 843-402-4775; Fax 843-556-7404
Web Site www.portergaud.edu
E-mail eleanor.hurtes@portergaud.edu

Porter-Gaud School traces its origins to Holy Communion Church Institute, founded in 1867 by an Episcopal priest to educate children orphaned by the Civil War. The present-day Porter-Gaud was formed by the 1964 merger of three earlier schools. While adhering to its Episcopal heritage, Porter-Gaud today welcomes 900 day students from diverse faiths and backgrounds. Its mission is to nurture each student's faith, curiosity, talents, integrity, humanity, and dreams through a dynamic Grades 1–12 college preparatory curriculum. Academic course work centers on the traditional liberal arts and sciences including Latin, three modern languages, and honors and AP courses in all departments. The campus and buildings are designed to create an environment that maximizes the educational experience for both students and faculty. Among the facilities are The Science, Information and Technology Center with science and computer labs and a spacious library. All classrooms are connected to the campus network and the Internet. Students take part in community service, leadership groups, music, drama, debate, interest clubs, and 18 sports. Tuition: $15,180–$17,480. Eleanor W. Hurtes is Director of Admissions; Dr. Christian Proctor is Head of School. *Southern Association.*

Trident Academy 1972

1455 Wakendaw Road, Mount Pleasant, SC 29464
Tel. 843-884-7046; Admissions 843-884-3494; Fax 843-881-8320
Admissions Fax 843-884-1483
Web Site www.tridentacademy.com
E-mail admissions@tridentacademy.com

Trident Academy, providing multisensory education for students with learning disabilities, enrolls approximately 100 day students in Kindergarten–Grade 12. A language-therapy program and a structured, individualized learning environment foster academic and personal development. The High School offers thorough preparation for postsecondary education. Sports, publications, Student Council, and clubs are offered. Participation in athletics or community service is encouraged. A summer day program provides tutoring. Restricted Boarding is offered. Tuition: $23,900. Financial aid is available. Patty Held is Director of Admissions; Joe Ferber (George Washington University, B.A.; American University, M.Ed.) is Headmaster. *Southern Association.*

TENNESSEE

Battle Ground Academy   1889

P.O. Box 1889, Franklin, TN 37065-1889
Tel. 615-794-3501; Admissions 615-567-9014; Fax 615-567-8360
Web Site www.battlegroundacademy.org
E-mail sparrish@battlegroundacademy.org

Located 16 miles south of Nashville, Battle Ground Academy is a college preparatory day school enrolling 980 boys and girls in Kindergarten–Grade 12. By combining the traditions of a 120-year-old institution with progressive academics, students and faculty are provided with a setting to maximize the educational experience. With state-of-the-art technology, including a 1:1 tablet program for upper school students, mobile labs, and SMARTboards, students in each division are given the tools to help them succeed in this technological age. Individual college counseling and personal counseling assist students and their families. Upper school academic offerings include accelerated or Advanced Placement courses in each discipline. Student life is enriched by a broad and diverse range of activities, including required community service. Tuition: $13,040–$15,890. Extras: $300–$600. Need-based Tuition Assistance: $1,200,000. Cathy Irwin is Director of Admissions; Dr. John Griffith (Middlebury College, B.A.; University of Oxford, M.Phil., D.Phil.; Columbia University, M.A.) is Head of School. *Southern Association.*

Brentwood Academy   1969

219 Granny White Pike, Brentwood, TN 37027
Tel. 615-373-0611; Fax 615-377-3709
Web Site www.brentwoodacademy.com
E-mail office@brentwoodacademy.com

Brentwood Academy is a coeducational, college preparatory school dedicated to nurturing and challenging the whole person—body, mind, and spirit—to the glory of God. Located 5 miles south of Nashville on a 49-acre campus, Brentwood Academy serves 780 students in Grades 6–12. Cocurricular activities include the Student Leadership Team, Fellowship of Christian Athletes, Winterim, Big Sisters-Big Brothers for new students, athletics, forensics, drama, chorus, band, Academy Singers, clubs, and publications. A summer program is available. Tuition: $16,500. Financial Aid: $1,010,000. Sue Gering is Director of Admission; Curtis G. Masters (Wheaton, B.A.; University of Puget Sound, M.S.) is Headmaster. *Southern Association.*

Christ Methodist Day School   1958

411 Grove Park, Memphis, TN 38117
Tel. 901-683-6873; Fax 901-761-5759
Web Site www.cmdsmemphis.org; E-mail office@cmdsmemphis.org

Established by Christ United Methodist Church, Christ Methodist Day School enrolls 400 boys and girls in Pre-Kindergarten through Grade 6. The School is committed to the task of helping each child develop to his or her potential academically, physically, socially, emotionally, and spiritually. The traditional curriculum is designed to provide a sound academic foundation supplemented by Bible, gifted education, Spanish, music, physical education, art, and computer studies. A complete recreational sports program, before- and after-school care, and a summer program are also available. The School is a member of the Southern Association of Independent Schools. Tuition: $2729–$9350. Alison Hinson is Admissions Director; Steven T. Jackson (Olivet College, B.A. 1982; University of Virginia, M.Ed. 1987) was appointed Headmaster in 2002. *Southern Association.*

The Ensworth School   1958

Pre-First–8: 211 Ensworth Avenue, Nashville, TN 37205
9–12: 7401 Highway 100, Nashville, TN 37221
Tel. 615-383-0661; Fax 615-269-4840
Web Site www.ensworth.com; E-mail moseleyw@ensworth.com

Ensworth is a coeducational day school enrolling 1030 students in Pre-First–Grade 12. The high school opened in 2004 on a new 127-acre campus. In small classes averaging 16, Ensworth promotes academic excellence and encourages students to be intellectually curious, to be people of integrity, to use their talents to the fullest, and to contribute to society. Programs include a full range of academics including Advanced Placement courses, athletics, visual and performing arts, Chinese, Spanish, Latin, and service learning. Summer programs feature academics, enrichment, sports, and young children's camps. Tuition: $15,720–$19,200. Need-based financial aid is available. Rebekah Capps and Pascha Swett are Admission Directors; William N. Moseley (Lake Forest, B.A.; Columbia Teachers College, M.A.) is Headmaster.

Episcopal School of Knoxville   1994

950 Episcopal School Way, Knoxville, TN 37932
Tel. 865-777-9032; Fax 865-777-9034
Web Site www.esknoxville.org; E-mail secor@esknoxville.org

Episcopal School of Knoxville is an independent elementary/middle school enrolling 292 boys and girls from many faiths in Kindergarten–Grade 8. In the Episcopal tradition, the School offers a challenging academic curriculum underscored by character education, religious studies, and inclusive chapel services and liturgies. Courses emphasize the acquisition of strong skills and an understanding of basic concepts. They include language arts, math, science, and social studies, Middle School Latin, Middle and Lower School French and Spanish, art, music, computer technology on a networked campus, and physical education. Strong extracurricular offerings include a full sports program and interscholastic activities such as Youth Legislature and Destination Imagination. Tuition: $10,875–$11,925. Financial aid is available. Peter Klekamp is Assistant Headmaster and Director of Admissions; James Jay Secor III (Virginia Wesleyan, B.A.; James Madison, M.Ed.) is Headmaster.

Franklin Road Academy   1971

4700 Franklin Road, Nashville, TN 37220
Tel. 615-832-8845; Admissions Ext. 304; Fax 615-834-4137
Web Site www.franklinroadacademy.com
E-mail matthewsc@franklinroadacademy.com

Franklin Road Academy is an independent, Christian, coeducational day school enrolling 862 students in Prekindergarten 4–Grade 12. The school prepares students intellectually for higher levels of education while also providing programs and facilities for their total development. While emphasis is on traditional disciplines, arts, and physical education, students are encouraged to participate in athletics, fine and performing arts, student government, publications, and interest clubs. Tuition: $11,625–$15,675. Jan Marshall and Alison Elliott are Associate Directors of Admissions; Dr. Margaret W. Wade (Vanderbilt, B.A.; Middle Tennessee State, M.Ed.; Peabody College of Vanderbilt University, Ed.D.) was appointed Head of School in 2001. *Southern Association.*

Harding Academy   1971

170 Windsor Drive, Nashville, TN 37205
Tel. 615-356-5510; Fax 615-356-0441
Web Site www.hardingacademy.org
E-mail arnoldb@hardingacademy.org

A nonsectarian school, Harding Academy enrolls 490 boys and girls in Kindergarten–Grade 8. The Lower School (K–5) features extensive arts facilities and a Discovery Lab with an indoor creek in a greenhouse environment. The Middle School (6–8) places 97 percent of its students in their first-choice high schools. Library, reading, and computer specialists work with all students on the fully networked campus. Band, music, art, drama, and dance are showcased yearly, and Harding offers 21 competitive sports teams. Extended-day care and summer camps are offered. Tuition: $13,360. Financial aid and payment plans are available. Rebecca Arnold is Director of Admissions; Ian L. Craig (Syracuse University, B.A.; New York University, M.A.) is Head of School. *Southern Association.*

Lausanne Collegiate School   1926

1381 West Massey Road, Memphis, TN 38120
Tel. 901-474-1000; Admission 901-474-1030; Fax 901-474-1010
Web Site www.lausanneschool.com

Enrolling 740 day boys and girls from diverse backgrounds in PreKindergarten–Grade 12, Lausanne Collegiate School is committed to preparing young people for success in higher education and in the global environment of the 21st century. Lausanne's rigorous curriculum includes honors and Advanced Placement courses, challenging electives, technology integration, modern languages, and the arts. Lausanne is a candidate school for the International Baccalaureate Program for the fall of 2010. One hundred percent of graduates are accepted to colleges and institutions around the world. Students follow a code of conduct that honors individuality and respects differences. Activities range from the arts and overseas travel to school government, Model UN, and sports. Tuition: $11,200–$14,400. Financial aid is available. Molly B. Cook is Director of Admission; Stuart McCathie is Headmaster. *Southern Association.*

Memphis University School   1893

6191 Park Avenue, Memphis, TN 38119-5399
Tel. 901-260-1300; Fax 901-260-1301
Web Site www.musowls.org; E-mail admissions@musowls.org

Set on 94 acres, Memphis University School is a nondenominational, college preparatory day school for boys in Grades 7 through 12. With an enrollment of approximately 650 students, MUS is dedicated to academic excellence and the development of well-rounded young men of strong moral character. The academic program includes 19 Advanced Placement courses with 100 percent college attendance in an average year. The Class of 2008 received more than $9,600,000 in merit-based aid from universities. The School has many extracurricular offerings and

fields athletic teams in 14 sports. Tuition: $15,950. Daniel Kahalley is Director of Admissions; Ellis L. Haguewood (Harding University, B.A.; University of Memphis, M.A.) was appointed Headmaster in 1995. *Southern Association.*

Montgomery Bell Academy   1867

4001 Harding Road, Nashville, TN 37205
Tel. 615-298-5514; Admission 615-369-5311; Fax 615-297-0271
Web Site www.montgomerybell.edu
E-mail ferrelg@montgomerybell.edu

Montgomery Bell Academy, enrolling 690 day students in Grades 7 through 12, seeks to prepare young men for college and a lifetime of learning, enabling each to reach his full potential as "gentleman, scholar, and athlete." The rigorous liberal arts curriculum features 20 Advanced Placement and 30 honors courses as well as a variety of challenging electives. The Debate Program, exchange programs at Eton and Winchester Colleges, and publications offer further academic enrichment. Students take part in extracurricular activities such as chorus, jazz band, varsity sports, drama, leadership organizations, and community service. An academic session and sports camps are available in the summer. Tuition: $18,900. Greg Ferrell is Director of Admission and Financial Aid; Bradford Gioia is Headmaster. *Southern Association.*

Overbrook School   1936

4210 Harding Road, Nashville, TN 37205
Tel. 615-292-5134; Fax 615-783-0560
Web Site www.overbrook.edu; E-mail admissions-os@overbrook.edu

The Dominican Sisters of the St. Cecilia Congregation founded this coeducational day school to provide primary education in the Roman Catholic tradition. Enrolling 350 students in PreKindergarten–Grade 8, Overbrook School seeks to "permeate students' entire day with Christ so that He will be the source of their strength, the goal of their actions, and the center of their lives." High standards of excellence dominate a curriculum that acknowledges and addresses individual differences and learning styles. In partnership with parents, dedicated teachers educate the whole child in all phases of intellectual, spiritual, athletic, aesthetic, personal, and social development. Good citizenship, responsibility, and character share equal emphasis with academic achievement. Classes in religion and special liturgies are open to children from all faith backgrounds. Activities include National Junior Honor Society, forensics (speech and debate), three choirs, three instrumental groups, MathCounts, soccer, basketball, cross-country, chess club, drama club, and more. Extended care and tuition assistance are available. Tuition: $5400–$10,275. Financial Aid: $150,000. Ellen Fernández is Director of Admissions; Sr. Marie Blanchette, O.P., is Principal. *Southern Association.*

St. Agnes Academy–St. Dominic School   1851

4830 Walnut Grove Road, Memphis, TN 38117
Tel. 901-767-1356; Admission 901-435-5819; Fax 901-435-5866
Web Site www.saa-sds.org; E-mail tforsythe@saa-sds.org

This college preparatory day school enrolls 895 students, with boys in Pre-Kindergarten–Grade 8 and girls in Pre-K–Grade 12. Ecumenical by charter and Catholic in tradition, St. Agnes Academy–St. Dominic School seeks to develop academic excellence, spirituality, leadership, and morality in young people from diverse faith backgrounds. Classes are coeducational in early childhood and junior high and single-gender in lower and upper schools. This configuration helps provide the School's teachers with ways to individualize and customize curriculum to match the students' developmental and gender-specific needs. The classical curriculum, which includes Advanced Placement opportunities, is enriched by technology, three languages, and the arts. The School is a leader in the integration of technology into the curriculum and the first in the area to provide laptops to every student in Grades 1–12. Traditionally, graduates attend four-year colleges and universities. Among the activities are drama, chorus, newspaper, Key Club, and sports. Extended care and summer programs are available. Tuition: $6045–$11,435. Financial Aid: $620,000. Terry Forsythe is Dean of Admission; Barbara H. Daush is President. *Southern Association.*

St. Cecilia Academy 1860

4210 Harding Road, Nashville, TN 37205
Tel. 615-298-4525; Fax 615-783-0561
Web Site www.stcecilia.edu; E-mail info@stcecilia.edu

This college preparatory day school was founded by the Dominican Sisters of St. Cecilia Congregation in 1860 to meet the need for a Catholic secondary school for young women. St. Cecilia Academy takes pride in offering a strong college preparatory education, "rooted in faith, rich in excellence," that equips girls for learning and leadership in the 21st century. The curriculum emphasizes the liberal arts, sciences, and humanities, with 23 AP courses typically enrolling about 70 percent of the 250-member student body. Religious studies, world languages, information technology, and the fine and performing arts complement the core academic program. Classes enroll an average of 13 girls, with a 12:1 student-teacher ratio. Qualified students may cross-enroll at Aquinas College. Virtually all St. Cecilia graduates go on to challenging four-year colleges and universities including, in recent years, Massachusetts Institute of Technology, Princeton, Yale, and the University of Notre Dame. Activities include student government, drama, forensics, National Honor Society, Science Olympiad, and varsity sports. Tuition: $13,500. Financial Aid: $450,000. Betty Bader is Director of Enrollment Management; Sr. Mary Thomas, O.P., is Principal. *Southern Association.*

St. George's Independent School 1959

PK–5: 8250 Poplar Avenue, Germantown, TN 38138
Tel. 901-261-2300; Fax 901-261-2311
PK–5: 3749 Kimball Avenue, Memphis, TN 38111
Tel. 901-261-3920; Fax 901-261-3999
6–12: 1880 Wolf River Boulevard, Collierville, TN 38017
Tel. 901-457-2000; Fax 901-457-2111
Web Site sgis.org

St. George's is a coeducational, college preparatory school for 1241 students in Prekindergarten–Grade 12. The School's culture rests on its dedication to meaningful relationships, an appreciation for the individual, and a foundation for lifelong learning. The academically rigorous curriculum is designed to relate student learning with real-life experiences. Technology is woven into all subjects. Preparing students for engaged citizenship in an increasingly diverse and interconnected world is a key component of the program. Founded in the Episcopal tradition, St. George's maintains an ecumenical atmosphere that counts all students as children of God. Through regular chapel services and religious education, students learn traditional Judeo-Christian values. Among the activities are Art Club, Band, Chorus, Drama, Knowledge Bowl, Model UN, and Youth and Government. St. George's students also make meaningful contributions through community service and fellowship to others. Summer programs are optional. Tuition: $7813–$14,094. Jennifer Taylor (Germantown/Memphis) and Julie Loftin (Collierville) coordinate admissions; William W. Taylor is President. *Southern Association.*

St. Nicholas School 1958

7525 Min-Tom Drive, Chattanooga, TN 37421
Tel. 423-899-1999; Fax 423-899-0109
Web Site www.stns.org; E-mail bdawkins@stns.org

St. Nicholas School, founded in 1958 in the Episcopal tradition, serves 230 day students age 4 through Grade 5. St. Nicholas addresses the whole, integrated development of the child and facilitates the unfolding of self-confident, independent learners. Its philosophy values diversity, fosters critical thinking among students, and uses age-appropriate approaches to meet the spiritual, intellectual, and physical needs of children. Extended school and summer camp programs are offered. Tuition: $8992–$12,092. Financial Aid: $200,000. Barbara B. Dawkins is Admission Director; Mark Fallo is Head of School. *Southern Association.*

TEXAS

Allen Academy 1886

3201 Boonville Road, Bryan, TX 77802
Tel. 979-776-0731; Fax 979-774-7769
Web Site www.allenacademy.org
E-mail admissions@allenacademy.org

John Hodges Allen founded this coeducational, college prepa-ratory school to provide a "rigorous and superior education in the humanities, arts, and sciences" while developing each stu-dent's moral and ethical values. Enrolling 295 day students in Pre-Kindergarten (age 3) through Grade 12, Allen Academy provides a dynamic learning environment in which students acquire the essential knowledge and skills required to succeed in higher education and in life. The curriculum includes honors and Advanced Placement courses, and all students are required to take part in service learning projects. English as a Second Language classes help international students adjust to the American language and culture. School activities include the visual and performing arts, student government, clubs, and interscholastic athletics. Allen Academy is accredited by the Southwestern Association of Colleges and Schools. Tuition: $4710–$9995. Financial Aid: $154,000. Dorcas Hohertz is Administrative Coordinator; Philip S. Deely (Hobart College, B.A.; University of Chicago, M.A.) is Interim Head of School.

All Saints Episcopal School 1954

4108 Delaware, P.O. Box 7188, Beaumont, TX 77706
Tel. 409-892-1755; Fax 409-892-0166
Web Site www.allsaints-beaumont.org
E-mail sclark@allsaints-beaumont.org

All Saints is a day school enrolling 400 boys and girls age 3–Grade 8. The School's challenging program, which empha-sizes the education and development of the whole child, men-tally, physically, and spiritually, has earned statewide academic recognition through participation in the Private School Inter-scholastic Association. Spanish is taught at all levels; Latin is introduced in the middle school, piano in Kindergarten–Grade 3. High school credit may be earned for Algebra I, Integrated Physics and Chemistry, and Spanish. A 17,000-volume library, networked computers with Internet access, three science labs, a full-size gym, new athletic fields, and daily chapel are features of the program. Tuition: $2610–$7360. Financial Aid: $100,000. Kathy Fisher is Admissions Director; Catherine "Scootie" Clark is Head of School.

All Saints' Episcopal School 1951

9700 Saints Circle, Fort Worth, TX 76108
Tel. 817-560-5746; Fax 817-560-5720
Web Site www.asesftw.org; E-mail admissions@aseschool.org

All Saints' Episcopal School, a coeducational day school set on a spacious 103-acre campus, is one of the largest independent parish schools in the United States. Welcoming more than 800 students from many religious, ethnic, and racial backgrounds, the School offers a dynamic, values-based academic program encompassing Kindergarten through Grade 12. The college preparatory curriculum balances the arts, sciences, and human-ities, combined with the development of moral values, character education, and ethical decision making. The Upper School pro-gram includes honors and Advanced Placement courses in all major departments. Students of all faiths attend chapel services in the Anglican tradition and take part in service outreach as a means of developing spiritual awareness. Among the activities are school government, honor societies, Students Against

Drunk Driving, publications, dance, theater productions, instrumental and vocal ensembles, 15 men's and women's inter-scholastic sports, cheerleading, and interest clubs formed in such areas as business, chess, physics, and literature. Tuition: $13,315–$14,460. Financial aid is available. Linda Sherlock is Director of Admissions; Dr. Thaddeus B. Bird is Head of School.

Annunciation Orthodox School 1970

3600 Yoakum Boulevard, Houston, TX 77006
Tel. 713-470-5600; Admissions 713-470-5611; Fax 713-470-5605
Web Site www.aoshouston.org; E-mail admissions@aoshouston.org

ANNUNCIATION ORTHODOX SCHOOL

In addition to preparing students for their next academic steps, Annunciation Orthodox School works in partnership with par-ents to lay solid foundations for life. Founded to develop "the whole child," AOS offers a challenging academic curriculum within a nurturing Christian environment for 668 students in Preschool–Grade 8. Programs encompass a balance of aca-demic, spiritual, physical, and social experiences that enrich students' lives and shape their hearts, bodies, and minds. Extracurricular activities include sports, student government, performing and visual art clubs, academic clubs, chess club, admissions club, and outreach service opportunities. Extended-day care and summer programs are available. Tuition: $11,850–$15,800; Fees: $500–$800. Financial Aid: $417,400. Maria Newton is Advisor to the Head of School and Director of Admissions; Mark H. Kelly is Head of School.

The Canterbury Episcopal School 1992

1708 North Westmoreland Road, DeSoto, TX 75115
Tel. 972-572-7200; Fax 972-572-7400
Web Site www.thecanterburyschool.org
E-mail admissions@thecanterburyschool.org

The Canterbury Episcopal School, serving 291 boys and girls from diverse racial, religious, and ethnic backgrounds, offers a college preparatory curriculum encompassing Kindergarten through Grade 12. Set on a 37-acre campus, the School pro-vides an academic program centered on the liberal arts, sci-ences, and humanities. Canterbury's Episcopal heritage is reflected in the School's ethnic, religious, and socioeconomic diversity, community service, chapel, and strong academics. English, math, history, science, modern and classical language, and the fine arts are integral to the curriculum, with honors and Advanced Placement courses in most subjects. Religious studies focus on the Hebrew Bible, New Testament, ethics, and theology. Students attend daily chapel, and an Episcopal chap-lain conducts Eucharistic services on a regular basis. Middle (Grades 6–8) and Upper School (Grades 9–12) athletes compete interscholastically in eight sports. Other activities include the

Texas

National Honor Society, publications, music and drama ensembles, academic and special-interest clubs, and community outreach. Tuition: $7700–$11,600. Financial aid is available. Lyn Baker is Head of School.

Cistercian Preparatory School   1962

3660 Cistercian Road, Irving, TX 75039
Tel. 469-499-5400; Admissions 469-499-5411; Fax 469-499-5440
Web Site www.cistercian.org; E-mail admissions@cistercian.org

Cistercian Preparatory School is a Roman Catholic, college preparatory day school enrolling 350 boys of all creeds in Grades 5 through 12. The curriculum is a fully integrated, eight-year honors program of English, theology, math, laboratory science, computer science, foreign language, and social studies, which is identical for all students. Electives, preparation for Advanced Placement exams, college-credit courses, and independent studies are offered in addition to athletics, activities, summer sports camp, and an academic summer school. Tuition: $13,200–$15,000. Need-based financial aid is available. Robert J. Haaser is Director of Admissions; Fr. Peter Verhalen is Headmaster.

Duchesne Academy of the Sacred Heart   1960

10202 Memorial Drive, Houston, TX 77024
Tel. 713-468-8211; Admissions Ext. 139; Fax 713-465-9809
Web Site www.duchesne.org; E-mail admissions@duchesne.org

DUCHESNE ACADEMY OF THE SACRED HEART

Duchesne Academy was founded by the Religious of the Sacred Heart to educate young women to an active faith, a respect for intellectual values, and a commitment to service, community, and personal growth. Enrolling 700 girls in Pre-kindergarten through Grade 12, the school is part of a worldwide Sacred Heart Network. State-of-the-art technology is integrated throughout a college preparatory curriculum that includes Advanced Placement courses, spiritual formation, and a strong community service component. Fine arts, athletics, summer enrichment opportunities, an advisory program, and interest clubs enrich the core program. Tuition: $10,430–$17,340. Financial Aid: $1,000,000. Beth Speck is Director of Admission; Sr. Jan Dunn is Headmistress.

Episcopal High School of Houston   1983

4650 Bissonnet, Bellaire, TX 77401
Tel. 713-512-3400; Admissions 713-512-3482; Fax 713-512-3603
Web Site www.ehshouston.org; E-mail akoehler@ehshouston.org

Founded in 1983 within the Episcopal Diocese of Texas, Episcopal High is a coeducational day school serving 659 students in Grades 9–12. The School's broad college preparatory program is comprised of four pillars that emphasize academic, religious, artistic, and athletic disciplines, nurtured by Christian values in a supportive environment. Daily chapel services reinforce the ethical and religious principles upon which the School was founded. The 35-acre campus is located in Bellaire, south of the Galleria. State-of-the-art buildings and wireless technology for the students' laptop computers enhance their total learning experience. Tuition: $20,634. Audrey Koehler is Director of Admission; C. Edward Smith (Princeton University, A.B.; Middlebury College, M.A.) is Headmaster.

The Episcopal School of Dallas   1974

4100 Merrell Road, Dallas, TX 75229-6200
Tel. 214-358-4368; Admissions 214-353-5827; Fax 214-353-5872
Web Site www.esdallas.org; E-mail admission@esdallas.org

The Episcopal School of Dallas was established to provide a strong classical education within the framework of Judeo-Christian principles. Its commitment places equal emphasis on character development and the acquisition of knowledge through a college preparatory curriculum centered on the liberal arts, sciences, and humanities. Enrolling 1120 day boys and girls from diverse backgrounds in Beginners (3)–Grade 12, the School aims to encourage the spiritual, intellectual, physical, and social well-being of its students through an academic program infused with enduring values. All students attend daily chapel and participate in social outreach. Core subjects are enhanced by world languages, computer technology, and the visual and performing arts. Students take part in school government, leadership committees, publications, dramas and musicals, vocal and instrumental ensembles, and interscholastic sports. Community service is required and may involve projects with local homeless shelters, nursing homes, Big Brothers/Sisters, and inner-city schools. Tuition: $9400–$22,600. Financial Aid: $2,000,000. Ruth Burke is Director of Admission and Financial Aid; the Reverend Stephen B. Swann is Founding Rector/Headmaster.

Fort Worth Academy   1982

7301 Dutch Branch Road, Fort Worth, TX 76132
Tel. 817-370-1191; Admission Ext. 603; Fax 817-294-1323
Web Site www.fwacademy.org; E-mail npalmer@fwacademy.org

Located in southwest Fort Worth, this nationally recognized prepreparatory day school enrolls 240 boys and girls in Kindergarten–Grade 8. In the belief that the curriculum is the catalyst to academic success, Fort Worth Academy offers a comprehensive program designed to develop strong skills in language arts, math, social studies, and science. One-to-one computing is a reality in the Academy's 21st Century School. All middle school (Grades 5–8) students are issued their own Tablet PC for classroom and home use. Lower school students have daily and immediate access to wireless laptop and desktop computers in their classrooms. Core subjects are complemented by enrichment courses and electives in foreign language, the visual and performing arts, and athletics. Small classes, inspiring teachers, shared values, and an active partnership with parents contribute to the success of the Academy's goals. Tuition: $12,750. Financial aid is available. Nancy Palmer is Director of Admission; William M. Broderick is Head of School. *Southern Association.*

Fort Worth Country Day   1962

4200 Country Day Lane, Fort Worth, TX 76109-4299
Tel. 817-732-7718; Admissions 817-302-3209; Fax 817-377-3425
Web Site www.fwcds.org; E-mail bjiongo@fwcds.org

Fort Worth Country Day aims to nurture the intellectual, physical, emotional, and moral development of its students through a comprehensive advanced curriculum grounded in the liberal arts, sciences, and humanities. The school prizes integrity, kindness, courage, scholarship, respect, and responsibility, and students and faculty alike adhere to an Honor Code. Fort Worth Country Day enrolls 1113 boys and girls from diverse backgrounds in full-day Kindergarten to Grade 12. FWCD offers a challenging college preparatory program, with AP courses in all departments, modern and classical languages, and required offerings in the performing arts and athletics. Nearly 70 percent of all faculty have earned advanced degrees. Community service is an integral component of the educational process for students in all grades. The 100-acre campus features 11 academic buildings, tennis courts, playing fields, and a stadium/all-weather track. FWCD students may participate in Breakthrough Fort Worth, a six-year, 12-month program of intense academic enrichment. Tuition: $14,955–$16,315. Financial aid is available. Barbara W. Jiongo is Admissions Director; Evan D. Peterson is Head of School.

Good Shepherd Episcopal School 1959

11110 Midway Road, Dallas, TX 75229-4119
Tel. 214-357-1610; Admission Ext. 230; Fax 214-357-4105
Web Site www.gseschooldallas.org; E-mail admissions@gsesdallas.org

Good Shepherd Episcopal School is a parish-affiliated school enrolling 600 boys and girls in Preschool–Grade 8. Its purpose is to equip students with Christian principles, a love of learning, a creative mind, and a giving spirit. In the lower grades, writing, language arts, social studies, math, science, and health are taught by classroom teachers, with specialized teachers for reading, art, music, Spanish, and physical education. In Grades 5–8, students take one class period each in core subjects and Spanish, and one semester each of art, music, and drama, all taught by specialists. Activities include Student Council, athletics, and Classroom of the Earth. Tuition: $9744–$13,448. Financial aid is available. Kathleen Whalen is Director of Admission; J. Robert Kohler is Head of the School.

The Hockaday School 1913

11600 Welch Road, Dallas, TX 75229-2999
Tel. 214-363-6311; Admissions 214-360-6526; Fax 214-265-1649
Web Site www.hockaday.org; E-mail jliggitt@mail.hockaday.org

THE HOCKADAY SCHOOL in Dallas, Texas, is an all-girls boarding and day school from Pre-Kindergarten through Grade 12 with a boarding program for Grades 8–12. At Hockaday, more than 1000 students of diverse backgrounds and cultures have the opportunity to realize their full potential and to be inspired to live the brilliant lives that await them. Situated in a residential neighborhood, the School affords students a secluded campus environment with access to several cultural and civic activities in and around Dallas.

Founded in 1913 by Miss Ela Hockaday, the School seeks to provide a college preparatory education to girls of strong potential and diverse backgrounds who may be expected to assume positions of responsibility and leadership in an increasingly complex world. Hockaday fosters a community of concern and friendship and instills in every girl a love of learning and an appreciation of excellence in all forms.

Hockaday is directed by a Board of Trustees that represents alumnae, parents, and the community. The School fosters relationships with approximately 6500 graduates and former students through the Hockaday Alumnae Association. Hockaday is accredited by the Independent Schools Association of the Southwest and holds membership in the National Association of Independent Schools, among other organizations.

THE CAMPUS. Located on 100 acres, the campus includes 16 buildings. The 52,000-square-foot Liza Lee Academic Research Center (2002) hosts two expansive libraries, academic classrooms, an audiovisual classroom, and computer labs for the student-run newspaper and yearbook. Middle and Upper School classrooms are equipped with Smartboard™ technology for use with the students' laptops, which are required for every girl in Grades 6–12. The campus is fully wireless. The Fine Arts facilities include a 600-seat auditorium, instrumental and voice studios, practice rooms, a painting studio, ceramics facilities with outdoor kilns, a photography laboratory, printmaking facilities, and an electronic music studio. The updated Science Center contains a lecture hall, study lounges, classrooms, ten major laboratories, a computer lab, and a greenhouse powered by solar energy. Facilities for the Lower School include classrooms for Pre-Kindergarten–Grade 4, art and music rooms, two commons areas, and science labs. The Wellness Center includes the 5000-square-foot Hill Family Fitness Center, an 1800-square-foot aerobics room and athletic training facilities fully equipped for the treatment of sports-related injuries.

THE HOCKADAY SCHOOL

The residence halls have recently updated lounges and kitchens with new furniture, appliances, and large-screen televisions for a home-away-from-home feeling. Boarders are encouraged to personalize their rooms. The infirmary is adjacent to the living quarters. A large common lounge with a fireplace and TV/study/sitting area leads to the outdoor pool.

Athletics facilities include two gymnasiums housing four basketball courts (convertible to three volleyball and indoor tennis courts), a climbing wall, two racquetball courts, a swimming pool, and a dance studio. On the grounds are six athletic fields, a softball complex, an all-weather track, a tennis center with ten courts and seating for 90, and several acres of open space.

THE FACULTY. Ms. Jeanne P. Whitman, the Eugene McDermott Headmistress, is a *magna cum laude* graduate of Wake Forest University. She earned a master's degree in English from the University of Virginia and a second master's degree in business from Wake Forest University.

The faculty is composed of 104 full-time teachers, most of whom have advanced degrees, with 12 holding doctorates. Hockaday instructors are recruited from around the world, providing a faculty that reflects the School's diverse student body. The average tenure is 10 years.

STUDENT BODY. In 2009–10, there were 1083 boarding and day students. The 76 boarding students come from 10 states and 11 countries. Hockaday's residence program begins in Grade 8 upward. Day students are enrolled from Pre-Kindergarten to Grade 12. Thirty-four percent are minority students. The average class size is 14.

ACADEMIC PROGRAM. Students are exposed to a rigorous academic curriculum that offers core educational subjects as well as unique offerings in technology, the arts, and leadership and personal development. Pre-Kindergarten girls are introduced to the basic elements of language, numerical reasoning, science, social studies, computers, art, music, and creative drama. An extended-day program is offered in the afternoons to provide cultural enrichment. In the full-day Kindergarten program, reading and mathematics become more structured, and emphasis is placed on a balanced reading program. In Grades 1–4, the program is divided into subject areas: language arts, mathematics, science, social studies, art, music, drama, and physical education, with Spanish or French introduced in Kindergarten.

THE HOCKADAY SCHOOL

Middle School (Grades 5–8) continues to strengthen and widen the foundation of the Lower School. In Grades 5–6, language arts, mathematics, science, social studies, art, music, Spanish or French, and physical education comprise the core curriculum. Students are taught and utilize their computer skills in all disciplines.

In Grades 7–8, the curriculum includes English, history, mathematics (pre-algebra in Grade 7 and algebra concepts in Grade 8), laboratory science, and foreign language choices in French, Spanish, Latin, or Chinese. Fine arts selections are photography, broadcast, drawing, painting, drama, speech, debate, dance, guitar, musical theater, and ceramics. The eighth-grade class produces a musical each year. Upper School credits may be earned in math and foreign languages by eligible students in Grade 8. Activities include athletics, beginning in Grade 7; Student Council; the literary magazine, *BANNER*; math, art, and science clubs; a school newspaper, *NEWSWAY,* the broadcast news class, *Daisy Days;* and chorus for Grades 5–8. There is a sixth-grade trip to Colonial Williamsburg and the District of Columbia and a seventh-grade environmental-education trip to Taos, New Mexico. The curriculum in Grades 5–8 is complemented by visits to museums, the opera, the ballet, the symphony, and other sites of interest.

The Upper School curriculum includes English at each grade level and such senior English seminars as "The Heroine's Journey—The Search for Wholeness," "Stones of the Heart: Literature of War," and "Autobiography and Memoir." French, Spanish, Latin, Mandarin Chinese; United States History, World History, Criminal Law, Government, Consumer Economics and Media Literacy; Algebra I–II, Geometry, Pre-Calculus, Calculus and Analytical Geometry, Finite Math, Probability and Statistics, Multivariable Calculus; Web Design; Physics, Chemistry, Astronomy, and a multimester course in Biology, including Classical Genetics, Human Evolution, and Micro-Biology and Human Diseases; History of Art and Music; Video-Media Production, Acting Styles, Studio Art, Ceramics and Sculpture, Photography, Concert, Show and Madrigal Choirs, Orchestra, Dance; Debate, Journalism, Broadcast Journalism;

and Physical Education and Health are also offered. Swiss Semester in Zermatt is available for Grade 10 and CITYterm in New York for Grades 11 and 12.

Advanced Placement courses are available in more than 18 subjects. A cooperative arrangement with St. Mark's School of Texas allows girls to select courses there. Some Hockaday courses are also open to St. Mark's boys.

An English as a Second Language program is offered on intermediate and advanced levels. Intensive language training in writing, reading, listening, and speaking skills is the focus. Students may continue at Hockaday after the first year, following acceptance into the regular academic program. First-year resident students take trips to Washington, D.C., Austin, and San Antonio, Texas.

Graduation credit requirements in years include English 4, mathematics 3, history 2.5, language 3, laboratory science 3, fine arts 1.5, physical education and health 4, and two additional academic courses from any department plus basic proficiency in computer usage.

Private lessons are available in piano beginning in Pre-Kindergarten; guitar beginning in Grade 1; flute, cello, violin, and brass from Grade 5; and voice beginning in Grade 7.

Hockaday has a 100 percent acceptance rate to colleges and universities nationwide. Graduates matriculated at such colleges and universities as Boston College, Bowdoin, Cornell, Dartmouth, Emory, Georgetown, Harvard, New York University, Princeton, Rice, St. Andrews, Southern Methodist University, Stanford, Vanderbilt, Wake Forest, Washington University, Yale, and the Universities of Southern California and Texas, among others.

STUDENT ACTIVITIES. The conduct and activities of the older girls are regulated by the Student Council, elected by Upper School students. Special-interest organizations, publications, and honor societies augment the academic program. Community Service committees organize volunteer activities in the community and with nonprofit organizations. Students in Upper School must complete 15 hours of community service yearly, but most complete additional hours.

Each year, two alumnae memorial fellowships bring outstanding persons to spend extended time with the Hockaday community.

Festive occasions include class dances, retreats for Grades 9 and 12, all-school mixers, the Winter Formal, Senior Prom, a musical, and parent drop-ins.

THE HOCKADAY SCHOOL

Hockaday's program of health, physical education, and recreation begins in Pre-Kindergarten. Designed to meet each girl's needs and to encourage her to develop a permanent pattern of physical activity, it offers daily instruction in the Middle School. Swimming begins in Grade 1 and continues through Grade 11 lifeguarding. In Grades 7–8, Green and White intramural teams compete in field hockey, basketball, volleyball, lacrosse, soccer, tennis, gymnastics, flag football, softball, track and field, and swimming. Interscholastic athletics are available in Grades 7–12. Varsity and junior varsity teams in Grades 9–12 compete in swimming, golf, tennis, field hockey, softball, basketball, volleyball, cross-country, track, crew, lacrosse, and soccer.

ADMISSION AND COSTS. Applicants are accepted on the basis of previous school records, results of aptitude and achievement tests, recommendations, and a personal interview. Hockaday welcomes students of all nationalities, races, and creeds. Entrance tests are given at the School on specified dates.

THE HOCKADAY SCHOOL

In 2009–10, day tuition and fees range from $15,805 for Pre-Kindergarten to $21,445–$22,580 for Grades 8–12. For the residence program, the charge for tuition, room, and board is $40,101–$44,759. Optional expenses include allowances, transportation, and private lessons. Tuition payment plans and insurance are available. In 2007–08, Hockaday awarded $2,500,000 in assistance based on need.

Eugene McDermott Headmistress: Jeanne P. Whitman
Assistant Head & Chief Financial Officer: Mary Pat Higgins
Assistant Head for Academic Affairs & Provost: Cathy Murphree
Head of Upper School: John Ashton
Head of Middle School: Linda Kramer
Head of Lower School: Lisa Holekamp
Dean of Students: Meshea Matthews
Director of Alumnae: Amy Spence
Director of Admissions: Jen Liggitt
College Counselor: Carol Wasden
Director of Athletics: Tina Slinker
Director of Development & External Affairs: Susan Swan Smith

The John Cooper School   1988

One John Cooper Drive, The Woodlands, TX 77381
Tel. 281-367-0900; Admissions Ext. 308; Fax 281-298-5715
Web Site www.johncooper.org

Enrolling 964 boys and girls in Pre-K–Grade 12, The John Cooper School offers a challenging, traditional college preparatory curriculum designed to foster a lifelong love of learning and to equip students for success in higher education. Core academic disciplines are supported by extensive visual and performing arts, technology, athletics, and community service. A full-time college counseling staff assists students throughout the

college planning and admission process, and all graduates enter four-year institutions. Activities include interscholastic sports, student government, leadership organizations, drama and

THE JOHN COOPER SCHOOL

music, and community service, including an annual schoolwide commitment to build a Habitat for Humanity home. Tuition: $12,250–$17,640. Craig Meredith is Director of Admissions; Michael F. Maher is Head of School.

The Kinkaid School   1906

201 Kinkaid School Drive, Houston, TX 77024
Tel. 713-782-1640; Admissions 713-243-5035; Fax 713-243-5055
Web Site www.kinkaid.org; E-mail admissions@kinkaid.org

Kinkaid, the first coeducational, college preparatory day school in Houston, seeks to enable students to develop their talents and fulfill their potential through a balanced program of academics, arts, community service, and athletics. Enrolling 1355 students in Prekindergarten–Grade 12, The Kinkaid School offers a challenging liberal arts curriculum enhanced by special lecture series, off-campus career internships, and overseas travel/study. Students take part in school government, academic competitions, publications, interest clubs, arts, and athletics. A summer remedial and enrichment session is offered. Tuition: $13,215–$17,950. Financial Aid: $1,420,000. Iris Bonet is Admissions Director; Donald C. North (Vanderbilt, B.A.; Middlebury, M.A.) is Headmaster.

Lakehill Preparatory School   1971

2720 Hillside Drive, Dallas, TX 75214
Tel. 214-826-2931; Fax 214-826-4623
Web Site www.lakehillprep.org; E-mail sseitz@lakehillprep.org

Enrolling 400 boys and girls from diverse backgrounds, Lakehill preparatory School is an academic community dedicated to the whole student. Lakehill combines a rigorous college preparatory curriculum with opportunities for personal growth, individual enrichment, and community engagement. From kindergarten through high school, every Lakehill student is encouraged to strive, challenged to succeed, and inspired to excel. Lakehill is celebrated for the breadth of activities it provides. Extensive academic, fine arts, athletic, and community service programs expose every child to new experiences. Students are encouraged to participate and are challenged to excel where they may not have thought possible. Lakehill is accredited by the Independent Schools Association of the Southwest. Tuition: $11,498–$15,176. Financial aid is available. Holly Walker is Director of Admissions; Roger L. Perry is Headmaster. *Southern Association.*

The Lamplighter School   1953

11611 Inwood Road, Dallas, TX 75229
Tel. 214-369-9201; Admission Ext. 347; Fax 214-369-5540
Web Site www.thelamplighterschool.org
E-mail mbrenner@thelamplighterschool.org

The Lamplighter School, enrolling 430 boys and girls in Preschool (age 3)–Grade 4, seeks to foster the love of learning and build a positive self-concept. Lamplighter offers a highly integrated curriculum that merges the fine arts with language arts, math, environmental science, social studies, physical education, and Spanish. Innovative groupings provide a warm and supportive environment that fosters enthusiasm, self-confidence, and a sense of belonging. The north Dallas campus features a fine arts complex, a media center, a greenhouse, and a health and fitness facility. A summer program is available. Tuition: $9670–$17,420. Matt Brenner is Director of Admission and Community Services; Dr. Arnold S. Cohen (Ohio State, Ph.D.) is Head of School.

The Oakridge School   1979

5900 West Pioneer Parkway, Arlington, TX 76013
Tel. 817-451-4994; Admissions Ext. 708; Fax 817-457-6681
Web Site www.theoakridgeschool.org
E-mail jadavis@theoakridgeschool.org

THE OAKRIDGE SCHOOL in Arlington, Texas, is a coeducational, college preparatory day school enrolling students in 15 grade levels (preschool through Grade 12). East of Fort Worth, Oakridge is centrally located in the greater Dallas/Fort Worth Metroplex. Students benefit from the many cultural resources of the Metroplex, including libraries, galleries, theaters, museums, and universities.

THE OAKRIDGE SCHOOL

The Oakridge School, founded in 1979, inspires students "to seek their full potential in academics, the arts, and athletics in a challenging and nurturing environment that cultivates social responsibility, mutual respect, and personal integrity."

The Oakridge School is a nonprofit institution governed by an independent Board of Regents. Oakridge is accredited by the Independent Schools Association of the Southwest and holds membership in the National Association of Independent Schools, among other organizations.

THE CAMPUS. The School's 83-acre campus consists of ten buildings. The Early Childhood Center houses preschool, pre-kindergarten, and kindergarten. The Lower and Middle School building contains classrooms, two computer labs, and four science labs. The Upper School building houses three science labs, a central commons area, and specialized classrooms. The Student Activities Center consists of two basketball courts, kitchen, an eating area, locker rooms, a weight room, a training room, and offices. The Multi-purpose Activity Center has been acoustically enhanced to serve as a performing arts facility as well as an additional gym. The Information Center houses the technology center, an expanded school library, a college counseling suite with conference space, and the administrative offices. The Fine Arts Center features a 385-seat auditorium, plus enhanced facilities for the visual and performing arts. The Parents' Club Building provides meeting and work space for parent volunteers. The Maintenance Building accommodates the needs of the building and grounds staff. The Security Center, located at the main entrance of the campus, houses monitoring technology. The campus includes two playground areas; a National Wetlands with observation bridge; a combination children's garden, greenhouse, and outdoor classroom; a golf practice facility; and multiple athletic fields adjacent to the Lake Arlington Golf Course.

THE FACULTY. Andy J. Broadus, appointed Headmaster in 1981 and President in 2007, is a graduate of Jacksonville University (B.S.) and the University of North Florida (M.Ed.) and has done advanced graduate work at the University of Georgia and Columbia University. Jon Kellam, Headmaster, is a graduate of Texas Christian University (B.S., M.Ed.). He has served Oakridge as administrator, English teacher, and varsity soccer coach. Betty Garton (Texas Tech, B.S.; Texas Christian, M.Ed.) is the Director of the Early Childhood Center; Corliss Elsesser (Texas Christian, B.S., M.Ed.) has been with Oakridge since its founding and is Head of the Lower School; Mike Cobb (University of North Texas, B.A.; Cambridge College, M.Ed.) is Head of the Middle School; Butch Groves (Southwest Oklahoma State, B.S.; University of Central Oklahoma, M.Ed.) is Head of the Upper School; Melissa Grubb (Austin College, B.A., M.A.) is Director of Studies.

THE OAKRIDGE SCHOOL

The faculty includes 97 teachers, 66 women and 31 men. They hold 97 bachelor's degrees, 47 master's degrees, and 3 doctoral degrees representing study at a variety of colleges throughout the United States and abroad.

First aid is provided by a full-time registered nurse with a fully equipped school infirmary. An emergency medical facility is located nearby.

STUDENT BODY. In 2009–10, the Oakridge School enrolled 876 boys and girls, from 3 to 18 years of age. Students come from 31 communities, including Arlington, Bedford, Burleson, Cedar Hill, Cleburne, Colleyville, Dallas, DeSoto, Duncanville, Euless, Fort Worth, Grand Prairie, Grapevine, Hurst, Irving,

Keller, Mansfield, Midlothian, Southlake, and Waxahachie. Also represented are 11 countries: Britain, China, Germany, India, Malaysia, Nigeria, Pakistan, South Korea, Spain, Taiwan, and Vietnam.

ACADEMIC PROGRAM. The school year is divided into four marking periods in all divisions. Parents are informed regularly of student progress through periodic reports, parent conferences, and report cards, which are sent to parents at the end of each marking period. Classes range in size from 4 to 22 students with a student-teacher ratio of 10:1. Self-discipline and clear, concise rules are emphasized in "an atmosphere of mutual respect." Faculty members provide extra help as needed, and tutoring can be arranged.

THE OAKRIDGE SCHOOL

The Early Childhood Center curriculum incorporates Mathematics, Language Arts, Science, Social Studies, Spanish, Computer, Visual Perception, Music, Art, and Physical Education. The entire curriculum is sequential from level to level.

The Lower School (Grades 1–4) courses include Language Arts, Social Studies, Math, Science, Spanish, Art, Music, Physical Education, Computer, and Library program.

The Lower House of the Middle School (Grades 5–6) curriculum is as follows: Language Arts, French or Spanish, U.S. and World History, Latin, Math, General Science, Earth Science, Life Science, Physical Science, Honors Physical Science, Art, Music, Strings, Creative Dramatics, and intramural athletics.

The Upper House of the Middle School (Grades 7–8) curriculum is as follows: English, Composition, French or Spanish, U.S. History, Pre-Algebra and Algebra I, Geometry, Life Science and Physical Science, Art, Choir, Drama, Strings, and Physical Education/Athletics.

The Upper School (Grades 9–12) curriculum includes Introduction to Literature and Rhetoric, Honors Introduction to Literature and Rhetoric, Introduction to British Literature and Rhetoric, Honors Introduction to British Literature and Rhetoric, Introduction to American Literature and Rhetoric, Introduction to World Literature and Rhetoric, Creative Writing; World History I–II, U.S. History, U.S. Government, Eco-

nomics, Honors Economics; Spanish, French, Chinese; Algebra I–II, Geometry, Pre-Calculus, Discrete Mathematics, Calculus, Statistics; Biology, Honors Biology, Chemistry, Honors Chemistry, Environmental Science, Physics, Honors Physics, Anatomy and Physiology, Honors Anatomy and Physiology, and Computer Science Programming. Electives include Anthropology and Archaeology, Survey of Religions, Acting, Art, Choir, Digital Production, Video Production, and Yearbook.

Advanced Placement courses are offered in English Language & Composition, English Literature & Composition, Calculus AB, Calculus BC, Chemistry, Statistics, Environmental Science, Biology, Physics C Electricity and Magnetism, Physics C Mechanics, U.S. Government, U.S. History, European History, French Language, Spanish Language, Spanish Literature, Computer Science, Music Theory, Studio Art 2D Design, Studio Art 3D Design, and Studio Art Drawing.

Students in Kindergarten–Grade 8 take the Stanford Achievement Test each year and the Otis-Lennon School Ability Test every other year.

College advising is a core component of an Oakridge education. Students in Middle School take practice college admissions tests and are eligible to participate in Duke University's Talent Identification Program. All students in Grades 9–10 take the PLAN test; the PSAT in Grades 10–11; and the SAT and ACT in Grades 11–12. College representatives from throughout the nation visit campus, and students attend college fairs in the Metroplex. The sophomore class goes on a college tour. College advising is conducted on a 1:1 basis, particularly in the junior and senior years, and includes financial aid counseling, computer resources, and field trips to nearby colleges. Oakridge students have been accepted at such colleges and universities as Barnard, Boston College, Carnegie Mellon, Duke, Georgetown, Harvard, Howard, Massachusetts Institute of Technology, New York University, Rice, Smith, Washington University, Wellesley, and the Universities of Pennsylvania and Southern California.

STUDENT ACTIVITIES. There are elected Student Council programs in the Middle and Upper schools. In the Upper School, the Student Council consists of elected officers and the officers of each class. Members of the Student Council are expected to serve as representatives, leaders, and good examples for the entire student body. A faculty sponsor advises and works with the Student Council.

THE OAKRIDGE SCHOOL

The Middle and Upper School Inter-Scholastic Sports Program offers baseball, basketball, football, golf, soccer, swimming, tennis, cross-country, track, and wrestling for boys, and basketball, soccer, tennis, golf, cross-country, softball, swimming, track, field hockey, volleyball, and cheerleading for girls. The Athletic Director schedules games with public and private schools in the Fort Worth/Dallas area. Other activities include the National Junior Honor Society, the National Honor Society, Math Teams, Computer Science Team, Literary Magazine, and the Drama,

French, Spanish, Art, and Whole Earth Clubs. Special social activities are scheduled on a monthly basis.

Traditional programs and events include Grandparents' Day, New Parent Orientation Dinner, Book Fair, the Super Supper and Auction, Homecoming, Sports Banquets, Parent Orientation Night, Owlfest, Living History Program, concerts, and awards programs.

ADMISSION AND COSTS. The Oakridge School seeks bright, college-bound students. Students are accepted in all grades, when openings exist, on the basis of an aptitude test, reading and math achievement tests, past academic and behavior records, recommendations, and an interview. Application should be made as early as possible, preferably by March 1; students who have recently moved to the Fort Worth/Dallas area may be admitted in mid-year. There is an application fee of $65, a testing fee of $80 for preschool–Grade 12, and upon acceptance, a registration fee of $500, which is applied toward tuition. The Director of Admission handles applications.

In 2009–10, tuition ranges from $5460 for the three-day preschool program to $15,360 for seniors. Monthly tuition payments are available. The Oakridge School subscribes to the School and Student Service for Financial Aid and provides limited financial aid to students who qualify.

Director of Admissions: Dr. Jerry Davis
Director of Development: Sharon LeMond
College Advisor: Sarah Kramer
Business Officer: Richard Horvath
Director of Finance: Kathy Gamill

Parish Episcopal School   1972

4101 Sigma Road, Dallas, TX 75244
Tel. 972-239-8011; Fax 972-991-1237
Web Site www.parishepiscopal.org
E-mail admission@parishepiscopal.org

Parish Episcopal School provides a college preparatory education within the Episcopal tradition. Currently enrolling 1180 boys and girls as day students in Pre-Kindergarten–Grade 12, Parish emphasizes academics and instills an awareness of obligations to fellow students and the community. All students attend daily chapel services, and religion is taught in Kindergarten–Grade 12. Younger children develop confidence, independence, and responsibility while focusing on language arts, mathematics, science, social studies, the arts, and foreign language through individualized hands-on learning. The Upper School offers Advanced Placement courses in all major subjects, college counseling, and electives such as Modern American Literature, Discrete Mathematics, History of Philosophy, Latin, and Environmental Science. Extracurricular activities include community service, school government, chorus, drama, publications, student vestry, special-interest clubs, a full range of athletics, and student leadership opportunities. After-school and summer programs enhance the regular school year. Tuition: $9990–$19,650. Financial aid is available. Marci McLean is Assistant Head of External Affairs; David Monaco is Head of School.

River Oaks Baptist School   1955

2300 Willowick, Houston, TX 77027
Tel. 713-623-6938; Fax 713-626-0650
Web Site www.robs.org; E-mail admissions@robs.org

River Oaks Baptist School enrolls approximately 870 coed day students throughout the three schools of Primary (2 years of age–Prekindergarten), Lower (Kindergarten–Grade 4), and Middle (Grades 5–8). The academic environment, which balances high expectations with nurturing, encourages children to maximize their potential and cultivates creativity, critical think-

ing, initiative, and respect for diversity and the dignity of others. Extracurricular opportunities include Student Council, competitive sports and intramurals, publications, musical ensembles, theater arts, community outreach, and field trips. Tuition: $9570–$18,400. Financial Aid: $813,795. Kristin Poe is Director of Admission; Nancy Heath Hightower (University of Texas, B.S. 1958; University of Houston, M.Ed. 1983, Ed.D. 1985) was appointed Head of School in 1989.

St. Agnes Academy   1906

9000 Bellaire Boulevard, Houston, TX 77036
Tel. 713-219-5400; Admission 713-219-5411; Fax 713-219-5499
Web Site www.st-agnes.org; E-mail ehoover@st-agnes.org

Founded by Dominican Sisters, St. Agnes Academy enrolls 875 girls as day students in Grades 9–12. The school strives to provide a demanding program in an atmosphere imbued with the values and principles of the Catholic faith. The college preparatory curriculum includes Advanced Placement courses and offerings in the arts. Some classes are shared with boys from Strake Jesuit Preparatory. Activities involve students in athletics, musical and theatrical productions, publications, debate, and community service. Tuition: $11,700. Extras: $300–$600. Financial aid is available. Deborah Whalen is Director of Admission; Sr. Jane Meyer (Dominican College, B.A.; Texas Woman's, M.S.) was named Principal in 1981 and is now Head of School. *Southern Association.*

St. Andrew's Episcopal School   1952

Lower/Middle School: 1112 West 31st Street, Austin, TX 78705
Tel. 512-299-9800; Fax 512-299-9822
Web Site www.sasaustin.org
E-mail dwilliams@sasaustin.org
Upper School: 5901 Southwest Parkway; Austin, TX 78735
Tel. 512-299-9700; Fax 512-299-9660
E-mail maycock@sasaustin.org

Encompassing Grades 1–12, St. Andrew's provides "an enriched academic program within a Christian environment" to more than 830 day students from various racial, national, and ethnic origins, creating a diverse and culturally rich atmosphere. The rigorous academic curriculum of this college preparatory school is balanced by daily chapel, fine arts, community service, and athletics. The Upper School was the first in Central Texas to set up a state-of-the-art wireless laptop system. After-school enrichment is offered. Tuition: $13,000–$18,000. Extras: $400–$1400. Financial aid is available. Diane Williams (Lower/Middle Schools) and Malia Aycock (Upper School) are Directors of Admissions; Lucy C. Nazro (University of Texas [Austin], B.A.; Episcopal Seminary of the Southwest, M.A.) is Head.

St. James Episcopal School   1946

602 South Carancahua Street, Corpus Christi, TX 78401
Tel. 361-883-0835; Fax 361-883-0837
Web Site www.sjes.org; E-mail proberts@sjes.org

St. James is an independent, coeducational day school enrolling 310 students from 2-year-old through Grade 8. Since its founding in 1946, St. James has followed its mission to provide a superior education that enables students to reach their full potential in a Christian environment. Course work is based on learning activities around a "Central Theme." The early grades emphasize discovery activities in preparation for the mastery of specific academic skills in the Middle School. At all levels, classroom learning is enhanced by field trips and outdoor education beyond the campus. Fine arts, drama, sports, and community service are an integral part of St. James. Life skills, spiritual formation classes, and regular chapel services support personal growth and achievement. Tuition: $3100–$9150. Virginia Craig is the Admissions Coordinator; Patrick H. F. Roberts was appointed Headmaster in 2008; Darla K. Montano was appointed Assistant Head of School in 2009.

St. John's School   1946

2401 Claremont Lane, Houston, TX 77019-5897
Tel. 713-850-0222; Admissions Ext. 320; Fax 713-850-4089
Web Site www.sjs.org; E-mail cplummer@sjs.org

Founded by civic leaders interested in providing a school of exacting standards, St. John's School is a coeducational, college preparatory day school enrolling 1210 students in Kindergarten–Grade 12. Since its inception in 1946, the School has aimed to "yield self-disciplined graduates schooled to a pride in superior achievement and to an active understanding to the individual's responsibility to society." Athletics, arts, and community service are included among the extracurricular activities. Tuition: $15,175–$18,170. Financial aid is available. Cheryl Plummer is Director of Admissions; Dr. James P. Hendrix (Davidson, A.B.; Louisiana State University, M.A., Ph.D.) was appointed Interim Headmaster in 2009.

St. Luke's Episcopal School   1947

15 St. Luke's Lane, San Antonio, TX 78209-4445
Tel. 210-826-0664; Fax 210-826-8520
Web Site www.saintlukes.net; E-mail admission@saintlukes.net

Now in its 62nd year of providing quality education in a Christian context, St. Luke's Episcopal School enrolls an average of 350 day boys and girls from many religious expressions in PreKindergarten–Grade 8. Its mission is to provide a curriculum that nurtures the whole child intellectually, spiritually, physically, and socially. This Nationally Recognized 2005 Blue Ribbon School of Excellence seeks to develop young people who contribute to their world and who possess the qualities of cooperation, good judgment, and leadership. Course work is based on the Core Knowledge Sequence featuring reading and language arts, math, science, history, and Spanish or Latin. Students adhere to an honor code and attend daily chapel services intended to nourish spiritual awareness and character development. Small classes, a 30,000-volume-capacity library, and state-of-the-art computers enhance the educational experience. Students may take part in the National Mythology Exam, national science fair competition, and declamation days. SLES participates in the Independent School Athletic League offering competitive sports such as volleyball, cross-country, basketball, soccer, tennis, golf, and track. Tuition: $7315–$14,567. Margaret Ann Casseb is Director of Admission; Dr. Mark Reford is Head of School.

St. Mark's School of Texas   1906

10600 Preston Road, Dallas, TX 75230-4000
Tel. 214-346-8000; Admission 214-346-8700; Fax 214-346-8701
Web Site smtexas.org; E-mail admission@smtexas.org

St. Mark's is a nonsectarian, independent day school enrolling 840 boys in Grades 1–12. Since its founding in 1906, St. Mark's has prepared a diverse population of students for each succes-

sive step of their academic careers. It is the mission of the School to educate the "whole boy," providing him with the tools necessary to be successful in and out of the classroom. The rigorous academic program is balanced with opportunities to pursue varied interests including athletics, the arts, debate, community service, and school leadership. Tuition: $18,551–$23,674.

ST. MARK'S SCHOOL OF TEXAS

Financial Aid: $2,100,000. David Baker is Director of Admission and Financial Aid; Arnold E. Holtberg (Princeton, A.B.; Lutheran Theological Seminary, M.A.R.) is Headmaster.

Strake Jesuit College Preparatory   1961

8900 Bellaire Boulevard, Houston, TX 77036
Tel. 713-774-7651; Admissions 713-490-8113; Fax 713-774-6427
Web Site www.strakejesuit.org; E-mail admissions@strakejesuit.org

Strake Jesuit, a Catholic, college preparatory day school enrolling 893 boys in Grades 9–12, carries on the 450-year tradition of Jesuit education worldwide. The school prepares its graduates to be men in service to others as well as being ready to succeed in college; the curriculum allows 100 percent of the graduates to move directly into college. There is a closed-circuit TV system and electives in TV production as well as 13 varsity sports and many other extracurriculars. Some cross-registration is available at an adjacent Catholic girls' college prep. Summer remedial courses are available. Tuition: $13,600. Financial Aid: $1,000,000. Ken Lojo is Director of Admissions; Richard C. Nevle is Principal; Fr. Daniel K. Lahart, S.J., is President.

Trinity Valley School   1959

7500 Dutch Branch Road, Fort Worth, TX 76132
Tel. 817-321-0116; Fax 817-321-0105
Web Site www.trinityvalleyschool.org
E-mail tvs@trinityvalleyschool.org

Trinity Valley is a nondenominational, coeducational day school serving 950 young people in Kindergarten to Grade 12. Its mission is to develop in students high standards of scholarship, diverse and constructive interests, intelligent citizenship, and leadership with character. The curriculum in the lower grades focuses on mastery of strong skills in core subjects in readiness for the challenging college preparatory program in the Upper School. A Trinity Valley education is enhanced by Student Council, honor societies, a visiting-artist program, interest groups, music, drama, community service, experiential education, programs in leadership and Chinese, and interscholastic

TRINITY VALLEY SCHOOL

athletics. Tuition: $14,995–$15,815. Financial Aid: $969,471. Judith S. Kinser is Director of Admissions; Dr. Gary Krahn is Head of School.

Vanguard College Preparatory School 1973

2517 Mount Carmel Drive, Waco, TX 76710
Tel. 254-772-8111; Fax 254-772-8263
Web Site www.vanguard.org
E-mail maryhelen_george@vanguard.org

Vanguard College Preparatory School welcomes highly motivated students in Grades 7–12. The School offers a rigorous liberal arts curriculum and a challenging learning experience. The 28 members of the Class of 2008 received more than $4,100,000 in college scholarship offers, while 11 students received National Merit recognition. The environment is one that prizes excellence and develops young community leaders. Enrolling 150 boys and girls from diverse racial, ethnic, religious, and economic backgrounds, Vanguard emphasizes a

broad-based education. Core offerings are complemented by Advanced Placement and honors courses as well as a wide variety of electives. Tuition: $11,995. Financial aid is available. Mary

VANGUARD COLLEGE PREPARATORY SCHOOL

Helen George is Director of Admissions and Development; Cindy Graves is Director of College Counseling; Bill Borg (Huntingdon College, B.A.; Jacksonville University, M.A.T.) is Head of School.

The Winston School 1975

5707 Royal Lane, Dallas, TX 75229
Tel. 214-691-6950; Fax 214-691-1509
Web Site www.winston-school.org
E-mail amy_smith@winston-school.org

Winston, a coeducational, college preparatory day school, enrolls 225 *bright students who learn differently*® in Grades 1–12. Based on diagnostic testing and ongoing monitoring, the School formulates individual academic profiles to help students address learning problems. More than 95 percent of graduates enter college. Computers, the arts, and community service enrich the core curriculum, which emphasizes English, math, science, history, and Spanish. Activities include publications, sports, student government, honor societies, class trips, and clubs. Fees: Available upon request. Winston is accredited by the Independent School Association of the Southwest and is a member of the National Association of Independent Schools. Tuition: $17,787–$24,124. Amy C. Smith is Director of Admission and Financial Aid; Dr. Polly Peterson is Head of School.

UTAH

of athletics, including a ski academy. For more information, visit www.rowlandhall.org. Full-day Tuition: $13,440–$16,235. Financial Aid: $1,500,000. Kathy Gundersen (Pre-K–Grade 5)

Rowland Hall-St. Mark's School   1867

Upper School: 843 Lincoln Street, Salt Lake City, UT 84102
 Tel. 801-355-7494; Fax 801-355-0474
 Web Site www.rowlandhall.org; E-mail karenhyde@rowlandhall.org
Middle School: Tel. 801-355-0272; Fax 801-359-8318
Lower School: 720 Guardsman Way, Salt Lake City, UT 84108
 Tel. 801-355-7485; Fax 801-363-5521
 E-mail kathygundersen@rowlandhall.org

Founded in 1867, Rowland Hall-St. Mark's is an independent school enrolling 1000 day students in Pre-Kindergarten–Grade 12. The traditional college preparatory program includes three languages and the study of ethics and world religion. Advanced Placement courses are offered in 17 subjects. Among the extracurricular activities are student government and a variety

ROWLAND HALL-ST. MARK'S SCHOOL

and Karen Hyde (Grades 6–12) are Admissions Directors; Alan C. Sparrow (Brown, B.A.; University of Rochester, M.A.) is Headmaster. *Northwest Association*.

ROWLAND HALL - ST. MARK'S SCHOOL

VIRGINIA

Bishop Ireton High School   1964

201 Cambridge Road, Alexandria, VA 22314-4899
Tel. 703-751-7606; Admissions 703-212-5190; Fax 703-212-8173
Web Site www.bishopireton.org; E-mail hamerp@bishopireton.org

The Oblates of St. Francis de Sales founded and remain affiliated with this coeducational, diocesan school serving 800 students from Catholic and non-Catholic families. The Salesian tradition of excellence aims to develop the spiritual, aesthetic, intellectual, and physical potential of each young person while instilling a sense of responsibility and service to others. The curriculum is college preparatory, with Honors and Advanced Placement courses, computer technology, and required religious studies integral to the program. With 41 athletic teams, nearly 70 percent of students participate in at least one sport; other activities include a comprehensive music program, yearbook, drama, and special-interest clubs. Tuition: $10,920–$15,000. Financial Aid: $500,000. Peter Hamer is Director of Admissions; Tim Hamer is Principal.

Blue Ridge School   1909

273 Mayo Drive, St. George, VA 22935
Tel. 434-985-2811; Fax 434-985-7215
Web Site www.blueridgeschool.com
E-mail admission@blueridgeschool.com

BLUE RIDGE SCHOOL in St. George, Virginia, is an all-boys, all-boarding, college preparatory school for Grades 9 through 12. Set in a region of great natural beauty, the School is a 20-minute drive from the Appalachian Trail, 25 minutes by car from Charlottesville, and less than 2 hours from Washington, D.C.

Blue Ridge began as an Episcopal mission school in 1909 to educate the children of local families. In 1962, it was reorganized as a college preparatory school dedicated to serving young men who thrive on personalized instruction, teaching students to reach their highest potential.

The School recognizes that every boy is unique, with different growth and development rates, learning styles, interests, objectives, and life paths. Responding to these differences, Blue Ridge focuses on individual needs to build success, self-confidence, and independence. With an average class size of 9 and a 5:1 student-teacher ratio, personalized academic support is a key element in empowering boys to achieve their goals.

While welcoming young men from all religious faiths, Blue Ridge is proud of its Episcopal heritage and requires school-wide participation in weekday and Sunday services. The Episcopal chaplain is committed to fostering the spiritual beliefs of students from Jewish, Buddhist, Islamic, and other world religions.

Life at Blue Ridge is guided by the Code of Conduct, which comprises the core values of the school community: being honorable and accountable, being willing to invest oneself and to try new things, persevering and maintaining a positive attitude, displaying mutual respect and tolerance, being a good citizen, and developing habits of mind, body, and spirit.

A nonprofit institution, Blue Ridge School is accredited by the Southern Association of Colleges and Schools and the Virginia Association of Independent Schools. The School holds membership in the National Association of Independent Schools, The Association of Boarding Schools, the Secondary School Admission Test Board, and other professional organizations.

THE CAMPUS. Adjacent to Shenandoah National Park, the School occupies 751 acres of ponds, streams, and woodlands in the eastern foothills of the Blue Ridge Mountains. The rural setting provides a learning environment free of the distractions of more populated areas.

BLUE RIDGE SCHOOL

Perkins Hall, which contains the David Brobeck Science Center, is the academic heart of the School, furnishing classrooms, study halls, laboratories, and the computer center. The science program is enhanced by the state-of-the-art, all-digital Blue Ridge Observatory, located on Flattop Mountain at an elevation of 3250 feet. Blue Ridge School has deployed fiber-optic cable within all of the major campus buildings, allowing for 100 MB connectivity to all desktops within the school network, and wireless access points within the library and computer lab. The newly renovated Academic Building houses the Fishburne Learning Center, Loving Hall classrooms, and the Hatcher C. Williams Library. The New York Auxiliary Student Center furnishes fine arts facilities, a game room, a viewing room with home theater, a snack bar, and space for dances and social events. Boys live in two dormitories staffed by resident house parents who are available *in loco parentis* on a 24-hour, seven-day-a-week basis.

The academic hub of the campus is supplemented by the Massey Athletic Complex, containing a basketball court and spectator seating as well as a field house with tennis and basketball courts and wrestling, training, and weight-lifting rooms. Outdoor facilities include a 400-meter all-weather track, a climbing tower, driving range, a swimming pool, and playing fields for football, baseball, soccer, and lacrosse.

THE FACULTY. John O'Reilly, Ph.D., was appointed Headmaster in June 2009 after the retirement of Dr. David A. Bouton. Dr. O'Reilly holds master's degrees in Education and Arts from Columbia University and a doctorate in Education from Pennsylvania State University. For the past four years, he has served as the Associate Headmaster for Academics at Blue Ridge. Prior to his service at the School, he was Upper School Head at Fort Worth Country Day in Texas. Dr. O'Reilly and his wife, Cynthia, who live on campus with their dog, Marley, have two grown children, a son in Dallas and a daughter in New York.

The 35 members of the teaching and professional staff hold baccalaureate degrees or the equivalent, and more than half have earned advanced degrees. Nearly all faculty live on campus.

Two full-time nurses staff the infirmary, and hospital facilities are located in Charlottesville.

STUDENT BODY. For the 2009–10 school year, 190 boys are enrolled in Grades 9–12 and actively engaged in life at Blue Ridge School. They come from 20 states and 15 countries and represent a wide spectrum of racial, ethnic, and religious backgrounds.

ACADEMIC PROGRAM. The school calendar, divided into trimesters, extends from early September to late May. Boys attend classes five days a week, with six 50-minute periods three days a week and three 75-minute periods on the other two. Saturday mornings feature a variety of fine arts productions, guest speakers, field trips, and other special programs.

The highly structured environment at Blue Ridge enables boys to focus on the mastery of skills fundamental to success in a challenging college preparatory curriculum. Professional staff at the Fishburne Learning Center work closely with faculty and students to ensure that every young man receives the appropriate level and range of support needed to achieve his academic objectives. Among the services provided are reviews of student files, consultation with teachers, and small-group instruction that emphasizes study strategies, reading comprehension, written expression, and math. Students can also utilize the Learning Center for help from classroom teachers with specific problems in core courses. With the approval of the Assistant Head for Administration and Academics, boys have the additional option of taking part in the Homework Assistance Program (HAP), which provides a focused, supportive environment in the Learning Center during evening study hours. Daily conference periods provide students with extra-help opportunities from classroom teachers, and two-hour supervised study halls are held each evening from Sunday through Thursday.

To graduate, boys must earn 4 credits in English; 3 credits each in social studies, math, science, and the same foreign language; 2 credits in physical education; and 1 in life skills. Students in Grade 9 and new 10th graders are also required to take a study skills program during their first trimester in attendance.

BLUE RIDGE SCHOOL

Among the core and elective subjects are Literary Genres and Composition 9–10, World Literature, American Literature; French I–V, Spanish I–V, Spanish Conversation and Culture; Algebra I–III, Geometry, Pre-Calculus, Calculus, Discrete Mathematics; Integrated Sciences, Biology, Chemistry, Physics, Astronomy, Environmental Science, Mountain Ecology; World History and Ancient Civilizations, Modern European History, United States and Virginia Government and History, U.S. History; and Studio Art, Advanced Art, Photography, Concert Choir, and Music Appreciation. Honors and advanced courses are available in all academic disciplines.

SAT/ACT Prep is integrated into English and math classes, with emphasis on format, content, and strategies to maximize student performance on these tests. Blue Ridge also offers SAT prep courses on campus.

The Outdoor Program provides opportunities for boys to earn credit by participating in leadership, environmental service projects, and activities such as mountain biking, skiing, canoeing, and outdoor living skills.

BLUE RIDGE SCHOOL

Typically, 100 percent of Blue Ridge graduates are accepted into four-year colleges and universities. Over the past four years, these have included such institutions as Boston College, Boston University, The Citadel, College of Charleston, College of William and Mary, Denison, Dickinson, East Carolina, Emory, Georgia Southern, Gettysburg, Gonzaga, Hampden-Sydney, Hofstra, James Madison University, Johnson & Wales, Kansas State, Lynchburg, Manhattanville, Marymount, Mary Washington, Michigan State, New England College, Ohio State, Pennsylvania State, Pepperdine, Presbyterian, Purdue, Rhode Island School of Design, Roanoke, Rollins, Syracuse, Trinity College, Tulane, Virginia Polytechnic, and the Universities of California, Houston, Maryland, Massachusetts, Mississippi, Notre Dame, and Virginia.

STUDENT ACTIVITIES. Cocurricular activities at Blue Ridge, designed to promote leadership, growth, friendship, and recreation, reflect the trust and confidence the School places in its young men. Leadership opportunities include positions such as prefect, proctor, and member of the Honor Council and/or Disciplinary Committee. Qualified students may join the National Honor Society.

Community service involves students in altruistic endeavors such as food and fund drives, and they also volunteer with the American Heart Association, local elementary schools, nursing homes, and animal shelters.

Boys take part in clubs formed around interests in astronomy, chess, drama and the performing arts, publications, conservation, and other pursuits.

In the athletic program, Barons teams compete in cross-country, track and field, football, indoor and outdoor soccer, mountain biking, basketball, wrestling, baseball, golf, lacrosse, and tennis.

The Social Activities Committee coordinates events on and off campus, including dances and mixers with girls' schools in the area. Boys enjoy trips to amusement parks, collegiate and professional ballgames, and theaters in Charlottesville, Richmond, and the nation's capital.

ADMISSION AND COSTS. Blue Ridge seeks young men of good character and potential who will thrive in the School's structured program and close-knit community. Acceptance is based on the candidate's application, questionnaire and essay, teacher recommendations, previous transcripts, and the results of standardized tests.

In 2009–10, tuition, room, and board is $36,000. The School's innovative tuition plan is designed to make a Blue Ridge education more affordable. The tuition rate charged in the first year remains the same throughout a student's four years if the fee is paid in full before August 1 each year. The financial aid program assists approximately 35 percent of the student body based on demonstrated need and good academic and social standing.

Dean of Faculty: James A. Niederburger
Dean of Students: Tony Brown
Director of Resident Life: Chris Rehm
Director of Alumni Relations: Dan Dunsmore
Assistant Headmaster for Enrollment & Marketing: William A. Darrin III
Assistant Headmaster for Advancement: Robert J. Murphy III
College Counselor: Jill Perlmutter
Assistant Headmaster for Finance: Ronald Floor
Director of Athletics: Carl Frye

Browne Academy   1941

5917 Telegraph Road, Alexandria, VA 22310
Tel. 703-960-3000; Fax 703-960-7325
Web Site www.browneacademy.org
E-mail ssalvo@browneacademy.org

This coeducational day school enrolling 300 students in Preschool–Grade 8 is dedicated to the development of the individual child as an independent, lifelong learner who embraces the core values of excellence, diversity, character, and community. These values form the basis for preparing students for competitive secondary schools in the metropolitan area. Browne's academic environment features an interdisciplinary curriculum that emphasizes creative problem solving and critical thinking skills; 11 acres of fields and streams offer outdoor learning opportunities. The school also features a foreign language program from Preschool through Grade 8. Browne's new state-of-the-art Center for Athletics and Performing Arts provides a versatile space that not only allows students to engage in indoor athletic activities but also supplies a venue for musical performances, class plays, school assemblies, and community gatherings. Activities include competitive team sports, tae kwon do, soccer, choir, handbells, band, drama, publications, Scouts, and student council. Extended day and an 8-week summer camp program are available. Tuition: $12,975–$21,505. Financial Aid: $500,000. Steve Salvo is Director of Admission; Margot Durkin is Head of School.

Burgundy Farm Country Day School   1946

3700 Burgundy Road, Alexandria, VA 22303
Tel. 703-960-3431; Admissions 703-329-6968; Fax 703-960-5056
Web Site www.burgundyfarm.org; E-mail info@burgundyfarm.org

Burgundy Farm Country Day School, enrolling 280 boys and girls in Junior Kindergarten through Grade 8, provides a family-friendly atmosphere in which children love to learn. A 25-acre campus of forest, field, farm, and pond is a natural setting imbued with rich traditions and a unique history. Classrooms serve as laboratories where students undertake hands-on learning and a developmental curriculum. The innovative, student-centered academic program integrates fine arts, music, drama, French and Spanish, multicultural studies, and physical education throughout core subjects. Burgundy offers a low student-teacher ratio, a 21,000-volume library, bus transportation, extended day programs, competitive sports, summer camps, and a 500-acre wildlife campus in West Virginia. Tuition: $20,575–$22,675. Financial Aid: $680,000. Kari Cafeo is Director of Admissions; Jeff Sindler is Head of School.

Cape Henry Collegiate School   1924

1320 Mill Dam Road, Virginia Beach, VA 23454
Tel. 757-481-2446; Fax 757-481-9194
Web Site www.capehenrycollegiate.org
E-mail richardplank@capehenry.org

CAPE HENRY COLLEGIATE SCHOOL

Cape Henry Collegiate School is a coeducational, college preparatory day school enrolling more than 1000 students in Prekindergarten (age 3)–Grade 12. Emphasizing academic, social, and physical development, the balanced educational experience involves challenging academics, athletics, arts, community service, and extensive extracurricular activities. A year-round extended-day program is available for Lower School students. Tuition: $10,485–$15,610. Richard J. Plank is Director of Admissions & Financial Aid; Dr. John P. Lewis (St. Peter's College, B.S., M.A.; Seton Hall University, Ed.D.) is Head of School.

Chatham Hall   1894

800 Chatham Hall Circle, Chatham, VA 24531-3085
Tel. 434-432-2941; Fax 434-432-1002
Web Site www.chathamhall.org; E-mail admission@chathamhall.org

CHATHAM HALL

Chatham Hall, an all-girls, boarding and day high school in southern Virginia, is known for its strong college preparatory program, community life based on an Honor Code, leadership initiatives, and social service programs, which extend worldwide. One in four Chatham Hall students participates in service in the townships of Cape Town through the School's annual service trip to South Africa. Its Leader-in-Residence Program brings major female world leaders to campus every year. Chatham Hall's students come from 14 international countries and 24 states, ensuring a diverse community. Its alumnae — among them the artist Georgia O'Keeffe and Pulitzer Prize-winning poet Claudia Emerson — are at the forefront in business, medicine, media, education, arts, and philanthropy. Chatham Hall is associated with the Episcopal Church but offers an open environment designed to encourage growth in all areas. All graduates enter four-year colleges and universities including Cornell, Duke, Georgetown, Vassar, Virginia Tech, and the Universities of North Carolina and Virginia. Boarding Tuition: $38,000; Day Tuition: $16,500. Financial aid is available. Vicki Wright is Director of Admission and Financial Aid; Dr. Gary Fountain is Rector/Head of School.

Collegiate School   1915

North Mooreland Road, Richmond, VA 23229
Tel. 804-740-7077; Admission 804-741-9722; Fax 804-741-9797
Web Site www.collegiate-va.org
E-mail "firstinitial""lastname"@collegiate-va.org

Collegiate School enrolls 1556 boys and girls in Kindergarten–Grade 12 on a 55-acre campus, with an additional 150 acres devoted to athletic facilities. Collegiate seeks to admit students who have the academic and personal potential to meet the high standards of a college preparatory program, who have diverse abilities and backgrounds, and who will make positive contributions to the School. Math, sciences, foreign languages, art, music, physical education, economics, and computer literacy are required. A fine arts building features a 620-seat theater and art and music facility. Tuition: $15,990–$18,770. Financial Aid: $2,022,000. Amanda Surgner is Director of Admission; Keith A. Evans (Davidson, B.A.; Harvard University, Ed.M.; University of Tennessee, M.S.) is Head of School. *Southern Association.*

The Covenant School   1985

Pre-K–Grade 6: 1000 Birdwood Road, Charlottesville, VA 22903
Grades 7–12: 175 Hickory Street, Charlottesville, VA 22902
Tel. 434-220-7329; Admissions 434-220-7330; Fax 434-979-3204
Web Site www.convenantschool.org
E-mail dharris@covenantschool.org

The Covenant School is a nondenominational, coeducational, Christian day school enrolling 600 students in Pre-Kindergarten through Grade 12. The School fosters learning grounded in the best traditions of classical and Christian education. The central goal of its program is to cultivate young people who can think, communicate, and make wise decisions that honor Christ and serve the common interests of their community and society. The School offers a liberal arts, college preparatory education that seeks to instill the joy and discipline of learning in language arts, mathematics, history, science, fine arts, and physical education. Tuition: $6600–$13,370. Financial aid is available. Donna B. Harris is Director of Admission & Financial Aid; Dr. Ronald P. Sykes is Head of School.

Episcopal High School   1839

1200 North Quaker Lane, Alexandria, VA 22302
Tel. 703-933-3000; Admissions 703-933-4062
Fax 703-933-3016
Web Site www.episcopalhighschool.org
E-mail admissions@episcopalhighschool.org

EPISCOPAL HIGH SCHOOL in Alexandria, Virginia, is a college preparatory boarding school for boys and girls in Grades 9 through 12. It is 15 minutes from the cultural and educational resources of Washington, D.C., and Washington's Ronald Reagan Airport. Alexandria (population 175,000) is situated in northern Virginia on the Potomac River. Once an 18th-century seaport, today it is a thriving business and residential area that offers a spectrum of cultural, social, and educational events.

Episcopal High School opened in 1839 as a school for boys. Episcopal grew to accommodate more than 100 boys until May 1861, when the Civil War forced its closing. In continuous operation since reopening in 1866, the School became coeducational in 1991 and remains a fully residential community.

Episcopal is committed to the spiritual, intellectual, moral, and physical development of students. In addition to a challenging and dynamic academic program, there are regularly scheduled chapel services, an array of athletics and arts offerings, and community service programs.

Episcopal High School is a nonprofit corporation directed by a 30-member Board of Trustees, 18 of whom are alumni. There are approximately 4600 living graduates. The School is accredited by the Virginia Association of Independent Schools and the Southern Association of Colleges and Schools and holds membership in the National Association of Independent Schools, among other organizations. The School-owned plant is valued at $150,000,000, and the endowment is $142,000,000.

THE CAMPUS. Situated on 130 acres near the western boundary of Alexandria, Episcopal is surrounded by wooded areas. The principal buildings are situated on tree-shaded lawns in the middle of the campus.

The centerpiece of Episcopal's campus is Hoxton House, originally called Mount Washington when it was built in 1804 by Martha Washington's eldest granddaughter, Eliza Parke Custis Law. The original drawing room has been carefully restored and continues to be used as the main reception room on campus.

EPISCOPAL HIGH SCHOOL

The School's academic facilities provide students with ample resources and state-of-the-art technology. The new 34,000-square-foot Baker Science Center (2005) includes laboratories for biology, chemistry, physics, and environmental science. The Computer Center houses a training center and a network operations center providing 20 servers. All students have laptops with wireless capability and access to the Internet via a T-1 line. Printers are distributed around the campus, including one in each dormitory. The Ainslie Arts Center (2003) provides extensive, state-of-the-art facilities, including visual studios; drawing, painting, and ceramics studios; a digital lab with 15 computers, large format printers, film scanners, and digital cameras; and a traditional darkroom facility. Stewart Gymnasium Dance Studio; Auditorium and Performing Arts Center; a bookstore; Bryan Library Reception Center; and meeting rooms and offices.

EPISCOPAL HIGH SCHOOL

Episcopal's outstanding athletic facilities include Hummel Bowl, a 2800-seat stadium for football and lacrosse; Flippin Field House with 3 tennis courts, 3 basketball courts, a 200-yard track, and a batting cage; Centennial Gymnasium with a basketball court and a newly renovated fitness center featuring a Cybex weight machine room and cardiovascular area; seven playing fields, including two new FieldTurf all-weather fields; Goodman Squash Center with 5 international courts; Cooper Dawson Baseball Diamond; a wrestling cage; Shuford Tennis Courts (12 all-weather tennis courts); an outdoor swimming pool; and Hoxton Track, a six-lane, 400-meter outdoor track.

Residential facilities include eight dormitories with single, double, and triple rooms, common rooms, and laundry facilities; Patrick Henry Callaway Chapel, where students attend services on most weekdays; Laird Dining Room; Blackford Hall, the main coed student lounge with a snack bar, vending area, television, and CD jukebox; and the McAllister Health Center, which is staffed by a registered nurse and visited daily by a full-time resident physician. Alexandria Hospital, two blocks away, provides emergency treatment, if needed.

THE FACULTY. F. Robertson Hershey was appointed the School's 11th Headmaster in 1998. He attended Williams College (B.A. 1970) and the University of Virginia (M.Ed. 1975). Mr. Hershey had previously served as Headmaster at Durham Academy from 1978 to 1988 and, most recently, at The Collegiate School in Richmond from 1988 to 1998.

The faculty of 77 men and women hold 89 advanced degrees, including 7 doctorates. Nearly 90 percent of all full-time faculty members live on campus with their families.

STUDENT BODY. Episcopal High School's 445 boarding students—approximately 55 percent boys and 45 percent girls—come from 30 states, the District of Columbia, and 20 foreign countries.

ACADEMIC PROGRAM. The school year, from early September through late May, includes two semesters with vacations at Thanksgiving, Christmas, and in the spring.

Classes meet five days a week. A typical daily schedule, from 7:15 A.M. to 10:30 P.M., includes chapel, class periods,

meals, a tutoring period, athletics and activities in the afternoon, and two hours of evening study.

There are 10 to 12 students in an average class, with a student-teacher ratio of 6:1. Homework is prepared during free periods in the morning and during the evening study halls, with these periods supervised by student leaders and faculty. Grades are issued and sent to families four times a year.

A minimum of 23 credits is required for graduation, with the following specific requirements: 4 credits in English, 3-3½ in mathematics, 2 in social studies, 3 in a foreign language, 2 in physical education, 2 in laboratory science, 1 in theology, and 1 in fine arts. Students also have the opportunity to experience Episcopal's unique Washington Program, which provides academic exposure to cultural and historical sites in Washington, D.C., and the surrounding area.

A wide variety of courses are available, including 40 honors and Advanced Placement courses. The curriculum offers courses in English, Chinese, Creative Writing, French, German, Latin, Spanish, U.S. and World History, Theology, Economics, Algebra, Geometry, Trigonometry, Pre-Calculus, AB and BC Calculus, Statistics, Ethics, Computer Studies, Electronic Publishing, Art History, Photography, Studio Art, Music Theory, Music History, and Theatre Arts.

Members of Episcopal's Class of 2008 will attend such colleges and universities as Boston College, College of William and Mary, Cornell, Georgetown, Harvard, Johns Hopkins, New York University, Princeton, Vanderbilt, Washington and Lee, Wesleyan, and the Universities of North Carolina, Pennsylvania, and Virginia.

STUDENT ACTIVITIES. An enduring tradition is the Honor Code, which Episcopal pioneered among secondary schools. Faculty and students strongly support this concept, which asserts that students will not lie, cheat, or steal, and that, out of a genuine concern for and responsibility to the student who does, they are asked to report violators to the Honor Committee.

The student body is led by student monitors who are nominated to the Headmaster by the faculty and students and who are responsible for discipline and orderliness in the day-to-day life of the High School. A student-elected dorm council offers additional leadership opportunities.

EPISCOPAL HIGH SCHOOL

Episcopal fields 45 teams in 15 sports for boys and girls, including junior, junior varsity, and varsity teams in many sports. Baseball, basketball, girls' crew, cross-country, field hockey, football, golf, lacrosse, soccer, softball, squash, tennis, indoor and outdoor track, volleyball, and wrestling are offered. All students can participate in dance, and older students may choose aerobics, weight training, cross training, and an outdoor program during some seasons. Episcopal's teams play a full schedule with other independent schools located primarily in the Virginia, Maryland, and Washington, D.C., areas. Boys' teams participate in the Interstate Athletic Conference, and girls' teams compete in the Independent School League.

Activities include the Art Club, Choir, Community Service

Program, Environmental Club, Honor Committee, International Relations Club, Model U.N., peer counseling, Quiz Bowl, Performing Arts Group, two literary magazines, newspaper, yearbook, Student Health Awareness Committee, Student Vestry, Tour Guides, and Service Council. In addition, the Activities Program involves students in cultural, historic, athletic, outdoor, and social activities throughout the Washington area. Qualified musicians may participate in the American Youth Philharmonic or Mount Vernon Youth Symphony orchestras. A formal Outdoor Program is also available.

EPISCOPAL HIGH SCHOOL

Students present two full-length plays—a drama and a musical—and several one-act plays. Special events include dances and social events with other schools, winter weekend skiing in Pennsylvania, fall Homecoming, and Parents' Weekends in both the fall and spring.

ADMISSION AND COSTS. Qualified candidates are accepted without regard to race, creed, or family financial resources. Admission is highly selective, and applicants are evaluated on the basis of their academic record—previous grades, teacher comments, and testing—as well as intellectual curiosity, personal qualities, and extracurricular interests and talents.

Tuition is $42,000, and students must also purchase a laptop computer through the School. Tuition insurance and a tuition plan are available. In the 2008–09 academic year, 30 percent of the student body receive scholarship grants or low-interest loans totaling $3,300,000. Episcopal High School subscribes to the services and principles of the School and Student Service for Financial Aid.

Assistant Head for Academics: Jacqueline E. Maher
Assistant Head for Student Life: Timothy C. Jaeger
Director of Faculty Development: Peter A. Jordan
Dean of Students: Leavenworth M. Ferrell
Director of Admissions: Emily Atkinson
Director of Development: Robert C. Eckert
Director of College Counseling: Robert M. Hedrick
Treasurer: William H. de Butts
Director of Athletics: Mark E. Gowin

Fredericksburg Academy   1992

10800 Academy Drive, Fredericksburg, VA 22408-1931
Tel. 540-898-0020; Fax 540-898-8951
Web Site www.fredericksburgacademy.org
E-mail admission@fredericksburgacademy.org

Fredericksburg Academy is a coeducational day school enrolling approximately 450 students in Prekindergarten through Grade 12. The Academy's curriculum utilizes both traditional and innovative approaches to reach its goals of preparing students

for college, helping them become active citizens in the global community, and developing an appreciation for learning throughout their lives. Students benefit from a challenging core academic program that is balanced with exciting and rewarding opportunities in drama, music, art, computers, physical education, and community service. Upper School students participate in a wireless computer laptop program that is used in all disciplines. Parents are considered important and valuable partners in the educational process. Tuition: $13,700–$15,500. Financial aid and extended care are available. Lori J. Adams is Director of Admission; Robert E. Graves is Headmaster.

Grymes Memorial School   1947

13775 Spicer's Mill Road, Orange, VA 22960
Tel. 540-672-1010; Fax 540-672-9167
Web Site www.grymesschool.org; E-mail info@grymesschool.org

The first students who attended what is now Grymes Memorial School were accommodated in the home of founder and teacher Emily Grymes. As enrollment grew, the School relocated twice, the second time to its present 32-acre campus facing the Blue Ridge Mountains. Serving approximately 165 boys and girls as day students in Junior-Kindergarten to Grade 8, Grymes offers a challenging curriculum rooted in traditional preparatory subjects and enriched by music, the arts, modern language, and electives. Lower school students (JK–4) learn basic phonemic awareness, reading, numeracy, and Spanish. In the upper school, students apply their acquired skills to more complex concepts in English, math, science, and social studies. Technology is available throughout the School for research, writing, and exploration. Character education and moral values are emphasized along with academic excellence. Children enjoy activities in music, art, and drama as performers, creators, and audience members. Physical education classes and participation in sports build fitness and promotes team cooperation and sportsmanship. Tuition: $8400–$10,950. Lee Berry is Director of Admissions; Elisabeth "Penny" Work is Head of School.

Hampton Roads Academy   1959

739 Academy Lane, Newport News, VA 23602
Tel. 757-884-9100; Admissions 757-884-9148; Fax 757-884-9137
Web Site www.hra.org; E-mail admissions@hra.org

Hampton Roads Academy, a nationally recognized Blue Ribbon school, was founded in 1959. It is an independent, coeducational, college preparatory day school enrolling 660 students in Prekindergarten–Grade 12, with a student-teacher ratio of 10:1. The school community works together to foster a safe environment for its students. One hundred percent of Hampton Roads graduates attend selective colleges across the nation. Hampton Roads Academy is committed to diversity and enrolls international students from several different countries. Tuition: $7400–$14,365. Kristen Glauner is Director of Admissions; Thomas D. Harvey (St. Peter's College, A.B.; Wesleyan University, M.A.L.S.; Rockhurst College, M.B.A.; Klingenstein Fellow of Teachers College, Columbia) is Headmaster.

The Hill School of Middleburg   1926

130 South Madison Street, P.O. Box 65, Middleburg, VA 20118-0065
Tel. 540-687-5897; Fax 540-687-3132
Web Site www.thehillschool.org; E-mail tlord@thehillschool.org

The Hill School is a coeducational, elementary day school enrolling 240 students in Kindergarten–Grade 8. It seeks to prepare students for academic success in secondary schools through a strong curriculum, an excellent faculty, and small class sizes. Hill also offers a range of opportunities for intellectual, artistic, athletic, and interpersonal growth within its cocurricular program of art, music, drama, athletics, outdoor education, field trips, and community service. Tuition: $14,250–$18,800. Financial Aid: $550,000. Treavor Lord is Director of Admissions; Thomas A. Northrup (University of Pennsylvania, B.A. 1968, M.S.Ed. 1981) was appointed Headmaster in 1981.

The Langley School   1942

1411 Balls Hill Road, McLean, VA 22101
Tel. 703-356-1920; Admissions 703-848-2782; Fax 703-790-9712
Web Site www.langleyschool.org; E-mail admission@langleyschool.org

The Langley School, a coeducational day school enrolling 480 students in Preschool–Grade 8, strives to discover, amplify, and embrace the talents of every child every day through an engaging program of rigorous academics, fine arts, athletics, and community service. By nurturing, supporting, and academically challenging its students, Langley's inclusive community builds quietly confident, independent thinkers who flourish as learners and individuals. Situated on a 9.2-acre campus, the School's facilities include a new arts center, a 20,000-volume library, science and computer labs, a creative media studio featuring green screen technology, art studios, an athletic center, and a new turf field. Langley offers a 7:1 student-teacher ratio, bus transportation, and extended day. Tuition: $12,950–$25,950. Financial aid is available. Kerry Moody is Director of Admission; Doris Cottam is Head of School.

Loudoun Country Day School   1953

20600 Red Cedar Drive, Leesburg, VA 20175
Tel. 703-777-3841; Fax 703-771-1346
Web Site www.lcds.org; E-mail info@lcds.org

Loudoun Country Day School, an independent, coeducational school enrolling 285 students in Prekindergarten–Grade 8, develops knowledge and skills in language arts, math, science, social studies, French, Spanish, physical education, athletics, computers, music, orchestra, and art. An 8:1 student-teacher ratio provides a nurturing environment and affords considerable individual attention. A character education program, which emphasizes respect, courtesy, kindness, cooperation, and consideration, permeates the School's culture and philosophy. Team sports, dramatic productions, and field trips are central to the program. A new campus and facilities on 70 acres opened in the fall of 2009. Tuition: $11,500–$17,900. Need-based financial assistance is budgeted each year. Pam Larimer is Admissions Coordinator; Dr. Randall Hollister is Headmaster.

Miller School   1878

1000 Samuel Miller Loop, Charlottesville, VA 22903
Tel. 434-823-4805; Fax 434-823-6617
Web Site www.millerschool.org; E-mail admissions@millerschool.org

MILLER SCHOOL in Charlottesville, Virginia, is a coeducational boarding and day school enrolling students in Grades 8 through 12 and Postgraduate. Historic Charlottesville lies in the foothills of the Blue Ridge Mountains, 74 miles northwest of Richmond and 122 miles southwest of Washington, D.C. The city is the site of the University of Virginia, Thomas Jefferson's "Monticello," and the homes of James Monroe and Patrick Henry. Founded in 1878, Miller School is one of the oldest coeducational boarding schools in America and the oldest one in Virginia.

The School's mission statement reads, in part: "With a unique emphasis on minds, hands, and hearts, Miller School prepares young women and men for success in college and life. Distinguished by a rigorous and supportive program, talented

faculty and staff, meaningful leadership opportunities, and small classroom settings, our congenial community builds responsible citizens, insightful thinkers, and compassionate individuals." The faculty believes that young people learn best in a community of trust that seeks to educate a student's mind, hands, and heart through a challenging program of academics, athletics, service, and the arts.

MILLER SCHOOL

A 14-member Board of Trustees oversees the operation of the School, which is accredited by the Virginia Association of Independent Schools and holds membership in the National Association of Independent Schools. Graduates are represented by the Miller School Alumni Association, and families may participate in the Parents' Auxiliary.

THE CAMPUS. Miller School is set on a 1600-acre campus, which includes woodlands, orchards, farmlands, and a 12-acre lake. Old Main, the Headmaster's residence, and the Arts and Science Building are on the Virginia Landmarks Registry and provide excellent examples of High Victorian Gothic architecture. Old Main (1878) contains classrooms, administrative and admissions offices, chapel, dining hall, health center, the boys' dormitories, and the Flannagan Center for Innovative Technology, which houses state-of-the-art computer and support services. Old Main also contains the library, which is linked by computer to the University of Virginia's electronic library system, local public libraries, and all appropriate Internet research sites. Additional buildings on campus include The Arts and Science Building (1882), with woodworking, music, photography, and science classrooms; the Math Building (1885); Wayland Hall and Haden-Hart Hall, the girls' dormitories; the Student Center, housing Sam's Bistro, the book store, the launderette, and the studio art classroom; Alumni Gymnasium, a fully equipped athletic center with basketball, wrestling, and weight training; and faculty residences.

The campus features an outdoor swimming pool, miles of cross-country running trails, tennis courts, and five athletic fields.

THE FACULTY. Walter W. "Winn" Price III was appointed 12th Headmaster of Miller School in 2008. A graduate of the U.S. Naval Academy and the U.S. Naval War College, he holds a master's degree in Business Administration from Harvard University.

There are 52 faculty and professional staff, 29 women and 23 men. In addition to baccalaureates, they hold 22 advanced degrees. Faculty represent such schools as Auburn, Bates, Bridgewater, Dartmouth, Denison, Florida State, Guilford College, Harvard, Hofstra, James Madison, Longwood, Mary Baldwin, Mary Washington, Middlebury, National University of Defense Technology, Radford, Sweetbriar, Universidad Metropolitana de Caracas, Université Denis Diderot, Université Laval, Virginia Commonwealth, Virginia Military Institute, Virginia Polytechnic, and the Universities of North Carolina, Utah, and Virginia.

STUDENT BODY. In 2009–10, Miller School enrolled 140 students, 94 boarding and 46 day, as follows: 7 in Grade 8, 21 in Grade 9, 36 in Grade 10, 35 in Grade 11, 40 in Grade 12, and 1 postgraduate. They came from diverse family backgrounds and cultures and represented nine states and 11 countries.

ACADEMIC PROGRAM. The school year, from early September until the end of May, is divided into semesters, with two grading periods in the fall semester and two in the spring. Vacations are scheduled at Thanksgiving, Christmas, and in the spring. Parents' Weekends are scheduled in the fall and spring. Each student takes six classes that meet five times a week. Class size averages 10 to 12, with a student-teacher ratio of 6:1 throughout the grades.

A typical day begins with breakfast at 7:00 A.M. Classes begin at 8:00 A.M. and run for 50 minutes. Students, faculty, and staff meet in the chapel daily for morning announcements. Wednesday classes are shortened every other week to accommodate school-wide participation in community service programs. Each afternoon, all students are involved in athletics, theater, or other sanctioned activities. Required, faculty-supervised study periods are held each evening, Sunday through Thursday, from 7:30 to 9:30 P.M.

The Miller School diploma requires 23 credits, including four years each of English and history/social studies; three years of mathematics (at least through Algebra II), three years of laboratory science, three years of a foreign language (Latin, Spanish, or French), and two years of fine arts, plus electives. Qualified students may take Advanced Placement courses in a variety of disciplines.

MILLER SCHOOL

The eighth grade offers a strong grounding in the foundational subjects of English (including spelling, grammar, and vocabulary building), mathematics, social studies, science, and the fine arts.

Miller School's Educational Support Services program ranges from educational assessment and support to specialized tutoring, SAT preparation, and, on a limited basis, a study skills class for students with certain identified needs. There is also an English as a Second Language program.

In 2000 through 2009, 100 percent of the graduates who sought to attend college were accepted at four-year colleges and universities including College of William and Mary, Dartmouth, Dickinson, Duke, Hampden-Sydney, Harvard, James Madison, Johns Hopkins, Providence, Purdue, Rhodes, Roanoke College, St. Bonaventure, Seton Hall, Sewanee, Stanford, Syracuse, Tulane, Virginia Polytechnic, Wake Forest, Wellesley, Yale, and the Universities of Pennsylvania, Richmond, Southern California, Virginia, and Wisconsin, among others.

STUDENT ACTIVITIES. The student government is on the prefect model, where elected and appointed students and faculty members serve on the Honor Committee and the Disciplinary Review Board.

"Service to others" is a long-standing Miller tradition expressed in a multifaceted Community Service program. Students choose between on-campus and off-campus opportunities, and these groups, chaperoned by faculty, meet for two hours of service every other Wednesday afternoon. Off-campus groups become involved with various community agencies such as hospitals, retirement homes, local elementary schools, Parks and Recreation, the SPCA, and many others. On-campus groups include Environmental Projects, Library Assistance, and the Recycling Program.

MILLER SCHOOL

Participation in athletics or other authorized activities is required of all. Students compete on varsity and junior varsity teams in the local Virginia Independent Conference or the Blue Ridge Conference. Fall offerings include girls' volleyball, boys' soccer, and girls' and boys' cross-country; winter term offers boys' and girls' basketball and wrestling; spring sports are boys' lacrosse and baseball, girls' soccer, and boys' and girls' tennis. Conditioning is offered as an alternative to team sports, drama is an option during the fall and winter seasons, and an equestrian program is available in the fall and spring.

On weekends, students engage in activities off campus ranging from white-water rafting and tubing to hiking, skiing, and enjoying regional theme and water parks. Trips have included athletic and cultural events at the University of Virginia and other locations as well as Baltimore Orioles and Richmond Braves baseball games. Miller coordinates dances and social events with other boarding schools, and students shop and attend movies regularly.

ADMISSION AND COSTS. Miller School welcomes students of all cultural and racial backgrounds. International students should have a working knowledge of both spoken and written English. Miller seeks students who possess above-average to superior intelligence, high moral character, and a desire to improve and excel. Candidates are evaluated on their willingness to participate in the Miller School program, character and academic references, and the ability to handle challenging academic material. Acceptance is based on academic record and test scores, letters of recommendation from a current English and math teacher, completed applicant and parent questionnaires, and an interview in person or by phone, depending on distance. A $50 fee ($100 for international students) must accompany the application. Admission is on a rolling basis. First-round decisions are made in early March, and classes can fill any time thereafter. International applicants should allow enough time for processing the appropriate I-20 forms and student F-1 visas.

MILLER SCHOOL

The cost in 2009–10 is $34,200 for seven-day boarding, $31,200 for five-day boarding, $39,950 for international students (including ESL), and $14,950 for day students. These fees include tuition refund insurance, room and board, and activities. There are additional charges for books ($200–$400), spending money for boarding students, and Educational Support Services when appropriate. Financial aid grants totaling $726,550 were awarded to 33 percent of the student body in the current year, with an average grant of $12,691 to boarding students and $7007 to day students.

Director of Academics: Rick France
Director of Admissions: Jay Reeves
Director of Finance: Gerri Stewart
Director of Operations: Dan Pugh
Director of College Placement: Hugh Meagher
Director of Athletics: Scott Willard
Director of Student Life: Kathie Cason
Registrar: Cindy DeNome

Norfolk Academy   1728

1585 Wesleyan Drive, Norfolk, VA 23502
Tel. 757-461-6236; Admissions 757-455-5582; Fax 757-455-3199
Web Site www.norfolkacademy.org
E-mail pmclaughlin@norfolkacademy.org

NORFOLK ACADEMY in Norfolk, Virginia, is a coeducational, college preparatory day school enrolling students in Grades 1 through 12. Situated on the border of Norfolk (population 245,000) and Virginia Beach (population 450,000), the Academy enjoys the advantages and diversity of this major metropolitan area, known as Hampton Roads. Site of the world's largest naval base, Norfolk is also the home of Old Dominion University, Norfolk State University, Regent University, Virginia Wesleyan College, and Eastern Virginia Medical School. The Academy is directly off Interstate 64 at Route 13 North and is easily accessible by car.

Founded in 1728, Norfolk Academy is the oldest independent secondary school in Virginia and the eighth oldest in the nation. At its founding, the Academy was a typical 18th-century classical school for boys. It became coeducational in 1966 when the Trustees of Norfolk Academy and the Board of the Country Day School for Girls in Virginia Beach merged the two schools and moved them to the present campus.

Norfolk Academy's program reflects the conviction that sound moral and spiritual values define an individual in a more significant way than academic success. The Academy's mission is to nurture each student's mind, body, artistic expression and appreciation, and sense of responsibility in accordance with the highest standards of excellence. Generations of Norfolk Academy students have exhibited intellectual and personal integrity, in large measure, through their ownership of and participation in the school's honor code. In its effort to develop responsible and productive citizens, the Academy provides leadership opportunities and encourages involvement in community activities, government, social service organizations, and cultural programs.

A nonprofit organization, Norfolk Academy is governed by a 30-member Board of Trustees that meets quarterly. The Alumni Association represents the more than 4350 living alumni, many of whom are active in school activities. The Academy has an endowment of approximately $38,500,000.

Norfolk Academy is accredited by the Southern Association of Colleges and Schools and the Virginia Association of Independent Schools. It holds membership in the National Association of Independent Schools and other educational organizations.

THE CAMPUS. The 70-acre campus includes 11 playing fields, 8 tennis courts, a 400-meter latex track, a football stadium, and an aquatic center. There are also seven single-family homes and one duplex housing administrators and senior faculty.

NORFOLK ACADEMY

There are six school buildings, which provide classrooms, science laboratories, computer centers, art and music rooms, a 375-seat auditorium, the refectory, the bookstore, and administrative offices. In addition, there are two libraries with a total of 50,000 volumes and an extensive collection of periodicals and audiovisual equipment.

The campus also includes two gymnasiums and an athletic pavilion, which provides three additional basketball courts, a fully equipped fitness center, a wrestling room, and expanded locker areas. The 50,000-square-foot Tucker Arts Center houses the 575-seat Samuel C. Johnson Theater, rooms for choral and instrumental music, and dance, art, and sculpture studios.

The school plant is valued at $65,000,000.

THE FACULTY. Dennis Manning, appointed Headmaster in 2001, is a 1984 graduate of Wake Forest University (B.A., M.A.). Most recently, he was Headmaster of The American School in England. Previously, Mr. Manning had been a teacher, coach, and administrator at Woodberry Forest School; Dean of Freshmen and Residence Life and instructor in English at Washington and Lee University; faculty consultant to the Education Testing Service; consultant to the North Carolina Governor's Institute; and, from 1996 to 2000, a member of the Wake Forest University Board of Visitors.

NORFOLK ACADEMY

The full-time faculty number 126—78 women and 48 men; 101 hold advanced degrees. Two or more degrees were earned at College of William and Mary, Dartmouth, Duke, George Washington, Harvard, James Madison, Johns Hopkins, Middlebury, Old Dominion, Princeton, United States Military Academy, United States Naval Academy, Vanderbilt, Washington and Lee, and the Universities of Florida, Georgia, Maryland, Massachusetts, Michigan, North Carolina, Pennsylvania, the South (Sewanee), Texas, and Virginia.

Norfolk Academy offers health insurance, life insurance, and a retirement plan. Leaves of absence can be arranged.

Two school nurses and two trainers are available on campus. An emergency-care center and four major hospitals are within a 10-minute drive of the school.

STUDENT BODY. In 2009–10, Norfolk Academy enrolled 634 boys and 608 girls as follows: 533 in the Lower School (Grades 1–6), 364 in the Middle School (Grades 7–9), and 345 in the Upper School (Grades 10–12). The students live in Norfolk, Virginia Beach, and other communities in the region.

ACADEMIC PROGRAM. The school year, from late August to early June, is divided into semesters and includes a Thanksgiving recess, and Christmas and spring vacations. A typical school day, from 8:10 A.M. to 3:25 P.M., includes six 40-minute class periods, a morning break, lunch, a fine arts period, and an activities period. Sports, drama rehearsals, and dance practice are scheduled after the close of the school day.

Classes, which are held five days a week, have an average enrollment of 20 students. There are daily supervised study halls; some students may be required to attend a special study session held on Saturday mornings. A resource coordinator offers help to Lower School students; the Cum Laude Society provides tutorials for Middle and Upper School students who are having academic difficulties. Grades are issued every nine

weeks; progress reports are sent to parents three times each semester.

The Lower School curriculum consists of reading, written and oral expression, spelling, handwriting, grammar, research skills, problem solving, listening skills, social studies, mathematics, science, and physical and health education. Spanish, computer education, art, music, and instruction in library skills further enrich the curriculum.

Core courses for Grade 7 are English, Introduction to the Social Studies, Latin I, Pre-Algebra, Life Science, and physical education. The Grade 8 curriculum consists of English, Latin II, Ancient History, Algebra, Physical Science, and health and physical education. Computer skills and library instruction are taught throughout the curriculum.

To graduate, students in Grades 9–12 must complete at least 20 credits, including 4 in English, 4 in mathematics, 3 in a foreign language, 3 in history, 2 in laboratory science, 3 in academic electives, and 1 in health and physical education. Seniors must also present an eight-minute speech to the student body and faculty.

Courses offered include English 1–4; French 1–4, German 1–4, Spanish 1–5, Latin 1–5, Italian 1–3, Homeric Greek; World Cultures, Modern European History, United States History, United States Government, Economics; Algebra 1–2, Geometry, Pre-calculus, Calculus, Statistics; Biology, Chemistry, Physics; Art History, Studio Art; Music Theory, Music History, Music Appreciation, Instrumental Music, Chorus; Dramatic Arts; Film Studies; and Dance. Advanced Placement courses are available in all major subject areas. All Upper School students participate in a seminar four times a year.

In 2009, 116 graduates entered such colleges and universities as Brandeis, Brown, College of William and Mary, Cornell, Middlebury, Princeton, Swarthmore, Virginia Polytechnic, Wake Forest, Washington and Lee, Williams, and the Universities of North Carolina (Chapel Hill), Pennsylvania, and Virginia.

Norfolk Academy offers special programs that include the Young People's Theatre, summer school, and sports and summer camps. Breakthrough-Norfolk, a partnership between Norfolk Academy and the Norfolk public schools, is an academic enrichment program for talented, motivated public school students who want to go to college but have limited educational opportunities. Breakthrough-Norfolk is affiliated with Breakthrough National, which began at San Francisco University High School in 1978 as Summerbridge.

STUDENT ACTIVITIES. Each division has an elected student council, which, under the direction of a faculty advisor, helps to plan activities. The Honor Council, made up of Middle and Upper School students, reviews infractions of the Honor Code.

NORFOLK ACADEMY

Students publish a newspaper for each division, a literary magazine, and a yearbook. Extracurricular activities include the Cum Laude Society, Honor Council, Student Council, Fine Arts

Council, Key Club, Peer Counselors, Academy Singers, Dance, Orchestra, Theatre, and the Chess, Engineering, language, Science Fiction, Scientific Research, Forensics, Debate, and Cultural, Environmental, and Ethnic Awareness Clubs. Through Habitat for Humanity, the Happy Club, the Reach/ Interact Club, Third World Grace, and tutoring programs, students actively participate in community service.

Norfolk Academy varsity teams compete with those of other schools in the Tidewater Conference of Independent Schools, the Virginia Prep League, and the League of Independent Schools. Girls' teams compete in basketball, crew, sailing, cheerleading, cross-country, field hockey, lacrosse, tennis, track, soccer, softball, swimming, and volleyball. Boys compete in baseball, basketball, crew, sailing, cross-country, football, golf, lacrosse, soccer, swimming, tennis, track, and wrestling. Supervised weight training is encouraged for both boys and girls.

There are frequent theater and music productions by student groups as well as lectures and performances by guest speakers and artists. Traditional events include Field Day, Charter Day, Arts Festival Day, Grandparents' Day, the winter musical, Multicultural Day, Vespers, the Lower School Holiday Pageant, and Homecoming.

ADMISSION AND COSTS. Norfolk Academy seeks to enroll students from a variety of social, economic, religious, ethnic, and racial backgrounds who demonstrate intellectual curiosity and promise of accomplishment. New students are admitted to all grades on the basis of school-administered testing, interviews with school administrators, and previous school transcripts. Campus visits are encouraged. The application fee is $85 for Grade 1 and $35 for Grades 2–12.

In 2009–10, tuition and required fees for Grades 1–6 total $15,700; for Grades 7–12, costs total $18,450. Included in the total are lunches, supplies, athletics, publications, and laboratory fees. Additional costs include bus transportation ($1135) and driver education ($275). Textbooks are provided in the Lower School but are purchased by students in Grades 7–12.

In the current year, Norfolk Academy awarded more than $2,000,000 in financial aid to 193 students solely on the basis of need. A tuition payment plan is available. Norfolk Academy subscribes to the School and Student Service for Financial Aid.

Assistant Headmaster for Development: Herbert P. Soles
Assistant Headmaster for Business Operations: Sandra T. Kal
Director of the Upper School: Linda R. Gorsline
Director of the Middle School: Garrett C. Laws
Director of the Lower School: Michael W. Silva
Director of Admission: Patricia A. McLaughlin

North Cross School   1944

4254 Colonial Avenue, Roanoke, VA 24018
Tel. 540-989-6641; Admission Ext. 330; Fax 540-989-7299
Web Site www.northcross.org; E-mail djessee@northcross.org

A college preparatory day school enrolling 540 students in junior kindergarten 3 through 12th grade, North Cross School seeks to develop young men and women of intellect, curiosity, purpose, discipline, and patience. A rigorous academic program and accomplished, committed faculty afford all students unequaled opportunities to challenge, strengthen, and learn about themselves. The innovative curriculum includes broad offerings in the arts and community service; starting in sixth grade, 28 interscholastic teams; and student government and publications, as well as a student-run honor council and disciplinary system. As all of its graduates attend four-year colleges and universities, the school offers 11 Advanced Placement courses along with a full-time college counseling program. Tuition: $2550 (Junior Kindergarten 3 – 3-Day)–$11,475

(Grade 12). Need-based financial assistance is available. Deborah C. Jessee is Director of Admission and Financial Assistance; Timothy J. Seeley was appointed Headmaster in 2008.

Oakcrest School   1976

850 Balls Hill Road, McLean, VA 22101
Tel. 703-790-5450; Fax 703-790-5380
Web Site www.oakcrest.org; E-mail admissions@oakcrest.org

OAKCREST SCHOOL

Oakcrest School, in partnership with parents, challenges 180 girls in Grades 6–12 to develop their intellect, character, faith, and leadership potential to succeed in college and throughout their lives. As an independent school, Oakcrest weaves together a rich liberal arts curriculum, character development, one-on-one advising, and service to educate the whole person. Middle School students explore new interests and develop friendships through mini courses, field trips, and club activities. Upper School offers AP courses across the curriculum and comprehensive, individualized college counseling. In addition to classes in Catholic theology and Christian philosophy, students are free to attend daily Mass, seek spiritual advice from the School's chaplain, and take time for prayer and reflection in the chapel. Science, computer and language labs, team sports, and the fine arts complete the program. Tuition: $15,360–$16,300. Susan O'Connor is Director of Admissions and Enrollment Management; Holly Hartge is Director of Admissions; Ellen M. Cavanagh is Head of School.

The Potomac School   1904

1301 Potomac School Road, McLean, VA 22101
Tel. 703-356-4100; Admission 703-749-6313; Fax 703-356-1764
Web Site www.potomacschool.org

The Potomac School is a day school enrolling 980 boys and girls in Kindergarten–Grade 12. Students come from throughout the Washington, D.C., metropolitan area utilizing the School's extensive bus service. Potomac's challenging college preparatory program encourages academic excellence, a love of learning, individual accomplishment, and diverse voices and ideas. The curriculum, designed to provide a substantial foundation in the liberal arts and sciences, includes elective and Advanced Placement courses in the Upper School. Students enjoy small classes,

THE POTOMAC SCHOOL

theatrical productions, weekly assemblies, character education and community service programs, and varsity athletics. Tuition: $24,765–$27,925. Financial Aid: $3,000,000. Charlotte H. Nelsen is Director of Admission; Geoff Jones is Head of School.

St. Andrew's Episcopal School   1946

45 Main Street, Newport News, VA 23601
Tel. 757-596-6261; Fax 757-596-7218
Web Site www.standrewsschool.com
E-mail standrews@standrewsschool.com

St. Andrew's offers a strong academic education within a Christian environment for approximately 165 children in Pre-Kindergarten–Grade 5. Each day begins with Chapel. The School provides a loving, caring atmosphere with small classes that assure individual attention by a qualified and dedicated faculty. Enrichment is provided by resource classes in art, music, French, physical education, and library as well as computer classes in the School's state-of-the-art lab. Pre-kindergarten and all-day and half-day kindergarten, extended-day, and summer programs are offered. St. Andrew's is fully accredited by the Virginia Association of Independent Schools. Tuition: $4140–$6155. Financial aid is available. Margaret Delk Moore is Head of School.

St. Christopher's School   1911

711 St. Christopher's Road, Richmond, VA 23226
Tel. 804-282-3185; Fax 804-673-6632
Web Site www.stchristophers.com; E-mail admissions@stcva.org

St. Christopher's is an Episcopal day school enrolling 940 boys in Junior Kindergarten–Grade 12. The School offers a college preparatory curriculum, with a wide choice of electives, in an atmosphere stressing Christian ideals. Small classes foster close student/teacher relationships, with emphasis on bringing out the best in each boy. There is a program of coordinate education with St. Catherine's School. The athletic program features 16 varsity sports. Academic, recreational, and athletic camps are offered in the summer. Tuition: $15,495–$19,925. Financial Aid: $2,500,000. Cary C. Mauck is Director of Admission; Charles M. Stillwell (Princeton, A.B. 1985; Brown, M.A. 1990) is Headmaster. *Southern Association.*

Saint Patrick Catholic School   2005

1000 Bolling Avenue, Norfolk, VA 23508
Tel. 757-440-5500; Fax 757-440-5200
Web Site www.stpcs.org; E-mail info@stpcs.org

SAINT PATRICK CATHOLIC SCHOOL

Saint Patrick Catholic School enrolls approximately 380 day boys and girls from many faiths in Pre-Kindergarten–Grade 8. During the 2008–09 school year, it received dual accreditation from the Southern Association of Colleges and Schools and the Southern Association of Independent Schools. Also named a "Quality School" as defined by educational reformer William Glasser, the School is committed to "the intentional foundation of students using a vision of 47 outcomes within five domains set forth in the School's founding document, *The Saint Patrick Catholic School Graduate at Graduation.*" The instructional process offers high curricular differentiation, cutting-edge technology, Catholic religious education, and service learning in an environment that identifies, nurtures, and celebrates the gifts of each child. Instructional methods in core subjects include project-based learning, cross-thematic learning, Socratic questioning, and discovery learning. High-level visual, musical, and performing arts instruction is integral to the students' total education. Clubs, leadership groups, team sports, community outreach, and fine arts are among the after-school opportunities. Tuition: $3815–$7155. Financial aid is available. Steve Hammond is Principal; Cathy Thaden is Director of Advancement.

St. Stephen's and St. Agnes School   1924

Upper School: 1000 St. Stephen's Road, Alexandria, VA 22304
Tel. 703-751-2700; Admissions 703-212-2706
Web Site www.sssas.org; E-mail admission@sssas.org
Middle School: 4401 West Braddock Road, Alexandria, VA 22304
Tel. 703-751-2700; Admissions 703-212-2706
Lower School: 400 Fontaine Street, Alexandria, VA 22302
Tel. 703-751-2700; Admissions 703-212-2705

This college preparatory, Episcopal day school enrolls 1141 students in Junior Kindergarten–Grade 12. It seeks to instill a passion for learning, enthusiasm for athletics and the arts, and commitment to service. An honor code, chapel, and service learning are central to the program. Providing a global perspective enables the School to prepare students for a complex and changing world. Foreign language begins in Junior Kindergarten. The curriculum includes 24 Advanced Placement courses and varied electives. Student Government, sports, technology, drama, publications, music, and interest and multicultural clubs are among the extracurriculars. Single-gender math and science classes are unique to the Middle School. A summer program, transportation, and extended day are also provided. Tuition: $21,063–$27,416. Financial Aid: $3,556,729. Diane Dunning is Director of Admission; Joan G. Ogilvy Holden (Tufts, B.A.; Harvard, M.Ed.) is Head of School.

The Steward School   1972

11600 Gayton Road, Richmond, VA 23238
Tel. 804-740-3394; Admission 804-565-2315; Fax 804-740-1464
Web Site www.stewardschool.org
E-mail scott.moncure@stewardschool.org

The Steward School, founded in 1972, is a fully accredited, independent, coeducational day school for 600 students from Kindergarten to Grade 12. Small classes, individualized attention, and extracurricular activities support the uniqueness of each child's growth and are essential to enabling students to reach their educational goals. The Steward School is a mission-driven school where education and relationships are anchored in a shared set of community principles. The goal of the School is to develop purposeful and contributing citizens who are aware of their responsibilities—to themselves, their school, and their society. Steward offers challenging and supportive experiences in academics, the arts, athletics, and community service to help students prepare for college and for life. Extended care, innovative minimesters, and summer sessions are also offered. Tuition: $16,665–$18,465. Financial aid is available. Debbie Robson is Director of Admission; Kenneth H. Seward (Middlebury College, B.A.; Case Western Reserve University, M.A.) is Headmaster.

Sullins Academy   1966

22218 Sullins Academy Drive, Bristol, VA 24202
Tel. 276-669-4101; Admissions Ext. 224; Fax 276-669-4294
Web Site www.sullinsacademy.org
E-mail mmjustis@sullinsacademy.org

Founded in 1966, Sullins Academy is a fully accredited, independent, coeducational day school offering an accelerated program for 210 students in Pre-School through Grade 8. Academic excellence is emphasized with a core curriculum of language arts, mathematics, social studies, foreign language, and computer instruction. Art, music, physical education, reading readiness, clubs, field trips, and athletics further support the nurturing of the whole child. Located on a beautiful 32-acre campus in southwest Virginia, Sullins Academy is committed to the development of minds and character. Tuition: $3050–$6750. Financial aid is available. Mary Margaret Justis is Director of Admissions; Ramona Harr is Head of School.

Trinity Episcopal School   1972

3850 Pittaway Road, Richmond, VA 23235
Tel. 804-272-5864; Fax 804-272-4652
Web Site www.trinityes.org; E-mail emilym@trinityes.org

A coeducational, college preparatory day school enrolling 415 students in Grades 8–12, Trinity Episcopal offers a strong academic program and a caring environment dedicated to the personal growth of each student. The International Baccalaureate Diploma Program is offered in Grades 11–12. Advanced Placement courses are available in 13 disciplines, and electives include Multimedia, Personal Finance, Politics and Film, Creative Writing, Theatrical Design, Human Biology, and Psychology. Tuition: $16,880. Financial Aid: $985,000. Emily H. McLeod is Admissions Director; Thomas G. Aycock (Barton College, B.S.; University of North Carolina, M.A., Ph.D.) was appointed Headmaster in 1990.

EPISCOPAL HIGH SCHOOL

WASHINGTON

The Bush School   1924

3400 East Harrison Street, Seattle, WA 98112
Tel. 206-322-7978; Admissions 206-326-7735; Fax 206-860-3876
Web Site www.bush.edu; E-mail elizabeth.atcheson@bush.edu

The Bush School enrolls 580 students in Kindergarten–Grade 12 on a 6-acre campus convenient to downtown Seattle and the Eastside. With a class size average of 15, the School provides a challenging, progressive educational program that balances rigor with close teacher relationships and experiential education opportunities. Programs emphasize high academic standards and the development of the whole child within a "culture of kindness" that values diversity; 29 percent are students of color and 15 percent receive financial aid. A full-time college counselor, an extended day program, and a wilderness/outdoor education program complement Bush's mission. Tuition: $18,050–$24,530. Elizabeth Atcheson is Director of Admissions and Financial Aid; Frank Magusin is Head of School. *Pacific Northwest Association.*

Charles Wright Academy   1957

7723 Chambers Creek Road West, Tacoma, WA 98467-2099
Tel. 253-620-8300; Admissions 253-620-8373; Fax 253-620-8431
Web Site www.charleswright.org
E-mail ssaalfeld@charleswright.org

A nonprofit, coeducational, college preparatory day school set on a 90-acre, wooded campus, Charles Wright Academy enrolls 730 students in Pre-Kindergarten–Grade 12. Advanced Placement, computer science, drama, art and music, outdoor education, and athletics are integral to the program. Each student's unique academic and artistic abilities, confidence, and sense of values are developed and nurtured by a carefully selected faculty within a community that respects and cares for the well-being of each member. Honesty, integrity, courage, and humor are essential to the school's individual and collective strength and growth. Tuition: $14,900–$20,125. Financial aid is available. Steve Saalfeld is Director of Admissions; Robert Camner (Oberlin, B.A.; Ohio State, M.S.) is Headmaster. *Pacific Northwest Association.*

Epiphany School   1958

3710 East Howell Street, Seattle, WA 98122
Tel. 206-323-9011; Admissions 206-720-7663; Fax 206-324-2127
Web Site www.epiphanyschool.org; E-mail annes@epiphanyschool.org

Epiphany School is an independent, nonsectarian day school enrolling 222 boys and girls in Pre-School–Grade 5. It seeks to help students achieve academic excellence through a traditional, structured approach to learning with strong emphasis on fundamentals. Music, art, French, physical education, drama, library skills, science, and computers enrich the basic curriculum. The School also offers an intensive tutoring program for its students with learning disabilities. Tuition: $12,920–$17,020. Financial Aid: $225,000. Anne Sarewitz is Director of Admissions; Matt Neely was appointed Head of School in 2008. *Northwest Association.*

Forest Ridge School of the Sacred Heart   1907

4800 139th Avenue SE, Bellevue, WA 98006
Tel. 425-641-0700; Admission Ext. 7103; Fax 425-643-3881
Web Site www.forestridge.org

FOREST RIDGE SCHOOL OF THE SACRED HEART

Now in its 103rd year of educating young women, Forest Ridge School of the Sacred Heart enrolls 390 day students in Grades 5 through 12 in a learning environment that prizes a long tradition of academic excellence. More than 30 percent of the student body is racially, culturally, socioeconomically, and ethnically diverse. As a member of the Network of Sacred Heart Schools — 200 schools in 80 countries worldwide — Forest Ridge seeks to develop faith in God, intellectual values, social awareness, and personal growth in each student. While promoting Catholic teaching, the School welcomes girls from all faiths. The curriculum includes religious studies, science and technology including the "Physics First" program the School pioneered, Advanced Placement in eight disciplines, and the visual, performing, and creative arts. The average class size is 15. All graduates go on to higher education, and 15 percent of seniors are National Merit Scholars and Commended students. Community service and varsity athletics are among the activities. Tuition" $24,000. Financial aid is available. Rosanne Tomich is Director of Admission; Mark J. Pierotti is Head of School.

St. Thomas School   1951

8300 NE 12th Street, Medina, WA 98039
Tel. 425-454-5880; Fax 425-454-1921
Web Site www.stthomasschool.org
E-mail admissions@stthomasschool.org

St. Thomas School is a nonsectarian day school enrolling 260 boys and girls in Preschool through Grade 6. St. Thomas School is well known for its commitment to a rigorous academic curriculum and the education of the whole child. The School develops students' full potential in a challenging academic environment that builds a foundation of basic skills and integrates technology, language arts, social studies, science, mathematics, foreign language, fine arts, and physical education. Children develop proficient writing and speaking abilities and acquire solid technological skills. The daily community meeting in Chapel emphasizes character development. Through the curriculum, through school climate, and through service, St. Thomas students are encouraged to apply lessons from the classroom to the world around them. A recently completed construction of its 55,000-square-foot, state-of-the-art campus accommodates the School's expanding enrollment. Tuition: $6475–$19,335. Financial aid is available. Lyn-Felice Calvin is Director of Admissions; Dr. Kirk Wheeler is Head of School. *Pacific Northwest Association.*

Seattle Academy 1983

1201 East Union Street, Seattle, WA 98122
Tel. 206-323-6600; Admissions 206-324-7227; Fax 206-676-6881
Web Site www.seattleacademy.org; E-mail jrupp@seattleacademy.org

Seattle Academy offers a demanding college preparatory program that incorporates academics with the arts, athletics, outdoor education, and community service. Enrolling 600 day boys and girls in Grades 6–12, the school provides a supportive environment that enhances the learning experience through hands-on activities and extensive use of classroom technology and Seattle's urban resources. The curriculum includes rigorous academic courses and visual and performing arts, all of which prepare graduates to attend some of the country's most selective colleges, universities, conservatories, and art schools. Student government, sports, and travel to such locales as Alaska, Africa, Europe, and Latin America enrich the program. Tuition: $22,776–$23,922. Extras: $750. Financial aid is available. Jim Rupp is Director of Admission; Joe Puggelli (State University of New York, B.A.; Pennsylvania State, M.A.) is Head of School.

Seattle Country Day School 1963

2619 Fourth Avenue North, Seattle, WA 98109
Tel. 206-284-6220; Admissions 206-691-2625; Fax 206-283-4251
Web Site www.seattlecountryday.org
E-mail kathymccann@seattlecountryday.org

Seattle Country Day School is an independent K–8 school serving 328 students of high intellectual and creative promise in the heart of Seattle. Experienced teachers, small class sizes, and an inquiry-based teaching model promote academic excellence and enthusiasm for learning. While the curriculum accentuates mathematics, science, and technology, every student's experience includes dynamic humanities, music, art, foreign language, and physical education programs. The learning environment is simultaneously challenging and developmentally age-appropriate. SCDS students enjoy strong after-school and special programs including extended-day, athletics, alpine skiing, ice skating, clubs, and instrumental music classes. SCDS welcomes students of all races, religions, economic backgrounds, and ethnic origins. Tuition: $17,912–$20,943. Financial aid is available. Kathy McCann is Director of Admissions; Michael G. Murphy is Head of School. *Pacific Northwest Association.*

University Child Development School 1976

5062 9th Avenue, NE, Seattle, WA 98105
Tel. 206-547-8237; Fax 206-547-3615
Web Site www.ucds.org; E-mail admission@ucds.org

University Child Development School is centered around the lives of children and dedicated to the development of their intellect and character. Enrolling 300 children in Preschool through Grade 5, the School actively encourages and everywhere reflects the process of joyful discovery that is central to meaningful and responsible learning. Teaching is individualized and responsive to the talents of each student, and the curriculum is rigorous and integrates the concepts and skills embedded within the major disciplines. Students are chosen for their promise of intellect and character and are selected from a cross-section of the community. Faculty members are leaders in their fields, supported in advancing their studies and encouraged to share their knowledge widely. Tuition: $12,305–$18,931. Financial Aid: $634,712. Tami Milles is Director of Admission; Paula Smith is Head of School. *Pacific Northwest Association.*

University Prep 1976

8000 25th Avenue, NE, Seattle, WA 98115
Tel. 206-525-2714; Admission 206-523-6407; Fax 206-525-5320
Web Site www.universityprep.org
E-mail admissionoffice@universityprep.org

University Prep, a day school with more than 480 students in Grades 6–12, is committed to developing each student's potential to become an intellectually courageous, socially responsible citizen of the world. The curriculum is designed to inspire students' natural curiosity and to instill within them the desire for lifelong learning. Small classes, exceptional teachers, and innovative course work challenge students to develop creativity and critical thinking skills. University Prep students learn to solve problems and make mature decisions as well as learn to value diversity and give back to their community. Tuition: $24,025–$25,255. Financial Aid: $1,704,770. Kathy Mitchell O'Neal is Director of Admission and Financial Aid; Erica L. Hamlin (Smith, B.A.; Wesleyan University, M.A.L.S.) is Head of School. *Northwest Association.*

THE BUSH SCHOOL

WEST VIRGINIA

The Linsly School   1814

60 Knox Lane, Wheeling, WV 26003-6489
Tel. 304-233-3260; Admission 304-233-1436; Fax 304-234-4614
Web Site www.linsly.org; E-mail admit@linsly.org

The Linsly School, a coeducational, college preparatory boarding and day school, provides a structured, disciplined program in a community environment that challenges young people to achieve their greatest potential. Enrolling 443 students in Grades 5–12, with 100 boarders in Grade 7 upward, Linsly emphasizes the liberal arts and sciences, enriched by opportunities for overseas travel/study and a unique outdoor education program, The Linsly Outdoor Center. One hundred percent of graduates attend college. Campus activities include interest groups, community service, honor societies, musical productions, and interscholastic sports. Boarding Tuition: $26,360; Day Tuition: $12,950. Financial aid is available. Craig Tredenick is Director of Admissions; Chad Barnett is Headmaster. *North Central Association.*

WISCONSIN

Brookfield Academy   1962

3460 North Brookfield Road, Brookfield, WI 53045
Tel. 262-783-3200; Fax 262-783-3213
Web Site www.brookfieldacademy.org
E-mail admissions@brookfieldacademy.org

Founded in 1962 to provide a strong liberal arts education within a nurturing atmosphere, Brookfield Academy enrolls 800 day students in Pre-Kindergarten to Grade 12. The school's Five Star system emphasizes the moral principles of a free society, and personal responsibility and ethics are promoted at all levels. The college preparatory curriculum also includes classics, languages, music, art, and numerous Advanced Placement opportunities. Upper School students experience a week of outdoor recreation and sports at the start of each academic year. Activities include yearbook, drama, international travel, Mock Trial, Academic Decathlon, and community service. Tuition: $7450–$14,535. Financial aid is available. Sharon Koenings is Director of Admissions; Robert Solsrud is Head of School.

University Lake School   1956

4024 Nagawicka Road, Hartland, WI 53029
Tel. 262-367-6011; Admission Ext. 1455; Fax 262-367-3146
Web Site www.universitylake.org
E-mail awenger@universitylake.org

University Lake School was founded by a small group of parents who envisioned a rigorous, college preparatory day school in Wisconsin's Lake Country. Set on 180 wooded acres, the School is committed to excellence in education through a challenging curriculum, high-caliber faculty, and a safe and supportive environment. University Lake School enrolls 324 boys and girls in Pre-Kindergarten (age 3)–Grade 12. Its academic program is designed to engender a love of learning, creativity, curiosity, leadership skills, and independent thinking. Classes are small, with a 9:1 student-teacher ratio. ULS integrates the traditional liberal arts, sciences, and humanities with the visual and performing arts, advanced technology, athletics, and service learning. College counseling begins in Grade 8, and virtually all University Lake School graduates go on to higher education. Students participate in school government, publications, vocal and instrumental ensembles, clubs, and sports, including a "no-cut" athletic program in Grades 5–12. A summer session of enrichment and recreation is offered. Tuition: $3365–$14,200. Tuition assistance and scholarships are available. Angela Wenger is Director of Admissions; Bradley F. Ashley is Head of School.

University School of Milwaukee   1851

2100 West Fairy Chasm Road, Milwaukee, WI 53217
Tel. 414-352-6000; Admission 414-540-3320; Fax 414-352-8076
Web Site www.usmk12.org; E-mail admissions@usmk12.org

University School of Milwaukee is an independent, college preparatory day school for students in Prekindergarten (age 3) through Grade 12. Enrolling approximately 1080 students, the School is divided into three academic divisions: Lower, Middle, and Upper. USM's faculty-to-student ratio of 1:9 and average class size of 15 allow teachers to provide individual attention. Students are given numerous opportunities to explore who they are and what they can do. Located on a beautiful 120-acre campus, the School includes a state-of-the-art science center, three libraries, a 5-acre outdoor environmental classroom, athletic fields, an indoor ice arena, a 395-seat theater, art and music studios, and facilities for band, orchestra, and chorus. USM promotes an atmosphere that supports the academic, artistic, and athletic achievements of all students, offering them the experience of a lifetime. Tuition: $7843–$19,146. Financial Aid. $3,200,000. Kathleen Friedman is Director of Admissions; Ward J. Ghory, Ed.D., is Head of School.

OTHER COUNTRIES AND UNITED STATES TERRITORIES

BERMUDA

The Bermuda High School for Girls 1894

19 Richmond Road, Pembroke HM 08, Bermuda
Tel. 441-295-6153; Fax 441-278-3017
Web Site www.bhs.bm; E-mail info@bhs.bm

Set on an 8-acre campus, The Bermuda High School for Girls is a Round Square School and enrolls 750 day students, predominantly young women, in Years 1–13. The School's rigorous college preparatory program is specially designed to enable young women to reach their potential in a safe, nurturing environment in which each is free to question, explore, and participate fully in the educational process. The island's first International Baccalaureate school, Bermuda High welcomes students from diverse racial, ethnic, religious, and economic backgrounds, including boys in Years 11–12 of the IB program. The core curriculum centers on English, math, sciences, world languages, and social studies. The arts, music, drama, and information technology complete the program. Students take part in school government, community service, publications, vocal and instrumental ensembles, dramatic productions, and a rigorous interscholastic sports program. Tuition: $16,400–$18,530. Financial aid, bursaries, and competitive scholarships are available. Tina Harris is Head of Primary Admissions; Levyette Robinson is Head of Secondary Admissions; Linda Parker is Head of School.

Saltus Grammar School 1888

P.O. Box HM-2224, HMJX Hamilton, Bermuda
Tel. 441-292-6177; Fax 441-295-4977
Web Site www.saltus.bm; E-mail admissions@saltus.bm

This coeducational school, established with funds left by Samuel Saltus, enrolls 1060 day students in Grades 1–12. Stressing "well-tried, traditional approaches" to education in a "lively and caring atmosphere," the School's goal is to prepare students mentally, spiritually, and physically to meet the demands of the modern world. A college preparatory program working toward Advanced Placement Exams is available. Activities include sports, drama, photography, music, and debate. A summer program is offered. Tuition: $17,224. Financial Aid: $350,000. Deputy Headmaster Malcolm Durrant (Oxford University, M.A., P.G.C.E.) coordinates admissions; E.G. (Ted) Staunton (B.A. [Hons.], B.Ed., M.Ed.) was appointed Headmaster in 2009.

CANADA

Collingwood School 1984

70 Morven Drive, West Vancouver, BC V7S 1B2, Canada
Tel. 604-925-3331; Admissions 604-925-3016; Fax 604-925-3862
Web Site www.collingwood.org
E-mail judy.wilson-neil@collingwood.org

Collingwood, a coeducational, university preparatory day school set on two campuses, enrolls more than 1200 students in Junior Kindergarten–Grade 12. It has built a reputation as a dynamic and progressive educational environment. Colling-

wood's four-stranded approach to education emphasizes academics, arts, athletics, and service to provide the foundation for developing the whole child. The broad academic curriculum is enhanced with honors and AP courses across all subject areas. Among the School's innovative programs are Explore, a challenging outdoor educational and leadership course, and Key, a

COLLINGWOOD SCHOOL

specialized program for children with learning disabilities. Collingwood is a member of The Round Square Conference, a worldwide association of schools whose students share a commitment, beyond academic excellence, to personal development and responsibility through service, challenge, adventure, and international understanding. In 2007, 40 percent of the 19th graduating class was offered more than $365,000 in scholarships to universities and colleges across Canada and the U.S. Tuition: $4960–$21,870 (CAD). Judy Wilson-Neil is Director of Admissions; Rodger Wright, M.Ed., is Headmaster.

The Country Day School 1972

13415 Dufferin Street, King, ON L7B 1K5, Canada
Tel. 905-833-1220; Fax 905-833-1350
Web Site www.cds.on.ca; E-mail admissions@cds.on.ca

The Country Day School, enrolling students in JK–Grade 12, is situated on a beautiful 100-acre campus in the heart of King Township, just north of Toronto. The CDS community is dynamic, friendly, down-to-earth, and involved. Its mandate is to equip students with what they need to make their way in the world with success. To this end, the School offers girls and boys a superior, balanced education that challenges the student, develops the mind, and strengthens the character. CDS has a clear vision for the future, a mission that it strives to make possible for every child, and a set of eight guiding principles to keep faculty and staff focused on the School's objectives and its students. The campus features outstanding athletic facilities, a modern performing arts center, and leading-edge technology, all of which enhance the ability to educate in innovative ways. The Country Day School seeks to ensure that every graduate leaves well prepared for university, confident, independent, intellectually curious, morally responsible, appreciative of the arts, physically fit, and globally aware. Tuition: (Cdn.) $18,450–$21,100. David Huckvale is Director of Admission; Paul C. Duckett is Headmaster.

Glenlyon Norfolk School 1912

801 Bank Street, Victoria, BC V8S 4A8, Canada
Tel. 250-370-6800; Admissions 250-370-6801; Fax 250-370-6811
Web Site www.glenlyonnorfolk.bc.ca
E-mail admissions@glenlyonnorfolk.bc.ca

A day school for more than 700 students in JK–Grade 12, Glenlyon Norfolk is one of only seven schools in Canada accredited to offer all three of the International Baccalaureate (IB) programs: Primary Years, Middle Years, and Diploma. The IB programs provide an inquiry-based, engaging approach to learning and develop students' skills in critical and creative thinking. It is a goal of GNS and the IB to foster in students a sense of responsibility for the well-being of their communities and to develop the leadership skills necessary for them to make a difference. It is expected that students will participate fully in the life of the School through involvement in the fine arts, athletics, clubs, and/or public speaking and debating. The GNS motto, "Do your best through truth and courage," lies at the very heart of everything Glenlyon Norfolk does, establishing the values by which students, faculty, and staff live every day. Tuition: $11,970–$14,835. Simon Bruce-Lockhart is Head of School; Deirdre Chettleburgh is Director of Admissions.

Greenwood College School 2002

443 Mount Pleasant Road, Toronto, ON M4S 2L8, Canada
Tel. 416-482-9811; Fax 416-482-9188
Web Site greenwoodcollege.com

Greenwood College School was founded by four inspired citizens who sought to provide an excellent academic program combined with experiential learning, outdoor education, and character development. Enrolling 380 young men and women as day students in Grades 7–12, Greenwood offers a strong academic program based on differentiated learning. The core program centers on reading and language arts, math, science, and social studies, enriched by modern languages, state-of-the-art technology, and a mandatory Outdoor Leadership component. The Student Success Center offers faculty assistance and advocacy, enrichment activities, and individualized academic support. Greenwood's committed teachers infuse the student community with purpose, engaging them by means of experiential and collaborative learning. Through the Greenwood@Acadia summer program, students have the opportunity to earn OSSD credits through Greenwood-sponsored courses held at Acadia University in Nova Scotia. Tuition: $26,500. Jamie Lougheed is Director of Admissions and Recruitment; Allan Hardy is Principal.

Halifax Grammar School 1958

945 Tower Road, Halifax, NS B3H 2Y2, Canada
Tel. 902-423-9312; Admissions 902-431-8550; Fax 902-423-9315
Web Site www.hgs.ns.ca; E-mail admissions@hgs.ns.ca

The Halifax Grammar School strives to educate "thoughtful, independent students prepared to take on the world." Located near Saint Mary's University, HGS is a leading IB World School where all graduating students study the full International Baccalaureate Program. Founded in 1958, this coeducational day school offers a challenging, balanced curriculum with enriched academics, competitive athletics, and vibrant arts programs. Since 2000, the School has expanded to two campuses, enrolling 540 students from Junior Primary to Grade 12. Students compete at the highest levels in soccer, basketball, and track and field and regularly win math league and debating honors. Scholarships and bursaries are available to qualified students. Tuition: $8500–$11,808. Ms. Ann Marie Kent is Admissions Officer; Mr. Blayne Addley is Headmaster.

The Mabin School 1980

50 Poplar Plains Road, Toronto, ON M4V 2M8, Canada
Tel. 416-964-9594; Admissions Ext. 251; Fax 416-964-3643
Web Site www.mabin.com; E-mail admissions@mabin.com

Enrolling 150 boys and girls as day students in Junior Kindergarten–Grade 6, The Mabin School is an educational leader committed to developing confident and independent learners through an innovative curriculum. The rich, hands-on program is organized around the learning needs of the students and set

in an intimate and vibrant environment where children love to come because they feel known, respected, and effective. Teachers provide a strong academic foundation by promoting classroom themes that are of intrinsic interest to the students. Children are encouraged to inquire, investigate, develop theories, and build knowledge. French, music, art, science, computer technology, and physical education are taught by specialists and round out the program. A 6:1 student-faculty ratio and small class sizes enable teachers to know and understand each child. Students are engaged daily in leadership opportunities and the cultivation of conflict resolution skills, resulting in a thriving school and family community where respect for oneself and others is valued. Tuition: $19,625 (Cdn.). Monica Barden is Admissions Coordinator; Lynn Seligman is Principal.

St. Andrew's College 1899

15800 Yonge Street, Aurora, ON L4G 3H7, Canada
Tel. 905-727-3178; Admission Ext. 303; [Toll-free] 877-378-1899
Fax 905-727-9032
Web Site www.sac.on.ca; E-mail admission@sac.on.ca

ST. ANDREW'S COLLEGE

St. Andrew's College is one of Canada's premier all-boys schools for Grades 6 to 12, with 570 students split between boarding and day. St. Andrew's seeks well-rounded students who display a strong sense of character and intellectual curiosity, want to participate in the school's extensive athletic program (55 teams in 24 sports), and can contribute to the arts, drama, or music programs. Activity-based learning is at the forefront of the academic curriculum, offering a learning environment that inspires and challenges boys with an expanding Advanced Placement program. The wireless laptop program allows students to take advantage of online daybooks, daily schedules, assignment calendars, and related websites. An award-winning Public Speaking team, robotics, Model UN, photography, video editing, SAC TV, and community outreach are among the many activities offered. Boys are encouraged to become involved in these extracurricular offerings which help develop lifelong leadership and independent learning skills. All students take part in the 104-year-old Cadet Corps, and 100 percent of graduates attend university in Canada, the U.S., and abroad. Boarding Tuition: $41,470; Day Tuition: $25,790 (Cdn.). Financial Aid: $1,500,000. Michael Roy '85 is Director of Admission; Kevin McHenry is Head of School.

St. Clement's School 1901

21 St. Clements Avenue, Toronto, ON M4R 1G8, Canada
Tel. 416-483-4835; Admissions 416-483-4414, Ext. 2259
Fax 416-483-8242
Web Site www.scs.on.ca; E-mail admissions@scs.on.ca

St. Clement's School, enrolling 450 day students in Grades 1–12, develops women of character by encouraging academic excellence, self-confidence, and independent thinking in an enriching, supportive environment. This approach provides success, as 100 percent of graduates gain university admission in Canada, the U.S., and abroad. St. Clement's opened a new facility (2006) that includes a theater-style performance and lecture hall, a dance/drama studio, a gymnasium, and science laboratories, reflecting the various activities of SCS students. The School has doubled in physical size but enrollment and spirit remain the same. SCS has the most extensive Advanced Placement program of any girls' school in Canada. All girls take leadership roles in school government, the House system, service, clubs, and sports. Each student, staff member, alumna, parent, and friend in this close-knit community contributes to the vital St. Clement's spirit. Tuition: $21,300 (Cdn.). Financial aid is available. Elena Holeton is Director of Admissions; Patricia D. Parisi is Principal.

Trafalgar Castle School   1874

401 Reynolds Street, Whitby, ON L1N 3W9, Canada
Tel. 905-668-3358; Admissions Ext. 227; Fax 905-668-4136
Web Site www.castle-ed.com; E-mail admin@castle-ed.com

Trafalgar Castle School, a day and boarding school established in 1874, educates university-bound young women in an environment that supports and challenges each individual to achieve her full potential. Trafalgar enrolls 240 students in Grades 6–12; 70 are boarders in Grades 7–12. The curriculum, featuring small classes, integrates the latest information technology across the disciplines. All classrooms are networked, and all girls are equipped with laptops. Field trips extend learning beyond the classroom, while the House System fosters a sense of community. Students take part in the arts, athletics, clubs, debate, robotics, and community service. Boarding Tuition: $37,400–$41,000 (Cdn.); Day Tuition: $17,500–$19,575. Irene Talent is Admissions Officer; Brian McClure is Principal.

Upper Canada College   1829

200 Lonsdale Road, Toronto, ON M4V 1W6, Canada
Tel. 416-488-1125; Day Admission Ext. 4123
Boarding Admission Ext. 2221
Web Site www.ucc.on.ca; E-mail admission@ucc.on.ca

UPPER CANADA COLLEGE

Upper Canada College enjoys a reputation as one of North America's great independent schools, with renowned politicians,

scholars, business leaders, artists, and Olympians among its alumni. UCC's main campus is in the heart of beautiful, ethnically diverse Toronto. The school comprises 1145 students in Senior Kindergarten–Grade 12 (IB2), with boarding from Grade 9. The campus blends heritage architecture with modern facilities, including a new twin-pad hockey arena, two large libraries, modern science and technology labs, and the Norval Outdoor School, a 400-acre nature sanctuary 50 kilometers northwest of Toronto. UCC offers "big school" opportunities and facilities combined with a "small school" approach to individualized learning. Within a diverse learning community, the school helps students develop their unique passions, be it history, jazz, or sports. Students also develop personal strength through international service trips and local community initiatives. Graduates receive both the IB Diploma and the Ontario Secondary School Diploma. Boarding Tuition: $46,430–$48,430 (Cdn.); Day Tuition: $26,020–$28,020. Financial assistance is available beginning in Grade 7. Chantal Kenny is Executive Director of Admission; Dr. James Power is Principal.

CHILE

Santiago College   1880

Lota 2465, Providencia, Casilla 130-D, Santiago, Chile
Tel. 56-2-751-3800; Fax 56-2-751-3802
Web Site www.scollege.cl
E-mail admiss@scollege.cl/master@scollege.cl

SANTIAGO COLLEGE

An American clergyman founded Santiago College to provide an education that reflects the values and traditions of the Chilean-American heritage. The mission of the College is to develop young people who will contribute to a democratic society in an interdependent world. Fluency in written and spoken English is a key goal for the coeducational school's 1800 students in Nursery–Grade 12. The integrated curriculum includes course work leading to the International Baccalaureate Diploma; 95 percent of graduates enter colleges and universities worldwide. Student Council, drama, debate, the creative arts, scouting, and interscholastic sports are among the activities. Santiago College is a member of the European Council of International Schools and the New England Association of Schools and Colleges. Tuition: $6085. Karen Thomas is Head of Admissions; Lorna Prado Scott is Headmistress.

CHINA

Chinese International School   1983

1 Hau Yuen Path, Braemar Hill, Hong Kong, China
Tel. 852-2510-7288; Admissions 852-2512-5915; Fax 852-2566-0239
Web Site www.cis.edu.hk; E-mail admissions@cis.edu.hk

Chinese International School was established as Hong Kong's first school teaching an international curriculum in English and Mandarin. With 1400 day students ages 4 to 18, the School aims to be a flagship institution for the region. A defining characteristic is that all students learn in English and Mandarin; however, prior knowledge of Chinese is not required for admission, and beginning Mandarin is available at many grade levels. Every Primary homeroom is headed by a pair of teachers, with native-language abilities in English and Chinese, who adopt a collaborative approach to planning and teaching the inquiry-based program. In the first four years, time devoted to each language is equal, with English gradually taking precedence by the Secondary years. All Secondary students pursue the International Baccalaureate Middle Years and Diploma Programs. Graduates continue on to leading universities around the world, with 40 percent studying in the U.S., 33 percent in the U.K., 15 percent in Canada, and 10 percent in Hong Kong. Tuition: HK$93,000–HK$147,600. Bonnie Chan is Admissions Officer; Dr. Theodore Faunce (Princeton, A.B., Ph.D.) is Headmaster. *New England Association.*

Hong Kong International School   1966

6 & 23 South Bay Close, Repulse Bay, Hong Kong, China
1 Red Hill Road, Tai Tam, Hong Kong, China
Tel. 852-3149-7000; Fax 852-2813-4293
Web Site www.hkis.edu.hk; E-mail admiss@hkis.edu.hk

Christian business leaders and members of the Lutheran Church Missouri Synod founded Hong Kong International School to nurture young people academically and spiritually. Situated on two campuses, the School enrolls approximately 2650 day students in Pre-School through Grade 12. More than 40 nationalities are represented in the American-style, English-language program, which includes religion, Mandarin, computer technology, and the arts. The curriculum is designed to prepare students for college, with 100 percent of graduates going on to higher education. Trips to mainland China and throughout Asia, community service, drama, Student Council, athletics, and special-interest clubs are among the activities. Tuition: HK$88,500–HK$183,000. Richard W. Mueller is the Head of School.

School Year Abroad   1994

BNU High School #2, 12, Xinjiekouwai Street, Beijing 100088, People's Republic of China
Tel. 8610-6235-4503; Fax 8610-6235-4505
Web Site www.sya.org; E-mail admissions@sya.org
U.S. Office: 439 South Union Street, Lawrence, MA 01843
Tel. 978-725-6828; Fax 978-725-6833

School Year Abroad's mission is to teach self-reliance, responsibility, resourcefulness, and respect for other cultures. Through this program, approximately 60 students entering their junior or senior year of high school travel to China and live with a host family for nine months, gaining a life-changing experience outside the traditional preparatory school setting. Students travel extensively on school-led trips to both urban centers and rural areas throughout China, and a winter break during the Chinese New Year allows for an extended study in the Tibet regions. All students enroll in $2\frac{1}{2}$ credits of Mandarin Chinese and develop speaking, listening, reading, and writing skills. English and math classes from Algebra II through Calculus are taught in English. American and Chinese faculty teach an average of 12 students in each class. Numerous extracurricular activities involve athletics, music, dance, painting, and community service and are available through both BNU High School #2 and the Beijing community. Tuition: $41,000. Financial aid is available. Roland Lemay is Director of Admissions; Jeff Bissell is President.

ENGLAND

ACS International Schools   1967

ACS Cobham International School: Heywood, Portsmouth Road, Cobham, Surrey KT11, 1BL, England
Tel. 44-1932-867251; Admissions 44-1932-869744
Fax 44-1932-869789
Web Site www.acs-england.co.uk
E-mail CobhamAdmissions@acs-england.co.uk
ACS Hillingdon International School: Hillingdon Court, 108 Vine Lane, Middlesex UB10 OBE, England
Tel. 44-1895-259771; Admissions 44-1895-818402
Fax 44-1895-818404
E-mail HillingdonAdmissions@acs-england.co.uk
ACS Egham International School: Woodlee, London Road (A30), Egham, Surrey TW20 OHS, England
Tel. 44-1784-430800; Admissions 44-1784-430611
Fax 44-1784-430626
E-mail EghamAdmissions@acs-england.co.uk

ACS INTERNATIONAL SCHOOLS, founded in 1967 to serve the expatriate community, today educate over 2500 pre-school through high school students from more than 70 nations on three suburban London campuses. The campuses are 30 minutes south and west of London, with easy access to excellent road and fast commuter rail links into the capital. All campuses accommodate day students, while ACS Cobham also offers boarding.

All ACS campuses are International Baccalaureate (IB) World Schools, offering the IB Diploma. In addition, ACS Egham is one of only three schools in the United Kingdom to also offer the IB Primary Years Programme (3–11) and the IB Middle Years Programme (11–16). All ACS campuses provide a traditional American high school diploma, with ACS Cobham and ACS Hillingdon also teaching Advanced Placement courses.

A proprietary institution, ACS International Schools are

governed by a Board of Directors, accredited by the New England Association of Schools and Colleges, authorized by the Independent Schools Association UK, and hold membership in the Council of International Schools and the International Baccalaureate Organization.

THE CAMPUSES. Situated on a 128-acre country estate, ACS Cobham has purpose-built Lower, Middle, and High School buildings, a gymnasium and cafeteria complex, an Interactive Learning Centre, and a boarding house. The Early Childhood Village is located in an 1804 stable block, expanded by a new purpose-built classroom and office structure that provides classes and recreation areas for children ages 2 to 5. Sports facilities include tennis courts, an Olympic-size track, practice golf course, separate adventure playgrounds for Early Childhood and Lower School students, and soccer, rugby, and baseball fields. The state-of-the-art Sports Centre houses a basketball/volleyball show court, 25-meter competition-class swimming pool, dance studio, fitness suite, and cafeteria.

The 11-acre ACS Hillingdon campus combines a stately mansion (1855), which is the setting for classes, concerts, art exhibitions, and receptions, with a modern, purpose-built wing housing classrooms, science laboratories, computer room, gymnasium, cafeteria, auditorium, and libraries. The campus also has off-site playing fields for soccer, rugby, and track. The facilities include a music center, complete with digital recording studio, rehearsal rooms, practice studios, and a computer lab for music technology.

ACS INTERNATIONAL SCHOOLS

The 20-acre ACS Egham campus features a stately mansion house (1876) as well as purpose-built science and computer labs, design technology, gymnasiums, adventure playgrounds, classrooms, tennis courts, and landscaped gardens. The campuswide wireless and cabled IT network makes working with laptop or desktop computers an integral part of the learning process.

THE FACULTY. ACS International Schools Superintendent Malcolm Kay holds a B.Sc. (Hons.), P.G.C.E., from Nottingham University and an M.A. from Bath University.

Thomas Lehman was appointed Head of School at ACS Cobham in 1992. Mr. Lehman holds a B.A. from Thiel College and a B.S. from Syracuse University.

Ginger G. Apple, Head of School at ACS Hillingdon, holds a B.S. from Miami University of Ohio and an M.Ed. from the College of New Jersey.

ACS INTERNATIONAL SCHOOLS

Peter Hosier, Acting Head of School at ACS Egham, is a graduate of the University of Nottingham and holds a postgraduate certificate in education from the University of Sussex.

The full-time faculty at ACS Cobham number 139. At ACS Hillingdon, there are 78 full-time teachers. There are 78 full-time teachers at ACS Egham. All teachers hold bachelor's degrees and are accredited; 120 have advanced degrees.

There are 13 part-time instructors; full-time nurses for each school provide health care.

STUDENT BODY. At ACS Cobham, enrollment is 1329—743 boys and 586 girls. The Boarding School has 58 boys and 33 girls. The student body at ACS Hillingdon numbers 496—258 boys and 238 girls. The ACS Egham campus enrolls 555 students—294 boys and 261 girls.

ACADEMIC PROGRAM. The school year, from late August to mid-June, is divided into two semesters with autumn, winter, midwinter, and spring recesses. The school day extends from 8:30 A.M. until approximately 3:10 P.M., followed by extracurricular activities.

Average class sizes range from 15 to 20 students. Teachers are available for extra-help sessions during and after school. School reports are issued every quarter (approximately every nine weeks). Regular parent-teacher conferences are scheduled twice per year and on an occasional basis as necessary.

Lower School students are in self-contained classes for their main academic areas; starting in the Middle School, students have separate subject-area teachers.

The academic program includes language arts, social studies, mathematics, science, art, music, library, information technology, and physical education. Modern foreign languages are studied on all campuses in the Lower, Middle, and High

Schools. Native language enrichment courses are offered as necessary on each campus. Starting in Grade 7, qualified students may take more advanced math classes.

Specialized learning support is available in all divisions for students with mild learning differences. English as an Additional Language (EAL) is offered on all campuses.

To graduate, High School students must complete 20 credits, including 4 in English, 6 in social studies and a foreign language, 6 in mathematics and science, 2 in art electives, and 2 in physical education. An Honours Diploma is awarded to graduates achieving additional requirements.

Among the full-year courses are English 9–12; French 1–4, German 1–3, Spanish 1–4; World History 1–2, United States History, Psychology, Economics; Algebra 1–2, Geometry, Algebra II, Precalculus; Biology, Chemistry, Physics; Drawing and Painting 1–3, Crafts, Ceramics and Sculpture, Advanced Art; Music, Chorus, Band, Drama; and Computer Science.

Semester or partial-credit courses include Advanced Composition, Journalism, Speech; Contemporary History, Economics, Psychology; Word Processing, Computer Sciences, Information Technology; and Photography. Courses vary slightly between campuses. The Schools reserve the right to add or delete courses according to student demand and staff availability.

At ACS Cobham in 2009, 61 students received the full International Baccalaureate Diploma, with a 97 percent pass rate. At ACS Hillingdon in 2009, 25 students achieved the full IB Diploma, with a 93 percent pass rate. At ACS Egham, 23 students achieved the full IB Diploma, with a 100 percent pass rate.

At ACS Cobham, Advanced Placement courses currently include English Literature and Composition, French Language and Composition, German Language and Composition, Spanish Language and Composition, U.S. History, European History, Calculus, Biology, Chemistry, Physics, Studio Art, Statistics, Psychology, Human Geography, Macroeconomics, and Microeconomics. At ACS Hillingdon, English Literature and Composition, French Literature and Composition, German Literature and Composition, Spanish Literature and Composition, Physics B, Chemistry, Biology, Calculus AB, Statistics, Microeconomics, Macroeconomics, U.S. History, Psychology, Comparative Government, Studio Art, and Music Theory are available.

Graduates attend such universities as Amherst, Baylor, Brown, Cornell, Dartmouth, Duke, Harvard, Johns Hopkins, Mount Holyoke, Stanford, Texas A&M, Tufts, and the Universities of California, Chicago, Michigan, Notre Dame, Pennsylvania, and Virginia. In the United Kingdom, graduates attend London School of Economics, Imperial College, and the Universities of Cambridge, Edinburgh, Oxford, and Warwick, among others.

ACS International Schools conduct various summer academic and recreational programs.

STUDENT ACTIVITIES. Lower School activities include arts and crafts clubs, scouts, choir, band, dance, chess, tennis, bowling, golf, and other sports. Middle School students enjoy a similar variety as well as cooking clubs, safe sitter programs, and a musical production. The High and Middle Schools also have student councils, peer counselors, cheerleaders, student newspapers, literary magazines, yearbooks, and recycling and environmental clubs. High School students may participate in three drama productions, math teams, Model UN, National Honor Society, International Schools Thespian Association, speech and debate competitions, quiz bowls, and service organizations such as Habitat for Humanity, The Duke of Edinburgh Award scheme, and World Challenge projects.

School teams compete with local American and British schools as well as international schools on the Continent. Middle School teams are fielded in baseball, basketball, soccer, swimming, tennis, track and field, and volleyball. Boys' and girls' varsity teams compete in basketball, cross-country, tennis, track and field, and volleyball. There are also boys' rugby and baseball teams, a girls' softball team, intramural sports, and noncompetitive physical activities.

Typical field trips include Stratford-upon-Avon; environmental or history centers in England; Outward Bound or pony-trekking in Wales; foreign language, ski, and arts trips in Europe; and community service in Africa and Asia. The Schools regularly host visiting artists, writers, and musicians and hold arts festivals, international celebrations, and a variety of community service events.

ADMISSION AND COSTS. ACS International Schools seek to enroll motivated students of all nationalities. New students are accepted in all grades throughout the year on the basis of the completed application form, previous school records, standardized test results, two recommendations from the previous school, and, in the Middle and High Schools, a student questionnaire. The School may administer diagnostic exams for new High School students; nonnative speakers may need to take an English proficiency test for entry. A nonrefundable £125 application fee must accompany each application.

ACS INTERNATIONAL SCHOOLS

Day tuition per semester for 2009–10 is £2865 for the half-day 2-year-old program; £3125–£4240 for Pre-kindergarten half-day or full-day program; £7080–£7755 for Kindergarten–Grade 4; £8175–£8590 for Grades 5–8; and £8850–£9325 for Grades 9–12. Boarding fees per semester at ACS Cobham campus only are £5225 for five-day boarders and £7155 for seven-day boarders. Bus service per semester ranges from £445 for shuttle service to £1110 for door-to-door busing.

Superintendent: Malcolm J. Kay
Heads of School: Thomas Lehman (Cobham), Ginger G. Apple (Hillingdon) & Peter Hosier (Egham)
High School Principals: Stephen Baker (Cobham), Monika Howick (Hillingdon) & Cathy Jones (Egham)
Deans of Admissions: Heidi Ayoub (Cobham), Julia Love (Egham), & Rudianne Soltis (Hillingdon)
Head of Marketing & Communications: Fergus J. Rose

The American School in London   1951

One Waverley Place, London NW8 0NP, England
Tel. 020-7449-1200; Fax 020-7449-1350
Web Site www.asl.org; E-mail admissions@asl.org

THE AMERICAN SCHOOL IN LONDON is a coeducational, college preparatory day school enrolling students in Pre-Kindergarten through Grade 12.

The mission of the School is to develop the intellect and character of each student by providing an outstanding American education with a global perspective.

The School is situated in St. John's Wood, a residential area of Central London just north of Regent's Park and is convenient to the underground and bus routes. In addition, a School-administered door-to-door bus service covers a large area of the city. The School's location, within easy reach of the theaters and art galleries of the West End as well as many historic sites, makes field studies in London, the United Kingdom, and Europe a central part of the curriculum.

THE AMERICAN SCHOOL IN LONDON

The American School in London was founded by Stephen L. Eckard in 1951 to provide the continuity of an American curriculum for children of U.S. business and government personnel on assignment in London. The American School in London is the oldest American-curriculum school in the United Kingdom and remains the only nonprofit American-curriculum school in London. The School is registered as a nonprofit organization in the United Kingdom and in the United States. It is governed by a Board of Trustees, with 19 full-time members of the educational, business, and professional communities.

The School is accredited by the Middle States Association of Colleges and Schools and the Council of International Schools. It holds membership in the National Association of Independent Schools, among other affiliations.

THE CAMPUS. The school building, located on a 3.2-acre site, houses all classes from Pre-Kindergarten through Grade 12. Eighty classrooms are supplemented with nine science laboratories, seven computer laboratories, five music rooms, five art studios, two theaters, a double gymnasium, craft shops, and two libraries containing 50,000 volumes and audiovisual and periodical departments. A major building program was completed in September 2001. The School's 21 acres of playing fields at nearby Canons Park include a baseball diamond, soccer fields, and rugby pitches as well as grass and all-weather tennis courts.

The School is committed to using technology to facilitate all aspects of education and has embarked on a long-term plan that combines the latest technology with innovative teaching strategies. A computer network with 1600 network outlets, a state-of-the-art, dedicated high-speed server, and a high-speed Internet connection links over 600 computers in the building.

THE FACULTY. Coreen R. Hester became the seventh Head at the American School in London in 2007. Most recently, Mrs. Hester served for 10 years as Head of The Hamlin School in San Francisco, California. Prior to that appointment, she was ASL's High School Principal from 1995 to 1997. Early in her career, Mrs. Hester taught English at University Liggett School in Grosse Pointe Woods, Michigan. Later, she spent 10 years at The Branson School as teacher, dean college counselor, Assistant Head, and Interim Head of School. Mrs. Hester is also a former Director of the Western Region of Independent Educational Services. She holds an A.B. in English and an A.M. in Education from Stanford University.

The full-time faculty consists of 46 men and 91 women. They hold 137 graduate degrees from schools and colleges such as Boston University, Brown, Columbia, Cornell, Harvard, Michigan State, Smith, State University of New York, and the Universities of California, Colorado, Hawaii, Illinois, London, Massachusetts, Notre Dame, Oregon, Redlands, Sussex (England), and Wisconsin.

Two full-time nurses at the School attend to minor injuries and illnesses. Emergency medical services are available minutes from the campus.

STUDENT BODY. In 2009–10, the School enrolled 1350 day students, 676 boys and 674 girls, as follows: 416 in the Lower School (Kindergarten 1–Grade 4), 460 in the Middle School (Grades 5–8), and 474 in the High School (Grades 9–12). Although the majority of the students are American, more than 45 nationalities are represented.

ACADEMIC PROGRAM. The school year, divided into two semesters, begins in early September and extends to mid-June. Vacations are scheduled in October, November, December, February, and in the spring. The School is in session Monday through Friday from 8:05 A.M. to 3:05 P.M. The average class has 16–20 students.

The Lower School program is highly personal and attempts to encompass all traditional values of education as well as proven and effective modern methods. The basic skills of language arts and mathematics are complemented by social studies, art, music, technology, physical education, and library use. The Middle School (Grades 5–8) responds to the needs and characteristics of young people during the transition from childhood to adolescence. Team teaching and integrated study encourage mastery with a depth of understanding.

In the High School college preparatory curriculum, students fulfill major discipline requirements in English, mathematics, social studies, science, and modern language. Elective courses are offered, and advanced courses are offered leading to Advanced Placement examinations in more than 14 subjects.

THE AMERICAN SCHOOL IN LONDON

To graduate, a student must complete at least 18 credits, including four years of English; two each of mathematics, visual and/or performing arts, and science; three of social studies and modern language; and one of physical education. One semester each of health and technology is also required. The School recommends at least an additional year of modern language, mathematics, and science. Students in Grades 9 and 10 must take five "solids" (English, modern language, history, mathematics, science) per year. Four "solids" are required in Grades 11 and 12; five are recommended.

The High School schedule is an eight-day rotating block schedule, with 80-minute periods divided over every two days.

Because the periods rotate, classes meet at different times of the day over the course of an eight-day cycle. A full team of college counselors, grade-level deans, faculty advisors, and a personal counselor ensure that each student receives personal attention.

Grade reports are sent to parents twice yearly for Lower, Middle, and High School students. The School has an "open-door" policy and communicates through parent conferences, the Parents' Newsletter, and the School magazine. Special events for ASL parents, sponsored by the Parent Teacher Organization, include an International Festival, a Book Fair, and a gala fund-raising auction.

THE AMERICAN SCHOOL IN LONDON

Student support services include reading recovery, language development, and speech therapy in the Lower School. There are Lower and Middle School English as an Additional Language programs as well as a school-wide program for students with specific learning difficulties.

All 120 graduates of the Class of 2009 were accepted to college, with 5 students taking gap years in 2009–10. Students are attending Brown, Cambridge, Columbia, Duke, Georgetown, Harvard, New York University, Princeton, Tufts, and Yale.

The School runs a Summer Camp, which concentrates on athletic and recreational activities.

STUDENT ACTIVITIES. The Lower School After School Program organizes classes in crafts, sports, and other activities. Lower School students also participate in scouting and Little League.

Students in Grades 5–8 can take part in the Middle School After School Program, which offers them the opportunity to develop lifelong hobbies and pursuits and to make friends with students in other grades.

Students in the High School elect officers and class representatives to the Student Council, which brings their interests and concerns to the administration and organizes social activities. Regular student activities include the yearbook, newspaper, literary magazine, drama productions, National Honor Society, prom committee, Model United Nations, Mock U.S. Senate, instrumental and choral groups, math teams, Amnesty International, and the Robotics, Writers, and Debate Clubs. Volunteer student groups serve hospitals, schools, the elderly, and other groups in the local community.

The School's varsity teams compete against local British, American, and international schools as well as American and international schools on the continent in rugby, volleyball, basketball, wrestling, swimming, soccer, track, tennis, baseball, crew, golf, and cross-country for boys. Girls compete in volleyball, field hockey, soccer, basketball, track, tennis, softball, swimming, crew, golf, dance, cheerleading, and cross-country. Some interscholastic competition is arranged for Middle School teams. The physical education program is directed toward recreational and lifetime sports.

ADMISSION AND COSTS. The School welcomes American and international students who can meet its academic standards. Students are accepted in all grades throughout the year, provided vacancies are available, on the basis of a completed application, the previous academic record, standardized test results, recommendations from the previous school, and payment of a £100 application fee and a £1000 tuition deposit. Applications should be made up to one year before the date of entry.

In 2009–10, tuition is £17,780 for Pre-Kindergarten–Grade 3, £18,100 for Grade 4, £20,330 for Grade 5, £20,970 for Grade 6, £20,940 for Grade 7, £21,500 for Grade 8, and £20,800 for Grades 9–12. Additional costs are £2300 per year for busing (per child) and £594 per year for food service in the Lower School. Approximately £716,500 in financial aid was awarded in 2008–09.

High School Principal: Paul Richards
Dean of Students: Joe Chodl
Dean of Admissions: Jodi Coats
Director of External Affairs: John G. Clark
Director of College Counseling: Patty Strohm
Business Manager: Christopher Almond
Athletics Director: Sandy Lloyd

FRANCE

School Year Abroad 1967

5, Allée Sainte Marie, 35700 Rennes, France
Tel. 33-299-382-333; Fax 33-299-636-894
Web Site www.sya.org; E-mail admissions@sya.org
U.S. Office: 439 South Union Street, Lawrence, MA 01843
Tel. 978-725-6828; Fax 978-725-6833

School Year Abroad's mission is to teach self-reliance, responsibility, resourcefulness, and respect for other cultures. Approximately 60 students entering Grades 11 and 12, who have at least two or more years of French, travel to Rennes, France, for two semesters and immerse themselves in French language and culture. All students live with a local family for nine months. Courses in French language, French literature, English, history, art history, math, and French society and culture are offered. Because only English and math classes are taught in English, prior knowledge of French is required. American and French faculty teach an average class size of 15 students. Extracurricular activities are abundant and organized by local schools and organizations, so students participate in athletics, the arts, and community service within the Rennes community. School Year Abroad also offers drama workshops and a chorus on campus. Trips with SYA take place on weekends and during regularly scheduled breaks and include school-led excursions to the Loire Valley, Paris, Normandy, and southern France. Independent travel is also an option. Tuition: $41,000. Financial aid is available. Roland Lemay is Director of Admissions; Denis Brochu is Resident Director.

GERMANY

Munich International School 1966

Schloss Buchhof, D-82319 Starnberg, Germany
Tel. 49-8151-366-0; Admissions 49-8151-366-120
Fax 49-8151-366-129
Web Site www.mis-munich.de; E-mail admissions@mis-munich.de

Founded in 1966, Munich International School enrolls 1260 day boys and girls from over 50 nationalities in Early Childhood (ages 4–5)–Grade 12. As an exemplary English-language, IB World School, MIS inspires students to be interculturally aware and achieve their potential within a stimulating, caring environment. The curriculum follows the framework of the International Baccalaureate Primary and Middle Year Programmes, culminating with the IB Diploma. MIS graduates enter such institutions as Brown, Cambridge, Columbia, Georgetown, Harvard, London School of Economics, Massachusetts Institute of

MUNICH INTERNATIONAL SCHOOL

Technology, Oxford, Princeton, and Yale. Competitive and noncompetitive sports with numerous teams participate in international tournaments. After-school activities include the fine arts, from painting, ceramics, and handicrafts to drama and dance, as well as school choirs, bands, and orchestral groups. Students take part in the International School Theatre Festival, Speech and Debate Team, math contests, and other international events. The 26-acre campus is 12 miles south of Munich. Tuition: €12,680–€15,930 + Entrance Fee. Ola Schmidt is Director of Admissions; Eif Phillips is Head of School. *New England Association.*

ITALY

St. Stephen's School   1964

3 Via Aventina, 00153 Rome, Italy
Tel. [3906] 5750605; Fax [3906] 5741941
Web Site www.ststephens-rome.com
E-mail ststephens@ststephens-rome.com
United States Office: 15 Gramercy Park, New York, NY 10003
Tel. 212-505-7409; Fax 212-505-7423

St. STEPHEN'S SCHOOL in Rome, Italy, is a nondenominational, coeducational college preparatory school enrolling boarding and day students in Grades 9 through 12 and a few postgraduates. Situated next to the Circus Maximus and a short distance from the Colosseum and the Roman Forum, St. Stephen's is easily reached by the city buses, streetcars, and Metro trains that run within a block of the School. Its location in the heart of the Eternal City offers students unique cultural, educational, and recreational advantages as well as frequent travel opportunities to other cities in Europe and the Mediterranean area.

Established by the late Dr. John O. Patterson, former Headmaster of Kent School in Connecticut, to "epitomize the best elements of the classical liberal arts education," St. Stephen's opened for classes in 1964; the first seniors graduated in 1966. Its founder chose Rome as the site because he believed

the city to be "the symbol and repository of the enduring ethical, cultural, and religious values of the West," as well as "one of the most cosmopolitan international crossroads of the modern world."

The curriculum is based on the American model and also offers the International Baccalaureate, which prepares students for colleges and universities worldwide. The student body includes young people from many nations and diverse cultural backgrounds.

ST. STEPHEN'S SCHOOL

St. Stephen's School, a nonprofit corporation registered in Connecticut, is governed by a Board of Trustees composed of 25 members who reside in the United States and Italy. The approximately 4000 alumni provide financial assistance and offer other support. The School is accredited by the New England Association of Schools and Colleges and the European Council of International Schools.

THE CAMPUS. The campus of St. Stephen's School occupies 2.5 acres in the center of historic Rome. Constructed around a central courtyard in the traditional Roman style, the school building contains three science laboratories, new sculpture and art studios, an audiovisual facility, a photo lab, physical education facilities, and a renovated performing arts center/assembly hall on the lower floors. The two upper stories house 21 student dormitory rooms, faculty apartments, a computer room, classrooms, a library containing 14,300 volumes, CD-ROMs, and an extensive collection of videos, records, and English and foreign-language periodicals. Also on the premises are the dining hall, snack bar, and offices. The campus has gardens, a barbecue pit, and newly renovated tennis, volleyball, and basketball courts.

THE FACULTY. Lesley Murphy (University of Sussex [England], B.A., P.G.C.E.) was appointed Head of School in July 2008. A former St. Stephen's faculty member, Head of English, and IB coordinator, Ms. Murphy has worked in international education for 25 years, 13 of which were at the Foundation of the International School of Geneva.

The faculty include 28 full-time and 15 part-time teachers, 29 of whom hold advanced degrees. They have attended Carlow College, Columbia, Dartmouth, Harvard, Haverford, Indiana University, Mount Holyoke, New England Conservatory of Music, Oberlin, Princeton, Stanford, Temple, Tyler School of Art, Vassar, Wellesley, Wesleyan, and the Universities of California, Chicago, Kansas, Nebraska, Pennsylvania, Rhode Island, San Diego, Santa Clara, and Tennessee in the United States; the University of Toronto in Canada; London Guild University, Warwick University, and the Universities of Cambridge, East London, Essex, Paisley, Portsmouth, Sheffield, Sussex, and Westminster in the United Kingdom; Monash University and the University of Technology (Sydney) in Australia; Ecole Normale de Musique de Paris, the Sorbonne, and the University of

Grenoble in France; the University of Rome in Italy; University Libanaise of Beyrouth; University of Belgrade; Bucharest Polytechnical University; and Université Libre in Belgium.

An infirmary is located on the school grounds, and a school psychologist is on staff. An American hospital is available for complete emergency medical care.

STUDENT BODY. In 2009–10, St. Stephen's enrolls 214 day and 35 boarding boys and girls as follows: 54 in Grade 9, 53 in Grade 10, 69 in Grade 11 and 73 in Grade 12. The diverse enrollment includes 86 students from the United States and Canada and 83 from Italy; 29 other countries are represented including Argentina, Australia, Bangladesh, Belgium, Brazil, China, Ecuador, Germany, Ghana, Greece, India, Iran, Ireland, Ivory Coast, Japan, Korea, Malaysia, Mali, Montenegro, the Netherlands, New Zealand, Russia, Spain, Sri Lanka, Sweden, Switzerland, the United Kingdom, Uruguay, and Zimbabwe.

ACADEMIC PROGRAM. The 39-week school year, which begins in early September and ends in mid-June, is divided into semesters, with a Thanksgiving break and vacations at Christmas and in the spring. All courses meet four periods per week, three of which are 45 minutes long, the fourth 90 minutes in length. Classes enroll 10 to 18 students to permit individual attention. In addition, each student selects a faculty advisor whose role is to offer guidance and support in personal and academic matters and to keep parents apprised regarding the student's progress. Tutorials in specific subjects and special counseling assistance are available upon request. On Sunday through Thursday evenings, supervised study halls are held for boarders in the library or in dormitory rooms.

The School's curriculum reflects the philosophy that "there is no substitute for a balanced and comprehensive preparation" in each of the six major subject areas: English, foreign language, history, mathematics and computer studies, experimental science, and the arts. Each student is expected to carry five full-time courses. Nineteen credits are required for graduation as follows: four in English; three each in a foreign language, history, experimental science, and mathematics; two in electives; and one in the arts. In addition, noncredit physical education is a yearly requirement, and seniors must submit a research paper (senior essay). Approximately two-thirds of the upperclassmen participate in the International Baccalaureate program.

ST. STEPHEN'S SCHOOL

Among the courses offered are English I–IV; Italian I–VI, French I–V, Latin I–IV; Roman Topography, Renaissance and Baroque Art History, Medieval Renaissance History, Classical Greek and Roman Studies, Art History, History of the United States, Islamic History and Civilization, Economics I–II, Contemporary History; Theory of Knowledge; Biology I–III, Chemistry I–III, Physics I–III, Environmental Systems and Society; Algebra I–II, Geometry, Mathematical Studies, Precalculus, Calculus, Computer Studies; and Studio Art, Sculpture,

Chorus, American Popular Music/Classical Music (alternate years), Drama, Photography, and Modern Dance. Special sessions are held for students who need assistance in English as a Second Language.

ST. STEPHEN'S SCHOOL

Recent graduates are attending such institutions as Bard, Barnard, Boston University, Brown, Columbia, Duke, Georgetown, Grinnell, Hampshire, Harvard, New York University, Reed College, Sarah Lawrence, Texas A & M, Tufts, Vassar, Wesleyan, Yale, and the Universities of Santa Clara and Wisconsin in the United States; McGill and the University of Toronto in Canada; Cambridge, Imperial College, King's College, London School of Economics, Oxford, School of Oriental and African Arts, University College London, and the Universities of Durham, Edinburgh, Glasgow, Kent, and Warwick in the United Kingdom; and Bocconi, LUISS, and the University of Rome in Italy.

STUDENT ACTIVITIES. The Student Council is comprised of representatives from each class, with juniors and seniors serving as elected officers. Members work with faculty representatives in the planning of social activities and serve as a liaison between students and the administration concerning all school matters. A variety of activities and clubs reflects the diversity of student interests and includes such groups as Model United Nations, Amnesty International, Community Service, Yearbook, Newspaper, Literary Magazine, and the Debate, Chess, Photography, Classics/Rome, Math, Computer, Recycling, and Art Clubs.

St. Stephen's Physical Education Department offers track and field, soccer, softball, volleyball, basketball, tennis, ultimate frisbee, yoga, and modern dance. Regularly scheduled games and meets bring St. Stephen's athletic teams into competition with other schools within the Rome community.

Weekly class-time field trips, weekend outings, and two mandatory excursions of three to seven days' duration are planned by faculty in the belief that Italy is an educational resource in itself and should be used accordingly. Students have visited historical and cultural sites in and around Rome, hiked in the Abruzzi, ascended Mount Vesuvius, and explored Etruscan sites. With parental permission, boarders may spend evenings or weekends with the families of day students.

St. Stephen's calendar of special highlights includes New Student Orientation and School Picnic, two Parent-Faculty Evenings, Treasure Hunt in Rome, and many student-organized events.

ADMISSION AND COSTS. St. Stephen's welcomes students of all races and religious backgrounds who are eager to undertake the School's academic challenges. Acceptance is based on the results of an admissions test, previous school records, and teacher recommendations. A personal interview with the prospective student and parents is recommended. Application should be accompanied by a fee of 100 Euros.

In 2009–10, day tuition is 18,800 Euros; tuition for boarders is 30,000 Euros. Additional charges include a capital assessment fee of 900 Euros for new students and 500 Euros for returning students, and a lunch fee of 1100 Euros for day students.

Head of School: Lesley Murphy
Director of Studies: Deborah M. Dostert
Admissions Office: Alessandra (Alex) Perniciaro
College Counselor: Alison Lewis
International Baccalaureate Coordinator: Jennifer Ferrara
Business Office: Alessandra Pisanelli
Director of Athletics: Fausto DiMarco
Director of Advancement: Michael Brouse

School Year Abroad   2001

Via Cavour 77, 01100 Viterbo, Italy
 Tel. 39-0761-326-856; Fax 39-0761-304-529
 Web Site www.sya.org; E-mail admissions@sya.org
U.S. Office: 439 South Union Street, Lawrence, MA 01843
 Tel. 978-725-6828; Fax 978-725-6833

School Year Abroad's mission is to teach self-reliance, responsibility, resourcefulness, and respect for other cultures. With SYA, 60 high school juniors and seniors travel to Viterbo, Italy, for nine months in order to live with an Italian family and embrace a different way of life. Courses in Latin, Greek, Italian, English, ancient history, art history, and mathematics are offered, with each class except Italian taught in English. Classes average 15 students. The intensive language courses allow students to learn Italian and Latin rapidly, while history courses address culture, philosophy, and politics during early civilization. School-led trips to Tuscany, Pompeii, and Greece occur during major breaks in the year, and weekend trips bring students to ancient, medieval, Renaissance, and modern sites throughout Italy, including Sicily. Independent travel is also an option. Because most extracurricular activities are organized by local schools and organizations, students involve themselves in athletics, the arts, and community service within the Viterbo community. Students have participated in soccer, rugby, drama, music, sculpture, ceramics, and fresco restoration. Tuition: $41,000. Financial aid is available. Roland Lemay is Director of Admissions; Patrick Scanlon is Resident Director.

JAPAN

St. Mary's International School   1954

1-6-19 Seta, Setagaya-ku, Tokyo 158-8668, Japan
Tel. 81-3-3709-3411; Fax 81-3-3707-1950
Web Site http://www.smis.ac.jp; E-mail michelj@smis.ac.jp

ST. MARY'S INTERNATIONAL SCHOOL in Tokyo, Japan, is a Roman Catholic, college preparatory day school enrolling boys in Kindergarten through Grade 12. The School is located in a greenbelt section of Setagaya-ku, Tokyo's largest residential district, and is easily accessible from other areas of the city.

Founded in 1954 by the Brothers of Christian Instruction, St. Mary's International School first opened its doors to 59 foreign boys in Kindergarten–Grade 3. By 1971, the rapid growth of the international community and the demands for quality college preparatory education in Tokyo required the Brothers to expand. In that year, St. Mary's moved to a new campus at its current location, a 9-acre site in the Setagaya district in one of Tokyo's rare green residential areas. In September 2009, St. Mary's enrolled 930 students from Kindergarten to Grade 12 and anticipates future development and expansion.

St. Mary's International endeavors to form free and responsible young men. As a Catholic school, it integrates the acquisition of knowledge, the establishment of responsible freedom, and the deepening of personal faith. Education is based on love and respect for the person in full recognition of the dignity of humankind, created in God's image and destined to live in union with Him.

ST. MARY'S INTERNATIONAL SCHOOL

Students are made aware of global issues as well as of the aspirations of people who work for peace, justice, freedom, and truth, in the hope that these may engender beliefs and actions conducive to the betterment of humanity. In this process, personal development is marked by empathy and mutual trust.

Academic programs are rigorous and challenging and are designed to prepare students for higher education within a safe, caring, and orderly atmosphere. The all-boy environment creates a place wherein positive self-esteem can fully develop and where learning is promoted at a pace appropriate for boys. A comprehensive and enriching cocurricular program is offered, which allows for individual expression to enhance self-worth. At St. Mary's, members of the international community in Japan can establish an identity respectful of both cultural and religious differences in an atmosphere that values diversity.

St. Mary's International School is a nonprofit institution operated by the Brothers of Christian Instruction. An active parent association provides fund-raising support through various benefit events.

The School is accredited by the Western Association of Schools and Colleges and the Council of International Schools. It holds membership in the Japan Council of International Schools, the East Asia Regional Council of Overseas Schools, Council of International Schools, and other professional organizations.

THE CAMPUS. The School is located on a 9-acre site in a lovely green residential area. The entire campus is currently being reconstructed in three phases. The new classroom and administration building (2009) includes all regular classrooms, two libraries, seven science labs, three computer labs, large play areas, and all administrative functions. The classrooms have wireless network access to give students all the advantages of the latest technologies for learning. Phase Two, to be completed in August 2010, will include a new gym, seven-lane swimming pool, cafeteria, fine arts classrooms, and a large athletic field. The final phase (March 2011) will include a new multipurpose facility. During the reconstruction period, the existing buildings continue to be used, negating the need for temporary facilities. The new buildings are designed to be 25 percent stronger than required by the latest, stringent Japanese seismic design codes. They are air-conditioned and have 24-hour ventilation to maintain good indoor air quality. The entire campus will be environmentally friendly, using recycled rainwater, solar panels, and "green" walls. More than 90 percent of the large trees on campus will be saved, and many new trees will be planted as well.

THE FACULTY. Br. Michel Jutras, a graduate of Laval University in Canada (B.Ed., B.A.), the University of Detroit (M.S.), and California State University at Northridge (M.A.), was named Headmaster in 1988. Brother Michel came to Japan in 1969 and served in other schools as teacher and administrator before accepting his present appointment.

There are 101 men and women on the faculty, 15 of whom teach part-time. Five are Brothers of Christian Instruction. All hold baccalaureate degrees or the equivalent, and 54 have master's degrees. The average length of service of the entire teaching staff is 11 years, and the average teaching experience of faculty members is 21 years.

A nurse is on duty through the school day, and hospital facilities are nearby.

STUDENT BODY. In 2009–10, the School enrolled 920 boys in Kindergarten–Grade 12. Of these, 292 were in the high school, 208 in Middle School, and 420 in the Elementary School. Students came from 55 countries, with the largest percentage from Japan.

ACADEMIC PROGRAM. The academic year, divided into semesters, begins in late August and ends in early June, with vacations at Christmas and one week in the spring. Classes are held 5 days a week between 8:30 A.M. and 3:15 P.M. Because the three school units share facilities, each operates on a different schedule, but, in the upper grades, a student normally has eight 45-minute classes. The library opens half an hour before the start of the class day and stays open for one hour after classes end to provide students ample study opportunities. Faculty members are involved in counseling and advising students. English as a Second Language support is available for students entering the School without full command of the language. Grades are issued four times a year.

ST. MARY'S INTERNATIONAL SCHOOL

The curriculum parallels the contemporary curricula of American international schools. At the elementary level, homeroom teachers lead classes in English, Social Studies, Mathematics, Science, and Religion. Specialist teachers provide instruction in Computer, Art, Physical Education, Vocal and Instrumental Music, and Japanese language. Three religion programs are provided: one for Roman Catholics, another for other Christians, and a third for non-Christians.

Middle School (Grades 6–8) students take English, Japanese or French, World Geography of Social Studies, Mathematics, Life Science or Physical Science, Physical Education, and Religion/Ethics. Electives available are Latin, Study Skills, Journalism, Band, Design Technology, Computer, Choir, and Art, among others.

To graduate, a student must complete a minimum of 22 units of credit in Grades 9–12, with each unit representing a full-year course. These must include 4 of English, 3 of a second language, 2 of social studies, 3 each of mathematics and science, 1 of religion/ethics, 1 of physical education, $1/2$ of fine arts, $1/4$ each of computer skills and health, and 4 of electives. In Grades 11–12, students may take the International Baccalaureate curriculum to qualify for a diploma that usually affords advanced standing in American universities.

ST. MARY'S INTERNATIONAL SCHOOL

Among the courses offered are English 1–4; French 1–5, Japanese 1–9; Economics, World History, Contemporary World History, International Relations, U.S. History, East Asian Studies, Social and Cultural Anthropology; Algebra 1–3, Geometry, Pre-Calculus, Calculus, Advanced Topics in Mathematics; Earth Science, Biology 1–2, Chemistry 1–2, Physics 1–2; Fine Arts, Ceramics 1–2, Photography, Yearbook, Concert Band, Choir, Creative Music, Student Television, Architectural Design 1–2, Design Technology; SAT Preparation, Journalism, Theory of Knowledge, Computer Science; and Physical Education. In the major subject areas, International Baccalaureate courses are available.

All 78 seniors who graduated in 2009 went on to further their education at the college level. They are enrolled at such institutions as Boston University, Brown, Columbia, Waseda (Japan), and the Universities of British Columbia, Notre Dame, and Southern California.

A coeducational three-week Summer School Program offering review courses in English and Mathematics, various courses in the arts, and recreation for Elementary and Middle School students will begin in June 2011.

STUDENT ACTIVITIES. In the secondary school, students elect representatives to a Student Council, which organizes social activities with St. Mary's "sister" schools, Seisen and Sacred Heart (all-girls schools).

A variety of activities are offered to meet student interests. Among those currently functioning are the student newspaper, yearbook, literary magazine, National Honor Society, drama, musical, speech, debate, Boy Scouts, Leo Club, concert band, choir, and boosters.

The School competes in the Kanto Plains Association against other international and Department of Defense schools at both varsity and junior varsity levels in soccer, basketball, tennis, track and field, cross-country, baseball, swimming, and wrestling. Similar sports programs are provided in both the Elementary and Middle Schools.

From January through March, classes from Grades 4–6 take four- or five-day trips to the ski lodge in Tsumagoi to receive instruction in skiing and strengthen ties with classmates. Other student groups make use of the lodge as well.

Special events on the school calendar, including those sponsored by the SMA, are Back-to-School Day for Parents,

New Mothers' Tea, Show Choir Dinner, Big Band Bash, Library Book Fair, Spring Luncheon, Christmas and Spring Band and Choir Concerts, Bingo, Musical, and Carnival.

ADMISSION AND COSTS. St. Mary's International School seeks students from the international community of Tokyo who will benefit from a college preparatory curriculum. Students are admitted on the basis of previous transcripts, standardized test results, and a personal interview with the student and parents. In some instances, an admissions test is administered. On acceptance, a registration fee of 300,000 yen must be paid and a medical certificate submitted.

In 2009–10, the tuition fee is 2,040,000 yen for all grades. Transportation and lunch fees are extra. Limited financial aid is available.

Headmaster: Br. Michel Jutras
High School Principal: Mr. Saburo Kagei
Middle School Principal: Mr. Andrew Cross
Elementary School Principal: Br. Lawrence Lambert
Elementary Assistant Principal: Mr. Michael DiMuzio
Curriculum Coordinator: Ms. Linda Wayne
Elementary/Middle School Counselor: Ms. Julie Gordon
Middle/High School Counselor: Mr. Charles Stanislaw
College Counselor: Mr. Christopher Polley
Business Manager: Mr. Kunihiko Takamichi

KOREA

Seoul Foreign School   1912

55 Yonhi Dong, Seoul, Korea 120-113
Tel. 82-2-330-3100; Admissions 82-2-330-3121; Fax 82-2-330-1857
Web Site www.seoulforeign.org; E-mail sfsoffice@seoulforeign.org

Seoul Foreign School, founded in 1912, provides excellence in education to the expatriate community within a caring, Christ-centered environment. The School serves nearly 1500 students in Preschool through Grade 12. An American curriculum is taught in all grades; a British curriculum is available for children age 3 through the equivalent of Middle School. The college preparatory high school program provides the IGCSE and the International Baccalaureate diploma. Among the activities offered are student government, publications, debate, Korean crafts, drama, bands, choruses, and interscholastic sports. Tuition: $7880–$21,610. Esther Kim Myong is Director of Admissions; Dr. John B. Engstrom is Head of School. *Western Association.*

PUERTO RICO

Commonwealth-Parkville School   1952

Upper School (Grades 7–12): Commonwealth Campus
Lower/Middle Schools (PPK–Grade 6): Parkville Campus
P.O. Box 70177, San Juan, PR 00936-8177
Tel. 787-765-4411; Admissions Exts. 32/33; Fax 787-764-3809
Web Site www.cpspr.org; E-mail jaranguren@cpspr.org

Commonwealth-Parkville School, a day school enrolling 700 boys and girls age 3–Grade 12, offers a program of academic vigor and varied activities including sports. With instruction in English, the School aims to prepare students for selective universities stateside and in Puerto Rico. It emphasizes interactive, hands-on experiences with exchange and travel programs abroad. The study of Spanish and Puerto Rican culture is required. Honors and Advanced Placement courses and a program for students with mild learning differences are offered. Summer program and camp are available. Tuition: $5620–$11,730. Financial Aid: $125,000. Jo-Ann Aranguren is Admissions Director; Richard Marracino (University of Connecticut, B.A.; University of California [Los Angeles], M.P.A.) is Headmaster. *Middle States Association.*

SPAIN

The American School of Madrid   1961

Apartado 80, 28080 Madrid, Spain
Tel. 34-91-740-1900; Fax 34-91-357-2678
Web Site www.asmadrid.org; E-mail admissions@asmadrid.org

This college preparatory, coeducational day school enrolls over 870 students from more than 50 nations in K1 (3-year-olds)–Grade 12. Its primary objective is to provide a traditional U.S. curriculum consistent with that of the best American schools. Students may also opt to complete the Spanish *Programa Oficial* and the International Baccalaureate diploma. Electives and the arts enrich the program. Classes are taught in English; Spanish and French are offered as second and third languages. "Experience Spain" allows students in Grades 10–12 from other schools to attend the American School for a semester or a year while living with host families. Tuition: €8094–€19,174. Ms. Sholeh Farpour Arab is Admissions Head; William D. O'Hale is Headmaster. *Middle States Association.*

School Year Abroad   1964

Plaza de Aragón 12, Principal, 50004 Zaragoza, Spain
Tel. 34-976-239-208; Fax 34-976-235-220
Web Site www.sya.org; E-mail admissions@sya.org
U.S. Office: 439 South Union Street, Lawrence, MA 01843
Tel. 978-725-6828; Fax 978-725-6833

School Year Abroad's mission is to teach self-reliance, responsibility, resourcefulness, and respect for other cultures. Approximately 60 rising juniors and seniors, who have taken at least two years of Spanish travel to Zaragoza, Spain, for the school year, live with a Spanish family, and immerse themselves in the country's language and culture. Spanish Language, Spanish Literature, English, History, Art History, Spanish Cinema, Spanish Journalism, Literature of the Theater, and math classes through Calculus are among the courses available. All classes except English and math are taught in Spanish. The average class size is 15 students. Student-exchange opportunities with schools in other cities are also offered. All students participate in over 20 days of school-led travel to Aragón, Navarra, Barcelona, Asturías, Valencia, and Andalucía and, with approval, are allowed to travel independently during breaks. Extracurricular activities are abundant and organized by local organizations or independent clubs. Tuition: $41,000. Financial aid is available. Roland Lemay is Director of Admissions; Griffin Morse is Resident Director.

VIETNAM

School Year Abroad   2009

Vietnam National University, Pham Van Dong Road, Cau Giay
 District, Hanoi, Vietnam
 U.S. Office: 439 South Union Street, Lawrence, MA 01843
 Tel. 978-725-6828; Fax 978-725-6833
 Web Site www.sya.org; E-mail admissions@sya.org

School Year Abroad's new Vietnam program introduces capable students to the history, language, and everyday life of the people of that nation. Approximately 30 boys and girls in Grade 10–Postgraduate attend classes in the heart of Hanoi for a year or a semester. The curriculum features college preparatory courses leading to an American diploma, including AP classes in economic and environmental science as well as math, English, and other traditional subjects. Classes in Vietnamese language meet five days a week and are taught by native speakers with focus on writing as well as intonation, speaking, and overall comprehension. Equal emphasis is placed on service learning, volunteer projects, and immersion in the culture and life of Vietnam. Students reside with local families and investigate critical issues such as water delivery systems; teach in orphanages and elementary schools; and work on issues that affect developing countries and economies. SYA's Resident Director coordinates extracurricular activities that students can share with Vietnamese students. Tuition: $41,000 (year); $22,000 (semester). Financial aid is available. Roland Lemay is Director of Admissions.

VIRGIN ISLANDS

The Good Hope School   1967

170 Estate Whim, Frederiksted, St. Croix, VI 00840
 Tel. 340-772-0022; Fax 340-772-0951
 Web Site www.ghsvi.org; E-mail mail@ghsvi.org

Celebrating more than 40 years of excellence in education, The Good Hope School is an independent, Pre-K–Grade 12 day school located on 32 seaside acres on St. Croix. A second campus on the island's East End serves children in Pre-K and Kindergarten. The Good Hope School offers its 318 students a rigorous college preparatory curriculum that includes Honors and Advanced Placement classes in all disciplines of study as well as participation in an Intel-affiliated science fair. A strong focus on the arts and athletics as well as a commitment to the individual child provide the well-rounded learning experience for which The Good Hope School is known. After-school and summer programs are offered. Good Hope is a member of the National Association of Independent Schools and the Caribbean Association of Independent Schools and is accredited by the Virgin Islands Department of Education and the Department of Human Services. Tuition: $7800–$11,520. Financial aid is available. Raquel B. Cedano is Head of School. *Middle States Association.*

St. Croix Country Day School   1964

R.R. 1, Box 6199 Kingshill, St. Croix, VI 00850
 Tel. 340-778-1974; Fax 340-779-3331
 Web Site www.stxcountryday.com
 E-mail bsinfield@stxcountryday.com

Established in 1964 by a group of parents who wanted an alternative to public and parochial schools, Country Day is now regarded as one of the premier college preparatory schools in the eastern Caribbean. At Country Day, the approximately 490 students in Nursery–Grade 12 are at the center of the community of learners, including parents, faculty, and staff, who are dedicated to academic and personal growth. The curriculum includes advanced courses in physics, marine biology, calculus, and world languages. Extracurricular activities include sports, theater, music, dance, fine arts, publications, academic competition such as Quiz Bowl, and service clubs. After-school care and a summer camp are offered. Tuition: $8700–$12,650. Tuition assistance is available. William D. Sinfield (Wilfred Laurier University, B.A.; Brock University, B.Ed.; Simon Fraser University, M.Ed.Ad.) is Headmaster. *Middle States Association.*

ST. CROIX COUNTRY DAY SCHOOL

A

Abbott, Andy, *John Burroughs School* (MO)
Abram, Percy L., Ph.D., *Gateway School* (CA)
Ackerly, Rick, *Children's Day* (CA)
Acquavita, Fred, *St. Thomas's Day* (CT)
Adams, Natalie R., *Washington Waldorf* (MD)
Addley, Blayne, *The Country School* (Canada)
Allan, Adrian, *Le Jardin Academy* (HI)
Allio, Matt, *The Walden School* (CA)
Allison, George K., *The Knox School* (NY)
Alvar, Concepcion, *Marymount School* (NY)
Amadio, Paul, *Besant Hill/Happy Valley* (CA)
Anderson, Laurance, *Grace Day School* (NY)
Appel, Maureen K., *Connelly/Holy Child* (MD)
Archer, Andrea, *Derby Academy* (MA)
Armstrong, David M., *Landon School* (MD)
Arzelier, Frédérick, *Lycée Français* (CA)
Ashley, Bradley F., *University Lake* (WI)
Assaf, Frederick G., *Pace Academy* (GA)
Austin, Donald M., *Newark Academy* (NJ)
Aycock, Thomas G., Ph.D., *Trinity Episcopal* (VA)

B

Bailey, Michael S., *St. Timothy's School* (NC)
Baily, Peter F., *Oakwood Friends* (NY)
Baker, Lyn, *Canterbury Episcopal* (TX)
Barnett, Chad, *The Linsly School* (WV)
Barr, Alan, *The O'Neal School* (NC)
Barr, Kathryn J., *Highlands School* (AL)
Barrengos, John, *Independent Day* (CT)
Barrett, Peter A., *St. Patrick's Episcopal Day* (DC)
Barrows, Craig, *Berkeley Hall* (CA)
Barton, Paul, *Avery Coonley* (IL)
Battle, Henry M., Jr., *Forsyth CDS* (NC)
Battles, Una S., *Advent Episcopal* (AL)
Bearss, Sr. Bridget, *Academy/Sacred Heart* (MI)
Beauregard, Joan, *The Oaks School* (CA)
Beecher, David Z., *Hillside School* (MA)
Beedy, Dr. Jeffrey P., *St. Martin's Episcopal* (LA)
Bell, H. Palmer, *Riverside Presbyterian* (FL)
Bellis, Steven J., Ed.D., *Pembroke Hill* (MO)
Benedict, Peter B. II, *Miami Valley* (OH)
Berkman, James S., *Boston Univ. Academy* (MA)
Berry, Kendell, *Evansville Day* (IN)
Bezsylko, Scott, *Winston Prep* (NY)
Biddulph, Karen, *The Mead School* (CT)
Bird, Dr. Thaddeus B., *All Saints Episcopal* (TX)
Bisgaard, Dennis, *Kingswood-Oxford* (CT)
Bissell, Jeff, *School Year Abroad* (China)
Blackburn, Greg, Ph.D., *Caedmon* (NY)
Blanchard, David Dennen, *The Craig School* (NJ)
Blanchette, Sr. Marie, O.P., *Overbrook* (TN)
Bland, Todd B., *Milton Academy* (MA)
Blumenthal, Richard M., Ph.D., *Francis Parker* (CA)
Bohlin, Dr. Karen E., *Montrose School* (MA)
Borg, William, *Vanguard College Prep* (TX)
Borgmann, Diane, *Sycamore School* (IN)
Borlo, Carolyn, *The Wilson School* (NJ)
Borst, Gina, *Grier School* (PA)
Bosland, Susan C., *Kent Place* (NJ)
Bowers, Reveta, *Center for Early Education* (CA)
Bowers, Stephen L., *St. James Episcopal* (CA)
Branch, Peter M., *Georgetown Day* (DC)
Branigan, Br. James, CSC, *Notre Dame/West Haven* (CT)
Brereton, Thomas G., *Galloway* (GA)
Bridenstine, Sheila, *Kalamazoo CDS* (MI)

Bright, Christopher, *Casady School* (OK)
Britton, Charles, *McDonogh School* (MD)
Broadus, Andy J., *Oakridge* (TX)
Brochu, Denis, *School Year Abroad* (France)
Broderick, Sr. Mary, SHCJ, *Rosemont/Holy Child* (PA)
Broderick, William M., *Fort Worth Academy* (TX)
Brooks, Fr. Dub, *St. Mark's Episcopal* (FL)
Broudo, Robert J., *Landmark School* (MA)
Brown, Frank D., *Brookstone School* (GA)
Brown, Neal, *Green Acres School* (MD)
Brown, Dr. Steven M., *Jack M. Barrack* (PA)
Brownley, Travis, *Marin Academy* (CA)
Bruce-Lockhart, Simon, *Glenlyon Norfolk* (Canada)
Brune, Jean Waller, *Roland Park Country* (MD)
Bryan, Richard C., Jr., *Nichols School* (NY)
Bull, Julian, *Campbell Hall* (CA)
Bur, Rev. George W., S.J., *St. Joseph's Prep* (PA)
Burger, James T., *Tuxedo Park* (NY)
Burke, William L. III, *St. Sebastian's* (MA)
Burner, Christopher D. '80, *Western Reserve* (OH)

C

Camner, Robert, *Charles Wright* (WA)
Campbell, Geoff, *Phoenix CDS* (AZ)
Campbell, Maryann, *Glenholme School* (CT)
Canadas, Frédéric, *Ecole Bilingue* (CA)
Cannon, Jonathan, *Charles E. Smith* (MD)
Carnabuci, Frank J., *Birch Wathen Lenox* (NY)
Carreiro, Paula, *Beauvoir, Natl. Cathedral ES* (DC)
Carter, Chris, *St. Mark's Cathedral School* (LA)
Casertano, Drew, *Millbrook School* (NY)
Cash, Steven J., *Mizzentop Day School* (NY)
Castro, Dr. Marjorie, *Eagle Hill School* (CT)
Cavanagh, Ellen M., *Oakcrest School* (VA)
Cedano, Raquel B., *The Good Hope School* (VI)
Celestin, Sonia, *The Cathedral School* (NY)
Chamberlain, Judith, *Calmont School* (CA)
Chapman, Paul D., Ph.D., *Head-Royce School* (CA)
Chase, Andrew C., *Eaglebrook School* (MA)
Chase, Nelson, *School Year Abroad* (MA)
Chinitz, Helen Stevens, *Storm King* (NY)
Christ, H. William, *Hathaway Brown* (OH)
Ciampoli, Robert, *Andrews–Lake St. Louis* (MO)
Ciancaglini, Dr. Joseph, *Convent/Sacred Heart* (NY)
Cikoski, Diane, *The Melrose School* (NY)
Cissel, John, *Dutchess Day School* (NY)
Clark, Catherine, *All Saints Episcopal* (TX)
Clark, L. Hamilton, *Episcopal Academy* (PA)
Clark, Martha S., *Riverfield CDS* (OK)
Clarkson, William IV, *Westminster Schools* (GA)
Cohen, Arnold S., Ph.D., *Lamplighter* (TX)
Cohen, Murray, Ph.D., *College Prep* (CA)
Colb, Norman, *Menlo School* (CA)
Collins, Richard G., Ph.D, *Brehm Prep* (IL)
Conard, Nathaniel, *Pingry School* (NJ)
Conklin, Kevin R., *Montgomery School* (PA)
Connor, James W., *Germantown Academy* (PA)
Connor, Virginia, *St. Hilda's & St. Hugh's* (NY)
Conway, Br. Leonard, OSF, *Saint Francis Prep* (NY)
Cooke, Sr. Suzanne, *Carrollton /Sacred Heart* (FL)
Coonrod, Theo W., *Saint Mary's School* (NC)
Cooper, John W., Ph.D., *Elgin Academy* (IL)
Costello, David J., *St. Peter's School* (PA)
Cottam, Doris, *The Langley School* (VA)
Cottrell, Dr. Timothy R., *The Harley School* (NY)
Cowan, E. Kay, *Nashoba Brooks* (MA)
Cowgill, Lourdes M., Ph.D., *Pine Crest School* (FL)
Cox, Joseph T., Ph.D., *The Haverford School* (PA)
Craig, Ian L., *Harding Academy* (TN)

Creeden, John E., Ph.D., *Providence Day* (NC)
Culbert, Sheila, *Loomis Chaffee* (CT)
Curtis, Dr. Alex C., *Morristown-Beard* (NJ)

D

Daggett, Clark, *Cape Cod Academy* (MA)
Dalton, The Rev. James E., OSFS, *Salesianum* (DE)
Daub, Walt, *Lowell Whiteman* (CO)
Daush, Barbara H., *St. Agnes-St. Dominic* (TN)
David, Deborah, *Marymount/Santa Barbara* (CA)
Davidson, Eileen, *The Ursuline School* (NY)
Davies, John P., Ed.D., *Miami CDS* (FL)
Davis, Mark, *Lexington Christian* (MA)
Davis, Dr. Mike, *Colorado Academy* (CO)
Deely, Philip S., *Allen Academy* (TX)
DeHaven, William, *Winston Prep* (NY)
Demartini, Phil, *Grosse Pointe Academy* (MI)
Dennis, Dr. Bruce, *Packer Collegiate* (NY)
Desjardins, Mark D., Ph.D., *Holland Hall* (OK)
Diamonti, Dr. Michael, *San Francisco Univ. HS* (CA)
Diamonti, Dr. Nancy, *Ring Mountain Day* (CA)
Dioli, Richard A., *Sacred Heart, Atherton* (CA)
Dodd, Jean C., *San Jose Episcopal Day* (FL)
Dominguez, Jaime, *Stuart Hall for Boys* (CA)
Dooman, Michael D., *Mooreland Hill* (CT)
Dougherty, David R., *The Hill School* (PA)
Douglass, Jody, *Buffalo Seminary* (NY)
Douglass, Robert G., *Stanley Clark* (IN)
Dressel, Leo P., *All Saints' Episcopal* (AZ)
Duaime, Rev. Jeffrey T., C.S.Sp. '76, *Holy Ghost Prep* (PA)
Duckett, Paul C., *Country Day School* (Canada)
Dunn, Sr. Jan, *Duchesne/Sacred Heart* (TX)
Dunn, Randall, *The Roeper School* (MI)
Dunnan, Rev. Dr. D. Stuart, *Saint James School* (MD)
Durgin, Janet, *Sonoma Academy* (CA)
Durham, Rev. DePorres, *Fenwick HS* (IL)
Durkin, Margot, *Browne Academy* (VA)
Dworkoski, Dr. Robert J., *Viewpoint School* (CA)

E

Eanes, Michael N., *Capitol Hill Day* (DC)
Ebeling, Dr. Michael J., *Summit School* (NC)
Edgerton, Nicholas M., *Pine Cobble* (MA)
Edwards, Michael, Ed.D., *Cliff Valley* (GA)
Elam, Julie, *Marin Primary/Middle* (CA)
Ely, W. Brewster IV, *Town School for Boys* (CA)
Enemark, Richard D., Ph.D., *Doane Stuart* (NY)
Engstrom, Dr. John B., *Seoul Foreign School* (Korea)
Erisman, Caroline, *Dana Hall* (MA)
Evans, Keith A., *Collegiate School* (VA)
Ewing, Richard T., Jr., *Norwood School* (MD)

F

Fader, Mark, *The Williams School* (CT)
Falkner, Thad M., *The Wilson School* (MO)
Fallo, Mark, *St. Nicholas School* (TN)
Farber, John S., *Old Trail School* (OH)
Farmen, Thomas W., *Rumsey Hall* (CT)
Farrell, Anthony, *Stuart Hall High* (CA)
Faunce, Dr. Theodore, *Chinese Intl. School* (China)

Faus, David C., *Falmouth Academy* (MA)
Featherston, Anthony G. IV, *Elmwood Franklin* (NY)
Felsen, David M., *Friends' Central* (PA)
Fenstermacher, Barry W., *Harvey* (NY)
Ferber, Joe, *Trident Academy* (SC)
Ferreboeuf, Michael, *Cathedral School/Boys* (CA)
Finch, John, *Chandler School* (CA)
Fleming, Allison, *Gillispie School* (CA)
Foecking, Bernd, *Hampshire Country School* (NH)
Ford, Darryl J., Ph.D., *William Penn Charter* (PA)
Foster, Shane, *The Barstow School* (MO)
Fountain, Dr. Gary, *Chatham Hall* (VA)
France, Frank A., *Kehoe-France* (LA)
Freund, Mark John, *Saint Mark's HS* (DE)
Frost, Les W., *St. Matthew's Parish* (CA)

G

Gambacorto, Sr. Lisa, *Mount Saint Mary* (NJ)
Garman, Dr. Bryan, *Wilmington Friends* (DE)
Garrett, Pritchard, *Delaware Valley Friends* (PA)
Garten, Christopher, *Seven Hills School* (OH)
Gately, Catherine H., *Charles River School* (MA)
Gehman, Richard H., *Oak Hall School* (FL)
George, Rev. William L., S.J., *Georgetown Prep* (MD)
Ghory, Ward J., Ed.D., *Univ. School/Milwaukee* (WI)
Gibbs, Debbie, *Lowell School* (DC)
Gilder, Thomas W., *Windward School* (CA)
Gill, Joseph J., *Mayfield Junior* (CA)
Gillespie, Dr. Monica, *St. Paul's for Girls* (MD)
Gillinger, Ann, *Chatsworth Hills Academy* (CA)
Gioia, Bradford, *Montgomery Bell* (TN)
Glass, Kevin, *Atlanta International School* (GA)
Goldberg, Robert S., *The Benjamin School* (FL)
Goodman, Carolyn G., *The Meadows School* (NV)
Goss, Dr. R. Mason, *Triangle Day School* (NC)
Gossage, Matthew E., *Cannon School* (NC)
Gould, Dr. Matthew A., *Community School* (MO)
Grabis, Christie B., *Gunston Day School* (MD)
Graves, Robert E., *Fredericksburg Academy* (VA)
Green, John F., *Peddie School* (NJ)
Green, Landis, *Wildwood School* (CA)
Greene, Wanda M. Holland, *Hamlin School* (CA)
Griffith, Dr. John, *Battle Ground Academy* (TN)
Griffith, Judith, *The Heritage School* (GA)
Grubbs, Denny, *Eliot Montessori School* (MA)
Gulla, John C., *The Blake School* (MN)
Gulley, Dr. Stuart, *Woodward Academy* (GA)
Gunther, Sr. Francine, SHCJ, *Cornelia Connelly* (CA)
Gurley, Sheila, *The College School* (MO)

H

Haberlandt, Susan M., *Providence CDS* (RI)
Hague, Dr. David, *Saklan Valley* (CA)
Haguewood, Ellis L., *Memphis Univ. School* (TN)
Hale, Mark, *Greensboro Day* (NC)
Hall-Mounsey, Michael, *Ojai Valley School* (CA)
Hamar, Rosalind, *Marin Horizon* (CA)
Hamer, Tim, *Bishop Ireton HS* (VA)
Hamlin, Erica L., *University Prep* (WA)
Hammond, Steve, *Saint Patrick Catholic School* (VA)
Hamner, Rev. Dr. James E. IV, *St. Martin's Episc.* (GA)
Hancock, Jonathan M., *Canterbury School* (IN)
Hardage, Cathy, *St. Mark's Episcopal Day* (FL)
Hardy, Allan, *Greenwood College* (Canada)
Harhager, Rev. John, *Marist School* (GA)

Harman, David B., *Poly Prep CDS* (NY)
Harr, Ramona, *Sullins Academy* (VA)
Harris, Susan G., *Harford Day* (MD)
Harrison, Stephen, *St. John's Parish Day School* (MD)
Hartwell, Janet M., *Greens Farms Academy* (CT)
Harvey, Thomas D., *Hampton Roads* (VA)
Hathaway, Dr. Laura, *Pegasus School* (CA)
Hayes, Pamela Juan '64, *Convent of the Sacred Heart* (CT)
Hayot, Dr. Patricia, *The Chapin School* (NY)
Healey, Joseph P., Ph.D., *University Liggett* (MI)
Hearn, W. Glyn, *Soundview Prep* (NY)
Heath, Richard L., *Sandia Prep* (NM)
Heim, William III, *Sage Ridge School* (NV)
Helm, Claire, Ph.D., *Academy/Holy Cross* (MD)
Henderson, Robert P., Jr., *Noble and Greenough* (MA)
Hendrix, Dr. James P., *St. John's School* (TX)
Henrichsen, B.H., *Robert Louis Stevenson* (NY)
Hernández, Sr. Carla, OSBM, *Saint Basil* (PA)
Hershey, F. Robertson, *Episcopal HS* (VA)
Hertrick, Charles F., *Allendale Columbia* (NY)
Hester, Coreen R., *American School/London* (England)
Hickman, Steve, *Episcopal Collegiate* (AR)
Hightower, Nancy Heath, Ed.D., *River Oaks Baptist* (TX)
Hill, Frederick T., *Chadwick School* (CA)
Hinds, Stephen T., *Meadowbrook of Weston* (MA)
Hogan, Arlene, *The Bentley School* (CA)
Holden, Joan G. Ogilvy, *St. Stephen's/St. Agnes* (VA)
Holford, Josie, Ph.D., *Poughkeepsie Day* (NY)
Hollister, Dr. Randall, *Loudoun CDS* (VA)
Holtberg, Arnold E., *St. Mark's of Texas* (TX)
Holyer, Christiana, *Queen Anne School* (MD)
Hood, Thomas G., *MMI Prep* (PA)
Horn, Kelly R., *Rohan Woods* (MO)
Horn, Todd R.W., Ph.D., *Kent Denver* (CO)
Hornung, Dr. Claire, *Wyoming Seminary LS* (PA)
Horton, Holly, *Live Oak School* (CA)
Horwitz, Alyson K. Ed.D., *Bernard Zell* (IL)
Hudnut, Thomas C., *Harvard-Westlake* (CA)
Hull, Marcia, *Savannah Country Day* (GA)
Hull, Stephanie J., Ph.D., *Brearley* (NY)
Hulse, Diane J., *Staten Island Academy* (NY)
Hulsey, Dr. Byron, *Randolph School* (AL)
Hunter, Catherine, *San Francisco Friends* (CA)
Hutcheson, Dorothy A., *Nightingale-Bamford* (NY)
Huybrechts, Jeanne, Ed.D., *Harvard-Westlake* (CA)

I

Iadarola, Dr. Antoinette, *Academy/Our Lady of Mercy* (CT)
Izzo, Robert J., *Hamden Hall CDS* (CT)

J

Jablon, William W., *Maclay School* (FL)
Jackson, Steven T., *Christ Methodist Day* (TN)
Jacobson, Marvin, *Laurence School* (CA)
Jamieson, Kathleen O., *Natl. Cathedral School* (DC)
Jaques, Herbert, Jr., *Friends School Haverford* (PA)
Jellig, Dr. Gerald M., *Summit CDS* (OH)
Jernberg, James Peter, Jr., *Jackson Academy* (MS)
Johnson, Brian, *Alexander Dawson* (CO)
Johnson, Dale T., *The Field School* (DC)
Johnson, Stuart H. III, *St. Bernard's School* (NY)
Johnson, Thomas, *Bayside Academy* (AL)
Johnson, Timothy J., *Bay School/SF* (CA)

Johnson, Dr. Timothy M., *Pingree School* (MA)
Johnson, Walter C., *Hackley School* (NY)
Jonathan, Jeff, *Cold Spring* (CT)
Jones, Geoff, *The Potomac School* (VA)
Jordan, Tony, *All Saints' Academy* (FL)
Judge, Molly, *Radcliffe Creek* (MD)
Juhel, Dr. Jean-Marc, *Buckley CDS* (NY)
Jutras, Br. Michel, *St. Mary's Intl. School* (Japan)

K

Kang, Laura, *Gibson Island Country School* (MD)
Karrels, Catherine Ronan '86, *Stone Ridge/Sacred Heart* (MD)
Katsouros, Rev. Stephen N., SJ, *Loyola School* (NY)
Katz, Jerrold I., Ed.D., *The Park School* (MA)
Katz, Dr. Lucinda Lee, *Marin CDS* (CA)
Kaufman, Ilana, *Windrush School* (CA)
Kaufman, Robert, *Fairfield Country Day* (CT)
Kay, Malcolm, *ACS Intl. Schools* (England)
Kelley, Robert A., *The Pennfield School* (RI)
Kelly, Doreen C., *Ravenscroft School* (NC)
Kelly, Mark H., *Annunciation Orthodox* (TX)
Kelly, Thomas M., Ph.D., *Horace Mann* (NY)
Kennedy, Michael, *Barrie School* (MD)
Kennedy, Stephen, *Trinity School* (GA)
Kerby, Damon H., *Saint Mark's* (CA)
Kerns, Daniel M., J.D., *Georgetown Visitation Prep* (DC)
Kestler, Br. Richard, FSC, *LaSalle College HS* (PA)
Kidd, Marie, *Crestview Prep* (CA)
Kim, Edward, *Breck School* (MN)
King, George N., Jr., *Moravian Academy* (PA)
King, John J., *Hebron Academy* (ME)
King, Molly H., *Greenwich Academy* (CT)
Kleger, Eve, *Village Community* (NY)
Klimas, Carol, *Lake Ridge Academy* (OH)
Kohler, J. Robert, *Good Shepherd Episcopal* (TX)
Kosasky, Robert, *St. Andrew's Episcopal* (MD)
Koskores, Theodore '70, *Thayer Academy* (MA)
Kost, Deborah, *The Janus School* (PA)
Kowalik, John J., *The Peck School* (NJ)
Krahn, Dr. Gary, *Trinity Valley* (TX)
Krieger, Paul, *Christ School* (NC)
Kuh, Edward, *Fayerweather Street* (MA)
Kuhn, The Rev. Michael, *Trinity Episcopal* (LA)
Kytle, Dr. Angél, *Saint Paul's School* (FL)

L

Lagarde, Douglas H., *Severn School* (MD)
Lahart, Fr. Daniel K., SJ, *Strake Jesuit College Prep* (TX)
Laird, Scott D., *St Mary's Episcopal Day* (FL)
Lambert, Eileen F., *Saddle River Day* (NJ)
Landry, Jacqueline, *Marymount High School* (CA)
Larrauri, Silvia, *St. Stephen's Episcopal Day* (FL)
Lauder, Robert, *Friends Seminary* (NY)
Lauricella, Chris, *Park School/Buffalo* (NY)
Lavelle, Br. Robert E., CSC, *Gilmour Academy* (OH)
Leahy, Rev. Edwin D., OSB, *St. Benedict's Prep* (NJ)
Leana, Lenesa, *Belmont Day* (MA)
Lecky, D. Mason, *St. Andrew's Episcopal School* (LA)
Lester, F. Martin, Jr., *St. Paul's Episcopal* (AL)
Levison, Lee M., Ed.D., *Collegiate School* (NY)
Lewis, John P., Ed.D., *Cape Henry Collegiate* (VA)
Lewis, Peter S., Ph.D., *The Winston School* (NJ)
Libbon, Rosemary, *Bishop Montgomery HS* (CA)
Lindsay, Susan, *Jackson Prep* (MS)

Lloyd, Cathie Field, *Ursuline Academy* (DE)
Loan, James, *Telluride Mountain School* (CO)
Locke, T.J., *Isidore Newman* (LA)
Loomis, Jeffrey P., *Saint Gregory's School* (NY)
Lopdell-Lawrence, Murray E., *Far Brook School* (NJ)
Lowry, David M., Ph.D., *Elisabeth Morrow* (NJ)
Loy, Steven A., Ed.D., *Rutgers Prep* (NJ)
Lyle, Lisa, *Mary Inst./St. Louis CDS* (FL)
Lynch, J. Harry, *The Newman School* (MA)

M

MacKelcan, Douglas, Jr., *Sanford School* (DE)
MacKenzie, John M., *The Columbus Academy* (OH)
MacMullen, William R. '78, *Taft* School (CT)
Magill, Dr. David W., *Univ. of Chicago Lab* (IL)
Maguire, Sr. Shawn Marie, SND, *Maryvale Prep* (MD)
Magusin, Frank, *The Bush School* (WA)
Maher, Michael F., *John Cooper* (TX)
Maher, Michael J., *Berkshire School* (MA)
Mahler, David V., *The Out-of-Door Academy* (FL)
Main, Thomas B., *King Low Heywood Thomas* (CT)
Malone, Nora, *Village School* (CA)
Manning, Dennis, *Norfolk Academy* (VA)
Maoz, Carol, *The Foote School* (CT)
Marblo, Christopher, *The Town School* (NY)
Marracino, F. Richard, *Commonwealth-Parkville* (PR)
Marshall, Joseph P., *The Orchard School* (IN)
Masters, Curtis G., *Brentwood Academy* (TN)
Maughan, Craig S., *Trinity Prep* (FL)
McBride, Rita Curasi, *Mayfield Sr. School* (CA)
McBrine, Judson L. III, *Washington Academy* (ME)
McCathie, Stuart, *Lausanne Collegiate* (TN)
McClure, Brian, *Trafalgar Castle* (Canada)
McCormack, Peter, *Rolling Hills Prep* (CA)
McGregor, Elizabeth J., *Westridge School* (CA)
McHenry, Kevin, *St. Andrew's College* (Canada)
McIntosh, Arch N., Jr., *Charlotte Latin* (NC)
McKee, Krista, *St. John's Parish Day* (MD)
McKee, Mark, *St. Matthew's Episcopal Day* (CA)
McKenzie, Malcolm H., *Hotchkiss School* (CT)
McKinney, Sr. Kathleen, *Mary Louis Academy* (NY)
McLaughlin, Rev. Joseph, O.Praem., *Archmere* (DE)
McNeill, Gordon, *Sage Hill School* (CA)
Mecca, Kathleen M., Ph.D., *Mount Tamalpais* (CA)
Meehl, John B., *Cape Fear Academy* (NC)
Melvoin, Richard I., Ph.D., *Belmont Hill* (MA)
Merluzzi, Joseph A., *Berkeley Prep* (FL)
Merry, Karan A., *St. Paul's Episcopal* (CA)
Mersky, Michael J., *Saint Edward's School* (FL)
Merz, Thya, *Corlears School* (NY)
Meyer, Sr. Jane, *St. Agnes Academy* (TX)
Michaud, Raymond R., Jr., *John Thomas Dye* (CA)
Miller, Dan B., Ph.D., *The Wheeler School* (RI)
Miller, William H., *The Seven Hills School* (CA)
Mixsell, Sally, *Stoneleigh-Burnham* (MA)
Mlatac, Laura Blackburn, *Guilford Day* (NC)
Moceri, Ellen Y., *Ransom Everglades* (FL)
Monaco, David, *Parish Episcopal School* (TX)
Montgomery, M.J., Jr., *Ridgewood Prep* (LA)
Moore, Margaret Delk, *St. Andrew's Episcopal* (VA)
Moran, Paul J., *Austin Prep* (MA)
Morse, Griffin, *School Year Abroad* (Spain)
Moseley, William N., *Ensworth* (TN)
Mueller, Richard W., *Hong Kong Intl.* (China)
Mullen, David, *The Nora School* (MD)
Mullins, Andrea A., *The Maddux School* (MD)
Murphy, Lesley, *St. Stephen's* (Italy)
Murphy, Michael G., *Seattle CDS* (WA)

N

Nafie, Robert W., Ph.D., *Clairbourn School* (CA)
Nance, Raymond, *Glen Urquhart* (MA)
Nazro, Lucy, *St. Andrew's Episcopal* (TX)
Neely, Matt, *Epiphany School* (WA)
Nelson, Marsha K., *Cathedral School/St. John the Divine* (NY)
Nelson, Scott A., *Rye CDS* (NY)
Newman, Suellen, *The Hudson School* (NJ)
Nichols, Dawn, Ed.D., *Convent of the Visitation* (MN)
Nierenberg, Steven R., *Newtown Friends* (PA)
Nikoloff, Christopher, *The Harker School* (CA)
Niles, Eric, J.D., *The Athenian School* (CA)
Nill, Dr. Michael, *Brooklyn Friends* (NY)
North, Donald C., *Kinkaid* (TX)
Northrup, Thomas A., *Hill School/Middleburg* (VA)
Nourie, Richard F., *Abington Friends* (PA)
Nygren, Kip P., Ph.D., *Wyoming Seminary* (PA)

O

O'Brien, John, *St Mary/All Angels* (CA)
O'Hale, William D., *American School/Madrid* (Spain)
O'Halloran, P. David, Ph.D., *Saint David's* (NY)
Olszamowski, Rev. Leon, s.m., *Notre Dame /Marist* (MI)
O'Melia, Gregory J., *The Buckley School* (NY)
Ora, John, *Woodland School* (CA)
O'Reilly, John, Ph.D., *Blue Ridge School* (VA)
Orenstein, Denise G., *Centreville School* (DE)
O'Shea, Brendan J., *Charleston Day* (SC)

P

Pacelli, Joseph A., *Oak Hill Academy* (NJ)
Packard, John, *Brooks School* (MA)
Parisi, Patricia D., *St. Clement's* (Canada)
Parker, Linda, *Bermuda HS for Girls* (Bermuda)
Patterson, Joseph C., *Andrews Academy* (MO)
Paulus, John Anthony II, *The Canterbury School* (FL)
Peebles, William S. IV, *Lovett* (GA)
Peirce, Dr. Nathaniel, *East Woods School* (NY)
Perez, Joseph, *Country School* (CA)
Perry, Roger L., *Lakehill Prep* (TX)
Pesci, Rev. Thomas A., S.J., *Loyola Blakefield* (MD)
Peterman, John C., *Brookwood School* (MA)
Peters, Dane L., *Brooklyn Hgts. Montessori* (NY)
Peters, Robert G., Ed.D., *Hanahau'oli* (HI)
Peterson, Evan D., *Fort Worth Country Day* (TX)
Peterson, Dr. Polly, *The Winston School* (TX)
Peterson, Robert R., *Oakwood School* (NC)
Phelps, Douglas E., *Harbor Day* (CA)
Philip, Thomas W., *Brunswick School* (CT)
Phillips, Eif, *Munich International* (Germany)
Phinney, William F., *Dexter & Southfield Schools* (MA)
Piechota, Dr. Mark, *The Crefeld School* (PA)
Pierotti, Mark J., *Forest Ridge/Sacred Heart* (WA)
Piltch, Neal, *Manzano Day* (NM)
Piltch, Steven S., Ed.D., *Shipley* (PA)
Piñero, Kristina, *Overbrook Academy* (RI)
Pleasanton, Tami, *Saint Joseph's Episcopal School* (FL)
Plumb, Louise K., *Primary Day* (MD)
Pollina, Ann S., *Westover School* (CT)

Powell, Lynne, Ed.D., *Seacrest CDS* (FL)
Power, Dr. James, *Upper Canada College* (Canada)
Powers, Benjamin N., *The Kildonan School* (NY)
Powers, William, *The Country School* (CT)
Pratt, Dr. Michael, *Brentwood School* (CA)
Price, Walter W., *Miller School* (VA)
Proctor, Dr. Christian, *Porter-Gaud* (SC)
Pryor, Christopher, *Harbor CDS* (NY)
Puggelli, Joe, *Seattle Academy* (WA)
Pullen, Janet S., *Saint Stephen's Episcopal* (FL)
Purpur, Dr. Harry, *Academy of the Holy Names* (FL)

R

Ralston, Matthew, *The Leelanau School* (MI)
Randolph, Dominic A.A., *Riverdale Country School* (NY)
Reed, Deborah, *Polytechnic School* (CA)
Reed, Mark, *Charlotte Country Day* (NC)
Reel, Kevin, *Colorado Springs School* (CO)
Reenstierna, Anne C., *Brimmer and May* (MA)
Reford, Dr. Mark, *St. Luke's Episcopal* (TX)
Regan, Dale, *Episcopal HS of Jacksonville* (FL)
Reisinger, Scott R., *Bancroft School* (MA)
Rench, Michele M., *All Saints' Episcopal Day* (CA)
Riley, Barbara Masters, *Hopkins School* (CT)
Roberts, Michael, Ph.D., *Catherine Cook* (IL)
Roberts, Patrick H.F., *St. James Episcopal* (TX)
Robertson, Donald B., *The Walker School* (GA)
Robinson, Michael, *Lake Forest CDS* (IL)
Roche, Aimeclaire, *The Bishop's School* (CA)
Rode, Gordon R., *St. John's Episcopal Parish Day* (FL)
Rogers, M. Bradley, Jr., *The Gow School* (NY)
Ruoss, Eric G., Ed.D., *The Tatnall School* (DE)
Russell, Dr. John J., *Windward School* (NY)

S

Saburn, Timothy J., *Oak Knoll/Holy Child* (NJ)
St. Laurent, Richard, *Rivermont Collegiate* (IA)
Salkind, Mark, *Urban School/San Francisco* (CA)
Sands, Priscilla G., Ed.D., *Springside School* (PA)
Scanlon, Patrick, *School Year Abroad* (Italy)
Schafer, Michael J., *Kimball Union* (NH)
Schantz, Katherine, *The Lab School* (DC)
Scheindlin, Rabbi Laurence, *Sinai Akiba* (CA)
Schmick, John F., *Gilman School* (MD)
Schrader, Fr. Tom, *Crespi Carmelite HS* (CA)
Schuck, Christopher, *La Jolla CDS* (CA)
Scott, Lorna Prado, *Santiago College* (Chile)
Secor, James Jay III, *Episcopal School/Knoxville* (TN)
Seeley, Timothy J., *North Cross School* (VA)
Seery, James L., *The Windsor School* (NY)
Seligman, Lynn, *The Mabin School* (Canada)
Seward, Kenneth H., *The Steward School* (VA)
Sgro, Beverly H., Ph.D., *Carolina Day* (NC)
Shanahan, Edward J., Ph.D., *Choate Rosemary Hall* (CT)
Shapiro, David, *Edmund Burke* (DC)
Shatlock, Kathleen, *PACE-Brantley Hall* (FL)
Shaw, Pamela, *Canton CDS* (OH)
Shepardson-Killam, Martha, *Seacoast Academy* (NH)
Sheridan, Rev. Paul, S.J., *Bellarmine College Prep* (CA)
Shipley, Patricia A., *Rossman School* (MO)
Shirley, J. Robert, Ph.D., *Charleston Collegiate* (SC)
Shlachter, Irwin, *Claremont Prep* (NY)

Shon, Betty, *Chinese American Intl. School* (CA)
Shurley, Andrea, *Convent/Sacred Heart HS* (CA)
Siebert, Bob, Ed.D., *Churchill School/Center* (NY)
Sindler, Jeff, *Burgundy Farm CDS* (VA)
Sinfield, William D., *St. Croix CDS* (VI)
Sipus, Ronald G., Ph.D., *Village Christian* (CA)
Skrumbis, Jim, *Sierra Canyon* (CA)
Slade, Whitney C., *St. Michael's CDS* (RI)
Smailes, Peter W., *Curtis School* (CA)
Small, Dr. Chad B., *Rumson CDS* (NJ)
Smethurst, Jacqueline, Ed.D., *Pegasus School* (CA)
Smiley, Alan, *St. Anne's Episcopal* (CO)
Smith, C. Edward, *Episcopal HS of Houston* (TX)
Smith, Paula, *University Child Development* (WA)
Soghoian, Richard J., Ph.D., *Columbia Grammar/Prep* (NY)
Solsrud, Robert, *Brookfield Academy* (WI)
Sommer, Peter, *Cambridge Friends* (MA)
Southard, Thomas N., *Shady Side* (PA)
Spahn, Stephen H., *Dwight School* (NY)
Sparrow, Alan C., *Rowland Hall-St. Mark's* (UT)
Speers, Elizabeth, *Ethel Walker* (CT)
Spinelli, Lydia, Ed.D., *Brick Church School* (NY)
Stanek, Mark J., *Ethical Culture Fieldston* (NY)
Stansbery, Todd P., *The Swain School* (PA)
Staunton, E.G. "Ted", Jr., *Saltus Grammar School* (Bermuda)
Steel, Francis P., Jr., '77, *Chestnut Hill Academy* (PA)
Steele, Paula G., *Collegiate School* (NJ)
Stein, Ellen C., *The Dalton School* (NY)
Stellato, Paul J., *Princeton Day School* (NJ)
Stencel, Marsha, *Princeton Montessori* (NJ)
Stephens, David B., *Meadowbrook School* (PA)
Stettler, Rachel Friis, *The Winsor School* (MA)
Stevens, Randy S., *St. Timothy's* (MD)
Stewart, Marilyn E., *The Red Oaks School* (NJ)
Stewart, Ronald P., *York Prep* (NY)
Stillwell, Charles M., *St. Christopher's* (VA)
Stockhammer, Paul R., *Brandon Hall School* (GA)
Stokes, Jeffrey, *Southfield School* (LA)
Straeter, Sue M., Ed.D., *The Hillside School* (PA)
Swann, Rev. Stephen B., *Episcopal School/Dallas* (TX)
Swartz, Albert J., *The Montessori School* (MD)
Swarzman, Dr. Joyce Burick, *Independent Day* (FL)
Sykes, Dr. Ronald P., *The Covenant School* (VA)
Sykoff, Lawrence S., Ed.D., *Ranney School* (NJ)

T

Talbott, Marjo, *Maret School* (DC)
Taylor, Clint, Ed.D., *Foothill Country Day* (CA)
Taylor, William W., *St. George's Independent* (TN)
Temple Eric, *The Carey School* (CA)
Thacher, Nicholas S., *Dedham CDS* (MA)
Theunick, Sandra J., *St. Andrew's Priory* (HI)
Thomas, Sr. Mary, O.P., *St. Cecilia Academy* (TN)
Thompson, Douglas C., Ph.D., *Mid-Peninsula HS* (CA)
Tobolsky, Stephen, Ph.D., *Chestnut Hill* (MA)
Tomlin, David, *New Garden Friends* (NC)
Townsend, Stephanie G., *Pennington School* (NJ)
Trigaux, David, *Pear Tree Point School* (CT)
Trower, David R., *Allen-Stevenson* (NY)
Turley, Kate, *City & Country* (NY)

U

Underwood, Jay, *Rio Grande School* (NM)

V

Vachow, Michael J., *Forsyth School* (MO)
van der Bogert, Dr. Rebecca, *Palm Beach Day* (FL)
Van Meter, Laurence R., *Moorestown Friends* (NJ)
Ventre, Gregory, *Glenelg Country School* (MD)
Verhalen, Rev. Peter, *Cistercian Prep* (TX)
Villatico, Paul, *Kerr-Vance Academy* (NC)

W

Wachter, Sr. Anne, RSCJ, *Convent/Sacred Heart ES* (CA)
Wade, Margaret W., Ed.D., *Franklin Road Academy* (TN)
Wagner, Barbara E., *Marlborough School* (CA)
Wales, Ralph L., *The Gordon School* (RI)
Walker, Stuart, *UN International School* (NY)
Walsh, Kate Burke, *The Willow School* (NJ)
Walter, H. John III, *St. Timothy's Prep* (CA)
Ward, Clair, *Valley School/Ligonier* (PA)
Ward, Gerard J.G., *The Fenn School* (MA)
Watson, Andrew T., *Albuquerque Academy* (NM)
Watters, Stephen H., *The Green Vale School* (NY)
Webb, Raymond, *Foxcroft Academy* (ME)
Webster, Andrew, *Wardlaw-Hartridge* (NJ)
Webster, Chuck, *University HS* (IN)
Weiss, Joel, *Crane CDS* (CA)
Weiss, Larry, Ph.D., *Saint Ann's School* (NY)
Welch, Robert W., *The Dunham School* (LA)
West, John Thomas III, *Mirman School/Gifted Children* (CA)
Wharton, William D., *Commonwealth* (MA)
Wheeler, Dr. Kirk, *St. Thomas School* (WA)
Whiteside, Sarah, *Altamont* (AL)
Whiting, Robert H., Ph.D., *Holy Nativity* (HI)
Whitman, Jeanne P., *Hockaday* (TX)
Wilkins, Stephen, *The Carroll School* (MA)
Wilson, Andrew, *Grier School* (PA)
Wilson, Vance, *St. Albans School* (DC)
Winn, Betty, *Abraham Joshua Heschel* (CA)
Wintrol, Jan, *The Ivymount School* (MD)
Woodhall, Matthew Campbell, *The Woodhall School* (CT)
Worch, Mary C., *The Woods Academy* (MD)
Work, Elisabeth, *Grymes Memorial* (VA)
Wright, Alexis, *Bank Street School* (NY)
Wright, Brian, Ph.D., *Williston Northampton* (MA)
Wright, Rodger, *Collingwood School* (Canada)
Wunner, Kathleen E., Ph.D., *Wyndcroft* (PA)

Y

Yedid, Marcella M., *The Key School* (MD)
Young, Pat, *The Stanwich School* (CT)

Z

Zacuto, Bradley, *Westside Neighborhood* (CA)
Zlotowitz, Debbie, *Mary McDowell Center* (NY)

A

Abramson, Ryan T. '94, *Holy Ghost Prep* (PA)
Acker, Elaine, *Elmwood Franklin* (NY)
Adams, Lori, *Fredericksburg Academy* (VA)
Albanese, Meghan, *Palm Beach Day Academy* (FL)
Altshul, Laura O., *The Foote School* (CT)
Alvarez, Josie, *The Bishop's School* (CA)
Anderson, Emily, *The Gordon School* (RI)
Aperavich, Mary, *Saint Joseph's School* (FL)
Aquino, Lisa Lau '81, *Hamlin School* (CA)
Arab, Sholeh Farpour, *American School/Madrid* (Spain)
Aranguren, Jo-Ann, *Commonwealth-Parkville* (PR)
Armstrong, Sara, *Cold Spring School* (CT)
Arnold, Rebecca, *Harding Academy* (TN)
Atcheson, Elizabeth, *The Bush School* (WA)
Atkinson, Emily, *Episcopal HS* (VA)
Aulicino, Christine, *The Country School* (CT)
Auwarter, Carrie, *Buffalo Seminary* (NY)
Axelbaum, Erica, *Forsyth School* (MO)
Axford, Dan, *Moravian* (PA)
Aycock, Malia, *St. Andrew's Episcopal* (TX)
Ayoub, Heidi, *ACS International* (England)

B

Babior, Dan, *Marin Academy* (CA)
Backlund, Lori D., *Stone Ridge/Sacred Heart* (MD)
Bader, Betty, *St. Cecilia Academy* (TN)
Baker, David, *St. Mark's School of Texas* (TX)
Barden, Monica, *The Mabin School* (Canada)
Barfield, Pam, *Independent Day School* (FL)
Barfield, Terri, *Savannah CDS* (GA)
Barnes, Christena, *Walden School* (CA)
Barry, Mary Beth, *Brentwood School* (CA)
Bartow, Elizabeth, *The Barstow School* (MO)
Bastrenta, Brigitte, *Ecole Bilingue* (CA)
Baty, Kristin, *Trinity School* (GA)
Beams, Judy, *Brooks School* (MA)
Beare, Rachael N., *Hotchkiss School* (CT)
Becker, Linda J.L., *Pine Cobble School* (MA)
Beeson, Christopher, *The Athenian School* (CA)
Behar, Barbara, *Friends' Central* (PA)
Below, Glynn, *Randolph School* (AL)
Belton, Michelle, *Lowell School* (DC)
Bentree, Barbara, *Rio Grande School* (NM)
Bernstein, Marina, *The Dwight School* (NY)
Berry, Lee, *Grymes Memorial School* (VA)
Bertin, Randy, *Besant Hill School* (CA)
Biehn, Jennifer, *The Shipley School* (PA)
Blair, Jeanne Marie, *Rosemont/Holy Child* (PA)
Bohrer, Cynthia, *Fayerweather Street* (MA)
Boisvert, Sara, *The Pingry School* (NJ)
Bonaparte, Yvette, *San Francisco Friends* (CA)
Bond, David, *Windrush School* (CA)
Bonet, Iris, *The Kinkaid School* (TX)
Bonnichsen, Gail, *All Saints' Academy* (FL)
Bonnie, Dr. Stephen A., *William Penn Charter* (PA)
Bonus, Sharman M., *Marin Horizon* (CA)
Booe, Kathryn B., *Charlotte Latin* (NC)
Borosavage, Wendy W., *Chestnut Hill* (MA)
Bowman, Jeannie, *Delaware Valley Friends* (PA)
Brady, Jennifer, *Park School of Buffalo* (NY)
Breen, Kevin, *University Liggett School* (MI)
Brennan, Jay, *Foxcroft Academy* (ME)
Brenner, Matt, *Lamplighter* (TX)
Breschi, Michael, *Loyola Blakefield* (MD)
Brewster, Paige, *Boston University Academy* (MA)
Briggs, Mary Jane, *Episcopal Collegiate School* (AR)
Brissenden, Deborah, *Belmont Day* (MA)

Brown, Barbara, *Mid-Peninsula HS* (CA)
Burke, Holly, *The Brick Church School* (NY)
Burke, Kathleen M., *The Pennfield School* (RI)
Burke, Ruth, *Episcopal School/Dallas* (TX)
Burnett, Harriet, *Friends Seminary* (NY)
Burnett, Steve, *Sierra Canyon School* (CA)
Burns, Tom, *The Melrose School* (NY)
Burr, Hacker, *Charleston Collegiate* (SC)
Byrne, James G., *Marist School* (GA)

C

Cabot, Raymond H., *Peddie School* (NJ)
Cafeo, Kari, *Burgundy Farm CDS* (VA)
Cain, Molly, *Harford Day School* (MD)
Caldwell, Jason, *Packer Collegiate* (NY)
Calixto, Judy, *Village Community* (NY)
Callahan, Beth, *Montessori School* (MD)
Callahan, Jennifer, *Ursuline Academy* (DE)
Calvin, Lyn-Felice, *St. Thomas School* (WA)
Capps, Rebekah, *The Ensworth School* (TN)
Carroll, Alan, *Allendale Columbia* (NY)
Carter, Helene, *Commonwealth School* (MA)
Casaccio, Francesca, *Fenwick High School* (IL)
Casey, Jackie, *Convent/Sacred Heart* (NY)
Casseb, Margaret Ann, *St. Luke's Episcopal* (TX)
Chan, Bonnie, *Chinese Intl. School* (China)
Chettleburgh, Deirdre, *Glenlyon Norfolk* (Canada)
Chibber, Nina, *Green Acres* (MD)
Chitjian, Jeanette Woo, *Marlborough School* (CA)
Clark, Elise, *City & Country School* (NY)
Clement, Cathy, *St. Timothy's* (NC)
Coats, Jodi, *American School/London* (England)
Coburn, Clare, *Southfield School* (LA)
Cohen, Susan, *Charles E. Smith Jewish Day* (MD)
Collins, Donna, *Brehm Preparatory School* (IL)
Colucci, Bill, *Bellarmine College Prep* (CA)
Cone, Tom, *Eagle Hill School* (CT)
Conklin, Nancy, *Pegasus School* (CA)
Conner, Judy, *Francis Parker School* (CA)
Convery, Deborah, *Montrose School* (MA)
Cook, Molly B., *Lausanne Collegiate* (TN)
Corbett, Erin, *Ethel Walker* (CT)
Core, Julie S., *Hackley School* (NY)
Cox, Laura, *Evansville Day School* (IN)
Craig, Virginia, *St. James Episcopal* (TX)
Cranford, Susan, *Bancroft School* (MA)
Crisan, Anne, *All Saints' Episcopal Day* (CA)
Croll, Ann, *The Stanwich School* (CT)
Crum, Beverly, *Hanahau'oli School* (HI)
Cunitz, Stacey, *The Crefeld School* (PA)
Curran, Caitlin, *Convent/Sacred Heart HS* (CA)

D

Damico, David, *Wyoming Seminary* (PA)
Danish, Jennifer S., *St. Patrick's Episc. Day* (DC)
D'Arcy, Cathie, *St. Stephen's Episcopal Day* (FL)
Darrin, William A. III, *Blue Ridge School* (VA)
Davis, Dr. Jerry, *The Oakridge School* (TX)
Dawkins, Barbara B., *St. Nicholas School* (TN)
DeBono, Denise, *Packer Collegiate* (NY)
DeHoff, Courtney, *Winston Prep* (NY)
Del Alamo, Elena, *Pine Crest School* (FL)
DeRose, Johnette, *Valley School/Ligonier* (PA)
DeRussy, Susie, *Trinity Episcopal* (LA)
Desmole, Isabelle, *Lycée Français La Pérouse* (CA)

Diaz-Imbelli, Lillian, *Loyola School* (NY)
Dickerman, William, Ph.D., *Hampshire Country School* (NH)
Diffley, Ray III, *Choate Rosemary Hall* (CT)
DiGuiseppe, Barbara W., *Brookwood* (MA)
DiPaolo, Steve, *Cape Cod Academy* (MA)
Douglas, Louise B., *Woodland School* (CA)
Driscoll, Kevin J., *Austin Prep* (MA)
Droppers, Alice, *The O'Neal School* (NC)
Due, Jill, *The Catherine Cook School* (IL)
Duffy, Ann V., *Buckley CDS* (NY)
Dun, Kelly, *Princeton Day School* (NJ)
Dunleavy, Jessie D., *The Key School* (MD)
Dunn, Casey, *Bishop Montgomery HS* (CA)
Dunning, Diane, *St. Stephen's and St. Agnes* (VA)
Durrant, Malcolm, *Saltus Grammar* (Bermuda)

E

Earley, Marion L., *Charles River School* (MA)
Earley, Michael, *Falmouth Academy* (MA)
Eccleston, Tom '87, *The Hill School* (PA)
Edel, Deborah, *Mary McDowell Center* (NY)
Edwards, Margie, *The Gillispie School* (CA)
Efter, Athena, *The Cathedral School* (NY)
Egan, Peter C., *Seven Hills* (OH)
Ehringhaus, Nancy, *Charlotte CDS* (NC)
Eidam, John R., *Wyoming Seminary* (PA)
Elliott, Alison, *Franklin Road Academy* (TN)
Epstein, Catherine, *Head-Royce School* (CA)
Epstein, Jeanette, *The Wheeler School* (RI)
Escabar, Jeffrey, *Marin CDS* (CA)
Evans, Mary Beth, *Princeton Montessori* (NJ)

F

Fanfelle, Donna, *Marin Primary* (CA)
Farquhar, Annie M., *Maret School* (DC)
Federico, Wendy, *Churchill School/Center* (NY)
Feeley, Susan F., *Lab School of Washington* (DC)
Fenlon, Cindy, *St. John's Episc. Parish Day* (FL)
Fernández, Ellen, *Overbrook School* (TN)
Ferrell, Greg, *Montgomery Bell* (TN)
Fisher, Becky Riley, *Mirman School/Gifted* (CA)
Fisher, Kathy, *All Saints Episcopal* (TX)
Fitzherbert, Kathi L., *Glenholme School* (CT)
Fleming, Alice, *Campbell Hall* (CA)
Flintoft, Kathy, *The Brick Church School* (NY)
Flynn, David T., *Storm King School* (NY)
Forsythe, Terry, *St. Agnes -St. Dominic* (TN)
Foster, Alan, *Bayside Academy* (AL)
Fox, Britton, *Riverfield CDS* (OK)
Fox, Peggy, *Episcopal HS of Jacksonville* (FL)
Francis, Shirley W., *Riverside Presbyterian Day* (FL)
Fredericks, Khadija, *St. Paul's Episcopal* (CA)
Frew, Peter A., *The Taft School* (CT)
Friedman, Kathleen, *Univ. School/Milwaukee* (WI)
Friend, Susan, *Green Acres* (MD)

G

Gagarin, Russ, *Landon School* (MD)
Gallo, Mario, *St. Benedict's Prep* (NJ)
Gamper, William H., *Gilman School* (MD)
Garcia, Robert, *The Gow School* (NY)
Gardner, Kim, *Washington Academy* (ME)

Garwood, Alice, *Oak Hall School* (FL)
George, Kai-Anasa, *Edmund Burke School* (DC)
George, Mary Helen, *Vanguard College Prep* (TX)
Gerber, Ingrid, *Moravian Academy* (PA)
Gering, Sue, *Brentwood Academy* (TN)
Gerrard, Myra, *The Country School* (CA)
Gersten, Tracey, *Live Oak School* (CA)
Gilbert, Brian J., *Georgetown Prep* (MD)
Giles, Aimee, *Children's Day* (CA)
Gilla, Andy, *Avery Coonley School* (IL)
Glace, Diane, *Rutgers Prep* (NJ)
Glausner, Kristen, *Hampton Roads Academy* (VA)
Goertz, Robin, *Carolina Day* (NC)
Goheen, Kelly, *Holy Nativity School* (HI)
Goldberg, Dana, *The Carey School* (CA)
Goldman, Susanne, *Seven Hills* (CA)
Gooden, Rosetta, *The Galloway School* (GA)
Goodhill, Barbara, *Sinai Akiba Academy* (CA)
Gordon, Erin K., *The Peck School* (NJ)
Gore, Heidi, *St. Bernard's School* (NY)
Graham, Monica C., *Maryvale Prep* (MD)
Grant, Michael R., *Belmont Hill* (MA)
Green, Michael P., *Doane Stuart* (NY)
Green, Molly M. '83, *Severn School* (MD)
Gregory, Elizabeth, *Harvard-Westlake* (CA)
Gruber, Susan, *Pace Academy* (GA)
Gundersen, Kathy, *Rowland Hall-St. Mark's* (UT)

H

Haaser, Robert J., *Cistercian Prep* (TX)
Hall, Barbara, *Notre Dame Prep/Marist Academy* (MI)
Hamer, Peter, *Bishop Ireton HS* (VA)
Haney, Louise, *Oakwood School* (NC)
Hansen, Alexa, *Lake Ridge Academy* (OH)
Harrell, Susan, *Cape Fear Academy* (NC)
Harris, Donna B., *The Covenant School* (VA)
Harris, Elizabeth Brode '91, *Springside School* (PA)
Harris, Jeffry, *Brunswick School* (CT)
Harris, Tina, *Bermuda HS for Girls* (Bermuda)
Hart, Richard, *Holland Hall* (OK)
Hartge, Holly, *Oakcrest School* (VA)
Hartung, Laura C., *Wilson School* (MO)
Haskins, Deborah, *St. Timothy's School* (MD)
Hasler, Susan, *St. Paul's School/Girls* (MD)
Hawes, Janice, *Pear Tree Point School* (CT)
Hay, Ellen, *The Episcopal Academy* (PA)
Hay, Sherryn M., *Trinity Prep* (FL)
Hayes, Kassandra, *Cathedral/St. John the Divine* (NY)
Hays, Julia, *Rudolf Steiner School* (NY)
Heard, Kristen J., *Tuxedo Park School* (NY)
Heaton, Jean Stahl, *Nashoba Brooks* (MA)
Hein, Kristen, *The Orchard School* (IN)
Held, Patty, *Trident Academy* (SC)
Hemmings, Joseph, *Hebron Academy* (ME)
Hendon, Louise, *Academy/Holy Cross* (MD)
Hendrickson, Alice, *St. Mark's Episcopal* (FL)
Henry, David, *Gunston Day School* (MD)
Herman, Tina I., *The Chapin School* (NY)
Heyman, Joanne P., *Collegiate School* (NY)
Higgins, Susan, *Eliot Montessori School* (MA)
Hilson, Anita, *McDonogh School* (MD)
Hines, Jennifer, *Noble and Greenough* (MA)
Hinson, Alison, *Christ Methodist Day* (TN)
Hirsch, Judy, *John Thomas Dye* (CA)
Hoeniger, Matthew S., *Rumsey Hall School* (CT)
Hohertz, Dorcas, *Allen Academy* (TX)
Holeton, Elena, *St. Clement's* (Canada)
Holt, Gayle, *The Williams School* (CT)
Holt, Todd A., *The Leelanau School* (MI)
Honeywell, Ashley, *Episcopal Collegiate* (AR)

Hopkins, Kathleen, *Wilmington Friends* (DE)
Hopper, Helen V., *Westridge School* (CA)
Howell, Mr. Shannon, *Elgin Academy* (IL)
Hristidis, Simone, *Columbia Grammar and Prep* (NY)
Huckvale, David, *The Country Day School* (Canada)
Hudenko, Judy, *Albuquerque Academy* (NM)
Hudnut, Deedie, *Center for Early Education* (CA)
Huebner, Mrs. Erica, *Marymount HS* (CA)
Humick, Nancy, *Kent Place School* (NJ)
Hurtes, Eleanor W., *Porter-Gaud School* (SC)
Hyde, Karen, *Rowland Hall-St. Mark's* (UT)

I

Irvin, Rebecca, *Kerr-Vance Academy* (NC)
Irwin, Cathy, *Battle Ground Academy* (TN)
Issa, Lillian, *Marymount School* (NY)
Ivanyi, Mary, *Soundview Prep* (NY)
Izzo, Janet B., *Hamden Hall CDS* (CT)
Izzo, Pasquale G., *Notre Dame of West Haven* (CT)

J

Jackson, Cory Jones, *Oldfields School* (MD)
Jacobs, Merle, *The Park School* (MA)
Jahn, Theodore, *Saint Francis Prep* (NY)
James, Aaron, *Casady School* (OK)
James, Jim, *Breck School* (MN)
Jameson, Julie, *St. Andrew's Episcopal* (MD)
Jamison, Pamela J., *Ravenscroft School* (NC)
Janiak, Alicia, *The Dwight School* (NY)
Jankoff, Ronnie R., *Allen-Stevenson* (NY)
Jankowski, Judy, *McLean School* (MD)
Jenkins, Sally Ann, *St. Michael's CDS* (RI)
Jensen, Lawrence, *Saint James* (MD)
Jessee, Deborah C., *North Cross* (VA)
Jiongo, Barbara W., *Fort Worth Country Day* (TX)
Johnson, Susan, *Canterbury School* (IN)
Johnston, Sarah L., *Hathaway Brown* (OH)
Jolly, Amy, *Fenn School* (MA)
Jones, Jamie, *Ursuline Academy* (DE)
Jordan, John J., *Archmere Academy* (DE)
Justis, Mary Margaret, *Sullins Academy* (VA)

K

Kahalley, Daniel, *Memphis Univ. School* (TN)
Kaplan, Joan, *Brearley* (NY)
Kaplan, Julianne, *Birch Wathen Lenox* (NY)
Katz, Abby S., *Greenwich Academy* (CT)
Keller, Janet D., *Georgetown Visitation Prep* (DC)
Kelly, Rose, *St. Anne's Episcopal* (CO)
Kenny, Chantal, *Upper Canada* (Canada)
Kent, Ann Marie, *The Country School* (Canada)
Khan, Shuja, *Stuart Hall High School* (CA)
Kindler, Karen N., *San Francisco Univ. HS* (CA)
King, Jenna R., *Riverdale Country School* (NY)
Kinser, Judith S., *Trinity Valley* (TX)
Klekamp, Peter, *Episcopal/Knoxville* (TN)
Klipstein, Tara, *Rutgers Prep* (NJ)
Kluttz, Cindy, *Forsyth CDS* (NC)
Knies, Jennifer, *Brooklyn Friends* (NY)
Kodama, Robert, *Crespi Carmelite HS* (CA)

Koehler, Audrey, *Episcopal HS/Houston* (TX)
Koenings, Sharon, *Brookfield Academy* (WI)
Krents, Elizabeth, Ph.D., *The Dalton School* (NY)
Krick, Beth, *Friends Haverford* (PA)
Kwartler, Susan, *St. Mark's Episcopal Day* (FL)

L

Lafferty, Sarah M., *Riverdale Country School* (NY)
Lake, Jasmine, *Miami Country Day School* (FL)
Lange, Debbie, *The Lovett School* (GA)
Laramie, Peggy B., *Mary Inst./Saint Louis CDS* (MO)
Larimer, Pam, *Loudoun CDS* (VA)
Laskey, Catherine, *Colorado Academy* (CO)
LaVigne, Caroline, *John Burroughs* (MO)
Lawson, Lezlie, *Washington Waldorf* (MD)
Layman, Will, *The Field School* (DC)
Leary, Catherine C., *Saint Mary's School* (NC)
Leas, Dawn, *Wyoming Seminary* (PA)
Leber, Jacqueline, *York Preparatory School* (NY)
Lee, Gretchen, *Saddle River Day* (NJ)
Leiser, Holly, *Saint Paul's School* (FL)
Lemay, Roland, *School Year Abroad* (China)
Lemay, Roland, *School Year Abroad* (France)
Lemay, Roland, *School Year Abroad* (Italy)
Lemay, Roland, *School Year Abroad* (MA)
Lemay, Roland, *School Year Abroad* (Spain)
Lemay, Roland, *School Year Abroad* (Vietnam)
Lemon, Thomas, *St. Mark's High School* (DE)
Lewis, Suzanne Kimm, *Oak Knoll/Holy Child* (NJ)
Liggitt, Jen, *Hockaday* (TX)
Loftin, Julie, *St. George's Independent* (TN)
Lohmar, Krista, *Canterbury School* (IN)
Lojo, Ken, *Strake Jesuit College Prep* (TX)
Lomask, Diana, *Saint Ann's School* (NY)
Lopez, Kathleen, *St. Mary's Episcopal Day* (FL)
Lopiccolo, Barbara, *Academy/Sacred Heart* (MI)
Lord, Treavor, *Hill School/ Middleburg* (VA)
Lordy, Paula, *The Winston School* (NJ)
Lougheed, Jamie, *Greenwood College* (Canada)
Love, Julia, *ACS Intl. Schools* (England)
Low, Theodore J., *Eaglebrook* (MA)
Luciano, Sr. Filippa, *Mary Louis Academy* (NY)
Lund, Priscilla, *Capitol Hill Day School* (DC)
Lundquist, Jill, *Poughkeepsie Day* (NY)
Lurie, Gretchen, *Chandler School* (CA)
Lutz, Linda, *Saint Stephen's Episcopal* (FL)
Lynch, Jo Ann, *The Buckley School* (NY)
Lynch, Patricia, *Newman School* (MA)
Lyons, Norm, *Saint Mark's School* (CA)

M

Mabley, Winifred, *Brearley* (NY)
Machir, Catherine, *Convent of the Sacred Heart* (CT)
Madison, Catherine, *Cathedral for Boys* (CA)
Malouf, Rosemary, *St. Matthew's Episc. Day* (CA)
Mandell, Peggy Klein, *Springside School* (PA)
Mantel, Irene, *Rudolf Steiner School* (NY)
Mantilla-Goin, Susan, *National Cathedral* (DC)
Marchesseault, Leslie, *Glen Urquhart* (MA)
Marrie, Megan, *Gilmour Academy* (OH)
Marsau, Blythe, *St. Martin's Episcopal* (GA)
Marshall, Duncan, *The Knox School* (NY)
Marshall, Jan, *Franklin Road Academy* (TN)
Martin, Katharine, *Rossman School* (MO)
Martin, Lara, *Abraham Joshua Heschel* (CA)

Martinelli, Camille, *Village Christian* (CA)
Masciale-Lynch, Susan, *Oakwood Friends* (NY)
Mattia, Elise, *Brooklyn Heights Montessori* (NY)
Mauck, Cary C., *St. Christopher's School* (VA)
Mayo, Meg, *Connelly/Holy Child* (MD)
McCaffery, Julie A., *Primary Day* (MD)
McCann, Kathy, *Seattle CDS* (WA)
McColl, Christopher T., *Hackley School* (NY)
McDermott, Molly, *The Grosse Pointe Academy* (MI)
McDonald, Judy Ladden, *Highlands School* (AL)
McGovern, Valerie, *Overbrook* (RI)
McIlvaine, Janie, *Berkeley Prep* (FL)
McKannay, Lynn, *Town School for Boys* (CA)
McKenna, Pamela R., *Hopkins School* (CT)
McKenna, Sally Jeanne, *Polytechnic School* (CA)
McLaughlin, Patricia A., *Norfolk Academy* (VA)
McLaurin, Pamela Parks, *Winsor* (MA)
McLean, Marci, *Parish Episcopal* (TX)
McLeod, Emily H., *Trinity Episcopal* (VA)
McNulty, Kim, *MMI Preparatory School* (PA)
McWilliams, Cynthia S., *Millbrook School* (NY)
Memory, Katherine, *Summit School* (NC)
Meredith, Craig, *The John Cooper School* (TX)
Metz, Margaret, *Nightingale-Bamford* (NY)
Mihm, Katherine H., *Shady Side Academy* (PA)
Mijalis-Kahn, Elaine J., *Sage Hill* (CA)
Miller, Karin B., *Moorestown Friends* (NJ)
Miller, Nathalie, *Berkeley Hall* (CA)
Milles, Tami, *Univ. Child Development* (WA)
Mitchell, Erby, *The Loomis Chaffee School* (CT)
Mitchell, James Irwin, *Alexander Dawson* (CO)
Mitchell, Marjorie, *Westminster Schools* (GA)
Mizell, Reid, *Atlanta International School* (GA)
Monks, Paul, *Canton CDS* (OH)
Montgomery, Tim, *Guilford Day* (NC)
Moody, Kerry, *The Langley School* (VA)
Moore, Caroline, *Carolina Day School* (SC)
Moreira, Lisa J., *Horace Mann* (NY)
Morrison, Tearson W., *Montgomery School* (PA)
Morton, Lesley, *Jackson Preparatory School* (MS)
Mosteller, Kelly, *Meadowbrook School* (PA)
Mozley, Patricia H., *The Walker School* (GA)
Mulligan, George, *Landon School* (MD)
Mulligan, Mimi, *Norwood School* (MD)
Munsterteiger, Brit, *St. Peter's School* (PA)
Muradi, Victoria, *Durham Academy* (NC)
Murphy, Carol, *Sage Ridge* (NV)
Murphy, Christine L., *Moravian Academy* (PA)
Murphy, Erin, *Marin Primary* (CA)
Murphy, Laura, *The Out-of-Door Academy* (FL)
Murray, Cindy, *Rivermont Collegiate* (IA)
Mynnti, Valerie A., *The Harley School* (NY)
Myong, Esther Kim, *Seoul Foreign* (Korea)

N

Naspo, Kristen, *Hillside School* (MA)
Nastro, Hillary, *Morristown-Beard* (NJ)
Neal, Carolyn, *Advent Episcopal School* (AL)
Neal, Kelsey, *Phoenix CDS* (AZ)
Nelsen, Charlotte H., *The Potomac School* (VA)
Nelson, Carolyn Orsini, *Landmark School* (MA)
Nesbitt, Lesley, *The Carroll School* (MA)
Newman, William J., *Univ. of Chicago Lab Schools* (IL)
Newton, Maria, *Annunciation Orthodox* (TX)
Nicoletta, Christine R., *Lake Forest CDS* (IL)
Nielsen, Nan, *The Harker School* (CA)
Niszczak, Rebecca, *Newtown Friends School* (PA)
N'Jie, Saphiatou, *Corlears School* (NY)
Nordeman, Anne, *St. Bernard's School* (NY)

O

Obrecht, Michael, *Maclay School* (FL)
O'Brien, Carney, *Mizzentop Day School* (NY)
O'Connor, Susan, *Oakcrest School* (VA)
O'Donnell, James E., *Kingswood-Oxford* (CT)
Offer, Kathleen, *Notre Dame Prep/Marist Academy* (MI)
O'Neal, Kathy Mitchell, *University Prep* (WA)
Orloff, Blair Talcott, *Elisabeth Morrow* (NJ)
Owens, Katie, *Convent of the Visitation* (MN)

P

Palmer, Nancy, *Fort Worth Academy* (TX)
Pananos, Janet, *Kehoe-France* (LA)
Pansano, Susan, *St. Martin's Episcopal* (LA)
Papir, Erica L., *The Caedmon School* (NY)
Papp, Leah, *The Swain School* (PA)
Park, Suzanne, *The Craig School* (NJ)
Parker, Elizabeth, *Tower School* (MA)
Patterson, Janette, *Nora School* (MD)
Payne, Robin, *The Janus School* (PA)
Pearline, Sharon, *Windward School* (CA)
Pehlke, Jane C., *Gibson Island* (MD)
Perniciaro, Alex, *St. Stephen's School* (Italy)
Peters, Julie, *The Canterbury School* (FL)
Petrie, Mimi, *Curtis School* (CA)
Phillips, Clemmie, *Mayfield Senior/Holy Child* (CA)
Pickrell, Ann C., *Williston Northampton* (MA)
Pierre, Chantelle, *Wildwood School* (CA)
Pillsbury, Kendall, *Sierra Canyon School* (CA)
Plank, Richard J., *Cape Henry Collegiate* (VA)
Plummer, Cheryl, *St. John's School* (TX)
Pochet, Courtney, *Queen Anne* (MD)
Poe, Kristin, *River Oaks Baptist School* (TX)
Popeil, Pamela, *Bernard Zell Anshe Emet Day* (IL)
Porter, William, *The Harvey School* (NY)
Post, Suzanne R., *Rumson CDS* (NJ)
Poteet, Michele, *Crestview Prep* (CA)
Potter, Ellen, *Dutchess Day School* (NY)
Primm, Mary Lou, *The Benjamin School* (FL)
Prokopiak, Madonna, *Manzano Day School* (NM)
Purviance, Linda, *Jackson Academy* (MS)

Q

Quattlebaum, Wendy, *Sacred Heart, Atherton* (CA)
Quinto, Patricia, *Grace Day School* (NY)
Quiring, A. Lee, *St. Matthew's Parish School* (CA)

R

Ramos, Bobby, *Urban School/San Francisco* (CA)
Randall, Caroline, *Seacrest CDS* (FL)
Rapp-Seguel, Molly, *Marymount/Santa Barbara* (CA)
Rattew, Amelia, *UN International School* (NY)
Rebuck, Paul, *Milton Academy* (MA)
Redell, Lori W., *Poly Prep CDS* (NY)
Reeves, Jay, *Miller School* (VA)
Reilly, Maria, *Stanley Clark School* (IN)
Rieck, Br. James, FSC, *La Salle College HS* (PA)
Riley, Amy, *The Heritage School* (GA)
Risner, Jennifer, *St. Mary and All Angels* (CA)
Robinson, Levyette, *Bermuda HS for Girls* (Bermuda)

Robson, Debbie, *The Steward School* (VA)
Roesch, Marcia, *Bank Street School* (NY)
Rogers, Carol, *East Woods School* (NY)
Roper, Hart, *St. Albans School* (DC)
Rosen, Jennifer, *Isidore Newman* (LA)
Rowe, Kristin H., *Harbor Day* (CA)
Rowe, Vincent, *Georgetown Day School* (DC)
Roy, Michael '85, *St. Andrew's College* (Canada)
Roye, Ana J., *Carrollton of the Sacred Heart* (FL)
Rudisi, Heather, *Ranney School* (NJ)
Runkel, Richard, *Fairfield CDS* (CT)
Rupp, Jim, *Seattle Academy* (WA)
Rusbarsky, Adrienne, *The College School* (MO)
Ruth-Williams, Barbara, *Village School* (CA)
Ryerson, Rich, *Kimball Union Academy* (NH)

S

Saalfeld, Steve, *Charles Wright* (WA)
Sadlon, Jay K., *Derby Academy* (MA)
Sahadi, Natasha, *The Town School* (NY)
Salvatore, Carrie, *King Low Heywood Thomas* (CT)
Salvo, Steve, *Browne Academy* (VA)
Sarewitz, Anne, *Epiphany School* (WA)
Sarkisian, Keith, *Brentwood School* (CA)
Saulsberry, Dana Scott, *Community School* (MO)
Saunders, Mark, *Pennington* (NJ)
Sayfie, Amy, *Ransom Everglades* (FL)
Scheidt, Steve M., *Gilmour Academy* (OH)
Schenck, Robin, *Greensboro Day School* (NY)
Schenken, Susan, *Ridgewood Preparatory* (LA)
Schiavenza, Lisa, *Menlo School* (CA)
Schiess, Kelley K., *Summit CDS* (OH)
Schmidt, Maureen K., *Wyndcroft* (PA)
Schmidt, Ola, *Munich International* (Germany)
Schuler, Nancy, *Westminster School* (VA)
Secor, Wendy Sibert, *Dana Hall* (MA)
Seits, Kevin, *The Haverford School* (PA)
Serrill, Barbara, *Germantown Academy* (PA)
Sheffer, Andy, *Saint Edward's School* (FL)
Shelburne, Cathy, *Menlo School* (CA)
Sheppard, Anne, *Western Reserve Academy* (OH)
Sherlock, Linda, *All Saints' Episcopal School* (TX)
Shine, Kathleen, *Academy/Our Lady of Mercy* (CT)
Shinkle, Adaline, *The Blake School* (MN)
Shoolman, Barbara, *Brimmer and May* (MA)
Shuffman, Linda, *Staten Island Academy* (NY)
Siegfried, Scott, *Providence Day* (NC)
Silk, Erika, *The Bentley School* (CA)
Sills, Robin, *Westside Neighborhood* (CA)
Simon, Gregory P., *Notre Dame Prep/Marist* (MI)
Skiff, James J., *Providence Country Day* (RI)
Slider, Russell L., *Woodward Academy* (GA)
Smith, Amy C., *The Winston School* (TX)
Snyder, Barbara B., *The Woods Academy* (MD)
Snyder, Mary S., *Brookstone School* (GA)
Soll, Sara, *Brooklyn Friends School* (NY)
Soltis, Rudianne, *ACS International* (England)
Somerville, Bobbie, *Hilton Head Prep* (SC)
Southwick, William H., *Dexter & Southfield Schools* (MA)
Spahr, Christine, *Harbor Country Day School* (MA)
Spear, Linda, *The Dunham School* (LA)
Speck, Beth, *Duchesne Academy* (TX)
Spence, Rebecca, *The Red Oaks School* (NJ)
Spencer, Leon, *The Tatnall School* (DE)
Stacey, Eric '81, *Pingree School* (MA)
Stack, Sandy, *Sonoma Academy* (CA)
Stewart, Mary Lou, *Independent Day* (CT)
Stewart, Philip A., Ph.D., *The Windsor School* (NY)
Stokes, Denis, *Christ School* (NC)
Strowd, Claire, *Pace Academy* (GA)

Sullivan, Carolyn, *Pembroke Hill* (MO)
Sullivan, Colleen, *Gateway School* (CA)
Surgner, Amanda, *Collegiate School* (VA)
Suzuki, Matthew, *Rye CDS* (NY)
Swartzentruber, Eric, *Stoneleigh-Burnham* (MA)
Sweeney, Maureen A., *Windward School* (NY)
Swett, Pascha, *The Ensworth School* (TN)
Sykes, Julie B., *Saint David's School* (NY)
Symonds, Kate, *St. Hilda's & St. Hugh's* (NY)

T

Talent, Irene, *Trafalgar Castle* (Canada)
Taubar, Rich, *Centreville School* (DE)
Taylor, Jennifer, *St. George's Independent* (TN)
Taylor, Susan L., *Le Jardin Academy* (HI)
Taylor, Willard L., Jr., *Newark Academy* (NJ)
Templin-Page, Samantha, *Rohan Woods* (MO)
Tew, Laurel Baker, *Viewpoint School* (CA)
Thaden, Cathy, *Saint Patrick Catholic School* (VA)
Thielen, Averyl, *Mayfield Junior School* (CA)
Thomas, Karen, *Santiago College* (Chile)
Thompson, Nicole A., *Triangle Day School* (NC)
Thompson, Taisha, *Ethical Culture Fieldston* (NY)
Thorp, Pamela, *Convent/Sacred Heart ES* (CA)
Thorp, Pamela, *Stuart Hall for Boys* (CA)
Ting, Cheryl, *The Bentley School* (CA)
Tolen, Jane, *St. John's Parish Day School* (MD)
Tomelloso, Ester, *Sandia Prep* (NM)
Tomich, Rosanne, *Forest Ridge/Sacred Heart* (WA)
Toomer, Vikki, *Abington Friends* (PA)
Torjesen, Cynthia, *Lexington Christian* (MA)
Toryak, Donna Venezia, *Mount Saint Mary* (NJ)
Travaglione, Vincent, *La Jolla CDS* (CA)
Tredenick, Craig, *The Linsly School* (WV)
Tretter, Ellen, *Dedham CDS* (MA)
Tsang, Annie, *Bay School/San Francisco* (CA)
Turekian, Roxanne, *St. Thomas's Day School* (CT)
Turner, Sarah M., *Cambridge Friends School* (MA)
Tuttle, David J., *The Kildonan School* (NY)
Tyau, Garret, *The Oaks School* (CA)

V

Vakulchik, Christopher, *The Wilson School* (NJ)
Valenzuela, Vincent, *Chestnut Hill* (PA)
Vanausdoll, Abby, *Cornelia Connelly* (CA)
Vann-Adibe, Linda, *Chinese American Intl. School* (CA)
Vigeant, Charlotte, *Wardlaw-Hartridge* (NJ)
Vincent, Barbara, *Meadowbrook of Weston* (MA)
Vitale, Megan, *Cliff Valley School* (GA)
Volovski, Laura Nash '83, *Westover School* (CT)

W

Waage, Dan, *All Saints' Episcopal Day* (AZ)
Wachtel, Brooke, *The Mead School* (CT)
Walker, Holly, *Lakehill Prep* (TX)
Walker, Karen, *Telluride Mtn. School* (CO)
Wall, Kay, *The Stanwich School* (CT)
Walpole, Andrew R.N., *Sanford School* (DE)
Walsh, Maureen McKeown, *Saint Basil* (PA)
Wargo, Sue Ann, *St. Andrew's Priory* (HI)
Waters, Brenda H., *Norfolk Collegiate* (VA)
Watters, Anne B., *Green Vale* (NY)

Webster, Nancy, *University High School* (IN)
Wenger, Angela, *University Lake* (WI)
Whalen, Deborah, *St. Agnes Academy* (TX)
Whalen, Kathleen, *Good Shepherd Episcopal* (TX)
White, Jonathan, *Thayer Academy* (MA)
Whitney, Stephanie, *Greens Farms Academy* (CT)
Wilkinson, Charlotte, *St. Mark's Cathedral* (LA)
Williams, Andrea, *The Barrie School* (MD)
Williams, Debbie, *Crane CDS* (CA)
Williams, Diane, *St. Andrew's Episcopal* (TX)
Williamson, Tiffany, *The Colorado Springs School* (CO)
Wilson, Andrew, *Grier School* (PA)
Wilson, Jacqueline D., *Academy of the Holy Names* (FL)
Wilson, Tracy, *Ojai Valley* (CA)
Wilson-Neil, Judy, *Collingwood School* (Canada)
Winchell, Mark '98, *Salesianum* (DE)
Winchester, Chris, *New Garden Friends* (NC)
Windsor, Janna, *Clairbourn School* (CA)
Winter, Barbara, *PACE-Brantley Hall* (FL)
Wishart, Gregory W., *St. Sebastian's School* (MA)
Witter, Lisa, *St. Andrew's Episcopal* (LA)
Wiygul, Jimmy, *Altamont* (AL)
Wolf, Peggy K., *Roland Park* (MD)
Wolke, Lauren, *Laurence School* (CA)
Wolstan, Judith S., *Chadwick School* (CA)
Wootton, Karen, *Glenelg* (MD)
Worthington, Annette, *The Willow School* (NJ)
Wright, Vicki, *Chatham Hall* (VA)
Wuorinen, John S., *The Columbus Academy* (OH)

Y

Young, Vivian, *Jack M. Barrack Hebrew Academy* (PA)
Yusick, Laura Lombardo '96, *Nichols School* (NY)

Z

Zazyczny, Jason, *St. Joseph's Prep* (PA)
Zinser, Lori, *The Roeper School* (MI)
Zondervan, Denise, *Foothill CDS* (CA)
Zucker, Jonathan, *College Preparatory* (CA)

A

Adams, Sonya, *Kingswood-Oxford School* (CT)
Adler, Joan, *Green Acres School* (MD)
Ahlborn, Carolyn R., *St. Patrick's Episcopal Day* (DC)
Alexander, Terry Pink, *Head-Royce School* (CA)
Aliquo, Judy L., *Wilmington Friends School* (DE)
Alpert, Suzanne, *Ring Mountain Day School* (CA)
Amatulli, Jodi, *Hamden Hall Country Day* (CT)
Andersen, Steven, *Poly Prep Country Day* (NY)
Anderson, Liz, *Holland Hall* (OK)
Angelbello, Patty, *St. Mark's Episcopal School* (FL)
Angeletti, Robert, *Saint Francis Prep* (NY)
Anthony, Robert W., *Millbrook School* (NY)
Argenio, Mandy, *Greens Farms Academy* (CT)
Arms, Richard F., *St. Sebastian's School* (MA)
Ashworth, Ken, *Landon School* (MD)
Ashworth, Lele, *Georgetown Day School* (DC)

B

Bailey, Cindy, *River Oaks Baptist School* (TX)
Baker, Beth, *Evansville Day School* (IN)
Balk, Jahna, *The Hudson School* (NJ)
Banks-Sims, Denita, *The Roeper School* (MO)
Barden, Monica, *The Mabin School* (Canada)
Barry, Maureen, *Saint David's School* (NY)
Bartzen, Gretchen, *Seven Hills School* (CA)
Bates, Jerry, *Riverfield Country Day* (OK)
Battista, Miriam, *St. Thomas's Day School* (CT)
Battles, Craig, *Advent Episcopal School* (AL)
Bauman, Melissa, *The Town School* (NY)
Bebla, Jim, *MMI Preparatory School* (PA)
Bennett, Kristin, *Clairbourn School* (CA)
Benson, Jennifer, *East Woods School* (NY)
Berkeley, Amy Sullivan, *Brookwood School* (MA)
Berrigan, Julie, *The Elmwood Franklin School* (NY)
Berry, Mary Elizabeth, *Sacred Heart Schools Atherton* (CA)
Bertin, Randy, *Besant Hill School* (CA)
Beskind, Marcie, *Cliff Valley School* (CA)
Binney, Diane, *Polytechnic School* (CA)
Bizzarri, Jennifer, *Greenwood College School* (ON)
Block, Annie, *Campbell Hall* (CA)
Blum, Adam, *Bay School/SF* (CA)
Boig, Patricia Gedney, *Pine Crest School* (FL)
Bolt, Sage, *St. Paul's Episcopal Day* (AL)
Boone, Crisler, *Jackson Preparatory School* (MS)
Borden, John, *Bank Street School for Children* (NY)
Boster, Drew, *Rivermont Collegiate* (IA)
Bowater, Laurie, *Bancroft School* (MA)
Bowen, Myra, *The Oakwood School* (NC)
Bowman, David, *Forsyth Country Day* (NC)
Boyd, David, *The Heritage School* (GA)
Brady, Brisen, *Urban School of SF* (CA)
Bridenstine, Sheila, *Kalamazoo Country Day* (MI)
Brienza, Leigh Ann, *Saint Basil Academy* (PA)
Brouse, Michael, *St. Stephen's School* (Italy)
Brown, Barbara, *Breck School* (MN)
Brown, D. Andrew, *The Hill School* (PA)
Brown, Kathy, *St. Paul's Episcopal School* (CA)
Brunsvold, Lisa, *St. Luke's Episcopal School* (TX)
Buchholz, Ken, *Forsyth School* (MO)
Budd, Claire P., *Rohan Woods School* (MO)
Bugliari, Elizabeth, *Kent Place School* (NJ)
Bullock, Vera, *The Chapin School* (NY)
Bunis, Lynn, *Packer Collegiate School* (NY)
Burger, Courtney, *Collegiate School* (NY)
Burke, Valerie, *St. Stephen's and St. Agnes School* (VA)
Burks, Michelle, *Canterbury Episcopal School* (TX)

Burlingham, Barry A., *Derby Academy* (MA)
Burnett, Steve, *Sierra Canyon School* (CA)
Burnett-Herkes, Andrew, *Saltus Grammar School* (Bermuda)
Burns, Tom, *Melrose School* (NY)
Butler, Critt, *Ransom Everglades School* (FL)
Byrnes, Donna, *Greenwich Academy* (CT)

C

Cady, Alison, *Morristown-Beard School* (NJ)
Callahan, Karen, *Brooks School* (MA)
Cantelou, Dexter, *St. Nicholas School* (TN)
Carabello, Christopher, *La Salle College HS* (PA)
Carnes, Wyndi, *The Steward School* (VA)
Cash, Steven J., *Mizzentop Day School* (NY)
Cathcart, Marty, *The Lab School of Washington* (DC)
Chamberlain, Judith, *Calmont School* (CA)
Chapman, Dennis, *The Out-of-Door Academy* (FL)
Chang, Margaret, *Independent Day School* (CT)
Chapman, Nicholas, *The Janus School* (PA)
Cheung, Virginia, *Chinese American Intl. School* (CA)
Chiang, Jenny, *National Cathedral School* (DC)
Christopher, Michael, *Lausanne Collegiate School* (TN)
Clark, John G., *The American School in London* (England)
Clausen, Diane, *Menlo School* (CA)
Clerici, Sandi, *Charleston Collegiate School* (SC)
Cole, Kathy, *The Winsor School* (MA)
Constantine, Jane, *Buffalo Seminary* (NY)
Conti, Bekah, *Saint Edward's School* (FL)
Cornell, Greg, *Crespi Carmelite HS* (CA)
Corley, Beth, *La Jolla Country Day* (CA)
Corman-Hall, Meg, *Gateway School* (CA)
Costello, Joanne M., *The Mead School* (CT)
Coull, Kim, *The College Preparatory School* (CA)
Courcey, Daniel J. III, *Choate Rosemary Hall* (CT)
Cove, Rosemary, *Palm Beach Day Academy* (FL)
Coyne, Paula, *Cold Spring School* (CT)
Crawford, Rob, *The Park School* (MA)
Curran, Liz, *The Woods Academy* (MD)
Custodio, Ria, *The Bishop's School* (CA)

D

Daley, Rhonda, *Trafalgar Castle School* (ON)
Dallman, Christine, *Sycamore School* (IN)
Danielewski, Christina, *Marymount School* (NY)
Darby, Peggy, *Highlands School* (AL)
Davenport, Sharon, *Williston Northampton School* (MA)
Dean, Joanna, *Saint Ann's School* (NY)
deButts, Dorsey, *Hill School of Middleburg* (VA)
De Falla, Emily, *The Athenian School* (CA)
Decker, Donna, *Harford Day School* (MD)
Denson, Mary, *Pace Academy* (GA)
Derheim, Holly, *St. Mary and All Angels School* (CA)
Diamond, Sandy, *The Lamplighter School* (TX)
Diaz, Michele, *The Wheeler School* (RI)
Dicovitsky, Laura, *Foothill Country Day* (CA)
Dini, Mark, *St. John's School* (TX)
Doherty, Lisa, *John Thomas Dye School* (CA)
Dominic, Andrea, *Friends School Haverford* (PA)
Donahue, Kerrie, *The Gordon School* (RI)
Donovan, Catherine, *Savannah Country Day School* (GA)
Doornick, Deb, *King Low Heywood Thomas* (CT)
Dopman, Kelly, *Mary Institute/Saint Louis CDS* (MO)
Doran, Leonard, *Cape Henry Collegiate* (VA)
Dowd, James, *Austin Prep School* (MA)

Dowlen, Lauren, *St. Stephen's Episcopal Day* (FL)
Dowley-Blackman, Tammy, *Fayerweather Street School* (MA)
Driggers, Susan, *The Altamont School* (AL)
Drourr, Nancy, *Brimmer and May School* (MA)
Duffy, Erin, *The Orchard School* (IN)
Dunkelburger, Sally, *Maret School* (DC)
Dunn, Sally, *McDonogh School* (MD)
Durkin, Janet, *Sonoma Academy* (CA)

E

Eberly, Alison, *St. Mark's Episcopal Day School* (FL)
Eckert, Robert C., *Episcopal High School* (VA)
Edelman, Karen, *Brooklyn Friends School* (NY)
Eichelberger, Elaine, *St. Agnes Academy* (TX)
Ekstrom, Gigi, *Lakehill Preparatory School* (TX)
Ennist, Bill, *King Low Heywood Thomas* (CT)
Evans, Tom, *Trinity Prep* (FL)
Ezuka, Linda, *Holy Nativity School* (HI)

F

Farr, Chris, *The Shipley School* (PA)
Farrar, Jim, *Gilmour Academy* (OH)
Fender, Pell, *St. Paul's School for Girls* (MD)
Fenlon, Cindy M., *St. John's Episc. Parish Day School* (FL)
Fenoglio, Carole Sue, *Episcopal HS of Houston* (TX)
Fenton, Linda, *Charles River School* (MA)
Ferrara, Kenneth, *Holy Ghost Preparatory School* (PA)
Fix, Kimberly Kouri, *Marin Horizon School* (CA)
Foard, Lynn, *Gibson Island Country School* (MD)
Fogarty, Thomas, *Hebron Academy* (ME)
Foster, Tricia, *San Francisco University HS* (CA)
Fountain, Melissa, *Chatham Hall* (VA)
Fowler, Lisa, *The Carey School* (CA)
Franceschino, Carmen, *Archmere Academy* (DE)
Frantz, Kathleen, *The Meadows School* (NV)
French, Christopher R., *The Hotchkiss School* (CT)
Friborg, John, *Boston University Academy* (MA)
Furubayashi, Bethany, *Epiphany School* (WA)
Fusco, Chris, *The Canterbury School* (FL)

G

Gaddis, Sue, *Rio Grande School* (NM)
Gage, Sharra, *The Country School* (CA)
Gallagher, Stacy, *The Hillside School* (PA)
Gavalas, Debbie, *Academy of the Holy Names* (FL)
Gemgnani, Cathy, *Westside Neighborhood School* (CA)
George, Mary Helen, *Vanguard College Prep* (TX)
Gibson, Brooke Hutson, *The Wilson School* (MO)
Goetting, Matthew, *The Pennington School* (NJ)
Goetz, Jeri, *Chestnut Hill School* (MA)
Golden, Rosaria, *Rudolf Steiner School* (NY)
Gonzales, Melinda, *The Harker School* (CA)
Gould, Matt, *Porter-Gaud School* (SC)
Grammer, Shoshanna, *Sage Hill School* (CA)
Grams, Laura, *Berkeley Preparatory* (FL)
Gray, Julie, *Dana Hall School* (MA)
Green, Molly, *Severn School* (MD)
Greif, Joyce, *Chandler School* (CA)
Grider, Lisa, *Newark Academy* (NJ)
Groat, Annie, *Brooklyn Heights Montessori* (NY)

Guest, Andrew, *Notre Dame Prep/Marist* (MI)
Gundy, Jay, *Western Reserve Academy* (OH)
Gugerty, Patrick, *The Tatnall School* (DE)
Gundlach, Jeanie, *Christ Methodist Day School* (TN)
Gurney, Elilzabeth S. Stevens, *Nichols School* (NY)
Gutierrez, Mark, *Thayer Academy* (MA)
Gwynn, Sharon, *Kerr-Vance Academy* (NC)

H

Hagan, Julie, *Dedham Country Day* (MA)
Haku, Unryu, *St. Mary's International School* (Japan)
Ham, Lisa, *St. Timothy's School* (NC)
Hammett, Grace, *Ursuline Academy* (DE)
Hanchett, Anne, *St. John's Parish Day School* (MD)
Handalian, Linda, *St. Matthew's Episcopal Day* (CA)
Haney, Peggy, *Annunciation Orthodox School* (TX)
Hannon, Jenny, *Montgomery Bell Academy* (TN)
Hantman, Denise, *Corlears School* (NY)
Harbinson, Beth, *Barrie School* (MD)
Hargrove, Brian H., *St. Mark's School* (TX)
Harmon, Mike, *Village Christian Schools* (CA)
Harris, Jon, *Abington Friends School* (PA)
Harrison, Laura, *Saint Paul's School* (FL)
Harrison, Stephen, *University Child Development* (WA)
Harrison, Sue, *The Pegasus School* (CA)
Hart, Erin, *Cistercian Preparatory School* (TX)
Hartmann, Patti, *Marymount High School* (CA)
Haynie, John, *The Benjamin School* (FL)
Hazell, Susan, *Collingwood School* (BC)
Hedgepeth, Laurie, *Trinity Episcopal School* (VA)
Heidinger, Anna, *Marin Academy* (CA)
Heissenbuttel, Beverly J., *Tuxedo Park School* (NY)
Henderson, Hillary, *Dutchess Day School* (NY)
Henry, Emilie, *Trinity School* (GA)
Henson, Darlene, *Duchesne Academy* (TX)
Higginbotham, Carlton, *Riverside Presbyterian Day* (FL)
Higginson, Phil, *Ravenscroft School* (NC)
Hitchcock, Naomi, *The Carroll School* (MA)
Ho, Pat, *Hanahau'oli School* (HI)
Hoblin, Bob, *Delaware Valley Friends School* (PA)
Hoch, Kate Ratcliffe, *Gilman School* (MD)
Hoffmann, Melanie, *The Pingry School* (NJ)
Hoglund, Melissa, *The Stanwich School* (CT)
Hollis, Barbara, *The Winston School* (TX)
Holt, Alison, *Greenwood College School* (ON)
Hopke, Dawn, *Browne Academy* (VA)
Hopley, Janine, *The Birch Wathen Lenox School* (NY)
Horn, Carolyn, *Westridge School* (CA)
Howard, Stephen, *Harbor Country Day School* (NY)
Howell, Angela, *Mayfield Sr./Holy Child* (CA)
Howes, Meg, *The Avery Coonley School* (IL)
Hu, Ed, *Harvard-Westlake School* (CA)
Huang, Dede, *Chinese International School* (Hong Kong)
Hubbard, Margaret, *Harding Academy* (TN)
Hudgins, Mary Ellen, *Seattle Academy* (WA)
Hudner, Thomas J., *The Fenn School* (MA)
Hudson, Joan, *Seattle Country Day School* (WA)
Hunt, Denise, *Canton Country Day School* (OH)
Hurd, Anne, *Greensboro Day School* (NC)
Hutton, Gayle, *The Gow School* (NY)
Hyde, Debra Coleman, *Kingswood-Oxford School* (CT)

I

Iafrate, Jayne, *Falmouth Academy* (MA)
Ishon, Jane Jordan, *St. Andrew's Episcopal School* (VA)

J

Jackson, Brenda, *The O'Neal School* (NC)
Jackson, Jeffrey, *Saint Mark's High School* (DE)
Jackson, Kathleen, *Harbor Day School* (CA)
Jackson, Lorrie, *Lausanne Collegiate School* (TN)
Jagodowski, Stacy, *Derby Academy* (MA)
James, Aaron, *Casady School* (OK)
James, Bedell, *The Ensworth School* (TN)
Jamieson, Daniel H., Jr., *St. Albans School* (DC)
Janssen, Patty Healy, *Convent of the Visitation* (MN)
Jantsch, Beth, *Summit Country Day School* (OH)
Jenkins, Jeanne, *The Bush School* (WA)
Johner, Diane, *Rossman School* (MO)
Johnson, Jill, *The Ensworth School* (TN)
Johnson, Melanie, *Southfield School* (LA)
Johnston, Abby, *Saint Mary's School* (NC)
Johnston, Brent, *The Country Day School* (Canada)
Johnston, Rebecca, *The Heritage School* (TN)
Jones, Michael Barrett, *Staten Island Academy* (NY)
Justis, Mary Margaret, *Sullins Academy* (VA)

K

Kang, June Elizabeth, *Seoul Foreign School* (Korea)
Kasof, Emily, *The Dalton School* (NY)
Keen, Sharon, *St. Timothy's School* (NC)
Kephen, Steve, *University Prep* (WA)
Kelley, Mary, *Live Oak School* (CA)
Kellogg, Bede, *The Walden School* (CA)
Kelly, Jean, *Fort Worth Academy* (TX)
Kemp, Jim, *The John Burroughs School* (MO)
Kenny, Mary Nelson, *Forest Ridge School/Sacred Heart* (WA)
Kent, Emily, *The Hillside School* (MA)
Keogh, Ellen, *Fairfield Country Day* (CT)
Kidd, Andy, *Episcopal HS/Jacksonville* (FL)
Kilduff, Kelley, *Maryvale Preparatory School* (MD)
Kiser, Linda, *St. Andrew's Episcopal School* (MD)
Knapp, Julia, *St. Clement's School* (Canada)
Knuth, Bob, *The Blake School* (MN)
Koles, Susan, *Rowland Hall-St. Mark's* (UT)
Kraeger, Susan, *The Good Hope School* (VI)
Kragen, Florence, *Ecole Bilingue de Berkeley* (CA)
Kramer, Margaret, *Trinity Valley School* (TX)
Krejci, Marina, *University School of Milwaukee* (WI)
Kulyla, Todd, *Ivymount & Maddux Schools* (MD)
Kussin, Karl, *Nashoba Brooks School* (MA)

L

LaClaire, Cathy, *The Walker School* (GA)
LaForge, Ann, *Cathedral School/St. John the Divine* (NY)
Landini, Mark, *The Linsly School* (WV)
Larkins, Christina, *Oak Hill Academy* (NJ)
Latham, Christopher, *The Taft School* (CT)
Lawrence, Nancy, *Good Shepherd Episcopal School* (TX)
LeGrand, Paige Peters, *The Episcopal Academy* (PA)
Lathan, Stewart, *Atlanta International School* (GA)
Leardi, Margaret, *Centreville School* (DE)
Ledford, Rita Rice, *New Garden Friends School* (NC)
Lee, Barbara, *Storm King School* (NY)
LeMond, Sharon, *The Oakridge School* (TX)
Leskin, Shannon, *Triangle Day School* (NC)
Levine, Wendy, *Saint Mark's School* (CA)
Levy, Linda, *The Galloway School* (GA)
Lieberman, Cathy, *Bernard Zell Anshe Emet Day* (IL)
Lippe, Penny, *Elisabeth Morrow School* (NJ)

Lopez, Kathleen, *St. Mary's Episcopal Day School* (FL)
Lordan, Gerald, Ph.D., *Fenwick High School* (IL)
Lough, Kathy, *Grace Day School* (NY)
Lovelock, Julie A., *St. James' Episcopal School* (CA)
Lucaire, Lewise, *The Brearley School* (NY)

M

MacPherson, Craig, *Convent of the Sacred Heart* (NY)
Maley, George, *Noble and Greenough School* (MA)
Malone, Lane, *Lowell Whiteman School* (CO)
Manley, Carol, *Rosemont School of the Holy Child* (PA)
Manuel, Shelly, *St. Martin's Episcopal School* (GA)
Marafino, Andy, *Bishop Montgomery HS* (CA)
Markus, Faith, *The College School* (MO)
Marshall, Duncan L., *Riverdale Country School* (NY)
Martin, Lydia, *Friends' Central School* (PA)
Martin, Sage, *Telluride Mountain School* (CO)
Mateus, Sandy, *The Hamlin School* (CA)
Mathews, Sue, *Nightingale-Bamford* (NY)
McEnery, Joanie B., *Trinity Episcopal* (LA)
McFarling, Andrea, *Marymount of Santa Barbara* (CA)
McGrane, Eric, *The Miami Valley School* (OH)
McHugh, Jennifer, *Springside School* (PA)
McKay, Sarah, *Marin Country Day School* (CA)
McKillop, Janet, *St. Matthew's Parish School* (CA)
McLean, Marci, *Parish Episcopal School* (TX)
McMahon, R.J., *Fenwick High School* (IL)
McWilliams, Tim, *Jackson Academy* (MS)
Meadows, Polly, *The Pennfield School* (RI)
Meadows, Yukiko M., *Lycée Français La Pérouse* (CA)
Meighan, Judi, *The Willow School* (NJ)
Melvin, Sarah, *The Steward School* (VA)
Merrick, David, *The Haverford School* (PA)
Merrigan, Louise, *The Newman School* (MA)
Merrill, Karen, *The Covenant School* (VA)
Merrill, Mary, *Belmont Day School* (MA)
Metzger, Cerise, *Cornelia Connelly School* (CA)
Miles, Elaine, *Oakwood Friends School* (NY)
Miller, Pam, *The Nora School* (MD)
Miller, Susan, *Alexander Dawson School* (CO)
Minahan, Greg, *The Caedmon School* (NY)
Minor, Susan, *Battle Ground Academy* (TN)
Mitchell, L.J., *Mary McDowell Center* (NY)
Mitchell, Peggy, *Town School for Boys* (CA)
Mlatac, Laura, *Guilford Day School* (NC)
Mohi, Susan, *St. Hilda's & St. Hugh's* (NY)
Moloff-Gautier, Robin, *Washington Academy* (ME)
Monahan, Barbara Price, *Hopkins School* (CT)
Monnier, Gary, *The Seven Hills School* (OH)
Moody, Regina, Ph.D., *Stoneleigh-Burnham School* (MA)
Moore, Kimberley, *Pingree School* (MA)
Moore, Tom, *The Kinkaid School* (TX)
Mora, Aleida, *Commonwealth-Parkville* (PR)
Morgan, Jeffrey, *Albuquerque Academy* (NM)
Morrison, Patricia Reilly, *Norwood School* (MD)
Morse, Kathleen, *The Eliot Montessori School* (MA)
Murphy, Megan, *Marlborough School* (CA)
Murphy, Robert J., *Blue Ridge School* (VA)
Murray, Tom, *Brunswick School* (CT)
Myles, Eileen, *The Mary Louis Academy* (NY)

N

Neale, Mal, *Berkeley Hall School* (CA)
Neff-Henderson, Laura, *North Cross School* (VA)
Newton, Beth Ann, *Oakcrest School* (VA)
Nicol, Molly A., *Saint Gregory's School* (NY)

Directors of Development

Niedzwiecki, Eileen, *The Ursuline School* (NY)
Nuland, Jane, *Lowell School* (DC)

O

Olson, Sara, *Newtown Friends School* (PA)
Oppenheimer, Pat, *Barstow School* (MO)
Oroszlany, Antal, *Loyola School* (NY)
Ormiston, John, *Berkshire School* (MA)
Otto, Joan, *Sierra Canyon School* (CA)
Overbye, Christopher, *Meadowbrook of Weston* (MA)

P

Packer, Rachel, *Mid-Peninsula High* (CA)
Page, Janet, *Saint Joseph's Episcopal School* (FL)
Palmer, Mark, *Community School* (MO)
Park, Suzanne, *The Craig School* (NJ)
Parke, Jennifer H., *The Grosse Pointe Academy* (MI)
Parker, Reid, *Lakehill Preparatory School* (TX)
Parrish, Paula, *Fort Worth Country Day* (TX)
Pasciuto, Ray, *Cambridge Friends School* (MA)
Pate, Barbara, *Bayside Academy* (AL)
Patrykus, Katie, *Ojai Valley School* (CA)
Pepe, Ann Baker, *The Foote School* (CT)
Perry, Melinda, *Canterbury School* (IN)
Pesch, Larry, *Brookfield Academy* (WI)
Pfaff, John R., *Carolina Day School* (NC)
Pilant, Sabrina, *Isidore Newman School* (LA)
Piper, Sheryl, *Miami Country Day School* (FL)
Pollack, Whitney Namm, *Ethical Culture Fieldston* (NY)
Pricer, Michelle, *The Dunham School* (LA)
Prichard, Laura, *The Harvey School* (NY)
Pugh, Kim, *Rumsey Hall School* (CT)
Pundyk, Colleen, *Wildwood School* (CA)

Q

Quinones, Marion, *Children's Day School* (CA)

R

Rae, Linda S., *Soundview Prep* (NY)
Rainey, Terry, *Bishop Ireton High School* (VA)
Randall, Ted, *Foxcroft Academy* (ME)
Rawlings, Jennifer, *Edmund Burke School* (DC)
Read, Linda, *PACE-Brantley Hall School* (FL)
Reed, Lach, *Windward School* (CA)
Remsen, Liz, *Green Vale School* (NY)
Rhoades, Mary, *Sacred Heart Schools SF* (CA)
Rice, Doreen, *The Pembroke Hill School* (MO)
Richardson, Debbie, *The Key School* (MD)
Richter, Mary, *The Allen-Stevenson School* (NY)
Riis-Culver, Eva, *Glenlyon Norfork School* (BC)
Riordan, Karen, *Sanford School* (DE)
Rizzo, Becky, *Charlotte Country Day School* (NC)
Roberts, Mary E., *Loyola Blakefield* (MD)
Rogers, John T., *William Penn Charter School* (PA)
Rogg, Catherine, *University Liggett School* (MI)
Roman, Sheila, *Allendale Columbia School* (NY)
Rooney, Patricia J, RSM, *Academy of Our Lady of Mercy* (CT)
Rose, Fergus J., *ACS International Schools* (England)

Rosen, Beverly, *Jack Barrack Hebrew Academy* (PA)
Rowen, Virginia, *Rye Country Day School* (NY)
Roy, Jeanne, *The Country School* (CT)
Ruotolo, Tara, *The Buckley School* (NY)
Ryan, Marcia, *Cornelia Connelly School* (CA)

S

Sager, Jeannie, *University High School* (IN)
Saludo, Karen, *The Harley School* (NY)
Santarcangelo, N.J., *Strake Jesuit College Prep* (TX)
Sarasin, Warren, *The Langley School* (VA)
Sarkissian, Daniel, *Salesianum School* (DE)
Scales, Brian P., *Cannon School* (NC)
Schalk, Velda, *St. James Episcopal School* (TX)
Scheele, Anne, *The Orchard School* (IN)
Schiller, Jennifer, *Montrose School* (MA)
Schlotterbeck, Mike, *Moorestown Friends* (NJ)
Schmidt, James, *Cathedral School for Boys* (CA)
Schmitt, Dabney, *The Potomac School* (VA)
Schmitz, Bob, *Colorado Academy* (CO)
Schroth, Shelley, *Windward School* (CA)
Schultheis, Jenice, *All Saints' Episcopal Day* (CA)
Selby, David, *St. Thomas School* (WA)
Sewall, Gordon, *Milton Academy* (MA)
Shadle, Selena, *Friends Seminary* (NY)
Shafer, John H., *Wyoming Seminary* (PA)
Shaffer, Charlie, *The Westminster Schools* (GA)
Sheeline, Susan, *East Woods School* (NY)
Sherman, Molly, *St. Andrew's Episcopal* (TX)
Sibal, Lisa, *St. Martin's Episcopal School* (LA)
Sidell, Mary, *Brentwood School* (CA)
Silverman, Gay, *Halifax Grammar School* (NS)
Simmons, Barbara, *Burgundy Farm CDS* (VA)
Singletary, Isabel, *Carrollton School/Sacred Heart* (FL)
Skiff, James J., *Providence Country Day* (RI)
Skinner, Judy, *The Swain School* (PA)
Skipworth, Troy, *The John Cooper School* (TX)
Sloger, Marlene, *San Francisco Friends School* (CA)
Slotnick, Sue, *Village School* (CA)
Smith, Alex, *Collegiate School* (VA)
Smith, Audrey, *Hampton Roads Academy* (VA)
Smith, Bennett, *Sonoma Academy* (CA)
Smith, Carri, *Maclay School* (FL)
Smith, Delores, *St. Christopher's School* (VA)
Smith, Devereaux, *The Bentley School* (CA)
Smith, Nancy, *Glenelg Country School* (MD)
Smith, Steve, *Washington Waldorf School* (MD)
Smith, Susan, *The Catherine Cook School* (IL)
Smith, Susan Swan, *The Hockaday School* (TX)
Smithwick, Elizabeth, *Brookstone School* (GA)
Soles, Herbert P., *Norfolk Academy* (VA)
Sopic, Connie, *Village Community School* (NY)
South, Damaris, *The Wyndcroft School* (PA)
Spencer, Andy, *The Lovett School* (GA)
Spicer, Ellen, *Grymes Memorial School* (VA)
Spring, Ellen, *The Williams School* (CT)
Stahl, Gregory, *Georgetown Preparatory School* (MD)
Stephens, David B., *Meadowbrook School* (PA)
Stevens, Carolyn Hoyt, *Park School of Buffalo* (NY)
Stevens, Kristen, *Montgomery School* (PA)
Stiff, Angie, *Franklin Road Academy* (TN)
Stockton, Shana, *Charleston Day School* (SC)
Stone, Mimi, *St. Anne's Episcopal School* (CO)
Stringfellow, Janetta, *The Commonwealth School* (MA)
Stuart, Harrison, *Episcopal School of Knoxville* (TN)
Struthers, Timothy G., *The Loomis Chaffee School* (CT)
Sullivan, Jackie, *The Pingry School* (NJ)
Summers, Jennifer, *St. Timothy's School* (MD)
Sylvester, Tom, *Phoenix Country Day* (AZ)

T

Taylor, Janet, *Mount Tamalpais School* (CA)
Taylor, Tracey, *The Winston School* (NJ)
Tevlin, Patrick, *Shady Side Academy* (PA)
Thaden, Cathy, *Saint Patrick Catholic School* (VA)
Thomas, Sarah, *Lake Forest Country Day School* (IL)
Thompson, James, *Chadwick School* (CA)
Thornton, Carol, *St. Agnes Academy-St. Dominic School* (TN)
Thornton, Paul, *St. Benedict's Prep* (NJ)
Thorsen, John, *Francis Parker School* (CA)
Thurston, Lesley, *St. Michael's Country Day* (RI)
Tilney, Rachel, *Kimball Union Academy* (NH)
Tornehl, Kimberly, *University Lake School* (WI)
Torns, Nancy, *The Gillispie School* (CA)
Toth, Cynthia, *Robert Louis Stevenson School* (NY)
Trautner, Rebecca, *Mount Saint Mary Academy* (NJ)

U

Urban, Brook, *Eagle Hill School* (CT)

V

Valyi, Katherine, *The Hackley School* (NY)
Veneziano, Maria, *The Crefeld School* (PA)
Vigne, Jennifer, *Saint Stephen's Episcopal School* (FL)
Vulevic, Catherine, *St. Paul's Episcopal* (AL)

W

Wahler, Pat, *Bellarmine College Prep* (CA)
Wakefield, Louise, *Bermuda HS for Girls* (Bermuda)
Wakild, Susan, *Cape Fear Academy* (NC)
Walther, Celeste, *Sandia Prep* (NM)
Ward, Nancy, *Clairbourn School* (CA)
Waters, Bobbie, *Episcopal Collegiate* (AR)
Watson, Courtney, *Capitol Hill Day School* (DC)
Wells, Susannah, *Pine Cobble School* (MA)
Wenning, Jane, *Saddle River Day School* (NJ)
West, Kathryn, *Mooreland School* (CT)
Whitney, Stephanie B., *Greens Farms Academy* (CT)
Wielk, Kathleen, *Notre Dame of West Haven* (CT)
WiesemanLeader, Marcy, *St. Peter's School* (PA)
Wigley, Karla K., *Episcopal School of Dallas* (TX)
Williamson, Kimberly, *North Cross School* (VA)
Winick, Lisa, *Peddie School* (NJ)
Witter, Lisa, *St. Andrew's Episcopal* (LA)
Wolfram, Suzanne, *All Saints Episcopal-Beaumont* (TX)
Wong, Liz, *Abington Friends School* (PA)
Wood, Mary, *Saint James School* (MD)
Woodin, Jennifer, *Landmark School* (MA)
Woodward, James, *The Field School* (DC)
Wright, Danny, *Christ School* (NC)

Y

Young, A. Kay, *Wyoming Seminary* (PA)
Young, Dori, *Charles Wright Academy* (WA)

Z

Zaiser, Robert, *Moravian Academy* (PA)
Zimmerman, Al, *St. Joseph's Preparatory* (PA)
Zink, Evelyn, *Roland Park Country School* (MD)

A

Aceves, Jennifer, *Guilford Day School* (NC)
Adams, Jane, *St. Paul's Episcopal School* (CA)
Adams, Jenny, *Hebron Academy* (ME)
Adams, Sonya, *Kingswood-Oxford School* (CT)
Aiello, Kathy, *The Benjamin School* (FL)
Alexander, Phyllis, *The Dunham School* (LA)
Alfieri, Rosemarie, *Saint David's School* (NY)
Anderson, Lauren, *Friends School Haverford* (PA)
Anderson, Rebecca, *Friends' Central School* (PA)
Angorola, Jane, *Capitol Hill Day School* (DC)
Ankrom, Robert, *Chatham Hall* (VA)
Arnstein, David, *Georgetown Day School* (DC)
Avington, Bill, *St. Joseph's Preparatory* (PA)

B

Bailey, Kristen, *Urban School of SF* (CA)
Balk, Jahna, *The Hudson School* (NJ)
Ball, Liz, *Trinity School* (GA)
Ballantine, Danielle, *The Academy of the Holy Cross* (MD)
Banning, Dawn, *All Saints' Academy* (FL)
Barnes, Cynthia, *Saltus Grammar School* (Bermuda)
Barone, Nina, *Nichols School* (NY)
Battista, Miriam, *St. Thomas's Day School* (CT)
Beeson, Jennifer, *The College Preparatory School* (CA)
Belcher, Karen, *Canterbury School* (IN)
Bell, Peggy, *Green Vale School* (NY)
Bennett, Rachel, *The Dwight School* (NY)
Bernas, Ronald, *University Liggett School* (MI)
Bica, Adrian, *Saklan Valley School* (CA)
Bienvenour, Ginger, *The Orchard School* (IN)
Bizzarri, Jennifer, *Greenwood College School* (ON)
Blake, Shirley, *Brentwood School* (CA)
Blasdell, Rachel, *Duchesne Academy* (TX)
Blass, Kim, *The Lovett School* (GA)
Bogad, Molly, *Abraham Joshua Heschel* (CA)
Borden, Ann, *Marin Country Day School* (CA)
Bowen, Leslie, *Dedham Country Day* (MA)
Boyd, Brian, *Woodward Academy* (GA)
Braxton, Jennifer, *Montgomery School* (PA)
Bremner, Ellen, *John Burroughs School* (MO)
Brennan, Julia, *Kimball Union Academy* (NH)
Bridenstine, Sheila, *Kalamazoo Country Day* (MI)
Brin, David, *Marin Academy* (CA)
Britton, Sara Kassabian, *Oak Knoll School* (NJ)
Brodnick, Bonni, *Brunswick School* (CT)
Broughton, Joseph, *The Winsor School* (MA)
Brown, Evan, *Elisabeth Morrow School* (NJ)
Bryant, Beth, *The Pembroke Hill School* (MO)
Budd, Claire P., *Rohan Woods School* (MO)
Burke, Kathleen, *The Pennfield School* (RI)
Burns, Carol, *The Swain School* (PA)
Burns, Tom, *Melrose School* (NY)
Byrnes, David, *Cathedral School/St. John the Divine* (NY)

C

Calfo, Stacy, *Greensboro Day School* (NC)
Callahan, Dan, *Brooks School* (MA)
Campbell, Carole, *Collegiate School* (NY)
Carney, Tracey Quillen, *Wilmington Friends School* (DE)
Carroll, Alan, *Allendale Columbia School* (NY)
Casanave, David, *Thayer Academy* (MA)
Casey, Sean, *Peddie School* (NJ)

Castagna, Peter, *Salesianum School* (DE)
Castle, Brenda, *The Country Day School* (Canada)
Catalano, Laura, *Good Shepherd Episcopal School* (TX)
Chamberlain, Judith, *Calmont School* (CA)
Chapman, Judy, *The Meadows School* (NV)
Chernoff, Naina Narayana, *Burgundy Farm CDS* (VA)
Ciccarelli, Maura, *The Haverford School* (PA)
Clark, Andrea, *Academy of the Sacred Heart* (MI)
Clark, Megan, *St. Agnes Academy* (TX)
Clerici, Sandi, *Charleston Collegiate School* (SC)
Cluxton, Linda Doll, *Christ School* (NC)
Cogar, Elizabeth, *Collegiate School* (VA)
Cohen, Liza, *Dana Hall School* (MA)
Cooper, Leslie, *Polytechnic School* (CA)
Coraggio, Cristina, *Upper Canada College* (ON)
Creely, Stacey, *The Linsly School* (WV)
Crockett-Bunch, Kellye, *Barstow School* (MO)
Curwen, Ginger, *Ethical Culture Fieldston* (NY)

D

Davies, Tristan, *The Commonwealth School* (MA)
Dawkins, Barbara, *St. Nicholas School* (TN)
DeCell, Florri, *Georgetown Day School* (DC)
Delaney, Megan O'Hare, *St. Hilda's & St. Hugh's* (NY)
Dhue, Hutton, *The Westminster Schools* (GA)
Dianetti, Trish, *St. George's Independent School* (TN)
Dianis, Laura, *The Stanwich School* (CT)
Dickinson, Pam, *The Harker School* (CA)
Donohoe, Cecilia, *Windward School* (NY)
Dorrill, Melisa, *The Lamplighter School* (TX)
Dugan, Jan, *Christ Methodist Day School* (TN)
Duggan, Laura, *Marin Horizon School* (CA)
Durkin, Janet, *Sonoma Academy* (CA)

E

Earl, Christy, *The Hockaday School* (TX)
Earley, Marion, *Charles River School* (MA)
Ekstrom, Gigi, *Lakehill Preparatory School* (TX)
Elba, Vivian K., *Ethel Walker School* (CT)
Ellman, Holly, *Fort Worth Country Day* (TX)
Erstling, Jean, *Landon School* (MD)
Esteves-Moore, Barbara, *Overbrook & St. Cecilia* (TN)
Everett, Cathleen, *Milton Academy* (MA)

F

Failla, Kathy, *Convent of the Sacred Heart* (CT)
Falk, Laura, *Community School* (MO)
Farley, Malcolm, *Poly Prep Country Day* (NY)
Faulkner, Debra, *Harding Academy* (TN)
Ferrante, Deanna, *The Pennington School* (NJ)
Ferrera, Andrei, *Head-Royce School* (CA)
Field, Jill, *Breck School* (MN)
Fisher, Robert, *Marist School* (GA)
Fite, J.D., *The Galloway School* (GA)
Fleming, Cheryl, *Sanford School* (DE)
Fletcher, Claire, *Episcopal HS of Houston* (TX)
Flynn, Laurie, *The Wheeler School* (RI)
Fowler, Courtney Payne, *Atlanta International School* (GA)
Freeland, Alison, *Greens Farms Academy* (CT)
Freeman, Jill, *Cliff Valley School* (GA)
Frost, Darrel, *Nightingale-Bamford School* (NY)

G

Galayda, John, *Friends Seminary* (NY)
Garrison, Libby, *Sycamore School* (IN)
Gesualdo, Nicole, *The Chapin School* (NY)
Gibson, Brooke Hutson, *The Wilson School* (MO)
Giles, Aimee, *Children's Day School* (CA)
Gillert, Maura, *Kerr-Vance Academy* (NC)
Gnatt, Brian, *Georgetown Preparatory School* (MD)
Goyette, Elli, *Hampton Roads Academy* (VA)

H

Haas, Olivia, *Marlborough School* (CA)
Hackett, Ilene, *St. Mark's Episcopal Day School* (FL)
Hakoun, Celine, *Lycée Français La Pérouse* (CA)
Halpin, Tina, *Mayfield Junior School* (CA)
Hammers, Carri, *The Roeper School* (MI)
Handalian, Linda, *St. Matthew's Episcopal Day* (CA)
Hanley, Laurie, *Chadwick School* (CA)
Harrell, Susan, *Cape Fear Academy* (NC)
Harrison, Stephen, *University Child Development* (WA)
Hart, Erin, *Cistercian Preparatory School* (TX)
Hassel, John, *Saint Francis Prep* (NY)
Hay, Sherryn M., *Trinity Prep* (FL)
Hayes, Estelle, *Bellarmine College Prep* (CA)
Heap, Paula, *Saint Stephen's Episcopal School* (FL)
Heard, Jaqueline, *Edmund Burke School* (DC)
Held, Patty, *Trident Academy* (SC)
Helms, Kristy, *The Walker School* (GA)
Higgins, Deborah, *Mary Institute/Saint Louis CDS* (MO)
Hightower, Melanie, *River Oaks Baptist School* (TX)
Hill, Judy, *Abington Friends School* (PA)
Ho, Pat, *Hanahau'oli School* (HI)
Holt, Alison, *Greenwood College School* (Canada)
Holt, Christina, *Episcopal High School* (VA)
Honeywell, Anne, *St. Martin's Episcopal School* (VA)
Hoskins, Leah, *Brentwood Academy* (TN)
Howe, Jennifer, *Providence Day School* (NC)
Hsu, Lee, *Chinese American Intl. School* (CA)
Huang, Dede, *Chinese International School* (Hong Kong)

I

Ifft, Sharon, *The Langley School* (VA)

J

Jackson, Lorrie, *Lausanne Collegiate School* (TN)
James, Jessica, *The Colorado Springs School* (CO)
Janssen, Patty Healy, *Convent of the Visitation* (MN)
Jarzab, Sally, *The Elmwood Franklin School* (NY)
Jenckes, Roberta, *The Hotchkiss School* (CT)
Johner, Diane, *Rossman School* (MO)
Johnson, Linda, *The Maret School* (DC)
Johnson, Stephen, *Windward School* (CA)
Johnson, Susan M., *Canterbury School* (IN)
Jordan, Ginger, *St. Agnes Academy-St. Dominic School* (TN)
Jordan, Rena, *Staten Island Academy* (NY)

K

Kane, Jill, *Millbrook School* (NY)
Kang, June Elizabeth, *Seoul Foreign School* (Korea)
Kaz, Maia, *The Bush School* (WA)
Keller, Matthew, *The Orchard School* (IN)
Kenny, Kathy, *Gilmour Academy* (OH)
King, Vicki, *Jackson Preparatory School* (MS)
Kinsella, Julie, *Academy of Our Lady of Mercy* (CT)
Kiser, Linda, *St. Andrew's Episcopal School* (MD)
Klein, Judith, *Pingree School* (MA)
Klobetanz, Jack, *Lowell Whiteman School* (CO)
Kodama, Robert, *Crespi Carmelite HS* (CA)
Kolmen, Lora, *University Prep* (WA)
Krizan, Kate, *Connelly School of the Holy Child* (MD)
Kuhn, Kristyn, *Severn School* (MD)
Kulyla, Todd, *Ivymount & Maddux Schools* (MD)

L

Lamb, Elizabeth, *All Saints' Episcopal-FW* (TX)
LaPine, Kate, *The Park School* (MA)
Larkins, Christina, *Oak Hill Academy* (NJ)
Latimer, Irfan, *The Key School* (MD)
Lee, Barbara, *Storm King School* (NY)
LePoidevin, Michelle, *Wardlaw-Hartridge* (NJ)
Letts, Michael, *The Episcopal Academy* (PA)
Lewis, Aimee, *The Harley School* (NY)
Loffredo, Linda, *Bishop Ireton High School* (VA)
Long, Barbara, *Summit School* (NC)
Long, David L., *Cannon School* (NC)
Lopez, Kathleen, *St. Mary's Episcopal Day School* (FL)
Lovelock, Julie, *St. James' Episcopal School* (CA)
Lucas, Jill, *The Potomac School* (VA)
Lum, Hope, *The Kinkaid School* (TX)
Lynch, Patty, *Stone Ridge School of the Sacred Heart* (MD)

M

Maas, Melissa, *St. Stephen's and St. Agnes School* (VA)
Mackin, Heather, *Berkeley Preparatory* (FL)
Mahoney, Bill, *Belmont Hill School* (MA)
Malloy, Jennie, *Montrose School* (MA)
Manning, James, *Hong Kong International* (China)
Marr, Debra, *Newark Academy* (NJ)
Marshall, Toni, *Pine Crest School* (FL)
Martin, Joan, *Brooklyn Friends School* (NY)
Martorana, Amanda, *Glenelg Country School* (MD)
Matthews, Carleen, *Franklin Road Academy* (TN)
Mayer, Judith, *Charlotte Latin School* (NC)
Maynard, Matt, *The Miami Valley School* (OH)
McCoy, Cynthia, *All Saints' Episcopal School* (CA)
McDermott, Kathleen, *Gilmour Academy* (OH)
McKain, Lynn, *McDonogh School* (MD)
McLane, Cathy, *The Blake School* (MN)
McLean, Marci, *Parish Episcopal School* (TX)
McQuilton, Koreen, *Belmont Day School* (MA)
Mendoza, Mark, *St. Matthew's Parish School* (CA)
Menez, Monica, *Westridge School* (CA)
Merriman, Katy, *Southfield School* (LA)
Metzger, Cerise, *Cornelia Connelly School* (CA)
Mimms, Christina, *St. Martin's Episcopal School* (GA)
Minahan, Greg, *The Caedmon School* (NY)
Minor, Susan, *Battle Ground Academy* (TN)
Mitchell, Polly, *Wyoming Seminary* (PA)
Monahan, Jennifer, *Ecole Bilingue de Berkeley* (CA)
Moore, Laura, *Annunciation Orthodox School* (TX)

Moore, Rebecca B., *Randolph School* (AL)
Moore, Sandra, *Poughkeepsie Day School* (NY)
Morgan, Jenny, *St. Andrew's Episcopal* (TX)
Morgan, Louise D., *Loomis Chaffee* (CT)
Morgan, Michael F., *The Tatnall School* (DE)
Morris, Kacey, *Brookwood School* (MA)
Morrison, Cathy, *Francis Parker School* (CA)
Morrissey, Michelle, *Brooks School* (MA)
Morse, Kathleen, *The Eliot Montessori School* (MA)
Mosteller, Kelly, *Meadowbrook School* (PA)
Mott, Holly, *Stoneleigh-Burnham School* (MA)
Moxsom, Catherine, *Halifax Grammar School* (NS)
Mugele, Nancy, *Roland Park Country School* (MD)
Murphy, Charlotte, *The Foote School* (CT)
Myers, Kim, *The Montessori School* (MD)

N

Naggar, Rachel, *Kent Place School* (NJ)
Navarro, Kevin, *The College School* (MO)
Neff-Henderson, Laura L., *North Cross School* (VA)
Nelms, Dr. Lee, *The Langley School* (VA)
Norell, Kelly, *Episcopal School of Knoxville* (TN)
Norton, Brink, *Porter-Gaud School* (SC)
Nowak, Dave, *Mary Institute/Saint Louis CDS* (MO)

O

O'Connor, Peggy, *Forest Ridge/Sacred Heart* (WA)
Overton, Keir, *The Mabin School* (Canada)

P

Pasciuto, Ray, *Cambridge Friends School* (MA)
Patchett, Steve, *Morristown-Beard School* (NJ)
Patton, Warren, *Rosemont School of the Holy Child* (PA)
Peterson, Andi, *The Out-of-Door Academy* (FL)
Petringa, Dina, *Marymount High School* (CA)
Pluznik, Jodi L., *Gilman School* (MD)
Prokopowicz, Emily, *The Oakwood School* (NC)

R

Racine, Wynne, *Colorado Academy* (CO)
Rasak, Jennifer, *Rolling Hills Prep* (CA)
Rautio, Febecca, *St. John's School* (TX)
Reardon, Shannon, *Miami Country Day School* (FL)
Reitz, Timothy, *The Williams School* (CT)
Reuter-May, Mary, *Princeton Montessori* (NJ)
Rhodes, Allison, *Savannah Country Day School* (GA)
Rieff, Julie, *The Taft School* (CT)
Riekstins, Karyn, *St. Clement's School* (Canada)
Rivers, Rick, *Strake Jesuit College Prep* (TX)
Robertson, Loren, *Browne Academy* (VA)
Robinson, Robert J., *Loyola Blakefield* (MD)
Rogers, Luke, *Munich International School* (Germany)
Rogers, Penny, *Ravenscroft School* (NC)
Rose, Fergus J., *ACS International Schools* (England)
Rosecrans, Kristen, *The Kildonan School* (NY)
Rosen, Beverly C., *Jack Barrack Hebrew Academy* (PA)
Rossi, Veronica, *American School of Madrid* (Spain)
Rottman, Elaine, *Brookfield Academy* (WI)

Roupe, Jennifer, *Shady Side Academy* (PA)
Rowland, Jennifer, *Wildwood School* (CA)
Rucci, Debbie, *Pear Tree Point School* (CT)
Ruess, Phoebe, *Forsyth School* (MO)
Runyon, Michelle, *Oak Hall School* (FL)

S

Sanders, Nanci, *The Stanley Clark School* (IN)
Santini, Elizabeth, *Convent of the Sacred Heart* (NY)
Scafati, Pamela A., *Meadowbrook School of Weston* (MA)
Schlotterbeck, Mike, *Moorestown Friends* (NJ)
Scholer, Liz, *St. Stephen's Episcopal Day* (FL)
Sexton, Sharon, *William Penn Charter School* (PA)
Shain, Jo Ann, *Convent of the Sacred Heart HS* (CA)
Shelffo, Andrew, *Williston Northampton School* (MA)
Sigel, Marlene, *Albuquerque Academy* (NM)
Siladi, Elizabeth, *Bancroft School* (MA)
Sillcox, Kim, *St. Andrew's College* (Canada)
Smith, Amelia, *Episcopal HS/Jacksonville* (FL)
Smith, Ashley, *Blue Ridge School* (VA)
Smith, Beth, *St. Paul's School for Girls* (MD)
Smith, Carri, *Maclay School* (FL)
Smith, Devereaux, *The Bentley School* (CA)
Smith, Joyce, *Viewpoint School* (CA)
Smith, Linda, *Pace Academy* (GA)
Snellgrove, Pamela, *Bay School/SF* (CA)
Softness, Beth, *The Dalton School* (NY)
Sopic, Connie, *Village Community School* (NY)
Speiss, Deb, *The John Cooper School* (TX)
Stokes, Beth, *Harvard-Westlake School* (CA)
Straley, Michael, *Saint James School* (MD)
Stringham, Anne, *The Ensworth School* (TN)
Strobel, Cristina, *St. Mark's Episcopal School* (FL)
Strunk, Taylor, *Bayside Academy* (AL)
Stubbendieck, Leslie, *Beauvoir* (DC)
Sullivan, Debra, *Chestnut Hill School* (MA)
Sullivan, Mark, *The Pingry School* (NJ)
Sweet, Elaine, *University School of Milwaukee* (WI)

T

Taylor, Kathy, *The O'Neal School* (NC)
Taylor, Lisa, *Berkeley Hall School* (CA)
Temple, Vicky, *Barrie School* (MD)
Thomason, Elizabeth, *Saint Edward's School* (FL)
Thompson, Nicole, *Triangle Day School* (NC)
Toth, Cynthia, *Robert Louis Stevenson School* (NY)
Tracy, Karen, *Springside School* (PA)
Travaglione, Vincent, *La Jolla Country Day* (CA)
Tyler, Vicki, *Memphis University School* (TN)

U

Unrot, Michelle, *Chandler School* (CA)
Urban, Brook, *Eagle Hill School* (CT)

V

Vanausdall, Jeanette, *University High School* (IN)
Vaux, Trina, *The Shipley School* (PA)
Veneziano, Maria, *The Crefeld School* (PA)

Verselli, Mary G., *Choate Rosemary Hall* (CT)
Verver, Jeff, *Fenwick High School* (IL)

W

Wadeson, Aimee, *Green Acres School* (MD)
Wagner, Marcy, *Grymes Memorial School* (VA)
Waksman, Karen K.B., *Independent Day* (FL)
Walcoff, Nellie, *Providence Country Day* (RI)
Walker, Betsy, *St. Michael's Country Day* (RI)
Walsh, John B., *The Fenn School* (MA)
Walton, Brian, *Besant Hill School* (CA)
Warner, Amy, *Loudoun Country Day* (VA)
Waters, Bobbie, *Episcopal Collegiate* (AR)
Watson, Denise, *Glenholme School* (CT)
Weinberg, Jody, *Brimmer and May School* (MA)
Whelehan, Andrea, *Buckley Country Day School* (NY)
White, Christine, *Oakcrest School* (VA)
White, Kristin Martinkovic, *Westover School* (CT)
Wilcox, Faith, *The Carroll School* (MA)
Willingham, Angela, *Parish Episcopal School* (TX)
Winshel, Robin Keith, *Curtis School* (CA)
Wolfe, Jennifer, *Saint Mark's School* (CA)
Woodworth, Suzanne, *Gunston Day School* (MD)
Worthing, Glen, *St. Anne's Episcopal School* (CO)
Worthington, Samantha, *Windrush School* (CA)
Wright, Julia, *Lake Forest Country Day School* (IL)

Z

Zaiser, Robert, *Moravian Academy* (PA)
Zondervan, Denise, *Foothill Country Day* (CA)

Summer Programs 2010

What are you and your child looking for? A traditional summer camp? Creative and artistic opportunities? Hands-on computer and technology training? A sports clinic? Study in another country? Outdoor adventure opportunities? Do you want your child to learn about different cultures or to participate in community outreach? Perhaps your child needs support in an academic area or seeks college credit.

From coast to coast and overseas, the programs listed in these Yellow Pages offer a wide variety of ways to spend the summer in exploration, relaxation, growth, and renewal. Begin your search by reviewing the Yellow Pages Grid, which will help you prepare a list of appropriate offerings. Be sure, as well, to read the Blue Pages Grid, which references additional summer programs conducted by the schools in this book.

Time spent in summer learning, whether it's one week or two months, is exciting and rewarding. Make the summer count. Find the program of your choice in the Yellow Pages.

Bunting and Lyon, Inc.
238 North Main Street   Wallingford, Connecticut 06492
1-203-269-3333 Fax 1-203-269-8908
E-mail: BuntingandLyon@aol.com
www.BuntingandLyon.com

MAKE YOUR SUMMER COUNT! CHOOSE FROM THESE OPPORTUNITIES IN 2010!

Academic Courses

enrichment
college credit
high school credit
computer technology
study skills & strategies
learning differences
English as a Second Language
SAT preparation

Fine & Performing Arts

drawing, painting & sculpture
photography & film
dance & movement
drama & theater production
vocal & instrumental ensembles

Travel & Adventure

cultural & language studies
foreign travel
leadership training
wilderness & survival training
oceanography & marine science

Sports & Recreation

skill-building & healthy competition
specialized clinics
archery to windsurfing
   & every activity between

Field Trips

environmental/ecological excursions
college exploration
historical sites
cultural enhancement
sporting events & fun

GEOGRAPHICAL

WASH.

MONT.

N. DAK.

ORE.

IDAHO

S. DAK.

WYO.

CAL.

NEV.

UTAH

NEBR.

COL.

California
Ojai Valley School

KANS.

ARIZ.

N. MEX.

OKLA.

TEXAS

DISTRIBUTION OF SCHOOLS

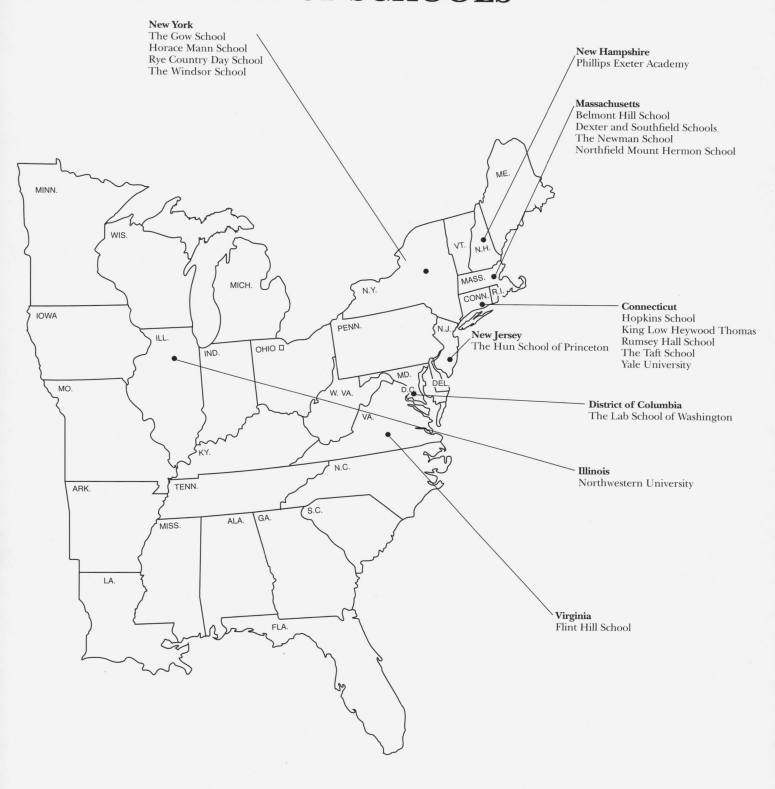

New York
The Gow School
Horace Mann School
Rye Country Day School
The Windsor School

New Hampshire
Phillips Exeter Academy

Massachusetts
Belmont Hill School
Dexter and Southfield Schools
The Newman School
Northfield Mount Hermon School

Connecticut
Hopkins School
King Low Heywood Thomas
Rumsey Hall School
The Taft School
Yale University

New Jersey
The Hun School of Princeton

District of Columbia
The Lab School of Washington

Illinois
Northwestern University

Virginia
Flint Hill School

BELMONT HILL SCHOOL

Belmont Hill School Summer Programs
Janice Campisi, Coordinator

350 Prospect Street
Belmont, Massachusetts 02478
Tel. 617-993-5215
Web Site www.belmonthill.org

Day, Coeducational

Summer School: 600 Students, Grades 6–12
Sport Camps: 650 Campers, Ages 6–15

BELMONT HILL SCHOOL SUMMER PROGRAMS offer academic courses for credit and enrichment as well as art programs and tennis for students entering Grades 6 to 12. The courses, which enroll private and public school students, extend from late June to early August.

Course offerings include classes in math, science, history, English, Latin, Spanish, French, and SAT preparation. There are also courses in ESL, computer programming, and speech and debate.

The art workshops enable students to refine familiar skills or develop new interests in photography, theater, painting and drawing, cartooning, jewelry making, woodworking, and pottery. Courses are taught by teachers proficient in their respective media.

Belmont Hill's tennis program is tailored to all ages and skill levels. The tennis program is a fine complement to the academic classes.

The weeklong Sport Camps for boys and girls ages 6–15 include baseball, field hockey, wrestling, and separate boys' and girls' basketball, lacrosse, and soccer camps. There is a Junior Sports Camp for children ages 6–9. Each camp is directed and staffed by experienced adult coaches.

Belmont Hill is located 5 miles west of Boston.

Contact Belmont Hill for more details; see listing on page 100.

DEXTER AND SOUTHFIELD SCHOOLS

Briarwood Marine Science Camp
Jason Cassista, Director

Summer Office: 20 Newton Street
Brookline, Massachusetts 02445
Tel. 617-454-2725; Fax 617-522-8166
Web Site www.dexter.org
E-mail summer@dexter.org
Boarding, 30 Boys and 30 Girls, Grades 5–9

DEXTER AND SOUTHFIELD SCHOOLS' MARINE SCIENCE PROGRAM at Monument Beach on Cape Cod is designed to encourage young people to explore and appreciate the natural environment. In four one-week sessions, for boys and for girls separately, learning takes place through hands-on activities under the guidance of specialists in their fields.

Campers focus on several major areas of environmental study. In Marine Biology, they learn about deep- and shallow-water sea creatures; collect, examine, and photograph specimens; and manage a saltwater aquarium. In Ecology, they explore the food web and relationship among species; monitor water for pH, salinity, and temperature; study the effects of pollution and over-fishing; conduct a census of spawning horseshoe crabs; and screen plankton and benthic samples. By observing the weather, students learn to interpret signs, patterns, and prevailing winds as they come to understand how the atmosphere affects the marine world and the water cycle. Kayaking combines learning and recreation as campers explore the coastline, visit a nearby island, and learn the use of nautical charts and the compass. Shallow-water snorkeling is also part of various research studies.

A fully equipped marine laboratory contains saltwater tanks, sampling and collecting instruments, and microscopes. Other facilities include a pier, beach, classrooms, dining hall and lodge, recreational areas, and heated cabins. The 8-acre property is adjacent to 90 acres of conservation land and has 2000 feet of shoreline and nature trails through the woods.

Contact the schools for more details; see listings on pages 104 and 111.

FLINT HILL SCHOOL

Summer on the Hill
Mia Burton, Director

3320 Jermantown Road
Oakton, Virginia 22124
Tel. 703-584-2392; Fax 703-242-0718
Web Site www.flinthill.org
E-mail summerprograms@flinthill.org

Day, Coeducational, Ages 5–18

SUMMER ON THE HILL welcomes Flint Hill and other public and private school students to participate in up to six weeks of academics and enrichment, athletics, creative arts, and various specialty camps. The program, from mid-June to the end of July, includes counselor-in-training opportunities, fun field trips in the Baltimore/Washington, D.C. area, and, for high school students, a three-week ecological trip to Ecuador, five-day river-rafting excursions, and backpacking in the American West.

Academic offerings range from reading and math clinics in Grades 2–6 and, for older participants, credit and refresher courses in Pre-Algebra Prep, Algebra I, Geometry, Art, Chemistry, Photography, and Ceramics. Students can also prepare for taking the SAT and brush up on skills such as note taking and active reading.

Among the options in the creative arts are drawing, painting, sculpting, Japanese art, acting, drumming, and dance.

Athletes interested in learning and developing skills and strategies may enroll in age-appropriate camps conducted by seasoned coaches. Girls play soccer, basketball, volleyball, lacrosse, tennis, weightlifting, and speed and agility training. Boys compete in most of these sports as well as in baseball and football.

Breakfast Club and Snack Pack offer extended care and activities for children in Kindergarten– Grade 8.

Summer on the Hill participants enjoy the use of Flint Hill's two campuses, extensive outdoor athletic facilities, two NCAA-regulation-size gyms, art and dance studios, theater, music halls, and computer labs.

Contact Flint Hill for more details.

THE GOW SCHOOL

The Gow Summer Program
Eric Bray, Director

Emery Road
South Wales, New York 14139
Tel. 716-652-3450
Web Site www.gow.org; E-mail summer@gow.org

Boarding, 100 Girls and Boys, Ages 8–16

THE GOW SUMMER PROGRAM was developed to allow children to benefit from summer academics without feeling as if they have lost their summer vacation. The five-week program, from late June to the end of July, provides solid academics with athletic, social, cultural, and recreational activities. The session includes morning academics, afternoon traditional camp, and weekend overnight trips. Gow strives to develop the skills and natural abilities of each camper while encouraging a sense of enthusiasm and positive self-image.

To best fit individual needs, camper-students and their families are assisted in the selection of four courses in the Academic Focus Programs. These programs, which enroll three to six students, meet five days per week. During a predinner period, camper-students have the option of reading for pleasure in the library, using the computer resource center, attending a film festival, playing challenging games such as chess and Trivial Pursuit, or attending a tutorial. Academics focus on reconstructive language, mathematics, organization and study skill development, humanities, studio art, computer literacy, and other courses offered according to student need.

Campers take part in afternoon camping and trip activities through Activity Instruction Clinics, Group Periods, and Focus Periods. There is also a Counselor in Training Program for older camper students.

The Gow Summer Program's 100-acre campus features a computer center, library, gymnasium/activities center, indoor-outdoor climbing walls, a challenging ropes course, and modern dormitories.

Contact Gow for more details; see descriptive article on page 152.

HOPKINS SCHOOL

Hopkins Summer School
Thomas Parr, Director
Kevin Cronin, Assistant Director

986 Forest Road
New Haven, Connecticut 06515
Tel. 203-397-1001, Ext. 540; Fax 203-392-0267
Web Site www.hopkins.edu
E-mail tparr@hopkins.edu

Day, 75 Boys, 75 Girls, Grades 3–12

HOPKINS SUMMER SCHOOL offers academic courses for credit and noncredit in a six-week program extending from late June to early August. A six-week sports camp is offered during the same period. It can be coordinated with the academic program.

Academic courses meet in 60-minute classes scheduled between 8:00 A.M. and 1:15 P.M., five days a week. Among the courses offered are Expository and Creative Writing, Atlantic Communities, Arithmetic Review, Pre-Algebra, Algebra 1–2, Geometry, Functions, Statistics and Trigonometry, Pre-Calculus, Developmental Reading, SAT Preparation, and Study Skills. Credit courses require 90–180 hours of intensive study and noncredit courses 30–60 hours.

The elementary school program provides Developmental Reading, a Writer's Workshop, Mathematics and Computer, Science, and a sports camp.

The sports camp, meeting from 8:00 to 11:00 A.M. daily, includes six one-week coeducational sessions in fencing, swimming, and tennis for Grades 3–12.

Contact Hopkins for more details; see descriptive article on page 45.

HORACE MANN SUMMER PROGRAMS

Horace Mann Summer Programs
Linda Dowling, Administrative Assistant of
Summer School

231 West 246th Street
Bronx, New York 10471
Tel. 718-432-4170; Fax 718-432-3616
Web Site www.horacemann.org
E-mail summer@horacemann.org

Day, Boys and Girls, Nursery–Grade 12

HORACE MANN SUMMER PROGRAMS offer diverse academic, athletic, and recreational activities for students age 3–Grade 12. Most programs take place on the Horace Mann campus.

The June Program, beginning at the end of the school year, helps students make the transition to vacation with a series of traditional and studio arts camps for the Nursery and Lower divisions and sports camps in wrestling, football, and basketball for boys; girls play volleyball, field hockey, lacrosse, basketball, and cross-country.

Students in Grades 6–12 from Horace Mann and other schools may enroll in the Summer School and take academic courses for review, reinforcement, make-up, or advancement. English, Spanish, French, Japanese, Chinese, U.S. history, math, sciences, and the visual, performing, and technical arts are offered. With approval from the appropriate school and department personnel, students may receive full credit for three daily classes and half credit for two daily classes by fulfilling department requirements. Classes are small to ensure individual attention.

Six weeks of day camps for students ages 5–11 offer a full day of activities such as swimming, team sports, tennis, arts and crafts, games, and gymnastics. There are also special days that feature cookouts, aquatic water play, and field trips.

For gifted students in Grades 2–8 who come from lower-income families, Summer on the Hill provides academic enrichment classes on Saturdays during the school year as well as a six-week summer session.

Contact Horace Mann for more details; see listing on page 157.

THE HUN SCHOOL OF PRINCETON

The Hun School of Princeton Summer Session
Donna O'Sullivan, Director of Auxiliary Services

176 Edgerstoune Road
Princeton, New Jersey 08540
Tel. 609-921-7600; Fax 609-921-0953
Web Site www.hunschool.org
E-mail dosullivan@hunschool.org

Boarding, Ages 13–17; Day, Ages 11–17 (Middle School)

THE HUN SCHOOL OF PRINCETON'S SUMMER SESSION offers five weeks of enrichment, refresher, and full-credit courses. In addition, Hun's American Culture and Language Institute provides international students a unique introduction to the American way of life through ESL classes and cultural trips.

Enrichment courses are designed for those who wish to get a head start on a class they will take in the fall. Preview or review courses (60 hours) are for students who need to complete credits or overcome a specific academic problem. Full-credit courses (120 hours) are given in Pre-Calculus, Chemistry, Algebra I–II, and Geometry. Enrichment courses include English, writing, math, biology, chemistry, physics, and SAT Math and Verbal Prep. Middle school students may take math and English and can choose from four courses. Resident students participate in two hours of afternoon activities; the evening schedule includes study hall and free time. Visits to nearby Princeton and Rider Universities and The College of New Jersey are arranged for resident students.

The American Language and Culture Institute, run by an experienced ESL teaching staff, combines intensive course work with frequent trips to museums, historical sites, and social events in the mid-Atlantic region. In 2009, international students from 16 countries prepared a CD-ROM and a collection of short stories and poetry.

Hun's facilities include an Athletic Center with a fitness center and gyms, air-conditioned classrooms, activity center, dining hall, snack bar, tennis courts, and playing fields. Resident students enjoy afternoon sports, organized group activities, weekend fun, and off-campus trips.

Contact The Hun School of Princeton for more details.

KING LOW HEYWOOD THOMAS

King Summer Institute

1450 Newfield Avenue
Stamford, Connecticut 06905
Tel. 203-322-3496, Ext. 500; Fax 203-461-9988
Web Site www.klht.org/summerinstitute
E-mail bschwartz@klht.org

Day, Coeducational, Pre-K–Grade 12

KING SUMMER INSTITUTE provides students from more than 45 private, parochial, and public schools a wide range of opportunities that combine fun and sports with academic acceleration, enrichment, and remediation. Programs run between one to six weeks, depending on grade level, from mid-June through early August.

Children in the Lower School (Pre-K–Grade 5) take classes from 8:00 A.M. to 2:30 P.M. Studies are related to such topics as story-telling, math, robotics, etiquette, crafts, and technology.

Students in Grades 6–8 may enroll in Introduction to Spanish, Pre-Algebra, Money Matters, Writer's Craft, Advanced Lego Robotics, Speaking With Confidence, and Explorations in Art, among others. Classes range from 50 minutes to 2 hours.

King Summer Institute offers Upper School (Grades 9–12) courses that include honors-level classes and SAT preparation in Math and Verbal to facilitate the college application process. Students may also choose among Expository Writing, Chemistry, Physics, Algebra 1, Algebra 2/Trigonometry, Art Explorations 2, and instruction in Spanish or French. Students may earn academic credit for work completed with prior approval from their home school.

Vikings athletic camps encourage children of all ages to develop a love of sports while acquiring specific skills and strategies in an atmosphere of teamwork, cooperation, and friendly competition. Among the sports offered are baseball, basketball, volleyball, and lacrosse.

Contact King for more details; see descriptive article on page 48.

THE LAB SCHOOL OF WASHINGTON®

Summer Session
Katherine Schantz, Director

4759 Reservoir Road, NW
Washington, D.C. 20007
Tel. 202-965-6600
Web Site www.labschool.org
Day, 120 Boys, 102 Girls, Ages 6–18

THE LAB SCHOOL OF WASHINGTON SUMMER SESSION provides a six-week program for children, ages 6 to 18, of average to superior intelligence who have learning disabilities or are in need of remedial academic work. The session begins in the middle of June and ends in late July. A five-week Summer Session is also held at Baltimore Lab, a division of The Lab School of Washington.

The Lower School Program is for children ages 6–12½ who have mild to severe learning disabilities. Individualized remedial instruction is given in all academic areas and through drama, music, woodworking, dance, and visual arts. Swimming and computer classes are optional.

The Junior High (Grades 7–8) level addresses students who have moderate to severe learning disabilities. Small-group instruction is offered in reading, spelling, written language, mathematics, science, computer skills, and study skills. Optional sports, computer, and arts programs are offered during the afternoon.

The High School Program (Grades 9–12) focuses on developing reading skills utilizing assistive technology. Executive functioning strategies are emphasized. Diagnostic services, individual tutoring, college counseling, occupational therapy, and speech/language therapy are available. Each summer's activities are built around a different program theme, such as "Green Summer at The Lab School" or a "Mediterranean Summer."

Contact the School for more details; see listing on page 61.

THE NEWMAN SCHOOL

Summer Programs
J. Harry Lynch, Headmaster

247 Marlborough Street
Boston, Massachusetts 02116
Tel. 617-267-4530; Fax 617-267-7070
Web Site www.newmanboston.org
E-mail plynch@newmanboston.org

Boarding & Day, Coed, Grades 9–12

THE NEWMAN SCHOOL, an International Baccalaureate Organization "World School," offers summer enrichment and academic preparation related to the IBO Diploma Programme as well as academic enrichment courses for international students who are building fluency in English.

Students entering Grades 9–12 may participate in the Summer Introduction to IB Session from July 12 to 30, 2010. This integrated course enables students to become acquainted with IB Programme components such as The Learner Profile and the Core Curriculum. They also take introductory sample IB lessons in English, Social Studies, and Science. Sample exam essay questions and answers from past years will be introduced, and students will become acquainted with various opportunities to pursue the IB Diploma at approved schools in New England.

From July 12 to August 6, students entering Grades 11–12 may participate in IB Revision Sessions in English, Math, and History. The primary focus is to allow them to prepare for the second year of IB studies. A limited number of students entering IB studies in Grade 11 who want an introduction to the courses will be enrolled.

For international students learning English, Literature, American History, and Math courses are academically oriented, providing high school credit to those who maintain excellent attendance and academic achievement. Newman diploma credits may be earned, and appropriate documentation of work performed will be provided to sending schools for determination of credit recognition. Course work is geared toward the needs of students in Grades 10–11. The session is from June 7 to July 9.

Contact the school for more details; see descriptive article on page 109.

NORTHFIELD MOUNT HERMON SCHOOL

NMH Summer Session
Debra J. Frank, Dean of Summer Admission

One Lamplighter Way
Mount Hermon, Massachusetts 01354
Tel. 413-498-3290; Fax 413-498-3112
Web Site www.nmhschool.org
E-mail summer_school@nmhschool.org

Boarding and Day, Coeducational, Entering
Grades 7–12

NMH SUMMER SESSION welcomes committed students from the United States and abroad who want a challenging academic experience. College Prep and Middle School Programs as well as English as a Second Language provide five weeks of instruction with master teachers and interns.

College Prep is designed for students entering Grades 10–12 who seek credit or enrichment. Each student takes one major course that meets for three hours Monday through Saturday mornings, plus an afternoon lab or minor course and a sport. Major courses include U.S. History, Economics, Algebra I, Algebra II, Geometry, Precalculus, Biology, Chemistry, Expository Writing, Literature and Composition, and Psychology. Among the minor courses are Art Studio, Community Service, Drama, Reading and Study Skills, and Public Speaking.

The Middle School Program develops skills and self-confidence for students entering Grades 7–9. Each student takes two major courses in the morning and a minor course and sports in the afternoon. Major courses include Drama Literature, Pre-Algebra, Algebra I, Beginning Spanish, Field Biology, Writing, and Skills in Literature.

Dances, movies, and talent shows complement trips to museums, amusement parks, and beaches. Students enjoy the use of the 40,000-volume library, a computer center, a language lab, a student center, and a gymnasium with fitness center.

Contact Northfield Mount Hermon for more details.

NORTHWESTERN UNIVERSITY

College Preparation Program
Stephanie Teterycz, Director

405 Church Street
Evanston, Illinois 60208-0001
Tel. 847-467-6703; Fax 847-491-3660
Web Site www.scs.northwestern.edu/collegeprep
E-mail cpp@northwestern.edu

Boarding and Day, Coed, High School Students

NORTHWESTERN UNIVERSITY'S COLLEGE PREPARATION PROGRAM 2010 is designed for high school students who want new academic challenges and the experience of real college life. This summer program offers three-, six-, and nine-week options as part of Northwestern's Summer Session. Students will earn college credit for the courses they take.

With more than 350 undergraduate courses to choose from, the College Preparation Program provides a great opportunity to explore a variety of academic areas and get a head start on a college career. Specialized tracks in Biological Sciences, Chemistry, Engineering, Physics, and a number of different languages enable students to lay the foundation for more advanced study once a degree program is started and earn up to a full year of university credit in one summer.

The weekly Get Ready Seminars prepare students for the transition between high school and college life and help them navigate the college admissions and application process with direct access to University admissions counselors, financial aid officers, and student services representatives. Writing consultants provide the guidance needed to develop strong application essays and to write with greater complexity, confidence, and interpretive savvy in preparation for college course work.

Students can experience the fun and excitement of college life in the College Preparation Program as residents or commuters. Residential scholars live on campus in Northwestern dorms.

The application deadline for the 2010 College Preparation Program is April 3, 2010. Late applications will be accepted until May 22, 2010.

Visit www.scs.northwestern.edu/collegeprep to apply and learn more.

OJAI VALLEY SCHOOL

Summer Programs
Eleanora Burright, Director
Tracy Wilson, Director of Admission

723 El Paseo Road
Ojai, California 93023
Tel. 805-646-1423; Fax 805-646-0362
Web Site www.ovs.org; E-mail admission@ovs.org

Residential, Day, Coeducational,
Pre-K–Grade 12

OJAI VALLEY SCHOOL SUMMER PROGRAMS give young people various opportunities to strengthen academic skills, discover new interests, and experience outdoor education in a warm and supportive environment.

Lower Camp for ages 3 to 14, with boarding for children beginning at age 8, provides four morning academic periods daily. These classes focus on building and reinforcing skills in reading, writing, and mathematics through hands-on involvement that combines learning with fun. In the afternoons, summer school teachers supervise campers in a wide variety of athletic and recreational activities. Participants may choose from swimming, basketball, archery, tennis, yoga, cooking, computers, and many other interests. Lower Camp students ages 9–14 may enroll in the School's summer equestrian program, spending a half-day developing balance and coordination skills, or, for more advanced riders, dressage, jumping, and competing in regional shows. A "camp within a camp" emphasizes the performing arts, with experiences in acting, singing, and movement as well as backstage involvement with lighting, sound, and set design. Upper Camp for Grades 9–12 enables students to earn credit in English, Algebra I–II, and Geometry, or choose from courses such as Creative Writing, Film Studies, Photoshop, Science Seminars, or Study Skills. A Counselor in Training program is available.

Residential international students benefit from the four-week English Language Camp. ESL sessions, TOEFL preparation, peer tutors, and programs that introduce the American culture are marked by individual attention and skill building. Students visit nearby theme parks and take part in typical camp activities.

Contact the school for more details; see listing on page 26.

PHILLIPS EXETER ACADEMY

Exeter Summer School
Ethan W. Shapiro, Director

20 Main Street
Exeter, New Hampshire 03833
Tel. 603-777-3488; Fax 603-777-4385
Web Site www.exeter.edu/summer
E-mail summer@exeter.edu

Private Boarding and Day School, Coeducational,
750 Rising Grade 8–Postgraduate

EXETER SUMMER SCHOOL welcomes to its campus some 700 students for five weeks of academic study, athletics, and exploration that carry participants far beyond the classrooms and playing fields. Typically, students come from more than 40 states, Puerto, the District of Columbia, and several world nations. They are public and private school students. Most reside in campus dormitories; others travel daily from their homes in the New Hampshire seacoast area. Together, they embody a rich diversity of language, culture, religion, and race and possess that particular mix of intellectual curiosity and adventurous spirit that holds the promise of glimpsing new horizons and making new discoveries.

The UPPER SCHOOL offers more than 100 courses of study for high school students entering Grade 10 and beyond. UPPER SCHOOL students have the freedom of designing their own program of study by simply selecting any three courses they find appealing. In designing their academic programs, they may immerse themselves in several disciplines. Among the numerous choices are *Observational Astronomy, Introductory Latin, Great Books/Great Reading, Digital Photography, Marine Biology,* and *Great Issues in American History.*

ACCESS EXETER is open to students entering Grades 8 and 9. The ACCESS EXETER curriculum consists of six academic clusters. Each cluster includes three courses organized around a central theme. The academic clusters are Project Exeter: A Greener Earth; The Land and the Sea; Problem-Solving: An Odyssey of the Mind; A Global Community; The Creative Arts: Let Your Spirit Soar; and Exeter C.S.I.: Crime Scene Investigation.

Exeter Summer School seeks bright, highly motivated students to participate in this program from July 4 to August 7, 2010.

Contact Phillips Exeter for more details.

RUMSEY HALL SCHOOL

Rumsey Hall School Summer Session
Thomas W. Farmen, Headmaster
Matthew S. Hoeniger, Assistant Headmaster/
   Director of Admission

Romford Road
Washington Depot, Connecticut 06794
Tel. 860-868-0535; Fax 860-868-7907
Web Site www.rumseyhall.org
E-mail admiss@rumseyhall.org
Coeducational
Grades 3–9 (Day), Grades 5–9 (Boarding)

RUMSEY HALL SCHOOL SUMMER SESSION is a five-week program of academic review and preview for students entering Grades 3–9. English as a Second Language is offered for international students. The program runs from the beginning of July to early August 2010 on a beautiful 147-acre campus bordering the Bantam River.

Academic courses are available for students who wish to review previous material or preview new material in English, mathematics, study skills, and computer skills. Average class size is ten students. Classes are available in language skills and developmental reading with trained specialists on a one-to-one basis. The schedule includes approximately four hours of coursework, with afternoon activities and recreation and evening study halls. Summer school participants spend at least an hour a day reading and must complete two book reports during the session. Parents receive biweekly progress reports and a comprehensive written report at the conclusion of the program.

English as a Second Language focuses on vocabulary and conversation in everyday situations. Students practice speaking skills with one another, keep journals, and discuss topics in American language and culture. Participants may also work with Language Skills faculty on a one-to-one basis.

Students live in dormitories and dine family style with their peers and faculty members. They enjoy swimming, various sports, hiking, mountain biking, and excursions to cultural events, historical sites, and amusement parks.

Contact Rumsey Hall for more details; see descriptive article on page 51.

RYE COUNTRY DAY SCHOOL

Rye Country Day School Summer Session
Corinne Grandolfo, Associate Head of School

Boston Post Road at Cedar Street
Rye, New York 10580
Tel. 914-925-4570
Web Site www.ryecountryday.org
E-mail corinne_grandolfo@ryecountryday.org
Day, 200 Boys and Girls, Grades 5–12

RYE COUNTRY DAY SCHOOL SUMMER SESSION offers a program of remedial and enrichment courses for students seeking to develop new areas of interest, earn course credits, or review subjects in which they need strengthening. The six-week session begins in late June and ends in early August.

Classes, enrolling 4–15 students, meet five mornings a week; normally, a student has one class and one study period, each 45 minutes long, for each course. The curriculum includes review courses in English, Mathematics, French, Latin, Spanish, United States History, Global Studies, Biology, and Chemistry; and enrichment courses in Reading and Study Skills, Summer Reading, Writing Clinic, SAT Review, and Art. The Performing Arts Center offers courses in Jazz Band and Electronic (MIDI) Music. Students wishing to take certain courses for advanced credit double the class time in each subject. A minimum enrollment of four students is necessary for the course to be offered.

Some math and science courses provide preparation for the New York State Regents examinations.

Visit the school's web site at www.ryecountryday.org for more information; see descriptive article on page 165.

THE TAFT SCHOOL

Taft Summer School
Stephen McCabe, Director

Watertown, Connecticut 06795

Tel. 860-945-7961

Web Site www.taftschool.org

E-mail summerschool@taftschool.org

Boarding and Day, 75 Boys, 75 Girls

Entering Grades 7–12

TAFT SUMMER SCHOOL provides an opportunity for motivated students to review course material, prepare for future courses, or enrich their school experiences by taking courses not available to them during the school year. High school students enroll in the Liberal Studies Program, which offers a broad selection in all academic disciplines. The Young Scholars Program, aimed at younger men and women who intend to take on the challenges of rigorous public and private secondary schools, focuses on building essential skills and on instilling students with confidence as they look ahead to Grades 7, 8, and 9, and, later, to the demands of a college preparatory program.

The five-week, on-campus session runs from late June to late July. Classes meet six days a week; afternoons are reserved for athletics. Evening room study is supervised.

Offerings include Literature & Composition, Algebra, Geometry, Precalculus, Biology, Physical Science, French, Spanish, English as a Second Language, U.S. History, Creative Writing, Current Events, Public Speaking, Art History, Acting, Photography, Studio Art, SAT Preparation, SSAT Preparation, and Testing, Reading & Study Skills. Advisors report to parents at session's end with a description of work covered, a progress report, and achievement and effort grades.

Weekend activities are organized on campus, and trips to New York and Boston are planned. Taft's 220-acre campus includes a 53,000-volume library, a computer center, an arts/humanities building, a state-of-the-art modern language lab, and the Cruikshank Athletic Center. The School is located 55 miles from Hartford and 90 miles from New York City.

Contact Taft for more details; see listing on page 53.

THE WINDSOR SCHOOL

Summer School Program 2010
Dr. Philip A. Stewart, Director

Administration Building
136-23 Sanford Avenue
Flushing, New York 11355

Tel. 718-359-8300; Fax 718-359-1876

Web Site www.windsorschool.com

E-mail admin@thewindsorschool.com

Day, Coeducational, Grades 5–12

THE WINDSOR SUMMER SCHOOL PROGRAM 2010 gives students of middle and high school ages the opportunity to preview, enrich, repeat, or advance in academic subjects. Participants may earn credit in as many as four classes.

Students interested in preparing for the PSAT or SAT may enroll in classes that cover the math, verbal, and writing sections of these tests. Students applying to special high schools may take preparation classes for the entrance exams in both English and math. International students may take English as a Second Language and prepare for the Test of English as a Foreign Language (TOEFL).

Many courses are offered in the major disciplines. English selections include English 7–12, Remedial Reading, and Reading Skills. The math selections offered are Algebra, Intermediate Algebra, Geometry, Trigonometry, Precalculus, General Math, Business Math, and Advanced Placement Calculus. Social studies students may enroll in Government, Economics, United States History, Global Studies, or World History. Sciences include Biology, Living Environment, Environmental Science, Chemistry, Physics, and Earth Science. Each of these courses requires laboratory work. Other subjects include Health Education, Physical Education, Spanish, and required art or music. High school students take final examinations and the Regents Examinations at the end of the six-week program.

Classes in all subject areas are also offered at the middle or junior high school level.

Gifted students in Grades 5 and 6 may enroll in enrichment classes in all subjects.

Contact the school for more details; see listing on page 173.

YALE UNIVERSITY

Yale Summer Session
William T. Whobrey, Dean

P.O. Box 208355
New Haven, Connecticut 06520-8355
Tel. 203-432-2430; Fax 203-432-2434
Web Site www.yale.edu/summer
E-mail summer.session@yale.edu

Boarding and Day, 250 Boys and Girls
Rising High School Seniors

YALE SUMMER SESSION offers an array of challenging, college-level academic courses for students who have completed their junior year. Most precollege students enroll in two courses in Session B, from July 5 to August 1, 2010. They choose from Yale College courses in the humanities, social sciences, and sciences taught by regular Yale faculty or other qualified instructors.

Among the areas of study are anthropology, astronomy, archaeology, architecture, art, biology, chemistry, computer science, creative writing, drama, expository writing, film, history, history of art, literature, music, philosophy, political science, psychology, and religious studies.

Students are required to reside on campus in one of the Yale dormitories, called residential colleges, unless they live with their families within commuting distance of the University. The residential atmosphere provides precollege students with an introduction to college life and

the opportunity to interact with other participants from across the country and around the world. Students enjoy a full range of recreational activities, many of which take advantage of Yale's relative proximity to New York, Boston, and the Atlantic coast.

All summer students have the use of Yale's academic and cultural resources including the 4,000,000 volumes housed in Sterling Memorial Library, the Yale University Art Gallery, Yale Center for British Art, and Peabody Museum of Natural History. During the summer, New Haven and Yale offer an abundance of activities including theater, concerts, and other cultural events.

Contact Yale for more details.

Summer Programs Grid

The Grid that follows is a quick reference to the summer opportunities in the Yellow Pages. Programs are arranged alphabetically by state or country, with a page number for locating the descriptive material. Summer programs are categorized in the following areas:

English/Reading

Mathematics

Science/Computers

History/Social Studies

Foreign Language

English as a Second Language

SAT Preparation/Study Skills

Dyslexia/Learning Differences

The Arts

Travel/Cross-Cultural Programs

Service/Outreach Programs

Wilderness/Survival Training

Sports Camps/Clinics

Summary Programs Grid

School	Page	English/Reading	Mathematics	Science/Computers	History/Social Studies	Foreign Language	English as a Second Language	SAT Preparation/Study Skills	Dyslexia/Learning Differences	The Arts	Travel/Cross-Cultural Programs	Service/Outreach Programs	Wilderness/Survival Training	Sports Camps/Clinics
CALIFORNIA														
Ojai Valley School — *Ojai*	S15	X	X	X			X			X				X
CONNECTICUT														
Hopkins School — *New Haven*	S11	X	X	X	X	X	X	X		X				X
King Low Heywood Thomas — *Stamford*	S12	X	X	X		X		X		X				X
Rumsey Hall School — *Washington Depot*	S16	X	X	X			X		X					
The Taft School — *Watertown*	S17	X	X	X	X	X	X	X		X				
Yale University — *New Haven*	S18	X	X	X	X	X	X			X				
DISTRICT OF COLUMBIA														
The Lab School of Washington — *Washington*	S13	X	X	X	X	X		X	X	X				
ILLINOIS														
Northwestern University — *Evanston*	S14	X	X	X	X	X				X				
MASSACHUSETTS														
Belmont Hill School — *Belmont*	S9	X	X	X	X	X	X	X		X				X
Dexter and Southfield Schools — *Brookline*	S9		X											
The Newman School — *Boston*	S13	X	X	X	X									
Northfield Mount Hermon School — *Northfield*	S14	X	X	X	X	X	X	X						
NEW HAMPSHIRE														
Phillips Exeter Academy — *Exeter*	S15	X	X	X	X	X				X				
NEW JERSEY														
The Hun School of Princeton — *Princeton*	S12	X	X	X	X	X	X	X		X				
NEW YORK														
The Gow School — *South Wales*	S10	X	X	X	X	X	X	X	X	X	X			X
Horace Mann School — *Riverdale/New York*	S11	X	X	X	X	X		X		X				X
Rye Country Day School — *Rye*	S16	X	X	X	X	X	X	X		X				
The Windsor School — *Flushing*	S17	X	X	X	X	X	X	X						
VIRGINIA														
Flint Hill School — *Oakton*	S10	X	X	X			X			X	X	X		X

Classification Grid

These pages give the reader an outline of the schools described in our book. The schools are arranged alphabetically by state or country, together with a page number for locating more descriptive material on each school. Use it as a quick reference for categorizing schools in the following areas:

Boarding or Day

Boys, Girls, or Coed

Secondary or Elementary

Junior Boarding

Postgraduate Program

Summer Program

English as a Second Language

Learning Differences Program

Preprofessional Arts Training

Religious Affiliation

Military Program

The Classification Grid is the best place to begin your search for the right school. We find this section to be invaluable in our counseling sessions in the Bunting and Lyon offices.

Classification Grid

Column headers (left to right): Boarding Boys · Boarding Girls · Day Boys · Day Girls · Elementary · Junior Boarding · Secondary · Postgraduate Program · Summer Program · English as a Second Language · Learning Differences Program · Preprofessional Arts Training · Religious Affiliation · Military Program · Page

ALABAMA

Board. Boys	Board. Girls	Day Boys	Day Girls	Elem.	Jr. Board.	Sec.	Postgrad.	Summer	ESL	Learn. Diff.	Preprof. Arts	Relig.	Military	Page	School
		X	X	X				X				E		3	Advent Episcopal School† *Birmingham*
		X	X	X		X		X						5	The Altamont School *Birmingham*
		X	X	X		X		X						5	Bayside Academy† *Daphne*
		X	X	X		X		X						5	Highlands School† *Birmingham*
		X	X	X		X		X						5	Randolph School *Huntsville*
		X	X	X		X		X		X		E		6	St. Paul's Episcopal School† *Mobile*

ARIZONA

Board. Boys	Board. Girls	Day Boys	Day Girls	Elem.	Jr. Board.	Sec.	Postgrad.	Summer	ESL	Learn. Diff.	Preprof. Arts	Relig.	Military	Page	School
		X	X	X		X		X				E		7	All Saints' Episcopal Day School *Phoenix*
		X	X	X		X		X						7	Phoenix Country Day School *Paradise Valley*

ARKANSAS

Board. Boys	Board. Girls	Day Boys	Day Girls	Elem.	Jr. Board.	Sec.	Postgrad.	Summer	ESL	Learn. Diff.	Preprof. Arts	Relig.	Military	Page	School
		X	X	X		X		X				E		7	Episcopal Collegiate School *Little Rock*

CALIFORNIA

Board. Boys	Board. Girls	Day Boys	Day Girls	Elem.	Jr. Board.	Sec.	Postgrad.	Summer	ESL	Learn. Diff.	Preprof. Arts	Relig.	Military	Page	School
		X	X	X				X				J		8	Abraham Joshua Heschel Day School *Northridge*
		X	X	X				X				E		8	All Saints' Episcopal Day School *Carmel*
X	X	X	X			X		X	X					8	The Athenian School *Danville*
		X	X			X				X				8	The Bay School of San Francisco *San Francisco*
		X				X						RC		8	Bellarmine College Preparatory *San Jose*
		X	X	X		X		X						8	The Bentley School *Oakland/Lafayette*
		X	X	X										9	Berkeley Hall School *Los Angeles*
X	X	X	X			X		X	X	X	X			9	Besant Hill School of Happy Valley† *Ojai*
		X	X			X		X				RC		9	Bishop Montgomery High School *Torrance*
		X	X			X		X				E		11	The Bishop's School *La Jolla*
		X	X	X		X		X						11	Brentwood School *Los Angeles*
		X	X	X										11	Calmont School *Calabasas*
		X	X	X		X		X		X		E		12	Campbell Hall *North Hollywood*
		X	X	X										12	The Carey School *San Mateo*
		X						X		X		E		12	Cathedral School for Boys† *San Francisco*
		X	X	X				X						12	The Center for Early Education *West Hollywood*
		X	X	X		X		X						13	Chadwick School *Palos Verdes Peninsula*
		X	X	X				X						13	Chandler School *Pasadena*
		X	X	X				X						13	Chatsworth Hills Academy *Chatsworth*

NOTE: The dagger (†) denotes those schools with learning-differences programs that are cross-referenced in the Learning Differences Grid on page 351. Some elementary school classifications include Grade 9; secondary school classifications usually begin at Grade 9 although some commence at Grade 7. Junior Boarding indicates programs for middle school students and, in some instances, elementary school students. The following abbreviations designate formal religious affiliations or historical association: A—Anglican; B—Baptist; C—United Church of Christ Congregational; CS—Christian Scientist; E—Episcopal; J—Jewish; L—Lutheran; NC—Nondenominational Christian; P—Presbyterian; Q—Quaker; RC—Roman Catholic; O—Other.

Boarding Boys	Boarding Girls	Day Boys	Day Girls	Elementary	Junior Boarding	Secondary	Postgraduate Program	Summer Program	English as a Second Language	Learning Differences Program	Preprofessional Arts Training	Religious Affiliation	Military Program	Page	School
		X	X	X				X						13	Children's Day School *San Francisco*
		X	X	X				X	X					13	Chinese American International School *San Francisco*
		X	X	X				X				CS		14	Clairbourn School *San Gabriel*
		X	X			X		X						14	The College Preparatory School† *Oakland*
		X	X					X				RC		14	Convent of the Sacred Heart Elementary School *San Francisco*
			X			X						RC		14	Convent of the Sacred Heart High School *San Francisco*
			X			X						RC		14	Cornelia Connelly School *Anaheim*
		X	X	X					X					14	The Country School† *Valley Village*
		X	X	X										15	Crane Country Day School *Santa Barbara*
		X				X		X				RC		15	Crespi Carmelite High School *Encino*
		X	X	X				X		X				15	Crestview Preparatory School† *La Cañada*
		X	X	X										15	Curtis School *Los Angeles*
		X	X	X										17	Ecole Bilingue de Berkeley *Berkeley*
		X	X	X				X						17	Foothill Country Day School *Claremont*
		X	X	X		X		X						17	Francis Parker School *San Diego*
		X	X	X				X		X				17	Gateway School† *Santa Cruz*
		X	X	X				X						18	The Gillispie School *La Jolla*
			X	X				X						18	The Hamlin School *San Francisco*
		X	X	X										18	Harbor Day School *Corona del Mar*
		X	X	X		X		X						18	The Harker School *San Jose*
		X	X			X		X						19	Harvard-Westlake School *Los Angeles/North Hollywood*
		X	X	X		X		X						19	Head-Royce School *Oakland*
		X	X	X										19	The John Thomas Dye School *Los Angeles*
		X	X	X		X		X						21	La Jolla Country Day School† *La Jolla*
		X	X	X				X		X				21	Laurence School† *Valley Glen*
		X	X	X				X						21	Live Oak School *San Francisco*
		X	X	X		X		X	X	X				21	Lycée Français La Pérouse† *San Francisco*
		X	X			X								22	Marin Academy *San Rafael*
		X	X	X										22	Marin Country Day School *Corte Madera*
		X	X	X				X						22	Marin Horizon School *Mill Valley*
		X	X	X				X		X				22	Marin Primary & Middle School† *Larkspur*
			X			X								22	Marlborough School *Los Angeles*
			X			X						RC		22	Marymount High School *Los Angeles*
		X	X											23	Marymount of Santa Barbara *Santa Barbara*
		X	X	X				X				RC		23	Mayfield Junior School *Pasadena*
			X			X						RC		23	Mayfield Senior School of the Holy Child *Pasadena*
		X	X			X								23	Menlo School *Atherton*
		X	X			X		X		X				23	Mid-Peninsula High School† *Menlo Park*
		X	X	X						X				23	The Mirman School for Gifted Children† *Los Angeles*
		X	X	X										24	Mount Tamalpais School *Mill Valley*
		X	X	X										26	The Oaks School *Hollywood*
X	X	X	X	X	X	X		X	X	X				26	Ojai Valley School† *Ojai*
		X	X	X				X		X				26	The Pegasus School† *Huntington Beach*
		X	X	X		X		X						26	Polytechnic School *Pasadena*
		X	X	X				X						27	Ring Mountain Day School *Mill Valley/Tiburon*

Boarding Boys	Boarding Girls	Day Boys	Day Girls	Elementary	Junior Boarding	Secondary	Postgraduate Program	Summer Program	English as a Second Language	Learning Differences Program	Preprofessional Arts Training	Religious Affiliation	Military Program	Page	School
		X	X			X	X	X						29	Rolling Hills Preparatory School† *San Pedro*
		X	X	X		X						RC		29	Sacred Heart Schools, Atherton *Atherton*
		X	X			X								29	Sage Hill School *Newport Coast*
		X	X	X		X						E		29	St. James' Episcopal School *Los Angeles*
		X	X	X										29	Saint Mark's School *San Rafael*
		X	X	X		X						NC		29	St. Mary and All Angels School *Aliso Viejo*
		X	X	X								E		30	St. Matthew's Episcopal Day School *San Mateo*
		X	X	X		X						E		30	St. Matthew's Parish School *Pacific Palisades*
		X	X	X	X	X						E		30	St. Paul's Episcopal School *Oakland*
		X	X	X	X	X						E		30	St. Timothy's Preparatory School *Apple Valley*
		X	X	X		X								30	Saklan Valley School *Moraga*
		X	X	X								Q		30	San Francisco Friends School *San Francisco*
		X	X			X		X						31	San Francisco University High School† *San Francisco*
		X	X	X		X								31	The Seven Hills School *Walnut Creek*
		X	X	X		X		X						31	Sierra Canyon School *Chatsworth*
		X	X	X								J		31	Sinai Akiba Academy *Los Angeles*
		X	X			X		X						32	Sonoma Academy *Santa Rosa*
		X		X				X				RC		32	Stuart Hall for Boys *San Francisco*
		X				X		X				RC		32	Stuart Hall High School *San Francisco*
		X		X		X		X						32	Town School for Boys *San Francisco*
		X	X			X		X						32	The Urban School of San Francisco† *San Francisco*
		X	X	X		X		X						33	Viewpoint School† *Calabasas*
		X	X	X		X						NC		33	Village Christian Schools *La Tuna Canyon*
		X	X	X										33	Village School *Pacific Palisades*
		X	X	X		X								35	The Walden School *Pasadena*
			X	X		X		X						35	Westridge School *Pasadena*
		X	X	X		X								35	Westside Neighborhood School *Los Angeles*
		X	X	X		X								35	Wildwood School *Los Angeles*
		X	X	X		X		X						35	Windrush School† *El Cerrito*
		X	X			X								36	Windward School *Los Angeles*
		X	X	X		X								36	Woodland School *Portola Valley*

COLORADO

Boarding Boys	Boarding Girls	Day Boys	Day Girls	Elementary	Junior Boarding	Secondary	Postgraduate Program	Summer Program	English as a Second Language	Learning Differences Program	Preprofessional Arts Training	Religious Affiliation	Military Program	Page	School
		X	X	X		X								37	Alexander Dawson School *Lafayette*
		X	X	X		X		X						37	Colorado Academy *Denver*
		X	X	X		X								37	The Colorado Springs School *Colorado Springs*
X	X	X	X			X								37	The Lowell Whiteman School *Steamboat Springs*
		X	X	X				X				E		37	St. Anne's Episcopal School *Denver*
		X	X	X		X								38	Telluride Mountain School *Telluride*

CONNECTICUT

Boarding Boys	Boarding Girls	Day Boys	Day Girls	Elementary	Junior Boarding	Secondary	Postgraduate Program	Summer Program	English as a Second Language	Learning Differences Program	Preprofessional Arts Training	Religious Affiliation	Military Program	Page	School
			X			X						RC		39	Academy of Our Lady of Mercy, Lauralton Hall *Milford*
		X		X		X		X						39	Brunswick School *Greenwich*
X	X	X	X			X	X	X						39	Choate Rosemary Hall *Wallingford*
		X	X	X										41	Cold Spring School *New Haven*
			X	X		X						RC		41	Convent of the Sacred Heart *Greenwich*

Classification Grid

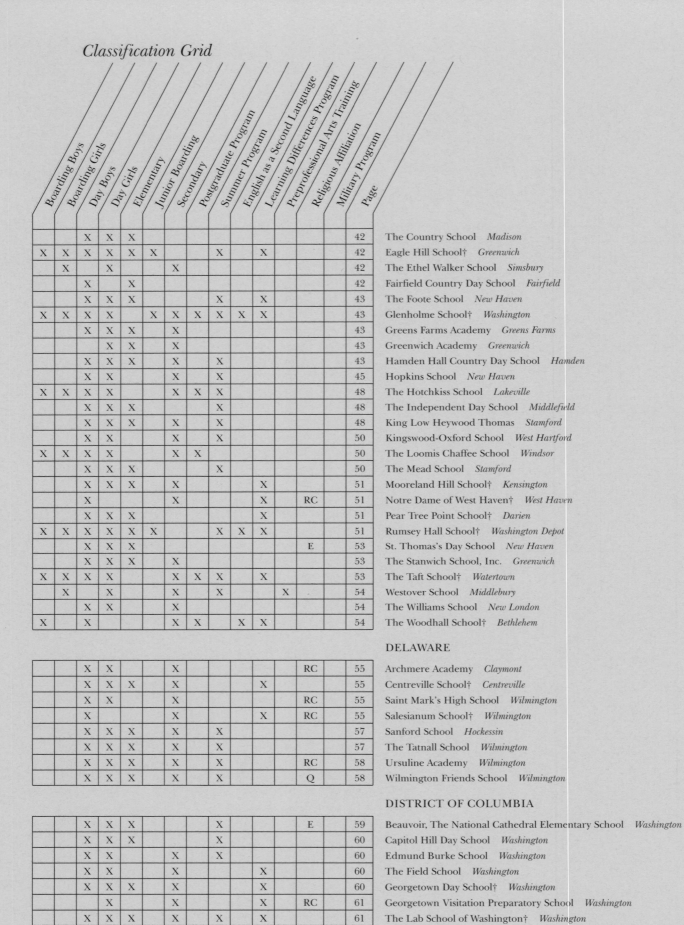

Boarding Boys	Boarding Girls	Day Boys	Day Girls	Elementary	Junior Boarding	Secondary	Postgraduate Program	Summer Program	English as a Second Language	Learning Differences Program	Preprofessional Arts Training	Religious Affiliation	Military Program	Page	
		X	X	X										42	The Country School *Madison*
X	X	X	X	X	X			X		X				42	Eagle Hill School† *Greenwich*
	X		X			X								42	The Ethel Walker School *Simsbury*
		X		X										42	Fairfield Country Day School *Fairfield*
		X	X	X				X		X				43	The Foote School *New Haven*
X	X	X	X		X	X	X	X	X	X				43	Glenholme School† *Washington*
		X	X	X		X								43	Greens Farms Academy *Greens Farms*
		X	X			X								43	Greenwich Academy *Greenwich*
		X	X	X		X		X						43	Hamden Hall Country Day School *Hamden*
		X	X			X		X						45	Hopkins School *New Haven*
X	X	X	X			X	X	X						48	The Hotchkiss School *Lakeville*
		X	X	X				X						48	The Independent Day School *Middlefield*
		X	X	X		X		X						48	King Low Heywood Thomas *Stamford*
		X	X			X		X						50	Kingswood-Oxford School *West Hartford*
X	X	X	X			X	X							50	The Loomis Chaffee School *Windsor*
		X	X	X				X						50	The Mead School *Stamford*
		X	X	X		X				X				51	Mooreland Hill School† *Kensington*
		X				X				X		RC		51	Notre Dame of West Haven† *West Haven*
		X	X	X						X				51	Pear Tree Point School† *Darien*
X	X	X	X	X	X			X	X	X				51	Rumsey Hall School† *Washington Depot*
		X	X	X								E		53	St. Thomas's Day School *New Haven*
		X	X	X		X								53	The Stanwich School, Inc. *Greenwich*
X	X	X	X			X	X	X		X				53	The Taft School† *Watertown*
	X		X			X		X			X			54	Westover School *Middlebury*
		X	X			X								54	The Williams School *New London*
X		X				X	X		X	X				54	The Woodhall School† *Bethlehem*

DELAWARE

Boarding Boys	Boarding Girls	Day Boys	Day Girls	Elementary	Junior Boarding	Secondary	Postgraduate Program	Summer Program	English as a Second Language	Learning Differences Program	Preprofessional Arts Training	Religious Affiliation	Military Program	Page	
		X	X			X						RC		55	Archmere Academy *Claymont*
		X	X	X		X				X				55	Centreville School† *Centreville*
		X	X			X						RC		55	Saint Mark's High School *Wilmington*
		X				X				X		RC		55	Salesianum School† *Wilmington*
		X	X	X		X		X						57	Sanford School *Hockessin*
		X	X	X		X		X						57	The Tatnall School *Wilmington*
		X	X	X		X		X				RC		58	Ursuline Academy *Wilmington*
		X	X	X		X		X				Q		58	Wilmington Friends School *Wilmington*

DISTRICT OF COLUMBIA

Boarding Boys	Boarding Girls	Day Boys	Day Girls	Elementary	Junior Boarding	Secondary	Postgraduate Program	Summer Program	English as a Second Language	Learning Differences Program	Preprofessional Arts Training	Religious Affiliation	Military Program	Page	
		X	X	X				X				E		59	Beauvoir, The National Cathedral Elementary School *Washington*
		X	X	X		X								60	Capitol Hill Day School *Washington*
		X	X			X		X						60	Edmund Burke School *Washington*
		X	X			X		X						60	The Field School *Washington*
		X	X	X		X		X						60	Georgetown Day School† *Washington*
			X			X		X				RC		61	Georgetown Visitation Preparatory School *Washington*
		X	X	X		X		X		X				61	The Lab School of Washington† *Washington*

Boarding Boys	Boarding Girls	Day Boys	Day Girls	Elementary	Junior Boarding	Secondary	Postgraduate Program	Summer Program	English as a Second Language	Learning Differences Program	Preprofessional Arts Training	Religious Affiliation	Military Program	Page	School
		X	X	X				X						61	Lowell School *Washington*
		X	X	X		X		X						61	Maret School *Washington*
			X	X		X						E		61	National Cathedral School *Washington*
X		X		X		X						E		61	St. Albans School *Washington*
		X	X	X				X				E		62	St. Patrick's Episcopal Day School *Washington*

FLORIDA

Boarding Boys	Boarding Girls	Day Boys	Day Girls	Elementary	Junior Boarding	Secondary	Postgraduate Program	Summer Program	English as a Second Language	Learning Differences Program	Preprofessional Arts Training	Religious Affiliation	Military Program	Page	School
		X	X	X		X		X				RC		63	Academy of the Holy Names *Tampa*
		X	X	X		X		X	X	X		E		63	All Saints' Academy† *Winter Haven*
		X	X	X		X		X						63	The Benjamin School *North Palm Beach/Palm Beach Gardens*
		X	X	X		X		X				E		63	Berkeley Preparatory School *Tampa*
		X	X	X		X		X						65	The Canterbury School *Fort Myers*
			X	X		X						RC		66	Carrollton School of the Sacred Heart *Miami*
		X	X			X		X				E		66	Episcopal High School of Jacksonville *Jacksonville*
		X	X	X		X				X				66	Independent Day School—Corbett Campus *Tampa*
		X	X	X		X		X						66	Maclay School *Tallahassee*
		X	X	X		X					X			66	Miami Country Day School† *Miami*
		X	X	X		X		X						67	Oak Hall School *Gainesville*
		X	X	X		X								67	The Out-of-Door Academy *Sarasota*
		X	X	X		X				X				67	PACE-Brantley Hall School† *Longwood*
		X	X	X										67	Palm Beach Day Academy *Palm Beach/West Palm Beach*
		X	X	X		X		X						67	Pine Crest School† *Boca Raton/Fort Lauderdale*
		X	X			X		X						68	Ransom Everglades School *Coconut Grove*
		X	X	X				X				P		68	Riverside Presbyterian Day School† *Jacksonville*
		X	X	X		X		X		X		E		68	Saint Edward's School† *Vero Beach*
		X	X	X								E		70	St. John's Episcopal Parish Day School *Tampa*
		X	X	X								E		71	Saint Joseph's Episcopal School *Boynton Beach*
		X	X	X				X		X		E		71	St. Mark's Episcopal Day School† *Jacksonville*
		X	X	X								E		71	St. Mark's Episcopal School *Fort Lauderdale*
		X	X	X							X	E		71	St. Mary's Episcopal Day School† *Tampa*
		X	X	X				X				E		71	Saint Paul's School *Clearwater*
		X	X	X								E		72	St. Stephen's Episcopal Day School *Miami*
		X	X	X		X		X				E		72	Saint Stephen's Episcopal School *Bradenton*
		X	X	X		X								72	Seacrest Country Day School *Naples*
		X	X			X		X				E		74	Trinity Preparatory School† *Winter Park*

GEORGIA

Boarding Boys	Boarding Girls	Day Boys	Day Girls	Elementary	Junior Boarding	Secondary	Postgraduate Program	Summer Program	English as a Second Language	Learning Differences Program	Preprofessional Arts Training	Religious Affiliation	Military Program	Page	School
		X	X	X		X								75	Atlanta International School *Atlanta*
X		X	X	X		X	X	X	X	X				75	Brandon Hall School *Atlanta*
		X	X	X		X								75	Brookstone School *Columbus*
		X	X	X										75	Cliff Valley School *Atlanta*
		X	X	X		X		X						75	The Galloway School *Atlanta*
		X	X	X		X								76	The Heritage School *Newnan*
		X	X	X		X		X						76	The Lovett School *Atlanta*
		X	X			X						RC		76	Marist School *Atlanta*

Classification Grid

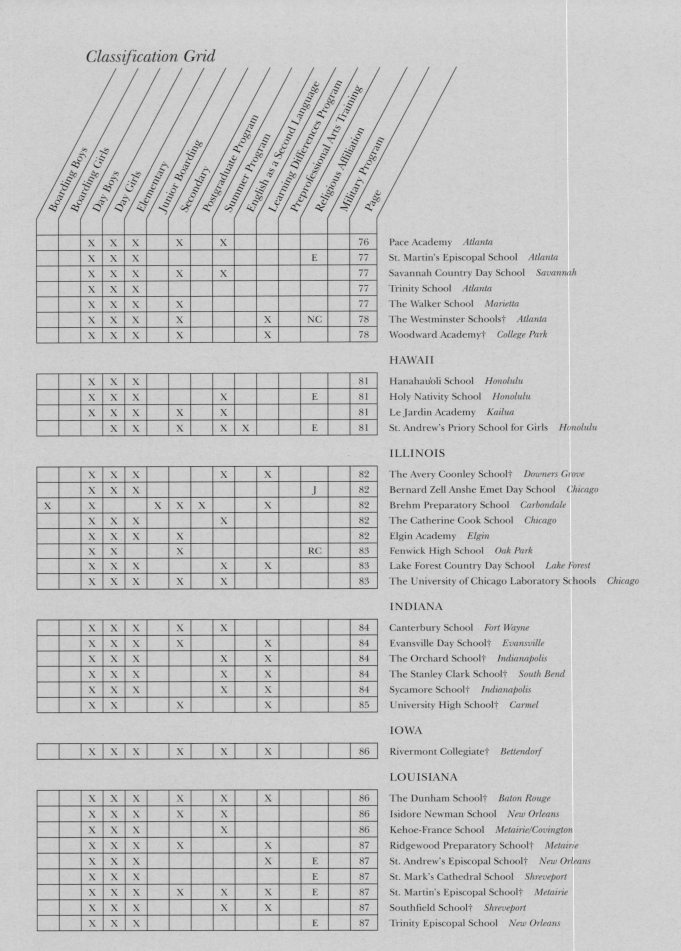

Boarding Boys	Boarding Girls	Day Boys	Day Girls	Elementary	Junior Boarding	Secondary	Postgraduate Program	Summer Program	English as a Second Language	Learning Differences Program	Preprofessional Arts Training	Religious Affiliation	Military Program	Page	School
		X	X	X		X		X						76	Pace Academy *Atlanta*
		X	X	X								E		77	St. Martin's Episcopal School *Atlanta*
		X	X	X		X		X						77	Savannah Country Day School *Savannah*
		X	X	X										77	Trinity School *Atlanta*
		X	X	X		X								77	The Walker School *Marietta*
		X	X	X		X				X		NC		78	The Westminster Schools† *Atlanta*
		X	X	X		X				X				78	Woodward Academy† *College Park*

HAWAII

Boarding Boys	Boarding Girls	Day Boys	Day Girls	Elementary	Junior Boarding	Secondary	Postgraduate Program	Summer Program	English as a Second Language	Learning Differences Program	Preprofessional Arts Training	Religious Affiliation	Military Program	Page	School
		X	X	X										81	Hanahau'oli School *Honolulu*
		X	X	X				X				E		81	Holy Nativity School *Honolulu*
		X	X	X		X		X						81	Le Jardin Academy *Kailua*
			X	X		X		X	X			E		81	St. Andrew's Priory School for Girls *Honolulu*

ILLINOIS

Boarding Boys	Boarding Girls	Day Boys	Day Girls	Elementary	Junior Boarding	Secondary	Postgraduate Program	Summer Program	English as a Second Language	Learning Differences Program	Preprofessional Arts Training	Religious Affiliation	Military Program	Page	School
		X	X	X				X		X				82	The Avery Coonley School† *Downers Grove*
		X	X	X								J		82	Bernard Zell Anshe Emet Day School *Chicago*
X	X			X	X	X				X				82	Brehm Preparatory School *Carbondale*
		X	X	X				X						82	The Catherine Cook School *Chicago*
		X	X	X		X								82	Elgin Academy *Elgin*
		X	X			X						RC		83	Fenwick High School *Oak Park*
		X	X	X				X		X				83	Lake Forest Country Day School *Lake Forest*
		X	X	X		X		X						83	The University of Chicago Laboratory Schools *Chicago*

INDIANA

Boarding Boys	Boarding Girls	Day Boys	Day Girls	Elementary	Junior Boarding	Secondary	Postgraduate Program	Summer Program	English as a Second Language	Learning Differences Program	Preprofessional Arts Training	Religious Affiliation	Military Program	Page	School
		X	X	X		X		X						84	Canterbury School *Fort Wayne*
		X	X	X		X				X				84	Evansville Day School† *Evansville*
		X	X	X				X		X				84	The Orchard School† *Indianapolis*
		X	X	X				X		X				84	The Stanley Clark School† *South Bend*
		X	X	X				X		X				84	Sycamore School† *Indianapolis*
		X	X			X				X				85	University High School† *Carmel*

IOWA

Boarding Boys	Boarding Girls	Day Boys	Day Girls	Elementary	Junior Boarding	Secondary	Postgraduate Program	Summer Program	English as a Second Language	Learning Differences Program	Preprofessional Arts Training	Religious Affiliation	Military Program	Page	School
		X	X	X		X		X		X				86	Rivermont Collegiate† *Bettendorf*

LOUISIANA

Boarding Boys	Boarding Girls	Day Boys	Day Girls	Elementary	Junior Boarding	Secondary	Postgraduate Program	Summer Program	English as a Second Language	Learning Differences Program	Preprofessional Arts Training	Religious Affiliation	Military Program	Page	School
		X	X	X		X		X		X				86	The Dunham School† *Baton Rouge*
		X	X	X		X		X						86	Isidore Newman School *New Orleans*
		X	X	X				X						86	Kehoe-France School *Metairie/Covington*
		X	X	X		X				X				87	Ridgewood Preparatory School† *Metairie*
		X	X	X						X		E		87	St. Andrew's Episcopal School† *New Orleans*
		X	X	X								E		87	St. Mark's Cathedral School *Shreveport*
		X	X	X		X		X		X		E		87	St. Martin's Episcopal School† *Metairie*
		X	X	X				X		X				87	Southfield School† *Shreveport*
		X	X	X								E		87	Trinity Episcopal School *New Orleans*

Boarding Boys	Boarding Girls	Day Boys	Day Girls	Elementary	Junior Boarding	Secondary	Postgraduate Program	Summer Program	English as a Second Language	Learning Differences Program	Preprofessional Arts Training	Religious Affiliation	Military Program	Page	
															MAINE
X	X	X	X			X		X	X					88	Foxcroft Academy *Dover-Foxcroft*
X	X	X	X			X	X	X	X					88	Hebron Academy† *Hebron*
X	X	X	X			X		X	X	X				88	Washington Academy† *East Machias*
															MARYLAND
		X				X		X				RC		89	The Academy of the Holy Cross *Kensington*
		X	X	X		X		X						89	Barrie School *Silver Spring*
		X	X	X		X						J		89	Charles E. Smith Jewish Day School *Rockville*
		X				X						RC		89	Connelly School of the Holy Child *Potomac*
X		X				X		X	X			RC		89	Georgetown Preparatory School *North Bethesda*
		X	X	X										90	Gibson Island Country School *Pasadena*
		X		X		X								90	Gilman School *Baltimore*
		X	X	X		X		X		X				90	Glenelg Country School† *Ellicott City*
		X	X	X				X						91	Green Acres School *Rockville*
		X	X			X		X		X				91	Gunston Day School† *Centreville*
		X	X	X										91	Harford Day School *Bel Air*
		X	X	X		X		X		X				91	The Ivymount School† *Rockville*
		X	X	X		X		X						91	The Key School *Annapolis*
		X		X		X								91	Landon School *Bethesda*
		X				X		X				RC		92	Loyola Blakefield *Towson*
		X	X	X						X				92	The Maddux School *Rockville*
		X				X						RC		92	Maryvale Preparatory School *Brooklandville*
X	X	X	X	X		X								92	McDonogh School *Owings Mills*
		X	X	X				X						92	The Montessori School *Lutherville*
		X	X			X				X				93	The Nora School† *Silver Spring*
		X	X	X				X		X				93	Norwood School† *Bethesda*
		X	X	X										93	The Primary Day School *Bethesda*
		X	X			X		X				E		93	Queen Anne School *Upper Marlboro*
		X	X	X						X				93	Radcliffe Creek School† *Chestertown*
		X	X	X		X		X						94	Roland Park Country School *Baltimore*
		X	X	X		X						E		94	St. Andrew's Episcopal School *Potomac*
X	X	X	X			X				X		E		96	Saint James School† *St. James*
		X	X	X								E		96	St. John's Parish Day School *Ellicott City*
		X	X			X						E		96	St. Paul's School for Girls *Brooklandville*
	X		X			X		X	X			E		97	St. Timothy's School *Stevenson*
		X	X			X		X	X					98	Severn School *Severna Park*
		X	X	X								RC		99	Stone Ridge School of the Sacred Heart *Bethesda*
		X	X	X		X				X				99	Washington Waldorf School *Bethesda*
		X	X	X								RC		99	The Woods Academy *Bethesda*
															MASSACHUSETTS
		X	X			X						RC		100	Austin Preparatory School *Reading*
		X	X	X		X								100	Bancroft School *Worcester*
		X	X	X				X						100	Belmont Day School *Belmont*
X		X				X		X						100	Belmont Hill School *Belmont*

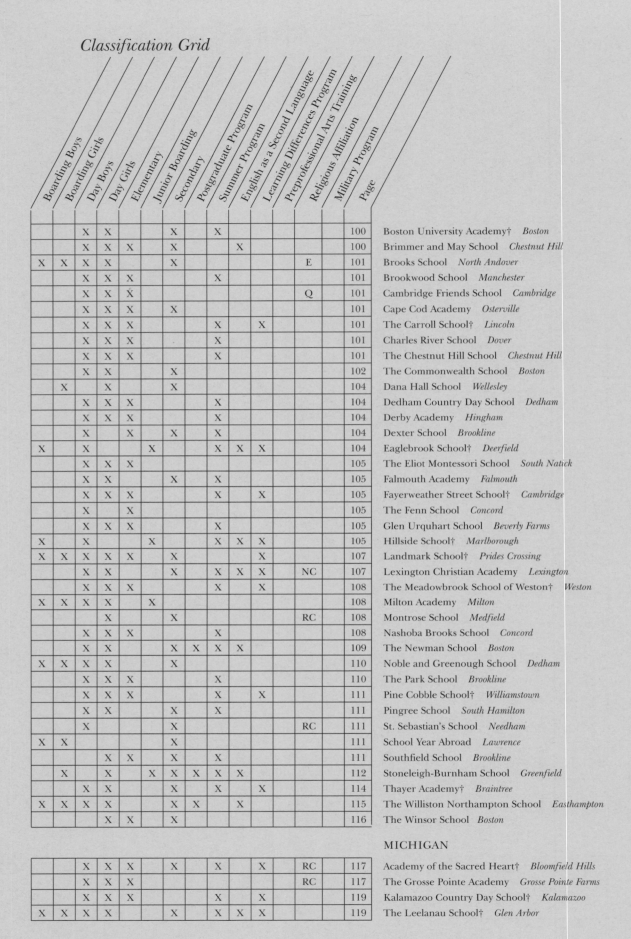

Boarding Boys	Boarding Girls	Day Boys	Day Girls	Elementary	Junior Boarding	Secondary	Postgraduate Program	Summer Program	English as a Second Language	Learning Differences Program	Preprofessional Arts Training	Religious Affiliation	Military Program	Page	
		X	X			X		X						100	Boston University Academy† *Boston*
		X	X	X		X			X					100	Brimmer and May School *Chestnut Hill*
X	X	X	X			X						E		101	Brooks School *North Andover*
		X	X	X				X						101	Brookwood School *Manchester*
		X	X	X								Q		101	Cambridge Friends School *Cambridge*
		X	X	X		X								101	Cape Cod Academy *Osterville*
		X	X	X				X		X				101	The Carroll School† *Lincoln*
		X	X	X				X						101	Charles River School *Dover*
		X	X	X				X						101	The Chestnut Hill School *Chestnut Hill*
		X	X			X								102	The Commonwealth School *Boston*
	X		X			X								104	Dana Hall School *Wellesley*
		X	X	X				X						104	Dedham Country Day School *Dedham*
		X	X	X				X						104	Derby Academy *Hingham*
		X		X	X			X						104	Dexter School *Brookline*
X		X			X			X	X	X				104	Eaglebrook School† *Deerfield*
		X	X	X										105	The Eliot Montessori School *South Natick*
		X	X			X		X						105	Falmouth Academy *Falmouth*
		X	X	X				X		X				105	Fayerweather Street School† *Cambridge*
		X		X										105	The Fenn School *Concord*
		X	X	X				X						105	Glen Urquhart School *Beverly Farms*
X		X			X			X	X	X				105	Hillside School† *Marlborough*
X	X	X	X	X		X				X				107	Landmark School† *Prides Crossing*
		X	X			X		X	X	X		NC		107	Lexington Christian Academy *Lexington*
		X	X	X				X	X					108	The Meadowbrook School of Weston† *Weston*
X	X	X	X		X									108	Milton Academy *Milton*
			X			X						RC		108	Montrose School *Medfield*
		X	X	X				X						108	Nashoba Brooks School *Concord*
		X	X			X	X	X	X					109	The Newman School *Boston*
X	X	X	X			X								110	Noble and Greenough School *Dedham*
		X	X	X				X						110	The Park School *Brookline*
		X	X	X				X		X				111	Pine Cobble School† *Williamstown*
		X	X			X		X						111	Pingree School *South Hamilton*
		X				X						RC		111	St. Sebastian's School *Needham*
X	X					X								111	School Year Abroad *Lawrence*
		X	X			X		X						111	Southfield School *Brookline*
	X		X		X	X	X	X	X					112	Stoneleigh-Burnham School *Greenfield*
		X	X			X		X		X				114	Thayer Academy† *Braintree*
X	X	X	X			X	X		X					115	The Williston Northampton School *Easthampton*
		X	X			X								116	The Winsor School *Boston*

MICHIGAN

Boarding Boys	Boarding Girls	Day Boys	Day Girls	Elementary	Junior Boarding	Secondary	Postgraduate Program	Summer Program	English as a Second Language	Learning Differences Program	Preprofessional Arts Training	Religious Affiliation	Military Program	Page	
		X	X	X		X		X		X		RC		117	Academy of the Sacred Heart† *Bloomfield Hills*
		X	X	X								RC		117	The Grosse Pointe Academy *Grosse Pointe Farms*
		X	X	X				X		X				119	Kalamazoo Country Day School† *Kalamazoo*
X	X	X	X			X		X	X	X				119	The Leelanau School† *Glen Arbor*

Boarding Boys	Boarding Girls	Day Boys	Day Girls	Elementary	Junior Boarding	Secondary	Postgraduate Program	Summer Program	English as a Second Language	Learning Differences Program	Preprofessional Arts Training	Religious Affiliation	Military Program	Page	School
		X	X	X		X		X				RC		119	Notre Dame Preparatory School and Marist Academy *Pontiac*
		X	X	X		X		X		X				121	The Roeper School† *Bloomfield Hills*
		X	X	X		X		X		X				122	University Liggett School† *Grosse Pointe Woods*
															MINNESOTA
		X	X	X		X		X						123	The Blake School *Minneapolis/Hopkins/Wayzata*
		X	X	X		X		X				E		123	Breck School *Minneapolis*
		X	X	X		X		X				RC		123	Convent of the Visitation School *Mendota Heights*
															MISSISSIPPI
		X	X	X		X		X						124	Jackson Academy *Jackson*
		X	X			X								126	Jackson Preparatory School *Jackson*
															MISSOURI
		X	X	X										127	Andrews Academy—Lake Saint Louis *Lake Saint Louis*
		X	X	X				X	X	X				127	Andrews Academy† *St. Louis*
		X	X	X		X								127	The Barstow School *Kansas City*
		X	X	X				X						127	The College School *Webster Groves*
		X	X	X				X		X				127	Community School† *St. Louis*
		X	X	X				X		X				128	Forsyth School† *St. Louis*
		X	X			X								128	John Burroughs School *St. Louis*
		X	X	X		X		X						128	Mary Institute and Saint Louis Country Day School† *St. Louis*
		X	X	X		X		X						128	The Pembroke Hill School *Kansas City*
		X	X	X										128	Rohan Woods School *St. Louis*
		X	X	X										129	Rossman School *St. Louis*
		X	X	X				X		X				129	The Wilson School† *St. Louis*
															NEVADA
		X	X	X		X		X						130	The Meadows School *Las Vegas*
		X	X	X		X								130	Sage Ridge School *Reno*
															NEW HAMPSHIRE
X				X	X	X				X				131	Hampshire Country School† *Rindge*
X	X	X	X			X	X	X	X					133	Kimball Union Academy† *Meriden*
		X	X	X				X						133	Seacoast Academy *Hampton Falls*
															NEW JERSEY
		X	X	X		X		X						134	Collegiate School† *Passaic Park*
		X	X	X		X		X		X				134	The Craig School† *Mountain Lakes*
		X	X	X				X	X					134	The Elisabeth Morrow School *Englewood*
		X	X	X		X		X	X					134	The Hudson School† *Hoboken*
			X	X		X		X						134	Kent Place School *Summit*
		X	X	X		X						Q		134	Moorestown Friends School *Moorestown*
		X	X			X								135	Morristown-Beard School *Morristown*
			X			X						RC		135	Mount Saint Mary Academy *Watchung*
		X	X			X								135	Newark Academy *Livingston*

Classification Grid

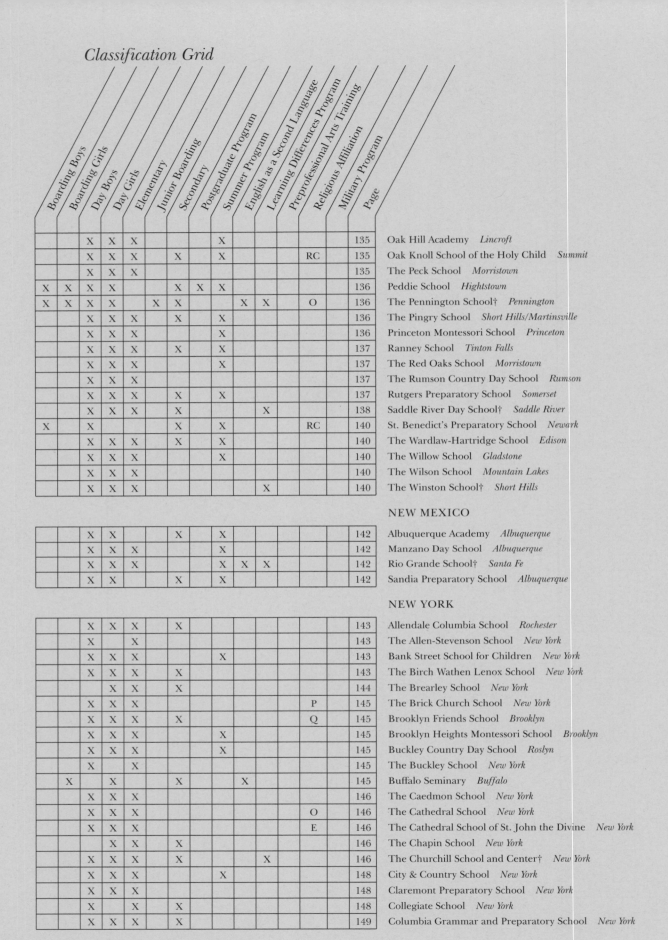

Boarding Boys	Boarding Girls	Day Boys	Day Girls	Elementary	Junior Boarding	Secondary	Postgraduate Program	Summer Program	English as a Second Language	Learning Differences Program	Preprofessional Arts Training	Religious Affiliation	Military Program	Page	School
		X	X	X				X						135	Oak Hill Academy *Lincroft*
		X	X	X		X		X				RC		135	Oak Knoll School of the Holy Child *Summit*
		X	X	X										135	The Peck School *Morristown*
X	X	X	X			X	X	X						136	Peddie School *Hightstown*
X	X	X	X		X	X			X	X		O		136	The Pennington School† *Pennington*
		X	X	X		X		X						136	The Pingry School *Short Hills/Martinsville*
		X	X	X				X						136	Princeton Montessori School *Princeton*
		X	X	X		X		X						137	Ranney School *Tinton Falls*
		X	X	X				X						137	The Red Oaks School *Morristown*
		X	X	X										137	The Rumson Country Day School *Rumson*
		X	X	X		X		X						137	Rutgers Preparatory School *Somerset*
		X	X	X		X					X			138	Saddle River Day School† *Saddle River*
X		X				X		X				RC		140	St. Benedict's Preparatory School *Newark*
		X	X	X		X		X						140	The Wardlaw-Hartridge School *Edison*
		X	X	X				X						140	The Willow School *Gladstone*
		X	X	X										140	The Wilson School *Mountain Lakes*
		X	X	X						X				140	The Winston School† *Short Hills*

NEW MEXICO

Boarding Boys	Boarding Girls	Day Boys	Day Girls	Elementary	Junior Boarding	Secondary	Postgraduate Program	Summer Program	English as a Second Language	Learning Differences Program	Preprofessional Arts Training	Religious Affiliation	Military Program	Page	School
		X	X			X		X						142	Albuquerque Academy *Albuquerque*
		X	X	X				X						142	Manzano Day School *Albuquerque*
		X	X	X				X	X	X				142	Rio Grande School† *Santa Fe*
		X	X			X		X						142	Sandia Preparatory School *Albuquerque*

NEW YORK

Boarding Boys	Boarding Girls	Day Boys	Day Girls	Elementary	Junior Boarding	Secondary	Postgraduate Program	Summer Program	English as a Second Language	Learning Differences Program	Preprofessional Arts Training	Religious Affiliation	Military Program	Page	School
		X	X	X		X								143	Allendale Columbia School *Rochester*
		X		X										143	The Allen-Stevenson School *New York*
		X	X	X				X						143	Bank Street School for Children *New York*
		X	X	X		X								143	The Birch Wathen Lenox School *New York*
			X	X		X								144	The Brearley School *New York*
		X	X	X								P		145	The Brick Church School *New York*
		X	X	X		X						Q		145	Brooklyn Friends School *Brooklyn*
		X	X	X				X						145	Brooklyn Heights Montessori School *Brooklyn*
		X	X	X				X						145	Buckley Country Day School *Roslyn*
		X		X										145	The Buckley School *New York*
	X		X			X		X						145	Buffalo Seminary *Buffalo*
		X	X	X										146	The Caedmon School *New York*
		X	X	X								O		146	The Cathedral School *New York*
		X	X	X								E		146	The Cathedral School of St. John the Divine *New York*
		X	X											146	The Chapin School *New York*
		X	X	X		X				X				146	The Churchill School and Center† *New York*
		X	X	X				X						148	City & Country School *New York*
		X	X	X										148	Claremont Preparatory School *New York*
		X		X		X								148	Collegiate School *New York*
		X	X	X		X								149	Columbia Grammar and Preparatory School *New York*

Boarding Boys	Boarding Girls	Day Boys	Day Girls	Elementary	Junior Boarding	Secondary	Postgraduate Program	Summer Program	English as a Second Language	Learning Differences Program	Preprofessional Arts Training	Religious Affiliation	Military Program	Page	School
		X	X			X						RC		150	Convent of the Sacred Heart *New York*
		X	X	X				X						151	Corlears School *New York*
		X	X	X		X								151	The Dalton School *New York*
		X	X	X		X								151	Doane Stuart School *Rensselaer*
		X	X	X										151	Dutchess Day School *Millbrook*
		X	X	X		X		X	X					151	The Dwight School† *New York*
		X	X	X				X						151	East Woods School *Oyster Bay*
		X	X	X				X		X				152	The Elmwood Franklin School† *Buffalo*
		X	X	X		X		X						152	Ethical Culture Fieldston School *New York/Bronx*
		X	X	X		X		X				Q		152	Friends Seminary *New York*
X						X	X	X		X				152	The Gow School† *South Wales*
		X	X	X				X				E		154	Grace Day School *Massapequa*
		X	X	X										154	The Green Vale School *Old Brookville*
X	X	X	X	X		X								154	Hackley School *Tarrytown*
		X	X	X				X						156	Harbor Country Day School *St. James*
		X	X	X		X		X						157	The Harley School *Rochester*
X	X	X	X					X						157	The Harvey School *Katonah*
		X	X	X		X		X						157	Horace Mann School *Riverdale/New York*
X	X	X	X	X	X	X	X	X		X				157	The Kildonan School† *Amenia*
X	X	X	X		X	X			X	X				157	The Knox School† *St. James*
		X	X			X						RC		158	Loyola School *New York*
			X			X				X		RC		158	The Mary Louis Academy† *Jamaica Estates*
		X	X	X						X				158	Mary McDowell Center for Learning† *Brooklyn*
			X	X		X						RC		158	Marymount School *New York*
		X	X	X				X				E		159	The Melrose School *Brewster*
X	X	X	X			X		X						159	Millbrook School *Millbrook*
		X	X	X				X						159	Mizzentop Day School *Pawling*
		X	X	X		X		X						159	Nichols School *Buffalo*
			X	X		X								159	The Nightingale-Bamford School *New York*
X	X	X	X			X			X	X		Q		160	Oakwood Friends School† *Poughkeepsie*
		X	X	X		X								162	The Packer Collegiate Institute *Brooklyn Heights*
		X	X	X		X		X	X					162	The Park School of Buffalo *Snyder*
		X	X	X		X		X						162	Poly Prep Country Day School *Brooklyn*
		X	X	X		X		X						162	Poughkeepsie Day School *Poughkeepsie*
		X	X	X		X								162	Riverdale Country School *Riverdale*
		X	X			X	X	X		X				164	Robert Louis Stevenson School† *New York*
		X	X	X		X		X						165	Rudolf Steiner School *New York*
		X	X	X		X		X						165	Rye Country Day School *Rye*
		X	X	X		X		X						167	Saint Ann's School *Brooklyn Heights*
		X		X										167	St. Bernard's School *New York*
		X		X								RC		167	Saint David's School *New York*
		X	X			X					X	RC	X	168	Saint Francis Preparatory School *Fresh Meadows*
		X		X				X				RC		168	Saint Gregory's School *Loudonville*
		X	X	X				X				E		168	St. Hilda's & St. Hugh's School *New York*
		X	X		X	X	X							168	Soundview Preparatory School *Yorktown Heights*
		X	X	X		X		X						168	Staten Island Academy *Staten Island*

279

Classification Grid

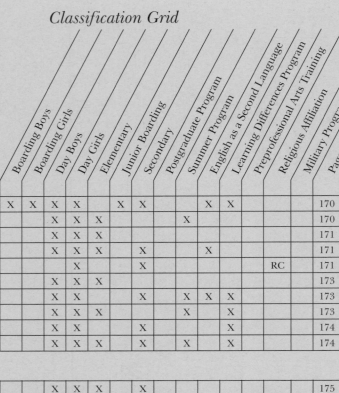

Boarding Boys	Boarding Girls	Day Boys	Day Girls	Elementary	Junior Boarding	Secondary	Postgraduate Program	Summer Program	English as a Second Language	Learning Differences Program	Preprofessional Arts Training	Religious Affiliation	Military Program	Page	School
X	X	X	X		X	X			X	X				170	The Storm King School† *Cornwall-on-Hudson*
		X	X	X				X						170	The Town School *New York*
		X	X	X										171	Tuxedo Park School *Tuxedo Park*
		X	X	X		X			X					171	United Nations International School *New York/Jamaica Estates*
			X			X						RC		171	The Ursuline School *New Rochelle*
		X	X	X										173	Village Community School *New York*
		X	X			X		X	X	X				173	The Windsor School† *Flushing*
		X	X	X				X		X				173	Windward School† *White Plains*
		X	X			X				X				174	The Winston Preparatory School† *New York*
		X	X	X		X		X		X				174	York Preparatory School† *New York*

NORTH CAROLINA

Boarding Boys	Boarding Girls	Day Boys	Day Girls	Elementary	Junior Boarding	Secondary	Postgraduate Program	Summer Program	English as a Second Language	Learning Differences Program	Preprofessional Arts Training	Religious Affiliation	Military Program	Page	School
		X	X	X		X								175	Cannon School *Concord*
		X	X	X		X		X						175	Cape Fear Academy *Wilmington*
		X	X	X		X		X		X				175	Carolina Day School† *Asheville*
		X	X	X		X		X	X					175	Charlotte Country Day School *Charlotte*
		X	X	X		X		X						175	Charlotte Latin School *Charlotte*
X		X				X		X				E		176	Christ School *Asheville*
		X	X	X		X		X		X				176	Forsyth Country Day School† *Lewisville*
		X	X	X		X		X	X					176	Greensboro Day School *Greensboro*
		X	X	X		X		X		X				176	Guilford Day School† *Greensboro*
		X	X	X		X								176	Kerr-Vance Academy *Henderson*
		X	X	X		X		X				Q		177	New Garden Friends School *Greensboro*
		X	X	X		X					X			177	The Oakwood School *Greenville*
		X	X	X		X		X		X				177	The O'Neal School† *Southern Pines*
		X	X	X		X		X		X				177	Providence Day School† *Charlotte*
		X	X	X		X		X						177	Ravenscroft School *Raleigh*
	X		X			X		X		X		E		178	Saint Mary's School† *Raleigh*
		X	X	X				X				E		178	St. Timothy's School† *Raleigh*
		X	X	X		X		X						178	Summit School† *Winston-Salem*
		X	X	X		X								178	Triangle Day School *Durham*

OHIO

Boarding Boys	Boarding Girls	Day Boys	Day Girls	Elementary	Junior Boarding	Secondary	Postgraduate Program	Summer Program	English as a Second Language	Learning Differences Program	Preprofessional Arts Training	Religious Affiliation	Military Program	Page	School
		X	X	X										179	Canton Country Day School *Canton*
		X	X	X		X		X						179	The Columbus Academy *Gahanna*
X	X	X	X	X	X	X						RC		179	Gilmour Academy *Gates Mills*
			X	X		X		X		X				179	Hathaway Brown School *Shaker Heights*
		X	X	X		X		X		X				179	Lake Ridge Academy† *North Ridgeville*
		X	X	X		X		X		X				179	The Miami Valley School† *Dayton*
		X	X	X		X		X						180	The Seven Hills Schools *Cincinnati*
		X	X	X		X		X				RC		180	The Summit Country Day School† *Cincinnati*
X	X	X	X			X	X	X						180	Western Reserve Academy† *Hudson*

280

OKLAHOMA

Boarding Boys	Boarding Girls	Day Boys	Day Girls	Elementary	Junior Boarding	Secondary	Postgraduate Program	Summer Program	English as a Second Language	Learning Differences Program	Preprofessional Arts Training	Religious Affiliation	Military Program	Page	School
		X	X	X		X						E		182	Casady School *Oklahoma City*
		X	X	X		X		X		X		E		182	Holland Hall† *Tulsa*
		X	X	X		X		X		X				183	Riverfield Country Day School† *Tulsa*

PENNSYLVANIA

Boarding Boys	Boarding Girls	Day Boys	Day Girls	Elementary	Junior Boarding	Secondary	Postgraduate Program	Summer Program	English as a Second Language	Learning Differences Program	Preprofessional Arts Training	Religious Affiliation	Military Program	Page	School
		X	X	X		X		X				Q		184	Abington Friends School *Jenkintown*
		X		X		X								184	Chestnut Hill Academy *Philadelphia*
		X	X			X				X				184	The Crefeld School† *Philadelphia*
		X	X			X		X		X		Q		184	Delaware Valley Friends School† *Paoli*
		X	X	X		X		X				E		184	The Episcopal Academy *Newtown Square*
		X	X	X		X		X				Q		185	Friends' Central School *Wynnewood*
		X	X	X								Q		185	Friends School Haverford *Haverford*
		X	X	X		X		X						185	Germantown Academy *Fort Washington*
	X				X	X	X	X	X	X	X			185	Grier School† *Tyrone*
		X		X		X								185	The Haverford School *Haverford*
X	X	X	X			X	X							186	The Hill School *Pottstown*
		X	X	X						X				187	The Hillside School† *Macungie*
		X				X		X				RC		188	Holy Ghost Preparatory School *Bensalem*
		X	X			X						J		188	Jack M. Barrack Hebrew Academy *Bryn Mawr*
		X	X	X		X		X		X				188	The Janus School *Mount Joy*
		X				X		X		X		RC		188	La Salle College High School *Wyndmoor*
		X	X	X										189	Meadowbrook School *Meadowbrook*
		X	X			X		X						189	MMI Preparatory School *Freeland*
		X	X	X										189	Montgomery School *Chester Springs*
		X	X	X		X		X				O		189	Moravian Academy *Bethlehem*
		X	X	X								Q		191	Newtown Friends School *Newtown*
		X	X			X						RC		191	Rosemont School of the Holy Child *Rosemont*
			X			X						O		191	Saint Basil Academy *Jenkintown*
		X				X		X				RC		192	St. Joseph's Preparatory School *Philadelphia*
		X	X	X				X						192	St. Peter's School *Philadelphia*
X	X	X	X	X		X		X						192	Shady Side Academy *Pittsburgh*
		X	X	X		X		X						192	The Shipley School *Bryn Mawr*
		X	X	X										192	Springside School *Philadelphia*
		X	X	X				X						193	The Swain School *Allentown*
		X	X	X				X						193	Valley School of Ligonier *Ligonier*
		X	X	X		X		X				Q		193	William Penn Charter School *Philadelphia*
		X	X	X										193	The Wyndcroft School *Pottstown*
X	X	X	X	X		X		X	X	X		O		193	Wyoming Seminary *Kingston*
		X	X	X								O		195	Wyoming Seminary *Forty Fort*

RHODE ISLAND

Boarding Boys	Boarding Girls	Day Boys	Day Girls	Elementary	Junior Boarding	Secondary	Postgraduate Program	Summer Program	English as a Second Language	Learning Differences Program	Preprofessional Arts Training	Religious Affiliation	Military Program	Page	School
		X	X	X										196	The Gordon School *East Providence*
	X				X	X			X			RC		196	Overbrook Academy *Warwick*
		X	X	X						X				197	The Pennfield School† *Portsmouth*

Classification Grid

Column key (diagonal headers, left to right): Boarding Boys · Boarding Girls · Day Boys · Day Girls · Elementary · Junior Boarding · Secondary · Postgraduate Program · Summer Program · English as a Second Language · Learning Differences Program · Preprofessional Arts Training · Religious Affiliation · Military Program · Page

Bd Boys	Bd Girls	Day Boys	Day Girls	Elem	Jr Bd	Sec	PG	Summer	ESL	Learn Diff	Preprof Arts	Relig	Mil	Page	School
		X	X	X		X								197	The Providence Country Day School *East Providence*
		X	X	X				X						197	St. Michael's Country Day School *Newport*
		X	X	X		X			X					198	The Wheeler School† *Providence*

SOUTH CAROLINA

Bd Boys	Bd Girls	Day Boys	Day Girls	Elem	Jr Bd	Sec	PG	Summer	ESL	Learn Diff	Preprof Arts	Relig	Mil	Page	School
		X	X	X		X			X					199	Charleston Collegiate School *Johns Island*
		X	X	X										199	Charleston Day School *Charleston*
		X	X	X		X			X			E		199	Porter-Gaud School† *Charleston*
X	X	X	X	X		X		X		X				199	Trident Academy† *Mount Pleasant*

TENNESSEE

Bd Boys	Bd Girls	Day Boys	Day Girls	Elem	Jr Bd	Sec	PG	Summer	ESL	Learn Diff	Preprof Arts	Relig	Mil	Page	School
		X	X	X		X		X		X				200	Battle Ground Academy† *Franklin*
		X	X	X		X		X				NC		200	Brentwood Academy *Brentwood*
		X	X	X		X						O		200	Christ Methodist Day School *Memphis*
		X	X	X		X								200	The Ensworth School *Nashville*
		X	X	X								E		200	Episcopal School of Knoxville *Knoxville*
		X	X	X		X		X				NC		200	Franklin Road Academy *Nashville*
		X	X	X		X		X						201	Harding Academy† *Nashville*
		X	X	X		X	X	X						201	Lausanne Collegiate School† *Memphis*
		X				X		X						201	Memphis University School *Memphis*
		X				X		X						201	Montgomery Bell Academy *Nashville*
		X	X	X		X						RC		201	Overbrook School *Nashville*
		X	X	X		X		X		X		RC		201	St. Agnes Academy-St. Dominic School† *Memphis*
			X			X						RC		202	St. Cecilia Academy *Nashville*
		X	X	X		X		X				E		202	St. George's Independent School *Germantown/Memphis/Collierville*
		X	X	X		X		X				E		202	St. Nicholas School† *Chattanooga*

TEXAS

Bd Boys	Bd Girls	Day Boys	Day Girls	Elem	Jr Bd	Sec	PG	Summer	ESL	Learn Diff	Preprof Arts	Relig	Mil	Page	School
		X	X	X		X		X						203	Allen Academy *Bryan*
		X	X	X								E		203	All Saints Episcopal School *Beaumont*
		X	X	X		X						E		203	All Saints' Episcopal School *Fort Worth*
		X	X	X				X				O		203	Annunciation Orthodox School *Houston*
		X	X	X		X						E		203	The Canterbury Episcopal School *DeSoto*
		X		X		X		X		X		RC		204	Cistercian Preparatory School† *Irving*
			X	X		X						RC		204	Duchesne Academy of the Sacred Heart *Houston*
		X	X			X						E		204	Episcopal High School of Houston *Bellaire*
		X	X	X		X						E		204	The Episcopal School of Dallas *Dallas*
		X	X	X		X								204	Fort Worth Academy *Fort Worth*
		X	X	X		X		X						204	Fort Worth Country Day *Fort Worth*
		X	X	X		X						E		205	Good Shepherd Episcopal School *Dallas*
	X		X	X	X	X		X						205	The Hockaday School *Dallas*
		X	X	X		X		X						207	The John Cooper School *The Woodlands*
		X	X	X		X		X						207	The Kinkaid School *Houston*
		X	X	X		X								207	Lakehill Preparatory School *Dallas*
		X	X	X				X						208	The Lamplighter School *Dallas*
		X	X	X		X		X						208	The Oakridge School *Arlington*

Boarding Boys	Boarding Girls	Day Boys	Day Girls	Elementary	Junior Boarding	Secondary	Postgraduate Program	Summer Program	English as a Second Language	Learning Differences Program	Preprofessional Arts Training	Religious Affiliation	Military Program	Page	School
		X	X	X		X						E		210	Parish Episcopal School *Dallas*
		X	X	X				X				B		210	River Oaks Baptist School *Houston*
			X			X						RC		210	St. Agnes Academy *Houston*
		X	X	X		X		X				E		210	St. Andrew's Episcopal School *Austin*
		X	X	X						X		E		210	St. James Episcopal School† *Corpus Christi*
		X	X	X		X								210	St. John's School *Houston*
		X	X	X				X	X			E		211	St. Luke's Episcopal School *San Antonio*
		X		X		X								211	St. Mark's School of Texas *Dallas*
		X				X		X				RC		211	Strake Jesuit College Preparatory *Houston*
		X	X	X		X		X		X				211	Trinity Valley School† *Fort Worth*
		X	X			X								211	Vanguard College Preparatory School *Waco*
		X	X	X		X		X		X				212	The Winston School† *Dallas*

UTAH

Boarding Boys	Boarding Girls	Day Boys	Day Girls	Elementary	Junior Boarding	Secondary	Postgraduate Program	Summer Program	English as a Second Language	Learning Differences Program	Preprofessional Arts Training	Religious Affiliation	Military Program	Page	School
		X	X	X		X								213	Rowland Hall-St. Mark's School *Salt Lake City*

VIRGINIA

Boarding Boys	Boarding Girls	Day Boys	Day Girls	Elementary	Junior Boarding	Secondary	Postgraduate Program	Summer Program	English as a Second Language	Learning Differences Program	Preprofessional Arts Training	Religious Affiliation	Military Program	Page	School
		X	X			X				X		RC		214	Bishop Ireton High School† *Alexandria*
X						X		X	X			E		214	Blue Ridge School† *St. George*
		X	X	X				X	X					216	Browne Academy† *Alexandria*
		X	X	X				X						216	Burgundy Farm Country Day School *Alexandria*
		X	X	X		X		X	X					216	Cape Henry Collegiate School *Virginia Beach*
	X		X			X						E		216	Chatham Hall *Chatham*
		X	X	X		X		X						217	Collegiate School *Richmond*
		X	X	X		X				X		NC		217	The Covenant School† *Charlottesville*
X	X					X		X	X			E		217	Episcopal High School† *Alexandria*
		X	X	X		X		X						219	Fredericksburg Academy *Fredericksburg*
		X	X	X										219	Grymes Memorial School *Orange*
		X	X	X		X		X						219	Hampton Roads Academy *Newport News*
		X	X	X										219	The Hill School of Middleburg *Middleburg*
		X	X	X				X						220	The Langley School *McLean*
		X	X	X										220	Loudoun Country Day School *Leesburg*
X	X	X	X		X	X	X	X						220	Miller School *Charlottesville*
		X	X	X		X	X	X						222	Norfolk Academy *Norfolk*
		X	X	X		X								224	North Cross School *Roanoke*
		X	X			X						RC		224	Oakcrest School *McLean*
		X	X	X		X		X						224	The Potomac School *McLean*
		X	X	X				X				E		225	St. Andrew's Episcopal School *Newport News*
		X		X		X		X				E		225	St. Christopher's School *Richmond*
		X	X	X								RC		225	Saint Patrick Catholic School *Norfolk*
		X	X	X		X		X				E		225	St. Stephen's and St. Agnes School *Alexandria*
		X	X	X		X		X	X					226	The Steward School *Richmond*
		X	X	X				X						226	Sullins Academy *Bristol*
		X	X			X						E		226	Trinity Episcopal School *Richmond*

Classification Grid

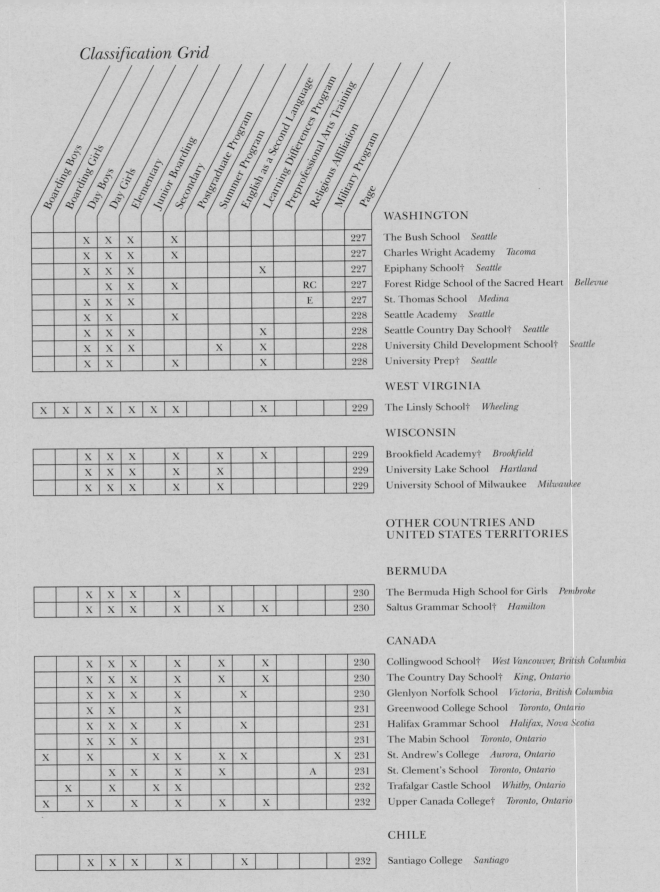

Boarding Boys	Boarding Girls	Day Boys	Day Girls	Elementary	Junior Boarding	Secondary	Postgraduate Program	Summer Program	English as a Second Language	Learning Differences Program	Preprofessional Arts Training	Religious Affiliation	Military Program	Page	School
															WASHINGTON
		X	X	X		X								227	The Bush School *Seattle*
		X	X	X		X								227	Charles Wright Academy *Tacoma*
		X	X	X				X						227	Epiphany School† *Seattle*
		X	X	X		X						RC		227	Forest Ridge School of the Sacred Heart *Bellevue*
		X	X	X								E		227	St. Thomas School *Medina*
		X	X			X								228	Seattle Academy *Seattle*
		X	X	X				X						228	Seattle Country Day School† *Seattle*
		X	X	X				X		X				228	University Child Development School† *Seattle*
		X	X			X		X						228	University Prep† *Seattle*
															WEST VIRGINIA
X	X	X	X	X	X	X				X				229	The Linsly School† *Wheeling*
															WISCONSIN
		X	X	X		X		X		X				229	Brookfield Academy† *Brookfield*
		X	X	X		X		X						229	University Lake School *Hartland*
		X	X	X		X		X						229	University School of Milwaukee *Milwaukee*

OTHER COUNTRIES AND UNITED STATES TERRITORIES

Boarding Boys	Boarding Girls	Day Boys	Day Girls	Elementary	Junior Boarding	Secondary	Postgraduate Program	Summer Program	English as a Second Language	Learning Differences Program	Preprofessional Arts Training	Religious Affiliation	Military Program	Page	School
															BERMUDA
		X	X	X		X								230	The Bermuda High School for Girls *Pembroke*
		X	X	X		X		X		X				230	Saltus Grammar School† *Hamilton*
															CANADA
		X	X	X		X		X		X				230	Collingwood School† *West Vancouver, British Columbia*
		X	X	X		X		X		X				230	The Country Day School† *King, Ontario*
		X	X	X		X			X					230	Glenlyon Norfolk School *Victoria, British Columbia*
		X	X			X								231	Greenwood College School *Toronto, Ontario*
		X	X	X		X		X						231	Halifax Grammar School *Halifax, Nova Scotia*
		X	X	X										231	The Mabin School *Toronto, Ontario*
X		X			X	X		X	X				X	231	St. Andrew's College *Aurora, Ontario*
			X	X		X		X				A		231	St. Clement's School *Toronto, Ontario*
	X		X		X	X								232	Trafalgar Castle School *Whitby, Ontario*
X		X		X		X		X	X					232	Upper Canada College† *Toronto, Ontario*
															CHILE
		X	X	X		X			X					232	Santiago College *Santiago*

Boarding Boys	Boarding Girls	Day Boys	Day Girls	Elementary	Junior Boarding	Secondary	Postgraduate Program	Summer Program	English as a Second Language	Learning Differences Program	Preprofessional Arts Training	Religious Affiliation	Military Program	Page	School
															CHINA
		X	X	X		X		X	X					233	Chinese International School *Hong Kong*
		X	X	X		X			X			L		233	Hong Kong International School *Hong Kong*
X	X					X								233	School Year Abroad *Beijing*
															ENGLAND
X	X	X	X	X		X		X	X	X				233	The ACS International Schools† *Cobham/Hillingdon/Egham*
		X	X	X		X		X	X	X				236	The American School in London† *London*
															FRANCE
X	X					X								237	School Year Abroad *Rennes*
															GERMANY
		X	X	X		X			X					237	Munich International School *Starnberg*
															ITALY
X	X	X	X			X	X							238	St. Stephen's School *Rome*
X	X					X				·				240	School Year Abroad *Viterbo*
															JAPAN
		X		X		X		X	X			RC		240	St. Mary's International School *Tokyo*
															KOREA
		X	X	X		X			X			NC		242	Seoul Foreign School *Seoul*
															PUERTO RICO
		X	X	X		X		X	X	X				242	Commonwealth-Parkville School† *San Juan*
															SPAIN
		X	X	X		X		X	X					242	The American School of Madrid *Madrid*
X	X					X								242	School Year Abroad *Zaragoza*
															VIETNAM
X	X					X								243	School Year Abroad *Hanoi*
															VIRGIN ISLANDS
		X	X	X		X		X		X				243	The Good Hope School† *Frederiksted, St. Croix*
		X	X	X		X		X		X				243	St. Croix Country Day School† *Kingshill, St. Croix*

Learning Differences Grid

The schools referenced in this grid are identified as offering programs for learning-different students. The grid is designed to help students, families, and counselors quickly find appropriate schools to fit specific learning needs.

The schools are arranged alphabetically by state or country with a page number for locating a full description on each school. The Learning Differences Grid can be used as a reference when searching for programs in the following areas:

Attention Deficit Disorder/Attention Deficit Hyperactivity Disorder

Dyslexia/Specific Learning Disability

Learning/Remediation Center

Talented/Gifted

Behavioral/Emotional Needs

Intellectual Handicap

Speech/Language Therapy

Physical/Occupational Therapy

Crisis Intervention

Career/Vocational Counseling

Transitional Living Skills

Substance Abuse Counseling

Parent/Professional Training

Learning Differences Grid

School	Page	ADD/ADHD	Dyslexia/Specific Learning Disability	Learning Disability Center/Remediation	Talented/Gifted	Behavioral/Emotional Needs	Intellectual Handicap	Speech/Language Therapy	Physical/Occupational Therapy	Crisis Intervention	Career/Vocational Counseling	Transitional Living Skills	Substance Abuse Counseling	Parent/Professional Training
ALABAMA														
Advent Episcopal School *Birmingham*	3			X										
Bayside Academy *Daphne*	5	X	X	X					X	X				
Highlands School *Birmingham*	5			X										
St. Paul's Episcopal School *Mobile*	6	X	X	X	X		X							X
CALIFORNIA														
Besant Hill School of Happy Valley *Ojai*	9	X	X			X								
Cathedral School for Boys *San Francisco*	12			X										
The College Preparatory School *Oakland*	14		X											
The Country School *Valley Village*	14	X		X										
Crestview Preparatory School *La Cañada*	15			X										
Gateway School *Santa Cruz*	17			X										
La Jolla Country Day School *La Jolla*	21		X				X							
Laurence School *Valley Glen*	21			X										
Lycée Français La Pérouse *San Francisco*	21		X		X		X							
Marin Primary & Middle School *Larkspur*	22	X	X	X	X									
Mid-Peninsula High School *Menlo Park*	23	X	X	X										
The Mirman School for Gifted Children *Los Angeles*	23			X										
Ojai Valley School *Ojai*	26	X	X	X										
The Pegasus School *Huntington Beach*	26			X										
Rolling Hills Preparatory School *San Pedro*	29	X	X											
San Francisco University High School *San Francisco*	31		X											
The Urban School of San Francisco *San Francisco*	32	X	X								X			
Viewpoint School *Calabasas*	33			X										
Windrush School *El Cerrito*	35			X										
CONNECTICUT														
Eagle Hill School *Greenwich*	42	X	X			X								X
Glenholme School *Washington*	43	X	X		X	X	X							X
Mooreland Hill School *Kensington*	51			X										
Notre Dame of West Haven *West Haven*	51	X	X	X	X	X			X	X			X	X
Pear Tree Point School *Darien*	51		X											
Rumsey Hall School *Washington Depot*	51	X	X	X	X									
The Taft School *Watertown*	53			X										
The Woodhall School *Bethlehem*	54	X	X											

Learning Differences Grid

	Page	ADD/ADHD	Dyslexia/Specific Learning Disability	Learning Remediation Center	Talented/Gifted	Behavioral/Emotional Needs	Intellectual Handicap	Speech/Language Therapy	Physical/Occupational Therapy	Crisis Intervention	Career/Vocational Counseling	Transitional Living Skills	Substance Abuse Counseling	Parent/Professional Training
DELAWARE														
Centreville School *Centreville*	55	X	X				X	X						
Salesianum School *Wilmington*	55	X	X	X					X	X			X	
DISTRICT OF COLUMBIA														
Georgetown Day School *Washington*	60				X									
The Lab School of Washington *Washington*	61	X	X	X	X		X	X				X		X
FLORIDA														
All Saints' Academy *Winter Haven*	63	X		X			X							
Miami Country Day School *Miami*	66	X	X	X	X									
PACE-Brantley Hall School *Longwood*	67	X	X	X							X			
Pine Crest School *Boca Raton/Fort Lauderdale*	67				X									
Riverside Presbyterian Day School *Jacksonville*	68				X									
Saint Edward's School *Vero Beach*	68			X	X									
St. Mark's Episcopal Day School *Jacksonville*	71		X	X				X	X					
St. Mary's Episcopal Day School *Tampa*	71								X					X
Trinity Preparatory School *Winter Park*	74				X									
GEORGIA														
The Westminster Schools *Atlanta*	78				X									
Woodward Academy *College Park*	78	X	X											
ILLINOIS														
The Avery Coonley School *Downers Grove*	82				X									
Brehm Preparatory School *Carbondale*	82	X	X				X							
INDIANA														
Evansville Day School *Evansville*	84				X									
The Orchard School *Indianapolis*	84	X	X		X	X	X							X
The Stanley Clark School *South Bend*	84	X	X	X	X	X	X							X
Sycamore School *Indianapolis*	84				X									
University High School *Carmel*	85	X												

Learning Differences Grid

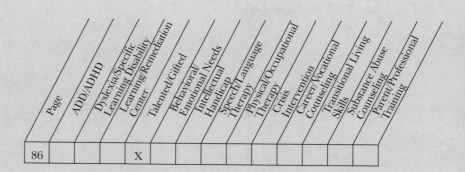

School	Page	ADD/ADHD	Dyslexia/Specific Learning Disability	Learning Disabilities Center	Learning Center/Remediation	Talented/Gifted	Behavioral/Emotional	Intellectual Handicap	Speech/Language Therapy	Physical/Occupational Therapy	Crisis Intervention	Career/Vocational Counseling	Transitional Living Skills	Substance Abuse Counseling	Parent/Professional Training
IOWA															
Rivermont Collegiate *Bettendorf*	86				X										
LOUISIANA															
The Dunham School *Baton Rouge*	86	X	X	X	X			X	X						
Ridgewood Preparatory School *Metairie*	87	X			X										
St. Andrew's Episcopal School *New Orleans*	87				X										
St. Martin's Episcopal School *Metairie*	87				X										
Southfield School *Shreveport*	87				X										
MAINE															
Hebron Academy *Hebron*	88	X	X	X											
Washington Academy *East Machias*	88	X	X	X	X	X	X	X	X			X	X		
MARYLAND															
Glenelg Country School *Ellicott City*	90				X										
Gunston Day School *Centreville*	91	X	X	X											
The Ivymount School *Rockville*	91	X	X				X	X	X	X		X			X
The Nora School *Silver Spring*	93	X													
Norwood School *Bethesda*	93				X										
Radcliffe Creek School *Chestertown*	93	X	X						X						
Saint James School *St. James*	96				X										
MASSACHUSETTS															
Boston University Academy *Boston*	100				X										
The Carroll School *Lincoln*	101		X												
Eaglebrook School *Deerfield*	104		X		X										
Fayerweather Street School *Cambridge*	105		X	X											
Hillside School *Marlborough*	105	X	X	X	X										
The Meadowbrook School of Weston *Weston*	108			X										X	
Pine Cobble School *Williamstown*	111	X	X	X	X										
Thayer Academy *Braintree*	114				X										

Learning Differences Grid

	Page	ADD/ADHD	Dyslexia/Specific Learning Disability	Learning/Remediation Center	Talented/Gifted	Behavioral/Emotional Needs	Intellectual Handicap	Speech/Language Therapy	Physical/Occupational Therapy	Crisis Intervention	Career/Vocational Counseling	Transitional Living Skills	Substance Abuse Counseling	Parent/Professional Training
MICHIGAN														
Academy of the Sacred Heart *Bloomfield Hills*	117		X	X						X				
Kalamazoo Country Day School *Kalamazoo*	119	X		X										
The Leelanau School *Glen Arbor*	119	X	X	X	X		X							
The Roeper School *Bloomfield Hills*	121			X										
University Liggett School *Grosse Pointe Woods*	122			X										
MISSOURI														
Andrews Academy *St. Louis*	127			X										
Community School *St. Louis*	127			X										
Forsyth School *St. Louis*	128			X										
Mary Institute and Saint Louis Country Day School *St. Louis*	128			X										
The Wilson School *St. Louis*	129			X										
NEW HAMPSHIRE														
Hampshire Country School *Rindge*	131	X		X	X									
Kimball Union Academy *Meriden*	133		X	X										
NEW JERSEY														
Collegiate School *Passaic Park*	134	X		X	X		X							
The Craig School *Mountain Lakes*	134	X	X				X							
The Hudson School *Hoboken*	134			X										
The Pennington School *Pennington*	136	X												
Princeton Montessori School *Princeton*	136												X	
Saddle River Day School *Saddle River*	138			X										
The Winston School *Short Hills*	140	X												
NEW MEXICO														
Rio Grande School *Santa Fe*	142	X	X	X			X							

Learning Differences Grid

School	Page	ADD/ADHD	Dyslexia/Specific Learning Disability	Learning Disability Center/Remediation	Talented/Gifted	Behavioral/Emotional Needs	Intellectual Handicap	Speech/Language Therapy	Physical/Occupational Therapy	Crisis Intervention	Career/Vocational Counseling	Transitional Living Skills	Substance Abuse Counseling	Parent/Professional Training
NEW YORK														
The Churchill School and Center *New York*	146	X						X						X
The Dwight School *New York*	151		X											
The Elmwood Franklin School *Buffalo*	152				X									
The Gow School *South Wales*	152	X												
The Kildonan School *Amenia*	157	X												
The Knox School *St. James*	157		X											
The Mary Louis Academy *Jamaica Estates*	158			X	X				X	X		X		
Mary McDowell Center for Learning *Brooklyn*	158	X												
Oakwood Friends School *Poughkeepsie*	160	X	X	X	X									
Robert Louis Stevenson School *New York*	164	X	X	X	X	X							X	X
The Storm King School *Cornwall-on-Hudson*	170	X	X		X									
The Windsor School *Flushing*	173				X									
Windward School *White Plains*	173	X											X	
The Winston Preparatory School *New York*	174	X	X	X		X								
York Preparatory School *New York*	174	X	X											
NORTH CAROLINA														
Carolina Day School *Asheville*	175	X												X
Forsyth Country Day School *Lewisville*	176	X	X	X		X								
Guilford Day School *Greensboro*	176	X	X	X							X	X		
The Oakwood School *Greenville*	177	X			X									
The O'Neal School *Southern Pines*	177	X	X	X										
Providence Day School *Charlotte*	177				X									
Saint Mary's School *Raleigh*	178				X									
St. Timothy's School *Raleigh*	178				X									
Summit School *Winston-Salem*	178	X			X									
OHIO														
Lake Ridge Academy *North Ridgeville*	179				X									
The Miami Valley School *Dayton*	179				X									
The Summit Country Day School *Cincinnati*	180				X									
Western Reserve Academy *Hudson*	180				X									

Learning Differences Grid

School	Page	ADD/ADHD	Dyslexia	Specific Learning Disability	Learning Remediation Center	Talented/Gifted	Behavioral/Emotional Needs	Intellectual Handicap	Speech/Language Therapy	Physical/Occupational Therapy	Crisis Intervention	Career/Vocational Counseling	Transitional Living Skills	Substance Abuse Counseling	Parent/Professional Training
OKLAHOMA															
Holland Hall *Tulsa*	182				X									X	
Riverfield Country Day School *Tulsa*	183				X										
PENNSYLVANIA															
The Crefeld School *Philadelphia*	184	X			X										
Delaware Valley Friends School *Paoli*	184	X	X												
Grier School *Tyrone*	185	X	X	X	X										
The Hillside School *Macungie*	187	X	X	X					X						
RHODE ISLAND															
The Pennfield School *Portsmouth*	197				X										
The Wheeler School *Providence*	198		X												
SOUTH CAROLINA															
Porter Gaud School *Charleston*	199	X													
Trident Academy *Mount Pleasant*	199	X	X	X					X	X					X
TENNESSEE															
Battle Ground Academy *Franklin*	200			X	X						X	X		X	X
Harding Academy *Nashville*	201				X										
Lausanne Collegiate School *Memphis*	201				X										
St. Agnes Academy–St. Dominic School *Memphis*	201	X			X										
St. Nicholas School *Chattanooga*	202				X										
TEXAS															
Cistercian Preparatory School *Irving*	204				X										
St. James Episcopal School *Corpus Christi*	210		X		X										
Trinity Valley School *Fort Worth*	211				X										
The Winston School *Dallas*	212	X	X	X											

Learning Differences Grid

	Page	ADD/ADHD	Dyslexia/Specific Learning Disability	Learning/Remediation Center	Talented/Gifted	Behavioral/Emotional Needs	Intellectual Handicap	Speech/Language Therapy	Physical/Occupational Therapy	Crisis Intervention	Career/Vocational Counseling	Transitional Living Skills	Substance Abuse Counseling	Parent/Professional Training
VIRGINIA														
Bishop Ireton High School *Alexandria*	214	X		X	X									
Blue Ridge School *St. George*	214	X	X	X										
Browne Academy *Alexandria*	216			X										
The Covenant School *Charlottesville*	217	X		X										
Episcopal High School *Alexandria*	217			X										
WASHINGTON														
Epiphany School *Seattle*	227		X											
Seattle Country Day School *Seattle*	228			X										X
University Child Development School *Seattle*	228			X										
University Prep *Seattle*	228	X	X											
WEST VIRGINIA														
Linsly School *Wheeling*	229			X										
WISCONSIN														
Brookfield Academy *Brookfield*	229			X										
INTERNATIONAL														
BERMUDA														
Saltus Grammar School *Hamilton*	230	X	X		X					X	X			
CANADA														
Collingwood School *West Vancouver*	230			X	X							X		
The Country Day School *King*	230		X											
Upper Canada College *Toronto*	232			X										
ENGLAND														
The ACS International Schools *Cobham/Hillingdon/Egham*	233	X	X	X	X			X	X					
The American School in London *London*	236		X					X						
PUERTO RICO														
Commonwealth-Parkville School *San Juan*	242	X	X											X

Learning Differences Grid

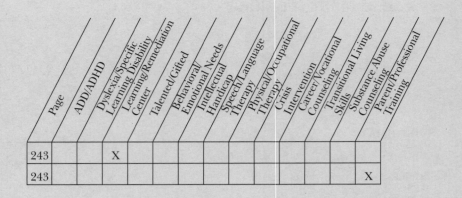

VIRGIN ISLANDS

The Good Hope School   *Frederiksted*

St. Croix Country Day School   *Kingshill*

Page	ADD/ADHD	Dyslexia/Specific Learning Disability	Learning/Remediation Center	Talented/Gifted	Behavioral/Emotional Needs	Intellectual Handicap	Speech/Language Therapy	Physical/Occupational Therapy	Crisis Intervention	Career/Vocational Counseling	Transitional Living Skills	Substance Abuse Counseling	Parent/Professional Training
243		X											
243												X	